JACKO, HIS RISE AND FALL:
The Social & Sexual History of Michael Jackson

by Darwin Porter

ISBN 0-9748118-5-8
ISBN13 978-0-9748118-5-7
ALL RIGHTS RESERVED
Copyright 2007, Blood Moon Productions, Ltd.
www.BloodMoonProductions.com

First edition published April 2007
Cover design by Richard Leeds (**www.bigwigdesign.com**)
Photo and page layouts by Theodora Chowfatt,
with special thanks to **www.Photofestnyc.com**

The author wishes to thank Monica Dunn for her tireless
assistance in the research of this biography.

"I think the story of Michael Jackson reflects our times perfectly and will be something historians in future centuries (provided there's still a planet) will explore. He has been destroyed by success. I worked on the fashion promotion of the movie The Wiz *in the 1970s and Michael was the scarecrow. Met him at the studio and found him to be normal, quiet and very sweet. Not a prima donna at all. But this was before the first nose job and the skin-bleaching."*

Virginia Haynes Montgomery
Montgomery Communications

"I'd have thought that there wasn't one single gossipy rock yet to be overturned in the microscopically scrutinized life of Michael Jackson. But Darwin Porter's exhaustive (but always zippy) hybrid of celebrity bio and solid reporting proves me quite wrong. It's all here: The abuse Jackson suffered as a boy from the fists of his father; rough early years on the "chitlin' circuit"; his rocky relationship with Diana Ross and his quirky relationship with Liz Taylor; his sham marriages and his oddly conceived three children; unflagging rumors of his homosexuality; and his scandalous affection for generations of adolescent boys. Definitely a page-turner. But don't turn the pages too quickly: Almost every one holds a fascinating revelation."

Richard Labonte
Books To Watch Out For

"When Michael Jackson sings, it is with the voice of angels, and when his feet move, you can see God dancing."

--Sir Bob Geldof

"I grew up in a fishbowl. I will not allow that to happen to my son."

--Michael Jackson

"Sure he's a little afraid of people. When you have people that from the time you're a little kid, want a part of you, they want your clothes, they want your hair--you're going to get a little nervous around people."

--Vince Paterson, choreographer

"He is one of the last living innocents who is in complete control of his life. I've never seen anybody like Michael. He's an emotional child star. He's in full control. Sometimes he appears to be wavering on the fringes of the twilight, but there is a great conscious forethought behind everything he does. He's very smart about his career and the choices he makes. I think he is definitely a man of two personalities."

--Steven Spielberg

"He really feels that the audience deserves the best he can give them. He really has a very strong sense of responsibility, a strong sense of showmanship."

--John Landis

"If it weren't for my desire to help the children of the world, I'd throw in the towel and kill myself."

--Michael Jackson

Michael Jackson at the peak of his "Thriller" fame in the 1980s was probably the most famous person on earth. Undeniably, thanks to his reign as the King of Pop, he was the world's biggest superstar. He was also the most famous African-American entertainer in the history of show business.

But after the turn of the millennium, the front pages of such tabloids as The New York Post were screaming: PETER PAN OR PERVERT?.

How could Michael Jackson's career and personal life have gone so wrong?

To answer that, you have to look at Michael's roots in the grimy industrial city of Gary, Indiana, "murder capital of the U.S." Here on the scorching night of August 29, 1958, Michael Jackson entered the world.

Chapter One

It can be said that Michael's musical career began when he was only three and a half years old. His soft-spoken mother, Katherine, was in her small kitchen in Gary, Indiana, washing clothes on an old Maytag wringer machine that squeaked, rattled, and rolled, having seen better days. She'd come home early from her dreary job as a clerk at Sears.

As she turned around, she noticed her toddler singing and dancing almost like a professional. For one brief moment, she flashed on his becoming a black version of Shirley Temple before quickly ruling that out. Like her older boys, her youngest son belonged to the world of music.

When her gruff husband, Joe, returned home from a hard day's work as a crane operator in a local steel mill, she planned to tell him that yet another of his sons was musically talented. She had a gut instinct that Michael's talents might one day surpass those of Jackie, Tito, Jermaine, and Marlon.

Michael was the seventh of her children, as she'd recently given birth to not only her boys, but to two girls, Maureen and La Toya. Randy and Janet were yet to come.

"I remember seeing Michael dancing like it was yesterday," Katherine recalled. "He was singing at the top of his voice with powerful lungs I didn't know he had developed. I sensed he was not only born to dance but to sing as well. There was a joy I saw on his face that afternoon that I was never to see again. His singing and dancing were spontaneous. When he was forced to sing and dance under threat of a beating from my husband, Joe, that same joy wasn't there. But there was enough of it left to thrill the world."

Since the day he'd entered the world, Michael had grown up listening to rock 'n' roll and The Blues. Little Richard's voice was often broadcast throughout the house, singing "Tutti Frutti" or "Good Golly Miss Molly." In his wildest dreams, Michael could not have imagined that he'd eventually own the rights to both of those songs. The sounds of Chuck Berry or Otis Redding also echoed throughout the small bungalow.

At that time in his life, Joe wanted to be a musical star himself. His R&B band was called "The Falcons," and the boys in the band, the members of which included Joe's brother, Luther, rehearsed almost nightly in the tiny two-bedroom bungalow already overcrowded with the burgeoning Jackson family.

Sometimes when her husband was away on gigs with The Falcons,

Young Michael

Katherine suspected that he was wasn't remaining faithful to her. But she'd decided long ago to overlook his transgressions as a means of salvaging her marriage.

One afternoon, Tito went to the closet in Joe's bedroom and removed his father's most precious possession, his guitar. Playing with the guitar in the small living room, the boy broke one of the strings. Later that night, after supper, when Joe started to play his guitar, he discovered what Tito had done. He grabbed Tito by his neck and forced him into the living room. Having repaired the string, Joe demanded that Tito play for him. "I wanna hear you play that guitar. And you'd better be good! If you're not good, I'm gonna beat the hell out of you!" Although prepared for violence, hard-to-please Joe was impressed with Tito's guitar playing.

It was on that night that Joe realized that all his sons had musical talent. If he couldn't make it in the music world himself, maybe his sons could bring in big paychecks with Joe managing their money. He began to rehearse not just with Tito, but with his oldest boys, Jackie and Jermaine. As soon as he was old enough—well, barely—the apple-cheeked Michael joined in pounding those bongos. "The kid is a dynamo," Joe told Katherine.

"What have I been telling you?" she asked.

A few weeks later, Joe decided that his own career with The Falcons was going nowhere. He threw all the energy he'd used for his own music into developing the careers of his sons—and he was a brutal taskmaster, even beating them with a switch or a belt when one of the boys missed a note or a dance step.

Joe told the members of The Falcons that he didn't practice birth control.

"One kid came right after the other. With all the hungry mouths to feed, I had to bring home a paycheck." He would later claim, "I sacrificed my own career for the sake of my sons. They were not grateful for what I did for them, especially Michael, the most ungrateful of them all."

"Even before our first record contract," Jermaine said, "we used to have to be in before the street lights came on. It was rehearse, rehearse, and then rehearse some more. We missed out on being kids. We could never play with the other boys on the block because we had to tend to business—and that meant making music."

Joe began to spend money he couldn't afford buying musical instruments for his children. This led to some bitter fights with Katherine, who needed the meager funds to put food on the table.

Joe used brutality to control his sons, Katherine preferring a more emotional and psychological approach in her possessiveness. Her family was her world. To lose her family would be tantamount to losing her reason for living.

Born in Arkansas but reared in dirt-poor rural Tennessee, where his dad taught school for fifteen dollars a week, Joe Jackson came up the hard way. He was determined to make it big. He learned to discipline his own children based on the harsh beatings and strict punishment he received from his own father, the iron-fisted Samuel, a devout Lutheran who "tolerated no sass from a snot-nosed kid."

The Jacksons (left to right) in the 70s:
Jackie, Janet, Michael, Tito, La Toya, Marlon, Randy, and Jermaine.

Joe's father had always proclaimed, "Spare the rod, spoil the child." Joe took his father's advice. Instead of a rod, he used leather belts, razor straps, and wire coat hangers evocative of Joan Crawford in *Mommie Dearest*. When none of those devices seemed to do the job, he balled up his fist and plowed it into one of his boys' noses. Blood would spurt out, but Joe succeeded in getting his point across.

Sometimes in the middle of the night, he would put on a fright mask and burst into the boys' room with a kitchen knife poised menacingly. The brothers' horrified screams could be heard throughout the working-class neighborhood.

Katherine was born in a small hamlet in Alabama that is no longer on the map. She sang spirituals in her church and listened to country music on the radio. Hank Williams was her favorite. Sometimes she'd take Michael in her lap and sing such old favorites as "Cotton Fields" or "Wabash Cannonball" to him.

Michael was about four years old when he noticed that his mother walked with a limp. When he asked her about it, she said that she'd been crippled with polio when she was a young girl growing up in the South. Claiming that musical talent was "a gift from God," she began to take him to the Sunday services of the Jehovah's Witnesses. Often only Maureen—nicknamed "Rebbie"—and La Toya would go with her. Her husband and her sons would rarely, if ever, accompany her.

Before she converted to the teachings of the Jehovah's Witnesses, Katherine had been a member of both a Baptist and a Lutheran church, until she learned that the ministers of each congregation were having extramarital affairs. As a Jehovah's Witness, she would eventually be confronted with evidence that her husband was also having extramarital affairs.

Even so, she steadfastly stood by her new faith that condemned "fornicators (in this case her own husband and later her children), idolaters, masturbators, adulterers, and homosexuals." Most of these labels—and more—would eventually be applied to members of her own family. But Katherine never lost the faith that condemned many of the pastimes of her own offspring.

Katherine, Michael, and Joe Jackson, circa 1972

Michael became an ardent disciple of the Jehovah's Witnesses and remained so until that religious cult "disowned" him.

When Michael turned five, Katherine once again caught him singing in the falsetto of a toddler, this time in front of a mirror. He perfectly impersonated Jermaine's lead vocal. For the second time, she was awed by her young boy's amazing talent. It was hard to admit it to herself, but she concluded that Michael's vocalizing, despite his age, surpassed that of Jermaine's. Jermaine had been Joe's favorite, and his father had been grooming the boy as the lead singer. That night, Katherine confided to Joe, "I think we have another lead singer." She didn't say "a replacement" but "another."

Michael was summoned into the living room. There Joe demanded that he sing for him. "Joe was really shocked when he heard our boy," Katherine said. "So young, so talented." To an increasing degree, his parents realized that they had given birth to a very special talent.

After the first week of rehearsing with Michael, Joe made an unusual prediction of stunning accuracy. "The kid is going to become the biggest entertainer in the world."

When his brothers finally heard Michael sing, "all of us were shocked," as Jackie remembered. "Michael was practically in diapers, but we knew he'd be our lead singer. Jermaine's days as lead singer were over." He was shunted aside, leading to a life-long resentment and envy of his more famous brother.

By the time Michael was six years old, he sang in public at the Garnett Elementary School. Singing *a capella*, he chose "Climb Ev'ry Mountain" from *The Sound of Music*, performing brilliantly enough to impress hard-to-please Joe and bringing tears to Katherine's eyes.

That same year, "Ripples and Waves," the first name of The Jackson 5, began to enter—and win—talent contests in Gary. Joe financed a comical record by them called "Let Me Carry Your Books to School."

Michael not only replaced Jermaine as lead singer, but he began to take over in other ways too. Soon he was choreographing their steps and even designing costumes for The Jackson 5.

By the age of seven, Michael was performing professionally with his brothers. At a talent contest at Roosevelt High School in Gary, the brothers won by

The Jackson residence in Gary, Indiana

singing "My Girl," a hit song from The Temptations.

"I was scared," Michael later recalled. "Afraid we'd be booed off the stage. The audience might not like us. I was untested. But I also felt I could do it. I knew I'd not forget the lyrics or make one big mistake. I was determined, and I pulled it off."

Joe continued to arrange bookings for his sons, the entire troupe hiring out for only eight dollars for a performance. That was only the base pay. Audiences were enthusiastic about the boys, and on a good night the sons brought back one hundred dollars, all derived from tips, to help Katherine run the household.

While still working at the steel plant, Joe drove his sons to gigs at night. Sometimes he'd take a leave from work and travel cross-country with his boys in a small van.

Although Joe privately told Katherine how talented he felt Michael was, he didn't let his son in on that. In front of his brothers, Joe often denounced Michael. "You're one ugly fucker. I'm handsome. You couldn't be my son. Your mama must have fucked the milkman. You're also the dumbest piece of shit that ever got up to entertain an audience. The only way you can get a squeal from a woman is to crawl on the floor and look up her dress. You're so clumsy I'm ashamed to call you my son." When Michael seriously angered him, Joe took out a pocket knife and held it to Michael's throat, threatening to slit it.

As a little boy, Michael performed in the wildest and raunchiest of the honky-tonks of "Sin City," the nickname for Gary.

"When not in Gary, the Jackson brothers were appearing in the seedy dives of Chicago, a van ride of around 90 minutes from Gary, where most known perversions could be catered to," in the words of one habitué of the nightlife scene in The Windy City.

Michael got his taste of female nudity watching strippers peel down and tossing their G-strings into the hard-drinking crowd of men, with a few "butch dykes," as they were called, in the audience seeking a thrill as well.

After The Jackson 5 performed musical numbers, Joe ordered Michael to crawl around on the beer-stained floor, looking up the dresses of screaming but compliant women.

After these antics, customers would throw money on the dirty floor. Michael would scamper around in the filth, collecting both coins and dollars. Even though it was illegal for the Jackson boys to perform in these joints, because they were minors, no police interference ever occurred.

In time, Michael himself would become an alluring, sexually ambiguous figure, but he got his first taste of drag in a Chicago club euphemistically called Guys & Dolls. An alluring blonde, who looked like Dolly Parton did in

Michael and Papa Joe

the Seventies, appeared on the bill. Michael remembered that she had "history's largest boobs," but when that G-string came off, "she" became a "he," "although not much of one."

Some sources claim that Michael deepened his appreciation of cross-dressing at the Apollo Theater on 125th Street in New York's Harlem. At the Apollo, performers merely pulled off their wigs to reveal that they were men. But at Guys & Dolls in Chicago, they actually flashed their male genitalia.

Some of the honky-tonks the boys appeared in were known as "blood buckets" because of the violence that would occur on a rowdy Saturday night, particularly after midnight.

Regardless of how late he stayed up on Saturday night, Michael always got up to go to the Sunday meeting of the Jehovah's Witnesses with Katherine. Afterward, he would join her on door-to-door canvassing of his neighborhood, trying to win new converts to their evangelical movement.

Even after fame came to Michael, he still joined La Toya and Katherine on proselytizing trips to knock on the doors of neighbors' houses, soliciting their enrollment in the "Kingdom of Heaven." Michael wore disguises and usually fooled the adults. But the children often shouted at him, "I know who you are! You're Michael Jackson!"

Rebecca Lowe, a neighbor of the Jackson family in Gary, remembered years later seeing Michael come to her door. "He was well scrubbed and righteous looking, like a black choir boy. He didn't grab his crotch to simulate masturbation. Nothing like that. He was always polite, even when we told him we were ardent Roman Catholics and wanted nothing to do with the Jehovah's Witness people."

Michael had just turned nine when Joe drove his sons to New York to perform at the fabled Apollo Theater. Louis Armstrong, Count Basie, Josephine Baker; each of those legends had appeared at the Apollo.

That night, the Jackson brothers won the Apollo's amateur night contest. "I have a date with destiny," Michael told the manager of the Apollo in one of the most melodramatic statements ever uttered by a nine-year-old. But, as those in show business and later the public were to learn, little pre-pubescent Michael Jackson was no average boy.

On one of the hottest August nights in New York, in 1967, The Jackson 5 faced "the toughest audience in the world," although the same is said for the patrons of La Scala in Milan.

Other "first timers" who broke in, appearing before the notoriously raucous audiences of the Apollo Theater, were Sarah Vaughan, Billie Holiday, Leslie Uggams, and Ella Fitzgerald.

To Joe's amazement, his boys got a standing ovation instead of being booed off the stage.

More bookings followed their win at the Apollo. The Jackson 5 hit Chicago, appearing at the Regal. In Philadelphia Joe got them a booking at the Uptown.

Upon their return to the Apollo, The Jackson 5 brothers were paid for their performance. On the same bill was Michael's role model, James Brown, the "King of Soul."

That night Michael stood in the wings, watching Brown's every move. It is said that Michael learned to "whiplash" a mike into place or "motorize a shuffle" across the stage by watching Brown do it first.

In *Rolling Stone*, writer Gerri Hirshey claimed that "Michael's kindergarten was the basement of the Apollo Theater in New York. He was too shy to actually approach the performers The Jackson 5 opened for. He crept downstairs, along passageways and walls and hid there, peering from behind the dusty flanks of old vaudeville sets while musicians tuned, smoked, played cards, and divided barbecue. Climbing back to the wings, he stood in the protective folds of the

James Brown

musty maroon curtain, watching favorite acts, committing every double dip and every bump, snap, whip-it-back mike toss, to his inventory of night moves."

The writer was right. The Jackson 5, especially Michael, studied all the top talent of the day, especially James Brown. Michael later recalled that seeing Brown perform for the first time was "a magical night."

Brown was an unlikely role model for Michael, but nonetheless he was called "the Godfather of Soul." Born in Barnwell, South Carolina, he once served 26 months in prison for leading police on a high-speed chase in Georgia in 1988.

Like Michael in the future, Brown too would face charges of sexual abuse. But Michael couldn't have cared less about Brown's personal troubles. Even though still a kid, he knew greatness in a performer when he saw it. His judgment about Brown came true when the performer Michael so admired was voted the seventh greatest rock 'n' roll artist of all time by *Entertainment Weekly*.

An icon of the music industry, Brown had a great influence on soul music in the 1960s, funk music in the 70s, and rap music in the 80s. Michael avidly followed his hero's career. In 1992 Brown received a Lifetime Achievement Grammy Award.

That night at the Apollo, when Brown learned that Michael was checking out his every move, he asked to meet "that kid watching me."

Introduced to Brown, Michael was so in awe of his idol that he couldn't utter a sound. Sensing the problem, Brown did all the talking, even taking time to give Michael some advice. "Always keep changing your hair style—that way, the public will keep noticing you. And always stay thin by taking a lot of laxatives. Shit away the fat!"

In the weeks to come, Michael would be hailed as a "pint-sized James Brown."

"Right from the beginning, audiences responded to Mike," Jackie later said. "At the time he was into that James Brown stuff. He was a born mimic. He stole ideas from entertainers everywhere. He could see a performer do some trick just one time, and then he could immediately do the same thing—it was amazing."

Michael and his brothers studied every move, every nuance the competition made. They often appeared on the same bill as The Temptations. With their close-cropped hair, The Temptations bounced onto the stage in their tight-fitting sharkskin suits and pointed Italian shoes. For their really big appearances, Motown's director, Berry Gordy Jr. insisted that the singers wear snappy, form-fitting tuxedos.

The Jackson brothers also appeared with such acts as Smokey Robinson and The Miracles, Little Anthony and The Imperials, and—more significantly—Gladys Knight and The Pips.

"Michael picked up all our dance steps," Gladys Knight recalled. "He was like a sponge taking it all in. It was amazing how he could watch a routine and then make it part of his own repertoire, giving whatever he'd learned an original twist."

The Jackson brothers struggled to acquire an education while constantly performing, often far away from home.

Gladys Knight and The Pips

"Most of our lives we had private schooling," Michael said. "I only went to one public school in my life—and that was in Gary. I tried another one in Los Angeles, but it didn't work out. We'd be in our class and a bunch of fans would break into the classroom. We'd come out of school and there'd be a bunch of kids waiting to take our pictures. Stuff like that. I stayed at that school for only one week. That's all we could take. After that, we had to enroll in private schools."

Katherine feared that time might be running out for her boys. "In a few years they'll look old and fat. They've got to make it now, especially since Michael looks so adorable." She forced her husband to record a demo tape and send it to Motown's founder, Berry Gordy Jr. But nothing ever came of it.

By July of 1968, success of a modest sort had come for The Jackson 5 when they made another appearance at the Regal in Chicago, opening for Gladys Knight and The Pips. That performance earned them their most recognition to date as well as acclaim in the press.

"Everyone thinks

Bobby Taylor and The Vancouvers

we started at the top," Marlon said. "But we traveled around for five years before that. Five brothers and two sisters, all crammed into a Volkswagen van."

Gladys even called Gordy, her boss at Motown, to come and look at the show. He agreed to attend just to see her perform. He arrived in time to catch the end of The Jackson 5 appearance. "A very derivative act," he later said. "I'm underwhelmed. Let them keep learning their trade on the chitlin' circuit."

He was referring to Apollo clone theaters across America that booked only black acts. On that chitlin' circuit, the Jackson brothers continued to find gigs—at least sometimes—but no stardom.

Over the years the accusation that Michael was a "midget" has been attributed to such popular acts as Sam and Dave or the Isley Brothers. It is not clear at this point who started the rumor, but word

Role model, Diana Ross

soon traveled the circuit that Michael was indeed a midget, and that Papa Joe was palming him off on audiences as a child.

In spite of Gladys Knight's promotion, Gordy at Motown sent word that "ol' Joe could take his boys and shove them where the sun don't shine." But another producer, Gordon Keith, agreed to sign the boys to his Steeltown label.

In April of 1968, their record, "Big Boy," was heard over WWCA radio in Indiana. "It didn't set the world on fire," Joe later recalled, "but it sold some copies."

Bypassing Gordy, Gladys Knight and performer Bobby Taylor got Ralph Seltzer, also a producer at Motown, to grant Joe's talented sons an audition in Detroit, not only headquarters of the U.S. automobile industry, but the home of Motown Records. In this unlikely setting, the studio was turning out hit records for Marvin Gaye, Stevie Wonder, and, of course, The Supremes with Diana Ross.

11

If Katherine became jubilant at the sound of Heaven, Joe responded in equal fashion to the word "Motown." It was not only the hottest record label in America, but evoked just how far a black entertainer could advance in show business. Joe once told Berry Gordy Jr.: "To me, Motown means that a black man can live in a fancy mansion with white servants, have money in his pocket, a hot pussy in his bed, and three big cars in the garage. It also means that my sons might one day have the name recognition of Frank Sinatra, Bing Crosby, and Dinah Shore."

Michael remembered "shakin' like a leaf in the wind" when he was brought before Seltzer to perform at the same sound studio where The Supremes, Stevie Wonder, and The Four Tops had scored big. After the band's performance of several songs was filmed, Seltzer thanked the boys for coming and shook Joe's hand. "We'll call you," he said, making it sound like a dismissal. Seltzer wasn't going to commit himself until he got the tape to Gordy.

Gordy was "forced" to sit through the film. At its end, he immediately instructed his staff to "sign them up. That little Michael's going to be a big star. *Bigtime*, that is."

When Gordy signed The Jackson 5, Michael was only ten years old. "But he had as much talent as Sammy Davis Jr., and Sammy boy was about as good as it gets," Gordy said. "In time, Michael will be even bigger than Sammy."

Thanks to earnings from their road trips, the Jackson family finally had a phone to receive the call from Seltzer, telling them to "get your asses back to Detroit," where boilerplate contracts awaited The Jackson 5. Without reading it, Joe signed for his sons on March 11, 1969. Gordy himself had bought out The Jackson 5 contract from Steeltown Records for a small amount of money. Gordon Keith later referred to the settlement as "peanuts."

If Joe had read the contract he'd signed, he would have learned that his boys would be getting a royalty of only 2.7 percent, the industry low.

Gordy mandated that, for the purposes of PR and media, he wanted it to be broadcast that The Jackson 5 had been discovered not by Gladys Knight but by Diana Ross. Ross had just achieved her 12th Number One hit for Motown, and was "hot." Already famous, Ross would, in time, become the best-selling female vocalist in music history. As such, her fictitious involvement in their "discovery" would add an attention-getting boost to Motown's introduction of The Jackson 5.

Michael idolized Ross. "She moves on stage like a panther and when she smiles her teeth shine like diamonds," he said. Before meeting her, he changed his clothing five times before arriving at a Christmas party at the Gordy mansion in Detroit. Gordy had booked the Jackson brothers to entertain his star-studded party held at this million-dollar residence with its marble floors and Grecian columns. Actually, at the time of the party, the house no longer functioned as Gordy's main residence, as he'd moved to Los Angeles where he was deeply involved in a romance with Ross.

In her white silk gown, with sparkling diamond earrings, Ross made her appearance before the Jackson brothers. She was truly "The Supreme" of The Supremes.

She immediately gravitated to Michael, sensing he was the star of the family. "Cute boys are so delicious," she said, bending down to plant a kiss on Michael's cheek.

"I'll never wash my face again, Miss Ross," he told her.

"I insist on most people calling me Miss Ross," she told him. "But to you, it's Diana."

"Yes, Miss Ross."

"As Humphrey Bogart told Claude Rains in *Casablanca*, I think this is going to be the beginning of a beautiful friendship."

"Who is Humphrey Bogart?"

"Bogie?" she asked in astonishment. "You've never heard of him? Kid, I've got to take you under my wing. You've got a lot to learn."

For the early part of the evening, Michael followed Ross around the mansion. He was shown a portrait Gordy had commissioned of himself as Napoleon, dressed in full military regalia.

The Jackson brothers, with Michael front and center

She felt uncomfortable with this young boy because of his constant stares. "He was soaking up my every move like a sponge with his wide eyes," she later said. Finally, she pinched his cheek aggressively, nicknaming him "saucer eyes."

Wandering through Gordy's mansion, Jackie was also awed. "I'm sure the Queen of England doesn't live in such a big place. Out back was a golf course. There was also an indoor swimming pool. I'd heard rumors about nekked swim parties. I was scared shitless. All the big Motown stars were there that night to hear us. And here we were. So many little black brothers singing the same songs these dudes had already made famous."

Miss Ross

The night was a success as the Jackson brothers performed before such Motown pros as Smokey Robinson and The Temptations. Joe later told Katherine, "I think these high-ridin' daddies were just a bit nervous hearing my boys for the first time. Maybe jealous, as they witnessed first-hand tomorrow's competition."

While the careers of the Jackson brothers were being launched, there was trouble brewing in the family, if published reports are to be believed. In 1994, Simon & Schuster published *Unauthorized*, a book about Michael Jackson by biographer Christopher Andersen, whose other works include *Madonna Unauthorized* and *Jagger Unauthorized*.

In this shocker, which we assumed was vetted by S&S's attorneys for libel, appears this quotation: "While La Toya lay shivering next to Rebbie in bed, Joe would, according to La Toya, climb in with them."

Around the time Ross was introducing the brothers in Detroit, Andersen quotes La Toya as claiming that her father molested her and her older sister, Rebbie. "My father was like an animal," La Toya allegedly said. "I was ten or eleven at the time," the quote continues. "He'd say dirty things and touch my body inside my clothes. And I had to touch him in certain places."

The older sister, Rebbie, as well as family members, have denied these accusations. On the surface, they are libelous. But no charges were ever brought against Joe, and he never sued Andersen or S&S for libel.

As serious as these charges are, there were even more explosive accusations that followed.

At the time of Michael's sham marriage to Lisa Marie Presley, his publicist, Bob Jones, had to deal not only with that make-believe union but with another story that a newspaper tabloid was set to reveal. A reporter had come upon charges that Joe also molested Michael when he was a small child. Jones categorically denied such charges and was able to suppress the story, even though accusations were aired over late-night talk radio.

Of course, Jones would have no way of knowing whether these accusations of molestation were true or not. In his book, *Michael Jackson: The Man Behind the Mask*, Jones did report on a confrontation he had with Michael.

He quotes the singer as saying, "How do you know that thing with Joseph never happened?" A valid question, of course. Not getting a straight answer from Michael, Jones asked himself a question: "Was he telling me the story was true? He certainly acted in a manner that wouldn't confirm or deny."

Jones, who knew Joe Jackson, found the molestation charges "hard to believe."

But the rumors persisted. Some pop psychologists in talk shows have pointed out that child molesters in case studies were often the victims of molestation in their youths. Like many other episodes in Michael's life, these molestation charges, including those from La Toya, remain a mystery.

No sooner had these charges that Joe molested Michael been suppressed than yet another shocking story emerged. Whether true or not, the Jackson family could be counted on by tabloids for a *scandal du jour*. Although much has been written about the family in "Second Coming headlines," some of the most explosive stories were never printed.

Also around the time of his marriage to Lisa Marie, there were allegations floating around that as a pre-pubescent, Michael was "pimped" to pedophiles within the record industry as a means of promoting the advance of The Jackson 5. There is no evidence that this is true but the rumors—some of them quite convincing—still persist.

To our knowledge, the only person who tried to sell such a story was a sleazy record producer we'll call John Stoffer, who worked the Detroit music industry for some twenty years. He approached the *National Enquirer* with a very detailed account of how a nine-year-old Michael was allegedly delivered to his hotel room in Detroit. His account didn't specify who made the delivery.

For a fee of ten thousand dollars, Stoffer was willing to tell all. In his report, he gave a very detailed and specific account of how he'd allegedly sodomized young Michael. "The boy cried through the ordeal and even bled," Stoffer claimed. "But I liked that. You see, I'm quite small down there. I used to be basically straight, but several women laughed at the size of my organ. I turned to young boys—very young—because I achieved great satisfaction in penetrating their tight, virgin butts. Michael was no exception. He was real tight. When I saw the pain I was causing him, it goaded me on and made me feel like more of a man."

Although Stoffer offered times, dates, and places that checked out, his charges could not be proven. The staff at *The Enquirer* decided not to publish the scoop, considering it too undocumented for publication. However, Stoffer did help promote and publicize The Jackson 5 and was instrumental in getting radio stations to play the group's records. In his dossier, Stoffer said that Michael was "delivered" to him on three different occasions, and that "each time the boy cried when he was penetrated."

A member of the *Enquirer* staff said, "We've published more stories about Michael Jackson than about any other modern celebrity, enough for our own book about the star called *Freak!* But what we've published is only a grain of sand on the beach. *The Enquirer* has been approached countless times by people trying to sell stories about Jacko. Some of them were obvious frauds. Others were quite convincing, but too shocking even for the *Enquirer*. Incidentally, I no longer work there."

On the road, traveling from "blood bucket" to "blood bucket," Michael learned about sex from his father. It wasn't exactly a healthy introduction.

Joe was a known womanizer. With Katherine safely tucked away at home, he could indulge his passions with other women, often quite young ones. Many women found him attractive, and he did possess sexual charisma.

Joe often flaunted his dates in front of his boys, sometimes bringing them back to his sons' bedrooms where the young women could give "my boys baby kisses and tuck them in for the night." Whenever that happened, Michael would turn over and bury his head in the pillow so he wouldn't have to kiss "one of Joe's whores." The other brothers were only too willing to be kissed on their mouths.

When the brothers stopped playing the honky-tonks, they were booked into black theaters as opening acts for performers who included James Brown, The Temptations, and Gladys Knight and The Pips. The Jackson 5 appeared in theaters from Boston to Kansas City, and from Washington, D.C., to Tucson.

Motown stardom wasn't forthcoming as month dragged into endless months. Gordy just wasn't pleased with any sound The Jackson 5 recorded. One song—a rip-off of The Temptations—was recorded forty times with no satisfaction. The boys still lived in Gary, whose streets were giving way to the violence of an increasingly powerful drug culture. One night two thieves cornered Joe staggering home in the early hours. Thugs hit him over the head, removing the fifty dollars he carried in his wallet.

In Gordy's bank vault rested the contract that Joe had signed without reading it. Motown's chief honcho was now ready to start exercising the options granted to him. He decided the time had come to order the Jackson brothers to Los Angeles, where they would be directed to start recording at Motown's new studio. Gordy told Ross, "If Jackson had read the fucking contract, he would have found that I owned his gold teeth and the air the Jackson boys breathe. The only one in the group that's got any talent is the midget." This was an obvious reference to Michael. "That one's gonna set the world on fire. Sooner than later."

In a large van—made in Detroit, of course—Joe drove to California carrying Johnny Jackson (no relation), the group's drummer, and Ronny

Rancifer, the keyboardist. Michael, along with three of his brothers, were given economy class air tickets to Los Angeles.

Along with eight-year-old Randy, the Jackson sisters as well as Katherine were left behind in Gary until Joe "could get the lay of the land," in Gordy's words. Later, a Motown executive in Los Angeles privately said, "California wouldn't be the only lay that Joe was scoping out."

As the plane flew over America's heartland, Michael was only ten years old with a birthday fast approaching.

On a smog-shrouded morning in Los Angeles—August 9, 1969 to be exact—Michael and his brothers landed in Los Angeles. On the way into town from the airport, Michael looked in awe at all the fast-moving cars, the palm trees, the oranges, the grand mansions. His eyes widened as he told Jermaine: "I have truly found Oz. No harm will ever come to me here."

One of Gordy's assistants delivered the boys not to a mansion but to a "hot bed" hotel on Santa Monica Boulevard, which was teeming with hookers, both male and female. Michael was given a room to share with Jermaine and Marlon. On the way to the dump, he heard through the paper-thin walls one woman telling someone: "That's twisted!"

In five weeks Gordy ordered that the boys be moved to another seedy address, the Hollywood Motel, which stood across from the famous Hollywood High, which so many children of stars had attended. By the late 1960s, the neighborhood had deteriorated. Drug pushers had moved in along with pimps recruiting the best-looking boys and girls to work as prostitutes. In a back alley, Michael spotted a blue-jeaned boy of sixteen or so standing against a wall while a balding, late middle-aged man performed fellatio on him.

It was while living at the Hollywood Motel that Michael began his famous practice of wearing sunglasses, even at night. "It's best to keep shaded day and night," he told Marlon. "That way no one can see the whites of your eyes. What you're really thinking. With sunglasses, you can hide from the world."

The boys worked almost constantly in Motown recording studios, although their songs still didn't please Gordy. On their first weekend off, Joe drove his sons to Disneyland. Michael fell under the spell of The Magic Kingdom. Joe laughed when Michael vowed that he was going to make so much money one day that he'd create a Disneyland just for his own pleasure.

On a command from Gordy, Joe drove his boys to the home in the Hollywood Hills where Diana Ross was living until Gordy could arrange for more luxurious digs in Beverly Hills—"a residence that is more fitting for a star of your magnitude."

As the boys sat in awe within Ross's living room, Gordy gave them the good news. "I know I haven't really liked anything you've recorded so far. But

17

hang in there. I'm gonna make you black brothers the greatest thing since shit on a stick."

Gordy was a genius in sensing the gap in American culture that the Jackson brothers could fill. As British critic Simon Frith put it: "What Gordy realized was that out there was a generation of black kids with money to spend and feet to dance and walls to hang pictures on. There had never been soul idols for clean-living black teens before, only sports figures and Martin Luther King Jr. Motown was going to give these kids idols and music and posters and fan magazines and T-shirts and TV shows and everything else."

At her home in the Hollywood Hills, Ross made a more spectacular appearance before Michael than she had at Gordy's Detroit mansion.

Michael would always remember her outfit, a black bolero jacket, a purple-colored lace blouse, and skin-tight toreador pants, along with towering stiletto high heels still known at the time as "Joan Crawford fuck-me shoes."

He compared her to a "Black Venus," whereas Jermaine told his brothers, "I got a hard-on that lasted for three days and nights."

Michael read that "the sensational eight-year-old Michael Jackson would be featured." "Miss Ross," he said. "There's a mistake. My age is given wrong here. On August 29, I'll be eleven years old."

As her surprise, Ross told the Jackson brothers that she was going to present them at the famous disco of the moment, Daisy, on North Rodeo Drive in Beverly Hills, the nighttime stamping grounds of stars that ranged from Mia Farrow to Peter Lawford. Ross handed Michael an invitation she'd sent out to *tout* Hollywood to attend the gala on the night of August 11, 1969.

"As an eight-year-old, you'll be even more of a sensation," Gordy said. "This is

Michael, aged 16

show business, kid. It's all about image. The press will think you're a child prodigy like Mozart."

"Darling," Ross told the impressionable boy, "a certain liberty must be taken with the truth. It's not exactly a lie. It's just a mask to wear. Everybody in Hollywood uses a mask to deceive the world. You'll get the hang of it. One day you'll be deceiving the world like a pro."

In addition to being a great entertainer, Ross could have made a decent living as a prophet.

"Speaking of images, kid," Gordy told Michael. "Forget all that crap about you little studs being discovered by Gladys Knight. What a pip! Forget Bobby Taylor. That dude's history. From now on, it was Diana Ross who discovered you. Chalk that one up for the history books."

By the official count, 312 "intimate" friends of Ross crowded into the chic disco cum private club known as Daisy. The fire department had posted a warning, allowing the club to hold only 250 patrons at one time. It was rumored that Frank Sinatra even slipped in that night unnoticed, although other reports placed him in New York.

Exactly at ten o'clock in their Sherwood Forest green suede boots with forest green vests, the "Jackson brothers looked like dancing black faggots as they zip-a-dee-do-dah-ed on stage," a stoned writer from *Rolling Stone* said privately. The audience of show biz veterans went wild in their enthusiasm.

The most unlikely guest in the audience was Charlton Heston, who would later become a friend of Michael in a case of "the odd couple." Heston, an advocate of "a gun in every home," later claimed that, "I was awed by their performance. The Jacksons project a squeaky clean image. They were making their debut at a time that rock-and-roll reigned supreme. All the hippies were taking drugs but the Jacksons proved there was hope for American youth yet. In my opinion, The Jackson 5 can be an antidote to all the poisonous shit going on."

As the chic crowd milled about after the show, Ross became a one-woman public relations factory for the Jackson brothers, especially for Michael, who was introduced as "the sweet one."

"Jermaine is the sexy one," she claimed.

In front of one woman from a Los Angeles magazine, Ross ran her hand through Michael's Afro. "Don't you just adore it?" she asked.

The greatest accolade came from a Hollywood newspaper which proclaimed: "We predict The Jackson 5, especially pint-sized Michael, will dominate popular music in the 70s."

"Whatever it took to get the song done right, he was willing to go the distance. And that was impressive, since he was still just a little kid."

--Hal Davis

"He spends a lot of time, too much by himself. I try to get him out. I rented a boat and took my children and Michael out on a cruise. Michael has a lot of people around him, but he's very afraid. I don't know why. I think it came from his early days."

--Diana Ross

"Just the other day, you were a 9-year-old kid auditioning for me, and now here you are, the greatest entertainer in the world. Here you are the greatest entertainer in the world, presenting me with an award. Michael, Michael, I believed in you when you were nine. I believe in you now. And I will never stop believing in you."

--Berry Gordy at the *Jackson Family Honors*

"When I see him dance and sing, it touches me, like a spirit; it moves me inside, sort of like the Holy Ghost. But it's more than singing and dancing; he manages to touch your soul."

--Isaiah Thomas

"Michael Jackson loves putting out the charity singles because they support his no. 1 charity in the world—himself."

--Richard Johnson

"If Michael Jackson came in this room right now, there would be no one in this room who could not stop looking at him. As long as you've got that power, you're never damaged. He has that power over anybody. If people can't stop looking at you, you're so interesting to people, there's no way you can be damaged."

--Jermaine Dupri

Chapter Two

In just a few short weeks, as the first winds of autumn blew into Southern California, The Jackson 5 would make their TV debut on ABC's *Hollywood Palace*. When asked about her alleged "discovery" of the Jackson brothers, Ross told the press, "I don't mind letting the boys ride to fame on my skirttails."

Wanting money and glory for his sons, Joe demanded twelve-hour daily rehearsals. He controlled the group's every move, utterance, song number, and first press conference. "You've heard of stage mothers," said Gordy. "Joe was the granddad of all stage fathers. At times I got so mad at the fucker, I thought he'd descended directly from Hell." Gordy also claimed that he felt Joe wanted to isolate his sons from the outside world.

Gordy wanted to launch the boys with a hit record, and Joe was determined to see that the Motown honcho got his wish.

Gladys Knight was not credited as the eagle eye who'd first spotted the talent of the Jackson brothers. She also saw a potential hit song, "I Want to Be Free," taken away from her by Gordy and reshaped for The Jackson 5. It was later retitled, "I Want You Back."

"I was angry," Knight recalled. "Really angry. I felt I'd become chopped liver at Motown. Ah, show business! It's all in the game."

Gladys Knight and The Pips had been added to the Motown "stable of Soul" in 1966. From Atlanta, they scored many hits and stayed with Motown for seven years. Ironically, their biggest hit, "Midnight Train to Georgia," would come after the group bolted from Motown and signed with Buddha.

Although he hadn't officially moved out of Detroit, Gordy had purchased a home from Tommy Smothers, also in the Hollywood Hills. That way, he could slip away for nights spent in the arms of Ross, who lived nearby.

One night as he was watching Michael rehearse with his brothers, Gordy told Joe: "Michael's just a kid but he sings James Brown's 'I Got the Feelin' with such feeling, inspiration, and pain. It's like he's experienced everything he's singing about, even though he's too young to know about adult emotions. Brown, on the other hand, knows all emotions."

That night, Gordy decided that Michael needed a lot more polish. At dinner the producer had noticed Michael still eating with his hands instead of using a knife and fork. "The kid is going to be a star," he told Joe. "To achieve that goal, he's gotta learn to behave like a star. I'm moving him in with Diana. He can watch what she does. Her polish and refinement will rub off on the boy. I just know it."

Although Katherine objected, Joe moved Michael into Ross's Hollywood Hills home. The self-absorbed diva had little time for a growing boy, as she was completely involved in her own career.

Miss Ross

She was at a pivotal point, breaking away from The Supremes to become a solo performer.

Katherine's primary objection involved having her impressionable young son live in the same household where Ross was carrying on "a tumultuous Ava Gardner/Frank Sinatra type of affair." Gordy was married at the time.

The first night Michael spent in Ross's house, she warned him about the dangers of show business. "I think you're going to make it in show business— and make it big. For a while, fans will build you up—even the media. But there's a dark side to all of this. The press likes to build up people only to tear them down. Show business brings many things, fame and fortune among them. But it also exposes you to the world. Your darkest secrets might end up one day on the front page of some tabloid. Show business can hurt you, it can devastate you. It can become your worst nightmare. Fame carries such a terrible price that I sometimes wonder if it's worth it."

In her warning to Michael, Ross might have been seeing a vision of her own future. In the years to come, it became popular to bash her in the press. Both her persona and her music were trashed. She was often referred to even in print as a "bitch." Many of her black fans attacked her for "losing her blackness" by marrying white men. In the words of a security guard at Chi-Chiz, a black men's gay bar on Christopher Street in New York City, "There are

22

three subjects so controversial, you should never, ever bring them up: Religion, politics, and Diana Ross."

Michael listened politely to his mentor, perhaps not truly believing her. Later he'd say, "To me, performing is like a dream come true. You live in grand mansions. You're driven around in fancy cars. You can buy all the clothes you want. You never have to go hungry again. No more settling for a bowl of tomato soup with a sweet roll for a meal. How can show business harm you? It can only reward you. As for the press, I think those guys will find me adorable. After all, I'm sorta cute. Besides, I have no dark secrets that would make tabloid headlines."

After a night spent in Ross's guest bedroom, Michael woke up refreshed and eager to get on with his career. Over breakfast, he told Ross, "I dreamed of a Neverland called California, never really knowing it existed. Maybe it was all a dream, like Oz." Once again, he compared California to Oz. "Now, this morning, my dream has come true."

Impatient to get to a recording studio, Ross patted his head after eating one scoop of low-fat cottage cheese and a dry piece of Melba toast. "Just you be careful that dream doesn't become a nightmare." As a final warning, she said, "And don't leave any doors and windows open. Stay in the house!"

Instead of "California Dreaming," most Hollywood celebrities at the time were obsessed with serial killings.

Ross herself seemed to live in fear and had stationed two security guards outside her home along with ferocious, man-eating guard dogs. The rich and famous of Hollywood, Bel Air, and Beverly Hills were also hiring body-guards. When the supply in Los Angeles was exhausted, many guards were flown in from as far away as Tennessee.

Sharon Tate and six of her guests had been slaughtered by the drug-crazed, Satan-worshipping "family" of a lunatic, Charles Manson, who origi-nally wanted to kill Doris Day and her son, Terry Melcher. Celebrities feared that other death squads in that drugged era would emulate the Manson family and also go on killing sprees, torturing and murdering victims. At every Hollywood party, the grisly tales of the murders were retold, even exaggerat-ed, with a vivid recounting of the tortures the victims were forced to endure before their slaughter.

"Imagine," actor Gregory Peck asked friends, "being forced to eat our genitals before dying."

Michael didn't listen to all this talk and felt no fear. "I feel California is the safest place in the world," he said. "I saw a lot of horrible things before coming here. Those terrible dives that Joe booked us into. Here the sun shines brightly on us. America's going to love us, especially me."

During his first week in Ross's home, Michael watched her rehearse

"Someday We'll Be Together," which would not only be her farewell song with The Supremes but would become a hit record.

Michael's first insight into heterosexual marriage had come from his own dysfunctional parents. In the Ross household, he learned about the rocky course of straight, off-the-record love affairs. When they weren't making love, Gordy and Ross were often fighting.

At Gordy's suggestion, her group was already being billed as Diana Ross and The Supremes instead of The Supremes. Under that label, the group with Ross as its lead singer had racked up at least a dozen hit records. Ross believed that she could do even better on her own.

Gordy and Ross had intense, often violent, arguments about the course of her career. He wanted her to be a crossover success, reaching more affluent audiences such as the largely white fans who flocked to hear big name entertainers in Las Vegas. She feared she'd lose her following of black devotees if she appeared to desert them. She also wondered about the future of The Supremes without her.

Perhaps Michael learned his lessons well . . . or not. He too would one day break from his brothers to pursue a solo career, and he, too, would be charged with deserting his black audiences in pursuit of pop—read that "white"—fans.

In the days ahead, little Michael hid behind draperies or behind a sofa as he watched Ross's every move performed before a full-length mirror. He was spying on her every gesture, her every subtle motion. She was the embodiment of feline grace. He listened for every note coming from her thin voice, and in time would incorporate every *oooh* into his own music.

"Michael was Eve Harrington to Diana's Margo Channing," Gordy later said. He was referring to the 1950 movie, *All About Eve*. In that film, Bette Davis played an aging actress, with Eve (Anne Baxter) waiting in the wings to go on stage in her place.

Michael was a fast learner. "He took the best of Diana Ross and the best of James Brown, and threw in every move Jackie Wilson ever made," Gordy recalled.

One day Smokey Robinson showed up at the Motown studios and watched the Jackson brothers perform. Having seen them on stage before, he was awed at how they'd improved and perfected their act since coming to California. In his autobiography, *Smokey—Inside My Life*, published in 1989, he wrote that Michael was the biggest talent since Ross—"and the accompaniment of his brothers, bad-ass singers and dancers themselves," only sweetened the stew pot.

On the few nights Ross was ever alone with Michael, she discussed her career concerns with him, especially about breaking from The Supremes. Even though he was at a tender age, she sensed he had a "gut instinct" about show business. After urging her to perform solo, he told her to "Go, girl go!" And she did.

On October 18, 1969, on *Hollywood Palace*, she introduced The Jackson 5 to America. Much of black America tuned in. So did millions of white Americans—potential new fans—hearing The Jackson 5 for the first time. A soul ballad, "Can You Remember?," was undistinguished. But when Michael sang, "Oooh, baby, give me one more chance," a line

The Jackson 5

from "I Want You Back," he went over big. At long last, black teenagers in America had someone to identify with in an era of black pride. "The kids identified with them not as stars, but as contemporaries fulfilling their own fantasies of stardom," said Steve Manning, a long-time Jackson family retainer.

When the song was released as a single, it climbed slowly up the charts, becoming number one in the nation by January of 1970, when it topped "Raindrops Keep Falling on My Head" on *Billboard* charts.

"'I Want You Back' took off like an aural steamroller," wrote Stewart Reagan. "It took off like a rocket and exploded with a nervous, frenetic pace that wouldn't let up. Its energy and freshness was made irresistible by the desperate passion of Michael's vocal. Here was a boy screaming for mercy as if his life depended on it. It reached the parts other records couldn't reach."

At first The Jackson 5 appealed to prepubescent jumpers and screamers.

Rolling Stone joined in high praise for Michael after the release of "I Want You Back," still considered one of his greatest records. "Catalyzed by a red hot performance from ten-year-old Michael," a critic wrote, "the record explodes off the turntable with an intricate Sly-influenced arrangement featuring some of the toughest bass, drum, piano, guitar playing on any soul record anywhere."

All the Jackson brothers, especially Michael, owe a debt to Freddie Perren, a writer-producer who worked on such hits as "I Will Survive,"

Sammy Davis Jr.

recorded by Gloria Gaynor. Perren produced and co-wrote that mega-seller, "I Want You Back." Assisting him to make pop music history for the Jacksons were his partners, Deke Richards and Fonce Mizell. Of course, Berry Gordy was also looking over the shoulders of his creative team, who were scoring one pop single hit after another for the Jacksons in the early 70s. The team that produced these early Jackson hits was nicknamed "The Corporation."

Sammy Davis Jr., whom Michael had always idolized, was also a host on *Hollywood Palace* that night, and Michael met him there for the first time.

Davis had already heard of the boy's prodigious talent, which evoked his own memories as a child entering show business when he was far too young.

"Did anyone ever tell you you have Shirley Temple dimples?" he asked Michael. Michael was dumbfounded at meeting Davis and couldn't immediately formulate an answer.

Davis invited the boy to his dressing room. Around Davis, Michael didn't have to talk . . . only listen.

"I paved the road for you, kid," Davis told him. "When I started out, I was told that a nigger could never make it big in show business, except on the chitlin' circuit. I crossed over and won over whitey. You can do the same. Of course, you'll always have the haters and hecklers in the audience. I face those nightly."

"But I want people to like me because of my talent, not judge me by the color of my skin," Michael said.

"A worthy ambition," Davis said. "Keep that thought."

At the end of their talk, there was a knock on Davis's door. It was the stage manager, announcing the arrival of the performer's date for the evening. Michael stepped aside as a shapely young woman, who evoked Marilyn Monroe, brushed past.

"One thing a crossover career means," Davis said, "is that after you've made it you can always fuck white. Which brings up the big question of the night: Are you gay?"

"If you mean homosexual, I am not!" Michael said adamantly. "I'm a Jehovah's Witness. Our religion is strongly opposed to any form of homosexuality. It is against God's teaching."

Davis laughed. "I didn't expect such an answer. Not in show business

26

where all of us guys, even the straight ones, get our dicks sucked from time to time. Even Sinatra told me he lets a gay stagehand occasionally cop his joint."

"Good night, Mr. Davis," Michael said. "An honor meeting you."

As Davis watched Michael rush off to join his brothers, he turned to the stage manager and said, "The kid's definitely gay, even if he don't know it yet."

As Michael departed, Davis called to him, "This is the last time I'm gonna share the stage with a scene-stealing, thirty-five-year-old midget. Try to upstage me, will you?"

When a startled Michael turned back, Davis smiled, claiming, "I was just joking!"

Only fifteen minutes earlier, Michael had kept dancing when Davis clearly wanted him off the stage. Davis practically had to take the boy by the nape of his neck and shove him out of the spotlight.

There would always remain a friendly rivalry between Davis and Michael, but they became friends of a sort.

In an interview with *People Extra*, Davis said of Michael: "He takes a step that you've been doing and then by the time he switches it around, you don't even recognize it. There is nothing new about thrusting your hips out, but when he does that with quick moves, the high kick out and that slow back-up step he does, people say, 'Jeez, what is he doing?' And he never lays on a move long enough for you to figure it out. I'm sure if he worked with Nureyev or Baryshnikov, he would come close to that level. Can he tap dance? I don't know. But then again I'd hate to leave my dancing shoes in his vicinity."

In Davis's autobiography, *Why Me?*, he said: "Michael used to come by my house—'Can I borrow some of your tapes, Mr. D.?' And he'd go to my library and take what he wanted of the shows I'd done. Visiting me in Monte Carlo in July of '88, he said, 'Y'know, I stole some moves from you, the attitudes.' I'd known that. It's terribly flattering for the young to feel that way about you. Especially Michael, who I think is the ultimate professional. A lot of young performers have become multimillionaires on ten big records, but they don't know how to bow and get themselves off a stage. Everything Michael does on a stage, though, is exactly right."

After his boys appeared on *Hollywood Palace*, an angry Joe confronted Berry Gordy. "What is it with Ross?" he asked. "She introduced my boys as Michael Jackson and The Jackson 5. Michael is no more a star than any of my other sons. All my kids are stars. Jermaine one day will sell more records than Michael."

Gordy later asked Ross why she'd made such an introduction, virtually renaming the group. She said: "You've heard of Diana Ross and The Supremes? Now you've heard of Michael Jackson and The Jackson 5." She turned and walked away.

One night when Ross came home late, she was startled to hear the sound of her own voice. *Live.* She had to pause for one minute before she realized that wasn't her voice but that of Michael. She slowly slipped into the room where she rehearsed her music.

There in front of her full-length mirror was Michael dressed as herself in her red toreador pants and bolero jacket. He even wore her Joan Crawford fuck-me stiletto heels. He was singing in perfect imitation her "Rock-A-Bye Your Baby with a Dixie Melody," just as he'd heard it in 1966.

Ross walked over and abruptly cut off the music. Frightened, Michael turned around so fast he almost fell from his perch on those stiletto heels.

"Forget it, kid!" she said harshly. "There's room on this planet for only one Miss Ross." She stormed off toward her bedroom to call Gordy. "The kid's gotta go!" she shouted into the phone when she reached her lover.

In spite of this rejection, Michael was not to be deterred. In the years to come, he would continue to imitate Ross. When he became the chatelain of Neverland, he even insisted that his staff refer to him as "Miss Ross."

As the years went by, Michael began to rewrite the history of his stay at the home of Ross.

When he was in his late teens, he carried his imagination too far by suggesting that he had shacked up with Ross. "Diana Ross was my mother, my lover, and my sister—all combined in one amazing person." Mother, perhaps. Sister, perhaps. But not lover.

When Ross heard that, she was more amused than angry. "In his dreams!" was her only comment.

Gordy was shocked. "That's like Liberace claiming he had a long affair with Ava Gardner, and she told Twinkle-Toes that he was better in bed than Sinatra."

The story about a physical relationship between Michael and Ross is pure bunk. For starters, Ross is not a child molester. She never possessed any sexual interest in Michael, who was only eleven years old when he lived under the same roof with her. "He was just a cute kid I helped along the road to stardom," Ross said—and accurately so.

Even though she has never publicly commented on Michael's sexuality, as a very hip woman she must have known for years where Michael's inclinations lay.

Ross had a more believable story to tell

Motown Records'
Berry Gordy, Jr.

28

years later. "I looked at this little kid whirling around up there on stage, and I thought I was looking at myself. I couldn't believe it. I saw so much of myself as a child in Michael. He was performing all the time. That's the way I was. He could be my son."

After years of struggle, fame at last came to The Jackson 5. By December of 1969, the brothers made their debut album, trading once again on the fame of their sponsor, Diana Ross. Released in time for the Christmas buying market that year, the album was called *Diana Ross Presents The Jackson 5*, although she'd wanted to call it, *Diana Ross Presents Michael Jackson and The Jackson 5*. The album became the fastest-selling group record in the history of Motown.

To prick this promotional balloon, a critic for *Rolling Stone* wrote: "Given any kind of decent material at all, The Jackson 5 should be able to give us many years of good tight music. Who's this 'Diana Ross' anyway?"

The opening sounds of "Zip A Dee Doo Dah" on their first album were played around the world. James Barker, a business traveler, remembered hearing the song at Heathrow Airport in London. When he got off the plane in Lagos, Nigeria, the same "Dee Doo Dah" sounds were heard. "My God," Barker said, "this Michael Jackson was just a kid and he could deliver a song with the evocative emotion of Marvin Gaye."

Barker, among millions of others, sensed what was happening. In spite of his age, the voice of Michael Jackson, a magnificent instrument, was destined to become an icon of pop music in the 1970s. Long before the release of his bestseller album, *Thriller*, Michael became a powerhouse at Motown, turning out some of its most memorable music. The Jackson 5 helped create a type of music called "bubblegum soul." Other "bubblegummers" included their white rivals, the Osmond Brothers, and the Partridge Family with David Cassidy and his stepmother, Shirley Jones.

While making *Diana Ross Presents The Jackson 5*, the entire Jackson family moved into a house that Gordy had leased for the brood at 1601 Queens Road in Los Angeles. Katherine and the other children arrived from Gary to hook up with family members. Ross personally drove Michael to his new home and said a brief "hello" to Katherine, who flown to Los Angeles with La Toya, Janet, and young Randy.

For Katherine, it was her first plane ride and her first palm tree. She hugged Michael to her breast. "With your real mother now in California, you will no longer need a substitute mother like Miss Ross. There's nothing like the real thing."

Less than two weeks before Christmas, Michael and his brother appeared on *The Ed Sullivan Show* singing not only "I Want You Back" but "Can You Remember?" It wasn't quite the sensation that Elvis Presley and The Beatles created. But all eyes were on Michael that night, which was fortunate because his brothers performed awkwardly—Jermaine, for example, warbling off-key. At his TV set, Berry Gordy, along with sixty million Americans, watched the program with avid interest. He later said, "Their tempo was off. I was devastated." As always, Gordy was being too much of a perfectionist. The public ate it up, heralding the arrival of a phenomenal new group.

Gordy demanded that the Jacksons come up with a second hit, and that's what he got when Michael and his brothers recorded "ABC." Michael's perfect voice sang, "Shake it, shake it, baby." Michael knew the moment he heard the lyrics that "ABC" was going to be another hit. Gordy was skeptical. Michael turned out to be right.

On February 24, 1970, "ABC" was released. The song featured a rapid and driving bass line underneath a shrill but dynamic vocal by Michael. Amazingly, he could be surprisingly convincing when he sang about love, even though sounding like a *castrato*.

In less than two months, it had knocked The Beatles' song, "Let It Be," off the top of the chart. Bubblegum boys or not, The Jackson 5 sold nearly 2½ million recordings of that solo. The third recording of the Jackson boys sold nearly two million copies.

In Las Vegas when he heard all three songs, Frank Sinatra was livid.

"Teenybopper shit!" he proclaimed in anger, forgetting that in the early 40s, he, too, was a favorite of bobbysoxers.

From his suite, Sinatra asked two of his henchmen, "What do I think of Michael Jackson? I'll tell you: he's a God damn faggot pickaninny!"

When he heard of that insult from Sinatra, Michael shot back:

"Sinatra's very overrated. I just don't understand why he has fans. He might be a living legend, but it's not because of his voice, 'cause he's not much of a singer. When was the last time he had a hit? Back in 1942?"

By June, the third solo of The Jackson 5, "The Love You Save," broke out at the top of the *Billboard* chart, knocking out The Beatles with their "The Long and Winding Road."

Jacksonmania swept America. With success came bookings all over the country, beginning with their first concert appearance on May 2, 1970 in Philadelphia. "My God," one policeman said, "you'd think Elvis has arrived in town with The Beatles as his back-up. I've never seen such pandemonium. I rescued one girl, no more than thirteen, who was almost trampled to death."

The same hysteria greeted the Jackson brothers wherever they went. In one case, police foiled the plot of some overeager girls to rush the stage and strip the brothers "buck-assed naked." At some of their more unruly concerts, fans disrupted the performance. One night, a loud-voice teenage girl shouted: "Whip out your big black dicks!"

With the release of their next album, also called *ABC*, The Jackson 5 continued the tour. The hysteria mounted. Michael tried to get used to screaming fans, the flashing dome lights, the sirens wailing, and limousines pushing forward into dense crowds. But he couldn't quite seem to adjust. His brothers adapted but he didn't, often breaking into tears or else sobbing screams when he felt he was going to be killed by the mobs.

In contrast, the older brothers enjoyed the adulation, especially from hysterical female fans eager to get laid by one of the brothers. "We are big-time. We'll be on top forever. Legends in the making, and pussy lined up from New York to California, all a man would ever want. Islamic men who sacrifice themselves for Allah are promised forty virgins in Heaven. Hell, man, that many virgins are available to each of us in every town." This quote, most often attributed to Jermaine, may be apocryphal.

When the neighbors got a petition together complaining about the noise from the Jackson's Queen Road house, Gordy moved them to an ugly but comfortable motel-like house on Bowmont Drive. The stucco house rested on stilts and was filled with chocolate brown shag carpeting and plastic furniture in neon colors of green and pink.

Even though reunited under one roof with his family again, Michael years later admitted the depth of his loneliness. "I used to sit in my room and cry. It was so hard to make friends. I was cut off from kids my own age, except for my brothers and sisters. They never had the same interests that I did. I had a lot of feelings in me that I could never talk about. I didn't even understand some of my own yearnings. I wanted to talk about them with someone understanding. I certainly couldn't go to my father. He would understand nothing, maybe even beat me up if I confided too much. I loved my mother but she was bound by her faith, one of the most faithful of the Jehovah's Witnesses. If I told her things, she might think the Devil had taken over my soul."

"An understanding heart" was on the way. When both Katherine and Joe were out of the house late one afternoon, Michael was sitting alone in his bedroom staring vacantly out the window.

All of a sudden, a Lincoln Executive limousine pulled into the driveway of the Jackson home. A pink-uniformed chauffeur in black boots with a gold hat got out from behind the wheel to open the door

Frank Sinatra, bobbysoxer favorite of the 40s.

31

for the passenger in the rear. It was the next door neighbor, Liberace, at the time one of the world's most famous entertainers. Stepping out of the limousine, he was a vision in white silk lamé. In the foyer, he announced to a Jackson household servant that he'd arrived to "see the wee one."

Michael rushed downstairs to meet one of his show biz idols. But Katherine didn't trust the effeminate, flamboyant entertainer alone with her son, although she was eventually persuaded to leave them together in the living room.

Holding Michael's hand, Liberace told the young boy that he couldn't stay as he was already late for a party at the home of Rock Hudson. He giggled at the thought of it. "I'll probably be asked to play an organ or two tonight." He giggled away, then flashed a wide grin. Michael was almost overcome by the heavy intoxicating smell of Liberace's perfume.

He invited Michael to come to dinner next week to "meet a special friend—she's more outrageous than *moi*," he said, "if that's possible." He jotted down Michael's phone number. "I'll call you to set up a night. Toodle-loo!" The performer sashayed out of the living room, descending toward the driveway where the dashingly handsome chauffeur already had the rear door open.

Michael could not contain himself with excitement waiting for the invitation to come through. He kept wondering who the special guest would be, figuring that Liberace by himself would be entertainment enough.

Knowing that Katherine would never let him attend a dinner party at Liberace's house, Michael kept the news of the invitation from his family. When Liberace called and set the date, Michael still remained mum. On the Tuesday night of the dinner, he pretended to have a headache and went to his bedroom early. But he slipped out of his room and walked down the street to the entertainer's house.

The young man who opened the door was the chauffeur, except this time he was attired in forest green slacks with a white shirt open to his six-pack waist. He introduced himself as Paul Richardson, and it is because of him, and his later revelations, that the world knows what transpired that night.

Emerging from the rear of the house was Liberace himself, wearing scarlet-colored lounging pajamas. To Michael, he extended a hand on which rested a large jewel-encrusted ring on each finger.

Before his special guest arrived, Liberace insisted on taking young Michael on a tour of the house. As he made his way toward the garden down a long hallway, Liberace pointed out the pieces of value, including a desk he claimed once adorned Versailles, the property of Louis XV. He also showed Michael his sumptuous bedroom. "The bed belonged to Rudolph Valentino. He was before your time. The great lover of the silent screen. Both of his wives were lesbians." Michael was impressed with the garden, particularly its large piano-shaped pool.

Back in the house, Michael had to go to the bathroom. Paul led the way. After carefully locking the door, Michael took in the chandelier-lit room, the walls covered with murals of naked men, some with excessively large genitalia.

Michael waited alone in the living room. Paul stood nearby ready to take the drink orders. Michael noticed the young man observing him closely. It was fifteen minutes before Liberace appeared again. "I had to change into something more spectacular," he said. "I called my guest, and she's wearing red. I decided to get rid of my own red and wear these champagne-colored lounging pajamas. That way, I'll blend in." Michael couldn't help but notice that the entire room was in champagne colors.

Liberace pounced on the sofa next to Michael, and took the boy's hand. "First, let me tell you that I love your music. You're gonna be a big star. Not as big as me, darling. But real big."

"Thank you, sir." Michael checked out the ruffled silk. "You look great!"

"Thanks," Liberace said. "After Elvis came along, I have to appear more outlandish than ever, topping him every time. Of course, my onstage outfits are far more fabulous. I have a different outfit designed every month because they tarnish so fast. I do, however, remove the diamond buttons from suit to suit."

Liberace

"When I start having stage clothes designed for me, I'll stick to sequins," Michael said. "Right now Katherine buys for my brothers and me off the rack."

Liberace looked over at Paul and winked lasciviously. "A Scotch for me and a Shirley Temple for Michael." When Paul came back, Liberace was lamenting about how many charity events he was asked to play at every week. "The same will happen to you," he predicted to Michael. "Don't do any. Never... but never associate yourself with some kind of disease."

Liberace had more advice. "Never take sides in anything, especially politics. If you take sides, you'll alienate large segments of your audience. No one knows if I'm a Republican or Democrat. Come to think of it, I don't know that myself."

"I'll remember that, sir."

"Just call me Cuddles, dear boy."

At that point the doorbell rang, and Paul went to answer it. Michael could hear the sound of male voices, but only a lady was ushered into the living room. He stared in awe as a bejeweled Mae West in a floor-length red gown with a white sable coat pranced in. "Liberace invited me to come up and see him sometime," West said, just assuming Michael knew who she was. "Tonight I'm here to check out Liberace's gold organ." Liberace was at her feet kissing a white-gloved hand. Taking note for the first time just how young Michael was, she issued a command. "Kid, write down everything I say tonight. When you grow up, read it. You'll understand it then."

As West seated herself in a winged armchair across from the two men, she carefully arranged herself. "I saw Liberace on one of his early TV shows and fell in love. When reporters asked me what I wanted for my birthday, I said Liberace. One day he shows up on my doorstep wearing a large red bow. 'Here I am!' he said. 'Your birthday present.'"

A dog ran into the room and headed for Michael where he proceeded to raise his leg and issue a squirt of piss. Liberace looked on, amused. "This is my favorite pet. A Lhasa Apso."

"I think he likes me," Michael said.

"I like you too," West cooed. "I caught your act on TV with that Ross creature. That one is a bit too uppity for her own good, but you were terrific."

Liberace seemed jealous that he was no longer the center of attention. Reclaiming the floor, he jumped up and headed for a 19th-century piano. "It once belonged to Frédéric Chopin." He sat down and played "Mad About the Boy" from Noël Coward's repertoire, beaming his famous smile at Michael.

When Paul signaled that the butler was serving dinner, Liberace took a bow. Michael applauded. West did not. "Tonight we're having dear ol' Mum's potato pancakes," Liberace said. "I made the rock Cornish game hen with cherry sauce myself. All these recipes are going to be in my new book, *Liberace Cooks!*"

"I'm not the domestic type," West said, rising to her feet. "The boudoir is where I show my expertise. How about you, kid?"

"I just sing and dance," Michael said, following Liberace and West into the dining room lit by three antique Venetian chandeliers, one of which depicted a series of faces, each fashioned from black glass, that resembled Aunt Jemima.

Before seating Michael and West, Liberace pointed out the K on his silverware. "The set once belonged to President John F. Kennedy."

Somehow West made a romantic link in her head. "You know, that Marilyn Monroe bitch–speak of the dead–stole her whole act from me. I was singing about diamonds before she was born."

Over dinner and champagne—Michael was allowed to have one glass of bubbly—Liberace, his eyes twinkling, leaned over toward West. "There's this one rumor I want to know about. Do you have African-American roots? Did one of your ancestors pass for white?"

"I've heard that one a million times," she said, smiling at Paul who hovered nearby. "I'm not black. The rumor probably started because of my affinity for black music." She leaned over and patted Michael's hand. "Black music is the best there is."

"My parents always had progressive racial attitudes," she said. "We once entertained Bert Williams—of course, he was famous. I was just a little gal when I realized that black people are just like us, only of a different color. I've always believed that white men should not exploit women, black people, or gays." She smiled at Liberace.

"I grew up listening to ragtime," she said, continuing her monologue. "Ragtime is certainly rooted in African music. I remember when the Cakewalk, created by blacks, was the rage of the nation." She leaned toward Michael again. "Let me give you some advice, kid. You should develop a distinctive walk on the stage."

Did Mae West inspire Michael's future Moonwalk?

"I was a champion of blacks before it became fashionable," she went on.

Mae West

"I fought to get Duke Ellington cast in *The Belle of the Nineties*. I even was seen dining alone with Louis Armstrong, my reputation be damned. When a black performer was injured in a car accident in Las Vegas, I intervened and got treatment for the poor soul in a whites-only facility."

When dessert arrived, West shooed it away, although Michael went in a big way for the baked Alaska.

West almost never drank alcohol except on this rare occasion. The champagne had made her tipsy. As the three of them settled into the living room, with Paul still hovering nearby, she provocatively asked Liberace: "Are you still against homosexuality like you said in that British court a decade ago?"

"Just because I wear fancy clothes and am a nonconformist, people always judge me," Liberace said.

"Let's cut out this horse manure," West said, "You're talking to your mama here. You're just as gay as those male chorines I cast in my play, *Drag*, way back when. Without you boys, I wouldn't have any fans left."

"You must understand, Mae, I'm trying to set a fine example before this impressionable young boy here."

He looked over at Michael. "You're just a little boy, and already I'm hearing rumors about you. Regardless of what the press writes about you, no matter how cancerous the innuendo, deny that you are a homosexual."

"Liberace's got a point," West chimed in. "I've spent years denying I'm a drag queen! Personally, I adore homosexuals. You might say I launched the gay movement by writing the first gay play. But, to me, homosexual sex is just a form of masturbation. A temporary relief of tension. No real satisfaction."

"Oh, Mae darling, if the boys could hear you say that," Liberace said. "They'd take away your crown as Queen of Sex."

"Not bloody likely, dearie," West said defensively. Ignoring Liberace, who seemed to have angered her, she focused once again on Michael. "Clean livin', kid, that's the answer, for a long career in show business. No drugs. Take an enema once or twice a day. There's putrid, poisonous matter in your body. I can't stand to take a shit that smells. Bad for my image. What if someone followed me into the crapper and it was all smelly? When you've cleaned yourself with an enema, and then you answer nature's call, your wastes are fresh – not putrid."

"Mae, are you trying to tell us your shit don't stink?" a drunken Liberace asked.

"It ain't Chanel Number 5," West said. "At its worst, perhaps the smell of beef stew."

"This has been a most enlightening evening for me," Michael said, "and I thank you for it. My parents might discover I'm missing, so I'd better be leaving. Miss West, meeting you and Mr. Liberace has been the grandest evening of my life. From now on, both of you in separate ways will be my role models."

"Thanks, dearie," West said. "The impersonators always do me."

"You couldn't have made a wiser choice than the two of us," Liberace said.

Michael, of course, never became another Liberace and certainly not another Mae West. But he passed his interest in West onto his younger sister, Janet, who in the future would deliver a brilliant impersonation of the fading star.

After his secret visit with two of the biggest legends in show business, it was back to work for Michael.

Michael's single, "Got to Be There," was released by Motown in 1970, following in the wake of the hit solo album by Donny Osmond, Michael's main competitor with young white girls. Michael later called it his "real break-through song; it was the one that said, 'I'm here to stay!'"

Even though some Motown brass, including Gordy himself, feared that the song would fail, it, like the previous three singles, zoomed to number one on the charts, staying there for five weeks. "Got to Be There" was a ballad, and had "tender soul," in the words of one reviewer. Gordy liked the record but feared it wasn't a sound the public wanted to hear coming from the throat of Michael.

Michael's solo debut sparked jealousy among his brothers, especially Jermaine. A love song, it sold some 1½ million copies. "It showed the world that Michael could do it on his own," Gordy said. "I felt he could be a big star just like Diana became when she broke from The Supremes. It must have sent a fright through his brothers, deflating their perpetual hard-ons." A month or so went by, but "Got to Be There" scored a bull's eye when *Cash Box* named it their number one hit.

One Motown executive claimed that "the Jackson brothers, especially that talented little Michael, in spite of his being a bit girlish, had become a meal ticket for Katherine and Papa Joe. He couldn't make it on his own as a musi-cian, but he was living like a fat cat off his sons. He didn't relax either. He wanted more and more, and pushed his sons even harder than he had done in Gary. Michael had been out there on that stage shaking his ass since he was five years old. He was deprived of a childhood. I'm sure the experience ruined his life, as subsequent scandals proved."

In 1972, Michael used this hit song as the title of his first ever album, "Got to Be There," which also included "Rockin' Robin" and "Ain't No Sunshine." Sales were a modest 355,000 albums, although Gordy at Motown had antici-pated a larger volume.

The Jackson 5 went on the road to promote their special sound and even broke attendance records at the Los Angeles Forum, selling almost 20,000 tickets. That night Michael did not endear himself to The Beatles, when he introduced "The Love You Save" as: "Here it is, the tune that knocked The Beatles out of number one." Even so, Michael and Paul McCartney would later become friends, then enemies.

Although their music was different, The Jackson 5 evoked The Beatles in the hysteria and pandemonium they caused on the road. One policeman in Los Angeles said, "The problem with The Jackson 5 was keeping them from being trampled to death. Kids pushed and shoved. If one of them fell to the ground, they were practically crushed under foot."

When The Jackson 5 stayed at a hotel, the manager had to double securi-ty. Young girls or even young women tried to break into their bedrooms, using any ruse or disguise. Often these impressionable fans pretended to be maids. Even the hotel's legitimate maids would steal the jockey shorts of the boys, not necessarily for themselves but to sell to fetish collectors. If a piss stain or a "skid mark" remained on the underwear, so much the better.

The Jackson 5 launched 1971 with a hit single, "Mama's Pearl," a return to bubblegum. Michael was extremely disappointed that after four number one hits, their latest release peaked at number two. Gordy told the brothers, "This is predictable. There's always next time."

Early in the year, the brothers made a sentimental visit back to Gary. Fans lined the streets of their old neighborhood, as their black limousine pulled up at 2300 Jackson Street, a thoroughfare which had carried that name long before the Jackson family ever made the address famous. After all the grand mansions they'd seen, their family home looked like a small hovel. Outside on the lawn, the neighbors had posted a big sign: WELCOME HOME, JACKSONS. KEEPERS OF THE DREAM.

That same year marked the biggest touring months ever for the brothers, as they played 45 cities that summer, plus another 50 cities before Christmas, an amazing feat. Wherever they went, they were hailed as "The Black Beatles." Berry was overheard telling associates at Motown: "Every time these brothers take a shit, gold nuggets drop out of their assholes!"

When they played Milwaukee, they attracted 115,000 fans to their concert. At New York's Madison Square Garden, all tickets to hear The Jackson 5 disappeared two weeks before they hit town. The night the brothers opened in New York, their show was disrupted after only ten minutes. According to *The New York Daily News*, "the barriers protecting the stage were smashed like so many pieces of kindling before the idol-crazed charge of pre-teen and teenage girls. Order had to be restored before the Jacksons could finish the concert."

As the 1970s dawned, Joe Jackson – the ultimate "stage father from Hell," as he was called – took pride in his accomplishments. All the beatings, all the rehearsals, all the terrorizing of his sons, had not made them love him. But he'd fine tuned the lavish talent of his sons. He had no regrets about his history of violence toward his children. "If I had it to do over again, I'd do it the same way," he said. "I don't want to brag, but looking at the kids, I think I've done a good job. It was hard,

Donny Osmond

but it sure paid off."

In spite of their hysterical touring schedule, the brothers had time in 1971 to release two albums for Motown: *The Third Album*, featuring the hit record "I'll Be There," and *Maybe Tomorrow*, with such hit singles as "Never Can Say Goodbye."

The actor and composer Clifton Davis wrote "Never Can Say Goodbye." Unknown to Michael at the time, Davis would later become a key player in a *faux* scandal with Michael that would sweep the nation and cause consternation among Jacko's fans.

"With their gaudy, psychedelic clothes, their trendy Afros, and their love beads, I thought The Jackson 5 was a hoot," said critic David Breen. "I gave them about eighteen months before they faded into oblivion. I saw no staying power in the group at all. Michael came across as a little faggy, and I thought he'd be too effeminate when he matured. In a way, I was right. But what I didn't understand was that the world was changing. Macho would not always prevail. Johnny Mathis wasn't the most masculine of men – and there were rumors – but he did all right. That 'Stormy Weather' was a great hit. But the funniest act in show biz was Michael himself imitating Mathis doing 'Stormy Weather.'"

Even though he was only at the dawn of puberty, some press members were writing that Michael was "androgynous." One writer claimed that "the first time I ever heard Michael Jackson sing, I thought he was a young girl. I still think that. Except he grew up to become a woman." Such press put-downs of Michael and rampant speculation about his ambiguous sexuality would in time become media fodder.

Although Berry, a black man, was one of the sharpest judges of pop music in the business, he failed to see the appeal of a new group, sometimes called the "white Jacksons"–that is, the Osmond brothers. This group originated in the closing year of the Eisenhower presidency as a barbershop quartet. By the Kennedy era, they were a regular feature on *The Andy Williams Show*.

George Osmond, the father of the brood, submitted a song to Gordy but was turned down. Eventually Osmond signed with MGM Records. With the baby of the family, Donny Osmond, imitating Michael's high-pitched voice and sound, the record, "One Bad Apple," became a megahit. Papa Joe went ballistic when he first heard the Osmonds. "They're stealing our act! Those little Goodie Two Shoes with their small white dicks!" He was furious at Berry for turning down "One Bad Apple," feeling it would have been an ideal record for his sons to record.

Executives at MGM Records plotted to launch the "lilywhite Osmonds" in direct competition to The Jackson 5. The word went out to promote Donny Osmond, then only thirteen years old, as a direct challenger to Michael.

Not to be outdone, Berry began to prepare a number of solo releases for Michael to put on the market. "Michael had so much more talent than Donny Osmond – and was so much cuter," a fan, Betty Barkin, said. "At first I loved the Osmonds and had a big crush on Donny, but Michael won my heart. I came to feel that the Osmonds were vanilla, Michael and his brothers chocolate – and I've always gone for chocolate."

The upcoming year, 1972, would see the music market saturated with Michael Jackson singles. His brothers, especially Jermaine, were very envious. "It's called sibling rivalry," Gordy said, pointing out the obvious.

On the road, Michael shared a room with Jermaine, perhaps the most sexual of his brothers, although Jackie too was known as a "ladies man." Disputes and jealousies would eventually drive Jermaine and Michael apart, but they nevertheless bonded together as boys.

Four years older than Michael, Jermaine was a sexual opportunist, as has been reported by many of the people who knew and worked with him on the road. At this point, Michael may have been too young to even know what his sexual proclivities were, but he learned his lessons in sex first hand from observing Jermaine.

In his startling 1994 biography published by Simon & Schuster, Christopher Andersen reported on an explosive claim made by Johnny Jackson. Johnny was called a "cousin" and originally had played drums with the Jackson brothers. "He shared our name but not our blood," Katherine said. Johnny reportedly told the chief of Steeltown Records, Gordon Keith, that he'd once walked in on a male relative of the Jackson family, catching him "sexually aroused" with Michael, who was only twelve years old at the time. The older relative, who was allegedly molesting young Michael, was not named. Of course, "evidence" such as this, even though reported in a book by one of the nation's leading publishers, must still be considered hearsay.

Unlike many stars, Michael has never claimed that he was molested as a boy. He has been enigmatic in his responses, although on more than one occasion he has held out the possibility, without any definitive confirmation, that he was indeed

Jackson 5

40

molested. At this point, the truth may never be known.

What really happened while the Jackson brothers were touring together on the road has now become the stuff of legend, as various people have come forward with tantalizing stories. In his vanilla whitewash and boring so-called autobiography, *Moonwalk*, Michael portrays life on the road as harmless fun – "pillow fights, tag-team wrestling matches, shaving cream wars, you name it."

A favorite pastime for the boys was dropping balloons and paper bags filled with water off hotel balconies to burst onto innocent pedestrians below, giving them an unexpected shower.

In a rare confession, Michael did admit spying on women while they were on the toilet. In various clubs and chitlin' circuits in which he appeared, male performers would often cut or drill little holes as a means of looking into women's dressing rooms or else their toilets. "You could peek through one of these holes," Michael said. He admitted that he did. "I saw stuff I've never forgotten," he confessed, but left out mention of what kind of "stuff" he witnessed.

Michael's most notorious peep-hole vision occurred when the group was performing in London. One of his brothers urged him to "get a look at this!" Peering through the hole, Michael saw a vision of a completely nude Carol Channing.

At this point in her career, Channing no longer looked as she did when she played Lorelei Lee in the original *Gentlemen Prefer Blondes* on stage in 1949, the 1953 movie role going to the sexier Marilyn Monroe.

"Ugh!" Michael reportedly said when viewing the aging Channing's fallen breasts. "That's disgusting."

A writer for *Rolling Stone* later jokingly said, "The sight of Carol Channing in the nude turned Michael off women for life."

Like Mick Jagger and the Rolling Stones, like Elvis Presley, like John Lennon and the other Beatles, the Jackson brothers took advantage of their sex appeal in whatever city they were appearing. Female groupies followed the Jackson brothers back to their hotel suites where all the brothers, except Michael, enjoyed their sexual favors. "I was first seduced by the father, Joe Jackson," confessed Petula Robin, "in Philadelphia. He introduced me to both Jermaine and Jackie, and they seduced me too. I met Michael but seducing him was out of the question. I heard he didn't like girls all that much, and he was far too young."

In some respects, the brothers used their father as a role model. Away from Katherine, Joe reportedly slept with some of the more attractive Jackson groupies, both white and black, as if he were one of the performers himself. Perry Elkins, a stage manager in Milwaukee, claimed that "Joe used his sons as bait – in other words, 'you sleep with me and I'll fix you up with Jermaine or Jackie,'" or whichever brother they fancied. "At his young age, Michael was off-limits," Elkins claimed. "One night I heard Michael lecturing his brothers that they were violating the tenets of their religion as Jehovah's Witnesses. If I recall, Jackie, or maybe it was Jermaine, just laughed Michael off. Except for Michael, I never knew one Jackson brother from the other."

It appears that Jermaine, from the age of 15 or 16, seduced far more girls and women than even his promiscuous brother, Jackie. "Jackie would have his pick of the girls," Elton Jenkins, who once worked for Motown in Los Angeles, claimed. "He'd pick out the most beautiful and bring her back to his hotel room. But Jermaine would

The Jackson children

top him. On any given night, he'd line up at least three girls – one for midnight, one for one o'clock, and one for two o'clock."

Since Michael often shared a room with Jermaine, he would watch his older brother in action. Jermaine may have been deliberately showing off his sexual prowess to his younger brother. "I think it was part of that sibling rivalry Gordy was always talking about," Jenkins said. "Jermaine might have been trying to show Michael that although his kid brother was the star on stage, in the boudoir, Jermaine was the king."

Adele Ferguson, a secretary who lived in Tampa at the time, claimed that Jermaine was the greatest lover she'd ever experienced "before or since. He must have read the *Kama Sutra* from cover to cover. In one night he taught me sexual positions I'd never heard of. Until Jermaine, my boyfriends had been the missionary position types. While Jermaine and I were going at it, I just knew that Michael, with his saucer-wide eyes, was taking in all the action. In some ways, it made it more exciting for me to know that we were educating the kid about how to do it. After that night with Jermaine, my husband never really satisfied me. What a lover Jermaine was!"

Jermaine and Michael joined their other brothers on April 18, 1971 to appear on *Diana!* a TV special featuring Diana Ross. The highlight of the

42

Carol Channing

show was when Michael, only 12 years old at the time, came out to do his impression of Frank Sinatra in a tuxedo with a raincoat slung over his shoulder. Like Blue Eyes himself, Michael wore the characteristic Sinatra brown fedora, tilted at a rakish angle. Michael parodied "It Was a Very Good Year."

After the song, Diana, a vision in a metallic silver lamé gown, and Michael presented a skit in which he played her lover who was leaving her.

In a hotel suite, Sinatra watched the skit in disgust. One of his henchmen reported that the singer was so outraged by Michael's imitation, that he took a bottle of bourbon and tossed it at the TV screen. "If I ever catch up with that little fag, I'll break his legs," Sinatra shouted. "No, not that! I'll hire two guys from Jersey to do it for me."

In addition to their career bursting into full bloom, the Jackson brothers experienced another milestone in 1971. They moved into a mansion at 4641 Hayvenhurst in affluent Encino, California, a property Joe had purchased for a quarter of a million dollars. Their Encino neighbors included such celebrities as Mike Connors, Dick Van Dyke, Dennis Weaver, and, Michael's favorite, "Soul Sister" Aretha Franklin.

On beautifully landscaped two-acre grounds, studded with orange and lemon trees, the estate contained six bedrooms, which meant that the Jackson siblings would have to double up.

Katherine herself made the room assignments, saving the master bedroom for Joe and herself. Michael's younger brother, Randy, became Michael's new roommate. La Toya and Janet shared a room, as did Marlon and Jermaine, and so it went. "For me, it would become an Alcatraz instead of a real home," La Toya was quoted as saying later in life when she fled Encino.

In the beginning, Michael was enchanted with the property, which included an Olympic-size swimming pool. He would live for years at Encino until there were too many eyes spying on his increasingly secret private life.

"I once delivered some demos to the Jackson family," Motown's Elton Jenkins claimed. "I must have arrived after a free-for-all. There was evidence of violence. I got out of there as soon as I could. That Joe Jackson had some temper. I didn't want to become a victim. As the years went by and more and more scandals were revealed, I came to realize that the address in Encino housed America's most dysfunctional family."

"Only in America can you be born a black man and end up a white woman."

--Truman Capote

"I would kill myself if I couldn't be close to young boys."

--Michael Jackson

"You can't say somebody's guilty of a crime when you have no evidence to prove it...I hate the media for what they do to Michael, I do hate them."

--Whitney Houston

"He wasn't at all sure that he could make it on his own. And me too. I had my doubts."

--Quincy Jones before *Off the Wall*

"Michael Jackson is like a skyscraper built on eggshells."

--Former *CBS Records* executive (name withheld)

"He had a real intensity...People take him for a simpleton with a head full of silly songs, but he's a complex young man, curious about everything, who wants to go further and further. He behaves like an adolescent and, at the same time, like a wise old philosopher."

--Quincy Jones

"Michael would rather cut his wrist than harm a child."

--Elizabeth Taylor

Chapter Three

Michael would spend the rest of his life fretting over and eventually altering his appearance. His obsession with his looks began in 1971 when he broke out with "history's worst case of acne." At the same time, his body shot skyward. No longer was he mistaken for a midget.

"My years as a cute kid were suddenly over," he said. "I was a gangly adolescent at almost five feet ten inches." He spent a good part of the day staring at his reflection in the mirror. Every night seemed to bring a fresh pimple or two. "It was like having measles," he later said.

He became even shier around people. Some of the business associates in the record business Joe introduced Michael to didn't even believe he was who he said he was, but one of his "uglier brothers." For the first time in his life, he began to think of himself as "disfigured," and he longed to be beautiful like Diana Ross. He was all right as long as he was on stage, because heavy coatings of makeup obscured his bad complexion. "At night I lived with my demons," he said. "I came to hate mirrors as my pimples got worse." He gave up greasy processed foods such as hamburgers and French fries and began to consume a healthier diet, concentrating on fresh fruits and vegetables.

In addition to his acne, Michael had to endure the taunts of his brothers, who, for some reason, had taken to mockingly calling him "Liver Lips" or "Big Nose."

At the same time, Berry Gordy Jr. was putting pressure on Michael to make solo recordings. At first Joe opposed it, seemingly not wanting Michael to be a star on his own. Perhaps Joe thought he'd lose control of his boy if he broke away from his singing brothers. Berry went so far as to urge Michael to start rehearsals for an album all his own.

There were some bright moments along the way. In 1971, *The Jackson 5 Show*, a Saturday morning cartoon film, was launched on network TV. The brothers recorded the musical numbers for this animated series. Michael later said, "I couldn't wait to wake up on a Saturday morning and see myself in a fantasy cartoon." He was less enthusiastic when he learned that the entire group, including himself, was being paid less than $4,000 per episode. With this series on his own family, Michael began his lifelong fascination with animated motion pictures. He developed a consuming passion for all the commercial products inspired by founding father Walt Disney.

Someone at Motown, the identity of the person not known, showed Michael a Hollywood newspaper with its "Second Coming" headline: WALT DISNEY WAS A HOMO. The underground newspaper was published right before Christmas in 1966, following Disney's death on December 15. Michael apparently had no immediate reaction, but friends reported that he was almost in a state of shock, particularly when he read that Disney preferred to seduce young boys.

Someone suggested that Michael couldn't believe that the one artist responsible for bringing so much joy to young boys all over the world could also be capable of molesting them. At this point in his life, Michael could not have known that the same charges leveled against Disney would one day be brought against him.

Michael's watching of endless cartoons, his fondness for pets, and his silly little pranks, such as locking his brothers out of their hotel rooms without their underwear, were relatively harmless.

Many young performers pursued more dangerous games. At the start of the 1970s, Michael was often compared to the ill-fated young singer, Frankie Lymon, nicknamed "The Golden Throat." He was the first black teenage singing idol, and his success had inspired The Jackson 5 back in Gary.

In the 1950s Lymon was the lead singer for "The Teenagers," a popular group at the time, scoring such hits as "Goody, Goody." By the time he was only thirteen, Lymon could travel anywhere in America and hear his own voice on the jukebox singing "Why Do Fools Fall in Love?"

Michael's adolescent voice in the early 70s evoked Lymon's soprano sounds. But their lives would take different turns as Lymon succumbed to drug addiction. At the age of eighteen, his career was all but over. In 1968, and only twenty-five years old, Lymon was found dead from a heroin overdose in New York, a syringe by his bed.

Walt Disney

46

Frankie Lymon & The Teenagers

When he died, Lymon was survived by three wives. A polygamist, he never divorced any of his wives and remained married to three women up to his death.

When he heard of Lymon's death, Michael vowed that, "That will never happen to me." At this early age, he saw how drugs or alcohol could destroy promising careers. It is not known if he was also familiar with how a sex scandal could destroy a career as it had done with silent screen comedian Fatty Arbuckle and many other performers.

Instead of acquiring a drug habit, Michael remained deeply religious and committed to his faith as a Jehovah's Witness. He spent a lot of time reading the Bible. When he wasn't doing that, or rehearsing, he escaped into a fantasy world of cartoons or motion pictures that definitely carried the family seal of approval.

When Joe built a 32-seat screening room onto the 22-room Encino mansion, Michael began to spend hours there watching films that an eight-year-old could enjoy. He was addicted to Shirley Temple movies, and he saw *The Wizard of Oz* with Judy Garland thirty-five times, little knowing that one day he'd be cast in the black version of this classic. He also began to collect animals as pets, and was particularly fond of snakes. Both he and Jermaine owned their own boa constrictors. "Mine is bigger than yours," Michael reportedly told his brother Jermaine, referring to his pet snake. "Dream on, girl!" Jermaine said. "I'm the best hung of all the Jackson brothers. Just ask any gal."

As the Jackson coffer filled with gold, Katherine no longer insisted that her children perform chores around the house. Servants began to appear— maids to keep the place clean, chauffeurs to drive them around Los Angeles (often to the recording studio), gardeners to tend the landscaped grounds and feed the animals, and cooks to prepare their favorite foods. Even though Michael had switched to a healthier diet, his siblings still preferred the soul food that Katherine had once fed them back in Gary.

Because fans held the Encino property under siege virtually day and night, the Jacksons had walls, iron gates, and police dogs to keep them out. Even so, the most ingenious fans found ways of getting onto the property. Occasionally, they even managed to invade the Jackson living quarters, and had to be forcibly ejected by armed security guards.

Michael's efforts to attend public school failed. He had been enrolled for less than two weeks as a sixth grader at the Gardner Street Elementary School in Los Angeles when fans crawled through the windows to get at him, seeking his autograph or a piece of his clothing.

When he was enrolled in Emerson Junior High School in elegant Beverly Hills, some fanatic called the principal of the school and threatened to bomb one of Michael's classrooms, killing him and all the other students. Subsequently, Katherine made a decision to withdraw Michael from Emerson. After that, a chauffeur drove him more or less regularly to The Buckley Private School in Sherman Oaks, where wealthy Californians, including an assortment of movie stars, placed members of their brood.

"That school had more faggots-in-training than Bill Gates today has quarters," said Buddy Epson, years later. He attended the school very briefly. "When we first met Michael, we just assumed that he was gay like us. I checked him out. If it walks like a faggot, talks like a faggot, acts like a faggot, and looks like a faggot, then what were we to assume? We had circle jerks in those days. We also went into the heavy stuff. A friend asked Michael to join one of our parties. Apparently, Michael not only turned down my friend but lectured him on the evils of being gay. He even brought religion into it. He was a Jehovah's Witness, or some such shit. Michael got really offended—at least according to my friend—when he was asked if black dicks are bigger than the pricks on white boys. We had some really big boys at that school, even though they were still pubescent, and we wanted to know how Michael measured up. But he came on like a preacher's son. We didn't pursue him after that. We got the impression he was some religious fanatic."

Actually, Michael only attended class occasionally, living on the road with his brothers most of the time. Joe had hired Rose Fine, a white tutor who gave the brothers private lessons, even traveling with them to and from their bookings. "I feel I was a mother to the boys in another life."

Michael never really got an education. To this day, his spelling is atrocious, as is his grammar, unless it's written out for him. (A rather scurrilous article in *The New Republic*, published in 1984, claimed that Michael was illiterate, which isn't true.)

When he did go to school, Michael was delighted to see his unpimpled image marketed on everything from T-shirts to lunchboxes. "I liked the red lunchboxes," he later said, "not the yellow or blue ones."

Newly organized fans waited outside their schoolroom doors or massed to ambush them when the brothers emerged from the Cow Palace in San Francisco or the Convention Hall in Philadelphia. "There is an explosion of adolescent chemistry that rivals the first teen bombs detonated by The

Beatles," wrote author Albert Goldman. "Sheets of screams hang in the air, hysterically contorted mouths and hands rise to the lights, scrimmages clog the aisles—the air of the *corrida*, the cockfight, the gladiatorial combat fills the plastic vastness."

Katherine called her son "sensitive," and Bob Jones, who once was charged with hyping Motown's stars, referred to Michael as an "introvert," who stayed alone in his hotel room or in his Encino bedroom while his brothers were often out "raising hell." Sensitive and introvert are words often used to describe a young homosexual in the making, but Jones and Katherine apparently didn't mean to suggest that.

Sammy Davis Jr. had been right in fearing future competition from the "midget." Originally, Davis was to have recorded *Maybe Tomorrow*.

Gordy intervened and gave the song to The Jackson 5, thinking it would be a mega-hit for the brothers. He was disappointed, although the song did make it to the Top Ten but at the bottom of *Billboard's* chart.

Davis was "seriously pissed." But Sinatra, who liked to tease his pal, found it amusing. "You're being replaced as the hottest dancing Jungle Bunny in show biz," he jokingly chided his friend. Davis always hated it when Sinatra called him a Jungle Bunny, but smiled as if those words didn't hurt him.

In the wake of their successful album, *Maybe Tomorrow*, taking its title from the hit single, The Jacksons also recorded another album, sentimentally called *Goin' Back to Indiana*, which included a single with that name as well as their hit, "I Want You Back," and once again, "Maybe Tomorrow."

Goin' Back to Indiana was also the name of an ABC-TV special, which included, among other footage, film of the Jackson brothers during their triumphant return to Gary.

A comedy and variety show, it featured Diana Ross (then pregnant), Bill Cosby, Tommy Smothers, and a badly shaken Bobby Darin who arrived at the studio after a violent fight with the alcoholic star, his ex-wife, Sandra Dee, whom he'd foolishly married in 1960, divorcing her in 1967.

The Jackson home in Encino

Michael was delighted when Katherine applauded the show, although Joe told his sons that they "could have done better." Before Katherine's eyes, her sons were growing up and trying to break away from the harsh influence of Joe. Michael avoided his father whenever he could, but

49

"stayed tied to his mama's apron strings," Gordy said.

It would take Michael a long time to escape the bondage of his family. The way out for many of the older siblings was marriage. At the age of eighteen, Tito broke away to marry Delores Martes on June 17, 1972. Called "Dee Dee," she was only seventeen at the time. He'd met her at Fairfax High School in Hollywood. Katherine and Joe only reluctantly agreed to welcome this *Mexicana* into the family and were turned off by her ghetto upbringing in the Dominican Republic and in New York's Harlem. Fearing that she might be "a gold digger," they insisted that Tito force her into a prenuptial agreement.

Maureen (Rebbie) had been the first sibling to flee the nest when in 1968, at the age of eighteen, she fell in love with Nathaniel Brown, another Jehovah's Witness. Joe opposed the marriage, but Rebbie stood firm, marrying Brown and moving to Kentucky. "She fled Joe's prison," La Toya claimed.

After he'd crashed his Datsun 240-Z, and incurred Joe's violence, Jackie didn't marry right away but moved out into his own "bachelor pad."

It was only natural that the older brothers spent more and more time thinking about girls—or, in some cases, their wives—and less and less about their music.

Michael was only thirteen when a reporter for *Crawdaddy* magazine inquired about his love life. He claimed he was "not old enough" to have a girlfriend. But even at that age, he could have had one if he wanted to. But he wasn't interested.

Female groupies were readily making themselves available to the Jacksons, even to Joe himself. One girl, Elizabeth Ashe, claimed that "I had Jackie first, then the daddy, then Jermaine. Jermaine was the best in spite of lover boy Jackie's reputation. Joe didn't turn me on at all. I just went along with it to get to the brothers."

Many of the sexual adventures of Jackie and Jermaine were conducted directly in front of Michael, in the same room. He feigned sleep, but the moans would have awakened the soundest sleeper.

Although Jermaine often preferred more than one girl per night, Jackie would select "someone special in the audience." That object of his eye would then be invited backstage and introduced to Jackie. In almost every case the girl ended up in Jackie's hotel room for the night.

Michael tried in vain to uphold the morality of his brothers. Often he would approach girls going to his brothers' bedrooms and beg them to go home. "It's against the teachings of God," he would tell a startled groupie. "It's a sin."

"Get out of my way," one determined fan, Betty Pittsfield, told Michael in Cincinnati, pushing him aside. "What are you? Some little faggot? I'm gonna sleep with both Jackie and Jermaine tonight."

Where "WILLARD" ended...

BEN

begins.

And this time, he's not alone!

A poster for *Ben*, the movie

Before heading for one of the bedrooms, Betty turned to Michael. "I bet you want to sleep with your older brothers yourself. You're such a little wimp." All she remembered was Jackie answering the door in tight-fitting white jockey shorts, nothing else. She looked back at Michael. Sobbing, he turned from her in disgust and ran down the hallway.

Over the years many female fans have come forward to discuss their one-night stands with the Jackson brothers. Some have claimed the boys were gentle, skilled lovers; others have spoken of violence.

One white girl, who was only sixteen at the time, claimed that she was brutally raped—"both front and back. I was a virgin. I was also made to perform oral sex on the brothers. Michael was in the room at the time watching everything. At four o'clock I left the room in tears. I felt used. They were no longer the sweet, clean-cut brothers they were on stage. They were monsters. I went home and found that I had bled all over my pants. I was afraid they'd made me pregnant. But I switched my loyalty. From then on, it was Mick Jagger and the Rolling Stones for me. No more Jackson brothers. After that ordeal, I never had sex with another black man."

It was not as a sexual adventurer but as a singer that Michael had a breakthrough as a solo artist when he turned fourteen in 1972. He followed "Got to Be There" with another hit, "Rockin' Robin," a revival of Bobby Day's 1958 rock 'n' roll novelty song. "Rockin' Robin" shot to number two on the charts, proving once again that Michael, like Diana Ross herself, could make it without a group.

His next big single, *Ben*, also in 1972, was actually a paean to a rat. Most of his fans who bought the record didn't know that. Michael always had an affinity for rats or mice, feeding the hapless creatures live to his pet boa constrictor. In spite of its dedication, the song was a beautiful ballad, winning a Golden Globe award and an Academy Award nomination. Michael also recorded the theme song for the film version of *Ben*, which was released in 1972, telling the story of a boy who befriended a rat, the leader of a pack of

The Jackson brothers meet Queen Elizabeth II

vicious rodents. *Ben* was a sequel to another film, *Willard*, released in 1971. In an understatement, Michael said, "A lot of people thought the movie was a bit off," referring to *Ben*, "but I was not one of them."

At one point in *Ben*, it sounds as if Diana Ross is singing. And for a few brief moments, especially in the melodrama of the lyric, Michael evokes Barbra Streisand.

Michael made *Ben* the title of his second solo album, released by Motown in 1972. This album included such favorites as "People Make the World Go 'Round," "Everybody's Somebody's Fool," and "Shoo-Be-Doo-Be-Doo-Da-Day." Even so, sales remained at the same relatively modest 350,000 or so that his first album, *Got to Be There*, generated. Three years would go by before Michael released another solo album. This time the results would be disastrous.

Michael was furious that in his acceptance speech on Oscar night, the writer of "Ben" didn't "thank me for singing the song that made it a success."

As an artist, Michael was growing increasingly rebellious. He complained to Gordy that, "They want me to sing in a certain way, and I know they are wrong." In *Moonwalk*, his autobiography, he claimed, "No matter what age you are, if you *have* it and you *know* it, then people should listen to you."

Joe regarded Michael's newly found independence with a certain dread. He welcomed the extra money that Michael was earning for the family through his solo recordings, but he feared that if his young son became too successful he might break away from his brothers. Actually the group could have been renamed "The Jackson 6," as "Baby Randy" had joined his brothers on stage.

Before Thanksgiving in 1972, The Jackson 5 (plus Randy) moved onto the world stage, as they flew to London's Heathrow Airport for a royal command performance in the U.K. for Queen Elizabeth II. Unaware of their popularity abroad, the brothers did not anticipate the extent of their fame. Jacksonmania in London reached mass hysteria, even threatening lives. Michael later reported that he was nearly strangled to death at the airport when two strong girls grabbed different ends of his bright red scarf. Show biz vets, facing screaming, souvenir-collecting fans, had long ago learned never to wear a scarf into a crowd. It was rumored that Michael nearly lost more than a scarf. One London commentator noted that a fanatical young girl had "grabbed Michael's weenie and had held onto it for life" until a security guard pushed her aside.

"There wasn't enough security," Marlon was quoted as saying. "Screaming fans completely blocked our silver Rolls Royce limousine. The car couldn't move forward without killing someone. Finally, we were forced out of the Rolls just in time. The screamers tipped it over. We could have been killed. We were grabbed everywhere—and I mean *everywhere*—as the police hustled us off to different transportation out of the hellhole. I was practically choked to death by one girl. Our Afros were pulled out by wads of hair. I was scared shitless."

From the very beginning, Michael was never good at interviews, and often ended up being ridiculed. In London, he told a reporter for *The Daily Mail*: "I'm glad to be in England because I've always wanted to learn more about Napoleon."

Fans surrounded the Churchill Hotel in London where the brothers had been booked. On the night of their appearance at Albert Hall, the brothers feared they could not get through the crowds and into their limousine. The hotel's security called the London police. Officers arrived with water hoses to turn back the crowds.

To complicate matters, "some insane fool" booked the Osmond brothers into the Churchill at the same time. Fights broke out between the two warring camps of fans: the Osmond devotees vs. the Jackson fans. A doorman at the Churchill was knifed by a rabid twelve-year-old girl who'd run away from her home in Lincoln.

Things went more smoothly when The Jacksons flew to Glasgow for a command performance at King's Hall in honor of Queen Elizabeth II's Silver Jubilee, and the brothers performed brilliantly. "We're making history," Michael said gleefully.

Her Majesty was ushered backstage to greet personally each member of the group, including its star, Michael. He was shy and embarrassed in the presence of Her Royal Highness. One London reporter claimed that Michael "curtsied like a girl" when introduced to Queen Elizabeth.

Michael seemed even more jubilant when The Jacksons performed in Liverpool, hometown of the "Fab Four." The brothers broke even the attendance records set by The Beatles themselves. When they appeared at the London Palladium, The Jackson 5 concert was sold out. In the future, whenever the name of Elton John would come up, Michael was arrogantly dismissive of the performer. "Oh, yeah, him! He was our opening act at the Palladium."

Flying out of Heathrow and once again facing hysterical fans, The Jacksons met "wild mobs" in such cities as Amsterdam, Frankfurt, Brussels, and Munich. In Munich, a limousine carrying the brothers was overturned and stripped so bare by souvenir hunters that it was left as a piece of junk. Fortunately, the brothers had been ushered out of the vehicle before it was ripped apart.

The mobs greeting The Beatles on the Continent of Europe years before showed some similarities in the mobs who turned out for a viewing of The Jacksons. But whereas the mass hysteria associated with the arrival of The Beatles translated into platinum records, it didn't apply to sales for The Jackson 5.

In fact, sales of The Jackson 5's singles began to fall on *Billboard* charts. Their song, "Sugar Daddy," barely made the Top Ten, appearing at the bottom of the list.

"Little Bitty Pretty One," a rhythm-and-blues number, had been a big hit when Bobby Day recorded it in 1958. By ripping off another Bobby Day number, also introduced in 1958, Michael had scored a hit single with "Rockin' Robin." But lightning did not strike twice. "Little Bitty Pretty One" never got beyond number thirteen on the charts.

The band's next single, "Lookin' through the Window," sold about a half-million copies, the same as "Little Bitty Pretty One." "Corner of the Sky," from the Broadway musical, *Pippin*, was a complete disappointment, selling about 350,000 copies, never moving beyond number 18 on *Billboard's* charts.

"What's happening?" Joe asked Gordy, blaming him for his lack of promotion. Joe, with some degree of accuracy, suspected that Gordy was devoting most of his creative energies to the launching of Diana Ross as a big-time black film star. "The fans are mad for my sons," Joe said. "I just know the public is buying their singles."

Back in the United States, even a special for CBS didn't help their record sales. "The Jackson brothers are aging, becoming men, and they seem to have lost their special appeal," wrote critic Gavin Spacey. "Michael is the only one with any real talent. He seems dedicated, his brothers distracted, just going through the motions. The kid should break away from his brothers and become a bright star in his own right. His brothers are just extra baggage he has to carry onto the stage."

Ross had made a film, *Lady Sings the Blues,* a biography of jazz vocalist Billie Holiday, which had been financed by her lover, Gordy. The film opened in the autumn of 1972 at Loew's State in New York, breaking the attendance record previously established in 1970 by the sappy *Love Story* starring Ryan O'Neal and Ali MacGraw.

Michael reportedly resented Ross's success with "Good Morning Heartache," a single release from the film's track album. "Gordy should have given me that number," Michael said. "I could have done it so much better."

Early in 1973, *Lady Sings the Blues* received five Oscar nominations, including a Best Actress nomination for Ross. Michael was envious, plotting to become a movie star himself. Gordy and Ross were heartsick when it was announced at the Dorothy Chandler Pavilion in Los Angeles that the Best Actress Oscar had been won by Michael's future friend and confidant, Liza Minnelli, for her brilliant performance in *Cabaret.* Michael reportedly danced a jig upon hearing the news, although in public he said that "I'm rooting for Diana. She deserves it!"

Whenever he could break free from his rehearsals, Michael visited Ross on the set of *Lady Sings the Blues.* "He gave me a creepy feeling when he stood watching Ross perform," said Larry Winsfield, who'd worked on the film in a lowly job. "Mostly I brought coffee to the crew. But I was fascinated by watching Michael's face. He seemed oblivious to everyone else. He was studying Ross with such concentration that it looked like he was stealing her soul. It was obvious to all of us who saw Michael on the set that he wanted to be in front of the cameras like Ross, not watching from the sidelines."

Long after the Oscar ceremonies, Michael was overheard telling a sound crew, "If I'd been given a chance like Diana, I wouldn't have lost the Oscar to nobody. I have the talent to re-create any black male entertainer. Can you imagine how great I'd be in *The Sammy Davis Jr. Story*? For that matter, if they ever film *The Diana Ross Story*, I'd make the ideal choice as the star even though I'm a man. With the proper makeup and some plastic surgery, I could create Diana. When the movie of her life is made, she'll be too old to play herself. But I have the kind of face that will be forever young."

A movie career lay in Michael's future. But in the meantime, there were serious career problems that faced both him and his brothers. The release of "Hallelujah Day" in February of 1973 had been a disappointment, generating a sale of only 200,000 copies. That same year, another single, "Doctor My Eyes," went nowhere.

Michael himself, in his autobiography, *Moonwalk*, wrote of his own disappointment in such Jackson 5 singles as "Skywriter." In spite of its advanced musical arrangements for strings, Michael maintained that the song was not a good choice for his brothers. "Skywriter" also became both the lead song and the name of the latest Jackson album, released in 1973 and featuring such other songs as "The Boogie Man" and "I Can't Quit Your Love." Sales of the *Skywriter* album were disappointing, coming in under 120,000 copies.

As Michael moved deeper into the mid-seventies, he feared that The Jackson 5 might be on the road to becoming a "Golden Oldies" act, playing Las Vegas clubs and going on nostalgic tours. "I had this fear even when I was a *young* teenager," Michael claimed.

Joe shared Michael's concerns, despite the initial success of The Jackson 5 and their screaming fans. "If we don't play it right from now on, my boys might end up a flash in the pan," he warned Gordy. Joe had grown increasingly resentful of Motown, complaining that the company did not let them choose their own songs or even play their own instruments. He began to plot a means of breaking away from Motown and signing with another record company.

One possible explanation for the fall-off in sales was oversaturation of the market. Between Thanksgiving of 1969 until Christmas of 1971, Motown flooded the market with eight Jackson singles, plus a solo by Michael. They also released an astonishing five Jackson 5 albums, a total of 54 songs. Another factor involved the product's pricing: Teen fans of The Jackson 5 could afford the one dollar price of a solo recording, but not the five dollar cost of an entire album.

The rapid rise and almost fall of The Jackson 5 was not unique in the music business, where most teenage groups rarely last more than two years. The critic Pablo Guzman explained it: "The basic problem of teen idolatry is that teens grow up. Subsequent waves of new teens usually consider last year's model *passé*."

Selma Davis worked briefly at Motown, but overheard some heated discussions when Gordy was overseeing the filming of *Mahogany*, starring Diana Ross. "First, I learned that Jackie, Marlon, and Tito were viewed as having no talent, certainly not as solo artists. The bosses (at Motown) thought that Jermaine and certainly Michael could be successful as solos. But even before Joe Jackson bolted from Motown, the brass there knew that the end was coming. It was just a matter of time."

Along the way, and at an unexpected moment, came some hope. When "Get It Together" was released following "Skywriter," sales picked up. There was talk of a comeback for The Jackson 5. Michael himself liked "Get It Together," and it became the group's biggest success in the past two years. Discos throughout the land played the song. "It had a good, tough, low harmony," Michael wrote, "a sharper wah-wah guitar, strings that buzzed like fireplaces." Released in time for Michael's fifteenth birthday in 1973, "Get It Together" sold more than 750,000 copies, but reached only number 28 on *Billboard's* charts. Even so, The Jackson 5 were back—sort of—thanks partly to the promotional efforts of producer Hal Davis.

At one point, Gordy may have dreamed of creating black versions of Paul McCartney and John Lennon out of Michael and Jermaine. But that dream, of course, was never to be realized. From the beginning, Jermaine was called the sexiest of the Jackson brothers. That seemed especially accurate when Jermaine's charms were compared to the boyish appeal of the androgynous Michael.

As critic Dave Marsh wrote: "Jermaine was cute, but his voice lacked the expressiveness of Michael's, and since he was not much of an instrumentalist and the group wrote none of its own music, it was difficult to present him and Michael as black analogues of Lennon and McCartney."

In spite of this, Jermaine later claimed "I had everything that Michael had and more," perhaps a reference to his sex appeal. That claim was an idle boast. His first album, *Jermaine*, was not as successful as Motown had hoped. Writing in *Rolling Stone*, Vince Aletti said: "Jermaine simply doesn't have the range and assurance of Michael—he's just right on the upbeat, bright number. But he's out of his depth, sometimes desperately, on other types of songs."

In 1973 the press was still writing about the Jackson brothers and their parents as "the ideal American family, a role model for other black families to emulate." But this fantasy was about to come to an end.

Scandal was brewing when Tito was arrested on April 17, 1973 by the Los Angeles Police Department. The charge was the purchasing of stolen TVs and stereos. Johnny Jackson, the group's drummer, was also arrested. Freed on $2,000 bail, along with Johnny, Tito was arraigned on October 12.

He refused to talk to the press that day. There were rumors that Joe had severely beaten him for destroying "the image of The Jackson 5."

By February, 1974, charges against Tito were dropped when Johnny pleaded guilty. There was speculation—pure heresay—that the drummer took the rap for Tito. Michael was horrified that one of his brothers "would even get messed up in something like this," and he vowed to Joe and Katherine that his own good name would never be attached to any scandal.

Joe might have worried about the reputation of The Jackson 5, but he had marital problems of his own. Michael was horrified when on March 9, 1973 Katherine filed for divorce in the Los Angeles Superior Court. She had been willing to overlook her husband's one-night stands, but not his ongoing affair with Cheryl Terrell, a fan of The Jackson 5 who reportedly had had a crush on Jackie, before Joe, then 46, grabbed her instead. Gordy warned Katherine that a nasty divorce would "kill your sons' careers." Katherine held firm in her insistence on divorce, even though she'd agreed to tour Japan with her family, including Joe, that summer. Later that year she would hear reports that Terrell was pregnant with Joe's kid.

In spite of threatened parental divorce, and sagging sales of their records, the Jackson brothers still remained a world phenomenon. They played to record audiences in Japan, China, and Australia, and traveled during a break in their schedule into Africa.

Japan and its people made a deep impression on Michael, who claimed that the country put him more in touch with his spiritual side. He discovered Buddhist temples, serene and beautiful "Teahouse of the August Moon" gardens, and Japanese art.

His brothers discovered Japanese girls, to whom they quickly became addicted. In their suites at the Takanawa Prince Hotel in Tokyo, the brothers reportedly stayed up late watching Japanese porn flicks on closed circuit TV. A picture was taken of the brothers at the Tokyo airport when they were leaving. The photo editor for *Soul* magazine later claimed that "Jackie still had a hard-on in the picture. Before I could feature it on the cover, I had to do a little air-brushing."

While in Tokyo, Michael had a reunion with Sammy Davis, Jr., who was appearing in a sold-out engagement there. Apparently, Joe had informed Davis that he was negotiating to book his sons into Las Vegas. Davis told Michael that, unlike his pal, Frank Sinatra, who was fascinated with Mafia dons, he, Davis, didn't like them at all. "But don't cross them," Davis warned Michael, "or else you might end up with cement shoes."

The entertainer warned Michael never to borrow money from club owners against future appearances. "I do that all the time to meet current expenses," Davis said. "I'm a big spender. Then when it comes time for me to appear, I've collected all the green ones and end up with nothing. I have to borrow against future earnings. That way, they always have me."

Michael promised him he'd never live beyond his means and go into debt. Obviously, in the future, Michael would not take "Mr. Wonderful"'s advice.

In spite of some jealousy, Michael and Davis would remain friends until the end. When Davis was fighting cancer in 1989, a tribute was hosted by Eddie Murphy. Michael encountered Davis who weighed only 92 pounds at the time. Both men knew that death was near for the entertainer. Michael sang "You Were There," a song that paid homage to Davis's role in helping to carve out a niche for black entertainers.

Backstage, Michael met some of the best-known African-Americans in the country, including Jesse Jackson, Mike Tyson, Richard Pryor, Magic Johnson, and Ella Fitzgerald.

Whitney Houston and Stevie Wonder were also on the bill, which included Sinatra as well. At the end of the tribute, Sinatra knocked on the door to Michael's dressing room and was ushered inside. Michael had heard some of the singer's more sarcastic remarks about him, and didn't look forward to a face-to-face confrontation.

Sinatra was full of compliments for Michael's music. Perhaps Sinatra didn't mean what he said. But when he wasn't mad or feuding, as was often the case, he had a great deal of personal charm, which won over Michael, at least temporarily.

"Kid," Sinatra was overheard telling Michael, "The press will build you up today, because they like to tear you down tomorrow. In show business, you're hot and then oblivion. Very few entertainers can make a successful comeback. I'm the comeback kid. Frankly, I thought you were washed up in the 70s. But who would have predicted *Thriller*? I'll tell you the truth. I didn't get off on that album. Not my kind of music. But I'm impressed by sales, and you are mighty impressive in that department."

"I think you're the greatest singer in America, Mr. Sinatra," Michael said.

"Thanks, but let's face it: The world doesn't want a voice anymore. They want loud songs. If there's enough noise in the background, anybody can make it today as a singer."

If Michael took that as an insult, he didn't let on. He smiled politely and gave Sinatra a wet, soft handshake, before heading for the next encounter.

Mike Tyson, one of the most frightening human beings ever to step into the boxing ring, was standing next to Goldie Hawn. They were watching a taped tribute from President George Bush (*primero*). As Michael came into their presence, Tyson extended his hand.

At last the two Michaels had met—one the supreme gladiator, the other a slightly effeminate singer with a soprano voice. Each was a king of pop culture.

Mike Tyson

When Tyson and Michael met that day, their big troubles and super disgraces were just months ahead of them. Tyson would lose his world championship to James (Buster) Douglas in Tokyo in February of 1990, and he'd be jailed for rape in 1992. Like Michael, in his future, Tyson too would face bankruptcy.

A hardened ghetto kid, born

in Brooklyn in 1966, Tyson was actually eight years younger than Michael, although Michael looked more the kid. Michael and Tyson bonded at least for that day. "At twelve you were a big-time star," Tyson told Michael. "At twelve I was arrested for purse snatching." After chatting for fifteen minutes, Tyson offered Michael a chance to teach him to box.

"I'm a lover—not a fighter," Michael said. "You should know that."

"Lover of what?" Tyson asked.

"Don't believe the rumors," Michael said.

"Believe me, I don't judge anybody," Tyson said. "All holes are black at night."

Before Michael bid *adieu*, Tyson grabbed him in a bone-crunching embrace. "Your *Thriller* was the biggest-selling album in history. I was the biggest draw in the history of boxing. But life isn't about what you acquire. Life is about losing everything." "Iron Mike" could have been predicting both his own future—and that of Michael.

Throughout their careers, the names of Mike Tyson and Michael Jackson were invariably linked in such stories as WHO'S THE BIGGEST NUT JOB IN POP CULTURE? Columnist Gino Bona wrote: "While these two celebrities couldn't be further opposites on the exterior, their careers have shared a common pattern over the past twenty years. Both Tyson and Jackson reached the pinnacle of their popularity in the 80s, plummeted into dire times in the 90s, and have spent the first couple years of the new millennium as undeniable weirdos."

Bona mockingly suggested that Michael wants to share his bed with children, whereas Tyson "wants to eat 'em." The columnist also suggested that both men faced startling transformations, Michael going "from black man to white hermaphrodite" and Tyson "from the youngest heavyweight champ to America's second most beloved cannibal."

Writing for Knight Ridder News Tribune News Service, Sam Donnelton said that, "One sleeps with little boys, dyes his skin and has shrunk his nostrils to the size of two straws. The other went to jail for rape, has offered to make another man 'my girlfriend,' had a big tattoo etched across his face, and disappeared from training one week before his latest comeback fight." Donnelton filed this column in May of 2006, and was referring to Tyson's Showtime and pay-per-view fight with Clifford Etienne, in Memphis, Tennessee. After disappearing, Tyson, at least according to a London tabloid, was seen with an impressive erection at a wild orgy at his Las Vegas residence.

On September 13, 2003, Michael invited Tyson to Neverland for a charity event, although the press would not be allowed inside the gates. Tickets sold for $5,000 each.

This was the first time Michael had ever opened Neverland to members of the public. Reportedly he staged the event to re-establish a positive view of himself in the media.

Looking for but never finding Michael, Tyson showed up with a new girl-friend. He flashed a wide smile but warned photographers he didn't want his picture taken. "The gold in my teeth might interest the bankruptcy creditors."

After touring the grounds of Neverland, Tyson told the press: "I love the gorillas, and the camels in there are just amazing." To end the day, Tyson watched a title fight broadcast from Las Vegas and shown on the super-wide TV screens in Michael's den. As Tyson was leaving, one reporter called out to him: "Did you see Jacko-Wacko?"

"Maybe next year," Tyson said.

Back at the Sammy Davis tribute, and after his encounter with Tyson, Michael was greeting a star around every corner. When asked, however, he said that he didn't want to meet yet another Michael that night.

Michael Jordan.

"Never heard of him," Michael said.

"I guess I'm not Jacko's type," Jordan laughingly remarked when he later heard what Michael had said.

When Clint Eastwood, whom Michael had heard of, explained to him that Jordan was the world's greatest basketball star, Michael went up to Jordan and introduced himself.

By 1996 Michael had become more familiar with at least one aspect of Jordan's career. At Neverland, Michael watched *Space Jam* six times. In the film, Jordan appeared with some of Michael's favorite "actors": Bugs Bunny, Daffy Duck, Elmer Fudd, and Tweety Bird.

Michael had also been impressed by Jordan when he was chosen by *People* magazine as "One of the 50 Most Beautiful People in the World." In 1997 *People* also named Jordan one of "The Most Intriguing People of the Century." Michael was further impressed—and perhaps jealous—when he learned that at the peak of his career, Jordan was earning $80 million annual-ly from Nike and another $35 million a year playing in the NBA.

Michael was astonished when *Fortune* cited Jordan as sitting on a vast $400 million reserve of cash. "He's a virtual endorsement cash cow," Michael reportedly said. "I should have made those millions. So many of my endorse-ment deals, unlike Jordan's, didn't work out—and I'm plenty mad."

Michael was particularly impressed that Jordan had developed his own line of sports clothing, called JORDAN in the 1997-98 season. Although they didn't really fit him, Michael ended up acquiring—by means not known— three of Jordan's custom-tailored silk shirts monogrammed either with "Michael" or just "MJ." They were in the colors of pumpkin, magenta, and midnight blue.

On the way out of his dressing room at the Davis tribute, Michael encountered another survivor of Hollywood's Golden Age: actor Gregory Peck. They talked pleasantly for a few minutes and seemed to genuinely like each other. Peck gave Michael his telephone number and asked him to call him some time. Michael agreed. He'd begun his love affair with stars of Hollywood's heyday. His passion for the older stars would only intensify as he got older himself.

Michael ran into Sinatra once again at the Davis funeral on May 18, 1990 at the Forest Lawn Memorial Park in the Hollywood Hills. Sinatra was talking to Shirley MacLaine and Dean Martin. "Kid," Sinatra told Michael, "we're laying to rest the best black male entertainer America has ever seen. He had more talent in his little finger than all the other small pricks who followed him."

Again, if Michael took this as an insult, he gave no indication. He didn't have to say anything. He was rescued from a response by the sudden appearance of Janet Leigh. She kissed Martin and Sinatra on the cheeks and turned to Michael to shake his hand. "I loved you in *Psycho*," he said to Leigh.

Before she could thank him, Liza Minnelli appeared, linking her arm with Michael's. "C'mon," she said. "I'll introduce you to Milton Berle if you haven't met him before. He's got the biggest cock in Hollywood, but don't take my word for it. Have you met Burt Reynolds? I hear he's got one of the smallest."

Michael seemed to ignore her remarks, but joined her anyway, mainly to escape from Sinatra. He looked around. "I wonder if this many people will attend my own funeral."

Michael's funeral lay far in the future. After winding up their tour in Japan, the Jackson brothers flew to Australia in the summer of 1973. Once there they would appear at concerts not only in Sydney and Melbourne, but in smaller towns such as Adelaide and Brisbane. While in Australia, The Jacksons also visited the Outback, meeting members of aborigine tribes. Michael later claimed that "they treated us like brothers."

When they returned to America, Joe continued to plot his break from Motown, which he thought would free his sons from bondage—at least musically. Then the unexpected happened.

The Gordy and Jackson families became linked through marriage on a gray, rainy day on December 15, 1973 in Beverly Hills. Hazel Gordy, Berry's daughter, married Jermaine Jackson at a gaudily expensive wedding at the Beverly Hills Hotel. "It was more about showing off than love," said a disgruntled member of Motown who was not invited.

The wedding ended up costing Gordy more than a quarter of a million dollars. Both the bride and groom were only nineteen years old. In its next issue,

Ebony proclaimed the Gordy/Jackson link "the wedding of the century." Jermaine chose Marlon as his best man, and Michael was relegated to the role of an usher, a humiliation for him.

In a pearl white tuxedo with bugle beads trimming his lapels, Jermaine said his "I do" to Hazel, who wore a white satin gown with a white mink train "that stretched to Sacramento," one member of the wedding observed. When pictures were taken, the couple almost got lost against an all-white backdrop of 7,500 white camellias and white carnations, with nearly a hundred caged white doves and mounds of artificial snow.

"For a black dude's wedding to a black chick, this was the whitest wedding ever recorded on film," wrote a reporter for *Ebony* magazine. His words were censored as sounding "too racist." As if all this ostentation wasn't enough, the guest appearance of Smokey Robinson was greeted with loud applause. For the wedding of his friends, he'd written a special ballad for the occasion. Jermaine hugged Robinson, and Hazel gave him a kiss for his efforts.

Under heavy pressure from Gordy earlier that morning, Katherine, a vision in sapphire blue, agreed to drop her impending divorce from Joe to protect the careers of her sons. A vision in mauve and gray, Joe tried to address Katherine at the wedding, but she pointedly ignored him, even when they posed together as the "happy" parents of the groom.

Coretta Scott King, a friend of the Gordy family, was seen mingling with such celebrities as Lola Falana, Billy Dee Williams, Diahann Carroll, and even the Los Angeles mayor, Tom Bradley.

Mrs. King caused a lot of excitement among The Jacksons, particularly with Katherine, who admired her greatly. Michael didn't seem impressed, and Mrs. King may have sensed his alienation.

The widow of the slain civil rights leader, King was overheard talking privately and confidentially to friends. Media had bribed certain staff members of the hotel to report on any indiscretions being uttered by either the Jacksons or their guests.

"Michael is acting very petulant," Mrs. King remarked. "Dare I say jealous? He told me he was 'not gaining a sister, but losing a brother, his best friend.' If you ask me, I think Michael has a crush on Jermaine. I could swear that Hazel's future husband doesn't think of Michael in that way at all. If I didn't know better, I would say that

Hazel Joy Gordy marries Jermaine

63

Michael is behaving like a jilted girl who has lost out to another woman. Surely my impression is wrong. Tell me I'm wrong!"

When Hazel—"my first born"—was only fifteen, Gordy discovered that she was in love with Jermaine. Someone on his staff showed him a fan letter his daughter had written to Jermaine: "I love you, Jermaine. You are my prince, my dream. I need you, Jermaine. I will love you forever."

Hazel would not love Jermaine forever, but she did not outgrow what Gordy called "puppy love" and continued her passion for Jermaine until he reluctantly agreed to marry her. At the time of his wedding, Jermaine was "playing the field," having almost any girl he wanted for the night. Some of his brothers speculated that Jermaine would not let a mere wedding band deny him the pleasures that came so easily to him every night.

Michael also had professional fears about the future direction of The Jackson 5. Tito's wife had been rather milquetoasty, never interfering. But Hazel was known for being strong-willed. She could use her influence as the daughter of the boss to push Jermaine into a role as the group's lead singer, thereby relegating Michael to a subservient role.

The sun finally came out, breaking through the overcast sky of southern California. But it didn't brighten Michael's spirit. He confided to Katherine and to others that "no good will come of this marriage."

Hazel and Jermaine flew to Europe for a four-week honeymoon, living in lavish suites and dining at only the most *luxe* restaurants from Paris to Rome. They spent the most time in Switzerland. Jermaine flew back to join his brothers, including Michael, on a ten-day tour of Senegal in West Africa. "The boys were determined to have a close encounter with their roots," wrote one Senegalese journalist.

And so they did. Michael was especially moved by the native music and the rhythms. He called it "eye-opening," as he experienced the sight of native Africans in tribal dress performing with drums, their music filling the air and mesmerizing him. "I've come back!" he shouted at the top of his lungs at the airport in Dakar. He didn't kiss the ground, but burst into tears of joy instead. In the years ahead, Michael would be accused of trying to change his skin color to white. But during those heady days in Senegal, he "became an African," in the words of the same Senegalese journalist.

From Dakar, the day after their arrival, the brothers took a thirty-minute ferry trip to Gore Island where thousands of slaves were imprisoned during the late 18th century and for nearly

Coretta Scott King

half of the 19th century after they'd been captured in the wild. Here these wretched souls were detained under the most horrid of conditions before shipment to the New World, where they'd become slaves. Many of these hapless victims died in chains before reaching America. Reportedly, Michael became so upset at seeing the *Maison des Esclaves,* the prison for slaves constructed in 1775, that he vomited.

Michael's romance with Senegal was of short duration. He was appalled at the living conditions, especially when he visited a hovel in which a family of nine was crowded. "I've seen where they lived and slept on a dirt floor," he told reporters. "I've seen bigger doghouses in America." He was also horrified when he saw what the family had for dinner. The mother had bought three chicken heads which she boiled in an earthen pot over an open fire for some broth to feed her brood.

Later that night, Michael suffered an attack of diarrhea so devastating that he had to be hospitalized. He told his brothers that he "couldn't wait to get back" to the luxuries of their Encino estate. Their own accommodations in Senegal were horrid. Their bedrooms were not clean, and they didn't even have hot water.

"Stevie might want to live here, but count me out!" Michael was referring to Stevie Wonder, who announced to the press that he was planning to "fly away" from America and settle in Africa. After this grandstand play, the announcement of which was printed in newspapers across America, Wonder decided Africa wasn't that wonderful and canceled his plans to go into exile.

Before leaving Senegal, Michael announced to the press that, "Blacks are the most talented race on earth. They've got the beat. They've got the rhythm. Our music comes from Africa, and we musicians, especially in the United States, owe these tribes an enormous debt of gratitude. We must always remember that."

After making that lofty pronouncement, Michael was overheard by a flight attendant telling one of his brothers: "Now let's get the hell out of here!"

Upon their return to the United States, The Jackson 5 recorded "Dancing Machine," released as a single by Motown in 1974. "Spit out the bubblegum soul and record a song that America can dance to," Gordy told them.

Michael's voice was more mature—"he no longer sounded like *castrati,*" wrote one critic—and the single went double platinum. It shot up to number two on *Billboard's* charts. Young America could actually dance to Michael's high-octane "watch her get down, watch her get down." The more mature sounds coming from Michael's throat ended an ugly rumor that Joe was going to have his son castrated in the tradition of Italy back in the 1600s.

Rumors of Michael's castration became so widespread that on some occasions when he was mobbed by fans, overzealous girls—and in some cases, gay boys—reached out to grope him to see if his male genitals were still intact. Or if he'd become transgendered.

"Boy soprano becomes a high-pitched tenor," said a *Rolling Stone* critic. "Dancing Machine" was played around the country as much as their former hit, "Never Can Say Goodbye."

Dancing Machine also became the title of The Jackson 5's latest album, which also featured such songs as "The Mirrors of My Mind" and "Whatever You Got, I Want." Producer Hal Davis, not always a winner, assembled the track for the album *Get It Together*. He built The Jackson's first disco concept album around this, and it reached only number sixteen on *Billboard's* charts. This album marked the end of The Jackson 5 being called "teenyboppers," although they still fitted that age category. Critic Pablo Guzman wrote, "Through disco, the Jackson brothers found a way to grow with their audience without puncturing teen fantasy."

On Cher's television series, "Dancing Machine" was heard by much of the nation, who tuned in to watch Cher and her guest, Michael, perform the number as robots. "Both Cher and Michael had hair that would stretch along the full length of the California coast," wrote one critic. "Both of them seemed in dire need of a hairdresser. Cher's pantsuit and a halter top seemed designed by a demented drag queen. Michael in his midnight black cutaway jacket, accented with silver accessories, seemed like a reject from Harlem's Apollo Theater."

Nearly all critics agreed that Michael was practically a Fred Astaire when it came to dancing, but Cher was no Ginger Rogers. "As a Cherokee she could perform tribal dances—and that was about it," another critic unkindly proclaimed.

At the end of the broadcast, Cher was exhausted from the strenuous workout the Jackson brothers had put her through. She was amazed at their seemingly boundless energy. To pay his respects, Michael visited her in her dressing room.

"So tell me, Michael, who in the fuck is the world's top diva: *Moi* or Diana Ross?"

"You both are big talents," he said, embarrassed at being put in such a spot.

"Okay, I'll concede that she's a better singer. Hell, I don't like the sound of my own voice that much. I'm a much better actress than I am a singer. Singing is like going to a party at someone else's house. Acting is like having the party at your own house." Cher would repeat this sentiment to various figures in show business. "What about you, kid? Plan to stick to singing?"

"I never told this even to my family, but I want to become a movie star like Diana. And not just in singing roles either. I want to win an Oscar."

"A noble ambition, but I don't know about that Oscar," Cher said. "Winning little baby Oscars with their cute butts is my fantasy. My ambition is to win as many Oscars, or as many nominations, as Katharine Hepburn."

"Who is she?" Michael asked. "Another singer?"

"You're in show business and you don't know Kate Hepburn?" Cher asked in astonishment. "Fuck, kid. Get real!" As a joke, she said, "Hepburn, my favorite actress, was Scarlett O'Hara in *Gone With the Wind.*"

Not knowing that Cher was joking, Michael took this as gospel. "I'm gonna see that movie some day."

Again joking, Cher said, "Have the Butterfly McQueen part rewritten for you. You'd be great at it. Repeat after me, 'Miss Scarlett, Miss Scarlett, I don't know nothin' 'bout birthin' babies.'"

"I could do that!"

"Listen, take some advice from your *mamma mia* here. At first people laughed me off as a joke when I was breaking into the business. Some fucking joke! Before my career is over, I'll have one hundred million in the bank." Cher underestimated her potential, ending up with a vast fortune of $600 million.

"I was a shy kid living in a fantasy world," she said.

"I still live there," Michael said.

"Fine," Cher said. "But live in the real world too. I've heard stories about you. You're gonna be ridiculed like I was. But stand up to your critics."

"How can I do that?"

"By becoming so God damn successful that even your harshest critics can't hurt you. You can become so rich and powerful in show business that the

Cher

hecklers won't matter any more."

"I hate it when people tell lies about me," he said.

"Deep down, we all do, but don't tell anybody I said that." She looked at the time. "Gotta go now. I've got a date with a hot young boy. A little older than you. You're still a bit young for me. You like girls, don't you?"

"I can take 'em or leave 'em," Michael said.

"Yeah, right! There's nothing wrong with liking boys.

Who in hell wouldn't like boys? The world is filled with holes to stuff. Finding the perfect prick is like looking for the Holy Grail."

Appalled and intimidated, Michael thanked her profusely for letting his brothers appear on her show and quickly hurried from her dressing room.

Cher called after him. "Seriously, boy, I wasn't planning to seduce you."

In spite of their initial introduction, Cher and Michael saw each other from time to time, but never really became friends. Eventually, the publicity about child molestation and other accusations turned her against Michael.

By 2003, she was telling the press, "I don't really care what he does to his face. He could just erase it as far as I'm concerned. I don't like him anymore. And it's because of his children. I cannot imagine putting my children through what he puts his children through. I once saw him with one of his kids rolled up in a blanket, and I was thinking, 'What kind of life is this?' He and I were friends when he was little. I watched him grow up and all that, but, you know, you dangle a baby over a balcony, that's it for me. If it was up to me, he wouldn't have those babies now. This guy is nuts. As an artist, I can't fault his art because he was brilliant. I wouldn't buy anything now."

Cher avoided a question about Michael's plastic surgery. Fans of Cher and Michael on the web asked this provocative question: "Which one has had more plastic surgery?"

Appearing on more and more TV specials such as Cher's was only one of Joe's schemes.

To show Gordy that he too could be an impresario, Joe established his own record company, calling it Ivory Tower International Records. "Ivory is not a good name for black groups," Gordy warned him. The first group Joe signed was an "all-gal" singing quartet from Ohio. It took as its name the awkward-sounding "M.D.L.T. Willis." As Gordy predicted, the group bombed. One member of the troupe bombed in more ways than one.

Joe told Jermaine that he felt Michael "is old enough to lose his virginity." Joe persuaded one of the members of M.D.L.T. (the exact identity of whom is not known) to go to Michael's hotel room and seduce him. The singer was only too willing. She also agreed that it was about time that Michael "knew the taste of a woman."

From all reports, the evening was a disaster. Joe secured a pass key and gained admittance to Michael's bedroom. The girl slipped in and apparently tried to get physical with Michael, but a row developed. There was pushing and even wrestling, with Michael fleeing to the balcony. He screamed at the girl to leave his bedroom and even promised "to pray for you." He told her that he wasn't like his other brothers, "seducing every slut in Los Angeles." Highly insulted, the attractive singer stormed out of Michael's bedroom and spent the next few years telling anyone even remotely interested that "Michael

Jackson is a fag!"

Joe failed in this attempt to get Michael to surrender his virginity to a woman. But where daddy didn't make it, Michael's brothers hoped to succeed. One night they hired two of the best-looking hookers they could find—one blonde, one black—and sent them to Michael's hotel bedroom. Jackie, in a phone call to Michael, claimed the young women were friends of The Jackson 5 and wanted Michael's autograph.

Up until then, the brothers had been telling reporters that "Michael's no virgin." Tito even claimed that "my little brother's had more girls than all the other brothers combined." Of course, that was gross exaggeration. Perhaps it was done to camouflage the fear that Michael might be a homosexual. Even when he was fifteen, the whispering campaign had only begun and would greatly intensify in the years ahead.

Details are lacking but when the hookers were allowed inside Michael's room, they apparently let their intentions become known, especially when they tried to take off Michael's clothes. In panic, he tried to flee the room, only to find his bedroom door bolted from the outside. His brothers stood in the hallway, catcalling into Michael. "After you've finished with them, we get sloppy seconds," one of the brothers called.

To protect himself from the voracious women, Michael burst into tears. "What a turn-off," one of the hookers said. "Have you ever tried to seduce a guy who's crying like a five-year-old baby? No fun at all!"

The black hooker told one of the brothers, "Your pansy brother was reading the Bible when we left him."

"Getting Michael to surrender his cherry was a daunting task that no woman—and I mean that literally—would ever be able to accomplish," claimed a Motown executive. "Even when they invented Viagra, it wouldn't cure Michael. Not that one!"

"Michael just wasn't interested in the opposite sex," the executive continued. "I suspected that he was gay from the first day I met him. I truly don't know how Joe Jackson felt on the subject. I knew that homosexuality was against Katherine's religion. I also saw that the brothers were embarrassed by all this gay talk. They wanted Michael to be a lady-killer. But he wasn't. He just wasn't. Nor would he ever be. Let's face it: unlike his older brothers, Michael is no pussyhound."

Although just beginning his teenage years, Michel became the one Jackson brother that the girls, and even older women, pursued now that Jermaine was married. "I have a son older than Michael," said Alexis Klucker of Alabama, "but I still wanted to seduce that little boy. I don't know why, but I wanted him. Pimples and all, it didn't matter."

One woman, Betty Scaff, was arrested on the grounds of the Jackson's

Encino mansion. Somehow she'd managed to elude security and even the guard dogs. When Michael came out through the back door and headed for his own private zoo, she jumped out from her hiding place in the bushes. She attacked Michael and ripped off most of his clothes, demanding that he impregnate her.

Before she was hauled away by security, the woman proclaimed that if Michael would father a child with her, the kid would grow up "to become the second Jesus Christ."

In tears, Michael retreated to his bedroom to nurse his wounds and to brood for three days over this violent attack.

"I think Michael had every reason to fear women from that point on in his life," said Lennox Biggs, who once worked for Motown. "Girls grabbed his groin. They took wads of his hair. They demanded sex from him. And this one bitch even tried to rape him. How could he grow up viewing women as objects of love? To him, all women were sexual predators trying to take his precious virginity. Michael held onto that virginity—at least with women—like it was something worth protecting."

Joe failed to hook Michael up with a woman, but he got all his boys a booking into Las Vegas for the winter of 1974. Conditions were much improved for black entertainers there following the efforts of Sammy Davis Jr. When Davis first appeared in Las Vegas, he couldn't stay in the same hotel where he entertained all-white audiences.

Even during the mid-70s, Vegas audiences were still mainly white. Black acts didn't succeed very well there, unless they were crossovers, as The Supremes had demonstrated. Vegas nightclubs were also a showcase for the stars of yesterday, often booking nostalgic acts like pompadoured Frankie Avalon who sang "Venus" every night.

Gordy predicted that the Jackson brothers would bomb before the all-white audiences, but Michael was more enthusiastic. "If Sammy can be a hit there, so can I!" he said.

Joe wanted his boys to open at "the top joint," which means the MGM Grand. The Osmonds had been a big hit there, and Michael felt he and his brothers could top them.

For their opening night, Joe ordered La Toya to go on the stage with her brothers. She was only seventeen. Imitating the Osmond act, he also brought in Randy, who was only twelve, and even Janet at seven years old. Joe created novelty acts, having Janet and Randy impersonate Sonny and Cher in a satirical skit.

On her own, little Janet got a standing ovation with her take on the "Come Up and See Me Sometime" gal, Mae West. To hear a seven-year-old say, "It's not the men in my life but the life in my men that counts," made for a hilarious evening.

La Toya wanted to have more of a star role, but Joe wasn't impressed with her vocal range. He ordered her to lip sync. "Don't let one sound escape from your throat," he demanded, causing La Toya to burst into tears and run from the rehearsal hall. But on opening night, she obeyed her father's commands.

The Jackson 5 wooed the audience, especially Michael's acts, including his brilliant impersonation of Diana Ross. Later, when Ross heard what he'd done, she was "furious" at Michael for holding her up to public ridicule.

Another highlight of the show came when The Jackson 5 imitated The Andrew Sisters, the favorite singers of the boys who won World War II.

Caught unaware by the sudden success of The Jacksons in Vegas, Gordy told the press, "I wanted to see the boys expand their musical horizon." Joe was furious when word got back to him. "The fucker predicted we'd bomb. Now he's taking credit for *my* success."

When the show opened at Radio City Music Hall in New York, Vince Aletti, a critic, was one of the first to write about the "new" Michael on stage. "No matter how much I love the other Jacksons, it is Michael who is the group's aesthetic focus. His stylized show-biz posing (the bends and turns, arms outstretched and sweeping the air in front of him; little self-hugs with his head thrown back) is becoming a little disturbing, at moments even grotesque for a boy who's still a very skinny sixteen. But when he isn't being Engelbert Humperdinck, he's supreme and so controlled it's almost frightening. In his motel room, when he tells you he's in the 11th grade, it might seem strange, but it's believable. Seeing him onstage, dancing, and striding confidently out to the edge, you just know he's lying."

In the wake of the Cher special, the Jackson brothers continued to appear on national television, including a Bob Hope special. The Jackson brothers were booked to go on with John Denver and Ann-Margaret. One Jackson brother was overheard backstage telling what he'd like to do with busty, leggy Ann-Margaret should he ever get her alone. "I don't think she's all that sexy," Michael said petulantly. "Just because you can't handle it," Jermaine said, "doesn't mean your older brother can't. Never call in a kid to do a man's work."

Although he had middle-of-the-road humor before the camera, and never said anything offensive on stage, Hope could be raunchy once he was in his dressing room. He could also tell very indiscreet stories about his rivals.

He informed Michael that Milton Berle always stole his best jokes. "Uncle Milty dresses in drag all the time," Hope said. "Putting on women's clothes comes natural to him. He's got a real gay streak in him. In New York years ago, when we were both struggling, I shared a hotel room with Berle. He came on to me. Don't ever let him get you alone, kid. You'll be in for a surprise."

On their night off, Joe booked a private plane to fly his sons from Vegas to Lake Tahoe to the Sahara Hotel and Casino to hear one of their all-time favorites, Elvis Presley.

Elvis appeared dazed on stage that night, at one point looking in vain for his band but not really sure where they were. He wandered about bloated and drugged in a white jump suit. But the fans were loyal. One critic wrote, "Elvis Presley could have appeared last night with his big belly in a wheelbarrow, and his devoted fans would still adore him." One critic was even harsher: "Presley on stage last night looked like a bloated go-go girl from the 60s who had just been gang-raped by a rock band."

At one point Elvis stopped the show and walked forward toward the stunned audience. "You know where I might have ended up?" he asked the silent audience. "Flipping burgers in Memphis." That's all he said before launching into "Hound Dog," the lines of which he'd seemingly forgotten after having sung them countless times.

Michael was particularly shocked by the sound of Elvis's voice. "I didn't recognize it. It was not his 'Hound Dog' voice of the 50s. More a childlike voice. Almost like I used to sound. He talked, instead of sang most of his song."

"Elvis was up there on that stage last night like a man crying out for some-one to come and save him—yet knowing that no help would ever come," Joe said.

After the show, the manager personally came to the Jackson table to escort Michael backstage. He was terribly shy and almost shaking with nervousness, but Michael followed the director.

"The King wants to meet you," the manager told Michael.

As he was ushered into the dressing room of Elvis Presley, Michael could hardly have known that he was meeting his future father-in-law.

"Kings are supposed to compete with their predecessors and kings are supposed to marry other royals. Elvis's widow, Priscilla Presley, makes clear that she saw Michael Jackson as a scheming pretender, building Neverland to top Graceland, then courting Elvis's daughter to secure his lineage. But why shouldn't Lisa Marie Presley want the only man in the world as famous and powerful as her father? A man who might help her find her own way as a singer-songwriter, yet keep her in the royal arena to which she was accustomed?"

--Margo Jefferson

"When dancing, I felt touched by something sacred. In those moments I felt my spirit soar and become one with everything that exists. I became the stars and the moon, I became the lover and the loved."

--Michael Jackson

"I've recorded a whole lot of these pop musicians and Michael's the straightest of the goddamn lot. Ok, Michael's got a few quirks but everybody in California does."

--Bruce Swedien

"One of the oddest things about Michael Jackson is that this 45-year-old former Motown child prodigy has remained a superstar despite all the Peter Pan fantasies, Potemkin marriages, cosmetic surgery, spending sprees and now criminal charges of child molestation. He is both a popular entertainer and a tabloid freak show. In that sense he is the perfect icon for the shame-free age: a television twofer."

--Alessandra Stanley of *The New York Times*

"I feel guilty having to put my name on the songs I write. I do write them and compose them, and I do the scoring, lyrics, and melodies. But still. It's a...it's a work of God!"

--Michael Jackson

Chapter Four

Freddy Briggs, who worked at the Sahara, has been the only one who has come forward to give a personal account of the historic first and only meeting between the King of Rock-and-Roll and the King of Pop. Briggs attended to Elvis's wardrobe and other personal needs. "I even made him several peanut butter and jelly sandwiches," he said. "Elvis liked creamy peanut butter and preferred blackberry jam, at least during his stay at Lake Tahoe."

As Briggs later revealed, Michael was "tongue-tied around Elvis," calling him "Sir" and letting Elvis do most of the talking through slurred speech. Ironically, Elvis used to address men as "Sir" in his earlier days, but no more. "After he became King, he didn't need to be subservient to anyone," Briggs said.

Elvis greeted and was polite to all the Jackson brothers, but he knew where the talent lay, so he paid most of his attention to Michael, whom he spoke with privately.

The Elvis Presley that Michael encountered in Lake Tahoe was in a foul mood, although respectful of Michael. He'd just taken some unknown medication which seemed to wake him up and put him in a talkative mood. Based on his performance on stage, Michael expected Elvis in private to be a zombie, but instead the singer was strangely articulate, at least as long as the medication lasted.

"They all come to me for advice," Elvis, according to Briggs, told Michael. "If I have any advice to give you, it's 'go solo.' You're the star of the act, the only real talent. You're letting your brothers and all that background music drown you out. I never let that happen to me, and you shouldn't either. Tell them to go fuck themselves. You're the show, boy, and don't forget it."

Michael politely thanked Elvis for this advice, looking at Elvis with a devotion that seemed so genuinely sincere that Briggs believed that it had touched Elvis in some deep way. At one point during their encounter, Elvis reached for Michael's hand. "I owe a debt to all you black boys and your music. Without the music of 'the brothers' I heard back in the Forties, there would be no Elvis Presley today." He turned around and looked at himself in the mirror. It appeared that he couldn't formulate his next thought. "Who am I kidding? There is no more Elvis Presley. Like yesterday, Elvis Presley is dead and gone. The bastards killed him long ago. This bag of shit you see before you is all that's left of the great Elvis Presley."

"To me, you'll always be the greatest," Michael said in a soft voice. "Your music will live forever."

"That sounds like a suck-up to me, boy," Elvis said. "But even if you're lying, what you just said is appreciated."

"Do you have any other advice to give me," Michael said. "I mean, you've gone so far in the business."

"Sure, I have more advice, but I don't expect you to follow it. No one ever does. Don't become a really big and famous star. If you do, you'll live to regret it. Stardom—I mean really big stardom, not the Ann-Margaret stuff— makes you pay such a price that it will destroy you. Nearly all really big stars have to suffer indignities and invasions of their private lives to such a degree that it's not worth it. If you become super famous, every little asshole in the world will be out to get you. They'll resent your fame and want to turn it into infamy, particularly if they can make a buck off you. Speaking of bucks, if you make the big ones, the world—or at least someone in the world—will figure out how to take it from you. It's happened to me. It'll happen to you. The press used to say I was a sweet Southern boy. No more. Have you read the shit written about me?"

"I don't read stuff like that," Michael said.

"I don't read it either," Elvis said. "If you do become big, don't read the papers, the tabloids, and those magazines. If you start reading what the fuckers write, it can destroy you. You won't even have enough courage to go on the stage if you read the shit."

There was a knock on Elvis's door, which Freddy went to answer. Joe, along with his other sons, was waiting to take Michael away.

"Gimme your phone number, boy," Elvis said to Michael. "I'd

Elvis: The Farewell Months

76

like to call you some night, real late, and talk more with you. There are so many things I could tell you. I have this great hunch that in the 80s you're gonna become what I was in the 50s. Revolutionary. But with a totally different kind of music than mine."

As Michael headed for the door, Elvis reached to shake his hand but decided instead to lock him in a warm embrace. "Be good now, you hear?"

"I stayed up with Elvis until late in the night after Jackson left," Briggs said. "He seemed lonely and I was a big fan. At first when he invited me up to his hotel suite, I thought it was for sex, and I was most willing, even though I'm basically straight. You don't turn down a star. He didn't want sex. He wanted company. During the night he had me place several calls for him around the country. I called numbers but I didn't know who they were to. On the phone, Elvis talked for hours. He was incoherent. I think he made up a lot of things. He was paranoid, claiming the FBI was trying to kill him because 'I knew too much.' He also claimed that everybody who even remotely knew him was writing a book to expose him. There were three phones in the suite. At one point Elvis ripped one phone out of the wall and tossed it at the television set. I forgot what program was on, but Elvis didn't like what he was seeing."

From all reports, and there have been dozens, Elvis continued his habit of calling people in the middle of the night and babbling into the phone. At times he was completely irrational. Acquaintances reported that there would be long periods of silence before he started talking again. "Perhaps some of Elvis's stories were true—perhaps not," Briggs said. "Those I heard sounded far-fetched to me. But, considering Elvis and all the crap that happened to him, they just might have been true."

"I know for a fact that Elvis planned to call Jackson," Briggs said, "even though he referred to him as 'the little nigger boy.' That was such a put-down of Jackson, but the way Elvis said it—and I know this sounds crazy—it was an affectionate reference."

"Like, would you tell your secrets to Michael Jackson?" Briggs asked Elvis.

"There's no way that Michael Jackson is gonna write a book about me," Elvis told Briggs. "No way. You can trust people who don't write books. From what I know, the kid can't even read and write. I hear his brothers never went to school. Not that I got much education myself. Living a life like I've lived is all the education I need. I've seen it all!"

"I don't get it," Briggs said. "Why would you tell Michael Jackson your secrets?"

"The kid has an honest face, and I know I can trust him with my most private secrets," Elvis told Briggs.

"Secrets are dangerous things," Briggs warned Elvis. "Why tell them to anyone? They might use them against you."

"Don't you think I know that?" Elvis asked. "But I've got to confess them before I die. It's a compulsion with me. I can't stop myself. I know it's crazy. I have to unburden myself, and I'm playing with fire telling all this shit about myself. I know it'll get in print one day for the world to learn about. There's a war going on inside myself. The good side of me wants to protect myself from all harm. But there's another side of me that is trying to destroy Elvis Presley. Not only abusing his body, but telling his darkest secrets so my fans will know what's really going on and will be revolted by me."

It was seven o'clock in the morning before Briggs finally left Elvis's hotel suite. Dawn had come, but you wouldn't know it if you were in the suite, because heavy black velvet curtains blotted out the day.

"When I was putting Elvis to bed, I couldn't resist," Briggs said. "I just had to slip off his jockey shorts and see what it looked like. After all, he'd been the sex symbol of the 50s, and I wanted to see what drove all those girls crazy—and also how I stacked up against the King. The first voyeur who's willing to give me five-thousand dollars will get a complete description of it, in all its uncut glory, even a description of Elvis's balls. So that I would never forget, I even sketched what I'd seen that morning. Before becoming a 'gofer' at some fucking hotel, I had wanted to be an artist. Here was my chance. I plan to sell reproductions of my sketches of Elvis's privates for big bucks to collectors."

Contrary to what he had told Elvis, in the months leading up to the death of the singer on August 16, 1977, Michael read every item he could find that had ever been written about Elvis. But calls from Elvis to Michael, spilling out dark secrets, never came to be.

After Elvis's demise, Michael became even more obsessed with the circumstances surrounding the death of the former truck driver from Memphis. In the immediate hours following Elvis's death, Michael repeatedly played such hit songs as "Jailhouse Rock" and "Love Me Tender." And ghoulishly, Michael became obsessed with learning the most minute details of the autopsy performed on Elvis by Dr. Eric Muirhead, chief of the department of pathology at the Memphis hospital where Elvis was taken. Michael learned that Dr. Muirhead, in an inch-by-inch study of Elvis's corpse, found that the skin was "pitted" with numerous needle marks, almost too many to count accurately.

What allegedly fascinated Michael even more was when he learned that Elvis's rib cage had been cut open with a saw, exposing his lungs and heart. Painstakingly, each organ was examined after removal from the body cavity. The organs were weighed and studied carefully. Elvis's much-abused liver was found to resemble "pâté de foie gras," the French goose liver specialty served in *luxe* restaurants.

The large intestine was clogged with fecal matter. One intern at the hospital morbidly joked, "The doctors learned that the King was full of shit, maybe forty feet of it."

Michael also learned that Elvis's heart was greatly enlarged. More than a dozen drugs, including significant amounts of codeine, were detected in Elvis's blood stream. Quaalude appeared in a toxic amount.

The staff at the hospital seemed particularly concerned that the autopsy on Elvis would not become the source of scandal the way it had on the one performed on the slain John F. Kennedy in 1963. Therefore, they proceeded to conduct the procedure on Elvis with extreme caution and meticulousness. Even so, the debate over Elvis's death would rage for at least a quarter of a century and beyond, evoking the usual lawsuits, book exposés, and even medical disbarment.

The usual procedure in an autopsy is to examine each organ exhaustively and remove tissue samples, placing them into bottles filled with preservatives. After that gruesome procedure, the brain is returned to the skull and the displaced organs "stuffed" back into the body the way a cook might assemble a Thanksgiving turkey.

In the wake of Elvis's death, there was a rumor that his body parts had not been returned to his corpse, but were still preserved in a laboratory. Rumors also spread that Michael made an attempt to secretly purchase Elvis's enlarged heart. Allegedly Michael also wanted Elvis's large intestine with the fecal matter intact. These stories may have been just scurrilous gossip at the time, and they cannot be confirmed. But in his future, Michael would be accused of similar ghoulish acts with the dead.

After his now legendary meeting with Elvis, Michael's life began to spin out of control. A fan, Theresa Gonsalves, pursued Michael to Las Vegas. Only sixteen, she was invited by Katherine to stay with the Jackson family. At first she was disappointed with Michael, finding him "arrogant and stuck up." But she finally warmed to Michael and they became friends, a relationship that would last for four years. Finally, when The Jacksons went to dinner and Michael stayed behind, Theresa got to be alone with her idol. As dreams of romance played out in her head, she was disappointed when Michael took out his Jehovah's Witness Bible and lectured her. "It's a sin to have sex outside of marriage," he told her, promising to pray for her redemption.

Following Michael's appearance with his brothers in Las Vegas, he was eager to abandon the group. He decided to pursue another solo album, *Forever Michael*, which would be released in January of 1975.

But he was distracted in rehearsals when Joe announced to his sons that they had a half-sister. Cheryl Terrell had given birth to a daughter, Joh Vonnie. Joe was the proud father.

Still married to Joe, Katherine referred to the Terrells as "that whore and her bastard child." Michael later claimed that the news of the addition to the Jackson family "made me want to vomit."

Not to be deterred, Joe purchased a midsize but tasteful home for his unmarried girlfriend and his new daughter only a short drive from the Jackson's Encino mansion. After enduring her humiliation for weeks, Katherine finally exploded. She drove to the Terrell household and attacked her rival when she appeared in her driveway. Her husband's baby was fastened into the Terrell car for a shopping expedition. Katherine yanked the hair of Joe's mistress, slapped her face, and knocked her down on the gravel.

Hearing the news an hour later, Michael rushed to Katherine's bedroom to console his mother, to whom he was still devoted. He pleaded with his mother to call her attorneys and reinstate her divorce proceedings against Joe. Katherine agreed to do that and packed her luggage, flying to stay with her mother. Three weeks later, after Joe pleaded with her on the phone, telling her that "You are the only woman I've ever loved," Katherine reluctantly returned to the household. Michael was disappointed at her capitulation to Joe.

The Jackson family continued to expand when Jackie married Enid Spann, age twenty. Her father was black but her mother had been born in Korea. The family, especially Joe, opposed Jackie's marriage, which was eventually celebrated on December 6, 1974. Jackie was extremely casual about his wedding, showing up in denim and gym shoes, with a wedding band he'd purchased at K-Mart.

Even though he'd recorded *Forever Michael* during a period of turmoil, Michael hoped for its success. But the album bombed, never going beyond 101 on *Billboard's* charts, selling fewer than 100,000 copies. Joe was furious when he heard of the disappointing sales. "No more solo albums for Michael," he said. Joe blamed the failure of the album on Gordy and his lack of promotion.

Forever Michael would be the singer's last album for Motown. Although the album was a failure, one song surfaced: "One Day In Your Life."

In a rare act of defiance, Michael called Gordy and arranged to meet with him alone. This had never happened before. Eager to hear what the real star of the Jackson family had to say, Gordy set up an appointment with Michael and didn't let Joe know what was going on.

Michael himself has admitted that his reputation is one of shyness. Although that is true, when he wanted something, he could have the resolve of a steel magnolia. The day Gordy met with Michael, the promoter saw a determination he'd never seen in any of The Jacksons, certainly not in his son-in-law, Jermaine, and a resolve unmatched by that of Joe himself.

"After that day, I never thought of Michael as a wimp," Gordy later said.

The secret rendezvous took place at the Gordy manse in Bel Air, California, on May 14, 1975. The meeting went badly, with Michael threatening to organize his family's abandonment of Motown, in spite of family ties through marriage. He poured out his frustration and unhappiness with the way Motown had controlled the group, not letting the brothers chart their own course with their own songs and instrumentation.

"Listen to me, kid," Gordy shouted at Michael in anger. "I picked you boys up in some Rust Belt hellhole in Indiana. You were playing stripper joints before I discovered you. Remember, without Berry Gordy, you'd be flipping burgers."

Finally, Gordy sighed. "I even let your brothers live in my own home. I moved you in with Diana Ross, a class act. I treated you like family. How can you even contemplate walking out on me after all I've done for you?"

That angered Michael. "Let me restate that. I respect you greatly. You're a genius in the business. But it's not a question of what you've done for us. It's what we've done for you. We worked our hearts out for one of the lowest royalty rates—perhaps the lowest in the business. A pathetic 2.7 percent." With that, Michael stormed out of Gordy's home. Their face-to-face encounter had utterly failed, and had, in fact, led to a lot of damage.

When Michael arrived home after the meeting, Joe had been tipped off by one of Gordy's household staff. He was waiting to beat Michael with a large thick leather belt with a steel buckle. When Michael came into the house, Joe didn't wait to have an argument. The sting of the whip slashed across Michael's face. When he realized what was happening, he fled from the house, outrunning his father. His whereabouts remained unknown for ten days.

To this day, no one knows where he went. But he was seen on Hollywood Boulevard three days later in a large sedan driven by an older man. When Michael finally did return home, Joe had cooled down considerably. He told Michael that he had decided that The Jackson 5 was "bolting Motown. It's our fuck-you to Jermaine's father-in-law."

Michael had nothing to say.

Joe called a meeting of all his sons, except Jermaine. Because of his marriage to Hazel, Joe didn't think he could trust Jermaine since "he's in the enemy camp." Michael joined in a vote with Jackie, Marlon, and Tito to split from Motown. Joe promised his sons that there was big money to be made at a much higher royalty rate at another record company. "You guys are big now because of me," Joe boasted. "I can make the deal of the century for you."

But other companies were not forthcoming with deals. The failure of Michael's recent album and the hit-or-miss sales racked up by the Jacksons didn't impress Atlantic Records, which nixed any hopes of linking their future to The Jackson 5.

Joe found a more receptive home at CBS Records, especially at its branch, Epic Records, which specialized in African-American entertainers.

Joe was happy to receive a check for $750,000 in upfront money. He also walked away with another half-a-million dollars for a development fund to produce Jackson 5 albums. Not only that, but he managed to negotiate an astonishing $350,000 per album as a guarantee against future sales, even if those sales didn't happen.

The advances were to be recouped from royalties, in a style that mimicked procedures that were prevalent in book publishing, but that rate was raised from 2.7 percent to 27 percent. "The decimal just disappeared," Joe boasted. And if sales shot up beyond the half million mark on an album, The Jackson 5 would get a 30 percent return. Epic did not grant complete artistic freedom, however, but allowed the brothers to select a trio of songs for each of their albums.

The bolting of The Jackson 5 from Motown was hailed as "the divorce of the century." Already in decline, Motown had lost such stars as Gladys Knight and The Pips, The Isley Brothers, The Four Tops, and The Temptations. Gordy had also witnessed the decline of his other acts, including the once-supreme Supremes.

Gordy told a reporter, "The Jacksons say they aren't being paid enough. Hell, they've made millions off me."

Jermaine faced a painful dilemma: To remain, professionally speaking, with his wife, Hazel, and her father, or else break from Motown, following Joe and his brothers. "Jermaine voted with his dick," said a raunchy Motown exec. "He stayed in Hazel's bed and told old Daddy-Pooh to go fuck himself, which he should have done long ago. Besides, I heard that Gordy had promised to make Jermaine a star in his own right, instead of appearing in Michael's shadow."

Jermaine explained it differently to the press. "I wasn't choosing between two families. I was making a selection between two rival recording companies. Motown or Epic."

Angered by Jermaine's decision, Joe blasted back. "It's my God damn blood that flows through Jermaine's body—not Berry Gordy's."

The farewell performance of The Jackson 5 occurred in Las Vegas in a final show in the summer of 1975. Michael suffered more from Jermaine's loss than his brothers. "I *depended* on being next to Jermaine. And when I did that first show without him there, with no one next to me, I felt totally naked onstage for the first time in my life."

Berry Gordy had been a smart executive. Even though he lost the Jackson brothers, he still owned the entire Jackson 5 catalogue. He was also sitting on a mountain of unissued recordings that the group had stockpiled over the years. Had he wished, he could have flooded the market with these recordings, potentially wiping out the sales of future Jackson 5 records through oversaturation of the marketplace.

That didn't happen, and The Jacksons, especially Michael, were set to move on into what one critic called "a record-busting future."

Regrettably, Joe had to abandon the name "The Jackson 5." Thanks to not having read the fine print when he'd signed the contract with Motown, Motown owned the rights to the use of the singing group's name. Consequently, Joe had to rename his boys "The Jacksons."

At a somber press conference during the summer of 1975 at New York's Rainbow Grill, the Jackson brothers, along with Joe, but without Jermaine, announced to the world they were leaving Motown. The announcement was premature, as The Jackson 5 contract would continue until March of 1976. The brothers had jumped ship before they were actually free to do so, an act of disloyalty that wasn't lost on the ever-sharp Gordy. Nonetheless, at the conference, Joe claimed that Epic, unlike Motown, which had often focused on the release of their songs as singles, would concentrate on issuing albums.

Gordy fought back, ordering his attorneys to file a $5 million breach of contract suit. Later, in his rage, he upped the ante to $20 million, his claim for damages. Almost immediately, Joe countersued.

To show he was still in control of The Jackson 5, Gordy ordered the release of a new Jackson 5 album, called *Moving Violation*. As if to show that Joe was wrong in his charges of neglect, Gordy worked personally to promote and distribute the album. But even so savvy a promoter as Gordy could not make *Moving Violation* a hit.

Gordy had hoped for a breakthrough single on the album—perhaps the solo version, "Moving Violation" itself—or else "All I Do Is Think of You." But no such luck.

That September, Gordy, exercising the rights of his contract, demanded that Joe bring the brothers back to Motown for another recording session. Joe adamantly refused, calling Gordy "a bastard," "an asshole," and a "son of a bitch." Wiser than his father this time, Michael urged caution. "A contract is a contract," he told Joe.

Michael was right. It would take years for Motown's lawsuit to be resolved, but it finally was, when Gordy got $600,000—not $20 million—in damages he'd legally sought.

Gordy later said, "At that time, I didn't know the full extent of what losing an act like The Jackson 5 would mean. I also did not know that in the industry it was hunting season, and Motown was the biggest game in town.

They were all after us."

Joe had been savvy about moving over to Epic. Their first Jackson single, "Enjoy Yourself," sold a million copies. Their second recording, "Show You the Way to Go," topped the charts in Britain, the first time the brothers had ever accomplished that. Randy, by this time, had joined the group, playing the bongos.

Billed as The Jacksons, the brothers released their first album for Epic in 1976. To introduce America to the group's new name, the album was entitled simply *The Jacksons*. "Enjoy Yourself," a rollicking disco-style song, was the number one single on the album. The album only reached number 36 on *Billboard's* charts. And as if he wanted to intentionally sabotage sales, Motown released *Joyful Jukebox Music*, another Jackson album compiled from previously recorded songs. Despite the fact that the competing album failed, it nonetheless diluted the allure of Epic's release. Meanwhile, on his own, Jermaine recorded his first Motown release, *My Name Is Jermaine*. It never got beyond number 164 on the charts.

Without Jermaine, Papa Joe moved ahead with what he thought would become "a big deal" for his sons.

Over Michael's objections, Joe signed his sons to star in their own TV series for CBS. Michael called it "that stupid summer replacement," fearing that overexposure on the tube would damage sales of their recordings. He protested the "ridiculous outfits" he and his brothers wore and the "silly comedy routines" played to canned laughter.

In spite of Michael's complaints, the four-week series of 30-minute programs was a groundbreaker for black entertainers, as no African-American family had ever starred in a series for TV.

The funniest moments on the show involved Janet's impersonations of Mae West. She stole all the lines West, with her hourglass figure, had made famous: "When I'm good, I'm very good. But when I'm bad, I'm better." After watching Janet on TV, producer Norman Lear cast her in the sitcom *Good Times*. A new star had emerged in the Jackson family.

After an initial flurry of success, CBS canceled the Jackson TV series in January of 1977. It had landed at the bottom of the Nielsen chart, ending up in 70th position. Michael later claimed that the show was canceled because he wouldn't agree to a new contract, but that was not true. The Jacksons weren't the only series booted. Variety show after variety show was canceled, including *Sonny and Cher*.

In New York the Jackson brothers performed at the Nassau Coliseum, setting box office records there. In spite of their hit-and-miss career so far, plenty of fans, often black teenagers, were willing to shell out big bucks to get a look at the Jackson brothers.

With the obvious sex symbol of the group, the more studly Jermaine, out of the picture, the girls began to fantasize about a date with Michael, in spite of his impossibly thin figure and fey manner.

Michael had seen *The Wiz* on Broadway an astonishing five times, little knowing that he'd eventually co-star in the movie version. Backstage he'd been introduced to Stephanie Mills, a small package of talent with a voice that was sometimes compared to that of the Broadway legend, Ethel Merman.

Promoters for Michael had been advising him to invite a girl out on a date to combat rumors of homosexuality, but Michael had steadfastly refused. Under growing pressure, he decided to give in and pop the question—a request for a date, that is—to the petite Mills, considering her harmless enough.

Stephanie was only fifteen when she starred as Dorothy in *The Wiz*, and was very disappointed when she lost the film role to Diana Ross, who was "far too old to play Dorothy." As a performer, Stephanie had been discovered by Michael's brother, Jermaine, and she had signed with Motown in 1974. Even after her eventual break from Motown, Michael continued to listen to Stephanie's songs, as, for example, when she recorded the highly danceable "Put Your Body In It" and "What Cha Gonna Do With My Lovin'?" Before their date was over that night, she'd told Michael: "God touched my soul and told me he was going to make me a star!"

Amazingly, perhaps to protect himself in case Mills got "too familiar" on their date, Michael also invited a most unlikely guest, Andy Warhol.

It's not exactly clear how Michael met the pop artist. The introduction perhaps had occurred through their mutual friend, Liza Minnelli, but there have been other claims as well.

The setting for the late-night outing of this "threesome" was Régine's on Park Avenue, then the most sophisticated nightclub in New York.

Of Sephardic North African descent, Régine was already of "a certain age" as she greeted Mills, Warhol, and Michael at the door of her club. Warhol had already kept Michael waiting for one hour. In front of Régine, Warhol explained why he was so late and thanked her for holding their table. "When I went to take a shower, I thought I detected crabs. And it took some time to get rid of them. I have a special solution. All gay men who sleep around know about it."

Dubbed *La reine de la Nuit Parisienne*, Régine seemed enchanted by Michael, although most of her attention was directed to a table of Brazilian millionaires who were demanding her presence. They had paid one-million dollars for five people to fly from Rio to New York for a glorious weekend. One busty, blonde American movie star, whose career was fading, had agreed to fly in from Los Angeles and fuck all five millionaires for a fee of $100,000 per customer.

Michael seemed entranced to watch Régine "work the room," as she mingled with the famous and the infamous, including both American and British "royalty." She seemed as comfortable with titans of industry as she was with upscale hookers, the idle and bored, the terminally jaded, and the socially ambitious.

To Michael's dazzled eyes, the setting was a gathering of the *glitterati* on New York's *après*-midnight scene.

"It's all style without substance," Warhol told Michael. "A viper's nest of roiling ambition. All of it horrendously snobbish and artfully arch, and how I love it! A feeding frenzy for the tabloids."

On the way into Régine's, Michael had passed the *demimondaines* of Europe (later known as Euro-Trash), shivering in gossamer dresses for the signal that would let them come inside.

At table, Mills made several obvious plays for Michael, but as Warhol would later tell Bianca Jagger, "The boy showed no interest at all."

At one point in the evening, Warhol startled Michael by saying, "I understand you Jackson brothers have to work like niggers in the cotton fields because you have no real money."

Michael politely asked him not to use the word "nigger."

"*Please*, this is no civil rights rally," Warhol said. "I am using the word as a form of endearment. You see, I'm always in the avant-garde. One day the word 'nigger' will be perfectly acceptable. Right now queer is a bad word. But one day gays themselves will refer to themselves as queer. I know about such things."

Andy Warhol

When Mills got up to go to the ladies room, Warhol leaned toward Michael to whisper something confidential. "I want you to star in my next movie."

Michael's eyes lit up. The idea of making an Andy Warhol movie intrigued him. He wanted to know more.

"It's very experimental," Warhol said. "My film will show only your face in close-up for twenty minutes."

"And what am I to do for that long?" a perplexed Michael asked.

"Forgive me, but I understand you're a virgin. I mean, I was told that your rectum has never been penetrated. In my film, I want to photograph only your face as a young and well-endowed model penetrates you for the first time. I also want to record every sound coming from your throat, including your cries of pain as you lose your cherry."

Michael was rescued by Régine herself, who appeared in a stylish but old Chanel gown and asked him to step with her onto the dance floor. As

Stephanie Mills

she whirled around, she still greeted both friends and acquaintances. She even managed to continue dancing with Michael when one of her very handsome and blond French waiters handed her a crystal glass of champagne.

"No one can play the night as well as Régine herself," she whispered into Michael's ear.

Later, after Michael saw to it that Mills was delivered safely back to her room, Andy pressed an invitation onto him.

"It's a very special event I've been invited to, and I want you to go with me. Arnold Schwarzenegger is in town. He's German, maybe Austrian. He's got the world's most gorgeous body. He was Mr. Universe or something. Absolutely gorgeous. Tonight he's going to take off his posing pouch and appear nude in a number of poses for wealthy fans of body builders. It'll be thrilling. Tonight you'll get to see exactly what Mr. Universe is packing in that posing pouch. He's tantalized us long enough. I hear it's a thick, uncut Teutonic sausage."

"No, thank you!" Michael said abruptly. "I really must go. It's long past my bedtime."

Months later, Warhol would neither confirm nor deny if such a party for bodybuilder fans ever took place.

In the wake of Mills, Michael would soon be linked to another "girl-friend."

He may have brushed past actress Tatum O'Neal at a party Paul McCartney tossed in 1975 aboard the *Queen Mary* in Long Beach, California. She would have been only twelve years old at the time. Michael was seventeen—"and ripe for plucking, darling—that's plucking with a P," said a gay friend of Cher's who had unsuccessfully tried to seduce Michael. "I wanted to be the first, but, alas, I got a lecture on morality instead."

Michael's relationship with the famous Beatle, and with Tatum herself, lay in the future.

It wasn't until April of 1977 that Michael and Tatum launched a much misunderstood friendship. It began at Jack Nicholson's On the Rox Club on Sunset Strip when Tatum showed up with her handsome, sandy-haired father, actor Ryan O'Neal, still remembered for his portrayal in that drippy 1970 film, *Love Story*. Tatum's father was one of the great womanizers of Hollywood. His seductions had included Mia Farrow, Melanie Griffith, Anjelica Huston, Bianca Jagger, Ali MacGraw, Liza Minnelli, Joan Collins, Oona Chaplin (widow of Charlie), and even Margaret Trudeau, wife of the Canadian prime minister. His most famous affair was with Farrah Fawcett. Both Berry Gordy and O'Neal had competed for the favors of Diana Ross. Gordy claimed that O'Neal had "the whitest damn teeth I have ever seen in my life."

Michael and Ryan were talking confidentially about the need for privacy. O'Neal told Michael, "I'm as moody and complex and private as anyone I ever knew—except you!"

In *Moonwalk*, Michael recalled, "I was sitting at this table and all of a sudden I felt this soft hand reach over and grab mine. It was Tatum. *She touched me.*" He later claimed "I fell in love with her" and made the preposterous statement, "and she with me." Once again, as with Ross, Michael invented a love relationship that didn't really exist. Call his so-called "affair" with Tatum a friendship. She certainly characterized it as that.

Tatum had appeared in the 1973 film, *Paper Moon*, opposite her real-life father. She stole the picture from him as the tough-talking, cigarette-smoking orphan. At the age of ten, she became the youngest performer to win an Oscar. Before her subsequent decline and eventual marriage to tennis player John McEnroe, she was considered a "hot child actor."

As unbelievable as it sounds, twelve-year-old Tatum called Michael and asked him out on a date. He accepted. To his surprise, she took him to a dinner in Holmby Hills. It turned out to be within the notorious mansion of Hugh Hefner, the *Playboy* publisher. Ryan O'Neal was a frequent visitor to the mansion and a favorite of the "Bunnies," allegedly because of his great skill in the sack. On their first night together, Tatum and Michael watched part of the TV mini-series, *Roots*, by Alex Haley.

Michael was enthralled by *Roots*, relating his own experiences in Senegal to Tatum. At one point she became distracted and invited Michael to join her in Hefner's "hot tub," where male movie stars often cavorted in the nude with *Playboy* Bunnies.

When he protested that he didn't have a bathing suit, she called him a "square," but finally secured one for him from one of Hefner's waiters.

Apparently, a waiter at Hefner's mansion that night tried to sell a story to the *National Enquirer* that he'd spotted a "totally nude" Tatum and a "jaybird naked" Michael fornicating in the hot tub. The rumor spread like wildfire. One underground paper in Hollywood carried the headline: TATUM BUSTS MICHAEL'S CHERRY. Yet another scurrilous rag, skirting the laws of libel, proclaimed that GAY MICHAEL SAMPLES STRAIGHT SEX WITH UNDERAGE TEEN STAR.

Ryan O'Neal

Michael later suggested that all Tatum and he did that night was "look for shooting stars and share our deepest secrets." He later asked a question of a reporter for the *Los Angeles Times*: "Why do people insist on always finding something dirty in the most harmless pastimes?"

Tatum left early that night to go home, but Michael was invited to stay on by Hefner himself. The original Playboy had just emerged from one of the upstairs boudoirs where he'd been occupied for most of the evening.

"You're a virgin, I hear," Hefner asked Michael as a way of introducing himself.

Michael blushed but did not directly answer the question. "We've all got our dark secrets."

"I can introduce you to one of my 'Special Ladies' tonight," Hefner offered. "She will rob you of your virginity forever."

"No thanks," Michael said.

"Come on, boy, live a little," Hefner urged. "I never recommend a brunette for the job of cherry stealing. A brunette is a type of woman you marry or at least take for a mistress. For the initial seduction, blondes are preferred, as they are always dangerous and forbidden, whether bottle or natural. They represent the forbidden sexuality, danger. As for redheads, they are a mere variation of the blonde. Also, danger. So what will it be: blonde or redhead."

"Mr. Hefner, I'm sure your Bunnies are wonderful," Michael said in a soft voice. "But at my age, the only Bunny I'm interested in is Bugs Bunny."

"Oh, I get it," Hefner said. "You're gay. Don't worry, I have several handsome waiters here who are most accommodating."

"Excuse me, Mr. Hefner," Michael said, getting up. "But I've got to go. I really thank you for your hospitality."

Their personalities could not have been more different, but after that night at the Playboy mansion, Michael and Tatum developed an unlikely friendship.

Sassy and precocious, Tatum was the very opposite of Michael. She was hip whereas he was square. She was cynical, Michael dreamy-eyed. But nonetheless, Tatum and Michael bonded, perhaps because of the childhood trauma each had endured. Both had "distant" fathers.

But there were differences: Michael claimed that his mother, Katherine, was a saint. Tatum's own mother, actress Joanna Moore, was an alcoholic, drifting in and out of her daughter's life, often destructively.

As their friendship deepened, Tatum poured out her past *angst* to Michael. She described how her Darvon-addicted mother once left her and her brother, Griffin, locked away in a room for hours. "We had no choice but to defecate on the floor," Tatum said. One time Joanna went away for a weekend, according to Tatum, having locked Tatum and Griffin in a bathroom. "She simply forgot about us." Once Joanna left them locked in a garage where they had to eat dog food to survive. Tatum's life with her mother made Christina Crawford's upbringing with Joan Crawford, as related in the 1981 *Mommie Dearest*, seem like a garden party. In her memoirs, *A Paper Life*, Tatum claimed that Joanna "was freewheeling with her fists, coming from a generation that was big on beatings."

Oddly enough, both Michael and Tatum had adopted rats as pets. At a ramshackle ranch where Tatum lived with her mother, Tatum set out food for the rodents along with water. Her brother, Griffin, and Tatum adopted the rats as pets and gave them names.

Michael's love for his pet rats ended badly when he came home one day and saw Father Rat eating his young babies. Tatum's love affair with rodents ended when her mother's fifteen-year-old boyfriend claimed that rats had rabies and threw them in a pond "and made us watch them drown," Tatum claimed. "Since rats can swim, it took a very long time, and it completely freaked us out. I grieved for days."

With such an unlikely beginning, Michael and Tatum continued this "odd couple" relationship that he'd repeat with both genders throughout the rest of the 20th and 21st century.

Tatum did admit that she found her long drawn-out conversations with Michael so boring that she would often hand over the receiver of the phone to a friend who listened as Michael droned on and on.

She found Michael "incredibly sweet and innocent," surprising, she admitted for a world-renowned performer. "His usual subject was sex," Tatum said, although admitting that at the age of twelve, even though worldly for her years, she didn't have a lot to contribute on the subject, except what she'd heard coming from her father's bedroom next to hers.

If Tatum is to be believed, the so-called seduction that Michael once bragged about didn't really happen, and Tatum is most trustworthy, having written such a candid memoir. Having rarely, if ever, viewed a girl's bedroom before, Michael asked to see where Tatum slept. "He sat on my bed, and we kissed very briefly," Tatum confessed, "but it was terribly awkward." All she remembered was Michael, "sweating profusely," jumping up and apologizing, claiming he had to go.

At the time of Michael's so-called "affair" with Tatum, various publications were offering good money to the first girl—or woman—who seduced Michael, taking his virginity. Various bets were placed, and some incidents of dubious authenticity were reported in headline news in such national publications as *The Star*. Various actresses, models, and singers were said to have attempted to seduce Michael—but to no avail.

Even Margaux Hemingway got in on the act. Born in Idaho, she was the daughter of Jack Hemingway, son of the Nobel Prize winning author Ernest Hemingway. She met Michael at the height of her fame when she had a budding movie career and a one-million-dollar promotional contract with Fabergé perfume. Her face was appearing on magazine covers around the world.

In Key West, Florida, in 1996, a few months before her suicide by overdose in Santa Monica, California, Margaux told her hostess, Hazel Triplett, that she once had a standing bet with Tatum as to which one could seduce Michael first. Margaux, who stood six feel tall in her bare feet, claimed that she had encountered Michael on several occasions. She even took to calling him "Boopsie" and invited him to go hiking with her in Idaho—"I know all the best trails."

"I completely struck out, and as I understand it, so did Tatum," she said. "I tried everything, but Michael eluded me. I hear he was as fleet footed as Mercury and outran his father to escape beatings. He got away from me, too, even though I was fast on my feet in spite of my size."

Later in her life, as she plunged into drugs and alcohol, Margaux in her decline sent several urgent appeals to Michael to help her. It is not known if these letters were even delivered to him. Once she invited him to Cicada, one of Hollywood's hippest restaurants, to hear her sing the blues, but he never showed up. Margaux was desperate for money and was forced to declare bankruptcy and to appear in sexually kinky B-movies. At one point, she lent her endorsement to a psychic hotline and supported herself by autographing nude photos of herself in *Playboy*.

Margaux confessed that her last attempt to

Griffin O'Neal

91

seduce Michael occurred one night at Studio 54 in New York. "He was there with the Liza Minnelli and Warhol crowd, and I went for him but he didn't go for me, although he did dance with me. I loved to dance. But somehow after he rejected me, I ended up feeling like a big potato from Idaho."

"Many doors were open to me because my last name was Hemingway," she once told Michael. "But to tell you the truth, I never cracked one of Papa's books. I have dyslexia."

Although Michael attacked rumors about himself for most of his career, he deliberately encouraged speculation about a romance with Tatum. *Tout Hollywood* wasn't to be fooled. At cocktail parties, some insiders of the industry were circulating far different rumors about Michael and his involvement with the O'Neals. As one made the party circuit in those days, the word was out that Michael had fallen not for Tatum but for her cute little brother, Griffin. If there were a crush—and this is pure speculation and gossip—it was strictly on Michael's part, not on Griffin's.

Griffin admired Michael's musical talent, and perhaps a friendship developed, but that was it. Tatum herself called her brother a "musical savant," and he was known for his skill not only at the drums but on the guitar. "He wasn't Liberace, but he could play a mean piano," his father said. Even Michael was impressed with Griffin's talents, and he would play the drums with Griffin, seemingly enjoying time spent with him instead of with Tatum. Tatum didn't seem jealous in the least, since she harbored no romantic fantasies about Michael.

These concerts between Michael and Griffin took place at 9897 Beverly Grove Drive in a house that had once belonged to John Barrymore. At the time, Griffin was small for his age and had a slight frame. Since this was the type of young boy Michael was allegedly drawn to, rumors were rampant, although completely untrue. "When did rumors ever have to be true in Hollywood?" a future friend of Michael's, Marlon Brando, once asked. "In fact, rumors often reveal more about the people spreading them than the subject of the gossip."

According to Tatum, within the text of her autobiography, *A Paper Life,* Michael lectured Griffin on the evils of pot-smoking and tried to get him to give up the habit. But Griffin refused. An intimate of the O'Neals, Michael quickly learned the family secrets. It brought back painful memories of his own father when he witnessed Ryan physically striking Griffin. As the boy cried from his beatings, Michael tried to console him, wishing someone in his own family, especially Katherine, had done the same for him.

Also within her autobiography, Tatum revealed that her father had sometimes sent Griffin on drives in her BMW to secure drugs. Even though he was at the time too young to even legally drive a car, Griffin carried out these dangerous drug runs anyway, and was once returned to the Barrymore/O'Neal house by the police. Michael seemed horrified when learning of these stories. Griffin was just thirteen at the time.

Michael was saddened by later events in Griffin's life as he struggled with substance abuse. In 1986 that would lead to a tragic boating accident that snuffed out the life of Gian-Carlo, the son of Francis Ford Coppola. Griffin was indicted for manslaughter in connection with that accident. The charges were later reduced to negligent boat operation, of which Griffin was found guilty.

At the time, Ruth Joanna Coffine, a Toronto-based journalist, was attempting to write a book about the dysfunctional O'Neal family. She eventually abandoned the project, but not before completing a chapter devoted to the "Michael/Tatum affair," which she described like this:

"Michael was a virgin when he met Tatum, and a virgin when he left her," Coffine claimed. "There are two reasons Michael Jackson refuses

Margaux Hemingway

to have sex with a girl in spite of literally hundreds of offers, most often from white girls. First, he's afraid of sex. His mother, Katherine, taught him it's a nasty thing to indulge in. Secondly, he doesn't give a damn for it. When his interest eventually surfaces, it might not even be a girl that Michael is attracted to, and I don't mean an older woman either. Tatum was ripe for the plucking, and stunningly beautiful. Her soft blonde hair and 'bassinet pink skin' was desired by every Lothario in Hollywood who had a Lolita fantasy. I really feel Michael could have seduced her—certainly one of his brothers would have gone for her—but Michael is, if you can believe him (and I don't), saving it 'until the right woman comes along.' Yeah, right!"

Tatum was known as a "disco baby," dancing the night away at clubs, with older friends: the far more sophisticated Bianca Jagger, Cher, or Margaux Hemingway.

"Tatum was younger than Michael," Margaux once said. "In terms of experience, Michael seemed as naïve as a nine-year-old girl, whereas Tatum talked like she had a track record to match that of Jayne Mansfield."

The *faux* romance between Michael and Tatum ended when he invited her to the premiere in New York of *The Wiz*, in which he'd been cast as the Scarecrow. Michael wanted to show up with "arm candy"—in this case, Tatum—and asked her to go with him. Tatum claimed that her talent agency protested violently, telling her, "You can't go to a premiere with a nigger." Tatum turned Michael down, and he was so insulted he would go for months without speaking to her again.

Michael's relationship with Tatum had begun impulsively and it eventually flickered out. However, in 1980, he would write the song, "She's Out of My Life." It was said to have been inspired by his so-called love affair with Tatum.

In the years ahead, Tatum had an outing or two with Michael and that was that. But she resurfaced in his life in 2003 when she went public to deny—once again—Michael's seduction claims. In a documentary, *Living With Michael Jackson*, Michael told Martin Bashir, a British journalist, that Tatum attempted to bed him, but he couldn't go through with it because he was overcome with shyness. Jackson claimed, "She told me to go over and lie on the bed. I lay on the bed and she slowly walked over, and she touched the button on my shirt to open it."

In the interview, aired on both British and American television, Michael said he covered his face with his hands and wouldn't let them down. "She just walked away," Michael said. "I was afraid." Tatum lashed back, claiming "Michael has a vivid imagination. Michael did come over to my house when my father was home, but at twelve years old, there was no way I was capable of being as mature or as sophisticated as he claimed I was."

Michael's encounters with Tatum were mild compared to other rumors sweeping the nation. Another *faux* romance. Rumors even made the headlines that Michael was going to undergo a sex change operation and become the "bride" of Clifton Davis. These allegations first appeared in *Jet* magazine.

Davis was a most unlikely "husband" for a future transgendered Michael. Born in Chicago at the close of World War II, Davis is familiar to TV addicts who saw him in the lead role in *That's My Mama* in the 1970s and on *Amen* in the 1980s. He won a Tony Award for Best Actor in 1972 on Broadway for his performance in a musical version of *Two Gentlemen of Verona*. He was also a songwriter, writing The Jackson 5 hit, "Never Can Say Goodbye."

An ordained Seventh Day Adventist Church minister, Davis was astonished to be linked with Michael in a rumored homosexual relationship.

Marlon Brando, who always had his ear tuned to a good rumor, said, "If you're going to tell a lie, make it a big one. Whoever started this rumor wasn't satisfied with a potential same-sex marriage. They had to go all out and throw in the sex change. In a way, the rumor had a strange kind of logic. Davis is straight. If he ever were to marry Michael, he would insist that our friend transform himself into a woman."

Michael was unaware of the rumor until one afternoon on Hollywood Boulevard when he was casually browsing through a record store. One young man, perhaps no more than fifteen, rushed up to him: "Please, don't cut it off!

Don't become a girl."

Without an explanation, the young man then ran screaming from the store. Later that night, Michael learned of the rumor linking him with Davis and the sex-change operation.

At the time, Michael had never met Davis. That meeting came later, in Las Vegas, when Davis, accompanied by Leslie Uggams, came backstage to congratulate Diana Ross on her spectacular appearance at Caesars Palace. Davis shook Michael's hand.

Unlike Michael, Davis was confident in his own sexuality and could regard the rumors with a certain detachment after his initial astonishment. "Michael," he said at the time of their initial meeting, firmly shaking his hand, "I think you'd make an ugly girl. You really don't have to go to such an extreme to have me become your husband." He laughed at the absurdity of it all.

"I am not a homo," Michael announced heatedly to Ross, Uggams, and Davis.

"We're all God's children," Davis said. "Be what you want to be."

"There's nothing gay about me!" Michael was overheard saying.

In the years to come, much of the world would disagree with Michael's assessment of his sexual preference and label him gay whether he was or not.

Although rumors about the sex change and his upcoming "marriage" to Davis eventually died their predictable death, the gay charges would remain forever.

In the political correctness battle, Michael lost the first round when he told one reporter for the *Los Angeles Times* that he found "homosexuality disgusting, and it's completely against my religion."

Being a homosexual himself, the reporter was immediately offended.

Some officials at Epic were horrified as well. Market surveys had shown that homosexual men and women formed one of the largest blocs of record buyers. The day he pronounced homosexuality disgusting, thousands of gay men agreed to boycott any of his future records. Public relations men in the record business apparently got to Michael, warning him "to cool it."

In subsequent statements to the press, he toned down his inflammatory rhetoric. "I am well aware that plenty of my fans are gay, and I appreciate that. I am not bothered by their choice of lifestyle. However, such a lifestyle is not suitable for me—I'm not gay! And that's that! I know the media will print what they will, but when they print that I'm gay, they are lying to the American public. There's not even the slightest gay streak in me. Just because I have a high, soft voice doesn't mean I'm gay. Millions of men throughout the world have soft, high voices—and aren't gay but married with children."

At times throughout his career, Michael seemed sensitive about his speak-

Clifton Davis

ing voice. Naturally, its high pitch inspired more rumors, one being that he took sex hormones to heighten the pitch of his voice, if such a thing were possible. Again, these rumors—perhaps accurately—were vehemently denied. "What people spreading those rumors were really saying," said an executive at Epic, "is that Michael is not a real man."

Like many Jehovah's Witnesses, Katherine herself was a homophobe. "I go nuts when I hear people calling my son, Michael, gay. He is not! A mother knows. He follows the teachings of our church which condemns the homosexual life. Michael reads his Bible every night. In it he reads that homosexuality is a sin against God's wishes. Michael does not disobey the will of God."

These protestations fell on deaf ears. Hundreds upon hundreds of fans stopped buying Michael's records. "How could I have boyfriend .fantasies about him any more?" asked Alexis Philip, who was the president of Michael's fan club in one of its Ohio branches. "I was shocked to learn that he wanted to have a vagina instead of a dick—that's one of the most sickening things I have ever heard in my life. Before I learned the truth, I used to think Michael was a great singer. Today if I hear his voice on the radio, I cut off the station. I have also urged my girlfriends never to buy another Michael Jackson record."

Confronting a member of the press in Los Angeles, Michael faced a barrage of questions, all of which dealt with the gay issue. "I am not gay!" he shot back angrily, a denial he was repeating more and more. "I'm not a homo. Not in the least. People make up stories claiming I'm gay just to sell papers. The idea of me having sex with men is absurd. I would never do that. I refuse to cheapen myself like that. Just because I'm not seen in public with a lot of girlfriends doesn't mean that I don't have them. But I like to keep my private life private. I believe in protecting the privacy of the young girls I date."

The biographer, J. Randy Taraborrelli, once wrote: "Michael Jackson would never allow himself to have homosexual relationships, even if he did have feelings for other men. He is much too puritanical, a result of his religious background."

Of course, no one could ever make such a statement about another human being without inviting ridicule. As one more astute journalist put it, "We can never know what is going on inside the heart of another human being. We can't share their dreams and desires. Some people are homosexuals and haven't even faced up to it. It is foolish for one person to claim that another person does not have homosexual desires. How could we possibly know that? I've led a completely straight life all my years except for one or two very early and very tentative experiences with another boy when I was fourteen. It was nothing, really. But every few weeks or so, I ask myself if I'm not a secret homosexual. But I try to wipe it from my mind because I don't want to go there."

One night Michael Bennett and playwright James Kirkwood were discussing the casting of a Broadway musical, *A Chorus Line*, in a bar at the Astor Colonnade in New York. Kirkwood was the first to suggest Michael for one of the roles, and Bennett, after thinking it over for a while, finally agreed.

When the role was offered to Michael, he was thrilled but finally decided not to take the part of a dancer, who at the show's climax, reveals himself to be gay, with all the trials and controversies that his sexual preference has cost him. Michael's reason for turning down the role was "because people will think I'm actually gay myself—and not just playing the part of a gay in a musical." What Michael didn't seem to realize was that thousands of people were beginning to think he was gay whether he played gay on the stage or not.

The press speculation about Michael's alleged homosexuality began to reach unprecedented heights for an entertainer, a situation that would "become nuclear," as Kirkwood put it, in the years ahead.

In a cover story for *Time* magazine, Jack Cocks wrote that Michael's "high-flying tenor makes him sound like the lead in some funked-up boys choir, even as the sexual dynamism irradiating from the arch of his dancing challenges government standards for nuclear meltdown. His lithe frame, five-fathom eyes, and long lashes might be threatening if Jackson gave, even for a second, the impression that he is obtainable. But the audience's sense of his sensuality becomes quite deliberately tangled up with the mirror image of his life. Undeniably sexy. Absolutely safe. Eroticism at arm's length."

Michael spoke candidly to his vocal coach, Seth Riggs, about the popular conception that he was gay. "The other day a big, tall, blond, nice-looking fellow came up to me and said, 'Gee, Michael, I think you're wonderful. I sure would like to go to bed with you.' I looked at him and said, 'When's the last time you read the Bible? You know you really should read it because there is some real information in there about homosexuality.' The guy said, 'I guess if I'd been a girl, it would have been different.' And I said, 'No, there are some very direct words on that in the Bible, too.'"

If that statement were reported accurately, Michael was not only admitting that he would not practice homosexuality because "the Bible says not to," but would not partake of straight sexual encounters as well. His randy brothers obviously did not share Michael's reserve.

"Could it be true?" writer Phoebe Foggin asked. "Is Michael neither gay nor straight—but asexual? He sure sounds that way. Or does he use religion as a shield to protect himself from reporters' probing questions?"

As time went by, Michael was having a hard time reconciling his "notorious" show business career with a draconian "Armageddon-around-the-corner religion," as defined by the Jehovah's Witnesses. Not only were Easter and Christmas "outlawed," and homosexuality forbidden, but extramarital intercourse between heterosexuals was condemned as well. Of course, oral and anal sex were out of the question, because gays indulged in such pastimes. As Barbara Grizzuti Harrison wrote in her book, *Visions of Glory*, Witnesses make it clear that, "you don't have to perform a homosexual act to qualify as a homosexual. If you have homosexual fantasies, you are a homosexual in your heart and God sees your heart."

Michael couldn't spend all his days denying that he was a homosexual. He also had to make music—and so he did, either with his less-talented brothers or without them.

Still known as "The Jacksons," the brothers, with Michael as lead singer, released their second album, *Goin' Places*, for Epic in the winter of 1977. It reached only number 52 on *Billboard's* charts, which did a lot better than Jermaine's album at Motown. Consequently, executives at CBS began to have serious second thoughts about the Jackson brothers.

"*Goin' Places* performed dismally," said an officer at Epic. "We were bitterly disappointed as we had high hopes. Even so, we decided it was too early to boot The Jacksons. We rolled the dice and gave the boys much greater control over their next album. For all we knew, if it failed, it would be the last of The Jacksons. As for me personally, I never liked black music. I like my music just like I like my women and my coffee: White!"

Katherine particularly liked one single on the album, "Man of War," a plea for peace. She noted that when her sons were at Motown, Gordy steered them away from any kind of "black power" material, but she was glad to see her boys record a "message song," feeling it was a sign that the Jackson brothers, even Michael and Randy, were growing into men who took stands for what is right.

Tito claimed that people in the business began telling him that "your career, and that of your brothers, is history."

Everybody was disappointed except Michael. At least on the surface, he appeared both defiant and confident. "We'll come back bigger and better than ever," he assured both his mother and his brothers.

Greg Phillinganes, who had toured with Stevie Wonder, was recruited by CBS to work with The Jacksons on their new album, *Destiny*, helping them with the arrangements. Arriving at their Encino house, Phillinganes found the brothers "real enthusiastic and excited because this was the first time in their entire careers that they controlled the music. All of them could write, but I thought Michael and Randy were probably the strongest of the brothers."

Michael repaid the compliment by naming Phillinganes "Mouse," for some odd reason. The artist was anything but. The nickname was completely inappropriate, "except he did eat cheese," Joe claimed.

With hopes for a comeback, the Jackson brothers recorded their third LP for Epic. *Destiny* was released in 1978 and was reviewed as a "coming-of-age" album for The Jacksons. In that sense, it evoked The Beatles' album, *Revolver*. Michael himself selected the peacock as the symbol to use on the back of the album. "The peacock is the only bird that integrates all the colors of the rainbow into one. It can produce only this radiance of fire when it's in love. Love is what we're trying to represent in *Destiny*. To unite the races through the enduring symbol of love. Since politics can't save the world, give music a chance." The name of the production company handling The Jacksons' music became known as Peacock Productions.

"Ron Alexenburg of CBS Records made a total leap of faith in us," Michael later said, "and let us write and produce our own material, something Gordy at Motown had never done."

Alexenburg "showed the faith" that none of the other top brass at CBS had—in fact, the studio had seriously considered buying out The Jacksons' contract for $100,000 and assigning them to the dustpan of the music industry as a faded, not-very-significant act that belonged to yesterday. "We had about as much faith in the revival of the Jackson brothers as we did in reviving the so-called singing career of Tab Hunter," said one CBS executive.

Randy claimed that doing the *Destiny* album "was the greatest test for my brothers and me." Marlon Jackson vowed, "We'll show the fuckers that we're not washed up in the business."

All of The Jacksons were collectively credited for five of the eight songs on the album. The first single release on the album, "Blame It on the Boogie," flopped, but the brothers hadn't written that one. The song was written by three writers from Europe. One member of that trio, ironically, was named Michael Jackson (no relation).

Their own song in solo release, "Shake Your Body (Down to the Ground)" peaked at number seven on *Billboard's* pop chart, selling two million records. Dick Clark declared it "the great dance record of the 70s." It was a joint effort of both Michael and his younger brother, Randy, and it shot up to become a platinum disc, generating across-the-board play on radio, becoming one of the most requested disco singles of 1978. Even Truman Capote and Lee Radziwell (Jackie's sister) were seen dancing to it at New York's Studio 54.

The final song on the album, "That's What You Get (For Being Polite)" was almost about Michael himself, in that it laments the woes of a "sensitive" young man who remains emotionally unfulfilled, as Michael was in his own closeted life.

After the release of the *Destiny* album, The Jacksons went on a nationwide tour, which left Michael so terribly exhausted at one point that he lost his voice. A specialist pronounced that his throat was coated with blisters. Marlon, standing close to Michael, had to sing some of his words for him. The audiences didn't detect that Michael was merely lip-synching.

The tour grossed $750,000 but Michael claimed, "I was very unhappy and stayed in my hotel room when I wasn't on stage. I came alive only when I was performing. That's the only time in my life I'm happy."

Joe forced Michael to grant interview after interview to reporters or magazine feature writers. Michael agreed although the questions had to be funneled through Janet. Sitting next to her, Michael would listen to a reporter's question, then would hear Janet repeat it. He then told his answer to Janet, who relayed it to the reporters sitting across from Michael and his sister. "It was so bizarre," said Steve Demorest of *Melody Maker* magazine.

It was with Demorest that Michael first expressed his "very strong interest" in children, although he made the claim that, "I would never father one myself."

One reporter found that Michael offstage showed "no masculinity at all. He had mastered that breathless whisper of Jackie Kennedy which he interspersed with Marilyn Monroe's pre-coital, come-hither voice—with a few Minnie Mouse caught-in-a-mousetrap squeals thrown in for good measure. If he talked like that in a bar in Broken Bow, Nebraska, he would have been hauled out into a back alley and beaten up as a faggot. In other words, Michael didn't speak like John Wayne at all."

Despite the many rumors, instead of a hot sex life, Michael was devoted to his music. On the dawn of his 18th birthday, he found solace in his work.

Still fighting to gain more artistic control over his own voice and the words he sang, he said: "There's a lot of music inside of me that I haven't brought out. We put our hearts into other writers' songs but they're not the cure. They're not really us."

Michael used music to escape from his own personal insecurities about his looks. Acne continued to plague him. "I seem to have a pimple for every oil gland," he said. "My skin is too dark, my nose too wide." He knew that in time the pimples would go, but not his looks. He dreamed of having lighter skin. "As for the nose," he told his mother, "there are surgeons who can do something about that."

When Katherine told Joe that Michael might possibly be considering plastic surgery on his nose, he replied: "If he goes through with that, I'll bash his face in, new nose and all, and then he'll really need to go to one of those butchers."

His brothers continued to tease him, making him feel even more insecure. All of them had learned to drive except Michael. For some reason, he was petrified to get behind the wheel of a car. "In that case," Joe told him, "you'd better earn enough money so that you can always afford a chauffeur in your future." Michael finally got a driver's license. By then, he was twenty-three years old.

During the 70s, Michael lived in an escapist world. Unlike some performers, such as Warren Beatty or Barbra Streisand, he had no interest in politics or the outside world. Robert Redford might express concern over the polluting of the environment, but all Michael saw of America was a hotel suite or else an auditorium.

After Gerald Ford became president following Richard Nixon's resignation, one newspaper reporter was startled to learn that Michael still thought Nixon was president. "Just who is president now?" Michael asked. The astonished reporter told him it was Gerald Ford. "I didn't know that," Michael responded, "but I never read newspapers, not even *Variety*. I find cartoons more interesting."

Michael's lack of education also showed up in his speech. He was still using such expressions as "don't got no."

But during the filming of *The Wiz*, co-starring Michael, Diana Ross topped even Michael in her ignorance of American presidents. When he noticed that Ross was edgy and nervous about a scene, director Sidney Lumet told her: "You have nothing to fear but fear itself."

"Catchy line," she said. "Did you make that up or steal it from someone?"

Lumet admitted stealing it from Franklin Delano Roosevelt.

"Never heard of him, but you should hire him to rewrite all my lines in this film."

Not satisfied with being a "mere singer" (his words), Michael harbored a secret dream of becoming a movie star. His chance for film stardom came when Lumet offered him the key role of the Scarecrow in *The Wiz*, a 1978 black version of MGM's 1939 *The Wizard of Oz*. The Wiz had been a smash hit on Broadway, winning seven Tony awards. Budgeted at thirty million dollars, the film version of *The Wiz* would be the most expensive film ever produced with an all-black cast.

Jermaine was dead set against Michael accepting the role, even though at the time he was still married to Hazel and still at Motown with a career going nowhere. "You'll fuck it up!" he warned Michael.

Joe also was against Michael accepting the role, fearing that it might "make him into a big movie star—and then he'll bolt from his brothers." For years, Joe had been searching for the right film script in which "all my sons—not just Michael—would be the stars." So far, he'd come up with no acceptable script.

The role of the Scarecrow seemed ideal for Michael, who admitted that he was "too bouncy for the Tin Man and too light for the Lion."

Michael nearly lost out on the role right before filming began when he suffered a lung attack on the beach on July 4, 1977. "They had to rush me to the emergency hospital," he later recalled. "The doctor said it was pneumothorax. That's bubbles on the lungs. Many slim people have this condition. The doctor also told me I had a mild case of pleurisy." At the time Michael stood five foot nine, a mere 105 pounds spread across a skeletal frame.

When he recovered and arrived at the studio to shoot the movie, he found make-up a grueling task and a painful ordeal. It took five hours every morning for make-up artists to transform Michael into his role. When they were finished, Michael faced the camera in a fright wig with a tomato nose. The heavy makeup left his skin blotched and marked. "My eyes were red and sore," he said. "At the end of the day, my fans outside would point at me and say, 'Hey that guy's on drugs—look what it's doing to him!'"

The Wiz was inspired by the film that had brought fame to Judy Garland, who wandered far from Kansas and over the rainbow. Michael dreamed that *The Wiz* would launch him into a successful movie career as well. Even more than he wanted to be a singer, he craved fame on the screen, much as Madonna would do.

In *The Wiz*, Michael faced a tough act to follow. The Scarecrow role had brought screen immortality to actor Ray Bolger, who painfully had to see Michael's rendition of what had been his *pièce-de-la-résistance*. After watching it, Bolger said, "*The Wiz* shortened my life by five years."

A savvy show biz entertainer, Bolger instinctively knew that Michael had not been inspired by his own interpretation of the Scarecrow, but by Charlie Chaplin instead. Like Chaplin, Michael too would later be accused of child molestation. Chaplin remained his favorite actor. "I wanted some of the quality of The Little Tramp in my Scarecrow," Michael claimed.

Michael had seen all available copies of Chaplin's films, including his favorite, *The Gold Rush*, released in 1925. In the words of one writer, Michael borrowed Chaplin's "disjointed, floppy movements and his shy, retiring on-screen character."

"I love acting so much," Michael told a reporter from *The New York Daily News*. "It's fun. It's just neat to become some character on the screen, another person different from yourself. That's especially true when you really believe you're the Scarecrow and not just acting. At the end of the day, I hate

102

MJ with Miss Ross and Quincy Jones, 1973

to take my makeup off. Sometimes I go home and keep it on while I watch old movies starring Katharine Hepburn or Fred Astaire. I've always hated the word 'acting.' Or 'I'm an actor.' What one should say is not that but 'I'm a believer.'"

The filming of *The Wiz* began in October and lasted until Christmas of 1977. The site was the old Astoria Studios in Queens, where the early greats of the silent screen had emoted. "It had a lot of dusty memories and cobwebs," Michael said. The studio had not been used since the heyday of the Roaring Twenties and the virtual birth of the cinema on a grand scale.

Michael's "girl friend," Stephanie Mills, who had played Dorothy on Broadway, desperately wanted to do the movie version. But one night Diana Ross woke up and decided she wanted to play Dorothy. She had star power back in those days, and the studio was willing to pay her one-million dollars.

Her Svengali, Berry Gordy, pleaded with her to abandon the dream of playing Dorothy. "You're not the right age."

"Dorothy is ageless!" Ross countered. At the time of her signing for the film, Ross was thirty-three years old. Ross claimed she could "outdazzle" Judy Garland in the part. Fresh from directing *Equus* with Richard Burton, Sidney Lumet knew Ross was wrong for the role, but signed on as director of *The Wiz* anyway.

An all-star black cast was signed up, including Nipsey Russell as the Tin Man, Ted Ross as the Lion, Richard Pryor as The Wiz, and even the legendary Lena Horne as Glinda the Good. Quincy Jones, who was to play a vital role in Michael's future singing career, signed on as musical director.

From the very beginning of their relationship, Michael was impressed with Jones, who grew up on the mean streets of Chicago's South Side, watching his mother descend into madness.

His credentials were awesome, including having played backup for Billie Holiday and touring with Lionel Hampton. During the course of his long career, he would arrange albums for Ray Charles, Dinah Washington, Sarah Vaughan, and Count Basie, even Frank Sinatra. Jones would also master virtually every form of American popular music, including African, jazz, urban, gospel, and, later, hip-hop.

Michael's one command to his musical director was: "I don't want our music to sound like The Jacksons. I want to be different."

During the filming of *The Wiz*, Jones "saw a depth that was never apparent in Michael before. I saw that Michael was growing up right before my eyes."

Jones found that Michael "had the wisdom of a sixty-year-old and the enthusiasm of a child." He also said, "Beneath that shy exterior was an artist with a burning desire for perfection and an unlimited ambition to be the biggest entertainer in the world—make no mistake. He would watch tapes of gazelles, cheetahs, and panthers to imitate the natural grace of their movements. He wanted to be the best of everything—to take it all in."

Michael told Jones that "the curse of my life is that girls are always after me, even climbing over the walls in Encino to get at me." Later in their work together, he related an incident in which one young woman, escaping the Jackson security guards, slipped onto the property and lounged by the pool for hours before she was discovered and ejected. Later, the woman sued, claiming Michael was the father of "just one of my twins."

Although their dialogues would be fraught with future tension, the relationship between Ross and Michael went fairly smoothly during filming. "I owe her a lot—she was my 'mam' on the set," he said. "Always there for me with a helping hand or some advice. We were really close. I have to say, I love her!"

In spite of these protestations of devotion, jealousy reared its head between Ross and Michael. In the ballroom of the St. George Hotel in Brooklyn, Michael learned the dance steps too quickly to please Ross, who was struggling with even the simplest of routines. She called him aside one afternoon and charged him with deliberately trying to embarrass her. "I take much longer to learn the steps, and you get them right away. You're doing this just to show me up. Stop it!"

Michael apologized. In the next dance rehearsal, he deliberately flubbed the steps one time after another. Ross smiled proudly at his "mistakes."

Michael secretly watched in delight as two great divas, Lena Horne and

Diana Ross, came together and clashed. "It was not a love-in," Michael said, seemingly taking glee at the bitchery going on between them.

Michael had great respect for the Brooklyn-born Lena Horne, who was ethereally beautiful with a lucid singing voice. He knew the contribution she'd made to the advancement of black entertainers in America. During her early days as a performer, Horne had been identified as a *"café au lait* Hedy Lamarr" and "the chocolate chanteuse."

During her short time on the set with Michael, Horne shared with him some of her triumphs and failures in show business, going back to the days when she was a chorus girl in the famed Cotton Club in Harlem. "And, yes, darling," she told a wide-eyed Michael, "I was one of the *Blackbirds of 1939.*"

She explained to Michael that even when she appeared before the cameras in Hollywood of the 1940s, her songs did not blend with the plot. "That allowed racist theater owners in the Deep South to remove my segment without interfering with any of the action."

"You mean they wouldn't even let black singers entertain the devils?" Michael asked in astonishment.

Jackson and Ross,
Los Angeles, 1984

Horne also told Michael that when she was photographed for her original screen test at MGM, her face appeared so light that the studio feared that she'd be mistaken for a white woman.

"Is that cameraman still around?" Michael asked. "I want to photograph as white."

"Your own color is perfect the way it is," she told him. "I'm addicted to Godiva chocolates. Be what you are. It's a different time now for black entertainers."

Horne explained that the make-up genius, Max Factor, created a whole new line for her called "Dark Egyptian." Hedy Lamarr used this same make-up in *White Cargo* in 1942 when she played a half-caste African native.

Horne laughed that Lumet, her son-in-law—soon to be her ex-son-in-law—was married to her daughter, Gail Jones. "I'm the wicked mother-in-law. A little nepotism never hurt nobody, honey. If you got it, use it. Press on with it."

On her last day on the set, Horne took Michael's hand and sang to him her signature song, "Stormy Weather."

Before their final good-bye, she gave him some advice. "It's not the load that breaks you down, kid, but the way you carry it. And, remember, be smarter than the people who hire you."

Horne would resurface once again in the lives of the Jackson family. Following Janet's so-called "wardrobe malfunction" debacle at the 2004 Super Bowl, Horne demanded that Janet be dropped as the star in a television biopic portraying Lena Horne's life and career. At first ABC executives resisted Horne's demand, but Janet's representatives told *Variety* that she abandoned the role willingly after Horne and her daughter, Gail Lumet, asked that Janet not take the part.

Michael dreaded it when *The Wiz* was completed and "cried all day," according to a crew member. "You could hear him sobbing in his dressing room."

After watching the final cut of *The Wiz*, Lumet called Michael, praising him as "the most brilliant actor since James Dean."

"Who is this Dean?" Michael asked.

The Wiz opened across the country around Thanksgiving in 1978 and was one big disappointment. "About as airy as an elephant dancing in quicksand," wrote one reviewer.

Lena Horne

At least one hit song came out of it: "Ease on Down the Road," which Michael recorded with his mentor—"and my only one true love," Diana Ross.

Many critics praised Michael's performance as the Scarecrow, blaming Lumet and Ross for creating "the bomb."

Michael cried for days in his bedroom in Encino. Katherine tried to get him to eat, but he refused food, subsisting on fruit juices. "I dreamed of being a movie star. Now it's all over for me." There was even an unconfirmed report that Michael attempted suicide.

The movie did rather well among black audiences but most white film patrons stayed away. Some critics thought that *The Wiz* "suffocated in its own lavish production," and that it missed the freshness and sparkle of the stage show.

Michael loved the film, feeling that it was "far superior to the Garland version," which it obviously wasn't, of course. "We made the story and the point more recognizable," he said somewhat enigmatically.

Ross, commenting on the film's failure at the box office, claimed, "I don't care that it didn't make the big bucks. *The Wiz* wasn't about some stupid movie as much as it was about *moi!*"

That was her public front. Privately, she was reported to have been almost "suicidally disappointed" over the critics's attack on her interpretation of Dorothy.

Liza Minnelli went to see the film and privately told friends, "Thank God mother never lived to see this travesty." As an afterthought, she diplomatically added, "Michael was wonderful."

Despite the financial collapse of *The Wiz*, many film projects for Michael reached the planning stage. Michael himself felt he would be perfect cast as Bill Bojangles, the famous black dancer, but the movie was never made.

"I wanted the filming of *The Wiz* to last forever," Michael said three years later. "Working on the movie was the happiest time of my life. From now on, I'm going to dwell forever in the Land of Oz."

"It's the combinations that really distinguish him as an artist. Spin, stop, pull up leg, pull jacket open, turn, freeze. And the glide where he steps forward while pushing back. Spinning three times and popping up on his toes. That's a trademark and a move a lot of professionals wouldn't try. If you go up wrong, you can really hurt yourself."

--Dancer Hilton Battle

"You look like an angel; you walk like an angel, but I got wise; you're the Devil in disguise."

--Elvis Presley

"I see God in the face of children. And, man, I just love being around them all the time."

--Michael Jackson

"Often isolated from other kids when he was growing up, Michael learned everything he knew from TV. Everything he saw on television that represented class and glamour was white."

--Former aide to the Jackson family (name withheld)

"Pedophiles are often adults who never grow up and they have a unique ability to identify with children, a Pied Piper effect. Their homes are often shrines to children and exhibit a Disneyland like atmosphere."

--Ken Lanning
A Behavioral Profile of Pedophiles

"You want to see the boy next door? Then don't go see Michael Jackson, because he ain't the boy next door."

--Sammy Davis Jr.

Chapter Five

During the making of *The Wiz* in New York, Katherine moved La Toya and Michael to a luxurious rented apartment on chic Sutton Place on Manhattan's East Side. Here Michael was to enjoy the taste of freedom and independence for the first time in his chaperoned life.

He also arrived in the New York of 1977, which, arguably, was the most decadent year in that city's history in the entire 20th century. Right before the AIDS epidemic struck, hip New Yorkers—both gay and straight—were on a sex binge. "If you couldn't get laid in New York at that time," said Truman Capote, "you had two heads and a lizard's tail."

In the apartment, La Toya took the luxury suite, a showplace boudoir with a large bed and a mirror above it. The decorator had been inspired by Mae West's bedroom in Los Angeles. She assigned Michael to the simple "maid's room," although he—not her—was the star.

The leased apartment rented for $2,500 a month, and was located on the 37th floor of a *luxe* apartment building "It was the type of place Joan Crawford might have rented," said Quincy Jones.

The apartment opened onto a balcony with a railing. To distract La Toya from her new addiction to eating chocolates day and night, Michael tried to frighten her by dangling himself precariously over the balcony, threatening to let go and fall to his death. He would, of course, later become notorious for dangling one of his children over another balcony.

Reclusive and shy for most of his life, Michael, at least temporarily, became "fun, outgoing, and a dancing fool," in the words of *Wiz* director Sidney Lumet. "I heard that he and La Toya were going out to the clubs every night. I was concerned if Michael could get up for early call at the studio. But regardless of how late he stayed out the night before, he was always on time for his appointment with the makeup boys."

One night at the Rainbow Grill, Michael was introduced to Jacqueline

Kennedy Onassis, who would play an important role in his future. "All memories of his goddess, Diana Ross, were forgotten when he encountered Jackie O," said the gossipy Capote. "He developed a fixation on her. All he could talk about was her voice, which sounded a bit like Michael's own whispers. Her clothing. Her glamorous hair styling. Her manner. Her polite manners. Her sophistication. Until that meeting at the Rainbow Grill, I think Michael had wanted to transform himself into Miss Diana. But after meeting Jackie, I think then and there Michael raised the bar on his transgendered dreams. Instead of a black diva like Ross, he apparently decided that he wanted to transform himself into a white woman like Jackie. After all, she was the most famous and most admired woman in the world at the time. Who wouldn't want to walk, act, talk, and look like Jackie? Even *moi*. Actually, to tell the truth, if I could become a woman, I would want to be Marilyn Monroe. As Marilyn, I would fuck Warren Beatty, Robert Redford, Steve McQueen, Paul Newman, Burt Reynolds, Nick Nolte, Tom Jones—big dick that one—Robert Goulet, Rock Hudson, you name it. But I was more realistic than Michael. I knew I was trapped with my own voice and physicality and could never escape it. Even though a Little Black Sambo, Michael felt no such limitation. He truly believed the American Dream—in his case, that you could be born a poor black ghetto boy and grow up to become a rich white woman."

Michael's interest in Jackie was first piqued weeks before he actually met her. Bob Weiner, a reporter for the *New York Daily News*, invited Michael to his apartment for an interview and a home-cooked meal. While Weiner was in his kitchen preparing a chicken and rice dish, Michael amused himself by "grazing" through the wealth of books and photographs that were scattered across the apartment.

At one point, Weiner heard Michael let out a yelp. Rushing in from the kitchen, he spotted Michael staring at a celebrity nude calendar. One of the snapshots was of a nude Jackie. "I can't believe what I'm seeing!" Michael said. "Why would a woman like Mrs. Kennedy pose nude for the paparazzi?"

Weiner patiently explained that the picture had been taken on Skorpios with a hidden camera. Jackie had no idea that she was being photographed and that her privacy had been invaded.

Later, the former First Lady found out that her husband, Aristotle Onassis, had hired a Greek photographer to take the picture. Apparently, her husband felt Jackie was getting "too grand," and he hoped to embarrass her—"bring her back down to earth," as he allegedly said at the time.

Weiner later expressed surprise that he had "encountered an eighteen-year-old millionaire with his innocence intact."

After their first meeting, Michael virtually "stalked" Jackie, if the not always reliable Capote can be believed. "He showered her with invitations. If she had agreed, Michael would have taken her out every night. I don't know what she saw in this inexperienced black boy from somewhere in the Middle West, but Jackie told me that she was intrigued with Michael and his sheer audacity."

"Of course, Jackie was a pro at gracefully turning down invitations and keeping ardent pursuers at arm's length," Capote claimed. "Everybody tried to fuck her after John Kennedy died--some succeeded. Marlon Brando, William Holden, Frank Sinatra, and, of course, such 'family' as Robert Kennedy and Peter Lawford. She was far too hip to suspect that Michael's

Truman Capote

motives were sexual. That would have been laughable to her. But she was aware that she'd become his new role model."

"As of yet, I have no opinion of Michael Jackson," Jackie allegedly told Capote. "I am just formulating one. I can't figure him out. It seems he's stalled on the bridge between boyhood and manhood. He also seems strangely asexual. I honestly believe that even though Michael is an adult, he hasn't completely figured out for himself yet if he wants to be gay or straight. I, naturally, have my own ideas about where he's going, which road he'll take. I think his future sex life—that is, if he has a future sex life—is going to be very difficult for him. Fraught with hazards."

If Jackie did say that, and Capote maintained that she did, it was a perceptive observation about where Michael was heading in his future.

Jackie invited Michael to accompany her to the Robert Kennedy Tennis Tournament where she introduced him to her children, John Jr. and Caroline. Later, Michael would invite his newly formed friend, Capote, to escort him to another tennis match to watch young John play.

The son of the slain American president was just a teenager at the time, and had not come into his full male beauty with a chiseled physique that would contribute to his being referred to as "the hunk" in American media.

"Even though John-John was quite young at the time," Capote later recalled, "he was still a Prince Charming, even with all that long hair. It was obvious that afternoon that Michael was smitten with John-John. I was only becoming aware of Michael's interest in teenage boys. I'd met John-John once or twice through Jackie, but had not paid much attention to him until that afternoon."

After the game, Capote said that John invited both of them to join him at

John-John, grown up, with his brainchild, *George Magazine*, and Jay Leno

some grill along Ninth Avenue because he said he was ravenously hungry. "But, first, we were also invited to join him in the locker room where he had to shower and get dressed. At the time, I didn't know that John-John was an exhibitionist. The world learned that much later. Before both Michael and me, John-John peeled off. He might have been just a boy at the time, but that was a man's cock he was flaunting at us. The kid was hung . . . and hung big. Michael appeared fascinated. Jack Kennedy often took nude swims—Rose did too—at their estate on Palm Beach. Anyone who was interested knew that the President wasn't hung at all. So where did John-John get this octoroon dick? I think I know. From Jackie's daddy, Jack Bouvier—called 'Black Jack.' His many girlfriends claimed Black Jack was hung like a horse."

Capote admitted that he did not know the outcome of Michael's attempt to forge a relationship with the handsome young teenager. "I understand that Michael pursued John-John, and they were seen together on a few occasions. As everybody knows, President Kennedy's closest friend, Lem Billings, was a homosexual and was madly in love with John Kennedy all his life—a one-way affair, I might add. But John-John didn't seem ready, willing, or able to use his father's relationship with Lem as a role model for Michael and himself."

"Exhibiting himself in front of Michael was one thing—he did that in front of any number of gay guys—but carrying it farther than that was out of the question," Capote claimed. "Jackie always had homosexual panic fears about her son, especially when he wanted to become an actor. She may have intervened and nipped Michael's friendship with John-John in the bud. Somebody told her that Michael was collecting pictures of 'the hunk,' all

112

shirtless, and decorating his bedroom walls with them. I don't know for a fact if that were true or not. But it was enough of a rumor to cause concern in Jackie's head. In the future, she would continue to pursue her own relationship with Michael, at least on a professional level. But at a point not known to me, John-John faded from Michael's life. Unlike Madonna, Michael never really got a piece of John-John. In that kid's case, the line formed on the right and the left."

Capote, Michael's original guide to Studio 54, called the legendary dance club "very democratic, boys with boys, girls with girls, girls with boys, blacks and whites, capitalists and Marxists, and everything else—all in one big mix!"

And so it was.

In 1977, Studio 54 was the hottest night club in the entire world. You never knew who might show up on any given night: Jackie Onassis, Gregory Peck, or even Doris Duke, the planet's richest woman. Andy Warhol was a regular. During the making of *The Wiz*, Diana Ross appeared frequently, even Elizabeth Taylor, Betty Ford, and Mikhail Baryshnikov, who wanted to dance with Michael as a lark but was politely and shyly turned down.

One night, Capote invited Michael to his favorite spot, the deejay's booth overlooking the dance floor. From this crow's nest, he had an ideal viewing spot. He told Michael that, "Proust would have loved this place. Too bad he's not around to record it. I think about all the dead who would have loved 54: Toulouse-Lautrec, Baudelaire, Ronald Firbank, Carl Van Vechten, Oscar Wilde."

"Who are all these people?" Michael asked, "And what did they die from?"

Capote stared incredulously at Michael. "They were lost souls who died for love," he finally said.

Constructed in 1927, the building itself was an old theater and TV studio. Before that it was once the home of the San Carlo Opera Company. The address was at 254 W. 54th St., off Broadway. Steve Rubell and Ian Schrager were the welcoming hosts if you were rich, famous, infamous, or just merely gorgeous. They invited "the right people," turning all others away.

Around the dance floor were silver banquettes. Under the balconies was a mirrored diamond-shaped bar. Overlooking both the balcony and the large dance floor was the infamous "Rubber Room," designed with thick rubber walls so they could be washed down with soap and water after a night of sex and drugs.

In the basement was the very private, invitation-only VIP Room, called the "sanctum sanctorum." With chain-link fences lining its perimeter, it evoked a prison. But night after night it was the most sought-after den of those denizens of the night who came here to pursue private pastimes devoted to

Gloria Vanderbilt

drugs and raw sex.

The waiters from upstairs appeared frequently, but not to serve drinks down here. They were shirtless, wearing only white silk basketball shorts. Clients, both male and female, brought their toy boys of the night here to pull down those shorts and to fellate them. Minnelli got Rubell to let Michael enter into this chamber. He was reportedly shocked yet fascinated by the coke-snorting and the wild sex in various combinations of sexes, including three- or four-ways.

"The lounge made Sodom and Gomorra look like kindergarten," said a former employee.

"We just assumed that Michael was gay," said one of the busboys. "With that voice, that mincing manner, what else could he be? But he turned down guys who came on to him. It was rumored that even Calvin Klein invited Michael to his lair in the Pines on Fire Island but Michael rejected the invitation of the great underwear king."

Michael often spent hours on the dance floor. One night he was seen dancing with Gloria Vanderbilt, the heiress once known as "the poor little rich girl." Gloria was also known for her affairs, including liaisons with Marlon Brando, Howard Hughes, and Frank Sinatra.

Night after night, Michael watched in fascination as Rollerena, one of the most amusing drag queens in New York City history, endlessly circled the floor on her roller skates.

On the main floor on any given night, Madonna might be seen chatting with Salvador Dalí. Elton John might be spotted trying to pick up Patrick Taylor, a busboy who, regrettably, turned out to be straight. At the time, patrons treated the handsome busboys and waiters like *Playboy* bunnies. "Everyone, guys and dolls, tried to bed us, and most of them succeeded," said a former waiter.

The co-owner, Steve Rubell, personally welcomed Michael and La Toya to the club, where a cocaine-snorting, neon-lit man-in-the-moon would descend from the ceiling five or six times a night, his flashing red eye approving of all the coke-snorting going on. The smell of amyl nitrite cut the night air.

Michael and La Toya were there at the famous May, 1977, birthday bash for Bianca Jagger. She rode onto the main floor on a white horse led by a naked man.

A far greater tour guide to Studio 54 than Capote was Liza Minnelli. She became a "fixture" in Michael's life during the frenzied nights she spent at

Studio 54, doing cocaine and partying the night away. Her health was fragile, and she was deep into relationships with both Martin Scorsese and Baryshnikov. When Michael caught up with her, she'd already missed seven performances of the musical, *The Act*, simply because she was not able to go on.

On one of Liza's "good nights," Michael had gone to see her perform in the Broadway musical, and had been deeply moved by her voice and movements on the stage. The next day, someone, perhaps La Toya, showed him a review written by John Simon, theater critic for *New York* magazine. In the harshest terms, the acerbic Simon had attacked the look of Liza's face, mocking it, especially her wide eyes.

"Like myself, Liza has always been insecure about her looks," Michael said. "After reading that mean-spirited attack, she was devastated and didn't even want to go on the next night. I know how she felt. When I was fourteen, a so-called fan mocked me for my awful acne. I stayed in my room for days with the curtains drawn. I couldn't even stand to look at my own face in the mirror. I cried day and night. I was ashamed to show my face to the world again. Poor Liza. Poor me. A performer's appearance is everything. When your look is mocked, it cuts into your heart like a sharp knife."

Michael remained steadfastly loyal to Liza, even though he could obviously see the toll that alcohol and drugs were taking on her. He dared not ask her to change her lifestyle, even though he suspected she was heading for a fall. The designer Halston told Warhol, who then told Michael, that Liza had arrived one night at his Upper East Side townhouse. Her face was partially

Liza Minnelli 1984

concealed by a black felt hat to hide the damage. According to Halston, "Liza barged into my house and demanded that I give her every drug I had."

In spite of her drugs, heavy drinking, and her horrible appearance (at least according to John Simon), Liza still managed to snare what was then considered the sexiest man in New York. The Russian dancer, Baryshnikov, was hit upon by both men and women wherever he went. One night as Capote and Michael were observing Liza dancing with Baryshnikov on Studio 54's floor, Capote turned to

Michael. "Unlike Rudolf Nureyev, Mischa actually likes women. He's also notoriously virile. I'm dying to sample that thick Russian sausage for myself. So far, no luck. But one night when he's really drunk down in the basement, I'll get him yet."

"How do you know if he can perform if he's all that drunk?" Michael asked. "The word is out," Capote said. "Mischa can get it rock hard even if completely wasted. He's Russian, my dear boy. Russians are always soggy with vodka."

In their private moments away from the frenzied heat of Studio 54, Liza and Michael bonded. Their friendship was forged partly because of their equivalently horrid showbiz childhoods.

Michael might have scorned his chain-smoking, Scotch-and-Coke drinking new friend, but he found her the most fascinating woman he'd ever known. Liza entered that rare pantheon of "friends for life" that would eventually include Elizabeth Taylor.

Compared to Judy Garland, Michael's father, Joe, was a pillar of stability. By 1969 Judy had attempted suicide twenty times, finally dying alone in the bathroom of her London townhouse.

Michael was impressed with the intensity of Liza's survival instinct, even though she currently was on a self-destructive binge. She told him that once when she was sixteen, her mother kicked her out of the house. "I had my plane fare and a $100 left over," she told Michael. "I went to New York, and I've never taken another penny from my parents."

Michael was mesmerized by her stories of growing up in Hollywood. She told of the fabulous parties thrown by Judy and her then-husband, Sid Luft. "At one of them, Lauren Bacall sang while Humphrey Bogart looked on in amusement. Judy had invited this newcomer to Hollywood. At least I thought she was a newcomer. Turns out she'd been around for quite awhile. Her name was Marilyn Monroe. She sat alone. No one would talk to her. I felt lonely, too, and I came over to sit with her and talk to her. She was so grateful for the company she practically cried."

Michael confided that he too had moments of great loneliness such as that.

Sometimes Liza could be seen sitting alone even at Studio 54 with Michael, just holding his hand, although romance was not part of the equation. "I'm vulnerable," she told him.

"It's one of your most appealing qualities."

"But I don't want to be vulnerable," she protested. "It's a secret. I don't want the public to find out I'm vulnerable. Oh, my God, the last thing I want to become is the second Judy Garland."

Michael was once asked what had drawn him to Liza since they were such different personalities. "She gives. Everyone else in my life takes."

116

One night, high on cocaine, Liza turned to Michael and said, "I'm tired of talking about myself. What do you think of me?"

"I like the way you crawled out from behind your mother's shadow."

Michael's devotion to Liza even earned her a paragraph in his autobiography, *Moonwalk*. "Liza Minelli (sic) is a person whose friendship I'll always cherish. She's like my show business sister."

Michael, who claimed "I love her," loved her so much he never learned to spell her name. But his editor, Jackie O, should have known to spell Minnelli with two n's. The line, "my show business sister," was very revealing. Capote sometimes referred to Michael and Liza as "soul sisters."

"We get together and talk about the business," Michael wrote. "It comes out of our pores. We both eat, sleep, and drink various moves and songs and dances."

Michael, however, wasn't spending all of his time with his "soul sister." He was making the scene with other cultural icons eager to see what he was about. "Michael was on the long path to his own liberation and independence from his domineering family," Sidney Lumet allegedly said. "Michael was the meal ticket for the Jacksons, so they wanted to keep a close eye on him even though he was experiencing New York on his own terms."

At Studio 54, Michael met some of the cultural elite of the era, although he wasn't certain who some of the celebrities were. Truman Capote introduced him to Gloria Swanson. Michael was found under his Afro wearing a pale shantung-weave shirt and a scarlet-colored Ascot. The silent screen vamp, who immortalized herself by playing Norma Desmond in the 1950 *Sunset Blvd.*, said, "Young man, in my day men went to a barber."

He also met the great diva of modern dance, Martha Graham, who sat next to Betty Ford. By that time, Michael had come to realize that her husband, Gerald, had been president of the United States.

Escorted by her mother, Teri, Brooke Shields was pointed out to Michael, but their relationship lay in the future. Years later, he could not recall meeting a brunette Madonna, but he did wonder who that old man was sitting next to her. It was William S. Burroughs, that "literary outlaw," junkie, wife murderer, and author of the underground classic, *Naked Lunch*.

Studio 54 functioned as Michael's major "Combat Zone," but he was spotted at other venues as well. He appeared at avant-garde gallery openings on the arm of his "date," Andy Warhol. At one such gathering in Soho, Warhol was overheard talking to Michael about what he wanted to do as a filmmaker.

"I want to depict homosexuality, lesbianism, sadomasochism, masturbation, drug use—even douching, and most definitely every known sexual permutation in the universe."

On another night at Studio 54, Warhol confided to Michael, as he had

Mick Jagger

countless others, his plans to stage a musical on Broadway to be called *The Velvet Underground.*

"Mick Jagger and I have been planning this for years," Warhol said. "There's a great role in it for a black singer. In nearly all artistic productions today, you have to cast a token black. Perhaps you'll agree to take the part and make it your Broadway debut."

"As the token nigger?" Michael asked, seemingly offended by Warhol's remark. "I don't know about that."

"My protégé, Paul Morrissey, wants me to produce a film starring Mick and Bianca Jagger," Warhol said. "It's to be based on André Gide's *The Caves of the Vatican.* Bianca and Mick will be cast as brother and sister. I guess I'll have to rewrite Gide because I want Mick and Bianca to commit incest in the film. Of course, I haven't read Gide. Maybe he's already come up with the incest thing all by himself."

"Actually, I heard that David Bowie and Jagger are considering dressing in drag and doing a remake of *Some Like It Hot,*" Michael said. "I'm sure they'd be better than Tony Curtis and Jack Lemmon. *Some Like It Hot* is my favorite Marilyn Monroe movie."

"Mine too!" Warhol chimed in, as he cruised the main dance floor of Studio 54. Suddenly, he showed astonishment. "Speak of the Devil! Here comes darling Mick now. I'll introduce the two of you."

As Mick Jagger talked to Michael for less than twenty minutes, he seemed to grow bored and invited both Warhol and Michael to go with him to Max's Kansas City Dance Club. Michael only reluctantly agreed to go along.

At Max's, Jagger continued to drink heavily. At one point Jagger asked Warhol to dance with him, and the two men took to the floor, creating a spectacle. Michael sat on the sidelines.

Warhol returned to table, but Jagger headed for the men's room. He was trailed by a string of gay guys hoping for a "sighting."

"Mick is hot!" Warhol told Michael. "Every time he goes to take a piss, a lot of guys follow him inside the toilet, hoping to get a look at his dick. I don't have to revert to such tactics. I've slept with Mick on several occasions. In fact, I'm mad about the boy."

Michael didn't know if that were true or not. He'd learned that Warhol often exaggerated. But as he later confided to La Toya, among others, "I think this time Andy was telling the truth."

118

For his part, Jagger always seemed to have mixed feelings about Warhol. In Robert Frank's film, *Cocksucker Blues*, Jagger called Warhol "a fucking voyeur"—and did so with a certain accuracy.

After meeting at Studio 54, Mick volunteered to introduce Michael to "the scene" in New York, taking the innocent young man to clubs Michael had never heard of.

"There's no way in hell that Mick could have found a *simpatico* soul in Michael Jackson," Keith Richards was reported to have said as an explanation for the time they spent together. "Mick is very bright, and I think he sensed future competition in Jackson. He wanted to study his every move, figure out what he was up to, what he was like, what he had that the world wanted to buy."

A music industry insider, Butch Wohlin, who worked briefly with both Jagger and Michael, said, "Mick was worldly wise. To him, Jackson must have looked like a prissy little baby. Almost everything about Jackson must have turned off Mick. That religious fanaticism. That little girl voice. His fear of drugs. His fear of sex. Jackson was the very opposite of Mick."

After touring the New York clubs with Michael, Jagger told Richards, "Jackson is a limp-wristed bore. Or at least I think he is. I never heard one word he ever said in that whispery voice of his. At the clubs I took him to, the music was too loud, and I'm not a lip reader. The kid is a total lightweight. He's like froth on beer. I'm the golden liquid itself. The alcohol that makes you drunk. The kid doesn't drink. Doesn't do drugs. I think the strongest drink Jackson ever ordered was a Shirley Temple."

As time would reveal, Michael may have learned more from Jagger than the rock star did from him.

"Long before Madonna grabbed her pussy on stage, long before Michael fondled his dick in front of an audience, Mick was crotch-grabbing years before," Wohlin said. "In Mick's case, and I've seen it, he had a lot more to grab. Jackson experienced a meltdown if it was suggested that he was gay. He appeared like such a sissy on the whole subject. Throughout his career, Mick has been exposed as a bisexual in print. Whether he is or not is another matter. But he didn't give a damn. Did Mick sleep with David Bowie? How in the fuck do I know? I wasn't concealed under Mick's bed with a recorder. Mick has a certain androgyny. So does Jackson. But what Mick had and Michael never would have was raw masculine power. You inherit that. You're born with it. When God handed out those male genes in Heaven, Michael was at the end of the food chain that day and got none of them. Madonna is far more masculine than Michael. The kid just doesn't have it. There's a rumor going around that he was born a hermaphrodite—and I believe that. He's certainly caught in that twilight zone between the sexes—neither girl nor boy. On the other hand, Mick got more male hormones than he knows what to do with."

"Mick may have given Jackson a few lessons in androgyny," Wohlin claimed, "but the kid didn't learn his lessons well. I think Jackson envied that Mick could wear lipstick and sashay around like a queen, yet still keep his image as a macho rocker. Jackson desperately wanted to learn from Mick what his secret was. How did he get away with that? Jackson never learned the secret. When he went out on stage with all that lipstick, all that sashaying around, he still hadn't learned the secret. But I'll let you in on the secret. Mick's public knew that behind the androgyny was a rocker with balls. Mick has balls. Michael Jackson does not!"

One night at a club in the East Village, Jagger showed up with Rudolf Nureyev, whom he'd met years before when he'd gone backstage after one of the Russian dancer's performances with Margot Fonteyn. In the great heyday of ambisexual New York in the late 70s, rumors were all over town that Nureyev and Jagger were "sometimes lovers."

At the club, Jagger introduced Nureyev to Michael, who later told friends, "Those two even look alike. God gave both of them the same mouth."

That night Michael was fascinated to hear an argument between Jagger and Nureyev. Jagger maintained that it took more talent to be a pop star than a ballet dancer. Looking over at Michael, Nureyev said, "Anyone can be a pop star. It takes incredible talent to be a ballet dancer."

Nureyev, at least for that night, won the argument.

Michael turned down Nureyev's offer of marijuana, but Jagger went for it. Again . . . and again . . . and again. Within the hour, Jagger and Nureyev had taken to the dance floor, as the other dancers in all combination of sexes parted to make room for them.

"Those two pressed their bodies so close to each other that night I'm sure they both got erections," said Tom Felison, club manager. "They weren't dancing. They were fucking each other in front of everybody. It was the most overtly sexual dance I've ever seen. Nureyev ran his hands across Jagger's bare chest, then kissed him. It was Big Mouth meeting Big Mouth."

According to the manager, Michael witnessed the whole event with wide-eyed wonder.

Suddenly, Nureyev, showing a big erection in tight pants, broke from Jagger and headed for the table where Michael sat on the edge of his seat, taking in all the action. With the grace of a swan, Nureyev reached for Michael's arm, pulling him onto the dance floor.

As an amused Jagger stood by, Nureyev began "the dance of love" with Michael, rubbing his well-endowed crotch against Michael's flaccid package.

"It was the most suggestive dance I'd ever seen," Felison claimed. "And I've seen boys and girls, even boys and boys, fucking each other on my dance floor. I realized that night that the suggestion of sexual mating can be far more erotic than the actual fucking. In the midst of all that heat, generated almost entirely by Nureyev, not by Michael, Jagger moved in from the rear. He too had an erection which he rammed up against Michael's butt encased in jeans. God, what a hot scene. Nureyev reached into Michael's shirt and rubbed his skilled hand across the nipples as he'd just done with Jagger. From the rear, Jagger was plowing his fingers into Michael's hair before lowering them to Michael's lips, presumably for him to suck on them. Michael was having none of that shit."

When Michael tried to break away, Nureyev yelled, "We've got ourselves a virgin, Mick."

With a sudden force, Michael bolted from the "human sandwich" of which he was a part. Bursting into tears, he fled from the club.

Not missing a beat, nor even seeming to care about their friend's departure, Nureyev resumed his erotic dance with Jagger.

"From the looks of things, those two climaxed in their pants before leaving the dance floor that night," Felison said. "Talk about two hot men!"

A long time would go by before Jagger would enter Michael's life again.

When not out with Jagger or Liza, Michael would continue to accept "dates" from Warhol. He was proud of the friendship, viewing Warhol as "The King of Pop Art."

Michael told Warhol that when he'd lived with Diana Ross, "she taught me how to appreciate art, and we often painted together, going out to record scenes from nature."

Warhol laughed in amusement, not really believing Michael. "How could Ross have taken time out for that?" he asked. "The only art Ross appreciates is what is staring back at her in the mirror."

When Warhol heard that Michael was bragging about his friendship with the "King of Pop Art," he corrected him.

"I'm also an artist myself, a filmmaker, a writer, publisher, interviewer, photographer, fashion consultant, set designer, record producer, and the world's greatest jet-setting trendsetter," Warhol claimed.

"You left out dog lover," Michael jokingly chastised him.

Warhol seemed to mull that over for a moment. "That too!" he said.

Warhol took Michael to the Sanctuary, a former church on 10th avenue where the altar had been turned into a sound booth. The DJ was dressed as a priest. "Look at those hookers over at the bar," Warhol pointed out to Michael.

"They're nuns!" Michael said, astonished.

"They're merely dressed as nuns," Warhol said. "They're actually drag queen hookers."

Warhol also pointed out that most of the boys dancing with each other on the floor weren't gay. "They just look gay. Actually, the Sanctuary has pioneered a new lifestyle. Here straight boys can dance with straight boys, and no one ridicules them for doing what they want to."

Warhol also took Michael to the Tambourlaine, a Latino night club that flourished briefly in the East 50s. He told Michael that their mutual friend, Capote, once showed up at the club with both Jacqueline Kennedy Onassis and Lee Radziwell. "Those sisters were wearing Hermès scarves to disguise themselves, but they were spotted and mobbed before the night was out," Warhol said.

Later, Warhol sadly informed Michael that the Tambourlaine had closed when a drug dealer from Harlem castrated one of his clients, a drag queen from Havana, for failing to pay him the five hundred dollars she owed him. "I made the bitch into a real woman," the drug dealer bragged, as he emerged from the women's toilet. The screams from the transvestite could be heard throughout the club.

One night Capote took both Warhol and Michael to Stage 54, a gay bar near the United Nations that attracted mainly black homosexuals serving the UN staffs of such countries as Nigeria and Haiti.

"Michael was turned off by the place," Capote said. "I suspected that Michael's desire was to fuck white."

The Studio 54 era and the New York scene were just a brief interlude in Michael's life. "It was a momentary diversion for him," Capote recalled. "In time, we would learn that he was far more interested in taking little boys to Disneyland than he was in hanging out with denizens of the night such as Bianca Jagger, Andy Warhol, Liza, and Mick. Or even *moi* as far as that goes. Foolish boy! With me, he was with the best. Going high class. I'm invited only to A-list parties. I also introduced Michael only to A-list people. Regrettably, the child didn't know how to behave. He was not meant to conquer high society as I'd done before him."

Capote might have been referring to, among other incidents, the coming together of Michael with the great designer, Halston.

One night at Studio 54, if Truman Capote is to be believed, the fashion designer, Halston, was mesmerized as he watched Michael dance across the floor. Before the evening ended, Halston confided to Capote: "I'm in love with that boy. I'm taking him for my next lover."

Halston (actually Roy Halston Frowick, born 1932 in Des Moines, Iowa) was in his mid-forties when he first encountered

Halston

Michael. "A bit long in the tooth for Michael," Capote cattily remarked.

At the time, Halston was still being celebrated for the pillbox hat made famous by former First Lady Jacqueline Kennedy. "He's designed hats for everybody from Gloria Swanson to Deborah Kerr," Capote said. "I'm sure if he plays it right, he can become Michael's milliner."

Halston never ended up designing hats for Michael, although he'd designed masks for Capote's famous Black and White Dance in the Grand Ballroom of the Plaza Hotel in 1966.

Halston made a striking, somewhat mysterious appearance with his mirrored sunglasses and all black attire. In the years to come, society's top dressmaker was accused of "looking like Darth Vader."

On the first night of hawk-eyeing Michael, the singer disappeared before the designer could meet him. On another night at Studio 54, under pressure from Halston, Capote finally introduced Halston to Michael. On this night, it was Michael who was dressed entirely in black, Halston appearing in a russet-brown ultra-suede jacket and tight-fitting red suede trousers.

He didn't really have to, but Halston tried to impress Michael, who at first didn't seem to know who the designer was, at least according to Capote. "The talk was of scent…perfume, my dear. Halston's perfume was the rage of New York. I wore it myself. Halston told Michael and me that he expected sales in the coming year to go beyond one hundred million dollars."

"He filled Michael in on the secrets of the fashion industry," Capote claimed. "We learned—actually I already knew this—that only three thousand women in the world could afford to buy a designer dress. But he felt his scent could reach millions around the world. At one point, Halston asked Michael if he'd wear his new perfume, and Michael agreed. Halston promised to send him a case."

That night, as Capote remembered, Halston showed his disdain for other designers. Both Gloria Vanderbilt and Calvin Klein were at Studio 54. Halston looked at each of them with a sneer. "Only a pig would put his name on a pair of blue jeans," Halston sneered.

Capote said that he, at Halston's request, left the designer alone to talk to Michael. "I learned some of the details later," Capote said. "After a long, apparently harmonious chit-chat, Michael suddenly arose from a banquette and abruptly left the club."

"What happened?" Capote asked when he rejoined Halston.

"I don't know why he got so huffy," Halston said. "All I said was, I want to fuck your beautiful *café au lait* ass all night. What's wrong with that? I ask many boys the same thing. No one turns down Halston but this uppity boy."

One night at Studio 54, Nureyev introduced Michael to his friend, Sterling Saint Jacques, an Afro-Italian singer with whom the dancer was having a torrid affair. Son of the famous black actor, Raymond St. Jacques, Sterling was tall, handsome, and "lean and mean," as he put it. Michael seemed intimidated when the singer leaned in close to him as if he were going to kiss him. "And they call Frank Sinatra ol' blue eyes. I should be called young blue eyes. Have you ever seen eyes as blue as mine—and in a nigger's head too?" Michael quickly drifted away. Years later, Michael read of the singer's death of AIDS in 1984.

Michael had long since fled Studio 54 when "this mad, mad, mad world" ended abruptly. By the end of 1979, Rubell and Schrager were arrested by the IRS for income tax evasion and were sentenced to three years in prison. They served 13 months before parole. But Studio 54 would never be the same again.

A closeted homosexual, Rubell was diagnosed HIV positive in 1985, but denied his condition and continued his lifestyle of heavy drinking and drug taking. This led to his death in 1989. Calvin Klein wept openly at the funeral. Michael was invited but chose not to attend.

On January 22, 1979, months after Michael's flirtation with Studio 54, the Jackson brothers, with Michael as the lead singer, embarked on another world tour, beginning in Bremen, West Germany. It was on to Nairobi, Kenya, with stops in Madrid, Paris, and London to follow.

In London, Michael learned that the latest Jackson album, *Destiny*, had gone double platinum. Michael's prediction of a comeback for the Jackson brothers was now a reality—in fact, long before the 1992 presidential campaign of Bill Clinton, Michael was calling his brothers "the comeback kids."

In England Michael turned a dangerous curve in his personal life.

Somehow evading security, star-struck Terry George, a 13-year-old Yorkshire lad, came knocking on Michael's hotel door in mid-February of 1979. With his tape recorder, Terry had come to interview Michael, his favorite singer, although the boy may also have told Paul McCartney that he was the favorite.

At the Dragonara Hotel in Leeds in the north of England, Michael himself came to the door but didn't open it until Terry told him that he was "only a boy of thirteen."

Michael invited him in and chatted pleasantly with the boy for nearly an hour. When Terry got up to leave, Michael invited him to return to his hotel suite the following day. Terry came by and was there to say good-bye to Michael when he returned to London. Before he left, Terry gave Michael his home address and phone number.

Three days went by before Michael called from London. A series of phone calls followed after Michael returned to California, mostly trivial talk but with many specific references to religion. Michael told Terry that he was a Jehovah's Witness and promised to send him a Bible.

124

By April the long phone conversations between Michael and the boy, some of which stretched out to more than three hours, had turned to sex. "Do you ever play with yourself?" Michael asked. Terry later said that, although red-faced at first, he finally admitted to Michael that he did masturbate on occasion.

Terry later revealed that he and Michael engaged in what is the equivalent of phone sex. According to Terry, Michael admitted to him that he often masturbated during their marathon transatlantic phone conversations.

Today, a grown-up Terry George has a website in England. Among other pursuits, he is a photographer, and his website features some of the best-looking hunks in the UK, most often in tight-fitting, basket-revealing swimwear. He's only a photographer of males in his spare time; otherwise he owns several companies and is said to be a multi-millionaire. One of his most successful projects has been the "Mr. Gay UK" competition, a pageant which he sponsors with his partner, Michael Rothwell.

After molestation charges against Michael surfaced in the 1990s, Terry was contacted by the press. *The Mail on Sunday* ran revelations about Terry's friendship with Michael. Terry called his interview with *The Mail on Sunday* "more like an interrogation." Soon UK readers by the millions were treated to a headlined interview: I HAD PHONE SEX WITH JACKO.

"I do not feel like a victim and I never did feel like a victim," Terry told the press. "We only stopped talking on the phone when my mum got a £350 phone bill. That was what put an end to the relationship, not anything Michael did."

On his website, Terry admitted that he had been contacted by detective Paul Zelis of the Santa Barbara County Sheriff's department and told that Michael had pleaded not guilty to child molestation charges.

A defense of sorts is posted on the web. "It isn't illegal to love boys," the site claims. "It isn't illegal to hug and kiss them, unless they don't want you to. Even then it isn't illegal if you happen to be an older female relative. Ask any ten-year-old boy right after a family gathering. There is no age of consent law for hugging and kissing. It isn't illegal to sleep in the same bed with them, or for unrelated men and boys to see each other naked. Each person who is attracted to boys is different from every other, and some of these dissimilarities are important. There are some whose exclusive interest (or nearly so) is in their own gratification. They use a boy with little or no regard for the youth's well-being, satisfaction, or happiness. The kidnappers, torturers, murderers, and real as opposed to statutory rapists come from this group. For boy lovers, the boy's gratification is important. The pleasures the boy lover derives, in no small part, from his role in the well-being, satisfaction, or happiness of the boy. Those who have long-term, loving relationships with boys come from this group. If you call a dog's tail a leg, how many legs does a dog have? The correct answer is four. Calling a dog's tail a leg doesn't make it one. It is the same with statutory rape. The law may call it rape, but it isn't. The failure of society to make reasonable distinctions between these two groups creates gross injustices."

When reached by the press during Michael's child molestation scandals, Terry said, "I have not been in contact with Michael since 1983, but the way he has been treated by the media has been wrong. I do not know whether he is guilty of abusing the other boys. I hope he is not. It has been so sad to see a man with so much talent fall from grace like he has."

As the 70s neared its end, personal pleasures for Michael gave way to career concerns. "I want to show that I can make it on my own," he told producer Quincy Jones. "My talent is my own—not my brothers. It doesn't belong to anybody else but me, and it doesn't depend on anybody else. I owe it to myself to show the world who I really am without any backup singers."

Michael and Quincy had become friends during the making of *The Wiz*, and Michael was delighted when Quincy signed on to produce an album with him. Michael later revealed that he was so thrilled to snare Quincy that "I didn't sleep for three whole days and nights."

During their long, drawn-out sessions of working together, which often extended into the early hours of the morning, Michael told Quincy: "Give me the ballads like 'Mona Lisa' and 'Moon River'—they'll live forever. A funky rock 'n' roll song will be number one for three weeks and then it's gone forever. I want to record the songs that last forever."

Quincy described Michael as "writing music like a machine—he could really crank it up." For the album, three of the songs were written by Michael, and many more lay in his bright future which would virtually explode into phenomenal success in the 80s.

Quincy nicknamed Michael "Smelly," because of his habit of calling a piece of music he liked "Smelly Jelly."

Michael deserved the nickname Smelly for other reasons. While recording the album, he refused to change his dirty jeans and T-shirts, even his jockey shorts. The odor got so bad that his fellow musicians in the studio complained of having to work with Michael in close quarters.

During the long recording sessions, Michael experienced two separate panic attacks, crying out that "I'm dying—help me!" On two different occasions, ambulances with dome lights flashing rushed him to Inglewood's Centinela Hospital. Each time he was placed in an oxygen tent and given sedatives to calm him down. The first time he came to, he gripped Katherine's wrist. "If the album doesn't succeed, I'll die—I'll just die!"

The album was originally meant to be called *Girlfriend*, named after the

Paul McCartney song written just for Michael.

Michael and Quincy later agreed to change it to *Off the Wall*, named for what they speculated would be a hit single from the album.

It was Michael who solicited the former Beatle to write a song for his new album. McCartney's own version was released earlier, followed by Michael's later interpretation. In a surprise to fans, McCartney sings in a higher register than Jackson, and the English singer turned in a better recording in the opinion of *Steve and Abe's Record Reviews*. "Jackson's rendition is light disco, with an awkward saxophone solo and a routine vocal. McCartney gives the song a much broader emotional palette. McCartney's version of 'Girlfriend' triumphs all over Jackson's."

This brought world outrage from Michael's fans, including one, Nu On, who posted his opinion on the web. It was typical of the blasts against reviews comparing Michael unfavorably to McCartney. "So your conclusion is that McCartney is a better singer, performer and artist than Jackson? Get fuckin' real. Maybe McCartney was a greater 'artist' (his songwriting is amazing), but you can forget calling The Beatles better performers or singers. When it comes to their performances and singing, The Beatles (and McCartney) are untalented and lame, while Jackson is pure electricity. Have you ever seen The Beatles dance? They look like stiff, rhythm-less, epileptic puppets. And their 'live' singing is mostly screeching. The Beatles are mostly a studio band that relied on 'electronic chemicals' and a thousand different tricks to sweeten their sound. Next you'll claim that Paul McCartney is a better guitar player than Jimi Hendrix."

Ever the perfectionist, Michael worked for days to get the title track, "Off the Wall," just right. Within months, Michael introduced that song to the world with a piercing falsetto that his fans hadn't quite heard before.

Carefully directed by Quincy, Michael performed most of his vocals live.

"He wasn't at all sure that he could make a name for himself on his own," said Quincy before "Off the Wall" was released. "And me, too. I had my doubts."

Upon its release, "Off the Wall" sold eight or thirteen million copies, depending on which source you want to believe. Regardless of its actual sales, it is believed to be the largest selling album ever recorded by a black artist at that time.

The hit single from the album, suggestively titled "Don't Stop 'Til You Get Enough," was released as a single in September of 1979, shooting up immediately to number one on *Billboard's* charts. Unlike the other records on the album, this single featured Michael's own overdubbed vocals. In essence, he was doing his own backup singing. "You might call it Michael Jackson and the Michael Jacksons," one critic jokingly suggested.

Privately the musicians in the studio speculated that Michael was still a virgin—at least with women—when he recorded "Don't Stop 'Til You Get Enough." But as one musician said, "Michael had seen that sexy Jermaine pound enough pussy in those hotel rooms to understand the meaning of the song."

Quincy had a hard time getting Michael to complete "She's Out of My Life," because he'd weep before the song's finish. "This went on for a month," Quincy said. "He could never get through the record without crying. Finally, in desperation, I left in the crying bit."

"She's Out of My Life" went top ten on the pop Hot 100, as did "Rock With You." After the release of these hit singles from the album, Michael Jackson became the hottest male recording star in the world.

In spite of its sales, "Off the Wall" is hardly a Michael Jackson *tour de force*. As critic Nelson George put it: "'Off the Wall's' aura is sweet, sunny and bright—and characteristic of so much middle-of-the-road black 70s Pop—and offers philosophical bromides about rockin' the night away in place of any real personal vision."

Michael Jackson Album Reviews found their star giving off an aura of "undeniably adult sexiness." But then the critics later added a cautionary note—"that was before the words 'Michael Jackson' and 'sexy' became mutually exclusive."

The cover of the *Off the Wall* album pictured Michael nattily dressed in a tuxedo. As a unique touch, he wore white fluorescent socks, which were destined to become his trademark.

For the first time, fans were treated to a discernibly thinner nose. No longer could his brothers nickname him "Big Nose." "It wasn't quite Diana Ross's button nose," said an executive at Epic, "but Michael had obviously had some cosmetic surgery." In the years ahead Michael would become a regular customer of beauty butchers.

Later, it was revealed how this change in Michael's face came about. On the *Destiny* tour with his brothers, he'd had an accident, falling down on stage and smashing his nose. With his broken nose, Michael went to a plastic surgeon in Beverly Hills in the spring of 1979.

He ordered the surgeon to "transform my nose—I don't want my father's nose." When the bandages came off, "Joseph's nose"—at least on Michael's face—was history. It was the beginning of countless plastic surgeries in his future.

After the surgery, Michael asked the doctor, "What are you going to do with the part of my nose you removed?"

"Discard it, of course," the surgeon told him.

"No, I want to keep it," Michael protested. "It's my nose and it belongs to

128

me."

As he was driven to Encino to recuperate, Michael gripped in his hand a glass vial. In it was preserved a bloody purple-red piece of nose cartilage. Beginning with this simple vial, Michael would, over the years, expand his bizarre collection of preserved medical oddities.

At this same time he also began the bizarre habit of collecting mementos of his seven nephews and nieces, all fathered by his brothers. The collection ranged from a discarded plastic replica of Donald Duck to soiled diapers—or so it was reported—from each child. The crusted brown contents from each child were still intact and carefully labeled and dated by Michael, members of the household staff at Encino later testified.

Even though Michael had gradually matured into an adult, his music was still geared to the youth of the world.

The greatest fan of *Off the Wall* was a fifteen-year-old girl, Roberta Flackson, born of trailer camp white trash somewhere in the Florida Panhandle. Her mother was a prostitute, her father of "unknown origin."

Since her mother had had sex, often of the unprotected variety, with so many men, she could not be certain who the father was.

Roberta suffered a background of child abuse. Her mother was not only a whore, but a drug addict who allegedly prostituted her own daughter to johns who wanted someone really young.

Eventually, when she was thirteen, Roberta fled the Panhandle, arriving in New York with money stolen from her mother's nightly earnings. When that money ran out, Roberta herself became a prostitute, allowing middle-aged men to pick her up and carry her to seedy motels in New Jersey or else to one of the hot-bed hotels that used to exist in midtown Manhattan in the 1970s.

Once, when arrested and questioned by the police, Roberta admitted that she was a prostitute, a profession she pursued for two reasons: one, to make a living; another, to buy all the Michael Jackson records and memorabilia she could. In an apartment on the Upper West Side that she shared with a much older prostitute, Roberta had stuffed every room with Jackson memorabilia. She played Jackson records day and night, especially *Off the Wall*.

When not plying her trade, she'd show up frequently on the set of *The Wiz*, and had to be forcefully removed by security guards. Somehow she learned that Michael and La Toya were living on Sutton Place. Between her nightly rounds, she hung out in front of the apartment building, hoping to get a glimpse of her idol. Even though he tried to avoid his number one fan, Michael frequently had run-ins with her when he was attempting to flee from her presence.

Finally, thanks to the urging of his friend, Theresa Gonsalves, Michael invited Roberta up to his Sutton Place apartment for tea. The girl was mesmerized by Michael and didn't know what to say. Even so, it was difficult to get her to leave. Theresa had thought that once the fan met Michael, and her curiosity was satisfied, she'd leave him alone.

Not so. With money earned from whoring, Roberta flew to the West Coast. Whenever she wasn't working, she stood at the gates to the Jackson Encino mansion hoping for a glimpse of Michael coming and going. Her presence became such a problem for him that he slipped in and out of the Jackson manse without her detecting him. He even used disguises to throw her off his trail.

Three weeks after she'd flown to Los Angeles, Roberta was found dead in a seedy motel off Santa Monica Boulevard. In her room was found all the Jackson memorabilia she'd collected. It is not known if Michael was even informed of the apparent suicide of his number one fan.

After the success of the album, Michael retreated to his room and rarely ventured out, except for secret visits to Disneyland. He donned several disguises, but finally decided the best camouflage was the enveloping black *chador* of a traditional Muslim woman. The only incongruity were those white socks and tennis shows which appeared right below the hem. Ironically, that was the same disguise he'd wear in the 21st century as an expatriate in the Middle Eastern country of Bahrain.

At the Grammy Awards in 1980, Michael expected many more prizes but won only a single Grammy as the best male R&B performer. Bitterly disappointed, he burst into tears in front of the audience. "One sore loser," a member of the staff of *Rolling Stone* was overheard saying.

"I was robbed!" Michael shouted, making a public spectacle of himself. "It's racism!" He vowed with amazing accuracy that his next album would be "the biggest in history."

Following the awards, Michael entered a deep depression and wouldn't leave his darkened room. It took a family tragedy to drive him from the house.

It was almost four o'clock in the morning, March 4, 1980, when an emergency call came in to the family home at Encino. Police had used equipment called "The Jaws of Life" to rescue the mangled body of Randy from the wreck of a Mercedes-Benz. At the wheel, Randy had lost control of his girlfriend's car along Cahuenga Boulevard.

It had been raining during the early morning hours, and the road was extremely slippery. Apparently, Randy had been driving at ninety miles per hour when he'd lost control of the car. "Like sailing on ice," in the words of one policeman, the Mercedes had glided across the street and into a telephone pole before coming to a jarring stop. Without his safety belt on, Randy was thrown forward into the windshield, cracking his pelvis and crushing both of his legs.

When the call came in, only Janet, La Toya, and Michael, along with both Joe and Katherine, were at their Encino home. All five piled into a family vehicle for the nervous ride to St. Joseph's Medical Center in Burbank.

At the hospital, the presiding doctor told a stern-faced Joe, "Your son may have less than twenty-four hours to live. We're doing all we can to save him."

Upon hearing the news, Michael burst into uncontrollable sobbing. "My baby brother!" he shouted. "Randy!" A nurse was asked to sedate him.

After Michael was brought under control, Joe also learned that the doctors might have to "amputate one or both" of Randy's legs.

"He's a performer and a dancer," Joe shouted at the doctor. "How can he do that without legs? You'll amputate over my dead body."

When a sedated Michael was brought in to see Randy, he started to cry again. Randy lay on blood-soaked sheets, with shards of glass from the windshield still imbedded in his face. In fright, Michael turned from the sight of him.

Later, he joined the rest of his family for a deathbed vigil. By ten o'clock, Randy had rallied but only slightly. Later, Michael learned that a male night nurse had nearly killed Randy when he'd administered a dose of methadone to the crash victim. The injection had been intended for a black heroin addict two rooms down.

After two days and nights, doctors determined that Randy's legs would not have to be amputated after all. "But I doubt if your boy will ever walk again," the doctor told Joe. "He'll be forced to live in a wheelchair for the rest of his life."

"There goes the fucking tour," Joe shouted angrily at the doctor. He'd wanted to send his sons on a national tour that summer, hoping to considerably beef up sagging family finances.

Michael paced the hallways at the Jackson's Encino home at night. "Why Randy?" he kept asking out loud and to no one. "Why, God, couldn't the accident have happened to someone not important? Someone who doesn't need legs to go on stage?"

During the uncertain duration of Randy's recovery, Michael would often break into uncontrollable sobbing of the kind he'd displayed upon hearing of Randy's dire condition. "It could have been me. Everybody in this household has been urging me to get a driver's license. I might be the one who will never walk again."

Katherine maintained an almost constant ritual of prayer. But, of the siblings, Michael was the most loyal. He stood by Randy, offering moral support as he went through a therapy so painful that he often cried out. Bravely he told Michael, "Fuck what the doctors say. I will walk again! You'll see."

The months went by, and Randy's legs seemed to improve every day.

Katherine got to see her son not just walk on a stage again, but dance as well. "My prayers have saved my son."

When Katherine's mind wasn't occupied with Randy's recovery, she had to deal with an increasingly assertive Michael.

Now that he was a full-fledged adult, Michael decided to replace Joe as his business manager. He told Katherine what he planned to do. "It'll break your father's heart," she warned him, urging him not to fire Joe. Normally, Michael listened to his mother. Not this time.

He appealed to David Braun, hailed as one of the best attorneys in the music industry. Diana Ross had recommended Braun to Michael. His other clients included Neil Diamond, George Harrison, and Bob Dylan.

As president of PolyGram Records, Braun in the fall of 1980 recommended John Branca, an aggressive 30-year-old New York tax attorney, to handle Michael's account. At the time of his first meeting, Michael liked Branca and stated his ambition—"to become the wealthiest entertainer on the planet and, last but not least, the biggest star in the world."

If Branca was shocked by such bold ambition, his face gave no indication. On the way home that night, he stopped off in a record store and purchased both Jackson singles and albums. Previous to their meeting, he had never heard Michael sing.

From that night on, Branca became almost more familiar with Michael's music than the artist himself. He certainly knew more about Michael's financial affairs than Michael did himself. Branca would dominate Michael's career for more than a decade, and he'd become the single key figure in his success in the music industry. "Michael stated his goal to me on our first meeting," Branca later said, "and I saw that he achieved both those ambitions expressed to me."

Immediately after signing with Michael, Branca barged into the office of Walter Yetnikoff, the controversial monarch of CBS Records who ruled over

Walter Yetnikoff

John Branca

pop music's heyday in the 70s and 80s. Yetnikoff emerged as a key player in the careers of Bob Dylan, Billy Joel, Paul Simon, Barbra Streisand, Bruce Springsteen, and the Rolling Stones. In time he would become "the father confessor" to Michael.

One of Yetnikoff's secretaries confided, "He was in a constant state of blazing combustion," a condition usually fueled by alcohol and cocaine. Known as "the bully of the record industry," he was flamboyant, volatile, and tone-deaf.

"Two famous people came out of Brooklyn," he was fond of saying. "Mae West and Walter Yetnikoff. She's washed up. I'm still in there slugging away."

Yetnikoff originally had wanted to fire all the Jackson brothers, including Michael, but had become convinced that Michael could be turned into the biggest pop star of the 1980s. "Listen," he told Branca, "I can talk down Barbra Streisand, so I'm sure I'm up for any challenge the little Jackson boy will toss my way."

Before leaving Yetnikoff's office that day, Michael's new attorney secured for him an amazing contract. In an astonishing "giveaway" by CBS, Michael walked away with a 37% royalty rate. Michael had instructed Branca "to get me what Dylan gets," and that's exactly what Branca got.

Branca also negotiated with Johnny Mason, the lawyer representing Joe and his sons, a provision that Michael could break away from his brothers at any time without penalty. Joe ranted for days when he heard the terms, but didn't immediately confront Michael, fearing he might bolt from the group right away.

In addition to Branca and Yetnikoff, Frank DiLeo eventually became "the man behind Michael Jackson," forming a triumvirate that would take Michael to the zenith of his success in the 1980s. "Uncle Tookie," as Michael called him, would go on to orchestrate two hit albums for Michael, *Thriller* and *Bad*, plus two world tours that each met with overwhelming success.

A native of Pittsburgh—he once wanted to be mayor—DiLeo went from serving spaghetti and meatballs in a seedy Italian trattoria to becoming national director of promotions for RCA Records when he was only twenty-one. He was known for his foul mouth, "assholes" being one of his favorite epithets. With this blustering, outspoken record hustler, Michael would form yet another of the many "odd couple" relationships in his life.

Michael and DiLeo were a study in contrasts. A secretary who worked for DiLeo said, "to see the two of them together at lunch was a sight to behold. Michael would order a glass of carrot juice and a spinach salad. DiLeo preferred a 'triple bypass' burger smothered in onions, bacon, and Cheddar along with three Buds to help all that cholesterol go down his gullet."

In contrast to razor-thin Michael, the 275-pound DiLeo looked like a bookie left over from the cast of the film, *Guys and Dolls*, that had starred Michael's friend, Marlon Brando, and Michael's enemy, Frank Sinatra. "DiLeo smoked the kind of cigars Castro preferred, and at times I think he liked stogies better than women, although I'm not sure," said Luciano Pellegrini, who had met DiLeo in Pittsburgh. "He was more masculine than a bull in the ring, yet would be associated with the careers of two boys of dubious sexuality: Michael Jackson and Boy George." In addition to those artists, DiLeo also promoted Meat Loaf and Cyndi Lauper.

In time, Michael was so pleased with the promotional efforts of Uncle Tookie that he rewarded him with a Rolls Royce and a gold, diamond-studded watch among other prizes.

To celebrate signing a deal that granted him the highest royalty rate in the business, Michael joined the homeless.

Dressing up like a bum in soiled, ragged, and smelly clothing, he was driven to one of the seediest and most dangerous parts of Los Angeles. There he wandered among whores, pickpockets, winos, and bums, many of whom had contagious diseases. Attaching himself to a hobo who had managed to reach his 60s, Michael followed him on his rounds from garbage can to garbage can, scrounging for food or any object that could be used in an endless quest for survival. For some reason, the hobo had acquired the curious nickname of "Bearded Liver." Part of the pathetic figure's face seemed eaten away with cancer that was raging out of control and had never been treated.

When Katherine learned of Michael's disappearance, she sighed, "That Michael! He always was an inquisitive child."

"The next time he pulls a stunt like this, he's liable to get killed," Joe predicted.

When Michael later became friends with Marlon Brando, the actor confided in him that, "I did the same thing in the late 40s when I survived among the *clochards* of Paris. I didn't even have one franc on me. It was the happiest time of my life."

Michael got through his life as a hobo in seedy Los Angeles without incident. He wasn't so lucky months later in 1981 in Atlanta, Georgia, when he appeared in rags at an antique store, behaving strangely. He refused to halt when the store's owner, a Londoner, John Nolan, told him to. Instead of that, Michael concealed himself in a "Scarlett O'Hara armoire" rescued from some old plantation house.

Nolan called the police. Finally, Michael emerged and reached inside his breast pocket. The owner thought he was drawing a gun to shoot them. Nolan bashed his fist into Michael's reconstructed nose. Blood spurted out. While they were struggling, the police arrived. There was a station around the corner. Officer Jeff Green recognized Michael in spite of his disguise. "That's no hobo," Green said. "It's Michael Jackson in person."

When order was restored, Green considered charging Michael with criminal trespass, and Nolan with assault and battery, but charges were dropped.

Before leaving Georgia, Michael had another hostile encounter in the town of Macon. In a convenience store waiting for his vehicle to be filled with gasoline, a white man screamed "Nigger!" at him and accused him of stealing a candy bar. The man began to pound Michael, plowing his fists into him until his bodyguard rushed into the store and rescued the star. Assault charges were considered but never filed.

Back at Encino, enjoying the comforts of the Jackson mansion after his aimless wandering and countless disguises, Michael listened to the final cut of La Toya's first solo album, simply called *La Toya Jackson.*

Originally, Joe had pressured Michael to produce the album for La Toya, but he'd refused. "If my brothers and sisters want to strike out on their own," Michael said, "they are free to do so. But I'm not going to let them ride in on my coattails."

In spite of his refusal, Joe kept the pressure on Michael until he agreed to co-write and produce one song for La Toya's album, "Night Time Lover."

Suspicions were aroused when Michael heard the final mix and ordered that the song be recorded again. Katherine told La Toya, "Michael's jealous. He's scared that somebody in the family will be bigger than him, so he had to go back to the studio, make it different—and now it isn't as good." La Toya found that hard to believe.

Initially, La Toya had been dismayed when presented with some of the songs, especially her first single, "If You Feel the Funk." As a devout Jehovah's Witness, she feared that by recording some of the more suggestive lyrics, she'd be kicked out of her church. But Katherine, an even more devout Jehovah's Witness, told her to go ahead. La Toya reluctantly agreed.

Brett Stevenson was one of many who had observed La Toya when she was working on her first album. He claimed that, "All of us in the studio thought she was one hot pussy but had no talent as a singer. Instead of recording her songs, we wanted to go to bed with her. I felt that in spite of a poor voice, she had a fierce determination to become the female Michael Jackson. Old Joe showed up once or twice. I don't think he really had much faith in La Toya's talent as a singer either, although he kept goading her to move along with it. Actually, I heard that Janet is the only one in the family with enough talent to become a female Michael Jackson."

In the living room of the Encino home, Michael listened to the final album without saying a word. At its conclusion, he rose from his chair. "The album's a failure," he said to La Toya. "It'll bomb just like Jermaine did with his first solo album." Before heading upstairs to his bedroom, he assured his sister that she was beautiful and might have a better chance if she pursued a career as a model. Of course, Michael surely didn't mean she should pose nude for *Playboy*, which she would later scandalously do.

Randy's legs had miraculously improved, and he was walking on October 16, 1980, when he accompanied Janet and Katherine to the offices of Joe Jackson Productions at 6255 Sunset Boulevard. For months, Katherine had been hearing that her husband was having another affair, this time with one of his employees, a younger woman, Gina Sprague, who was descended from Mexican and Irish parents. She was only nineteen years old. Having confronted Cheryl Terrell, the mother of Joe's illegitimate daughter, Katherine was prepared to take on this younger and more beautiful woman. Although Sprague would later deny that she was having an affair with Joe, Katherine was convinced that they were lovers, enough so to take matters dangerously into her own hands as part of a public confrontation.

Based on her testimony to the Los Angeles Police Department, Sprague claimed that Randy, then 18 years old, and Janet, only 14, came into her office and attacked her.

In her testimony, Sprague told police that Katherine pulled her hair as Janet grabbed her wrist. Allegedly, Randy knocked Sprague from her desk chair, and she fell on the carpeted floor.

Apparently the victim was dragged out of the office, while Katherine pounded her face, calling her a "bitch" and threatening her if she didn't stop seeing her husband. Sprague also testified that Katherine took some blunt but unknown object from her pocketbook and hit Sprague nearly twenty times on her back and neck. Janet, Katherine, and Randy finally got Sprague to the stairwell of the office building, where her screams alerted security guard James Krieg, who came to her rescue.

The commotion created such hysteria that other employees began to gather to see what was the matter. Katherine, along with her son and daughter, fled from the building. Before going, she reached for a gold necklace around Sprague's neck, yanking it from her. "This belongs to me, bitch," Katherine was heard to shout at Sprague before running away.

When Michael was called and told what had happened, he was reading all the material he'd collected on "The Elephant Man." Upon hearing the news about his mother, he didn't believe it. He claimed that his "Kate would never do that," in spite of the fact that she'd once attacked Joe's other mistress, Cheryl Terrell.

"My mother would never harm anyone," Michael said. "There is no gentler person on the planet. This incident is a lie. It never took place. I know my Kate." To this day, Michael still insists that the attack on Sprague never occurred.

In the wake of the attack, Sprague filed a $21 million assault-and-battery lawsuit against Katherine, Janet, and Randy. Surprisingly, Sprague also named Joe in her lawsuit, although he was not one of the family members who ganged up on her. Later, Sprague testified that she was blackballed from working in the music industry. Five or perhaps six years went by before she was offered a job in the industry once more.

Michael refused to talk about the incident, although privately he voiced his concern, fearing that this scandal, which became the talk of Hollywood, could seriously damage his career as it was about to take off big-time.

In court, and in contradiction of eyewitness testimony, Katherine, Janet, and Randy maintained that the attack never took place.

That case could have been one of the sensational domestic trials of the decade, holding the Jackson family up to ridicule. Wisely, Joe's attorneys urged him to settle out of court. Various estimates have put the settlement as low as $75,000 or as high as $100,000. On July 21, 1983, Sprague's lawyers filed for a dismissal of the suit against the Jacksons.

When not agonizing over family woes, Michael buried himself into the story of John Merrick, the so-called Elephant Man, the English Victorian deformed by neurofibromatosis.

The story of Michael's fascination with the Elephant Man is a bit hard to piece together, because there has been so much written about it, so many misconceptions, and, last but not least, a series of lies from the Jackson camp itself.

During a live interview with Oprah Winfrey in 1993, Michael said that the story of the Elephant Man "touched me profoundly—it made me cry because I saw myself in the story. But, no, I never tried to buy the Elephant's Man's bones. What would I do with a bag of bones?"

He was being a bit disingenuous during that interview. On the question of bones and body parts, Winfrey might have asked, "Why do you need to keep a pickled human brain in your bedroom? Or a piece of preserved cartilage from your own nose?"

When director David Lynch released *The Elephant Man* in 1980, Michael is reported to have seen the film a dozen times. John Hurt played John Merrick, with other lead roles interpreted by Anthony Hopkins, Anne Bancroft, and John Gielgud. Michael was not alone in appreciating the film, as it was nominated for eight Oscars. But Michael seemed the most obsessive. He was reported to have purchased clothing and artifacts that had belonged to Merrick.

If a maid who worked at Encino is to be believed, Michael actually sat by his window for hours staring into space. He despondently and rhythmically tapped on the arm of his chair, holding his left hand in a distorted position. As the hours deepened, he pretended that a painful crippling was taking over his body. He kept repeating this verse:

'Tis true my form is something odd,
But blaming me is blaming God;
Could I create myself anew
I would not fail in pleasing you

"Merrick was a sideshow attraction," Michael is reported to have said. "Just what I am to the world. But in the end he was beloved by the Victorians. In time, I too will be loved, not by high society, but by the children of the world."

As the years went by and the world began to regard Michael more and more as a "Freak"—actually the title of a *National Enquirer* book about him—his identification with The Elephant Man grew and grew.

The Elephant Man would figure in Michael's future before the release of his album, *Bad*, in 1987. Wanting to attract bizarre publicity and make headlines, he arranged to view the bones of John Merrick kept in a glass case at the London Hospital Medical College.

Michael asked Frank DiLeo, Epic's production director, to announce to the press that he'd made a bid to purchase the skeleton for $500,000.

DiLeo sent ahead and even prepared a press release, claiming that "Michael Jackson has read and studied all material about The Elephant Man, and visited the hospital in London twice where Merrick's remains are found. His possible purchase of the skeleton of John Merrick is not for exploitation. Mr. Jackson cares about and is concerned with The Elephant Man as a dedicated and devoted collector of art and antiques."

John Merrick

The announcement generated millions of dollars of publicity. But an alert London reporter checked with the hospital and learned that no such offer had been made. The press announcement was a hoax.

Fearing a backlash, with his credibility on the line, Michael ordered DiLeo to make an actual offer of one million dollars for the bones.

"One million big ones for a sack of old bones," DiLeo reportedly told the hospital. The administration was offended, turning down the offer. "The Elephant Man is not for sale," said a hospital spokesperson. "In no way do we want to be part of a cheap publicity stunt."

Although free, the publicity generated by The Elephant Man ultimately boomeranged into headlines such as WACKO-JACKO'S IN THE CLOSET WITH THE ELEPHANT MAN.

Ultimately, the publicity campaign generated by Michael himself failed. He would never be taken seriously in the press again, and The Elephant Man only generated more press, most of it unfavorable, much of it devoted to ridiculing Michael as a public figure.

Although he was hardly grotesque like The Elephant Man, Michael himself still dreaded to look into the mirror. He decided that more surgical altering of his face was necessary, and he asked Dr. Steven Hoefflin to perform a second rhinoplasty. "With my new nose, I will never look like Joe ever again—no one will ever say that."

Abandoning the greasy "soul food" he loved, Michael became a vegetarian, losing his baby fat. He claimed he wanted to have a body as lithe as Rudolf Nureyev or Mick Jagger.

Eventually the dreaded acne that had plagued him for years began to clear up. With the second nose job, his face took on a different look. A remarkable transformation had begun. Those close to Michael privately voiced concerns that he was still not satisfied with his looks.

Speaking off the record, an executive of Epic said he felt that "deep down Michael just didn't want to be black like his brothers. He wanted to change his skin color. But how does a black boy become white? If there's a way, I predict Michael will find it, regardless of the cost."

As the 80s rolled in, Michael began to change his appearance drastically. His looks caused massive public interest, analysis, and an outcry from many of his fans, especially black ones.

Author David Buckley wrote, "If David Bowie was about psychic reconstruction through a personal style, then soul singer Michael Jackson was taking it all too literally and way too far. Jackson took home improvements literally and, by redesigning his face and skin tone, allegedly through elective cosmetic surgery, he gave the impression of being ashamed of his colour. Running through all this was a Peter Pan-esque androgyny. Jackson, with the body of a boy and the face of a strategically redesigned white/black, male/female hybrid, made a global impact in the 1980s through his plastic-surgery bisexuality. In a decade in which Western youths were subjected to increasing pressure to reconstruct their bodies through diet and exercise (with

139

often fatal results), Jackson set himself up as the ultimate example of an individual trying to cheat nature. At a time when hundreds of thousands developed eating disorders and became ashamed of their natural size and shape, Jackson's quest for bodily 'perfection' was another signal to youth that the current orthodoxy was both righteous and right."

With his increased earning power, Michael not only changed his face but financed the expansion and restoration of the Encino family home. The old lackluster ranch-style house, which Roy Rogers and Dale Evans might have called home, was completely gutted. In its place a Tudor-style mansion sprouted up, a far more luxurious retreat to the increasingly famous Jacksons. Michael owned fifty percent of the house, for which he paid half-a-million dollars, the rest belonging to his parents. Eventually Joe, strapped for cash, would sell his quarter interest to Michael as well, giving him three-fourths ownership with his mother sharing the rest.

Reconstruction of Hayvenhurst would go on for more than two years. While driving through West Sussex in England, Michael had spotted a country estate that intrigued him. He wanted it duplicated at Encino. The leaded stained glass with beveled panes would have made Elizabeth I feel at home.

When the estate was finished, black swans and flamboyant peacocks wandered the grounds along with llamas and deer, even a giraffe nicknamed "Jabar." His favorite pet was "Muscles," a ten-foot boa constrictor.

Michael's "folly," was the inclusion, within the reconfigured Encino estate, of an abbreviated version of Main Street U.S.A., his favorite part of Disneyland, which he continued to visit frequently.

Michael would also spend several hours every week watching films within the estate's on-site theater, a facility that provided plush scarlet-colored seating for 32 guests. His favorite film was *Fantasia*, which he is said to have seen one hundred times. For comedy, he preferred Charlie Chaplin or The Three Stooges. Fred Astaire movies like *Royal Wedding* were also among his favorites, as was Katharine Hepburn's *Little Women*.

The house itself was filled with Jackson memorabilia, including both gold and platinum albums used as wall decorations, along with family pictures, many depicting Michael with celebrities such as Liza Minnelli.

In all, Michael would spend nearly four million dollars "to turn Hayvenhurst into a fairytale."

While reconstruction was going on, Michael in February of 1981 purchased a three-bedroom condo at 5420 Lindley Avenue in Encino for $225,000, giving Katherine a share. Since the condo afforded privacy, Michael would later share it with a series of very young boys he'd invite for "sleepovers."

With his new estate at Encino and his increasingly celebrity status,

Michael began to seek out other celebrities, some of whom were the most famous on the planet. Or, rather, celebrities began to seek Michael out.

Unlike many pop stars of his age who had no use for the established stars of the industry, Michael in his future would court some of the biggest stars of the so-called Golden Age of Hollywood.

One night in Los Angeles the most controversial star in Hollywood—at that time—walked across a crowded room and extended her hand to Michael in a firm handshake.

At the time of their meeting, he was aware of her reputation, knowing that she'd been variously ridiculed as a sex kitten in the film *Barbarella*, and as a political activist for her views on the Vietnam War. Her enemies called her "Hanoi Jane."

Standing before him was one of the most self-assured and beautiful women he'd ever seen, definitely with an independent spirit and a "mind of her own," as he'd later tell Katherine.

She was one of the most recognizable faces in the world. Although they were hardly the type of films he normally liked to see, Michael had sat through *Klute* in 1971 and *Coming Home* in 1978, each of which had earned her an Oscar for Best Actress.

"Hello," she said in her perfectly modulated voice, "you must be Michael Jackson. I'm Jane Fonda."

"Michael has a heightened sensitivity for the crying needs of this world. Through his 'Heal the World Foundation,' he works to preserve this planet's most precious resources-children, and the environment. He feels much of the same responsibility a parent feels-his children are all of our children. Michael brings so much to so many, he is one of the world's most precious resources himself."

--Steven Spielberg

"The world sees me as this monstrous freak who abuses little boys."

--Michael Jackson to Elizabeth Taylor

"He's taken a lot more control of his own life. When I made 'Thriller' I dealt with thousands of managers and record people and all this stuff and it's pretty clear to me that Mike makes his own decisions now...He has a lot more pressure on him now. There's a lot more jealousy. Michael, you know, is an old pro. People still think of Michael Jackson as little Michael Jackson like little Stevie Wonder, but you're talking about someone who was on the Ed Sullivan show, I mean he was making live performances and working hard from the time he was little."

--John Landis

"Michael originally rang me up on Christmas day...and I didn't believe it was him. I didn't think it was Michael...eventually I said, 'Is that really you?' He was laughing on the phone, he said, 'You don't believe me, do you?'"

**--Paul McCartney,
On the first time Michael proposed they work together**

"Billy Joel and Michael Jackson."

--Taylor Hanson, on his favorite singers

Chapter Six

In Jane Fonda's 2005 autobiography, *My Life So Far*, you can look in the index under the Js, and you'll find Jackson State University. But no Michael Jackson. Since he was the biggest entertainer in the world during the height of their friendship, and they became close personal comrades, it can be assumed that Jane's omission of Michael was a deliberate choice.

Jane devoted several pages to the making of the 1981 film, *On Golden Pond*, and Michael was a frequent visitor to the set, yet he is not included in her memoirs. She introduced him to her father, Henry Fonda, who was near death at the time, and to the indomitable Katharine Hepburn, with whom Michael formed the unlikeliest of friendships.

Perhaps Jane, and this is pure speculation, was offended by all the subsequent child molestation charges whirling around Michael, and wanted to distance herself from him. Jane has had enough controversy in her life, without having to defend Michael in public as Elizabeth Taylor has done without apologies.

At least before she moved to Atlanta and became a "Born Again," Jane was worldly wise and sophisticated. Born to Hollywood royalty, Henry Fonda and Frances Brokaw, Jane had led a privileged life, meeting screen legends and moving in left-wing political circles. From reports, she was mesmerized by the naïveté of Michael. She might have considered him like a child, a very fragile individual, a wounded antelope in private life, but the epitome of a graceful panther on stage where every move is perfect. He might have seemed to be filled with a love for mankind, especially the children of the world.

Sharp, sexy, and strong, Jane could, in succession, play a call girl stalked by a killer, the writer Lillian Hellman, a timid wife involved in an erotic relationship with a paraplegic, a hardened newswoman, or a newlywed in a Tennessee Williams atypical stab at comedy.

Michael eagerly accepted her invitation to come to Squam Lake in New

Hampshire where *On Golden Pond* was being shot.

He recalled the time fondly as they sat "all alone on a boat in the water just talking, talking, talking. We talked about everything: racism, Vietnam, acting, politics, even philosophers. It was like wandering into the Magic Kingdom. Miss Fonda knew so much about everything. Even though young, she was informed about all things, especially politics."

Michael might have listened to Jane talk about politics, and he may have absorbed much, but he was never to commit himself politically. "Unlike Jane, I don't think Michael ever learned the difference between a Republican and a Democrat," Katharine Hepburn once said.

Jane opened up to Michael and shared some of the private trauma she'd experienced in her own life, including the suicide of her mother. She spoke of the coldness of Henry Fonda to her, and how difficult their father-daughter relationship had been.

"We had the same psychic scars," Jane later said of Michael. "The tissue had never healed. We bonded by talking about how emotionally distant our fathers were from us."

Michael shared his own trauma of growing up under Joe's thumb—the midnight terrorizing, the beatings, and the punishments inflicted if he didn't get all dance movements and notes right. At one time, Michael told Jane, "I was so afraid of displeasing Joe that my vocal cords froze."

Although Michael became a far better-known entertainer than even Jane

MJ and Jane Fonda

herself, she intervened and tried to help him launch a film career, the one form of the entertainment industry where success had eluded him. As Michael's chauffeur drove his sparkling new, cream-colored Rolls-Royce through the streets of Los Angeles, Jane conjured up the "perfect role for you—Peter Pan, a symbol of youth, joy, freedom."

Michael burst into tears. "How could you know?" he asked her. "You touched on my dream. I've always wanted to be Peter Pan, to lead lost children into a magical world of fantasy. My bedroom is filled with pictures of Peter and memorabilia. At times I dream I'm that lost boy of Never-Never Land."

"The more I think about it, the more I know you're Peter Pan. You wouldn't even have to act it since you *are* Peter."

Jane, who had her own production company, said she'd like to produce the film. Then she learned that Francis Ford Coppola of *The Godfather* fame was planning a spectacular and costly version of *Peter Pan*. Encountering the producer at a party, Jane pitched the idea of casting Michael as Peter Pan to Coppola, who had his doubts. "A black Peter Pan—what a novel idea!"

Quincy Jones felt Michael might be brilliant as Peter Pan on the screen. "There's a downside, though," he cautioned. "Michael might keep playing Peter Pan even when the camera is not on him. Children are supposed to grow up—that is, all but one."

Later, when Michael shared his dream of becoming the screen version of Peter Pan with friend Marlon Brando, the actor said, "Forget it! Peter Pan is a wimp. Go for the role of Al Capone instead!" Michael later wondered if Brando was sincere or merely being the prankster he so often was.

Eventually, Steven Spielberg entered the race to film *Peter Pan,* but ran into trouble securing the rights. He was receptive, however, to casting Michael as a young Peter Pan. Later, an original script, *Hook*, was written. In this film,

Steven Spielberg

the role of Peter Pan called for an older actor, the part going to Robin Williams. Michael was extremely disappointed. At grim times such as this, he retreated to his darkened bedroom at Encino, "where I cried my eyes out."

As the years went by, Jane would pop in and out of Michael's life, appearing at a dinner, a party, or a première. But in the 90s, when charges of child molestation against Michael became more shrill, she disappeared from the radar screen.

"She just wasn't there to lend her

moral support," David Geffen is reported to have said. "Neither was Katharine Hepburn, Brooke Shields, or Jackie Onassis for that matter. Jane no longer returned Michael's calls, or so I heard." As far as that goes, Geffen too disappeared from Michael's life.

When Henry Fonda published his memoirs, *Fonda My Life*, in 1981, he too omitted any mention of Michael Jackson. But he'd met Michael during the filming of *On Golden Pond*, and in some strange way had bonded with him for a few days.

Knowing that her father could be difficult and closed off to people, Jane had been hesitant to introduce him to Michael. "I was in awe of my Dad," Jane told Michael. "As a girl, I used to do naughty things just to get his attention." She related an amusing story about how, when she was cast in the sexually provocative film, *Barbarella*, in 1968, she discussed with Henry the possibility of his appearing in a cameo role in the movie. "Will I have to take my clothes off?" Henry queried his daughter.

Before Jane introduced them, Michael had never seen a Henry Fonda movie. The taciturn Henry was sitting by a boat dock fishing. During Jane's introduction, her father's face was partially covered by a wide-brimmed hat as he was allergic to too much sun. He didn't look up or even acknowledge Michael on the first meeting. Michael was heartbroken, as he wanted screen legends to like him. It isn't even certain that Henry even knew who Michael was.

"Dad, you must speak to Michael," Jane beseeched him. "He's one of the most important singers in the world."

"If he's so important, why haven't I heard of him?" Henry finally spoke up. "Frank Sinatra, Judy Garland I've heard of."

"People in the music industry think Michael is going to become the biggest star of the 1980s," Jane said.

"What do I care about the 80s?" Henry asked. "I won't be around to live through them."

At that point Michael walked up. "If you give me your address, I'll send you a postcard to wherever you are," Michael said.

Henry looked up at him as if he hadn't quite registered that remark. Finally, he broke into laughter. "Listen boy, I don't

Henry Fonda and Katharine Hepburn

want to put up with you today, but come around this time tomorrow and I'll teach you to fish."

Michael showed up at the appointed time, and there was Henry impatiently waiting for him. He wore a different hat. When Michael asked about it, Henry told him that he had been given the hat by his co-star on the film, Katharine Hepburn. "She said it had been Spencer Tracy's favorite hat. Tracy and Kate were supposed to have been lovers. Frankly, in my opinion, I think they were more beards for each other than lovers."

Michael didn't understand what that meant.

According to Jane, Michael and Henry went fishing together every day for three days before either of them opened up to each other. "They would sit for hours in silence as both of them were incredibly sensitive and private people—not really comfortable with strangers."

On the night of the third day, Henry told his daughter, "That Michael Jackson is one strange young man. But, so what?"

Jane granted an interview to Gerri Hirshey of *Rolling Stone*. "Like Michael, Dad was also painfully self-conscious and shy in life. He really only felt comfortable when he was behind the mask of a character. He could liberate himself when he was being someone else. That's a lot like Michael."

At first, Henry had been unnerved by Michael's falsetto whisper, but later he said, "I guess he can talk like he wants to talk."

On the fourth day of fishing, the normally crusty Henry opened up more to Michael, who wondered when they were ever going to catch a fish. "There are only two fish in this lake," Henry said, "and both of those fuckers are too smart to get caught by us."

Michael sensed that Henry was visibly upset by something, although he wasn't revealing why. Finally, Michael asked, "What's the matter? I can tell something's wrong."

Henry took off his hat and reached for a newspaper article he'd tucked away there. He showed it to Michael. Some supposedly well-meaning friend had sent him an article by one "John Evans," which had appeared in an underground Hollywood paper. It was the most scurrilous article ever written on Henry, and certainly the most invasive ever published on his private life.

Very slowly, Michael read some of the more shocking revelations.

"Just because we perform in public, showing our asses, or at least our faces, to the world, that same public thinks it owns a piece of us," Henry said. "It thinks it's entitled to know all about us, even the most personal things. You'll find that true as you hang around longer in the business."

The article had dredged up rumors about Henry's past, including a report that he and his best pal, Jimmy Stewart, had been lovers when they'd roomed together during their poverty days as struggling actors in New York. It also was reported that Henry had gotten his start in the theater when he'd been seduced by Marlon Brando's mother in Omaha when he was quite young.

The most viperish part of the article quoted his first wife, actress Margaret Sullavan, who claimed that Henry had been a premature ejaculator. She labeled him "the one-minute man," and Evans reported that in his article. He also reported Henry's alleged response: "Maggie can make a man feel like he has two inches."

Henry was known for making homophobic remarks. Once he'd mocked George Sanders for "running after Tyrone Power with his tongue hanging out." When Sanders heard that, he curtly responded, "Henry Fonda is a Don Juan homosexual who has to prove himself with one woman after another."

Crumpling up the article and throwing it in the lake, Henry told Michael, "All the women, except my present wife, Shirlee Adams, have been sexual predators. Joan Crawford, not one of my wives, once called me in my dressing and invited herself by. She told me to be waiting for her in a jockstrap. I'm not impressive in a jockstrap. I fled the studio."

Months later, Michael was watching when Henry won his first Oscar for his appearance in *On Golden Pond*. Regrettably, Henry was too ill to attend the ceremonies, and his statuette was accepted by Jane. All the Fonda family and Michael knew that the Oscar was the veteran actor's last hurrah.

Michael became so close to the Fonda family that on August 12, 1982, he arrived at their Bel Air home in a black Rolls-Royce to commiserate with family members after Henry's death. That night, Michael got to see his first Henry Fonda movie. It was the 1940s film *The Grapes of Wrath*. He vowed one day to watch *On Golden Pond*.

Before Michael had ended his stay with Jane on that New Hampshire lakeshore, he'd met yet another screen legend appearing in *On Golden Pond*, an actor even more formidable than Henry Fonda. Once again, the introduction was arranged by Jane.

If Michael needed a role model for a closeted life, or even an example of how to fool the world, he could find no better figure than Miss Hepburn herself. At the time of his meeting with her, she'd retired from the sexual wars and was an imperial diva who demanded that you play by her rules or else you'd be banished from her court.

Her youth was long behind her, and she often claimed that, "I wasted it in the idiot profession of acting."

When Jane had first introduced them, Hepburn had been put off by Michael's wimpy presentation of himself. "Men are worthless creatures," she later told Jane, "but if you are a man, then you should act like one—not some creature trapped in the twilight zone."

She did have one question for Jane, however. "Just who in the hell is

Michael Jackson, and why should I bother?"

Gradually she warmed to Michael, even though at first he annoyed her. "He followed me around the set like a puppy dog in heat," she claimed. In him, she found the perfect listener. He had almost nothing to say, at least nothing of importance, and she had "the wisdom of the ages to impart to him."

She delivered one *bon mot* after another to him, and sometimes he wrote them down. She told him, "If you obey all the rules, you miss all the fun!" She recommended that he live his life on his own terms, not bowing to the social pressures of the world.

When she'd been young—her own father had called her "a raging bull"— Hepburn had pursued the bisexual life, her longest affairs being with Laura Harding, the American Express heiress, and with Spencer Tracy, an abusive alcoholic who drank to escape the torment of his own closeted homosexuality. Hepburn invented *faux* romances with such unlikely candidates as Howard Hughes, while carrying on genuine affairs with women, many of them famous such as Claudette Colbert, Greta Garbo, Judy Garland, and Judy Holliday. Her male lovers had included Charles Boyer, John Ford, Leland Hayward, Van Heflin, George Stevens, and Jimmy Stewart.

"My privacy is my own, and *I* am the one to decide when it shall be violated," Hepburn told Michael. "Do whatever you want, but only behind closed doors. Don't let the world knock down your closed door. Bolt it if you have to."

Privately she told Henry Fonda and others that "Michael is a homosexual—only he doesn't know it yet. It's an obvious source of torment to him, and will cause him great grief unless he comes to terms with it. I know of such things." Was that a reference to her troubled relationship with the tormented Spencer Tracy?

There were things that Michael did that annoyed her. She didn't like him to wear sunglasses all the time. "A performer must show his eyes to the world. The eyes are the most important feature of the face. You can convey whatever the hell you're trying to just through the use of your eyes. It could be your most effective weapon. Sunglasses keep you hidden from the world. That's okay in private life. But on stage you must let the audience, however briefly, look into the mirror of your soul. Besides, those damn sunglasses make you look like a Harlem drug addict."

At the Grammy Awards in February of 1984 at the Shrine Auditorium in Los Angeles, Michael remembered Hepburn's advice. He removed his sunglasses "for the girls in the balcony."

Oddly enough, in a picture that Hepburn consented to pose for with Michael, it was she who was wearing the sunglasses—and Jackie Kennedy's 1960s style at that.

On the set of *On Golden Pond* in New Hampshire, Michael could sit patiently for hours, listening to Hepburn's "bits of wisdom" acquired over many a decade of what she called "my trials and tribulations. If you survive long enough, you're revered—rather like an old landmark building."

Long after Michael had left the set of *On Golden Pond*, he continued his phone dialogue with Hepburn. She said, "I always liked bad eggs, always, always—and always attracted them. I had a lot of energy and looked as if I was (and I was) hard to get. I wasn't mad about the male sex—perfectly independent, never had any intention of getting married, wanted to paddle my own canoe, didn't want anyone to pay my way."

In time, Hepburn introduced him to some of her grandnieces and grandnephews, some of whom belonged to the Jehovah's Witness clan. The actress held the cult in total disdain, but introduced her extended family members to Michael anyway. He often went door to door with them handing out pamphlets, many of which attacked "the sin" of homosexuality.

In 1981, at Michael's invitation, Hepburn agreed to go to her first rock concert, starring Michael himself, as staged at Madison Square Garden in New York. Thinking her grandniece would enjoy Michael's performance more than she would, Hepburn took the nine year old with her.

Hepburn wanted to see for herself what "all the fuss was about, all those hysterically screaming fans." Members in the audience that night included Andy Warhol, Victoria Principal, Tatum O'Neal, Jane Fonda, and Steven Spielberg.

"It's not my kind of music," Hepburn later admitted. "I prefer Judy Garland. But the boy can move about the stage. He's got the grace of Fred Astaire minus that bitch, Ginger Rogers, a woman I loathe to this day. That dyed blonde heifer and I competed for the queenly throne of RKO and also for the same beaus until I finally decided to let her have the worthless lot of them. I mean, who would want Lew Ayres for more than a night?"

Bob Jones, Michael's publicist, later claimed that "I saw a man who embarrassed himself at Katharine Hepburn's house." He was referring to the night when Hepburn gave a dinner party honoring Michael at her Turtle Bay residence in New York. Michael had ordered his photographer to wait outside. After dinner, the photographer asked her if she'd pose with Michael for a picture. "Absolutely not!" she virtually shouted at him. "This is a private affair—not something to make the front page of the *National Enquirer*."

Before the night was over, Michael told her that he'd seen all her films. Several writers, including biographer Scott Berg, later claimed that Michael was "caught with his pants down. He was unable to name any."

Actually that was not quite true. Everyone from Liza Minnelli to Tatum O'Neal, even La Toya, knew that Michael was addicted to Hepburn movies.

He loved her voice and her haughty air on camera. Of course, *Little Women*, with all its sentimentality, would forever remain his favorite but he also liked *Adam's Rib* and *The African Queen*. He didn't like *Suddenly, Last Summer*.

At the time of the Turtle Bay dinner, Michael had not seen the film, *Gone With the Wind*. When queried about which of her movies were his favorites, he included *Gone With the Wind* among his favorites. She looked flabbergasted. "That, my dear boy, was a role I lost to one Vivien Leigh. The producer, David O. Selznick, made the mistake of his life by not casting me as Scarlett O'Hara. Vivien won only one Oscar for her performance. I would have won three."

Now it was Michael's turn to look flabbergasted. "But I thought it was possible to carry home only one Oscar per performance."

She laughed at this and took his arm, leading him toward the door since it was her bedtime. "My dear boy, of course, you're right. I was speaking in hyperbole."

"What does that mean?" Michael asked.

"Go home and look it up in the dictionary," she advised.

Later, Michael did just that but never found the word. "How could I look it up in the dictionary if I don't know how to spell it?"

Irene Mayer Selznick, the daughter of Louis B. Mayer, was also invited to that dinner in Turtle Bay, at 244 West 49th Street, but politely turned down the invitation. Selznick told Bob Gottlieb, book editor: "Can you believe what she's done now?" Selznick asked Gottlieb, referring to Hepburn, with whom the bisexual Selznick had once had a love affair. "She's dared to invite me to dinner with—of all people—Michael Jackson! Just how low can she sink? Is Kate insane?"

To others of her friends, Selznick asked, "Just why is Kate hanging out with the likes of Michael Jackson? You've heard of white trash. Jackson and his whole family are black trash. The invitation to dinner is just another attempt of Kate's vulgar, even pathetic, desperation to keep herself in the news columns and to keep up with what she thinks is the current scene."

When Michael wasn't "hanging with" the elite of Hollywood, he was rehearsing, writing his own songs, or recording with his brothers. He still hadn't broken from them. Far from it.

In 1980, Epic released *Triumph*, the album that would be backed by a nationwide tour. "Can You Feel It?" was one of the hits from that album.

Carried to the far corners of America, the tour included the most intricate "lighting magic" and pyrotechnics of any of the Jackson road show appearances to date. After singing "Don't Stop 'Til You Get Enough" (not on the *Triumph* album), Michael seemingly vanished in a puff of smoke as a special effect created by the great magician Doug Henning.

151

In Atlanta, a major stopover on the tour, Michael told reporters: "I wish the world was full of children. I plan to have twenty children of my own and adopt kids, too." At the time of his appearance in that southern city, a series of unsolved murders of black children was mysteriously occurring. As a sign of solidarity, Michael requested that about a quarter of a million dollars from his two shows there go to help needy black families.

The tour began in Memphis on the hot summer night of July 9, 1981, ending in a record-breaking four-night performance on other hot nights at the Forum in Los Angeles. When Joe finally tallied up the gross for his sons, it came to an astonishing five million dollars. "My boys are here to stay—they ain't going nowhere," Joe said. "They are the top of the heap, and I'm gonna see that's where they remain."

On the tour, the Jacksons—with Michael, of course, as the star attraction—played 39 cities. Michael hinted that this might be his last tour with his brothers. In an uncharitable moment, he said, "I'm fed up with all the screaming fans, the security problems, the different environments every night. I plan to continue to do records, but I want to devote time to making movies. I plan to become an even bigger film star than I am a singer."

Throughout the tour, Michael was constantly asked by reporters if he planned to split from his brothers and establish himself as a solo recording artist. His answer to *Ebony* magazine was enigmatic at best. "Yes and no!" Michael said.

An oddity on the *Triumph* tour was a song called "This Place Hotel." When Michael had originally written it, he'd called it "Heartbreak Hotel," but executives at Epic had insisted on a change of name. Michael later said, "I swear that was a phrase that came out of my head, and I wasn't thinking of any other song when I wrote it." No one believed Michael. How could he not have thought of Elvis's big-time hit when he wrote "Heartbreak Hotel?"

"As important as Elvis was to music, black as well as white, he just wasn't an influence on me," Michael claimed. "I guess he was too early for me. Maybe it was timing more than anything else. By the time our song had come out, people thought that if I kept living in seclusion the way I was, I might die the way he did. The parallels aren't there as far as I'm concerned, and I was never much for scare tactics. Still, the way Elvis destroyed himself interests me, because I don't ever want to walk those grounds myself."

"Heartbreak Hotel" (Michael's version) opens with a scream. The voice was that of La Toya. Michael himself admitted that this was "not the most auspicious start to a recording career."

Michael said that his version of "Heartbreak Hotel" had "revenge in it and I am fascinated by the concept of revenge."

Michael, watching the 1975 Hepburn film, *Love Among the Ruins*, heard her utter a line that had stayed in his mind. "There's no harm in a little revenge," Hepburn said to movie audiences, perhaps meaning it in her private life as well.

The performance attended by Hepburn at Madison Square Garden was recorded and later distributed by Epic as a two-album set in 1981.

Jacksonmania was sweeping the land. Wherever you went in America, including driving in your own car, you could hear The Jackson 5, The Jacksons, or Michael as a solo artist singing such 70s favorites as "Rockin' Robin" or "Ain't No Sunshine."

Like a Nora Roberts novel recycled from the 1980s to capitalize off her subsequent fame, Motown continued to release Jackson records from its back-log. In 1981, the company reissued the previously recorded "One Day in Your Life," which became Michael's first solo hit in Britain. That same year, Motown also released Michael's single, "We're Almost There."

After seeing Michael perform at Madison Square Garden, Spielberg was impressed. He decided at the end of the show that he wanted to approach Michael about narrating the storybook for the E.T. album for MCA. Michael had seen *E.T. the Extra-Terrestrial* three times and had cried every time. He was delighted to accept the offer, especially when he learned that he would be working with his friend, Quincy Jones, on the album.

But, first, Michael had one request. He wanted to meet E.T. Spielberg arranged for him to meet the extra-terrestrial robot. "E.T. grabbed me in an embrace," Michael later said. "He was so real that I was talking to him. I kissed him before I left."

Michael told *Ebony* magazine that, "I really felt that I was E.T., and it was because his story is the story of my life in some ways. He's in a strange place and wants to be accepted, which is a situation I've found myself in many times. He's most comfortable with children, and I have a great love of kids. He gives love, and wants love in return, which is me."

He also made an astonishing statement in noting that E.T. could lift off and fly away when he wanted to get away from this Earth. "I can identify with that," Michael said. "I

MJ and ET

also believe that a human being can fly. We just don't know how to think the right thoughts and levitate ourselves off the ground."

In an interview with reporter Gerri Hirshey, Spielberg said, "I've never seen anybody like that Michael Jackson. He's an emotional star child. Those were Michael's actual tears heard on the recording when E.T. lays dying."

Although many in the business have derisively dismissed Michael as a "flighty faggot" or "for being out of touch with reality," others such as Spielberg sensed a strong business sense in him.

Since turning 21, Michael had managed his own affairs, earning more money than any other singer in the history of music. When his contract with Joe expired, Michael took over the reins of his own career.

The downside to Michael's show business savvy is that he also was launched into a lifestyle as a big-spending performer who in time would squander millions and millions of dollars. "As a big spender, Michael would in time cause Elvis to blush in his grave," said Bob Jones.

Michael wasn't thinking about Elvis but the biggest-selling female singing star of all time when he flew the Concorde from London to Los Angeles after a visit with Paul McCartney. Diana Ross needed a hit solo for her new album, *Silk Electric*, for RCA.

Michael had a pet snake at Encino—called "Muscles"—and as he flew across the Atlantic the nucleus of a song came to him. "I didn't have a tape recorder when the song popped into my head," he said. "So I had to suffer through the faster-than-sound flight until I reached Encino. As soon as I did, I whipped that baby onto tape."

Both Ross and executives at RCA were surprised at the message of the song. It wasn't an ode to a snake but extolled the joy of having the muscles of a man "all over your body."

"If written and sung by a male singer," said an executive at RCA, "'Muscles' would be as gay as a goose, as queer as a nine-dollar bill, as faggy as a drag queen at three o'clock in the morning at an all-male revue where the strippers show it hard. I don't give a fuck what Jacko says. The song is a paean to well-built hunks."

Whether Michael had a pet boa constrictor called "Muscles" or not, music critics found the

MJ and Paul McCartney

Martin, "Say Say Say" as a duet for the unlikely pair evolved into a 1983 hit single for both McCartney and Michael. As a single, it stayed for six weeks at the top of *Billboard's* "Hot 100" chart. Despite the high praise and glory it received, it contains such inane lines as "You know I'm crying oooh ooh ooh ooh ooh!"

This record was followed by "The Man," the third duet from Michael and McCartney, which was released on the former Beatle's *Pipes of Peace* album. "The Man" sounds like a Michael ballad with limited input from McCartney. But who knew what the lyrics were about? One critic found them "so vague they must have been written by McCartney."

During this second visit to Sussex, Michael did not reveal his intention, at least not to McCartney, of acquiring the rights to the greatest of The Beatles' songs. With his Machiavellian intentions completely hidden, Michael blended into the local neighborhood, meeting the children who lived nearby. They called him "Mr. Mum," and he always had treats for them. Later in the day, he would help Linda prepare vegetables in the farmhouse kitchen, and end the afternoon reading Winnie-the-Pooh stories to the kids who flocked around him.

Months later, long after Michael's departure from his home, McCartney received a phone call from a reporter seeking his reaction to Michael's purchase of the ATV Music Catalogue. McCartney was stunned by the news. A quick call to Lee Eastman, and McCartney knew the tip from the reporter was true. Michael had outbid Warners, the Coca-Cola Corporation, and CBS, thereby acquiring control over each of The Beatles' songs written or released between 1964 and 1971.

When he first became aware that The Beatles' songs were available for sale, Michael had done a "hop, skip, and a jump," eerily evocative of Hitler's dance steps after the fall of France.

Many years before, John Lennon and McCartney had foolishly sold their copyrights to a publisher, Dick James, when they were young and naïve about the music business. James went on to make a fortune from their music, which was controlled by a company called Northern Songs. In time James sold Northern Songs to Sir Lew Grade's ATV Music, Limited, for tax reasons.

McCartney himself had attempted to purchase this same catalogue for $20 million in 1981 when he tried to convince Yoko Ono to become his partner in the deal. But the widow of John Lennon turned him down.

Yoko thought her $10 million share was too much money. She would eventually have made tens of millions. One executive at ATV said Yoko's decision was one of the worst ever made in terms of money in the music industry. "With her profits, she could have fucking bought the Dakota." He was referring to the luxury apartment building on Manhattan's Central Park

West, in front of which her husband, John Lennon, was murdered.

Headlines in 1984 blared the news of Michael's acquisition of the songs for $47.5 million, the largest publishing takeover by one person in the history of the music industry.

Many Beatles fans around the world reacted with outrage when they heard that Michael now owned The Beatles' songs. One fan wrote, "It's a humiliating kick in the crotch to Paul. It's sickening to know that he has to pay that little twerp royalties every time he sings a Beatles song. Jackson stabbed him in the back—but good."

One music executive who didn't want to be named, said: "In spite of that little girl voice and that oh, so delicate manner, Michael Jackson is one hard-nosed son of a bitch in business. But whereas old Joe made one stupid decision after another, Michael is more calculating. The smartest move he ever did was to hire John Branca, one hot-shot lawyer, to acquire old standards and not just The Beatles' catalogue."

"A fish gets caught by opening its damn mouth," McCartney later said. "I should have kept mine shut."

McCartney went on to additional feelings of betrayal when he discovered that Michael even owned a $5 million insurance policy on his life. "My God, he'll make millions when I'm 64 and dead and gone." ATV itself had collected a life insurance policy on Lennon after he was assassinated.

McCartney was particularly enraged to learn that, as part of the deal, Michael would get fifty percent royalties for any performance, anywhere, on any Beatles' songs, with a 25% royalty going to him. Yoko took the final quarter-share, thanks to her role as Lennon's widow and heir.

The official date of Michael's acquisition was September 6, 1985. When he woke up the next morning, he owned 250 Beatles' songs, including such famous classics as "A Hard Day's Night," "Help!," "Eleanor Rigby," "Penny Lane," "Yesterday," "Strawberry Fields Forever," "Let It Be," "Good Day Sunshine," "Yellow Submarine," "Revolution," and "Hey Jude."

When Michael was told that he was now the owner of all of those Beatles' songs, he said, "I've found the Holy Grail, although I'm not sure what the Holy Grail is."

The ex-Beatle—and now "former friend" of Michael—felt betrayed and used. He was understandably bitter about the way Michael had done

Yoko Ono, "A later portrait"

158

business. "Our friendship suffered a bit of a blow," McCartney said in a statement noted for its restraint. "I've hardly spoken to Jackson since then, except to ask, 'Will you give me a deal? I'm under a slave agreement.' Talk about stonewalling! He's worse than all of them."

When Michael was in Los Angeles shooting a clip for "Dangerous" in 1991, years after the infamous deal was concluded, he agreed to meet with McCartney. "Jackson was friendly enough but hardly in a mood to accommodate my request," McCartney said.

"You know, I've cried so much about this," Michael whimpered.

"Ok, but please, Michael, see your people," McCartney beseeched. "Give me a promise that you'll talk to your people about this." According to McCartney, Michael said, "I've tried. I have told them." In reporting his meeting with Michael, McCartney did not make it clear exactly what compensation he was seeking from Michael, but no doubt it was an increased share of the royalties.

In an interview on ABC, McCartney said, "Michael's the kind of guy who picks brains. When we worked together, I don't even think he'd had the cosmetic surgery. I've got photos of him and me at our house, and he looks quite different. He's had a lot of facial surgery since then. He actually told me he was going to a religious retreat and I believed him. But he came out of that religious retreat with a new nose. The power of prayer, I guess."

Branca seemed to understand McCartney's position and why the ex-Beatle was sad. "Whether Paul likes it or not," Branca reportedly said, "he has to pay Michael every time he performs a song he himself wrote between 1964 and 1971. Of course, he's pissed. But that's the law."

Under his so-called "slave manifesto," McCartney was to face more disappointment, especially when a trio of "old favorites" from The Beatles were turned into commercials. "Revolution," for example, was used to promote Nike.

In a long, handwritten letter to Michael, the ex-Beatle complained that "my good name, the reputation of The Beatles themselves, is being blown on rubber soles." He pleaded with Michael to respect their music and "my wishes" and stop exploiting the catalogue he'd acquired. McCartney never received an answer from Michael.

When Michael was confronted with charges of exploiting The Beatles, he looked surprised. "Why, I don't understand what Paul is belly-aching about. After all, he taught me everything I know about acquiring copyrights."

"I heard that Michael had told Branca to turn a deaf ear to Paul's protests," a music executive claimed. "Apparently, Michael told Branca to 'let Paul rage, kick, and scream. Paul had his chance to buy the records. He was too cheap to part with $20 million of his $560 million fortune. He let that chance fly by. To hell with him. Exploit the catalogue! Make more money for me to add to the millions I already have.'" Branca did as he was told.

Michael continued to sell Beatles' songs to commercial concerns, with "All You Need Is Love" going to Panasonic. "Good Day Sunshine" went to Sunshine Bakeries. On hearing this, McCartney lamented, "My God, he's turning the song into an ode to an Oreo cookie—real cheeky of him."

"Jackson has trashed the reputation of The Beatles," McCartney charged. "He seemed so nice and polite when I met him. But he has a heart of gold, and I don't mean that as a compliment."

He also is reported to have said, "I'm in a shit deal and can't get out of it. Each day with Michael Jackson in charge, I take another bite from the shit sandwich he offers me."

Yoko Ono seemed comfortable with Michael's ownership of the catalogue, since it was generating millions for her, but not the potential millions she could have made with co-ownership with McCartney. She once was quoted as saying, "If I owned the catalogue, the press would say, 'the dragon lady strikes again.'"

McCartney, or so it was rumored, felt greatly betrayed by Yoko when she allowed her son, Sean, then 12 years of age, to appear as one of the "lost boys" saved by Michael in his 1988 film, *Moonwalker*. The video closed with a rendition of "Come Together" from The Beatles.

Even though losing on the deal, McCartney also revealed that he would go to court to prevent what he viewed as unfair use of his legacy. He did win a court order barring sales of three bootleg Beatles movies. He also denied the Beastie Boys the right to use The Beatles song, "I'm Down." The group wanted to add new lyrics to the song, which McCartney found "too salacious."

In spite of the bitterness that McCartney still felt over Michael's purchase of The Beatles' songs and his use of them, McCartney spoke kindly of Michael when he first faced child molestation charges in the early 90s. Speaking to the *Clarin*, a newspaper in Buenos Aires, McCartney claimed, "Michael is not *that kind* of person."

When asked about Michael's drug dependency, McCartney said, "It's all very L.A.—I mean, Judy Garland and Elizabeth Taylor—these are people who became stars at a very young age. We, The Beatles, we were ordinary guys. When fame arrived, we went a bit crazy, but even so we had our feet on the ground. We had roots. We knew about life. Michael, instead…Ah, well!"

As the years went by, McCartney became less reserved about Michael. In 2001, on *The Howard Stern Show*, McCartney claimed that Michael "won't even answer my letters, so we haven't talked and we don't have that great a relationship."

In a statement made in April of 2003, McCartney expressed greater reservations about Michael, calling him "an unusual guy" and questioning his parenting skills. The interview was broadcast over the BBC. He claimed he felt sorry for Michael's children "being brought up under those veils."

That remark seriously angered Michael, who shot back: "I like some of Paul's songs. But he's a lousy performer. I can pack a stadium. He can't."

Songs by the Beatles were not, by any means, the first that Michael acquired. Long before his purchase of the ATV catalogue, Michael had ordered Branca to buy the rights to recordings by Sly & the Family Stone, a group that began in San Francisco in 1969 and eventually achieved worldwide fame before they disbanded in 1975. The band is credited with a critical role in the development of soul music, funk, and psychedelia.

The group's fourth album, *Stand!*, had been a runaway success, selling more than three million copies and giving birth to one hit single, "Everyday People." The Jackson 5 had performed a number from Sly's album during their first appearance on *The Ed Sullivan Show*.

The success of Sly & the Family Stone peaked in the summer of 1969. Sly's intense drug abuse began to affect his career but not before he became celebrated as the "J.D. Salinger of pop music."

Michael also acquired the rights to some of the recordings of Dion & The Belmonts (named after Dion's neighborhood in New York City's northern Bronx). Dion's most memorable song, released in 1968, was "Abraham, Martin & John." Two of Dion's biggest hits, "The Wanderer" and "Runaround Sue," were also purchased by Branca for Michael, as was Len Barry's "1-2-3" and the Soul Survivors' "Expressway to Your Heart."

At Encino, in the wake of his massive purchases, Michael could be heard listening to some of his new acquisitions. He played "He's So Shy" several times, a recording made by the Pointer Sisters. An R&B group from Oakland,

Dion & The Belmonts

California, they were a big hit in the 70s and 80s. Michael had something in common with them, as both he and the sisters had come from archly conservative religious backgrounds and had been taught that rock 'n' roll was "the devil's music."

The ATV catalogue also contained some of the greatest hits of Little Richard, the self-proclaimed "Queen of Rock 'n' Roll." With a public persona marked by bisexual ambiguity, he would make his mark with such suggestive hits as "Tutti Frutti" and "Great Balls of Fire." He was voted the eighth greatest Rock 'n' Roll artist of all time by *Rolling Stone*, and *The New York Times* called this Georgia-born entertainer "the original wild man of rock 'n' roll."

Some critics claimed that both Michael and Elvis Presley "stole Fort Knox" from Little Richard's music and on-stage persona. When an interviewer once asked Michael what he thought of Little Richard, and if he were influenced by him, Michael delivered another one of his enigmatic responses: "Awop-bob-a-loo-mop-alop-bam-boom."

Although Michael surely has had conflicting feelings about Little Richard, Michael once said: "Without Little Richard's blueprint to follow, Elvis wouldn't have had a kingdom or been a king of anything."

When he acquired "Tutti Fruitti," Michael learned that the original lyrics contained this line: "Good goddamn, Tutti Frutti, good booty, if it don't fit, don't force it, you can grease it, make it easy." And all this from a Seventh Day Adventist minister "who devotes all my life to God."

The flamboyant Little Richard once told Michael, and the public in general, that "Rock 'n' roll is evil, because rock 'n' roll makes you take drugs, and drugs turn you into a homosexual." Aware of homophobia among his black fans, he renounced his own homosexuality, but since has back-pedaled in his anti-gay proclamations. Like Michael, he once was a Jehovah's Witness but only briefly. Like Michael's friend, Elizabeth Taylor, Little Richard also embraced Judaism.

On certain occasions, Little Richard and Michael ran into each other at social gatherings, but no great friendship ever seemed to develop between the two performers, often viewed as rivals. Little Richard could not have been happy when he heard the news that Michael had acquired the rights to some of his biggest hits and could exploit them any way he wished.

As Michael's career zoomed skyward, he faced family dilemmas. Once again, on August 19, 1982, Katherine quietly filed for a divorce from her errant husband, the man of many mistresses. She told Michael, "I can't take it any more." She was particularly infuriated that Joe was siphoning money from their joint funds to pay for his girlfriends.

During the divorce proceedings, Joe refused to move

The Pointer Sisters

Little Richard

out of the Encino house. Michael accurately predicted that his mother would never escape her marriage. And so she didn't, the legal maneuvering over a divorce eventually sputtering, unresolved, to an end. Joe continued on the same path he'd traveled before—that is, to other women.

At the same time, Marlon, who was a year older than Michael, was also filing for divorce from Carol, his wife of seven years. "I still love my husband…desperately" she testified. Michael believed that, unlike Joe and Katherine, Marlon and Carol had a chance to work out their marital difficulties.

Michael was right. Marlon and Carol managed to iron out their problems and are still married today, making him the only one of the Jackson brothers to avoid the divorce courts.

After the "Victory" tour, Marlon grew disillusioned about performing with his brothers, especially Michael. On the last Jackson album, *2300 Jackson Street*, he, like Michael, did not join in. Through a deal with Capitol Records, Marlon released his one and only solo album, *Baby Tonight*. It bombed, but in time he became a successful real estate agent in Southern California and a part owner of the Black Family Channel, a cable TV network.

Family problems were all but forgotten by Michael on one hot, muggy and overcast morning in Los Angeles when he was driven to Westlake Studios. The date was August 29, 1979.

Michael had once again teamed up with Quincy Jones to record an album. Only Michael seemed convinced at the time that they were going to make music industry history. From a stockpile of 600 songs, they narrowed the field to nine. At a cost of $850,000—perhaps a lot more when the final bills came in—they produced an album called *Thriller*.

Before he'd recorded the album's first song, Michael told Quincy and Rod Temperton, who was working with them, that "I want *Thriller* to not only do better in sales than *Off the Wall*, but to become the biggest selling album of all time." Both Quincy and Temperton smiled indulgently. Temperton, in the words of Quincy, was the only man in Hollywood whose body contained "not one drop of bullshit." But this breakthrough album Michael was demanding sounded like bullshit to him.

McCartney had already contributed "The Girl Is Mine," which was the first solo release from the album. The song peaked at number two on *Billboard's* chart, but it was a mere warm-up act, not a harbinger of what was about to happen to this album.

Songs written by Temperton ("The Lady In My Life" and "Baby Be Mine") were also selected for *Thriller*, as was "PYT (Pretty Young Thing)," a joint effort of Quincy and James Ingram. All these songs were solid pop numbers and contained in the words of Nelson George, "snappy rhythm tracks and bright, immaculate arrangements."

The title cut was another Temperton tune, and it appealed to Michael's fascination with the supernatural. The recording was climaxed by a camp horror rap by the actor Vincent Price, "king of the macabre." Despite his towering height, large body, and a propensity to marry, Price was quite effete. *Tout* Hollywod knew he was gay. Upon meeting Michael, Price was so attracted to him that he made a pass. Informing Price that he was a Jehovah's Witness, a cult that "abhorred homosexuality," Michael turned down the proposition.

The star of countless horror films, Price worked on both the song on the album and in the video of the same name. For his work, he agreed to accept a flat fee of $20,000. If Price's agent had made a deal for his client to get a percentage of the total sales, the actor would have "won lotto," as he himself later admitted.

"Jackson gave me the shaft," Price later charged, "and no pun intended." He recalled that two of the Jackson brothers—"I can't remember their names"—showed up at his doorstep with a gold record plaque. Price was gracious to the brothers. But once the door was closed in their faces, he went into a rage. "What in the fuck am I supposed to do with this shit? Erect a shrine to it?"

Although initially attracted to Michael, Price became more and more bitter as *Thriller* went on to become the biggest selling album of all time. In the early 90s, when a reporter asked Price if he thought the child molestation charges against Michael were true, Price had a sarcastic reply. "They must be true," he said. "After all, Michael Jackson fucked me too."

In "Wanna Be Startin' Somethin'," Michael rants against gossip and unwanted babies and compares himself to a vegetable on a buffet that fans can take a bite out of. He was obviously referring to fans grabbing and tearing at his hair and clothes.

The gorgeous dance ballad, "Human Nature," was the creation of John Bettis and Steve Porcaro. It allows Michael to express a certain sexuality. Back in those days he was still a handsome black man and could be taken seriously by young girls as a sex object.

But in retrospect, most of the success of *Thriller* as a whole was because of Michael's own songs, notably "Billie Jean," which even today is still his signature. In the song, Billie Jean is a bad lady, accusing Michael of fathering her child ("but the kid is not my son," the song claims). In real life, such an event would happen to Michael several times, as young girls showed up at the gates of Hayvenhurst with children in tow, each claiming that Michael was the father. One woman evaded security guards and was eventually discovered in a bikini and wearing sunglasses beside the family pool. She made an astonishing claim that Michael was "the father of my two girls."

Such women were said to be the inspiration for Michael to write "Billie Jean." But there is a more compelling story. "Ms. Paula Abdul is the infamous 'Billie Jean' of the song," Enid Jackson once charged. She was married to Michael's brother, Jackie. "Michael wrote the song to vent his anger against Abdul and Jackie for having an eight-year affair while Jackie was married to me."

Other critics have suggested that Michael wrote the song to deflect suspicion about his own sexuality.

Before she became one of the most famous pop singers in the world, Paula Abdul—known for such hits as "Forever Your Girl," "Rush Rush," and "Straight Up"—had been an LA Lakers cheerleader. One day at a basketball game, she approached Jackie to ask him for his autograph. It wasn't long before Abdul was getting more than Jackie's autograph.

Even while still a teenager, she was also making a name for herself as a very talented choreographer. Jackie hired her to do the choreography for the video of the song, "Torture," in which Michael did not participate. Janet was so impressed with Abdul's work on the video that she also hired her to do choreography on her album, *Control*.

By then, Michael had long ago heard of his brother's affair from Enid. Reportedly, he was "*über*-pissed" at what he felt was a betrayal from Janet.

Vincent Price

Enid alleged that Abdul once called her from the hospital, claiming that she was having an abortion and naming Jackie as the father.

When confronted with this allegation, Jackie denied the affair. But secretly, he continued to meet with Abdul. A suspicious Enid trailed her husband one night and caught Jackie with Abdul in the back seat of the Jackson family's Land Rover, a confrontation rumored to have ended in violence.

In time, this long-running affair would lead to Jackie's divorce from Enid in August of 1987.

Enid was Michael's favorite sister-in-law, and he deeply regretted the break-up of her marriage to his brother. Some of his bitterness about the affair definitely spilled over into "Billie Jean."

One of the most ridiculous rumors ever circulated about Michael was that Abdul had abandoned Jackie and moved in with Michael at Neverland. When questioned about this, Michael said, "I admire the talents of Miss Abdul on a professional level. As a person, I *hate* her!"

In 2005, Abdul made a comeback as a judge on Fox Television's Reality Show, *American Idol*.

Although he may not have admitted this lapse of musical judgment in his memoirs, Quincy Jones reportedly did not want to include "Billie Jean" in the *Thriller* album. Angered that his judgment was being questioned, Michael telephoned Yetnikoff, demanding that Quincy's name be removed from the album. The music mogul tried to pacify Michael, knowing that Quincy could have sued if his name had been erased.

In its own way, "Beat It" made history in the music industry. In a crossover move, "Beat It" was suddenly played throughout the land on "white rock stations" that rarely featured songs by black performers. "Beat It" was a heavy-hitting rock song that featured Eddie Van Halen, the rock guitar genius.

Quincy remembered that at one point the music was so hot that an electronic amplifier burst into flames. "I've never seen anything like that in forty years in the business." Ever since, "Beat It" has been singled out as the first song that cracked the rock radio color barrier.

Released as a single, "Billie Jean" began at a lukewarm number 47 on *Billboard's* chart of the top 100, but within six weeks shot to the top. The third single release from the album, "Beat It" also shot to number one on the charts. Michael became the first artist in *Billboard's* history to have number one records on both the black and pop charts.

But the phenomenal success of *Thriller* lay in the future. When Quincy, Michael, and the crew first assembled to hear the final mix of the album, Westlake Studios was permeated with gloom and doom. The album was pronounced a disaster.

"After all the great songs and the great performances and great mixes and a great tune stack, we

Paula Abdul with Maria Shriver, 1991

had a 24-karat sonic doo-doo," Quincy said. Sobbing hysterically, Michael ran from the studio. It was decided that the album was not releasable.

Quincy knew how to save the album. It was back to work for all concerned, especially Michael who seemed desperate to have a hit. "It was like he was going to make it this time or die trying," Quincy said.

When Walter Yetnikoff heard the final cut of *Thriller*, he told Michael, "You deliver like a mother-fucker." In a whispery little voice, Michael replied, "Please, Walter, don't use that word with me."

On hearing the album, critic Vincent Aletti of New York's *Village Voice* had an ominous prediction. "In *Thriller*, Jackson has begun to part the shimmering curtain of his innocence—it's magic, it's unreal—to glimpse darker, deeper things. Once that curtain is ripped down, the view could be astonishing."

The album that both Quincy and Michael were once too embarrassed to release went on to chalk up a worldwide sale of 50 million copies, outdistancing such mega-sellers as *Grease* and *Saturday Night Fever*. It would also spend more than seventy-five weeks at Number One on the *Billboard* album charts, longer than any other modern pop recording. It also produced seven Top Ten hits, beating the records previously held by Bruce Springsteen and Fleetwood Mac.

No other album in the history of music had ever sold like that. Ten-year-olds purchased the album, as did some seniors who were young in 1917. *Michael-mania* spread around the planet.

The decade of the 80s belonged to Jacko, "King of Pop," and to Ronald Reagan, who was president of the United States as the Soviet Union entered its twilight zone. The name of Michael Jackson became one of the most famous in the world—or, as his fans claimed, "*The* most famous."

In listening to the album today, the songs make for a good pop album music, fun to sing and dance to, but *Thriller* doesn't quite "live up to its legendary reputation," in the words of *Michael Jackson Record Reviews*. The success of the album depended largely on Michael's imaginative videos, much of the action inspired by his own visions.

Michael lived, breathed, and ate *Thriller*, devoting his entire life to guarantee its success. His "drive bordered on the psychopathic," in the words of Yetnikoff. Michael called the mogul day and night, demanding to know the latest figures of its worldwide sales. He was an artist obsessed with his own success, demanding more and more promotion. After weeks as number one, he wept uncontrollably when *Thriller* fell to number two position.

Quincy traveled with Michael on a world tour to promote *Thriller*, concentrating on Japan and Europe.

In Rome, Michael learned that his huge upcoming concert had been simultaneously scheduled for the same evening that Leonard Bernstein was conducting an orchestra at Vatican City. Michael had long been impressed with such smash hits as *On the Town* and *West Side Story*. Michael's own dance moves had been greatly influenced by *West Side Story* in particular. On a more personal level, perhaps Michael was intrigued by how a homosexual pursued a career—that of conductor of a symphony orchestra—that demanded a heterosexual facade.

Eddie Van Halen

The coming together of Bernstein and Michael did not exactly transpire as Michael had planned. When he met Michael, the conductor "virtually reached the bottom of Michael's throat" with what came to be called history's most prolonged tongue kiss. Michael should not have been flattered. Bernstein did that to many handsome young men he was introduced to.

When Michael finally broke away, he was astonished to hear Bernstein say: "I hear that AIDS can be contracted by an exchange of saliva. Let's hope that both of us are not entertaining something really wicked in our blood streams."

Bernstein invited Quincy to a private viewing of the Sistine Chapel which he'd arranged through his Vatican connections. Both men lay on the floor looking up at the Michelangelo masterpiece. Studying the artist's figures carefully, Bernstein exclaimed: "Look at that! Michelangelo doesn't know what a woman looks like. He was as gay as I am. Those are just guys with tits!"

At the end of the world tour, plans went forward to make a video of "Thriller." But the 14-minute video would be delayed by a year and a half after the release of the album.

Sales had slumped, but after the release of the video, the album once again repeated its steady climb up the charts. Fans around the world treated the arrival of the video like the première of a major film. Quincy Jones claimed that Michael's video "made a sensation in tandem with the rise of video as an art form."

In a very short time, Michael would become even more celebrated because of his videos. One eyewitness on the set where "Thriller" was filmed recalled the moment. "Jackson's body tenses. Energy shoots through his body like a bolt of lightning. As he faces the camera, he seems to spit out the lyrics. His usually fragile voice suddenly takes on a dynamic tone. He can be heard over the deafening playback. He grips his left sleeve with his right hand and jerks it upward. He growls the chorus to the camera. He doesn't dance but seems to glide. He launches into one of his famous spins—a trio of turns in succession."

In the video, Michael is transformed into both a zombie and a werewolf, thereby challenging its director, John Landis, who had previously directed *An American Werewolf in London*. Landis cast Ola Ray as Michael's girlfriend. Because of Michael's strong religious beliefs, she concealed from him that she had been a *Playboy* centerfold in 1980.

Before she was tapped to appear with Michael in the "Thriller" video, Ray, who came from St. Louis, had appeared as a hooker in the 1981 film, *Body and Soul*. She'd also appeared as hookers in the 1982 *Night Shift* and in *48 Hrs.*, released the same year. "Thriller" was obviously the highlight of her career, but she continued to do minor film and TV work, appearing as a *Playboy* playmate in *Beverly Hills Cop II*, released in 1987.

In the "Thriller" video, choreographed zombies perform with Michael. He and the "undead" stage a fantastic song-and-dance number, which the Pulitzer Prize-winning critic for *The New York Times*, Margo Jefferson, called "Walpurgisnacht in suburbia."

The choreography in the "Thriller" video would have taxed the talents of Jerome Robbins. The dance sequences were filmed within the underground concourse at the Rockefeller Center subway stop in Manhattan. The video cost a million dollars.

After the airing of "Thriller" on MTV, and its subsequent worldwide success, all major stars—both black and white—demanded a music video to promote their recordings. A tie-in video with the release of an album became mandatory. Michael single-handedly had revolutionized the music business.

Two shorter but still successful videos were released from the *Thriller* album, "Billie Jean" and "Beat It."

By the time of his release of the video "Billie Jean," Michael had a new "wet look" to his hair. He'd plucked his eyebrows, now heavy with eyeliner. His dancing was slicker, his clothing more "with it." On one occasion he wore black leather trousers and a black leather jacket like Elvis Presley himself.

The video, "Beat It," was a sort of mini-version of *West Side Story*, with the urban violence updated to the 1980s. It was the most viewed video during the summer of 1983.

With its theme of gang warfare, "Beat It" was as

"Thriller"

MJ in "Thriller"

stunning as "Billie Jean." Actual gang members from the streets of Los Angeles appeared in the video along with professional dancers.

The "Thriller" video had been paid for by Branca's skillful negotiations of distribution deals. Meeting with Michael, the two men conceived an even more daring plan: they'd make a documentary on the making of the hit video, and would call it "The Making of 'Thriller.'"

Yetnikoff was instrumental in getting MTV to participate financially. Before that, he'd denounced MTV as "racist assholes" for presenting only white performers. But MTV, recognizing the unprecedented appeal of Michael, finally came around, even putting up some of the money for the financing of the second "Thriller" video. These videos opened the doors of MTV to other emerging black performers.

Jerry Kramer was called in to direct "The Making of 'Thriller.'" "As a professional, Michael is like a Zen monk," Kramer later said. "He's focused on a singular goal, his work, his art, which he constantly tries to take to a celestial level."

Long after the release of the "Thriller" video, a story leaked out to the press that under threat of expulsion from the Jehovah's Witness cult, Michael once ordered Branca to destroy the "Thriller" video, even though it had been financed by Vestron, Showtime, and MTV. Branca, at least in front of Michael, agreed to do that, but he had no intention of actually destroying the video. Finally, a last-minute compromise was reached thanks to the insertion of a disclaimer: "Due to my strong personal convictions, I wish to stress that this film in no way endorses a belief in the occult—Michael Jackson."

Later on, to pacify the more fanatical of the Jehovah's Witnesses, Michael, in an issue of *Awake!* on May 22, 1984, tried to distance himself from "Thriller." He promised, "I'll never do a video like *that* again! In fact, I have blocked further distribution of the film over which I have control, including its release in some other countries. There's all kinds of promotional stuff being proposed for 'Thriller.' But I tell them, 'No, no, no. I don't want to do anything on 'Thriller.' No more 'Thriller.'"

Not all the Jehovah's Witnesses disapproved of Michael, although church leaders did. A radical cult within the sect itself came up with the startling belief that Michael was "an incarnation of the Archangel Michael, a symbol of the arisen Christ."

170

Leonard Bernstein

Wearing a pink shirt and a red bow tie, with black leather pants and a jacket, Michael appeared live at the 1983 hoedown celebrating Motown's 25th anniversary. Michael at first refused to appear, but was eventually cajoled into performing. He electrified audiences.

On stage Michael had a reunion with his errant brother, Jermaine, who had voiced criticism of Michael for "trying to be white" to the press. Berry Gordy pleaded with Michael to do a solo number from Motown's long list of hits, but Michael adamantly refused, preferring to lip-sync his rendition of "Billie Jean."

"It was take that choice or leave it," Gordy later said. "I caved in just to get Michael out there on stage."

Some fifty million people tuned in to watch *Motown 25: Yesterday, Today, and Tomorrow*. Michael startled audiences with his "Moonwalk." Actually he'd ripped off the dance, in which he seemed to be gliding in opposite directions simultaneously, from inner-city black break dancers in the 1970s.

From that night on, Michael also became known as "The Gloved One." Many fans thought he'd introduced the lone white-sequined glove that night. But he'd been wearing such a glove since the late 1970s. Sammy Davis Jr. thought Michael was paying homage to old-fashioned black minstrel shows, or making a tribute to Al Jolson. *Motown 25* turned out to be the highest-rated variety show in the history of TV.

In less than a decade after Michael's *Motown 25* appearance, *Entertainment Weekly* hailed the performance as one of the greatest entertainment moments of the 20th century. The article wrote of "a delicate young man with a choked voice, a white glove, and magic shoes. He took the microphone and began to write the next chapter of American music history. The moment Michael Jackson ripped into his single, 'Billie Jean'—squealing, moaning, spinning, and finally taking the viewer's breath away, with his Moonwalk—the music industry had to throw away its old yardsticks of success."

Two of the greatest dancing stars of all time, Fred Astaire and Gene Kelly, watched Michael's "Moonwalk." The next day, each of them called Michael, asking to meet him. Although shy about meeting two of his all-time favorites, Michael eagerly set up times to see each of these talented stars of the Golden Age, from whom he had stolen so many of his own dance steps, adapting them, of course.

Both Gene Kelly and Fred Astaire were idols to Michael, and he also understood the different artistry of each dancer. Critic Steve Vineberg once noted that the two performers were a study in contrasts with different personal styles. He called Astaire "a natural aristocrat, movie musicals' closest equivalent to Cary Grant."

"If Fred Astaire is the Cary Grant of dance, I'm the Marlon Brando," Kelly said.

"Astaire was astonishingly lithe, perhaps the most graceful man who ever walked—let alone danced—across a movie set," Vineberg claimed.

On the other hand, Vineberg found that Kelly evoked Jimmy Cagney. "Kelly's style was rooted in vaudeville and the brash, crowing apple-pie musicals of George M. Cohan," Vineberg said. "He was an athlete, a two-fisted Irishman."

The first telephone call of the morning to Michael at his Encino home was from Astaire. The dancer told Michael that he'd taped the show and had gotten up early that morning to watch the program again.

"You're a hell of a mover," Astaire told Michael. "Man, you really put them on their asses last night."

After Michael thanked him, Astaire said, "You're an angry dancer. I'm the same way. I used to do the same thing with my cane."

In the days to come, Astaire invited Michael over to his Beverly Hills home. There, Michael taught Ginger Rogers' former dance partner how to Moonwalk. Astaire was eighty-four years old at the time. So impressed was he with Michael's steps that Astaire asked Hermes Pan to come over one night, as he wanted Michael to teach the dancer/choreographer also how to Moonwalk.

Michael admired Astaire, but he also had great respect for the talent of Hermes Pan, the Nashville-born artist responsible for choreographing every one of the nine Astaire-Rogers 1930s gems as well as Fred and Ginger's 1949 screen swan song, *The Barkleys of Broadway*. Pan also choreographed Betty Grable musicals in the 40s and danced on screen with both the "Blonde Bombshell," as she was called, and Hollywood's princess, Rita Hayworth.

Michael asked Astaire how he climbed the walls and danced on the ceiling in the 1951 *Royal Wedding*.

Astaire finally admitted how this trick shot was done. "The whole room revolved, and I was on the ground the whole time. The camera, the cameraman, and the room all turn, and I'm the one who does the climbing. It required a special set. We called it the Iron Lung, and it was constructed by Bethlehem Steel. Not only did the camera and cameraman revolve 360 degrees, the light for the set revolved as well. It's too difficult to explain. But don't you dare copy it from me. That scene belongs just to me."

"I always remember the song you sang," Michael said, obviously in awe.

"You're All the World to Me," Astaire said. "I remember it well."

Long after he gave up dancing in public, Astaire still put on private shows, as he did one night for Michael. He sat at his drums and pounded out some rhythms, before getting up and performing a few dance steps for Michael.

"Better watch out!" Michael warned. "I'll steal those steps from you too."

"Feel free," Astaire said. "At my age, I'm glad to be walking."

Michael confessed that he used to sit in front of his television, using his video cassette's stop-and-rewind switches to dissect every dance step his mentor made.

"I stole that idea of going up on my toes from those classic movies you made back in the 30s," Michael told Astaire.

"Those were the days," Astaire said with a touch of nostalgia.

"Anybody who can sing and dance at the same time—and do both well—is pretty darned good," Astaire said. "And that's what Michael does."

Michael would later be nominated for an Emmy Award in the musical category. Even though he lost to Leontyne Price, he felt Astaire's compliment took away some of the sting of defeat.

When Michael's so-called autobiography, *Moonwalk*, was published, he dedicated it to Fred Astaire.

After Astaire's death in 1987, and when Michael was preparing his 1988 *Moonwalker*, a full-length feature film, he received a major disappointment. Michael choreographed a dance sequence in which he'd superimpose himself onto one of Astaire's films, becoming in essence the dancer's Ginger Rogers. It was a brilliant idea and would have made for a first-rate film memory. But the female jockey who Astaire married at the end of his life, Robyn Smith, refused to give Michael permission to use the footage.

When Sarah Giles composed her collection of remembrances about Astaire, she asked Michael to contribute. In *Fred Astaire: His Friends Talk*, Michael wrote: "I could only repeat what has been said and written about Fred Astaire's perfectionism and enormous, one-of-a-kind artistry. What I can reflect on is the inspiration he afforded me personally, being privileged as I was to see him work his magic. Nobody could duplicate Mr. Astaire's ability, but what I never stop trying to emulate is his total discipline, his absolute dedication to every aspect of his art. He rehearsed, rehearsed, and rehearsed some more, until he got it just the way he wanted it. It was Fred Astaire's work ethic that few people ever discussed and even fewer could ever hope to equal."

In the 1980s, many critics and writers called Michael the Fred Astaire of his era. Such a tribute was expressed by Sandy Duncan in *People Extra*: "Fred Astaire was to that era and that music, the way the music moved through him in the 30s, what Michael Jackson is to this era. You could put him behind a scrim and see his silhouette and you'd know who he was. It's like he's got a direct connection to God, because those moves just come from within him and through the music."

In the wake of Astaire's approval, Michael's other idol, Gene Kelly, also paid him a visit at Encino. Michael estimated that he must have watched Kelly dance with the cartoon figures, Tom & Jerry, at least a hundred times in the 1945 film, *Anchors Aweigh*.

Gene Kelly

In time Kelly would return the compliment, filming a taped tribute to Michael for his self-serving lovefest broadcast on Showtime cable TV.

Kelly enthralled Michael with his insider show business stories, admitting, "I wasn't nice to Debbie—it's a wonder she still speaks to me." He was referring to working with Debbie Reynolds on the 1952 *Singin' in the Rain*. Michael told Kelly that he thought this was the greatest movie musical of all time.

He warned Michael that if he ever became a musical star in films, he should get used to being overlooked by The Academy. "It's a form of snobbism," Kelly said. "Members feel that drama is more deserving of awards than comedy."

Michael complimented Kelly on his all-ballet film, *Invitation to the Dance*. "I was never allowed to complete the picture," Kelly said. "The plug was pulled on me. The version released in 1956 was never finished. I was furious. Of course, I got disastrous notices. I took to bed for three weeks."

He blamed the director, Vincente Minnelli, for the disappointing *Brigadoon*, released in 1954. "You see, Vincente was in love with me . . . always was. When you're in love, you can't be objective as a director."

Kelly expressed his regret at his treatment of Judy Garland during the shooting of *The Pirate* in 1948. "She and Vincente were breaking up, and she was on the verge of a nervous breakdown and the beginning of a long and protracted illness," Kelly said. "Vincente didn't help matters by spending all his time in my dressing room panting after me like a puppy dog."

Michael appeared shocked at these revelations.

Kelly warned Michael, "Don't get carried away with your own brilliance in the studio. Both Vincente and I thought *The Pirate* was going to be the greatest musical of all time. At least we thought that for forty-eight hours. Perhaps only six people in America understood where we were going. In fact, Vincente kissed and licked my toes in gratitude for the performance I gave."

Before departing, Kelly told Michael: "So many men—women, too— have fallen for me. Judy herself, Peter Lawford. Noël Coward. Every chorus boy I've ever danced with developed a crush on me. As a lover, I never returned love. An artist can only love himself, and I'm sure you agree."

"How do you cope with all those gay rumors," Michael said. "They say bad things about me. That I'm a homosexual, and I'm not! How do you answer such questions?"

"Enigmatically," Kelly responded. "I tell my inquisitors that I'm not gay. Merely an Irish leprechaun. There's a difference you know."

At the door, Kelly gave Michael a warm embrace and a theatrical kiss. "You're going to be king in the 80s. For Fred and me, there's not much left except accepting lifetime achievement awards."

"Can you believe it?" Michael endlessly asked of anyone even remotely concerned. "The great Fred Astaire, the great Gene Kelly told me that I was just as great a dancer as they were in their prime. What can any future award mean to me when I get praise like that?"

Astaire and Kelly might approve of Michael, but not the members of his church, The Jehovah's Witnesses.

Michael might have tried to appease members of Jehovah's Witnesses and distance himself from *Thriller*, but he wasn't going to let the fanatical religious sect deter "me from the greatest night of my life." He showed up at the 1984 Grammy Awards to receive all those accolades for *Thriller*, and it would mark the pinnacle of his career. It would also turn into one of his most infamous appearances, launching him on the long road toward a forever tarnished reputation.

When Michael walked into the auditorium to receive his Grammys, he had child star Emmanuel Lewis on his left and the beautiful Brooke Shields on his right. The trio was, in the words of Walter Yetnikoff, "a *ménage à trois* to make the Marquis de Sade blush."

"I didn't get destroyed by the press and fan mania and neither will Michael. He's very talented. He knows how to make records that people like. But he's a very straightforward kid. He has a great deal of faith. He's got a great deal of innocence and he protects that especially. Michael looks at cartoons all day and keeps away from drugs. That's how he maintains his innocence."

--Paul McCartney

"I did it as a favor. I didn't want nothing. Maybe Michael will give me dance lessons some day. I was a complete fool, according to the rest of the band and our manager and everybody else."

--Eddie Van Halen, on playing 'Beat It' for free

"No dope-oriented album ever sold as much as Thriller, and no vulgar artist ever became so famous as Michael has."

--The Rev. Jesse Jackson

"Thank God for Elizabeth Taylor. She protected me."

--Michael Jackson

"He wasn't ever really interested in money. I'd give him his share of the night's earnings and the next day he'd buy ice cream or candy for all the kids in the neighborhood."

--Papa Joe Jackson

"My Lord, he's a wonderful mover. He makes these moves up himself and it's just great to watch. Michael is a dedicated artist. He dreams and thinks of it all the time."

--Fred Astaire

Chapter Seven

The Grammy Awards in 1984 alerted keen observers to Michael's interest in young boys. In his future, these boys—with an occasional exception—would be white. Not so Emmanuel Lewis, an African-American who was born in Brooklyn in 1971, which made him thirteen years old when Michael took him and Brooke Shields as his "dates" to the Grammys.

Michael met the pint-sized actor—known at the time as "The Tallest 40 Inches in Hollywood"—at an awards ceremony. They became intense friends, a relationship that would last for many years. It was another odd coupling for

Michael. Lewis was rumored to be a midget, but endocrinologists claimed he had all the potential for normal growth.

Speculation about the relationship became rampant when Michael and Lewis appeared in public dressed alike. They spent many happy hours—even days—together. When Lewis went somewhere with Michael, he was often mistaken for Gary Coleman, the *Diff'rent Strokes* TV child star. Both of these performers are short, African-American in origin, and had starred in sitcoms about trans-racial adoptions.

Lewis was twelve years old when his sitcom, *Webster*, premiered in 1983. The series finale would come just one day after his 18th birthday. Michael was a faithful fan of the series.

Before hitting it big on *Webster*, Lewis had starred in TV commercials, hawking fruit

Emmanuel Lewis

177

juice, glue, soup, toys, stereos, coffee, puddings, pizzas, and Burger King. He told reporters, "Though I'm still little, my heart and dreams are as big as ever."

It was during the making of those TV commercials that Michael became "smitten" (La Toya's words) with Lewis. Brazenly, Michael called the talent agent, Margaret Lewis, the young actor's mother, and asked her permission to allow her son to spend time at Hayvenhurst. Not suspicious at the time, she seemed delighted that a big star like Michael had expressed an interest in her son.

It was all fun and games, as they wrestled on the lawn at Encino, played cowboys and Indians, or petted the animals, including the boa constrictor, "Muscles," in Michael's zoo. Michael claimed that although boa constrictors could not devour the average person whole, Lewis was "just the right size for a tasty snack." In response, the child actor would run screaming into the house. Much time was spent in Michael's darkened bedroom watching movies. Sleepovers—later to become a notorious fixture in Michael's life—followed.

Steve Howell, who became Michael's unofficial videographer, captured on film many intimate moments between Lewis and Michael. "Yes, hugging and the most intimate cuddling," Howell was quoted as saying. "It's all on home video."

In March of 2005, *In Touch Weekly*, a tabloid, shocked Michael's fans by publishing a photograph of him, along with Lewis, lying in bed sucking on the nipples of baby bottles. "How retro!" a fan wrote Michael. "How could you? Talk about trying to relive your second childhood."

When he turned thirteen, Lewis received a diamond-and-gold "friend-ship" bracelet from Michael that allegedly cost $15,000. "It weighed more than Emmanuel did," said a Jackson family member. This was a great exag-geration, of course, but at the time, Lewis weighed only forty pounds.

Freddie Mercury

Michael was twenty-five years old when he launched this strange friend-ship with a boy about half his age. Some family members, including La Toya, were often embarrassed by the whisper-ing and giggling between the two, but Michael refused to talk about Lewis and asked that the Jacksons not probe into his personal relationships.

Unlike La Toya, Michael's sister, Rebbie, always denounced those who speculated that her brother was gay. "That's inconceivable. Homosexuality

178

is against the tenets of our faith," she said, referring to the Jehovah's Witness cult. "Anyone who turned out to be gay would be disfellowshipped, cut off right away." The statement is only startling in its naïveté.

In 1983, Michael invited Lewis to attend a concert with him at the Los Angeles Forum to hear Freddie Mercury, the flamboyant lead singer of the group, Queen.

Previously, Michael had urged Mercury to release "Another One Bites the Dust" as a single. Soon after, it shot to number one on the charts, and since then, Mercury had been urging Michael to record a duet with him, as he had with Paul McCartney and Mick Jagger.

Michael and Mercury were often compared to each other, one critic claiming that, "Both artists have an androgynous image...their appearance has blurred the conventional and traditional barriers surrounding gender, race, and age in society."

Watching Mercury perform, Michael reportedly was awed by this British-Indian singer, who was impressive not only for his powerful vocal abilities but for his charisma as a live performer. Later Michael went backstage for a reunion with Mercury, in the process introducing him to Lewis.

In his dressing room, Mercury was on the phone talking to his cats—yes, that's not a misprint. The mercurial singer was devoted to his cats and even dedicated his solo album, "Mr. Bad Guy," to his felines. Michael noted that Mercury was wearing a vest on which he'd painted portraits of each of his cats. The song, "Delilah," was written about his favorite cat.

Slamming down the phone, Mercury turned to Michael and Lewis. "Don't either of you ask my hand in marriage. I can't cook, and I'd be a terrible housewife. I'm just a musical prostitute, my dear." He uttered those lines to many visitors. Perhaps in deference to the presence of the obviously under-aged Lewis, he didn't express another one of his favorite quips: "The bigger the better—*in everything*."

After Michael and the pint-sized actor had departed, Mercury turned to the stage manager. "I'm gayer than Michael, but I like my men six feet tall with twelve-inch dicks."

A reporter, David Rowland, once asked Michael who his closest friends were. He said, "Freddie Mercury, Diana Ross, Elizabeth Taylor . . ." Rowland claimed that Michael then added the name of a kid standing beside him. "I didn't get his name. He looked ten years old, very cute, very blond, and blue-eyed. It certainly wasn't Emmanuel Lewis."

Michael said, "My grown-up friends and this boy here are the only people in the world who don't want anything from me. They love me for myself."

When Mercury learned that he had AIDS, seven years before he eventually died from the disease, he was reported to have said: "I should have used

Michael as a role model and dated only ten-year-old virgins."

In public, Michael sometimes defended his unusual friendship with Lewis. "I was Emmanuel's form of inspiration—he loved my humor and just hanging out and having fun. Not just with me, but my whole family."

"Michael is not only my friend, he's my family," Lewis claimed.

Michael's nickname for Lewis was "Manny."

Initially, Margaret Lewis didn't think that there was anything wrong about her young son pursuing a relationship with a big star like Michael. But when reports reached her that Michael and her son had checked into the Beverly Hills Hotel, registering themselves as father and son, she moved to sever the relationship. "There was something wrong here," she reportedly said. "The friendship didn't seem right. Michael was getting obsessional about my son."

Years later, in 2003, when Lewis was on *The Howard Stern Show* promoting the TV series, *The Surreal Life*, the controversial interviewer noted that Michael used to carry Lewis around like he was a little baby. Stern asked Lewis if Michael had been in love with him. Lewis seemed to want to drop the subject but Stern was persistent, asking Lewis if Michael used to bathe him. Stern also wanted to know if Michael ever "came on to you or fondled you?" Lewis denied that any incident like that ever happened. He later said, "I was ready to go over and kick Howard's ass for asking such questions."

Michael's other "date" at the 1984 Grammy Awards was Brooke Shields. Respected in later years as a Broadway actress, she was known at the time as a young Hollywood goddess, a sex kitten, a sensual starlet, an undergraduate at Princeton, and the scandalous star of 1978's *Pretty Baby*, 1980's *The Blue Lagoon*, and 1981's *Endless Love.*

In some ways, their early lives had run along roughly parallel courses. Michael had Papa Joe beating, pushing, and shoving him into early stardom. Brooke had a small-time actress, Teri Shields, the ultimate stage mother, placing her daughter in front of the camera before she was even one year old. As the Ivory Snow pin-up, Brooke was once hailed as "the most beautiful baby in America." Francesco Scavullo, the celebrated photographer who changed her diapers for the Ivory Snow ads, once said: "Brooke was born beautiful, she stays beautiful, and she gets more beautiful every month."

Brooke's first biographer, Jason Bonderoff, described a startling event that happened to Brooke when she was only two years old. One afternoon in Central Park, Teri Shields was guarding the baby carriage containing Brooke. An elderly woman in large sunglasses and an Hermès scarf strolled by and peered inside the carriage. Teri thought that the woman's face looked vaguely familiar. Staring at the baby, the woman said, "The child is magnificent. She'll go far." Teri recognized the husky Swedish accent. Greta Garbo had predicted Brooke's future before walking on without another word.

180

Reportedly, Michael had refused to see *Pretty Baby*, a movie in which Brooke played a child prostitute living in a brothel. There were numerous nude scenes. The release of the film caused an outcry from right-wing fundamentalists and groups attacking child porn. Michael was also said to have boycotted *The Blue Lagoon* because of its nude scenes. The release of this film led to Brooke's testifying at a U.S. congressional inquiry, where she insisted that older body doubles had been used during the filming of her nude scenes.

Brooke had created a sensation, and made a cool million, when she'd posed for Calvin Klein in his jeans, plugging the slogan, "Nothing comes between me and my Calvins."

Neither Brooke nor her stage mother, Teri, seemed to have a problem with Brooke becoming romantically linked in the press with "a man of color," as one public relations agent privately commented years later. "Of course, in Michael's case, if a girl didn't like him black, he could switch to white," quipped one reporter.

Michael, perhaps because of his lower class origins, was intrigued by Brooke's aristocratic background. She was a descendant of Lucrezia Borgia, one of the Holy Roman Emperors (Charles V), King Henri IV of France, Prince Rainier of Monaco, and the Marquis de Sade.

Michael was said to have been jealous when he learned that Brooke was dating John Kennedy Jr. When Capote heard this, he said, "He's only jealous because he can't have John-John for himself."

Before her arrival at the Grammys, the actress had unsuccessfully sued photographer Garry Gross in an attempt to stop him from exhibiting or selling nude pictures of herself for which she'd (voluntarily) posed when she was only ten years old. She had tearfully testified in court that the photographs embarrassed her. But despite Brooke's tears, and despite the fact that some commentators had defined the pictures as "child porn," the court decided that Gross had the right to display the pictures.

After her 1983 disaster, the film *Sahara*, for which she'd been paid $1,500,000, Brooke took a four-year sabbatical from pictures to attend Princeton. Nonetheless, her promoters jockeyed, during that era, to keep her name in the press. What better person to date than Michael Jackson himself, as he rode the crest of his fame?

"Dating Michael was a way to get Brooke's picture on the front page of every newspaper in America," a publicist said. "And Michael needed to show up with a beautiful woman to prove he was straight. It was a match made in heaven."

Except it wasn't, as subsequent events on the actual night of the Grammys revealed.

Michael had already escorted Brooke as his date to the January 1984,

American Music Awards, produced by "eternally young" Dick Clark. She had to share Michael with his other escorts of the evening, Emmanuel Lewis and La Toya. All four of them sat smiling as Clark claimed, "If 1983 wasn't the year of Michael Jackson, it wasn't the year of anybody."

According to La Toya, Michael was very reluctant to take Brooke once again to the Grammy Awards in February. His sister remembered Michael coming into the kitchen of their Encino home, joining Janet and her for a "confessional." Meanwhile, Brooke sat in the living room of the Jackson home, "cooling her heels," as Janet remembered. La Toya's claim was that Brooke was trying to cajole Michael into taking her to the awards ceremony, which was destined to attract worldwide press coverage.

It isn't known why Michael was reluctant to take Brooke to the Grammys. Even if she were only "arm candy," he could use his association with her to defend against rumors that he was gay. And she would get national publicity. Even so, many members in the press, even thousands of Michael's fans, were suspicious of this coupling. Speculation appeared that Michael had paid Brooke anywhere from $10,000 to $25,000 for each of their joint appearances. None of the allegations from those provocative web postings was ever proven.

Janet Jackson may have referred to Brooke as "giraffe butt," but she was one of the most beautiful teenagers to emerge in the 1980s. Garbo had been right to an extent. Brooke did go far, but, as is usually the case in Hollywood, not as far as she dreamed. She did not, for example, become the next Ava Gardner, as some had predicted.

In one of the more fanciful paragraphs in his autobiography, *Moonwalk*, Michael falsely claimed that in addition to Diana Ross, "another love was Brooke Shields. We were romantically serious for a while."

Brooke has denied that there was any romance or love affair between Michael and herself, and she did so on national television. She'd met Michael when she was only thirteen, and they had bonded in their discussions over the difficulties associated with being a child star.

"There were a handful of child stars at the time—actress Jodie Foster, Michael, and myself among them—and we were friends because we shared an understanding of how difficult life was in the public eye," Brooke said. "When we were together, we were in a safe place. We could be ourselves."

Accompanied by both Emmanuel Lewis and Brooke, Michael arrived customarily late on the biggest night of his life, the presentation of the Grammys on February 28, 1984, at the Los Angeles Shrine Auditorium. The televised event would be watched by sixty million viewers.

Michael's major competition of the evening, Lionel Richie, spotted him backstage. Destined to become the big loser of the evening, Richie was overheard talking to Quincy Jones, "My God," he allegedly said upon seeing

Michael's costume, "It's Sergeant Pepper and he's wearing more makeup than Brooke Shields."

Michael arrived at the glitzy gala, the music industry's Oscars, in full military uniform, his thin waist encased in a gold sash. A black sequined jacket with wide lapels fitted tightly over a pair of black sequined pants. Across his chest he'd hung a gold bandolier, and on each shoulder rested a mammoth epaulette. He skipped the tie but wore a white wing-collared dress shirt. Of course, he had on his trademark white socks and a spangled glove on one hand as well as a spangled wrist band. His eyes were concealed from his millions of fans behind dark aviator sunglasses.

Michael had been nominated for a dozen Grammys, and no star in the history of the academy had ever received such accolades, not even Elvis Presley. Even The Beatles had received only four Grammys, which one critic of the music awards called "a scandal."

The evening began with Michael winning Best Rock Vocal Performance by a Male for "Thriller." He had fully expected to win Best Song of the Year for his rendition of "Billie Jean," but he lost to The Police for "Every Breath You Take."

He bounced back, hitting the stage with Quincy Jones to accept Grammys as Producers of the Year for the *Thriller* album.

In many ways, the most meaningful Grammy was Michael's win for Best Children's Album honoring his work on *E.T. the Extra-Terrestrial.* As he accepted the award, his fans in the balcony broke into hysterical screaming as they rose to their feet shouting, "We love you, Michael."

More Grammys waited in the wings for Michael to pick up. Best R&B vocalist went to Michael for "Billie Jean," and he also won the Best Record award for "Beat It" and Best R&B Song Award for "Billie Jean."

One of the biggest awards of the evening, Best Pop Male Vocalist, went to Michael for "Beat It." Sisters La Toya, Janet, and Rebbie joined him on stage in his great moment of triumph. He said, "My mother's very shy, she's like me, she won't come up." For this award, he even removed his sunglasses, as Katharine Hepburn had suggested to him. One male fan called from the balcony, "Take it all off, Michael."

The highlight of the evening, the Grammy for Record of the Year, also went to—guess who?—Michael. Before millions, he was like a happy kid, jumping up and down. One of the presenters, pint-sized Mickey Rooney, called the ceremony "the Michael Jackson Show." He also entered the history books, having won more Grammy awards than any other musician before him, breaking the record set by Paul Simon, who in 1970 had walked away with seven Grammys for his album, *Bridge Over Troubled Water.*

When Michael in his falsetto announced, "I love all the girls in the balcony," a member of the audience sitting behind Lewis and Brooke could be heard saying, "Yeah, right!"

This was also the night the infamous Pepsi commercials were aired for the first time. Since news of Michael's hair catching fire had been flashed around the world, more people watched his commercial than any other TV commercial in the history of the medium. "The executives at Coca-Cola were getting diarrhea watching it," said one of the producers of the Grammys.

Even as the commercial for Pepsi aired, lawyers for both Michael and the soft drink company were in negotiations about the fallout from this disastrous filming.

Despite the events transpiring on the stage, everyone in the auditorium seemed to be staring at the strange trio who sat up front: Michael, Lewis, and Brooke. What caused Brooke distress was Michael's insistence that Lewis remain perched on his lap. Finally, when she couldn't take the scrutiny any more, Brooke was seen tugging at Michael's arm. "Let's get out of here! Everybody's looking at us. I'm so embarrassed I think we should make a run for it."

Michael cuddled Lewis in his arms as he left the auditorium, heading for a waiting limousine surrounded by his bodyguards. An apparently enraged Brooke trailed them, looking neither left nor right as she made her getaway.

His previous "girlfriend," Tatum O'Neal, made two attempts to reach Michael, but was shoved aside by security guards. Behind his dark glasses, Michael either didn't see her—or didn't want to see her. "How quickly they forget," Tatum told her friends, perhaps jokingly. "Without me, there would be no Michael Jackson."

Later that night at the Rex, a deluxe restaurant, where a post-Grammy bash was held, Michael tasted caviar, drank a glass of champagne, and was embraced by Arnold Schwarzenegger, the future governor of California. He even received a kiss from Julio Iglesias, who was rumored to "have the hots" for his sister, La Toya. Orange-haired Cyndi Lauper greeted Michael with a wet kiss, as did Eddie Murphy, known to appreciate a "trannie" when he spotted one.

"Michael, darling," came a familiar voice. He turned to confront a still beautiful, but aging, Joan Collins. "Tell me, dear heart, the name of your plastic surgeon. I simply adore your nose job."

Neil Diamond approached him, reminding him that "your role models," Diana Ross and James Brown, had never received a Grammy—"and now you're carrying home eight." Music legend Bob Dylan also came up to Michael, expressing his ongoing disappointment that his revolutionary *Highway 61 Revisited* hadn't received a Grammy in 1965.

Michael not only won all those Grammys but over the years he would also bank a total take from *Thriller* that may have gone beyond the $150 million mark. "Move over Paul McCartney," Quincy Jones was reported to have said. "Show business is getting a new rich daddy—and he's black."

When Michael in his limousine dropped Brooke off at her hotel, L'Ermitage in Beverly Hills, she is reported to have said: "Why don't you, Emmanuel, and I get married? That will give the press something to write about!" The quote might have been apocryphal.

Back in his bedroom at Encino, Michael spent the rest of the evening talking to "my only true friends in life," a series of six mannequins. Brooke herself had considered the manufacture of a mannequin as a present for Michael until she learned that she'd have to devote three weeks of her life posing for it.

One week after the awards, one insulting reporter asked the question on everyone's lips, "Who do you love? Brooke or Emmanuel?"

Michael didn't answer but launched into an excuse for not marrying. "I don't like some of the things my brothers do to their wives. I'm never going to marry. I just can't take it. It's awful, marriage. I don't trust anyone enough for that."

Later, when he published *Moonwalk*, Michael had other comments about the lack of a woman in his life. "My dating and relationships with girls have not had the happy ending I've been looking for. Something always seems to get in the way. The things I share with millions of people aren't the sort of things you share with one. Many girls want to know what makes me tick—why I live the way I live or do the things I do—trying to get inside my head. They want to rescue me from my loneliness. But they do it in such a way that they give me the impression they want to share my loneliness, which I wouldn't wish on anybody, because I believe I'm one of the loneliest people in the world."

When Brooke was promoting a romance in the press with Michael, she suggested there was some "real boy-girl interest" there. Years later, she'd be very candid and admit it was "only a friendship." Before "dating" Michael, she'd had another highly publicized romance, this time with the *Saturday Night Fever* himself, John Travolta. Like Michael, Travolta would live to see rumors of his alleged gay life splashed throughout the tabloids in blaring headlines.

When Michael was seriously questioned about his romance with Brooke, he admitted that he was still a virgin at the age of twenty-five despite his dates with the so-called Sex Kitten.

For the Grammy Awards, Michael—hired by Pepsi Cola—agreed to film what was to become the most controversial and highly publicized commercial of the 1980s. This Pepsi ad received more publicity than the Grammy telecast itself. One of the two Pepsi commercials became such a news event that many TV stations ran it for free as part of the evening news.

Michael turned out to be a hard bargainer with the soft drink company. Katharine Hepburn and Paul McCartney had urged him not to do commercials, fearing it would cheapen his image, but he went against their advice. He wrote new lines for "Billie Jean," helped conceive the Pepsi lyrics, and agreed to perform the new jingle, "You're a Whole New Generation," in the ads. Privately, he told Pepsi executives that he didn't drink Pepsi and that he'd refuse to do so on camera. "For that matter, I also don't drink Coca-Cola—have no fears about that. I prefer natural beverages such as carrot juice or bottled water."

Michael's comments met a grim reception at Pepsi. "At the rate we're paying the mother-fucker," one disgruntled executive said privately, "he should down a whole God damn case of Pepsi in one gulp on camera. The arrogant little faggot." Even so, the company official emerged in public with a smiling face to welcome Michael aboard.

The commercials were to be filmed at the Los Angeles Shrine Auditorium in front of three thousand or so fans.

Throughout the filming and editing, Michael turned out to be a domineering diva. It was said that he made Bette Davis appear comparatively docile and cooperative. In complete dictatorial control, Michael demanded that Pepsi hire Bob Giraldi, who had directed him in the video, "Beat It." He also wanted and got the services of Michael Peters, who had worked on the videos for "Beat It" and "Thriller."

At first Michael refused to take off his sunglasses during taping. Giraldi urged, "But Michael, Pepsi is paying to see your face." He shot back that he would allow his face to be shown in close-up for only four seconds.

That too didn't go over with Pepsi executives. "If a TV viewer blinks, he'll miss the jerk's face," the same disgruntled executive said. "Jackson should take a lesson from Gloria Swanson in *Sunset Blvd.* about how to deliver a close-up."

Michael also complained about the lighting, claiming it was as dark as the "Thriller" graveyard scene. An early version of the sequence showed Michael in a dance step that incorporated two spins. He demanded that it be cut. "I will allow Pepsi to show me in only one spin." On seeing the first cut, Michael sent word to Pepsi, "I hate the commercials and everything about them." He cited one segment that "made me furious. I am smiling in one of my dances, and I am never known to smile when I dance."

The astonished executive asked, "But Michael, if you never smile while dancing, how did the camera catch you smiling?"

Michael slammed down the phone.

Before the beginning of that day's filming, Michael had dropped his glove in the toilet when he went to urinate and had "screamed bloody murder," in the words of one of the cameramen.

"It sounded like a shrill woman," said a sound engineer, "one who had just had a 14-inch black dildo shoved up her tight ass. It was even more convincing than Janet Leigh's scream for Alfred Hitchcock in *Psycho*."

The famous glove was fished out, dried off by wardrobe, and placed back on Michael's hand.

Michael later told Giraldi that the accidental dropping of the glove in the toilet "is a bad omen. Maybe God is telling me not to go through with this Pepsi thing. It is, after all, a lie since I don't drink Pepsi. Maybe God will punish me for lying."

The first commercial was filmed without incident, depicting a group of children dancing in the street, one of whom is dressed as Michael in a red jacket from his "Beat It" video. Suddenly, the young actor, Alfonso Ribeiro, confronts the Moonwalker himself, and looks absolutely astonished. Then Michael and his brothers join the children in a song-and-dance routine that honors the Pepsi generation.

Michael became enchanted with the handsome young boy, and the professional relationship blossomed into a private friendship. When Ribeiro released his first single, "Dance Baby," in 1984, it was dedicated to Michael. Ribeiro went on to TV sitcom fame when he played Carlton Banks in the 1990s series *The Fresh Prince of Bel Air*, produced by Quincy Jones. Because of their age difference, there was speculation about the relationship between Michael and the young boy, but nothing approaching the "scandal" caused by Michael's association with Emmanuel Lewis.

Ribeiro, who today has developed a passionate interest in auto racing, was descended from parents who immigrated to New York from the Dominican Republic. In January of 2002 he married his girlfriend, Robin, and they have a daughter named Sienna.

In the second commercial, it was agreed that Tito—not Michael—would be seen drinking a Pepsi. In lieu of his face, Michael agreed to allow his gloved hand and his sequined socks to be filmed. "My fans will know it's me just by looking at my glove and socks."

The re-shoot began as Michael appeared at the top of the stairs in his famous cocksure pose with hip jutting out "like a Saturday night whore" in the words of one critic. The writer for *Rolling Stone* would have a different slant, calling the celebrated stance "a whole physical catechism of cool."

It was 6:30pm on the night of January 27, 1984. Michael faced a worn-out crew, exhausted after four days of filming and reacting to his often outrageous demands. But it was Giraldi who was holding the crew after hours. He wasn't satisfied with the intensity of the flash bombs in the previously filmed sequences. After the first bomb went off, Michael headed down the steps, dancing to the tune of "Billie Jean." For the second blast, the technical staff increased the intensity of the pyrotechnics. Suddenly, a piercing scream came from Michael, a sound that dwarfed his earlier yell from the toilet.

"Tito, Tito, I'm flaming," Michael shouted.

After a magnesium bomb was detonated two feet from Michael's head, his face disappeared in a cloud of bluish smoke, like the kind of haze that filled New York speakeasies in the Twenties. The intense heat of the magnesium bomb, amplified by the klieg lights, had ignited his hair. Flames shot from Michael's head as he screamed in horror. Yanking his jacket up over his head, Michael attempted, unsuccessfully, to put out the fire.

Security guard Miko Brando rushed to rescue him, putting out the flames with his bare hands, but badly burning his own fingers in doing so.

Michael was in such panic that he fought off rescuers trying to save him. They had to wrestle him to the ground, spraying him with a fire extinguisher. Jermaine later recalled that he thought at first that Michael had been assassinated by some crazed fan.

Michael defied the men wanting to slip him out the back exit of the theater. Although in pain, he still had enough media savvy to demand that he be taken out the front. He wanted the medics to let him keep his sequined glove on. A video of him on a stretcher covered with blankets, his head bandaged and taped, but with the gloved hand protruding from the wrappings, was shown on television broadcasts around the world.

With dome lights flashing, Michael, with Miko at his side, was rushed to Cedars Sinai Medical Center.

"Michael Jackson was no brave soul," one of the ambulance drivers later told the press. "He screamed all the way like a pig at castration time. I thought he was a complete sissy. I'd served in Vietnam and had seen patients with missing arms and legs, with their guts split open, bravely enduring their death. From Jackson, we got screams loud enough to curdle blood. Forget about any macho image for that boy. The kid is a piece of lavender-colored cotton candy."

Inside the hospital, Michael was well enough to take charge, refusing to wear the standard open-at-the-back green gown. "He felt it would expose his ass," a nurse said, "and he absolutely wouldn't put it on. We found another gown for him without the opening. He also didn't like the color of the first gown, calling it a 'pissy green.' He told us he had to have a turquoise blue gown instead. He also refused a doctor who wanted to examine his entire body for any stray burns. Jackson was insistent that no one on the hospital staff be allowed to see his penis or ass. I don't know anyone who wanted to see them—I sure didn't."

Michael's plastic surgeon, Dr. Steven Hoefflin, arrived at the hospital and made a decision to transfer his client to the Burn Center of the Brotman Medical Center at Culver City. During the preceding months, Hoefflin had executed three separate nose job operations on Michael.

Later Hoefflin assured the press that his patient was doing fine and, except for some pain, was in no danger at all.

Under Hoefflin's skilled hands, Michael would later undergo laser surgery to burn off the scar tissue and presumably to allow his hair to grow back.

During his first night in the hospital, doctors tried to give him painkillers, but he fought them off, claiming, "I'm opposed to drugs of any type." But as the night lengthened, and his pain from the head burns grew more intense, he called one of the doctors back to administer those painkillers. Regrettably, Michael's decision to take the painkillers led to his becoming hooked on what Jacqueline Susann called "dolls" in her best-selling novel, *Valley of the Dolls*.

As Michael's most loyal fans maintained an all-night vigil outside his hospital, thousands of calls came in from around the world. Liza Minnelli, Diana Ross. Even Jackie Onassis, soon to be his editor, called to wish him well.

A special delivery arrived from President Ronald Reagan, dated February 1, 1984. "I was pleased to learn that you were not seriously hurt in your recent accident. I know from experience that these things can happen on the set—no matter how much caution is exercised."

Following the accident, Michael threatened "to destroy Pepsi-Cola." A colleague told attorney John Branca, "If you play this right, your client will end up owning Pepsi."

When Michael first watched the tape of his hair catching on fire, he claimed, "They wanted to turn me into a human torch. I could have been disfigured for life, my career ruined. Pepsi will pay for this! When my fans watch this video, they'll never drink another bottle of Pepsi again!"

"But Michael you can't release that video of you on fire," Branca protested. "It's grotesque. Your fans would be horrified."

"I want revenge!" Michael shouted at his lawyer.

In the days ahead, Branca prevailed upon Michael to drop his plans to release the video with "the halo of fire." The version that was eventually released to the Associated Press was a short version that was greatly blurred.

Fearing Michael might sue, lawyers at Pepsi worked overtime to investigate the accident, They concluded that Michael might have caused the accident himself by dressing his hair with a very flammable oil. This line of reasoning, more than anything else, enraged Michael, who swore he wore only natural products on his hair.

Michael threatened Pepsi with a lawsuit. When executives offered to settle for half a million dollars, Michael sent word, "I don't come that cheap."

After many negotiations, Pepsi finally agreed to give Michael $1.5 million in damages. That money came in addition to the most expensive celebrity contract in the history of advertising. For making the two commercials, Michael got $5 million. The commercials were so successful that they sent shock waves through Coca-Cola, the market leader. Privately, an official at Coca-Cola conceded that, "It was because of Michael Jackson that we agreed to come up with a new formula after nearly a century of towering success."

Less than ten days after Michael's release from the Burn Center, as a means of celebrating the ever-growing success of the album *Thriller*, CBS sent out invitations printed on white gloves to a $300,000 bash at the Museum of Natural History in New York The coveted ticket didn't quite equal the prestige of Truman Capote's black-and-white ball at the Plaza Hotel, but for *tout* New York, the party was the talk of the town.

More than 1,600 guests arrived, the men looking smart in designer tuxedos and the women in the latest couture. Michael showed up, most of his face concealed under a midnight black fedora, wearing a pair of jeans that contrasted with a commodore jacket that had more braid than that of the former dictator of the Dominican Republic, Rafael Trujillo.

Michael made a dazzling entrance, his recent burns concealed by a wig-maker's toupée which had cost $5,000 and was made with human hair that matched Michael's own.

Walter Yetnikoff had begged Michael to sing for the occasion, but he arrogantly refused. Instead of a song, Yetnikoff read a congratulatory telegram signed by both President Reagan and his wife Nancy. Michael did stand up to accept the latest edition of the *Guinness Book of World Records*, listing him as the hottest selling solo artist in the history of music.

Once again, Michael's "date" was Brooke Shields, all six feet one inch of her.

The black-and-white duo met, among dozens of other luminaries, Donald and Ivana Trump. "For more than five minutes, The Donald and Jacko stood talking to each other," said Barry Evanston, who'd attended the party as a security guard. "I think each of them was trying to figure out how they could use the other one—in other words, The Donald was wondering how much money he might one day make off Jacko, and The Gloved One was trying to figure out how he could get The Donald to part with some of his dough. It was a friendship made in a Heaven where The Jacko/Donald yellow brick road was paved with gold bars."

Michael found Trump, one of the world's richest men, debonair, extravagant, and cocky. The billionaire real estate developer was also smart, funny, and lived an extravagant lifestyle. Before Michael and Trump parted for the evening, he made a statement that startled Michael: "Let's face it, you and I are media fodder. You know, it really doesn't matter what the press writes about you as long as you've got a young and beautiful piece of ass."

At the party, Michael approached Calvin Klein, whom he'd known from his Studio 54 days, accompanied by Klein's favorite model, Brooke. "Calvin," Michael said, "I've got on a pair of your jeans. Unlike Brooke here, there *is* something that comes between me and my Calvins."

Brooke appeared delighted that she didn't have to share the evening with Emmanuel Lewis, who had stayed in Hollywood to film a segment of the TV sitcom, *Webster*.

As the evening progressed, she moved, with Michael to a private party, accessible only to the most important of the VIPs at the event, being held in Michael's honor within an inner sanctum of the museum.

There, her hopes were dashed when Brooke encountered Michael's other "date" for the night. Looking adorable in a custom-made tuxedo, an eight-year-old Sean Lennon rushed toward Michael for a big hug. Brooke looked around but found no Yoko Ono. Instead, young Sean was being protected by a bodyguard who looked like one of Al Capone's henchmen. Lewis would, in time, fade into history as the son of the slain John Lennon evolved into the role of Michael's new special friend.

"It's all too obvious," Brooke reportedly told Ivana Trump. "Michael prefers the company of young boys to me."

Bombshell Brooke, circa 1998

Ivana looked the statuesque Brooke up and down and suggested that, "You should get a real man, honey. I know at least eighteen at this party that would give their right nut to date you."

"Thanks, but no thanks," Brooke said.

Since the assassination of John Lennon on December 8, 1980 at 10:50pm in New York City, Michael had privately expressed a secret wish. "Some day I hope to become the second father to Sean."

In the months ahead, Michael's wish would come true.

A friendship would also emerge between Trump and Michael after that gala night. Associates of the highly artic-ulate Trump often wondered what the two friends talked about, as they seemed to have so little in common. But Trump often bragged about his close friendship with Michael, although intimates in both camps wondered if that were really true.

As the 80s rolled on, Michael and Trump called each other occasionally. Despite the fact that Trump was one of the richest and most publicized men on the planet, Michael felt no embarrassment about breaking appointments with him at the last minute. "Just call Donald and tell him I have a headache," Michael would order a staff member on more than one occasion.

"If Michael could stand up Jackie Onassis, why not Trump?" David Gessler, who once worked for Trump, said. At first, Trump would respond with fury, but always seemed to forgive Michael for his rudeness.

In 1990 Trump showed the world that he could get Michael to fly into Atlantic City to open his new Taj Mahal Casino.

The paparazzi delighted in the photo ops at this lavish event. Michael showed up with a "special friend" who was quickly hustled upstairs out of camera view. After posing for pictures, Michael retreated to the lavish $12,000-a-night Alexander the Great penthouse suite on the 50th floor. Of course, the most expensive suite in Atlantic City came compliments of Trump himself. He knew what a small price that was to pay for the publicity Michael's appearance would generate for him.

Throughout their long relationship, Trump was always protective of Michael, even granting him "a secure address," protected from the press and paparazzi, when he housed him at New York's Plaza Hotel during the child molestation scandal of 1993.

And when Michael went on trial in 2005 on child molestation charges, Trump defended him during an interview with Larry King. "He's lived in Trump Tower, and I know him very well. And I knew what was happening with Michael Jackson. You know what was happening? Absolutely nothing. I had many people that worked for me in the building, and believe me, they would tell me if anything was wrong. I'm going to stick up for him, because nobody else is. I don't believe the molestation charges filed against Michael."

As late as the summer of 2005, when news about Michael's scandals had spread around the world, Trump realized that he'd be a sell-out in Las Vegas. He offered Michael a long-term contract for a series of ongoing performances, and the establishment of a personal headquarters for him in Las Vegas, evocative of deals made by Wayne Newton and Celine Dion.

Trump's Las Vegas partners, Phil Ruffin and Jack Wishna, courted Michael aggressively, offering terms for performances at the New Frontier Hotel and Casino. Wishna warned that if Michael signed on with them, "There will be moral clauses in the contract." He predicted that Michael would draw more than the $80 million Dion grossed in 2004.

On his next trip to New York after the CBS party, Michael checked into the Helmsley Palace. He paid $2,000 a night for a triplex which only CEOs, oil sheiks, and A-list movie starts rented. Efforts were made not to alert the press that he was in New York.

Hoping not to be recognized on the street, he adopted various disguises. At a Kool and the Gang concert at Radio City Music Hall, he was spotted wearing a beard and a bushy Afro. His date was Tatum O'Neal, which came as a surprise to his fans, since earlier, he had dropped her.

During that trip, a staff writer for *The New York Daily News* spotted Michael shopping on Fifth Avenue dressed as a woman. Outfitted in a chic woman's pants suit, he wore false eyelashes, heavy coatings of pancake make-up, scarlet red lipstick, and mascara.

Soon after, Michael arrived in a chauffered stretch limo at a Manhattan recording studio. There, he offered Mick Jagger a limp handshake before their rehearsal for a duet, "State of Shock," which had been selected as the first single within the *Victory* album.

When the idea of their duet had first been proposed to him, Jagger—envious of Michael's success—had refused the offer of recording with him. "You've got your family—you don't need me. Ask Jermaine to record with you." But eventually, Jagger succumbed to Michael's whiny pleas and agreed to make the record at the A & R Studio.

"State of Shock" would go on to become a hit, the only really successful song from the lackluster *Victory* album. But neither artist left the studio that day with anything good to say about the other.

"Froth on the beer," Jagger told his friends. "The kid's a lightweight, as limp as his handshake and as boring as a pussy that's already been worked over ten times."

Two days later, when Michael heard the recording, he flew into a rage, claiming that "it's so bad it's unreleasable. I'm good. Mick's awful. He can't sing. I don't get it. How could someone with absolutely no talent become a star? Look at his record sales and compare them with mine." Actually, upon its release, "State of Shock" boosted Jagger's career, propelling him farther along on his road to independence from his fellow stoned Stones.

Partly because of Michael's phenomenal success, Jagger became obsessed with him, grasping every detail he could learn both about his private life and his financial deals. Mainly, he wanted to know how many records he sold. Arthur Collins, an executive at Atlantic Records, remembered Jagger storming into his office, demanding to know, for example, how many records Michael had sold in France.

Meanwhile, from her digs at Princeton University, where she was enrolled as a student, Brooke was bubbling with enraged jealousy. Michael had not called her, and it was only through the tabloids that she learned that Michael was in New York. Even worse, instead of selecting her as his date for the Kool and the Gang Concert, he had invited Tatum instead.

As it turned out, Brooke and The Donald weren't the only celebrities who wanted to pose for photographs with Michael. About this time, an invitation arrived from the Reagans, summoning Michael to the White House.

Brooke had a motive for calling Michael. She wanted to be his "date" for his meeting with the Reagans. When Brooke finally got through to him, and learned about his invitation to the White House, she proposed that she accompany him to Washington.

Michael adamantly refused, putting down the phone.

The story behind the story about why Michael had been invited to meet the Reagans was revealed years later.

The invitation to the White House had not originated from the Reagans, but had come about through Elizabeth Dole, the homophobic Secretary of Transportation and the wife of failed presidential candidate Robert Dole, who ran a lackluster campaign against Bill Clinton in 1996 before becoming a spokesman for Viagra.

Dole had called Michael's attorney, John Branca, asking permission to use "Beat It" as background music for a thirty-second TV commercial aimed against drunk driving. When Branca informed Michael of this, he flatly refused. But upon reconsideration, he granted permission, "But only if I'm invited to the White House to receive an award."

When Branca conveyed Michael's request to Dole, she said that she thought the award ceremony could be arranged.

To White House advisors, Dole suggested that Michael receive some kind of humanitarian award, as a means of thanking him for his role in showing young people how successful a life could be if it was "free from alcohol and drug abuse." Later revelations about Michael's own drug and alcohol abuse would make a mockery of this award.

At least one official at the Reagan White House bitterly opposed the idea of an award for Michael. That official would later become one of the most powerful men in America.

In 2005, long after Michael's presidential citation, researchers found several memos from a Reagan White House lawyer, John Roberts. Yes, *the* John Roberts who now presides over the U.S. Supreme Court. In his memo, he protested the idea of granting an award to Michael, stating that it would be demeaning to the President. "If one wants the youth of America and the world sashaying around in garish sequined costumes, hair dripping with pomade, body shot full of female hormones to prevent voice change, mono-gloved, well, then I suppose 'Michael'—as he is affectionately known in the trade—

is in fact a good example. Quite apart from the problem of appearing to endorse Jackson's androgynous lifestyle, a Presidential award would be perceived as a shallow effort by the President to share in the constant publicity surrounding Jackson."

Dole managed to short-circuit objections from Roberts by appealing directly to the more star-struck Nancy, who approved the granting of a citation for Michael. She believed that his appearance would benefit her "Just Say No to Drugs" campaign. Consequently, the path was officially cleared for Michael's arrival in Washington for the presentation, which was scheduled for May 14, 1984.

In preparation for his upcoming visit to Washington, Michael ordered several dozen military-style costumes, and spent many hours in his hotel suite trying them on, rejecting one after another.

In grand style, like a visiting head of state, Michael arrived at the White House in the first of three black limos. The other two contained members of his entourage.

Holding Nancy's hand, Ronald Reagan stepped onto a stage on the South Lawn of the White House to greet Michael. "Well, isn't this a 'Thriller.' Welcome to our eight-star hotel," President Reagan said. Reagan often called 1600 Pennsylvania Avenue by that name because of the White House's army of butlers, maids, and cooks. Shaking Michael's hand, the ungloved one, he said, "Nancy and I haven't seen this many people since we left China." He was referring to the hundreds of Michael's fans amassed at the gates to the White House. "Just think, you all came to see me! No, I know why you're here—to see one of the most talented, most popular, and most exciting superstars in the music world today."

Nancy stood a few feet from Michael and the President. "Doesn't he know to remove his sunglasses?" she asked in a loud whisper to two guards standing nearby. "You don't greet the President of the United States wearing sunglasses." A sudden thought occurred to her. "I bet he's had an eyelift."

Reagan read from prepared remarks actually written by Norman Winter, Michael's publicist.

Ronald, the King of Pop, and the former Nancy Davis

195

"At this stage of his career, when it would seem he's achieved everything a musical performer could hope for, Michael Jackson is taking the time to help lead the fight against alcohol and drug abuse." At the end of his brief speech, Reagan presented Michael with a hastily made plaque awarded for "your humanitarian efforts."

Michael thanked the President and told him how honored he was. Suddenly, he realized he'd ignored Nancy. In a whisper, he added, "Oh, *and* Mrs. Reagan too." Nancy beamed.

After accepting the award, Michael raised his white gloved hand to the fans outside the gates. The glove had been designed by Bill Whitten. It had taken 45 hours to sew on 1,500 round Viennese crystal rhinestones. The fans responded by screaming WE WANT MICHAEL.

After waving to the crowd, the President and Mrs. Reagan escorted Michael through the Rose Garden to the Oval Office. Reagan had to excuse himself to answer an urgent call in another room. Michael and Nancy sat together for a brief chat, even though there were several other people in the office, including members of Michael's entourage. Secretaries and other members of the White House had virtually deserted their posts that day to get a look at Michael. Phones went unanswered.

Nancy offered Michael a chocolate chip cookie, which he refused. "They are Ronnie's favorite. I keep them in every room of the White House."

Holding Michael's hand, Nancy told him she admired his bugle-beaded Sergeant Pepper jacket, though she had far too much taste to truly like it. She'd later tell friends that Michael looked like some potentate from a banana republic. He wore a sequined gold sash with sequined gold epaulets, a vision in electric blue.

He returned the compliment, admiring her outfit, which was a white, perfectly tailored, and endlessly chic Adolfo-designed suit.

"It's hard to know how to dress as First Lady," she confided. "If you dress like a low-paid soldier's wife, you're Mamie Eisenhower. The press calls you dowdy. If you don't smile enough, like Pat Nixon and Rosalynn Carter, you're a steel magnolia. If you dress up a lot, you're an Imperial Queen Bee. Take a political stance and you're labeled a control freak bitch. Only this morning, a paper in Washington reminded me that I'm not Eleanor Roosevelt and pointed out that I

MJ with Nancy Reagan

196

don't have Jackie Kennedy's beauty—or her style. That's not all. The article said that all my movies were bad."

"I didn't know you made movies before coming to the White House," Michael said.

"My movies weren't as good as Ronnie's," she said.

"He made movies too?" Michael asked in astonishment. "You and the President were in movies? I'm amazed this has been kept secret."

"Neither of us were as big a star as Ronnie's first wife. Jane Wyman. Oscar winner."

"The President was married before? Is his wife dead?"

"She's very much alive from what I hear," Nancy said.

"I didn't know a divorced man could become the President of the United States."

"Ronnie did."

"I'm a Jehovah's Witness," he said. "We don't believe in divorce."

"You're against Christmas too," Nancy said, "or so I heard. But don't quote me. Ronnie and I don't want to offend any religious groups. We need all the support we can get."

"I hear your son is a ballet dancer," Michael said. "I admire that. You don't expect the son of Ronald Reagan to be a ballet dancer and take all the heat from the press."

"We're proud of him," Nancy said. "You forget: We were performers too."

Michael and his entourage were escorted out of the room, and Nancy waited behind to join her husband.

Trailing Michael at the White House reception was a handsome young man, who appeared to be Michael's "date" for the event. "He looks very young," Nancy was heard to say. "A Billy Budd type. I was surprised that Michael didn't introduce us."

"He is Michael's personal assistant," Winter said.

"Oh, I know of such things," she said. "I should, after all those years in Hollywood. At any rate, the boy is certainly good looking, whoever he is."

Arriving at the Diplomatic Reception Room, Michael was horrified to see about eighty adults assembled there to greet him. He turned and fled to the privacy of the bathroom off the White House Library where a future president, Bill Clinton, would conduct a dalliance or two.

Chief Justice of the U.S. Supreme Court, John Roberts

Frank DiLeo, Michael's manager, ran after him, but the door had been locked.

"I won't come out until there are children here—not adults!" Michael threatened. "I was told I'd be greeted by children."

At this point, Nancy had heard about the commotion and was summoned. But Michael refused to open the bathroom door, even to the First Lady in her own house. Learning of his demands, she ordered the Secret Service to round up all the children he could find on short notice. "Even if you have to grab some toddlers waiting outside the gates."

The mysterious young man appeared and called out through the door to Michael. Michael opened the door just enough to let his special friend in before slamming it shut and bolting it again.

Within less than ten minutes, the men of the Secret Service had assembled nearly twenty children and had ushered all adults from the room.

When DiLeo told Michael that the children were waiting, he slowly emerged from the bathroom, followed by his young friend.

Along with Mr. and Mrs. Reagan, Michael greeted the children. Then, Nancy invited Michael into the Roosevelt Room to meet top White House aides and their families.

"Will there be children?" Michael asked Nancy.

"Yes, some."

At the end of the session, Michael was escorted to a waiting limousine. Nancy turned to two of her guards. In front of witnesses, she asked, "Is it true? Did he undergo a sex change? I think he did. And that mysterious young man. What about him?"

No one ventured an answer.

"I hope the kid is legal," she said, before heading to her bedroom to change. "We don't want any scandals coming from this White House."

As she was leaving, she turned to address her staff one more time. "The Duchess of Windsor once said that no one can be too thin. I'm pretty thin. But that Jackson boy, he must weigh only ninety-five pounds. That's not only dangerous, but makes one look cadaverous."

She was almost right. Michael's weight had dropped to 102 pounds, which his doctors defined as anorexic. On some days, it was reported that Michael existed on only one carrot and a dozen snow peas.

The following day, the Kremlin, reacting to Michael's visit to the White House, banned all of his music, especially the album *Thriller*, from the Soviet Union. Michael was attacked as "a singer who sold his black soul for white profit." In a statement, Soviet authorities claimed that Michael was serving the Reagan administration by diverting the American public's mind away from its real problems.

After the glories of Washington, back in Encino trouble was brewing within America's so-called "most perfect African-American family." Since 1978, Papa Joe had co-managed the Jackson brothers, assisted by the management team of Ron Weisner and Fred DeMann.

But as the months dragged on, the business relationship inevitably soured, Joe accusing the managers of "stealing from my boys." He made the accusation but offered no proof. Of course, those reckless charges were vehemently denied by Weisner and DeMann.

Michael's other brothers had always believed, with a definite resentment, that their managers were devoting most of their time to Michael. So when Michael became upset with DeMann and Weisner and fired them, his other brothers dismissed the management team as well. At this point, Michael more or less had already turned over management of his career to Frank DiLeo and John Branca.

Before agreeing on new managers, Michael had even had a secret meeting with the flamboyant Colonel Tom Parker, the money collector for Elvis Presley. The meeting ended badly after Parker looked Jackson up and down and appeared skeptical about the star's appearance, voice, and manner. Parker later told some of his cronies, "I don't manage faggot nigger boys."

Michael's heroine, Diana Ross, also pushed to manage his career, hoping to sign him with her own newly formed company, R.T.C. Management. Privately, Michael was horrified at the suggestion, feeling that she hadn't been that brilliant at managing her own career. Too cowardly to turn her down, he went for weeks refusing her phone calls until she finally gave up.

Joe went public with his charges, crying "leeches" to the press and accusing DeMann and Weisner of "trying to break up the brothers." In a startling statement, he claimed, "There was a time when I felt I needed white help in dealing with the brass at CBS."

DeMann claimed that Joe did not enjoy "a good relationship with anyone whose skin is not black."

Joe countered that he was not a racist. "I wouldn't have hired a lot of people that aren't black to work for me if I was a racist."

Michael was horrified that Joe was raising the race card. He issued a statement claiming, "To hear him talk like that turns my stomach. I don't know where he gets that from. I happen to be color blind. I don't hire color. I hire competence. The individual can be of any race or creed as long as I get the best performance. Racism is not my motto."

During their press war with their white management team, the other brothers met in private and decided not to renew their managerial contract with Papa Joe as well.

Given the boot by his sons, Joe forged ahead anyway, hoping to interest all his sons, including Michael, in "starring in the largest grossing tour of all time." Knowing that Michael would be a key to the success of the tour, Joe wisely asked Katherine to be co-promoter with him. "If anybody can persuade Michael to tour with his brothers, it's Katherine," Joe was quoted as saying.

Even though he'd been fired, Joe told the press, "I was there when it started, and I'll be there when it ends." To prove to the world that he was still in charge of his boys, and to make some much-needed money, he recovered quickly from his disappointment about being booted, and concocted the idea of another nationwide tour for his sons, including the hard-to-pin-down Michael.

As Joe could have predicted, Michael was the lone holdout, the other brothers agreeing to go on the road again with their parents as managers. Eventually, however, thanks partly to Katherine's careful persuasion, Michael finally agreed to join his brothers on the road.

The tour would be sponsored by Pepsi Cola. In return, the Jacksons had agreed to film two commercials, which eventually led to the disastrous hair-burning incident and the feud that resulted between Michael and the soft-drink company. But in spite of that, Pepsi was contractually obligated to sponsor the "Victory Tour."

Joe startled his entire family, especially Michael, when he announced that he was negotiating with Don King to manage the tour.

The flamboyant, Don King, who often wore a white fur coat, diamond rings, and a gold necklace, looked like the biggest pimp in Harlem. The silver-tongued promoter was ridiculed for his hair sticks that stood straight up, looking as if he'd been electrocuted. But he was even more famous for his spectacular boxing promotions, including Muhammad Ali's "Thrilla in Manila" and the Sugar Ray Leonard—Robert Duran fight that seemingly half the world watched.

Michael was fully aware of King's racy background. The promoter got his start in the illegal numbers business in Cleveland. In December of 1954, he shot and killed one of three men trying to rob one of his gambling houses. He didn't go to jail, as prosecutors determined that the death was a "justifiable homicide."

Trouble, also in Cleveland, came again for King. He beat a man to death twelve years later. He told police the victim owed him money. King was convicted of second-degree murder, but the trial judge reduced the conviction to manslaughter. King served only 3½ years of the sentence before he received a pardon from James Rhodes, the governor of Ohio at the time.

On November 30, 1983, King called a press conference in New York at Tavern on the Green, the highlight of which was a 15-minute documentary congratulating himself for his achievements. A Washington reporter, Cody

Shearer, labeled the event "media history's most abominable press conference."

Michael arrived cuddling Emmanuel Lewis in his arms, to the shock of some members of the press. "What's going on here?" one of them asked in a whisper so loud it could be heard throughout the room. "Something queer this way comes." He was told to shut up.

Even though King referred to Michael as "the golden voice of song," Golden Throat refused to take questions, after introducing his mother and his sisters. After that, he sat glaring at King, not even disguising his hostility.

King did most of the talking, as the brothers followed Michael's example and concealed part of their faces behind sunglasses. The *Victory* album was announced for release on July 2, 1984. Despite its inaugural hype, many fans were disappointed. The brothers performed songs individually and didn't follow their already proven success of having Michael or even Jermaine sing the lead vocals. Amazingly, the "Victory" tour would not include one single song from the album of the same name. For the tour, the errant brother, Jermaine, rejoined the brood. The tour could have been billed as the "Jackson Six."

Jermaine had sought his release from Motown after his career as a solo artist had gone bust. "Being the son-in-law of Motown's president was not a long-range missile launch for Jermaine," Marvin Gaye said. "Berry Gordy Jr. was glad to see Jermaine go."

Later, in his New York hotel suite, Michael watched the videotape of the press conference, and he was disgusted. Summoning his brothers to his suite, he announced, "I'm the biggest star in the world! There's no way I'm gonna be an opening act for this sleazeball," referring to King of course. "What a creep!"

After the press conference, Michael became increasingly furious at King, issuing instructions to Branca to define, as noted below, the terms of their dealings with King:

A. King may not communicate with anyone on Michael's behalf without prior permission.
B. All monies will be collected by Michael's representatives and not by King.
C. King may not approach any promoters, sponsors, or other people on Michael's behalf.
D. King may not hire any personnel or local promoters, book halls, or, for that matter, do anything at all without Michael's prior approval.

Later King was fired as the tour promoter and replaced by Chuck Sullivan, who caused more problems. Because of the terms within his contract, King stayed with the tour but in a figurehead capacity.

In an interview with *Playboy* in 1988, King discussed his frustrations promoting the "Victory" tour. "The suits went after me," he claimed. "They did their usual thing. They told Michael, 'You know, a black guy can't do this. And King is a racketeer. Michael, your image is at stake here.' His image? What Michael's got to understand is that *Michael's a nigger*! It don't matter how great he can sing and dance; I don't care that he can prance; he's one of the greatest mega-stars in the world, but he's still going to be a *nigger* mega-star."

King found it "ludicrous" how Papa Joe was pushed aside, not only by Michael but by all his sons. "There is no way Michael Jackson should be as big as he is and treat his family the way that he does. No way! *Nothing* can justify that. He feels that his father did him wrong. There can't be *so* much wrong his father did him—Michael, after all, is the biggest star there ever was in the music business. His father may have done *some* wrong, but he also had to do a whole lot of right. Whatever it was, Michael could reprimand, chastise, teach—'If you did it wrong, Dad, don't do it wrong no more.'"

King concluded his interview by claiming that, "I see that Michael has nobody black around him—*nobody*. So therefore, he is, in effect, a pseudo-white."

When Chuck Sullivan, owner of the New England Patriots of the National Football League, signed on as a promoter, he had harsh demands for Michael's fans. Each fan would have to order a total of four tickets and would have to send in a mail order for $120. There would be no guarantee of a specific date, a certain seat, or even a ticket itself.

This caused an outcry. Even though these high ticket prices had not been Michael's idea, he was the one accused of "greed."

"We thought you were kind and loving to your fans," wrote Betty Lou Garghrin of Long Island. "But I think you're just a bloodsucker." Michael was stunned, even deeply hurt by such criticism, blaming Sullivan for such bad press and disastrous public relationships.

Sullivan and King were an ill-fated duo at the negotiating table. The bombastic boxing promoter labeled Chuck Sullivan "Charlie the Tuna." Sullivan lost $20 million as promoter of the tour, and "Victory" was not a victory for him. His company, Stadium Management Co., was forced into bankruptcy, and the Sullivans eventually had to sell the New England Patriots.

Even though Michael "fought against it," and in spite of his reservations, he threw himself into rehearsals and the actual stage appearances, "giving each performance everything I could." Before setting out, Michael demanded yet a third rhinoplasty from Dr. Hoefflin. "The first two didn't really do the job—the nose must be even thinner," were his instructions.

The "Victory" tour by the Jackson brothers was one of the pivotal events of 1984, a year that saw Vanessa Williams resign as Miss America, the death of jazz great Count Basie, and the birth of *The Cosby Show* on NBC.

Between July and December of 1984, The Jacksons bombarded America, with more drama transpiring off stage than on. Fans suspected that it would be the last time Michael would ever tour with his brothers. When the tour ended in Los Angeles, Michael proved them right by proclaiming, "This is our final farewell tour as a family." In fact, he had wanted to call it "The Farewell Tour," but he'd been voted down by his brothers.

The "Victory" tour opened in the heart of America: Kansas City. Despite bouts of depression, Michael found amusements wherever he could. He laughed hysterically when a fully clothed Frank DiLeo lost his balance and fell into a hotel's swimming pool in Kansas. In Washington, DC, Michael grabbed a handful of money from DiLeo's pockets and tossed the hundred-or-so bills to screaming fans below, causing a riot. It was well known that DiLeo usually carried a wad of cash to handle "MJ emergencies," as he put it.

Michael chased DiLeo around a hotel suite with his boa constrictor, Muscles. Terrified of snakes, DiLeo pulled a gun and threatened to shoot the monster, even though the reptile was harmless. When boredom set in, Michael reverted to the old tricks of his childhood. He would take a bucket of water and run out to the edge of the atrium, tossing the liquid down onto people dining below, especially at Hyatt hotels.

Tensions between the brothers were rampant. Michael always got the best accommodations and the best transportation. And whereas the brothers flew commercial airlines, Michael traveled by private jet, including in one instance, a luxurious craft belonging to Meshulam Riklis, the zillionaire husband of Pia Zadora.

The darkest point of the tour came in August, 1984, when the *Knoxville News-Sentinel* published anonymous letters threatening to kill Michael and assassinate many of his fans. Three concerts had been scheduled in that Tennessee city, but because of those letters, they were abruptly canceled. Hours later, the telecast of the Olympics was interrupted to announce that the "tour was back on again." Under tightened security, the concerts were presented without incident. Michael was delivered to Neyland Stadium in an armored Wells Fargo truck.

Rumors that Michael was gay rose to a crescendo during the "Victory" tour. There was even wide speculation that Michael had been castrated to maintain his falsetto voice. In a new CBS comedy album, Eddie Murphy had a line, claiming—and accurately so—that Michael was "not the most masculine guy in the world."

Joan Rivers was at the peak of her fame in 1984, when she often hosted the Johnny Carson show. Her two favorite subjects of ridicule were an overweight Elizabeth Taylor and Michael's sex life. "Is Michael Jackson gay?" she'd ask her audiences. "*Please,* he's as queer as a three-dollar bill." One night she claimed, "Michael Jackson is gay. He makes Liberace look like a Green Beret." Her audiences burst into hysterical laughter.

Entering the fray was Louis Farrakhan, "National Representative of the Honorable Elijah Muhammad and The Nation of Islam," who did not find anything amusing about Michael. He urged his devoted followers "not to practice Michael Jackson's sissified ways." Many of Farrakhan's disciples felt that Michael was transgendered and was deliberately blurring the dividing line between male and female.

One black writer claimed: "The white man has always feared the black man's superior sexual power. As we know, black men are superior to white men in both the bedroom and in the boardroom. Along comes Michael Jackson portraying the black man as a faggot! He has set back African-American advancement twenty years. He is trying to take our power from us. Slave owners in the 19th century used to castrate their unruly black male slaves. By castrating himself and singing in falsetto, Jackson is playing into whitie's game plan for us: To rob us of our manhood and remove the black sexual threat."

Of course, charges that Michael Jackson had been castrated are ridiculous, as photographs taken by Santa Barbara police authorities—today resting in a bank vault—can prove.

The outspoken Joan Rivers continued her attack. One night she asked her audience, "Ever wonder what happened to Michael Jackson's other glove? It's in Boy George's pocket!"

Rivers was reacting to a story that had run in a late summer edition of the *National Enquirer*. In bold headlines, Michael and Boy George, the self-admitted "queen" and lead singer of Culture Club, were alleged to be immersed in a hot affair. In less bold headlines, Michael was also rumored to be having simultaneous affairs with Wham's George Michael and Queen's Freddie Mercury. It appears, however, that he was having affairs with none of those homosexual entertainers.

Michael was so upset by the headlines linking him with Boy George that he called his publicist, Norman Winter, and burst into tears. The publicist had seen stacks of mail pouring in from young men and girls from around the world.

A typical letter from an impressionable young girl read: "Michael, Michael, tell me it's not true. You and Boy George! How could you! That's disgusting! My great dream has been to grow up and marry you and have many beautiful children with you. Now the news about you and that horrible creature from Britain has destroyed my dream. I want to die!"

Another letter from a young gay man read: "Michael, I am so happy to learn you are gay. My greatest dream is to fuck you all night. My former lover said that I'm the best top he has ever had. I can go for hours. I know from the faggy way you move around the stage that you are a bottom. My goal in life is to become the dream-man of all bottoms and all size queens. I'm enclosing a nude picture of myself so you can see how impressive I am. It's all yours, baby. I'm ready and willing and able to send you to Paradise!"

In the middle of the "Victory" tour, and in a startling development in September of 1984, Michael, enraged and fed up with the gay rumors, called a press conference. But he didn't show up. However, his manager, macho, cigar-smoking Frank DiLeo did. He shocked reporters when he read from a two-page document.

For some time now, I have been searching my conscience as to whether or not I should publicly react to the many falsehoods that have been spread about me. I have decided to make this statement based on the injustice of these allegations and the far-reaching trauma those who feel close to me are suffering.

I feel very fortunate to have been blessed with recognition for my efforts. This recognition also brings with it a responsibility to one's admirers throughout the world. Performers should always serve as role models who set an example for young people. It saddens me that many may actually believe the present flurry of false accusations:

No! I've never taken hormones to maintain my high voice.

No! I've never had cosmetic surgery on my eyes.

Yes! One day in the future I plan to get married and have a family.

Any statements to the contrary are simply untrue.

I have advised my attorneys of my willingness to institute legal action and subsequently prosecute all guilty to the fullest extent of the law.

As noted earlier, I love children. We all know that kids are very impressionable and therefore susceptible to such stories. I'm certain that some have already been hurt by this terrible slander. In addition to their admiration, I would like to keep their respect.

While reacting to all these gay rumors, Michael also received some disturbing news from a couple of a more heterosexual nature.

His youngest sister, Janet, had eloped with James DeBarge. She was only eighteen at the time, her groom twenty-one. Michael was adamantly opposed to the marriage and told family and associates that "Janet betrayed me." He never explained just how her marriage had betrayed him.

When she was just sixteen, Janet had met DeBarge, and they'd become close friends. Tall, dark, and handsome, he seemed like an ideal candidate for marriage, except for the fact that each of the Jacksons knew some dark secrets about him. There had been reports of drug and alcohol abuse. Katharine insisted that "the boy is completely wrong for my Janet."

In a touch of irony, the singing DeBarge brothers had been groomed by Motown during the early 80s as heirs to the departed Jackson 5. Originally formed in 1978 and hailing from Grand Rapids, Michigan, the quintet was comprised of four brothers and one sister, "Bunny." Before he married into pop royalty in 1984, DeBarge had recorded such 1980s classics as "Who's Holding Donna Now?" and "All This Love."

In a terrible case of bad judgment, the newlyweds moved into the Jackson's Encino mansion. DeBarge would later call it "The House of Fear." Living with the Jacksons put a severe strain on the marriage, and DeBarge and Papa Joe often engaged in denunciations of each other that sometimes evolved into physical violence. At one point, or so it was rumored, Papa Joe threatened to kill his son-in-law.

When DeBarge was in residence at the Encino house, he reported that "Michael was a sad, lonely figure, wandering around looking for love, which he seems to find only in Bubbles."

Bubbles was not a stripper, as the name suggests, but Michael's pet chimp. As such, he became the most famous—and the most controversial—chimp in the world.

Michael might not have actually found love, but DeBarge reported that during his stay at Hayvenhurst he saw a number of boys coming in and out of Michael's bedroom. These boys, or so the Encino bodyguards reported, ranged in age from nine to fourteen. Michael's excuse to DeBarge was that he was auditioning the boys for future videos. Many of DeBarge's charges were later dismissed as "nonsense" or "fantasies" by loyal members of Michael's camp.

Nonsense or not, DeBarge, along with bodyguards at Neverland, were called to testify against Michael in 1993 when young Jordie Chandler brought charges of child molestation against his former friend.

In anticipation of his trial, when Michael heard that DeBarge was going to testify against him, he was furious. Michael recalled going into the newlyweds' bedroom late one night and slipping under the covers with Janet and DeBarge to discuss deep, personal secrets. He viewed DeBarge going public with those secrets as "a betrayal."

Joan Rivers

As Michael had predicted, his sister's marriage was doomed from the start. There were rumors that they'd had a child together, but this was never confirmed, and there was also much speculation about an abortion.

On January 7, 1985, after a tumultuous marriage, Janet's link to DeBarge was annulled. Over the years she has said little, at least publicly, about her brief, unsuccessful marriage. "You don't have to hold onto the pain to hold onto the memory."

On those nights alone with Janet and DeBarge, Michael would sometimes discuss how painful it was to have the tabloids publish their accusations of homosexuality.

"Michael Jackson made charges of being gay sound like a case of leprosy," said gay activist Kevin Macmillan. "He alienated the entire gay community the way that Tom Cruise would do in years to come. The signal that both Cruise and Jackson gave out was that to be gay was the most scandalous and horrible thing that could happen to a guy. Thanks a lot, fellows."

In contrast to Michael's petulant response to gay charges, his sister, Janet, would handle future gay rumors about herself with far more style and sophistication. Unlike Michael, Janet was far more savvy, knowing how to retain, and not alienate, large segments of her fans.

In 2001, she was asked by a reporter from *Ebony*, "There have been questions about your sexuality. Some have asked if you're gay or bisexual."

"I don't mind people thinking that I'm gay or calling me gay," she said candidly. "People are going to believe whatever they want. Yes, I hang out at gay clubs, but other clubs too. I go where the music is good. I love people regardless of sexual preference, regardless of race. No, I am not bisexual. I have been linked to dancers in our group because we grow close. I grew up in a big family. I love being affectionate. I love intimacy and I am not afraid to show it. We fall asleep in each other's arms. We hug, we kiss, but there is nothing beyond that. Because René and I broke up, it's like people need some sort of drama, some sort of gossip."

She was referring to her long-time Mexican companion, René Elizondo. It has been whispered that René was really her husband. Reporter Joal Ryan once claimed that Rebbie, Janet's older sister, said that Janet and René had "eloped years ago."

René often worked with Janet, co-writing songs for her 1997 release *The Velvet Rope*.

Rebbie's remarks, broadcast over an Atlanta radio station, exploded into a national issue. But a spokesperson issued a quick denial. Janet claimed, "We're not married, only in spirit."

Janet achieved notoriety when the 1993 cover of *Rolling Stone* came out. René is standing behind her covering her bare breasts with his hands. In 1997 she made another startling quote, this time to *Ebony*. "It was René's idea that I get my nipple pierced. I gave him a choice of two areas, and he chose the nipple."

During their thirteen-year relationship, some reporters referred to the duo as "Yin and Yang."

After what could hardly be called a restful interlude at Encino, it was time for Michael to hit the road again with the continuation of the ill-fated "Victory" tour.

In Philadelphia, Michael met Bruce Springsteen, who had come to see "what in hell is this Jacko shit all about?" Michael was awkward and tongue-tied around the American rock and folk singer, who was competing in world markets with rival tours and albums. Springsteen's *Born in the U.S.A.* was a big hit, selling 15 million copies in America alone. The album became one of the best-selling in music history, with seven singles hitting the top ten.

Boy George

Springsteen asked Michael about the recent grosses on *Thriller*.

"I never learned to count that high in school," Michael said. "All I know is that you, me, and Prince have gone to Pop Heaven."

Springsteen and Jackson would meet again in 1985 to record "We Are the World," but the two artists seemed to have little interest in each other.

Sensing an arrogance in Michael that was off-putting, Springsteen gave him some advice which he'd repeat often to other stars. "I believe that the career of an artist can last as long as you look down into your audience and can see yourself, and your audience looks up at you and can see themselves, and as long as those reflections are human, realistic ones." He turned and parted, leaving Michael somewhat bewildered at the words he'd just heard.

Watching Springsteen go on his way, Michael became petulant, even bitchy. "I don't know why they call him The Boss. Personally, I think he's much overrated. He can't dance, and he can't really sing. Off key at best. I'm bigger than The Beatles ever were. Not only that, but I'm much bigger than Elvis Presley. If they called Elvis the King, what about me?"

The stage manager raised an eyebrow and said: "The Queen, perhaps."

The next day he was fired.

The Jacksons' final show at Dodger Stadium in Los Angeles was not a sell-out. DiLeo had to give away hundreds of tickets. In his hotel suite, Michael was screaming in rage. On his final night of the "Victory" tour, right before he went on, he heard that a federal grand jury in New York had indicted Don King on twenty-three counts of income tax evasion. "Couldn't happen to a nicer guy," Michael said.

On stage that historic night of December 9, 1984, Michael stood in front of his brothers and shouted at the audience: "We love you all! It's been a long twenty years since my brothers and I have entertained you together. Love to all." In a gesture of brotherly love, Michael blew pretend kisses at his brothers on stage.

In his autobiography, *Moonwalk*, Michael unrealistically summed up his experiences on the "Victory" tour. "It was a nice feeling," he wrote, "playing with my brothers again. We were all together again." The actual gossip associated with the tour suggested at the time, however, that Michael wasn't even speaking to his brothers during the last weeks of the tour, and that Michael claimed privately that The Jacksons would have been washed up long ago without him.

Another segment of *Moonwalk* repeated a rehearsed, much-repeated response from Michael about the gay issue, a question which had repeatedly been raised during the "Victory" tour.

"I believe in relationships," Michael wrote. "One day I know I'll find the right woman and get married myself. I imagine myself with thirteen children."

When the "Victory" tour ended in Los Angeles, it had played to more than two million fans, grossing $50 million, breaking the $30 million record set by the Rolling Stones in 1981.

The success of the tour spilled over into the *Victory* album, which also sold more than two million copies.

Sean Lennon, son of the slain ex-Beatle, became Michael's new "best bud" in spite of the significant age difference. Sean had been only five years old when John Lennon was assassinated in New York, and the boy was only nine when he began to "hang out" with Michael.

In the wake of her husband's death, Yoko Ono, Sean's mother, ordered 24-hour security guard protection for her offspring, fearing kidnapping or something much worse. Despite her concerns for her children, Yoko seemed willing to entrust her beloved son to Michael, allowing the older entertainer to spend hours or even days and nights at a stretch with Sean.

Many mothers who delivered their young sons to Michael over the years might have been overwhelmed with the magnitude of his stardom, might have been swayed by money, or else might simply have been naïve. This was not the case with Yoko Ono, one of the most sophisticated women in the entertainment business. For most of her life she'd known and befriended homosexuals and was hip to what was going on. Obviously Michael didn't set off any alarm bells within her, or else she would hardly have sanctioned turning Sean over to his care and feeding.

For his part, Michael got to enjoy the company of a handsome and charming young boy. There must have been the added thrill of knowing that Sean was the son of the one Beatle that Michael most admired, considering John far more talented than his former friend, Paul McCartney. "As a musician, John's talent extended to his toenails," Michael told Yoko, who agreed, of course.

Although extremely protective of Sean's health and welfare, Yoko never tried to be a domineering, smothering mother. She prided herself on rearing her son without the normal restraints imposed on one so young. In other words, if Sean wanted to urinate in the back seat of a limousine, he was free to do so without fear of reprimand. Apparently, Yoko took the point of view that limousine covers could always be re-upholstered. Yoko had received death threats against her son, but she felt that because of Michael's heavy security at Neverland, she had nothing to worry about . . . except perhaps Michael himself.

To a journalist from the *St. Louis Post-Dispatch*, Yoko once said, "Every mother worries, but I want Sean to pursue what he wants to as long as it's good for him. I try to avoid a situation where mother and son stick to each other too much. He has many friends, he communicates with many people."

Suddenly, Sean and Michael were seen everywhere, popping up at Broadway shows—only musicals—and other events. The young boy often spent nights in hotel suites with Michael, even weeks at Neverland.

At Neverland, the staff would often hear Sean and Michael playing the song, "Beautiful Boy," which John Lennon had written for his son.

Sean once startled Michael by telling him that for many years he did not know about John's previous life as a Beatle, and he kept no memorabilia or records at The Dakota where they lived in New York. Sean claimed that he learned about his father's musical background when a babysitter showed him a copy of *Yellow Submarine* (1968).

Dark-haired and almond-eyed, Sean was amazingly bright, often making quotations unusual for one so young. In 1983, he said, "Peace is a good thing. So is smoked salmon."

Michael was obviously taken with the boy's Eurasian attractiveness and charm. He often spoke of Sean's "rosebud mouth." The youth did not resemble either Yoko or John Lennon, but had his own distinctive look and features.

The young boy told Michael of his "undying love" for his father. "I can't tell you how many times I walk into a store or mall and hear him singing," Sean said. "I get this really nice feeling, like he's still around. It's almost magical."

Once he showed Michael a photograph taken at his birthday party when he'd turned seven. On the picture, he'd superimposed a picture of John and then had superimposed two large tears on his father's cheeks. "He's crying because he couldn't be at the party too."

As Sean got to know Michael more intimately and to trust him, he admitted that he didn't want to be "just a clone of my father," but an artist in his own right, capable of making his own distinct music. "The whole 'son of John Lennon' thing was dumped on me, and I didn't ask for that. All my father's friends are waiting for me to fail in my dream, figuring I can spend the rest of my life living off the old man's money."

Sean told Michael that he (Michael) and John (his father) "had it easy when it comes to making music. To both of you, writing music and singing is second nature. To me, it's very hard to make music." He asked Michael if he'd teach him "the tricks of the business," and Michael agreed to, although he was far too self-absorbed in his own issues to really do that.

"One day my music will bring people up in the world," Sean said. "Just like your music does."

When Sean was thirteen, Michael cast him in his film, *Moonwalker*.

With Michael, Sean shared some of his deepest fears, mainly of being gunned down as John had been in 1980. One night Sean revealed something that he'd told only his closest friends. "I absolutely believe that my father was killed on orders from the CIA who was bossed around by Ronald Reagan. Revolutionaries like my dad are always historically killed by the American government—all except Castro, and they sure tried hard to get him. The belief that Mark Chapman was some crazy guy who killed my dad for personal reasons is insane—or naïve."

Later, during the 1990s, as child molestation charges against Michael were aired, one New York journalist tried to reach Yoko for her reaction, knowing her own son had spent a lot of time in private with Michael. The reporter wanted to know if Michael had ever been a substitute father for Sean and did Yoko consider the singer a good role model. She had no comment.

In 1993, Sean's relationship made blaring tabloid headlines in Britain. James DeBarge, the former husband of Janet Jackson, made some explosive charges in a taped conversation with a police informant. During the time he'd been married to Janet, he'd slept in a bedroom next to Michael's. He claimed that he'd walked in on Michael and Sean, catching them "together in a sexual way."

"All the boys who visited at the Encino house slept in Michael's bed," DeBarge reportedly said. He admitted to doing some spying on Michael.

Or so it was reported in the press. DeBarge could not be reached to confirm or

Bruce Springsteen

211

deny these reports.

As his young special friends matured, Michael most often lost interest, although with certain boys, such as Macaulay Culkin, a lasting friendship emerged.

The last known encounter between Michael and Sean occurred in 2001 during a reception at Tavern on the Green in New York City's Central Park. The invitation-only gala followed Michael's big 30th anniversary celebration at Madison Square Garden.

A reporter for the British tabloid, *The Sun*, was seated at a table next to Yoko and Sean. He noticed Michael enter the room and head immediately to greet Yoko and her son. Ignoring Yoko for the moment, he turned on Sean with an accusatory tone in his wispy voice. "You never return my calls," Michael charged. "I leave messages for you all the time, and you never call back."

In spite of what appeared to be a rebuff to Michael, Sean has always been respectful of him in the press. "If it wasn't for Michael Jackson, I probably wouldn't make music now," Sean once said. "*Thriller* changed my life completely."

In 1984 Michael stood at the zenith of his career. He was celebrated throughout the world, even in countries that many people had never heard of before. "He was not just the King of Pop, but King of the World," Quincy Jones said.

On a windy day in Los Angeles, when Michael came home again, there was a distinct chill in the air. He sensed something ominous, and he couldn't put his finger on it.

Wherever he went, whatever he did, the world was watching him and judging him. There seemed to be eyes everywhere, as if hidden cameras had been installed in every corner of Hayvenhurst. He once told Diana Ross that he had no dark secrets to hide, and therefore had no fear of the press.

But now, at the age of twenty-six, he had many secrets, none of which he wanted to share with the world, or even with intimate friends.

He could be himself only around children "because they have no masks," he told his mother Katherine. "Adults are filled with lies and deceit. Kids will tell you the truth. You can share your innermost secrets and desires with them."

What Michael didn't know then, but what he surely knows now, is that not all children are alike. It's true that some children will hide your secrets and never tell them to the world. Other kids will splash your innermost desires on the front pages of tabloids. At this early stage of his life, Michael hadn't learned to tell the difference between the two types of young boys he'd select for "special friendships."

Nor had he fully realized that adults have ways of prying secrets, sometimes with manipulative pressure, from the minds of children, revelations that could destroy certain people who engage in dark desires.

He knew that he was too famous to escape the voyeuristic attention of the world, so he decided that, unlike a child, he would wear a mask when he was *out there*—his reference to the world that existed outside the Encino compound. He would conceal his true nature and create a fake persona deliberately intended to deceive. "I want the world to see me not as I am, but as they want me to be," he once told Katharine Hepburn.

"Good luck," Hepburn told him. "I've been doing that for years and getting away with it. I don't really care what anybody writes about me, as long as it's not the truth."

Back at Encino, Michael was leaving the family compound with an unknown blond-haired boy of great beauty, a Tadzio, perhaps no more than twelve. He was going on a shopping expedition to buy the child as many toys as he wanted.

La Toya ran after him. She had an urgent message. "The First Lady of the World is on the phone, and she wants to speak to you," La Toya said.

"You mean, Nancy? I've already been there, accepted that award."

"More famous than Nancy," La Toya said.

"That could be only one person," Michael replied.

Racing back into the house, he nervously picked up the receiver. In a whispery voice, he said, "Hi, this is Michael."

On the other end of the phone, an even more famous whispery voice greeted him. "Michael, you dear. It's been far too long. As they say in the Garment District, have I got a deal for you. This is Jackie Onassis!"

"I think Michael appeals to the child in all of us. He has the quality of innocence that we would all like to obtain or have kept. I think he is one of the finest people to hit this planet, and, in my estimation, he is the true King of Pop, Rock and Soul. I love you Michael."

--Elizabeth Taylor

"When I met him, it was really love at first sight. I think when you get to know Michael, you understand the nature of his charisma. He looks at the world with the innocent eyes of a child."

--Sophia Loren

"Jackie twisted my arm to make me write Moonwalk."

--Michael Jackson on Jackie Kennedy Onassis

"To many people Michael Jackson seems an elusive personality, but to those who work with him, he is not. This talented artist is a sensitive man, warm, funny, and full of insight. Michael's book, Moonwalk, *provides a startling glimpse of the artist at work and the artist in reflection."*

--Jackie Kennedy Onassis

"I expected it to be difficult, and it was. Michael's a perfectionist."

--Colin Chivers, director of the 'Smooth Criminal' video

"I ripped off a couple of solos, and he liked the first one. It was my choice too. He seemed to go on emotion rather than technique, which is how I've always worked."

--Steve Stevens, guitarist for 'Dirty Diana'

Chapter Eight

In 1984, after the "Victory" tour, Michael returned to Encino's Hayvenhurst, which by then had become the best-known celebrity mansion west of Elvis's Graceland. From there, he would launch friendships with three of the most celebrated people of the 20th century: Jackie Onassis, Marlon Brando, and Elizabeth Taylor, while still hanging onto friendships with such media events as Katharine Hepburn, Liza Minnelli, and Jane Fonda, and such minor celebs as the much younger Sean Lennon.

When Michael accepted the call from Jacqueline Onassis, she was working for Doubleday in New York and was at the time the most celebrated editor in publishing. Her boss had given her a budget of $300,000 to offer Michael for his memoirs, although in his mid-twenties he was a bit young to be penning an autobiography. One editor at Doubleday told Jackie, "If Michael agrees to this, we should call his memoirs *An Unfinished Life.*"

After exchanging pleasantries about their few previous meetings, Jackie got down to business and pitched the offer of a memoir.

"My life has only begun," he protested.

"There's such a great interest in you—millions of fans around the world—that we at Doubleday wanted to hear your story as you saw your life. The early years. The struggles. The incredible success. What it's done to you."

"If memoirs are such a great idea, then why haven't you written one?" he asked provocatively.

"Doubleday has a standing offer with me of $5 million for my autobiography, but I possess too many secrets. A memoir from me couldn't be honest, and therefore I won't write one."

"I know you must have many secrets—not only your own but the intimate details of so many other famous lives. But what secrets do I have? I'm still a virgin. Never been kissed. At least not on the mouth."

"That's a unique story in itself," she said with a slight sense of mischief.

"Imagine a man living for a quarter of a century and still a virgin. You and my late husband, Jack, had a lot in common.

"Now you're pulling my leg," he said. "I'm told that when you let your hair down, you have a wicked sense of humor."

"If you only knew," she said. "One time at the White House, I was doing this really horrendous impersonation of Lady Bird Johnson. Guess what? In flies Lady Bird herself."

"I'm also told you like gossip."

"I don't deny that."

"Then I think you'd be very disappointed in any memoir I wrote," he said. "I have no gossip to share."

"Perhaps I would be disappointed," she admitted candidly. "But I don't really expect you to tell *everything*. But because you're the biggest star in the world, we at Doubleday want your story."

"I don't know..."

She'd later recall that he seemed so hesitant, yet wavering. "Let me fly to the coast and pitch this idea to you in person. As you know from having met me, I'm very persuasive."

"That you are." He hesitated again, leading her to conclude that he was one of the least articulate men she'd ever encountered.

"I'm not going to debase myself in any book," he warned. "The tabloids already do that for me. Do you know a good libel lawyer?"

"I never sue for libel," she said. "Let the jackals write what they wish. Just tell your story from your heart. Just be Peter Pan. That's all you have to do."

"I'd like that!" He agreed to a meeting in Los Angeles.

"I'm packing my bags," she promised.

After putting down the phone, he was eager to tell family and friends of this remarkable offer he'd just had from Jackie. "I remember every word of the dialogue," he claimed.

Privately he confessed that he had little or no interest in writing a memoir. "As for that $300,000 advance, that's peanuts in the music business," he said. "We count in the millions." He confided to his family that if he agreed to do the memoir, he would have a chance to solidify his friendship with Jackie. "Imagine me, Michael Jackson, born in a bungalow in Gary, and growing up one day to be friends with Jackie Kennedy Onassis. She gave me her private phone number in New York. Imagine that!"

Jackie and her assistant, Shaye Areheart, flew to Los Angeles in the autumn of 1983 to convince Michael to write his autobiography. Their initial meeting was to be a luncheon at Chasen's, a posh Los Angeles restaurant. Jackie and Areheart arrived on time and were kept busy as well-wishers came to their table. In a city known for famous movie stars, Jackie outdazzled all of

216

them—all except Michael. Their meeting was scheduled at one o'clock. By two-thirty, he hadn't shown up, and Jackie and Areheart went ahead and ordered lunch.

Jackie Onassis, hailed as the world's most desirable woman, wasn't used to be being stood up. Initially embarrassed, she decided to forgive Michael. "He's very shy," she told her colleagues. Privately she was enraged.

The woman who'd charmed Charles de Gaulle and Nikita Krushchev didn't give up that easily. She called Michael the following morning, using her most seductive voice. At first he seemed intimidated and didn't want to take her call. Finally, he relented. He came to the phone and pleaded for her to forgive him for his rudeness. "The idea of writing an actual book devoted to my personal life paralyzed me," he said. "I changed costumes three times that morning and was ready to go. Then at the last minute I got cold feet."

Before the end of their conversation, he invited her to tea that afternoon at Hayvenhurst. When a chicly dressed Jackie arrived at Encino, she found only two staff members. Michael had ordered the rest of the household to leave, including photographer Steve Howell, who wanted to capture the historic coming together of this famous pair on film. "He kicked us out. We didn't get to see her. All of us were horribly disappointed and mad at Michael for his insensitivity."

Michael was awed by Jackie, considering her the epitome of grace, style, and charm. Once he'd held Diana Ross in such awe, but seemingly had graduated from that, moving on to bigger game. "And what bigger game could there have been than Jackie Onassis?" Howell asked. "My God, she was the most famous person on Earth meeting the second most famous person on Earth."

"It was a lovefest," said a staff member who was allowed to remain behind to serve tea. "Jackie and Michael were practically cooing at each other.

Jacqueline Kennedy Onassis

I couldn't tell where Jackie's whispery voice ended and Michael's whispery voice began."

As Jackie would later reveal, "I didn't end up interviewing Michael. He ended up interviewing me."

"How do you live with the dread that every time you walk out your door fans or the paparazzi are waiting to take your picture?" he asked her.

"I consider the alternative," she said. "Life as a recluse. A Georgetown widow peering out through the draperies at throngs gathered on the street in front of my house. That wasn't an option for me, so I moved to New York. Of course, I can't take the rush of people at times. Perhaps that's why I married Ari. He could almost guarantee my privacy when he wasn't invading it himself." She was referring, of course, to her second husband, Aristotle Onassis.

"How do you handle being a celebrity?" he asked.

"I don't know anything else," she said. "It comes easy for me. I couldn't imagine being unknown. Almost from the beginning of my life, I was on stage or being exhibited somewhere. Of course, not the kind of notoriety that came later. Actually, I've often pondered your question myself. Maybe I would miss the fame. At first anonymity sounds wonderful, at least the freedom it would give you. Imagine going shopping on Fifth Avenue without the gawkers and the paparazzi. I've asked a few movie stars what it was like to have known world adulation, then neglect. Gloria Swanson once told me, 'It's like the parade has passed me by.' She said she missed the adoring fans and the hysteria they once generated for her."

At the end of the afternoon, Michael still hadn't agreed to write his memoirs. Instead he proposed *The Michael Jackson Scrapbook*. "You know, a picture of my boa constrictor, Muscles. My first report card. The first song The Jackson 5 ever recorded. Stuff like that."

"I once compiled a book devoted to memorabilia of an early trip to Europe with Lee," she said, obviously turned off by the idea of a Jackson scrapbook. She was referring to Lee Radziwell, her sister.

The next day Michael invited Jackie on a tour of Disneyland, with him serving as her personal guide. "He knew all the hidden corners, the names of all the animals, the thrill of every attraction," she said. "I found it boring, but he was mesmerized. I think he has the heart of an eight-year-old."

After that day at Disneyland, Jackie seemed fascinated by the subject of Michael's sexual orientation. For such a worldly woman, this was out of character. Among others, she discussed it with J.C. Suares, who would become the book designer for *Moonwalk*. According to Suares, "She repeatedly asked me if I thought Michael liked girls."

She even discussed it with Peter Lawford, thinking that as a Hollywood insider he might know something. "I have never known Jackie to be so intrigued with someone's sexual orientation," Lawford later said. "She was one of the most sophisticated women in the world. Both she and Lee included many homosexuals, especially those in the arts, among their best friends. Truman Capote. Rudolf Nureyev. Jackie even had a distant kinship with gay author Gore Vidal."

She confided to Lawford, who was to die the following year, that, "When I first met Michael in New York in the late 70s, I just assumed he was gay, but hadn't admitted that to himself yet. After seeing him so many years later on his home turf in Encino, I think he's figured out he's gay. But his gayness, I suspect, has a strange twist to it."

"What do you mean exactly?" Lawford asked her.

"I mean, it's not gay like two handsome men who look like Paul Newman and Rock Hudson getting together. I have great intuition about these matters. Michael is gay, but his gayness is different. There's something fishy going on here. Something he's hiding from the world, something that will never be revealed in *Moonwalk*. The book will hardly be a candid confession, but a glossy, glitzy thing. Michael's mythology of himself. But in spite of what I've said, I predict it'll be a bestseller."

The staff at Doubleday was eager to hear Jackie's impressions of Michael even before she eventually landed the deal to publish a memoir, not a scrapbook.

"He seems to have no perspective on his life" she claimed. "That's understandable. He's only twenty-five. Of course, I've met men his age who ruled kingdoms. I think he's more interested in projecting an image of himself than he is in telling any truth. Maybe his truth would completely destroy his image."

It took Michael two weeks to make up his mind to go ahead with his book and accept Jackie's offer. "Of course, I'll need a ghostwriter," he told her.

"I can arrange that," she promised. She confessed that she'd been less successful in pursuing other celebrities. "I even went to your rival, Prince, and tried to get him to write a memoir. He turned me down. There have been other rejections. Katharine Hepburn, Bette Davis, Greta Garbo, Ted Turner, Brigitte Bardot, Barbra Streisand, Barbara Walters, Rudolf Nureyev."

"I've heard of some of these people, but some of those celebs are too obscure," he said. "Their biographies won't sell."

She concealed her astonishment.

Jackie amused friends with her description of Hayvenhurst. "It's La La Land," she claimed, "with a damn chimpanzee running amuck. Jack would have hated it, and Ari would have called in moving vans to cart off every tasteless stick. I haven't seen such kitsch since I saw photographs of Mrs. Khrushchev's home. Animals in cages. Tacky awards and trophies. Jackson family pictures. Furniture that only a demented queen could have purchased. It wasn't even nouveau riche, not even 'Jewish Renaissance,' but artifacts from the Land of Oz. Let me put it this way: Michael decorates like he selects his wardrobe."

In the months ahead, Jackie, from her publishing base in New York, listened to Michael's endless demands and insecurities about the project. She also read one disappointing chapter after another. Finally, in despair, she told her staff, "Dealing with the mercurial Mr. Jackson is like being in a train wreck—worse, an airplane crash."

Prince may have turned down Jackie's offer to write his memoirs, but he accepted an invitation to visit Hayvenhurst. Perhaps curiosity propelled him to Encino, not the prospect of any friendship with his rival, Michael. Privately, he'd ridiculed Michael and was flabbergasted at his phenomenal success. Michael was equally jealous of Prince.

Michael poured out his frustrations over Prince to his attorney, John Branca. "Prince is darkly sexual, a man of mystery," Michael said. "Sinister even. In spite of that 'Thriller' video, I'm still known as Goody Two-Shoes. Squeaky clean. Why don't fans regard me as sexually dangerous?"

Prince

Branca reportedly did not have an answer for that.

Michael became upset when he learned that Branca's firm was also representing Prince. "There can be only one King of Pop," he warned. "I don't believe in sharing the throne."

The press constantly linked the two bizarre young megastars, and many music fans gravitated into either pro-Michael or pro-Prince cults. But whereas Prince was by reputation known as a sexy womanizer, Michael had to keep on fighting gay rumors.

"I don't understand it," Michael said. "He's very effeminate. He wears lots of makeup. His dress isn't macho. Far more girlie than my own clothing. But he's called a stud. How could he be? He's only a midget."

During the summer of 1984, *Purple Rain*, recorded by Prince and topping the charts, was even more successful than the *Victory* album. Reportedly Michael was so jealous of Prince that he'd go into a rage at the mention of his name. Dozens of people heard him making uncharitable remarks about the performer. "He's a copycat," was only one of Michael's charges. "He's ripping me off!"

Purple Rain made Prince a megastar, selling more than ten million copies in the U.S. alone and resting comfortably for 24 weeks as number one on *Billboard*'s charts. Critic Gabe Fowlkes said, "Catapulting off the *Purple Rain* soundtrack, Prince combined dance beats with powerful guitar riffs to create music that even Nancy Reagan could bust a move to. And unlike Michael Jackson, Prince does not sing as if he's been castrated."

Later, Michael was heard telling people "how weird" Prince was, little realizing that he would one day be known as WACKO JACKO. "I don't like anything about him. He can't sing, and there's an awful aura about him—a bit creepy."

The one thing that Michael especially resented was the film, *Purple Rain*. Prince had succeeded in the movies where Michael had failed with *The Wiz*.

Michael was seen slipping into a private screening of *Purple Rain* at Warner Brothers. Before the lights went on, he'd left the screening room and headed for his waiting limousine. He could only bite his lip in frustration as he watched *Purple Rain* with Prince become the "sleeper" of the summer. Prince had a hit movie, an achievement denied Michael. His jealousy was aggravated when the film won an Oscar for best score.

Later, when Michael was quizzed about the movie, he said, "I've already told you. Prince can't sing. Now I know he can't act. I acted in the role of the Scarecrow in *The Wiz*. That was real acting, not something you are likely to see in *Purple Rain*."

Michael told Quincy Jones that he found Prince's music offensive, "vulgar in the extreme. Imagine writing a song about mutual masturbation." He was referring to "Jack U Off" in Prince's *Controversy* album, released in 1981.

Down the road, Michael would not concern himself with Prince as much as with two new rivals who had emerged on the scene—notably Janet, his sister, and the outspoken Madonna.

At the door to Hayvenhurst, the five-foot-tall Prince presented himself to the Jacksons—in this case Michael was joined not only by La Toya but young Janet. Prince had not come to admire Michael, which he didn't do at all, but to try to learn "what makes the dude tick." Prince would not learn anything, as Michael remained almost silent for the entire evening, observing Prince with great skepticism. In lieu of confronting such a rude host, Prince turned his attentions almost entirely to La Toya, hoping—but failing—to seduce her.

Prince promised La Toya "a trip to Paradise!" She wasn't interested. Later, she asked her brother, "What did the little creep think? That I was some Saturday night whore hot to trot?"

Michael finally managed to speak when he showed Prince to the door after a disastrous evening. "Good night," he said in his whispery voice.

One of Prince's bodyguards came inside and presented him with a package, which he then gave to Michael. It was some twigs and leaves from a sycamore tree along with some metal charms and the tail feathers of a peacock. There was also a tape. Prince told Michael to play the tape backwards.

As the door closed on Prince, Janet came up to stand beside her brother. In her best Mae West impersonation, she said, "I chew little sausages like that for breakfast."

Upstairs in his bedroom, Michael played the tape. "It sounded satanic," he told Frank DiLeo in a late-night phone call. "I think it's voodoo. Prince has put a hex on me. I'm sure he's a warlock."

"Now, now, Michael, it'll be okay," DiLeo assured him. He also reminded Michael that thousands of people had accused him of being a warlock after *Thriller* was released.

"That's different," Michael said, dismissing such charges. "I think Prince's gift came directly from the Devil himself. I want you to round up someone to break the spell tonight—perhaps somebody from Haiti. Prince's hex on me has got to be lifted. Otherwise, my career will be destroyed."

DiLeo said he would, then turned off the light and went back to sleep. The next morning Michael had completely forgotten about his instructions to his manager.

A year later, Prince and Michael were set to record a duet for the *We Are the World* album. But Prince didn't show up. Michael was furious until he was reminded that he once stood up a person far bigger than Prince, Jackie Onassis herself. Michael didn't have an immediate response for that.

When asked why he didn't show up, Prince told his associates, "The guy is silly, a wimp."

Does Michael deserve credit for converting Prince to the Jehovah's Witness far-right cult? Prince himself claimed that it wasn't Michael, but his mother's dying wish that he convert to the controversial religion that rejects everything from blood transfusions to the occult.

Following in the footsteps of the former "King of Pop," Michael himself, Prince now proselytizes door to door trying to convert unsuspecting innocents to the draconian world of Jehovah's Witnesses.

"Michael Jackson got the boot from us," said one of the Jehovah's Witnesses—and Prince may be next." She noted a report about Prince in the *London Mirror* that the "androgynous performer promotes Jehovah's Witnesses in Minneapolis, wearing his trademark mascara and dressed in a tailor-made suit with stack heels. He arrives at doorsteps in a limousine surrounded by four bodyguards."

The last known comment Michael made about Prince was, "He's a cherry moon with too much mascara." Michael was no doubt referring to Prince's 1986 film, *Under the Cherry Moon*.

During their visits to Hayvenhurst, neither Jackie nor Prince had been impressed with the chimp, "Bubbles."

"But he had become the love of Michael's life," according to a former staff member at Encino who didn't want to be named. She didn't like the chimp either, especially when she had to round up his dirty diapers. Michael always insisted on changing Bubbles' diapers himself.

"I was fired for no apparent reason," she said. "Maybe I saw too much." She didn't reveal what "too much" meant.

Michael rescued the chimp, "Bubbles," from a cancer laboratory where he was about to be used for medical experiments—or he didn't, depending on which story or which sources you want to believe. Whether he faced certain death or not, Bubbles was brought to Hayvenhurst, where he became the most pampered chimp in history.

The Star introduced Michael and Bubbles to the world under the headline: MICHAEL JACKSON GOES APE. NOW HE'S TALKING WITH HIS PET CHIMP—IN MONKEY LANGUAGE. Other supermarket tabloids filed even more bizarre stories. *The National Enquirer* claimed that Prince was using ESP and mental telepathy to drive Bubbles insane.

Michael obsessed over the baby chimp, even dining with him at table or throwing occasional "Alice in Wonderland" tea parties for him. "He came to regard the chimp as a human being," said Bob Michaelson, who visited Hayvenhurst on several occasions. The chimp knew benefits no other monkey had ever known: Limousine rides, his own hotel suite during road trips with Michael, even a personal bodyguard. Two dozen sets of Michael/Bubbles matching outfits were designed. Bubbles was perhaps the only chimp in the world associated with a custom-made tuxedo.

As the years went by, and as Bubbles matured, Michael grew bored with the chimp, the same way he did with young boys as they aged. Bubbles had also gotten hard to manage, once jumping up on the bed and landing in Michael's face after he'd had another nose job.

Eventually, Michael would adopt two additional, and younger, baby chimps, Max and Alex. Bubbles had designer clothes named after him, even a line of toys. But eventually, he was sent away in disgrace from Hayvenhurst, and ended up sharing a cage with two dozen other chimps, his days of glory behind him.

On March 3, 2005, columnists for *The New York Daily News* startled readers with a gossipy item, JACKO AND CHIMP TALE: IT GETS HAIRY. Uncovered was a 1993 interview that James DeBarge, former husband of Janet, gave to a police informant in Britain back in 1993. Revelations were subsequently published in Britain's *Daily Star*.

"The sex charges against Michael Jackson grow more bestial by the day," a columnist wrote. "Just when you thought the King of Pop's reputation couldn't sink any lower, it turns out Jackson's former brother-in-law, James DeBarge, has claimed the singer was up to some inappropriate monkey business with his chimp, Bubbles."

"He was changing Bubbles' diapers and just got carried away," DeBarge claimed in the 1993 interview. When Bubbles dropped out of sight, rumors were spread at the time that Papa Joe shot the chimp after he caught him in bed with his son, but this gossip was not true.

The allegations brought an avalanche of letters to the newspaper and postings on the web. One reader facetiously wrote, "Parents of young boys who live near Michael's Neverland Ranch thank Bubbles for the sacrifices he made so that their sons could have a night or two off." Another reader jokingly asked, "Is anyone old enough to remember the old song, "I'm Forever Blowing Bubbles?" Many readers wrote in with outrage:

Miko Brando

"It's blatantly obvious that he is mentally ill. Padded cell, straitjacket, throw away the key."

The Bubbles and Michael stories weren't the only tales relayed through the tabloids during 1984. At the peak of his career, Michael received tributes as well as condemnations. *The News of the World*'s color supplement hailed him as "The World's Hottest Property." But Britain's *Melody Maker* magazine put him on its list of "Ten Fruitcakes," because he bathed in Perrier water and talked to inflatable geese. There was a report that he was working on a new project, a video in which he'd wear a purple dress that catches on fire.

The Fashion Foundation of America's 43rd annual survey of custom tailors and designers named President Reagan, The Catholic Archbishop of New York City, and Michael Jackson as America's best dressed men—all that in spite of the archbishop's gowns and Michael's tacky military outfits.

In Sevran, France, in July of 1984, an "obsessed" teenage boy committed suicide when his parents refused to finance plastic surgery to make him look like his idol, Michael Jackson.

Michael was extremely upset by this report of a suicide and turned to Miko Brando for support. (Miko happened to be not only Michael's security guard, but the second-eldest son of actor Marlon Brando and Marlon's second wife, Movita Castenada.) Michael had grown closer to Miko after his security guard had put out the fire in his hair during the filming of the Pepsi commercial.

With Miko Brando employed by Michael, it was inevitable that he would eventually meet *The Godfather* himself. He'd seen the film fifteen times, as he was as fascinated by crime pictures as he was by Disney cartoons. Michael told friends, "Now that I'm the biggest entertainer in the world, I need to associate with names as big as me. Jackie Onassis, and, yes, Marlon Brando. Perhaps Elizabeth Taylor one day."

The "odd couple" friendship of Michael and Marlon began in the living

Marlon Brando

room of Marlon's home on Mulholland Drive in Los Angeles. Before an astonished Michael, Marlon placed a $10,000 check on his coffee table. He asked Michael for an I.O.U. for the same amount. The request flabbergasted Michael until Marlon explained that it was a contest. "Whoever lets out the biggest fart takes home the prize," Marlon said. "I have to warn you, I've been eating beans all afternoon."

Michael giggled and covered his face, later claiming that Marlon "had a potty mouth." But he kept returning to Brando's home time and time again, and Marlon also became a frequent house guest at Neverland.

Sometimes Quincy Jones joined Michael for an evening with Marlon. Jones and Marlon had known each other since the late 1940s when the actor was appearing as Stanley Kowalski in Tennessee Williams's *A Streetcar Named Desire* on Broadway. With fellow actor Sidney Poitier, Marlon used to hang out with Jones late at night at Small's Paradise in Harlem. Marlon regaled Michael with stories of his early days in New York, when he always wore a red fedora hat. Jones was at Marlon's side when they attended the funeral of the assassinated Dr. Martin Luther King Jr. Jones always called Marlon "Leroy," and Michael was envious of the bond between the two long-time friends.

"Tennessee always confused the real me with the fictional character of Stanley Kowalski," Marlon said to Jones. "And Michael still thinks of me as Don Corleone."

When Michael told Marlon that Jackie Onassis was going to be the editor of his autobiography, *Moonwalk*, Marlon leaned back on his sofa. "I fucked her but just once. She told me that it was the best fuck of her life."

"Now, Marlon, you know she wouldn't talk dirty like that," Michael said.

Ignoring him, Marlon went on, "I fucked Nancy Davis before she married Ronald Reagan. But I never got around to Pat Nixon, Bess Truman, or Mamie Eisenhower."

"Oh, Marlon," Michael said, covering his ears, which he would always do whenever he thought Marlon was "talking vulgar."

Their friendship began gradually but deepened in the 1990s. Toward the end of his life, Marlon was telling his friends, "Michael Jackson is my best comrade-in-arms."

The biggest project between Marlon and Michael never got off the ground. Marlon worked on a screen treatment, which he hoped to present to director Martin Scorsese. In the proposed scenario, Marlon cast himself as

God, with Michael playing the Devil. "It's typecasting, of course," Marlon facetiously told Michael.

Alarmed over Marlon's burgeoning weight, Michael arrived one night bringing Marlon fresh vegetables from his organic garden. What made the evening rather bizarre was that Michael arrived dressed in a pink-and-chartreuse Pinocchio outfit, complete with a long nose.

"I'm astonished to see you as Pinocchio," Marlon said.

"I like to dress up," Michael said.

"I know that," Marlon said. "It's the big nose I don't get. I thought you'd spent millions of dollars on plastic surgery trying to get rid of a big nose."

Marlon found that a friendship with Michael had fringe benefits. It was reported that he used Michael as his personal bank, at one point borrowing a million dollars from him.

Regardless of the stress Marlon faced in his life, Michael was there for him. He idolized Marlon and came to regard him as a father figure.

Marlon was no great father, no more than Michael's real father, Papa Joe, had been. Except for Miko, Marlon had two dysfunctional children, Christian and Cheyenne. One night Christian shot Cheyenne's lover and was sentenced to ten years in prison for the assassination. Cheyenne was pregnant at the time of the slaying.

She'd later accuse Marlon of molesting her, and eventually, at the age of 25, she would commit suicide. Throughout this painful ordeal, Michael stood by Marlon. When charges of child molestation were raised against Michael, many of his other famous friends deserted him. Marlon, however, along with Elizabeth Taylor, was there for Michael. "He did the same for me," Marlon told his friends. "I can't turn my back on him now. Molestation charges have been raised against me too. I know what it feels like."

Michael had confided in Marlon that he was suffering emotional distress over Janet's marriage to James DeBarge and that he was delighted when Janet eventually filed a petition to nullify the marriage.

Marlon tried to soothe his nerves, telling him, "I'm emotionally distressed over my own marriages, such as they were. My final conclusion is this: No man should ever marry and obligate himself to a woman. A man should be free. Even when I was married, I still insisted on being a free man. Sometimes I brought my girlfriends home to meet my wife . . . or wives."

"I'll never get married," Michael promised him.

"You know, I can believe that." Marlon

Martin Scorsese

226

chuckled at his own humor.

Michael shared with Marlon his experiences in filmmaking and often asked the actor—sometimes hailed as the greatest of the 20th century—for advice. Francis Ford Coppola, who had directed Marlon in *The Godfather*, was also directing Michael in a 17-minute film for Disney, which would be released in 1986. Steven Spielberg, Michael's friend, was originally going to direct but had to cancel because of a conflict in his schedule. Cast opposite Michael as Captain EO was Anjelica Huston, playing The Supreme Leader.

Amazingly, the film took more than a year to shoot and cost $20 million, which, of course, was more than a million dollars a minute. It ranks as the costliest short ever made.

Michael was cast as an intergalactic song-and-dance man fighting to save a planet from the evil designs of the villain, Anjelica Huston. Disney characters such as Captain EO's flying space monkey, "Fuzzball," pop in and out.

Michael tested Coppola's nerves in this musical sci-fi short by refusing to work on Mondays. He would only rehearse while wearing his sunglasses on a stage that was completely dark. Coppola couldn't even see his moves, much less direct them. He couldn't have heard the director's cues anyway because Michael demanded that the background music be played at full blast.

He had an infuriating habit of disappearing right before he was to be in one of his scenes. Actually, he was often hiding behind a prop. After the crew had searched frantically for him, with production costs mounting, he would suddenly appear on the set. "I don't know why you're complaining," he told Coppola. "I've been right here all along, waiting to go on."

Other than getting overpaid, Michael found a fringe benefit in working on *Captain EO*. It came in a ten-year-old package named Jonathan Spence.

Members of the crew reported to Todd Gold, a reporter for *People*, that the cuddly twosome would "hug and nuzzle a lot." Reportedly, nothing sexual was going on, but that didn't stop crew members from gossiping behind Michael's back. The blond-haired actor was called "an early version of Macaulay Culkin."

Little Jonathan seemed a devoted companion to Michael during filming. Not only did he fetch him such delights as a freshly made glass of chilled passion fruit juice, but he could be seen mopping Michael's brow after rehearsal.

When not resting, Jonathan and Michael dueled with water pistols. One day a food fight caused $3,000 worth of damage in Michael's

MJ in *Captain EO*

expensive trailer. Michael was also fond of ordering custard pies. He and Jonathan would "ambush" crew members in ways that evoked slapstick comedies from the silent screen. "When I got a pie in the face, I wanted to choke the shithead," one crew member said in disgust. "But he was *the* Michael Jackson, and I didn't want to cross the faggot. He was a diva. There's never been a greater diva in all of Hollywood than *Miss* Jackson."

When Coppola's final cut for the ultra-expensive video was approved, Disney planned a release of the film at only two specially constructed theaters—one at the Epcot Center at Disney World in Orlando and the other at Disneyland in Anaheim.

At the September 21, 1986 premiere of *Captain EO* at Disneyland, a non-stop 60-hour party was staged that drew such names as Jane Fonda, Jack Nicholson (who showed up with co-star Anjelica Huston), Sissy Spacek, and George Lucas. The only no-show was Michael himself. Actually he was spotted at Disneyland that day, wearing a large black hat and hiding behind a heavy gray beard. He was seen boarding the roller-coaster called "Space Mountain."

Captain EO was hardly a triumph for Michael. One of his young fans, Joseph P. Ulibas, said, "I saw it and was disappointed even at my young age. Dude, they promised me a movie, and all I got was some singing, dancing, and overacting. They burned a ton of money on this 'movie.' What I would like to know is what did they spend it on? For one thing, it wasn't on acting lessons. I can tell you that for sure."

To generate news before the premiere of *Captain EO*, and in a moment of indiscretion, Michael launched a secret publicity campaign to show the world that he was "bizarre," not that anyone on the planet needed much convincing at this point.

That was the word he wanted to be characterized as, although later this campaign would spin out of control and backfire on him. He set out to tantalize the press with his eccentricities, and the media, especially the tabloids, not only bought his self-styled "bizarre" act but invented stories of their own, making Michael appear far more idiosyncratic than he already was.

One morning he woke up and ordered one-hundred surgical masks in various colors. From the moment he first appeared in public wearing this mask, he was photographed. Pictures of him in disguise appeared on the front pages of newspapers around the world. "Isn't this fabulous!" he told Frank DiLeo, "The whole world is talking about me and my mask." Although most often appearing in white, he sometimes chose a colored surgical mask to match his outfit of the moment.

"He looked really fetching in magenta," DiLeo was heard to say. His manager went along with Michael's affectations, although the gruff, macho professional secretly must not have approved. He did admit, however, that Michael knew how to attract the attention of photographers and reporters. "If he hadn't made it as a singer, he could have hired out as a publicist."

Michael actually needed the surgical mask to cover up his chin while recovering from another plastic surgery operation performed by Dr. Steven Hoefflin. Somewhere along the way, Michael had seen Kirk Douglas performing in the 1960 film, *Spartacus*. He'd been intrigued with the cleft in the actor's chin and wanted the facial feature for himself. Dr. Hoefflin agreed to perform the operation.

To come up with the famous Douglas cleft, the surgeon had to drill two tiny holes in Michael's jaw. Once this delicate procedure was carried out, a plastic prosthesis was inserted. After the wound healed, Michael hardly looked like the macho actor but at least he had his photogenic cleft.

Weeks later, Michael returned to Dr. Hoefflin's office to have a permanent eyeliner applied. This less-difficult operation involved the insertion of black dye injected directly into the eyelids. When that operation also succeeded, Michael surveyed the results and seemed pleased. "Now I'll have no more need of eyeliner. I'll mail all my mascara to Prince."

At this point in his life, Michael chose as a role model an unlikely candidate: Howard Hughes, "The Aviator." He had never heard of this former American hero until someone in a newspaper story suggested that Michael's wearing of the surgical mask evoked Hughes's phobia about germs. From that day on, Michael read everything he could about America's first billionaire, not only his accomplishments in aviation, but his private life too.

Michael read that he was not only a womanizer, according to press reports, but also learned that he was a closeted homosexual, carrying on a long-term affair with Cary Grant and other male stars who included Errol Flynn. Michael became intrigued with Hughes on many levels, especially in his success at leading a private life that wasn't exposed to public view until after his death. Michael wanted to learn how this hero managed to cover up his bedtime activities with men while "enjoying" a press that linked him to some of the most famous women of the 20th century, including Ava Gardner, Katharine Hepburn, and Ginger Rogers.

Michael also learned that in addition to breaking aviation records, Hughes had become a successful movie producer. He ordered a copy of Hughes's film, *The Outlaw*, that had starred Jane Russell and Jack Buetel. Michael learned that the world believed that Hughes had been hotly in pursuit of the busty and buxom Russell but that secretly he had the hots for Buetel, who played Billy the Kid.

Michael, too, wanted to be linked in the press with famous women dangling at his side like "arm candy," while indulging his private passions away from the prying eyes of the world.

Unless it was by the hand of a "special friend," most often a cute little boy, Michael, like Hughes, ordered that he never be touched. Like Hughes, he wanted doors opened for him, as he did not want to touch a knob that might be contaminated by germs.

Michael made such frequent appearances at toy stores that staff members wondered where he was stashing this vast array of items. He wasn't. Once Michael and one of his spe-

Howard Hughes

cial friends had played with the toys for one day, Michael's staff was ordered to destroy the toys as a means of protecting him from germs and contamination.

Throwing precautions aside, Michael would sometimes expose himself to germs, just like the eccentric billionaire. In spite of his obsession with germs, Hughes preferred oral sex, often servicing women who had several different partners a week. Michael too seemed to forget about hygiene when he "French kissed" Bubbles or seemed to delight in changing soiled diapers and wiping the chimp's ass.

He continued to visit Disneyland but made a new demand on park attendants, whose supervisors were willing to do his bidding because of all the publicity he generated for the amusement park. Michael was one of the world's most agile dancers on the stage, yet he demanded that he be transported around Disneyland in a wheelchair. Fans who recognized him thought that he'd injured himself during a dance rehearsal. He hadn't. When he arrived at an attraction of his choice, he'd jump out of the wheelchair and be as agile as he was when performing the Moonwalk.

Toys weren't the only items Michael was purchasing for his amusement. For display alongside a human brain in a jar of formaldehyde and his own nose cartilage also preserved in a jar, he purchased the mummy of a young Egyptian boy for $3 million. He also acquired the boy's mummified pets—a lion cub, a lizard, and a rat which were buried with this son of a noble family. The pets were entombed with the boy to keep him company in the afterlife. Michael became intrigued with that idea and asked his lawyers to draw up a codicil to his will. Upon his death, his pets at the time were to be killed and mummified to join him in his grave.

At this time in his life, he also commissioned a portrait for placement above the headboard of his bed. His own portrait appeared in the center, and he was surrounded by five figures he viewed as his "equals." Sharing the oil painting with him were Albert Einstein, Abraham Lincoln, George

230

Cary Grant

Washington, Mona Lisa, and E.T. Each of the figures, including Michael himself, was painted in Napoleonic poses in full military regalia. Each followed Michael's example of wearing a white sequined glove and aviator sunglasses.

Wanting to generate even more publicity before the opening of *Captain EO*, Michael conceived one of the most ingenious publicity stunts yet, the equal of the Elephant Man story. Behind the scenes, he enlisted the support of *The National Enquirer*, which would break the story. A photographer arrived to take a picture of him sleeping inside a tube-like hyperbaric chamber made of see-through plastic. The *Enquirer* ran the story—MICHAEL JACKSON'S SECRET PLAN TO LIVE TO 150. The story claimed that by sleeping in this $175,000 contraption, Michael could stave off the aging process and not die at the ripe old age of ninety but live for an additional six decades at least.

After its first exposure in the national tabloid, the picture of Michael in the chamber ran worldwide.

Michael had encountered the machine when he was at the Burn Center being treated for burns after his hair caught fire during the Pepsi commercial. The machine was none too safe, and because of its 100% oxygen content, hospital employees approached the chamber wearing fire-retardant clothes to assist burn victims who were temporarily placed in the chamber to flood their body tissues with life-giving oxygen. Trained personnel knew of the dangers associated with the chamber, including the possibility of an oxygen-fed fire breaking out or else oxygen toxicity to the patient.

The tabloids weren't the only publications writing about Michael. After the worldwide success of *Thriller*, even *Time* magazine wanted him for a cover story. Surprisingly for an entertainer who deliberately courted bizarre publicity, Michael rejected *Time*'s request for an interview. A reporter for *Time*, Denise Worrell, had to settle for interviews with Papa Joe and Katherine instead.

On a tour of the Jackson's Encino compound, Papa Joe, escorting Worrell, knocked on Michael's bedroom door. When there was no answer, he opened the unlocked door to show her Michael's mannequin-studded room.

To the surprise of both Worrell and Joe himself, they discovered Michael sitting in the dark room lit only by the glow of a TV set turned on low. Michael did not introduce his friend, who looked like a boy in his late teens. Michael seemed embarrassed at this invasion of his privacy and extended a weak handshake to Worrell, which she would later claim felt "like a fluffy cloud."

Michael had nothing to say to the correspondent, but averted his eyes and turned back to watching the television screen. Papa Joe seemed embarrassed. Worrell, although she really wanted to interview the reclusive star, turned and

MJ in hyperbaric chamber

left the room quickly, followed by Joe. "I'll have a word with you later," Joe was heard warning Michael. Joe turned apologetically to Worrell. "Michael has only just discovered who Greta Garbo was, and he's trying to imitate her."

As Worrell was leaving the Encino mansion, a perplexed Katherine came up to her. "Don't get the wrong idea!" she said. "Michael isn't gay!" As Worrell drove away, she remembered Papa Joe's final words to her. "Get it right in your article on Michael. He's definitely not gay! Joan Rivers is broadcasting lies about my son. He's gonna sue!"

Katherine might have put up a bold front to a journalist from *Time* magazine, but in private she often expressed her despair to her children. "Michael hangs out so much with all those white boys." She went on to assert that if he wanted to play with children, there were lots of nieces and nephews for him to pick from.

Bob Michaelson, who once worked as a business partner with Michael, said, "There is a popular misconception that Michael was always in the company of young boys. Actually he was often seen with many handsome guys in their late teens. They were always white, always good looking, and always discreet. He was not seen with any girls or young women. *Not that!*"

Except for those special friends, Michael continued to pursue friendships with his equals, an array of personalities that now firmly included Marlon Brando. He continued to see Liza Minnelli, although admitting privately, "I would have preferred Judy Garland but she's dead."

"Jackie Onassis is definitely my equal," he claimed, although he was beginning to wonder about the status of Diana Ross.

He did not include Brooke Shields on that list as an equal. "I love people like Brooke who are talented but who work so hard," he said. "Brooke is a nice gal but she's not Elizabeth Taylor. That's the kind of woman I want to be seen with."

The Oscar-winning actress, darling of divorce lawyers and diamond dealers, was about to enter Michael's life.

Elizabeth had certainly heard of Michael Jackson, but was not familiar with his music. Her son, Christopher Wilding, was a devotee, however. Like many stars of her era, Elizabeth's taste in music ranged from Judy Garland to Frank Sinatra, although she'd enjoyed Elvis Presley as well. The rock 'n' roll star had once sent her a note, "Would you like to shake, rattle, and roll with me?" But she'd never answered it.

In the 80s, Michael was enjoying—or else detesting—the same kind of scandalous fame she'd experienced during her love affair with her *Cleopatra* costar, Richard Burton, in Rome. But now, instead of her escapades, it was Michael's adventures—real or imagined—that dominated the headlines.

With the onset of age—Elizabeth was now fifty-two—her beauty was fading, although she still made a stunning presence.

Michael had even more money than she did, a reported $300 million in his coffers, most of it from his hit album, *Thriller*. He was only twenty-six years old. In spite of Elizabeth's long and successful career, she estimated, "I can scare up only $80 million, if that."

When a maid in her Bel Air home announced that "Mr. Michael Jackson is on the phone," the megastar was skeptical. "Why would Michael Jackson be calling little ol' me?" she asked the maid, not expecting an answer. "A duet, maybe? Tell him to call Diana Ross." The maid returned to the phone, but came back soon. "No, it's really Mr. Jackson," she said. "I'd recognize that girlie-man voice anywhere." Still thinking one of her friends was playing a joke on her, Elizabeth got up to answer the phone.

But even after talking to Michael, she still wasn't convinced. Some of her friends delivered great impersonations. But when fourteen tickets to Michael's concert at Dodger Stadium on February 27 arrived, she was convinced that she'd been talking to the star himself. "A perfect gift for Christopher," she told her maid, "and I didn't have to pay a cent for it. He can invite all his young friends."

When the concert began, Elizabeth was extremely disappointed with her seats. Even though given the VIP box, she did not have a good view. After twenty minutes, she rose to her feet and left.

When news of her walkout reached Michael backstage, he was devastated. He called her the next day and, as Elizabeth remembered, "We talked for three hours. About everything. Mostly about having to go into the business without having a chance to grow up first. We truly identified with each other. I found him sweet and sensitive, not at all bizarre like the stories I've read in the tabloids. Not that I read tabloids, of course, but stories—most often outright lies—are written about him. As you know, I've been a tabloid scandal for years, so I know what he feels like. I told Michael that reporters must have slept under my bed to write the crap they do."

In his biography, *Moonwalk*, Michael summed up his relationship with Elizabeth this way: "I'm inspired by her bravery. She had been through so much and she is a survivor. I identify with her very strongly because of her experiences as a child star. When we first started to talk on the phone, she told me she felt like she had known me for years. I felt the same way."

Michael and Elizabeth were so compatible over the phone that they agreed to meet in person. He invited her to the set of *Captain EO*. Later, she told her friend, Roddy McDowall, "Being with Michael brings back memories of Monty." She was referring, of course, to her loving relationship with her long-time companion, the homosexual actor, Montgomery Clift, with whom she'd appeared in the 1951 *A Place in the Sun*.

On the set of *Captain EO*, Elizabeth seemed to revert to childhood herself. She joined Michael and Little Jonathan in their messy food fights in his trailer.

A few weeks later, she invited Michael to her home, where he showed up with a "date," Bubbles. "I find Michael very dear," Elizabeth later recalled. "He was very childlike. Not childish. Childlike. I could identify with that. He took me back to the days when I was shooting *National Velvet* with Mickey Rooney. The only difference is that Mickey was sexually aggressive. I didn't know at the time any details of Michael's private life, but he came across as very asexual. In other words, I didn't think he was going to rape me. With Rooney, you could never be sure."

If Michael were indeed gay, as rumors had it, he could find no more supportive friend and champion than Elizabeth herself. She had always been the most gay-friendly actress in Hollywood, and in time she'd become an AIDS activist.

In the months to come, Michael was seen frequently at Elizabeth's Bel Air home, talking with her for hours at a time. He even established a "hot line" to her manse so that they could talk at any hour of the day or night without going through staff members.

Both Michael and Elizabeth liked ice cream and sampled various flavors. He told her that he was considering manufacturing his own brand of ice cream which "will be the tastiest on the market because of a secret ingredient."

"What secret ingredient? Mother's breast milk?" she asked facetiously.

"Something even more startling," he told her. "An ingredient I learned about in Africa. The saliva of a rhinoceros."

When she received an invitation from President Nelson Mandela to join Michael on his tour of South Africa, she gracefully declined, speaking to Mandela personally. After putting down the phone with Mandela, Elizabeth asked friends, "Why do famous people want to meet only famous people?"

When Michael returned from the tour, he resumed his friendship with Elizabeth. Her staff often reported seeing him cuddled in her arms on a sofa watching TV.

"It was hardly a love affair, as some tabloids have suggested," said Bert Overfield, who covered this burgeoning friendship. "No sex. But lots of love. Michael himself spoke publicly about Elizabeth. 'She's my Wendy.'" Michael was referring to Wendy Darling, one of the characters in Sir James M. Barrie's *Peter Pan*.

Michael believed so strongly in the Barrie story that he once confided a secret to Elizabeth. "We can fly, you know. We just don't think the right thoughts to levitate ourselves. I'm studying with these two gurus."

"Don't take me with you," she warned him. "I'm too much of a blimp to get airborne. And don't jump off the Empire State Building, thinking you're Superman. You might come crashing down to Earth."

In talks with Michael, Elizabeth learned of "deeper, darker secrets." He claimed that he had the power to foresee his own death, "just knowing" that it would come in the year 1998 when he turned forty. So confident was he in this myth that he started to sign his name, "M.J., 1998." Recipients of his notes did not know what the "1998" stood for, and rumors spread among Michael's fans that the world was going to end that year.

Elizabeth, who did not turn out to be a prophet, told him, "With my history of ill health, I fear my world will come crashing down on me long before 1998."

During their long hours of conversation, he shared with her his fascination with sideshow freaks of nature, those unfortunate souls who used to be showcased in circuses. He was especially intrigued with the lives of Siamese twins and how they lived together. He was also fascinated with bearded ladies, and he once showed her a picture of a two-headed baby. She found it grotesque. "Sometimes I feel like a freak too," he said.

In spite of all these oddities, Elizabeth would one day announce to the press, "He's the sanest person I know. There is nothing weird about him."

In describing his friendship with Elizabeth to friends, Michael claimed that she was "a combination of Queen Elizabeth II and Princess Diana in the same body." At one point he even compared Elizabeth (the actress, not the queen) to Mother Teresa.

When she heard that remark, Elizabeth said, "Michael had better check with Teresa herself before making a comparison like that. I've been called Jezebel, the Whore of Babylon, and a home-wrecker, but never Mother Teresa. How can he compare me with that prune-faced Mother Teresa?"

When a rail-thin and much-altered Michael flew to London in March of 1985, he attended Madame Tussaud's to unveil his wax model. Elizabeth turned down the invitation to accompany him. It was his first public visit to England since the Jacksons toured there in 1979.

One member of the ever-cynical London press, noting a photograph of

Michael displayed beside his wax figure, wrote, "I can't tell which one is the dummy."

That wasn't all. Michael began to look whiter in all his photographs. The press speculated that he was using Porcelana, a skin-bleaching cream. Several writers for magazines commented on his "new, feminine look." One reporter claimed, "Michael Jackson was never the most masculine of men. Now with all the tweezing of the eyebrows, all that makeup, that heavy lipstick, I could swear he's transgendered. I'm going to follow him to the toilet, assuming he still uses the men's loo. I bet he'll go in a booth and squat to pee. Stay tuned, dear readers."

Back in Los Angeles, Frank DiLeo referred to claims that Michael had had his skin lightened by chemical, even surgical, means as "preposterous."

Quincy Jones commented publicly about Michael's "strangeness." He said, "When you start in this business as young as he did, at age five, it's hard to get a realistic point of view on life. Considering the background, and what happened to him in recent years, he's surprisingly sane. I've seen dudes with one record go absolutely nuts. You've got to have a strong center to handle it, and I think Michael has that. I'd rather have a kid who's talking about the Elephant Man's bones than one with a pound of cocaine. Any day!"

Michael called Barbara Walters to attack a *20/20* report that he was a "plastic surgery addict." A hip, savvy news hen like Walters wasn't fooled for a minute, but she listened patiently as Michael explained that the change in his looks was because of a change in his diet.

Later, Walters, or so it was rumored, laughed off Michael's explanation, telling her staff, "It's all those fruits and vegetables he eats—the raisins, unsalted nuts. Or maybe it's the popcorn. Yes, definitely. It's the popcorn making him turn white."

In April of 1985, Michael also made the news with another Elizabeth, this one the Queen of England. Buckingham Palace announced that the image of the Queen could not appear with Michael Jackson on a stamp issued in the British Virgin Islands. The statement claimed, "The Queen will not appear on any stamp which portrays a living person." It was suggested, however, that if any image had to appear with the Queen, William Shakespeare would be an

MJ with his wax effigy

acceptable candidate.

This rebuff was a great humiliation to Michael and a setback to him in one of his desires. For years, he'd had a dream, as expressed to his aides, to have Her Majesty confer British knighthood onto him. "No one deserves it more than I do," Michael was alleged to have said.

The Queen had bestowed knighthood on such figures as Sir Winston Churchill. And in the future, she'd elevate Michael's friend, Elizabeth Taylor, to the status of Dame of the British Empire. Sources close to the Queen said privately that Her Majesty appreciated the Jackson brothers performing before her, but that she had no intention of granting him a British knighthood. If reports are to be believed, the Queen found the whole idea "horrid."

Teaming with Lionel Richie, Michael composed a song for African famine relief. With the help of Quincy Jones, Michael came up with the basic music for "We Are the World." Demo cassettes of "We Are the World" were sent to various artists who had agreed to participate in the recording. The initiative for the relief program was started by Bob Geldof with his "Band Aid" in Britain. He spoke of seeing "120 people die slowly in front of you" after a visit to Ethiopia.

To impress Richie with his A-list friends, Michael invited the star to join him for dinner with Elizabeth Taylor. "We talked about isolation and what you do when you're lonely," Richie later recalled. "Michael seemed amazed to learn that Elizabeth often went out alone without security guards."

They told Richie that they sometimes disguised themselves and went to see movies in Westwood. "We always sit in the back holding hands," Michael said. "She's my new best girl." Richie wondered, but then rejected the possibility that Michael and Elizabeth were having a May-December affair.

From the very beginning of their relationship, Elizabeth had to be aware of Michael's special friendships with young boys. She often saw Michael with these children. Years later, in 1999, when she was asked about this, she didn't really answer, but excused Michael by claiming, "He is magic. I've long known that magical people, especially artists, have genuine eccentricity. That is, perhaps, what drives them to create magic in media."

A friend of Elizabeth's, who did not want to be named, claimed, "Even if Michael is nabbed as the King of Child Porn, Elizabeth will stick up for him and make excuses. She's a gutsy broad, but also a very sweet woman and fiercely loyal to her friends—take Rock Hudson, Montgomery Clift, and James Dean, for example."

When Michael told Elizabeth he wanted to direct his next music video himself, she called her friend Eddie Dmytryk "to show Michael the ropes." A Ukrainian, the liberal director had made *Crossfire* in 1947. It had been one of the first Hollywood pictures to decry anti-Semitism, for which he earned an

Oscar nomination as best director. He later became a victim of the House Un-American Activities Committee and an infamous member of the blacklisted "Hollywood Ten."

At the time of his meeting with Michael, the director was teaching film at UCLA. Dmytryk would later recall several meetings with Michael at his Neverland ranch. "He had dolls everywhere—perhaps he never had a chance to be a kid himself. Little dolls, big dolls, life-size dolls, and lots of cuddly teddy bears. I met Jordie Chandler there, the same kid who would later bring a lawsuit against Michael. A nice kid and rather bright. Perhaps fourteen at the time. I didn't see anything sexual going on between them, but it might be possible."

Knowing that Dmytryk was a sophisticated man of the world, and a discreet one, Michael confided a secret in him. "I once wanted to look like Diana Ross and a lot of people say I do. But now I want a different look. I'm going to have my appearance altered to look like Elizabeth as she was when she appeared with Mickey Rooney in *National Velvet* in 1945. I've seen the picture fifteen times."

Although it was later denied, Michael did create a "shrine" to Elizabeth at Neverland. Michael's publicist, Bob Jones, confirmed the existence of the shrine to Elizabeth. Several visitors saw it before it was locked permanently, its exhibits ultimately removed and put into storage when the white-heat friendship between the two legends dimmed somewhat. Within the shrine, on giant video screens, Elizabeth's films such as *A Place in the Sun*, *Cleopatra*, and *National Velvet* played twenty-four hours a day. Michael refused to show *Butterfield 8*, the 1960 film in which Elizabeth won an Oscar for her portrayal of a prostitute. "It's okay with me," Elizabeth was quoted as saying. "I thought the picture was lousy too and didn't want to make it."

Michael designed the wallpaper himself. It portrayed a series of little heads of Elizabeth. For the walls not covered with paper, Michael demanded that the painters come up with the exact violet of Elizabeth's eyes, but they never were able to match the exact shade.

Elizabeth interested Michael in the cause of fighting AIDS, and he not only donated money for her charity but was her escort to functions in Los Angeles staged to raise money in the battle against a disease that was killing off many of her friends. It claimed Rock Hudson, her costar in *Giant*, on October 2, 1985.

Michael boycotted the 12th Annual American Music Awards ceremony. He sensed what was to come. Unlike his great success in 1985 with *Thriller*, he failed to win any of the awards for which he was nominated.

Many of the artists who attended the awards ceremony later showed up at midnight to meet Michael and to record "We Are the World."

Quincy Jones posted a sign outside the studio that read: LEAVE YOUR EGO AT THE DOOR. The artists came from the worlds of pop, R&B, country, whatever. Among those who appeared were Harry Belafonte, Ray Charles, Bob Dylan, Cyndi Lauper, Tina Turner, Bette Midler, Willie Nelson, The Pointer Sisters, Paul Simon, Stevie Wonder, Smokey Robinson, Dionne Warwick, Bruce Springsteen, and Diana Ross, who went around asking for autographs. "How could she embarrass me like this?" Michael asked. "She's too big a star to ask for autographs."

Leaving the studio after a long night, Michael confided that he hadn't had dinner. He was going home to demand that his chef prepare him a plate of steamed okra.

One critic of the video claimed that all the stars except Michael had, indeed, left their egos at the door that night. He demanded that his solo recording be taped privately and away from the rest of the stars. "He wanted to be different and set aside from the other celebrities," said one of the recording staff. "Like he was special, better than the rest of the singers. In the video, a shot begins at his sequined socks and his Bass Weejun shoes. He's so big he doesn't need to show his face right away."

Michael was overheard bragging, "Fans will know me the moment they see my socks. Try to photograph Bruce Springsteen's socks. No one will know who he is. *No one!*"

"We Are the World—The Video Event" became the ninth best-selling

Quincy Jones, Lionel Richie, and Michael Jackson, 1985

video cassette of 1985, and "We Are the World" as a single record became the first ever to go multi-platinum, staying number one on *Billboard*'s charts for a month. The song's sales raised more than $40 million. At the Grammy Awards at the Shrine Auditorium in Los Angeles in February of 1986, "We Are the World" won four awards.

In June of that year Michael celebrated his success with "We Are the World" by undergoing yet a fourth operation on his nose, demanding to have it made even slimmer, although it was quite thin as it was. He claimed that he would soon turn twenty-eight, and he wanted to celebrate with a thinner nose, even though Jehovah's Witnesses aren't supposed to observe birthdays.

After he'd recovered from the operation, Michael told friends, "I can hardly rehearse my music any more. I spend all day looking at my reflection in the mirror. Dr. Steven Hoefflin is a wonderful plastic surgeon. Because of me, he's called 'The Plastic Surgeon to the Stars.' Not just movie stars go to him. Even Ivana Trump uses him."

Michael also reminded anyone interested, even Paul Anka, who clearly wasn't, that "lots of famous stars in the past had nose jobs, even Elvis Presley. Marilyn Monroe not only had her nose done, but her breasts. You don't think for a moment that those breasts were actually hers, do you?"

At one point, Frank DiLeo wondered why his client bothered with such expensive nose jobs and then went out in public with a surgical mask. "The last time he was spotted, or so I heard, he was wearing a gorilla head mask with fur. King Kong all the way."

On May 12, 1986, it was announced at a press conference in New York that Michael's new look would be showcased in Pepsi commercials. Michael, according to a contract negotiated with the soft drink king, Roger Enrico, would be paid a record-breaking $15 million. This time he wouldn't have to split the millions with his brothers, and, according to his demands, would not have to be seen "drinking one drop of the vile soda." Pepsi also agreed to sponsor Michael's first nationwide solo tour, although no dates were announced for that momentous event. Under most endorsement deals, an artist is usually paid in installments. Michael demanded the entire $15 million up front.

When the mega-check cleared, Michael was not in a mood for celebration. No longer was he thinking of the competition from Prince, but a challenge coming from "down the hall," a reference to the Encino manse where he still lived

MJ and Bob Jones

240

on the same floor as his younger sister Janet. Family members had overheard the second-most talented member of the Jackson clan claiming that her new album, *Control*, was going to sell more copies than the record-busting *Thriller*.

Even Papa Joe had told her, "You'll be as big as Michael—not bigger, but as big." Janet was in the throes of her own management crisis, as she, like Michael and her other brothers, wanted to break from her father, turning to others, such as John McClain, a young executive at A&M, for career guidance, much to her father's rage and fury.

After studying the latest photographs of Janet, Michael was enraged. He stormed out of his bedroom and rushed downstairs to confront Katherine. "Janet's even stolen my nose and had a plastic surgeon build an exact copy for herself. Not only that, she sounds like me. She looks like me. She's stealing my dance steps."

Katherine was hardly reassuring. "You started a trend. Everybody in the family, even your father, is trying to look like you, with a little help from plastic surgeons. That is, all except Jackie. He's pleased with the face God gave him."

With *Control*, Janet showed the world that she was no longer Daddy's Little Girl. She finally sacked Papa Joe as her manager and teamed with Terry Lewis and Jimmy ("Jam") Harris, two multi-talented music men, to create the album. Joe predicted failure, but *Control* went on to sell eight million copies and won Grammys for Lewis and Harris. Reportedly, Michael was furious at the album's success, especially when it spawned such hit singles as "What Have You Done for Me Lately?"

Michael complained bitterly to his publicist, Norman Winter, that both La Toya and Janet were altering their faces to look more like him. "You've got to do something about it," Michael demanded of Winter.

"But I'm not a plastic surgeon," he protested. "Otherwise, I would make La Toya look like a female Little Richard and Janet Mike Tyson in drag."

Michael was not amused at Winter's sarcasm. "The way it is now, La Toya is often mistaken for me when she goes through airports or lounges of deluxe hotels. Why would anyone mistake La Toya for me? Do you think I look like a girl?"

Winter had no comment.

Michael's fury spilled over onto Diana Ross when he learned that she was marrying a white man, Arne Naess, the Norwegian shipping millionaire who lived in Oslo. At first there had been rumors that he'd attend their wedding the following February, even functioning as best man for Naess. But later, he sent word to Ross that he was turning down her invitation to the wedding—"and future invitations as well."

Ross suffered public humiliation. "He has Elizabeth Taylor now," she told friends. "What does he need with the woman who was responsible for launching his career. Fuck him! Instead of ordering his chauffeur to call him *Miss Ross*, he's probably demanding to be called *Miss Taylor* now."

When Elizabeth heard what Ross had said, she replied, "Meow!"

Ross got her revenge two years later when Michael broke his stonewall silence and requested her appearance on a Showtime special for television. It was to be a tribute from "loving friends" to Michael's career and life. Ross cabled that she could not make the commitment because of her busy schedule.

Janet

"What do I need her for?" Michael ranted. "I've got Elizabeth Taylor. Sophia Loren. Gene Kelly. And Quincy Jones and Sean Lennon, and anybody else I could get if I really wanted them. She turns me down and I'm a bigger star than Greta Garbo in her heyday!" He had been reading books about the reclusive Garbo.

At one point, Michael told Winter that he would "henceforth and forever more" associate only with celebrities who were his equal. He didn't want minor celebrities being photographed with him "and trying to get a big break by feeding off my fame."

He made some exceptions to that. Bodyguards at Hayvenhurst would later report a parade of young boys, ranging in age from nine to fourteen, being slipped into Michael's bedroom at night. In spite of this clandestine activity, Michael was still living with his parents at Encino. One guard estimated that over a three-year period "at least three dozen young kids were slipped in." He could not offer an explanation about why parents would allow their offspring to spend the night with an entertainer "approaching the big 3-0" in age.

One guard would later testify that all the boys were white—and often blond and blue-eyed. None of them was black, as was the case with Emmanuel Lewis. Sometimes these boys would stay in Michael's bedroom for almost a month. Other boys were sent packing after only a one-night "sleepover."

All meals were prepared for Michael and the toy boy of the moment and delivered on a tray which rested outside his door. Michael would issue orders that he not be disturbed for days at a time.

According to La Toya, Michael would often keep seeing the same boy on and off for more than a year at a time. After they got "too old," the boys were dropped. Some were not willing to get the boot, and often had to be bought off or coerced out of the house with expensive gifts.

In a disturbing revelation, La Toya reported that Katherine, in a search of Michael's room when he was out of town, discovered a stash of checks. To La Toya, Katherine called her son "a fucking faggot." As a devout Jehovah's Witness, she was homophobic, as were many other members of her cult.

Checks in varying amounts— $100,000, $200,000, $300,000, even $1 million—had been written to parents of boys Michael had entertained for prolonged sleepovers. Even checks for the purchases of Rolls-Royces were found. Apparently, Michael gave away these expensive vehicles the way Elvis gave away Cadillacs.

Sophia Loren

La Toya warned Michael that he was courting a potential public scandal and might also be setting himself up for future blackmail. "Some of these parents might come back in the future and demand more money when whatever you gave them is spent."

He turned a deaf ear to her. "I love kids," he said. "We're just playing games—that's all there is to it. Case closed."

When not entertaining young boys, Michael entertained lucrative proposals for various endorsement deals. He was offered nearly $30 million by entrepreneurs to sponsor a line of Michael Jackson clothing. Copies of the clothes he wore in such videos as "Thriller" or "Beat It" were approved by Michael, but there were so many delays and indecisions on his part that the clothing did not make an impact on the market. Rip-offs of Michael Jackson clothing, especially garments made in China and Japan, saturated the market, such a vast exploitation that it virtually destroyed the authentic MJ label.

Likewise, an attempt to launch a line of toys called "Michael's Pets" also failed. There would have been a talking Muscles and a talking Bubbles. At one point it was reported that Michael became so jealous of all the media attention focusing on his chimp—and not on himself—that he nixed the deal.

He sent word to the toy manufacturers, "Let us not forget that it is Michael Jackson—not Bubbles—who is the star of this show." The line of toys never took off either, although Michael was said to have kept nearly $25 million in various marketing advances, including a line of Michael Jackson sunglasses.

"Michael Jackson ended up screwing everybody," said entrepreneur Bob Michaelson, who called his would-be partner "a sleaze."

Rip-off Michael Jackson clothing—some of the garments bearing a label MADE IN TAIWAN—flooded America. Kids attending schools from Oregon to Florida were wearing Michael Jackson sneakers, Michael Jackson T-shirts, and even carrying Michael Jackson lunchboxes. All of this merchandise was unauthorized, and the legitimate promoters who had originally contracted with Michael to use his image "went belly-up," in the words of one failed clothing manufacturer.

Among entrepreneurs in the business world, Michael became known as a "ruthless son-of-a-bitch." One irate manufacturer said, "Behind that whispery little Marilyn Monroe voice, that face of supposed naïveté, there beats a heart of gold. Hold onto your shirts should you ever have the misfortune to cross his path. He'll take it off your back. Not only that, he'll take your pants, your shoes, your socks, and, as a final fuck-you, your jockey shorts."

The business community wasn't the only sector furious at Michael Jackson. Jehovah's Witnesses were still upset about *Thriller*. They were as yet unaware of the future accusations that would link Michael with molestation of young boys. By February of 1987, Michael and the Jehovah's Witnesses had had it with each other. Michael was deliberately promoting a self-styled "bizarre" lifestyle, which the ultra-conservative church leaders found "repulsive," in the words of one of their elders. "In our church, men do not wear lipstick and enough makeup to look like a Saturday night whore," a spokesman said. "Unlike his mother, Mr. Jackson is not a true Jehovah's Witness. His lifestyle is not compatible with the teachings of our church."

William Van De Wall, speaking for the Watchtower Bible Society, said it was Michael's wish to separate himself from the church. "For one violation alone, he could have been disfellowshipped," Van De Wall claimed. "He attended a birthday party for Elizabeth Taylor. Jehovah's Witnesses do not celebrate birthdays. This has been made perfectly clear to Mr. Jackson from the beginning. He deliberately mocked our beliefs by attending the party for this much-married and scandalous movie star."

According to the terms of the church, Katherine would go against church policy if she ever spoke to her son once he was "disfellowshipped." Even so devout a Jehovah's Witness as Katherine had no intention of obeying this rule. She was riding around Los Angeles in a maroon-colored Rolls-Royce, a birthday gift from Michael, with whom she'd maintain a loving relationship long after he withdrew from the church.

Freed from the heavy rules of his cult religion, one of the world's most intolerant and severe, Michael would increasingly pursue that self-proclaimed "bizarre" lifestyle that he wanted. But he didn't spend all his time with cute little boys locked away in darkened bedrooms. He actively added to his list of friends a growing number of the most famous names in Hollywood, deciding that Liza Minnelli, Elizabeth Taylor, and Katharine Hepburn, although good for openers, weren't enough.

Even Robert De Niro showed up at Michael's for dinner. "Except for Frank Sinatra, whom Michael detested, he loved all Italians, because of his continuing fascination with the Mafia," Brando said. "Even though I'm not Italian, I had made *that* movie—so I qualified. But Michael seemed to think every Italian had a link to the mob, and this utterly thrilled him. He once told me he loved his manager, Frank DiLeo, because of his Italian name. He even entertained Martin Scorsese. Believe you me, Scorsese has no links to the mob. The one entertainer who did have a link to the mob, that piece of wop shit, Sinatra himself, turned Michael off and was never invited to one of his Italian nights like I was. Of course, I'm sure Sinatra wouldn't have gone to Michael's had he been invited. Oh, didn't I tell you? Ava Gardner once said I was a much better lay than Sinatra. Apparently, at times he was impotent. My noble tool has never failed me and never disappointed any woman. Or man, for that matter."

As the 80s deepened, and work continued on his latest album, *Bad*, which was delayed for months, Michael befriended the rich and famous. All of these elite members of the "Old Guard" in Hollywood wanted to meet the most famous entertainer in the world. In fact, Ronald Reagan one time called Michael—not to give him another award—but to chat with him for about fifteen minutes.

When Brando heard that, he laughed. "Perhaps Reagan needed Michael's advice on how to run the planet," Brando said facetiously. Brando could not tolerate Reagan. "God knows someone sane should give Reagan some advice. Bad actor. Bad president."

To Michael's doorstep came a host of stars, all odd couplings for Michael. Gregory Peck. Charlton Heston. Sophia Loren. Cary Grant. "I think most of them were driven by curiosity," Brando said. "Let's face it: all of us are in show business. It's only natural for stars to want to meet fellow stars. Peck and Heston didn't show up for the stimulating conversation. I love Michael dearly, although I never got around to fucking him. But, let's face it, at the table he doesn't have much to say. But it's fun to watch him get through a dinner giggling into his white-starched napkin. His maids must have a hard time getting rid of the lipstick smears."

When macho Charlton Heston came to dinner, Michael wanted to impress "Moses" with his straight credentials. He told the preposterous story that at least once a week he retreated to Hugh Hefner's Playboy mansion "where I enjoy my own private harem."

Whether Heston fell for this is not known.

Heston may have been the most conservative A-list actor that Michael would ever meet. His name had never been linked to any woman other than his wife, Lydia Clarke, a former drama student.

Heston's advocacy of "two guns in every home" and his right-wing political conservatism did not open many doors to him in Hollywood. Michael may not have been aware of Heston's political positions, although he was familiar with some of Heston's films.

Michael had seen his 1968 *Planet of the Apes* five times. Heston once said, "Nudity is never erotic, except in the bedroom." Yet he became the first major American male film star to show his ass in a movie.

Heston himself admitted that he was "too dull, too square, and too Protestant." As such, he fitted in with the public image that Michael promoted of himself. He still used the excuse that he was a virgin because his church dictated no sex before marriage. Heston seemed to live by that rule too. "I'm not a drunk," Heston told Michael, "and I've had only one wife. I don't cheat on her, and my kids aren't runaways."

He seemed to like Michael, or at least the image that Michael was projecting of himself. Later, when Heston learned that Michael might be a molester of young boys, he retreated in horror from his former friend. "I have never been an advocate of the homosexual lifestyle," Heston said.

"No one ever accused me of being a champion of gay rights. Child molestation is perhaps the most evil form of sex known on the planet. If Jackson has been guilty of such crimes, he should be sentenced to prison for life. Once in prison, he may learn the evils of molestation first hand."

Heston even lectured Michael on the "necessity" of keeping firearms in the house. "It seems to me ethically questionable to expect a policeman earning $35,000 annually to risk his life to protect a citizen. We've got to protect ourselves, turn our homes into armed camps if necessary. Even women should be trained to use weapons." He offered to teach Michael how to shoot, and he also invited Michael to his own home to see his gun collection. Michael never accepted either offer.

Witty, urbane, and sophisticated, Gregory Peck was the very opposite of Charlton Heston. Michael had little to say to Peck, but was seemingly fascinated by his long career and stories of the personalities he'd encountered. With his deep, modulated voice, Peck could hold a listener *Spellbound*, the name, of course, of one of his first movies, released in 1945. During the making of that film, he'd enjoyed a torrid affair with Ingrid Bergman.

He told Michael stories about his life that he'd never told an interviewer.

Charlton Heston

"People talk about you wearing lipstick," Peck said. "I did you one better. Once I was a tour guide at Radio City in New York. As a gag, the manager had me dress up in drag one night and come out as one of the Rockettes."

Michael told him that he'd cried while watching his 1962 performance in *To Kill a Mockingbird*.

Peck thanked him for the compliment but preferred to speak of movies that were never made. "Two years before *Mockingbird*, I was cast opposite Marilyn Monroe in *Let's Make Love*," he said. "Believe it or not, I was cast in a singing and dancing role. Now don't get fired up. My singing and dancing—have no fear—would not have offered you any competition at all. I dropped out when Marilyn's hubby at the time, Arthur Miller, downgraded my part and built up Marilyn's. Even so, Marilyn and I really bonded. I saw she was self-destructing. I tried to save her. But making love to a woman every day isn't necessarily the way to save her. She told me that if I married her, we'd be the happiest couple on the planet. Dreams, my friend, are sometimes better left as such and never translated into reality."

"Marilyn Monroe would have frightened me to death," Michael said. "Too much woman."

Peck and Michael also talked about the increasing infringement of the media into a star's private life, and Peck sympathized with the ongoing invasions of Michael's privacy. "It's second rate to expose one's insides to the public," Peck said. "I don't like the tendency of all these actors to go on TV and tell all. It's in poor taste. The only self-revelation I go for is in my screen performance. The public doesn't need to know that I fucked Ava Gardner."

Michael wanted to know how Peck got his start, and the actor laughed. "On the stage. I once worked with the great Katherine Cornell, a famous stage actress long before your day. She told me that I'd never make it as a film star. 'One of your ears is larger than the other,' she said, as if I didn't already know that."

One night Peck arrived unexpectedly at Michael's door, asking for the copy of the 1987 film *Amazing Grace and Chuck* that Peck had made with Jamie Lee Curtis. As a good neighbor, he'd lent the film to Michael but had to pick it up because a film exhibitor had received a defective copy. Peck wanted to get a good print in time for an eight o'clock showing of the film in a neighboring town. Peck returned later for a visit with Michael.

He surprised Michael by telling him that political groups were being formed to run him for President in the 1988 elections. "These foolish people think the world will be improved considerably if I replace Reagan in the White House. Then there are those who think Paul Newman should run as president with me running as vice president."

"The day has come," Michael proclaimed. "Movie stars taking over the role of politicians."

Peck amused Michael by reading to him an article that suggested Charlton Heston should run as the Republican candidate for President, with Peck taking up the Democratic banner. "Peck has nothing to compare with Heston's Moses," the

Gregory Peck

actor read from the newspaper column, "although Peck's portrayal of Douglas MacArthur cannot be taken lightly."

Peck facetiously said he feared that if he ran for President, his previous roles, where he played "certifiable lunatics," would be used against him. He included Captain Ahab in *Moby Dick* and Dr. Josef Mengele in *The Boys from Brazil*.

"I also suffered traumatic anxiety in *Spellbound*, and in *Twelve O'Clock High* I went to pieces under the strain of sending bombers on missions where they might die."

"I don't know," Michael said. "I've watched with my friend, Bubbles, *Bedtime for Bonzo* many times. It didn't keep Reagan out of the White House. Incidentally, if *Bedtime for Bonzo* is remade, I want Bubbles to play the lead. Perhaps you'll take the Reagan role in the remake."

Peck told Michael that "about as close as I will ever get to the White House is a visit I paid there when Richard Nixon was president. He kept praising my performances in films, and told me that in all of them I stood for the American way of life. I asked Nixon, 'Which films were your favorites?' I fully expected him to say *To Kill a Mockingbird*. Everybody goes for that one. Nixon said he thought I was most memorable in *Red River, Fort Apache, She Wore a Yellow Ribbon*, and *Sands of Iwo Jima*. I didn't want to embarrass the President but he had confused me with John Wayne."

One night Peck informed Michael that he'd signed with Michael's dear friend, Jane Fonda, to make a movie called *Old Gringo*.

Michael and Peck remained friends for a quarter of a century. Peck often went riding with Michael on his ranch, Neverland, and the actor was amazed that Michael had seen *To Kill a Mockingbird* so many times that he had actually memorized all the dialogue.

Unlike most of Michael's fabled friends, Peck defended him when

248

charges of child molestation arose. He even called Michael "a model parent," and posted a letter on Michael's website, defending him.

During many happy visits to Neverland, Peck saw up close how Michael was with his children, Prince Michael I and Paris, from his marriage to Debbie Rowe, his dermatology nurse. Peck even lived to see Michael as a parent to Prince Michael II by a surrogate mother.

At Michael's 30th Anniversary Celebration at New York's Madison Square Garden in 2001, an aging and ailing Peck taped a glowing video tribute. He'd kept his good looks as he matured, but he died in June of 2003. When Michael heard the news broadcast on TV, he cried for hours at the loss of such a steadfast and loyal friend. "The others deserted me," Michael claimed. "They won't take my calls. But Gregory was always there for me."

On Monday, June 16, 2003 Cardinal Roger Michael Mahoney, archbishop of Los Angeles, held up funeral services for 20 minutes because of Michael's late arrival at Peck's funeral. The moment he walked into the church, Michael realized he was inappropriately dressed. For the occasion, he'd worn a red jacket. To his dismay, he discovered that all the ushers were wearing a similar red jacket. Michael demanded that the services be further delayed until he could send for a black jacket, but the archbishop refused to accommodate him any more.

After the services, Michael shook hands with Harry Belafonte and Anjelica Huston, with whom he'd costarred in *Captain EO*. He stepped up in front of Greta Konen Peck, the hairdresser Peck had married, and offered his condolences.

She was 92 years old, and she took Michael's hand and gently squeezed it. "My husband admired you very much." Holding back tears, she said, "The story is over. No more Kilimanjaros to climb." She was referring to the 1952 movie, *The Snows of Kilimanjaro*, that her husband had made with Susan Hayward and Ava Gardner.

The friendship that existed between Charlton Heston and Michael, or even Gregory Peck and Michael, surprised Hollywood. His forming a relationship with Sophia Loren shocked insiders. "What are those two doing at night together?" asked reporter Donald Wolper. "I can guarantee they're not getting together for sex."

For all the world to hear, the forever chic and still glamorous Neapolitan proclaimed, "When I met him, it was love at first sight," she said.

In 1988, when Michael performed in Paris, Loren, in stunning couture, showed up to greet him. To the show, she'd invited an entourage of two dozen guests. When Michael appeared in Switzerland that same year, the continent-hopping Loren was also there to greet him.

Loren also appeared at Neverland for dinner with Michael, but claimed she wouldn't show up if he invited his "best friend," Marlon Brando.

"When we made that 1967 disaster, *A Countess from Hong Kong*, your Mr. Brando told me that 'my tits and ass are too big,'" Loren confided to Michael. "What about his tits and ass being too big? Fatso!" The picture had been directed by a 77-year-old Charlie Chaplin, who still remained Michael's all-time screen favorite.

Marlon later said, "Michael Jackson is the only person in the world who appreciated that movie."

Anjelica Huston

When Michael expressed his admiration of Loren's performance in the film, she said, "How very kind. But one reviewer found that Brando and *moi* had 'about as much passion as that of a pair of love-wracked halibuts.' How right he was."

"Is it true that Marlon told Chaplin at the end of the shoot…" He hesitated, not wanting to say the words.

"Brando informed Chaplin, 'You can take this fucking film and stick it up your ass—frame by frame!' Your Mr. Brando has such a way with words."

Michael was fascinated by Loren's background and eagerly listened to stories of her private life. Her upbringing had been even more difficult than his own, as she'd been born in a ward for unmarried mothers in Naples. She went on to become a star and international sex symbol, cooking spaghetti for Marshal Tito of Yugoslavia and dining with the Queen of England.

Michael was particularly interested in Loren's impression of working with his movie star pals—not just Brando, but Gregory Peck in *Arabesque* in 1966, and even Charlton Heston in the 1961 *El Cid*. "I was going through my epic period," Loren said, making it sound like an apology.

Michael was eager to learn what he could about Cary Grant, with whom Loren had appeared in the 1957 *The Pride and the Passion* and the 1958 *Houseboat*. One of Michael's all-time favorite films was *Bringing Up Baby*. Grant made the film in 1938 for RKO opposite Michael's friend, Katharine Hepburn. "I like leopards—that's why I liked the movie," Michael said.

He asked Loren if she could arrange for him to meet Grant. "Ask your friend Katharine Hepburn to set it up," Loren said, somewhat dismissively.

Weeks later Michael learned that Grant had fallen for Loren, filling her dressing room with fresh roses every day during the making of *Houseboat*. "I knew he loved me," Loren later said, "but he never came right out and said so—that's not his style." In spite of her wooing by the handsome actor, Loren

250

chose to stay with Carlo Ponti, her husband. Michael later learned that Loren had even spurned the advances of President John F. Kennedy.

In March of 1987, when Motown Productions launched a special for Showtime's cable network, *Motown on Showtime: Michael Jackson*, Loren went on the air as an expert on Michael Jackson. So did Elizabeth Taylor, joining Yoko Ono and Gene Kelly. Two people refused to cooperate: Diana Ross, still angered by Michael's boycott of her wedding to Arne Naess, and Michael himself. Michael's refusal to participate in his own tribute could only be viewed as arrogance by Motown's Berry Gordy Jr.

When he heard that Ross had turned down Motown's request to host his tribute, Michael attempted a lame explanation to the press. "I was jealous—that's why I didn't go to the wedding," he falsely claimed. "I wanted to marry Diana myself. The fourteen-year difference between us doesn't matter to me."

At this point in Michael's career, not one member of the press, even the most gullible, believed him. To an increasing degree, his straight talk was met with greater and greater skepticism.

Michael got even with Ross. Even though he was not participating in the Showtime "lovefest," he had total control over the project. The American public heard that Ross had taken credit for discovering The Jackson 5, but Michael now began dismissing that claim as publicity hype. "Not a word of truth to it," Michael said in direct contrast to statements he'd made since the 70s.

Michael was once overheard backstage at a concert talking to people he perceived as stagehands, not knowing that Jonathan Reeves was a freelance reporter who lived and fed on the fringe world of celebrities. "I can't be seen with run-of-the-mill celebrities, people like Richard Gere or Cindy Crawford. With my status in the world, I need to hang out with Jackie, Elizabeth, or Marlon. Sophia Loren is definitely A-list. I mean, she even won an Oscar. I'm

An artist's portrayal of MJ and Sophia Loren

proud to be photographed with her. She's so elegant, so beautiful, and, also, the world's best chef."

Before the child molestation charges went public, Loren was always there for Michael, at least at public events. In January of 1990 she attended a star-studded event at the Beverly Hilton in Beverly Hills. Honorees included Michael's friends, Elizabeth

Taylor and Gregory Peck. But it was clearly Michael's night when he won The American Cinema Award as "Entertainer of the Year." Michael showed up in a midnight black military uniform. Parading to the podium with an army of six bodyguards, he was presented the great honor by Loren herself. She had been photographed accompanying Michael to the awards ceremony which was hosted by Michael Douglas.

"The 90s had arrived," said Peck years later, "and Michael was king. But his incredible world was about to end."

When Cary Grant learned that Michael wanted to meet him, he came to call. At first the coming together of Michael with Grant appeared to be another one of the singer's many "odd couple" relationships. Yet the two superstars had more in common than might be obvious at first.

Grant was witty, sophisticated and urbane, whereas Michael was inarticulate and lacking a social presence except when he was on stage. Grant was seductive and could even be menacing on the screen. Michael was not. But both could be mysterious, as each star led a closeted life. Both were born into poverty.

Seated before Michael and fifteen minutes into the conversation (with Grant doing most of the talking), he informed Michael that he used to perform in musicals. "Never could carry a tune, though. I used to stand on stage and mouth the words. A singer behind the curtain warbled for me. I was also an acrobat and a juggler if you want me to teach you some lessons."

"I want to have a screen presence like you have," Michael said. "How did you do it?"

"It was an accident," Grant confessed. "In my early pictures reviewers found I had an amazing asexuality. Of course, I was cast with all the wrong women. In *Blonde Venus*, there was no heat between Marlene Dietrich and me. At that time I didn't know that I was supposed to actually act a love scene. She had eyes only for her director, Josef von Sternberg, and certain ladies. She was later asked what she felt about me. 'I had no feelings,' Dietrich said. 'He was a homosexual.' Wasn't that a charming reply?"

"Other people have said the same thing about me," Michael confessed.

"I know that! They've spread fag rumors about me for years. If someone wants to say I'm gay, what can I do?"

Grant was not being candid with Michael. He cared a lot about "fag rumors," sometimes suing. Even at the end of his life, he sued comedian Chevy Chase for saying, "I understand he was a homo," on Tom Snyder's *Tomorrow* talk show. At one point, Chase, billed as "the next Cary Grant," referred to the actor as brilliant but added, "What a gal!" Grant sued Chase for slander for $10 million, settling out of court for perhaps a million.

Michael complimented Grant on his movie appearances, including his

252

favorite film, *Bringing Up Baby*. But he told him he also liked him in *North by Northwest*, a film Grant had made for Alfred Hitchcock.

"I turned down *Lolita* to make that one," Grant said.

"What's *Lolita* about?" Michael asked.

Grant looked stunned that he hadn't heard of it. "It was a degenerate film about child molestation. Do you think I could have played a child molester? It was based on a novel by Vladimir Nabokov. About a man lusting after a young nymphet. Sir Laurence Olivier also turned it down. James Mason took the role and made it a classic. Even so, I'm glad I turned it down. Originally, Nabokov's publisher wanted him to rewrite the book, having the older man lust for a young boy. A sort of Tadzio. You know, *Death in Venice* and all that. The first script I was shown had Lolita cast as a boy, a kind of Lolito. Like bloody hell would I ever appear as a homosexual in film, much less as a child-molesting homo. A chicken hawk we'd call it. I did enough of that when I got intimate with Katharine Hepburn in *Sylvia Scarlet*. Presumably in the film, I thought Hepburn, with short hair and trousers, a boy. Yet George Cukor in one scene had me undress for the bed I was supposed to share with her. I look her over, thinking it's a boy, and say 'It's nippy tonight. You'll make a proper hot water bottle!' Personally, I think child molestation is repulsive."

It is not known if Grant at the time knew of Michael's interest in young boys and was indirectly criticizing him.

As the evening progressed, Grant pointedly looked at Michael. La Toya that night was in and out of the room; otherwise, we'd know nothing of this encounter between Grant and Michael.

"I read the other day that you said you planned to get married and have a family," Grant said.

"Yes, that is my dream," Michael said. "Many children to love."

"I don't advise it," Grant said. "I forget how many times I've been married. Every one of my wives left me. I don't know why. Maybe they got bored, real tired of me. My first wife accused me of being a homosexual. All the women, except Betsy, have accused me of being a homosexual. Virginia was just the first."

He was referring, of course, to Virginia Cherill and Betsy Drake.

Although Michael's meeting with Gregory Peck developed into a long-time friendship, his association with Grant was relatively short. Neither performer seemed to have any desire to pursue the other after one evening.

The following morning, Michael called Katharine Hepburn to ask her about her long-ago costar.

Tight-lipped and uncooperative with the press, Hepburn could be surprisingly outspoken in private. "Oh, yes, Cary Grant," she said. "If I recall, he was a supporting player to me in a film or two. Cold as the Arctic night. Ego as large as Mount Rushmore. A tightwad, but so am I. A self-hating homosexual. Never told the truth in his life, a compulsive liar. Took LSD for psychiatric reasons, or so he said. Married unhappily so many times you'd think he would finally learn that he hates women. Such a charming presence on the screen. Such a lonely heart off screen."

Michael, when not "hanging with the stars," was under great pressure to come out with a follow-up album to *Thriller*.

With more than sixty songs written, he had ample material from which to make the final selections. Driving himself to the verge of a nervous breakdown, he had an almost pathological desire to top *Thriller*. "I want to be the *only* Jackson on the charts." He was referring, of course, to the runaway success of sister Janet's *Control* album. His resentment of Janet's success became so strong that he began to ridicule her physicality. "You have the fattest thighs in the family," he told her.

The *Bad* album would be long in the gestation period. Many of Michael's hopes and dreams for the album never materialized. Originally, he'd wanted to record a duet with Prince to determine which one was "really bad." Michael told his producer, "that Prince could do all those James Brown imitations I used to do, and I could do my famous Moonwalk." Quincy shipped Prince a tape of the song. "It's shit!" Prince told his aides. "Send word to that gal I want nothing to do with *her* album."

Michael was also rebuffed when he wanted to record a duet with Barbra Streisand called "I Just Can't Stop Loving You." The diva sent back word: "You've got to be kidding. Me in a love duet with Michael Jackson? Ronald Reagan and I would be more convincing."

Michael was also rejected by Whitney Houston. "I don't understand," she said. "Does Michael want me to sing the girl's part—or is he saving that for himself?"

Quincy suggested that Diana Ross be asked. "Why should I revive her career?" Michael said.

In lieu of Streisand or Houston, Michael chose the unknown Siedah Garrett, a protégée of Quincy's, for the duet.

Eight of the ten songs on the LP were written by Michael, who also sang both lead and background vocals. He also wrote "Leave Me Alone" on the CD bonus track. In addition, he duetted with Stevie Wonder in "Just Good Friends." An adaptation of a gospel song, "Man in the Mirror," was sung with Andraé Crouch.

During their work together, there were false rumors circulating about a romance between Michael and Siedah Garrett, perhaps spread by Michael himself. She looked a lot like him. One headline claimed JACKSON AND LOOKALIKE MULLING MARRIAGE.

A member of the *Bad* crew later sarcastically said, "About the only phallic image Siedah ever saw was an eighteen-foot python that Jackson had three guys carry to the studio to frighten the shit out of her."

A California singer two years younger than Michael, Garrett was a talented artist who had previously performed in a duet with Dennis Edwards of The Temptations. Released in 1984, "Don't Look Any Further" was a Top 5 R&B hit.

Michael liked this African-American singer and songwriter as a friend, never a lover, and even hired Garrett to tour with him from 1992 to 1993 in his *Dangerous* trek around the globe.

But he never really forgave her when she supported Madonna as a backup singer and dancer on the "Re-Invention" Tour in 2004. Garrett's signing with Michael's "nemesis," Madonna, should hardly have come as a surprise to Michael, as Garrett had also sung backup vocals for Madonna in "True Blue" in 1986 and "Who's That Girl?" in 1987.

The Jackson/Garrett duet, "I Just Can't Stop Loving You," was the first single release from the *Bad* album. Its release was a good omen for the success of the album itself. The song shot to Number One on *Billboard*'s charts, but, regrettably, fell fast. Within fourteen weeks, it was off the charts completely, a short run for such a big hit in the music industry.

Garrett is still known today for co-writing Michael's worldwide hit, "Man in the Mirror," which was included in the *Bad* album. A lot of fans thought Michael was the co-author of "Man in the Mirror," but it was really another songwriter, Glen Ballard.

The second solo from the album, the namesake song, "Bad," sold nearly 11 million copies around the world, climbing to Number One on the charts in twenty-three countries. It was released in October of 1987.

The *Bad* album would produce five Number One songs, including the wonderfully melodramatic "Smooth Criminal." "Another Part of Me" was also a hit, as was "The Way You Make Me Feel." Michael denied that his solo, "Dirty Diana," was a dig at Diana Ross, with whom he was on the outs. Steve Stevens, a former guitarist for Billy Idol, performed with Michael on "Dirty Diana." But, in the words of one critic, "These two talents couldn't rescue this song."

Evoking silent screen vamp Gloria Swanson, the original album cover depicted Michael's face covered with a patterned lace net. Walter Yetnikoff at CBS Records exploded when he saw this cover, "What in hell's going on here? The cover says 'Bad,' not 'faggot!'" A picture of Michael in street punk black leather was submitted instead.

After endless delays, the *Bad* album was completed by June of 1987 and released that September where it made its debut as Number One on the charts.

"What a way to celebrate your twenty-ninth birthday," Michael said. Now that he'd cut himself off from the Jehovah's Witnesses, he could celebrate birthdays, which he'd always adored anyway.

As one reviewer, in an attack on the album, put it: "Even when Michael's 'Bad,' he's good, at least in sales." The solo single, "Bad," shot to Number One but collapsed within a five-week period. As Frank DiLeo knew from the beginning, *Bad* was not going to be another *Thriller*.

Glowing reviews flooded the media, including *Rolling Stone*, its critic claiming that Michael "can out funk anybody anytime."

But was Michael the funkiest? His "Bad" solo was attacked by many critics from black magazines. "If this is the *blackest* Jackson can get, better bring out the tarbrush." That line for *Ebony* magazine was killed before printing. Allegedly, it was written by "one seriously pissed-off black dude."

Even if *Thriller* could not be topped in sales, *Bad* would sell twenty-five million copies worldwide, making it the second biggest selling album of all time, an impressive achievement for any performer, but one viewed as a failure by Michael, who had so desperately wanted to beat his own record.

In spite of its success and all those hit singles, *Bad*, as an album, when heard today, is rather disappointing. For example, one critic wrote that the song, "Dirty Diana," a moody techno-metal excursion, "could have used a little less fake crowd noise and a little more Eddie Van Halen." Another critic complained of the "programmed synthesizers and cheesy backing chants that are *everywhere*." Basically, *Bad* has emerged as a fine dance pop album with some "catchy (albeit lightweight) tracks," in the words of one reviewer. The sad news is that Michael by the year 2006 never did anything to top this minor effort. Not a good track record for the so-called "King of Pop."

In 1987 Michael hired a Texas-born publicist, Bob Jones, to take over as his head honcho of communications for MJJ Productions. Leaving Motown, Jones signed on with the King of Pop, a label he bestowed on Michael.

Bob Jones had worked with the Motown greats, including Diana Ross herself, along with Stevie Wonder, Lionel Richie, The Temptations, Smokey Robinson, and The Supremes. But he'd never encountered a performer like Michael Jackson before. In the weeks and months ahead, he would be forced to handle one bizarre episode

Siedah Garrett

after another, some of the best of which he recorded in a memoir, *Michael Jackson: The Man Behind the Mask*, published in 2005. The book claimed that "It was Jones who was forced to put out public relation fires and give a positive spin to each successive bizarre story relating to the superstar."

Jones occupied an eyewitness seat as he watched entertainment's biggest star destroy himself "with self-hatred and self-indulgence." His was the unenviable role of explaining and interpreting to the public Michael's "fraudulent marriages and poisonous family relations," as well as his drug abuse and voodoo ceremonies. But before things began to unravel, Jones got to jump aboard the bandwagon promoting Michael during the last great success of his career, the *Bad* album, the *Bad* videos, and the *Bad* world tour.

Millions tuned in on August 31, 1987 to watch *Michael Jackson: The Magic Returns*, a 30-minute TV special that traced his rise as a star. It was the sixth highest rated show of the week. *Forbes Magazine* named Michael as the ninth highest paid entertainer, with a two-year estimated earnings of $43 million.

Along with the success came minor annoyances. A woman calling herself "Billie Jean Jackson," a resident of Illinois, filed a $100 million lawsuit, claiming that Michael was the father of her three children. It turned out that her actual name was Lavon Powlis.

"My God," Yetnikoff proclaimed, "if this so-called 'Billie-Jean' proves her case, Michael's reputation as a straight-shooter is made." But, like all paternity suits brought against Michael, this one failed. There wasn't the slightest proof that Michael even knew who the strange woman was, much less had fathered her children.

For six weeks, Michael worked on the "Bad" video at Brooklyn's Hoyt Schermerhorn subway station. Rather unconvincingly Michael cast himself as Daryl, a kid from the ghetto who'd gone away to a private school. Upon his return, he finds he no longer fits in with his street gang. His old gang members taunt him singing, "You don't down with us no more, you ain't down, you ain't bad."

When the video switches from black and white to color, Michael appears wearing fingerless gloves. Along with his backup dancers, he sings and dances, eventually uniting these West Side Story rival gangs. The famous director, Martin Scorsese himself, was the helmer on the video, Steven Spielberg having turned down the job.

Michael looked bizarre and outlandishly overdressed in his black leather motorcycle outfit, a modern interpretation of Marlon Brando's more macho outfit in the 1953 film, *The Wild One*.

Dancers who worked in the video with Michael, including Greg Burge and Jeffrey Daniel, claimed that Michael was trying to rip off *West Side Story*, insisting that they watch the film time and time again.

One of the dancers, who didn't want to be named, ridiculed Michael's costume: "He came out like a dominatrix, dressed in black boots with silver heels and buckles, lots of buckles. The leather jacket made him look like a motorcycle mama, his metal-studded wristband a bondage queen, and there were enough zippers for every drag costume between San Francisco and New York City. And chains—yes, girl, chains—enough for any S&M parlor."

In spite of the ridicule the costume generated, Michael took credit for designing it. It was later revealed that James O'Connor, owner of a punk rock store on Hollywood Boulevard, not only designed the costume but sold it to Michael for $291.34. "Even with the black surgical mask he wore into my store, I knew who was buying the costume from me," O'Connor claimed. The costume would later be auctioned off for $30,000.

That Kirk Douglas cleft Michael had placed in his chin through surgery came as a shock to his loyal fans.

At least the Douglas comparison was a macho image. But with the release of the "Bad" video, Michael suffered through unwanted comparisons to Joan Crawford, especially in his heavy use of pancake makeup. This was the begin-

ning of the comparisons with Crawford. They would reach their peak, especially around the world, when he was photographed just before his infamous trial for child molestation. One headline at the time ridiculed him as THE DAUGHTER OF JOAN CRAWFORD.

The "Bad" video cost two million dollars, maybe a lot more, and Michael was largely blamed for the production going over the budget. One assistant on the film said, "Jackson spent most of his time telling the director of *Taxi Driver* and *New York, New York* how to direct." He was referring, of course, to Martin Scorsese.

Bob Jones

The "Bad" video marked the first time Michael was filmed tugging at his crotch. "Was his underwear too tight?" Quincy Jones asked facetiously.

"Maybe he wanted to see if it were still there, or had atrophied from lack of use," one of the dancers cattily remarked.

The "Bad" video shoot moved to the 125th street subway stop in Harlem. A few blocks away, Madonna was shooting her video of "Who's That Girl?" When a break came for her, she invited herself to Michael's set. It was while watching him that she first saw him grab his crotch. Madonna was no stranger to crotch grabbing herself. But she seemed shocked at Michael's doing that. She was overheard to remark sarcastically, "Maybe he's trying to find some non-existent balls!"

The release of the "Bad" video sparked a fire sale in Michael Jackson merchandise. From posters to coat hangers, MJ memorabilia was the rage of the hour. Michael Jackson was a subject of amusement, often ridicule, on all the late night talk shows, even making imaginary appearances (never in person) on such TV sitcoms as *The Golden Girls*.

In night clubs from San Francisco to Miami, Jackson impersonators ruled the night. One performer, Valentino Johnson, spent $50,000 to have his face surgically altered to look more like Michael. But, as Yetnikoff pointed out, "How is he going to keep up with Michael's ever-changing face?"

With a white sash tied around his waist like Astaire, Michael also shot the video for "The Way You Make Me Feel." In it he appeared with Tatiana Thumbtzen, a Florida-born dancer.

She auditioned and won the role for "The Way You Make Me Feel" video, beating out some two-hundred other girls. For her four days of dancing, she was paid $4,000, playing a mini-skirted seductress.

Tatiana took her very limited and very unromantic experiences with Michael and fashioned them into a book, *The Way He Made Me Feel*, which she dedicated to "My Savior, The Lord Jesus Christ," not Michael.

As a ballet student, she had dreamed of working and dancing with Michael. In 1987 that dream came true for her, but there would also be a downside.

In her confessional, she admitted that she had a "big crush" on Michael the day she met him. During the shoot, when she accidentally fell on her ass, Michael rubbed her butt. "I could not believe it!" she later said. "Michael was flirting with me. I thought if anyone had ever questioned his manhood, here was his or her answer."

In the video's final scene, Michael and Tatiana hug. Many fans were disappointed, as they'd wanted the romantic duo to kiss, but Michael was against that.

He complimented her walk, finding it "very sexy." In Tatiana's view at the time, that was a "compliment from a heterosexual male." Michael liked working with Tatiana so much he invited her to join him on the *Bad* tour. At the time, she was still hoping for some romantic involvement, although up to now he'd never asked her out. Their most intimate encounter came when he asked to borrow some of her face powder to touch up his makeup. Magazines began running articles calling Tatiana MICHAEL'S GIRL.

During the *Bad* tour, at New York's Madison Square Garden, Tatiana made a daring move. "I landed a kiss right on his smacker!"

In explaining why she kissed Michael, she said, "I looked into his eyes, and he did this really sexy thing—he bit his lip—and just looked at me with this look that was so incredibly sexy. I pulled him close and as I was about to kiss him I felt the hand on my hip and before I knew it we were locked into this kiss."

No one had ever seen Michael kissing a girl in public—or in private for that matter. Backstage, Michael's manager, Frank DiLeo, gave her the evil eye, but later, mother Katherine seemed to applaud her action, "giving me a big bear hug."

A different reaction came from Michael's security guard, Miko Brando. Enraged and shouting at her at the top of his lungs, he yelled, "How dare you fucking take advantage of him like that! You fucking bitch! Who the fuck do you think you are? I cannot believe you fucking took advantage of him like that in front of all those people!" Later, Tatiana was fired from the *Bad* tour. She was replaced by Sheryl Crow.

Months later, Tatiana dated Michael's rival, Prince, but claimed, "We curled up in bed like kittens, and simply fell asleep."

"Michael was the Peter Pan squeaky-clean one, and Prince was the sexually overt one," Tatiana claimed. But if he was such a sexual creature, why didn't Prince seduce her? Seduction was also something she'd never get from Peter Pan.

Tonia Ryan, the co-author of Tatiana's autobiography, said, "Every other red-blooded male in America was going after Tatiana—Eddie Murphy, Prince, Robert De Niro, Matt LeBlanc, but Michael didn't even go out on a date with her. You do the math!"

In the wake of the first child molestation charges against Michael in 1993, Tatiana was interviewed by everybody from Howard Stern

Tatiana Thumbtzen

260

to Maury Povich. The question was always the same, "Did you sleep with him?" Tatiana later claimed that she felt that if she'd admit to having had sex with Michael, it was "going to validate his manhood" and perhaps make it appear more likely that he was innocent of those child molestation charges. Although not admitting to sex, she lied and told TV audiences that she'd dated Michael for a year. "In my fairytale mind, I thought that he would come looking for me to thank me. Boy, was I wrong!"

Bubbles and MJ: Friends forever

Ultimately, although Tatiana had initially tried to defend Michael, she ended up feeling used by him. She became part of an image to make Michael appear straight to the public. Her "dream," of working with Michael turned into a "nightmare."

"I now realize that when you are blessed, you may be cursed as well," she said.

On the *Bad* tour, Michael preferred the company, not of Tatiana, but of some very "special friends."

Michael had a saying that became his guide to living: "No wenches, bitches, heifers, and hoes."

Instead of female company, Bob Jones claimed that the King of Pop favored blond-haired young boys. "In my experience with Michael, once a boy turned fourteen or fifteen years old, ties were severed."

Even though it was still the 1980s, Michael, as he went on the "Bad" tour, was already living the lyrics of his 1993 single, "Keep It in the Closet":

Whatever we do whatever we say now
We'll make a vow to keep it in the closet.

"He is very curious and wants to draw from people who have survived. People who have lasted the course. He is not really of this planet. If he is eccentric it is because he is larger than life. What is a genius? What is a living legend? What is a megastar? Michael Jackson-that's all. And just when you think you know him, he gives you more…There is no one that can come near him. No one can dance like that, write the lyrics or cause the kind of excitement that he does."

--Elizabeth Taylor

"There is a considerable 'ick' factor when it comes to Michael Jackson. Though acquitted of child molestation, most people have been repulsed by his admission to sleeping in the same bed with children, even if it was non-sexual. He also carries plenty of baggage given his eccentric behavior over the years and plastic surgery that has reduced him to a disturbing visual image."

--Nekesa Mumbi Moody

"Michael never really had a childhood and I think he is trying to experience it in later life. I would tell him to keep the knowledge that he is innocent and hold his head up."

--Frank DiLeo, Michael Jackson's former manager

"Michael can go out and perform before 90,000 people, but if I ask him to sing a song for me, I have to sit on the couch with my hands over my eyes and he goes behind the couch. He is amazingly shy."

--Quincy Jones

"In my heart, I was saying, 'I love you, Diana. Shine! And shine on forever because you are the true princess of the people."

--Michael Jackson on Princess Diana

Chapter Nine

Michael never forgave the magazine, *Rolling Stone*, for the way it embarrassed him in February of 1987. Its readers voted him worst artist in a staggering number of categories. Worst male singer. Worst album (*Bad*). Worst video ("Bad"). Worst dressed. Worst single ("Bad"). Worst hype. Most unwelcome comeback.

Other organizations, including the American Music Awards, were more indulgent with his output. "Bad" was chosen as Best Soul/R&B Single, though Michael lost to Paul Simon as Best Pop/Rock Male Vocalist. Janet won for Best Pop/Rock Video for "When I Think of You."

The gamblers in Las Vegas were betting heavily on Michael to make another clean sweep of the Grammys in 1988, for which he'd earned four nominations. *Bad* had been nominated for Album of the Year. Both Michael and Quincy Jones were nominated for Producer of the Year, and Michael was also nominated for Best Male Pop Vocal and Best Male R&B Vocal.

The night seemed to belong to Michael as he performed live at the 30th annual awards ceremony, his first TV performance in five years. He sang and danced to "The Way You Make Me Feel" and "Man in the Mirror." For his performance, Michael got a standing ovation, and Quincy Jones told him, "The night is yours."

In a startling development, Michael lost all four Grammys. As Diana Ross was presenting the award for Album of the Year to U2 for *The Joshua Tree*, Michael collapsed backstage and had to be revived.

A sore loser, Michael told his handlers, "I refuse to attend another one of these stupid award presentations. The backers are white racists. They want to use me just for ratings—not to get the honors I deserve."

Bob Jones, his publicist, claimed that Michael tended to play the race card any time he felt "victimized." Otherwise, as Bob suggested, "Michael seemed to want to join the white race."

Regaining his composure, Michael stormed out of the auditorium where the Grammys had been presented, vowing never to return.

As the star of the Pepsi commercials that were aired during the Grammy telecast, Michael was clearly the winner, at least financially. Along with the millions of dollars he earned, Michael met a new young friend with whom he'd launch another one of his "special relationships." His name was Jimmy Safechuck, and Michael would be so enchanted with the good-looking boy he'd invite him to go with him on the *Bad* tour.

When Michael met the blond, blue-eyed California-born boy, it was early in 1988. Jimmy was only nine years old, Michael a ripe 3-0.

The boy appeared with Michael in one of the Pepsi ads. In the commercial, Jimmy, cast in the role of a young fan, enters Michael's dressing room, finding it empty. He tries on Michael's sunglasses and even dons one of his fedoras and one of his sequined jackets. Suddenly, he looks up and is startled, seeing Michael in the doorway. "Looking for me?" Michael asks.

Jimmy had been told that Michael's appearance at the doorway would be shot at some later date and that he should look startled at an empty space. That look on Jimmy's face was for real when Michael, without Jimmy's knowledge, suddenly appeared in the frame.

From the moment of their first meeting, Michael became enchanted with Jimmy. The man and boy were seen together virtually all the time, often accompanied by Jimmy's parents. Once, when the parents invited Michael for dinner, he arrived in a Rolls-Royce with his own food.

A relationship of extreme intimacy between the boy and Michael was maintained on and off for parts of 1988 and 1989, although there were other "special relationships" going on at the time with other boys. Jimmy and Michael were often seen in public wearing the same costumes, man and boy identical designs.

Michael not only obtained the permission of Jimmy's parents to allow their son to go on the *Bad* tour, but he eventually hired both the mother and father as well.

On the *Bad* tour, Jimmy often appeared on stage with Michael, both wearing identical bondage outfits, apparel evocative of the S&M shops on Christopher Street in New York City. Michael at the time seemed oblivious to the speculation the two costumes generated.

A crewmember, who toured with the *Bad* troupe and didn't want to be identified by name, claimed that "Michael in those days thought he was King of the

Jimmy Safechuck
and MJ

World and did pretty much what he Goddamn pleased. He must have known about the rumors circulating about him and the kid, but he made no attempt to conceal his affection for the boy. Although the *Bad* tour crew felt they were underpaid, considering the grueling schedule and long hours, and those crowds, this Safechuck boy was getting a king's ransom spent on him. Michael would take him shopping in Europe—you name it, toys, games, clothing, anything the kid desired. Michael once rented an entire amusement park just for the kid and himself. There were reports it cost him as much as $50,000."

The sales department at Hamley's in London, the largest toy store in the world, still remembers the visit of Michael where he held Jimmy's hand. "Michael even bought puppets of himself for the boy," said one clerk. "And also some puppets of Stevie Wonder. They made off with at least three dozen dolls and teddy bears. Every computer game that fascinated the kid was purchased without objection by Michael."

He generously gave Jimmy's parents a stunning new 1989 Rolls-Royce. With all the gadgets and extras, the bill came to $200,000. That wasn't all. Jimmy's parents were also given, or so it was reported, "His and Hers" Mercedes. "Transportation won't be their problem in the future," said an aide to Michael.

When Jimmy, who turned ten years old during the *Bad* tour, caught the flu, so did Michael. Two performances of the *Bad* road show had to be cancelled while Michael and his young friend recovered in a hotel suite.

Michael had learned to dance the Moonwalk sideways, and he taught its intricate steps to the very talented Jimmy, who appeared on stage dancing the same routines as the star himself. The *Motown 25* TV special showed pictures of Michael and Jimmy trading dance steps with each other.

On his shopping spree with Jimmy in Los Angeles, Michael ran into trouble when he visited the Zales Jewelry Store in the Simi Valley Shopping Center. Appearing in a wig, with false teeth and a mustache, Michael aroused the suspicions of the manager, who telephoned the police.

Michael was on the verge of being arrested until he took off the disguise and showed the officers who'd been summoned to the scene his identification. He explained that he had to wear disguises or else he'd be mobbed and the store overrun. The police let him go, and the manager was filled with apologies. But by this time Michael, who had come in to make large purchases, refused to patronize Zales.

It was said that Frank DiLeo urged Michael to break off his relationship with Jimmy because of the ugly rumors. In London, one member of the press actually suggested, in print, that the relationship was "perverted." By now, his fame was so great that Michael couldn't appear in public, even in disguise, and not attract unwanted public scrutiny.

Michael forced himself to separate from Jimmy after putting up a strong fight to stay with the boy. He later claimed, "I'm so terribly lonely without him. It's a sad day when my public determines who I can have for a friend. The difference in our age is not a problem for me."

It was later reported, and widely distributed on the web, that when Jimmy and Michael went their separate ways, the boy received a "large cash gift."

At the time of Michael's trial on a charge of child molestation in 2005, prosecutors sought Jimmy out to question the young man as a potential witness. Reportedly, he claimed that "nothing happened" during his short friendship with the star.

The *Bad* world tour was launched on September 12, 1987, coming to an end on January 27, 1989. In his first-ever solo tour, Michael appeared on stage 123 times, playing to an audience of nearly 4.5 million fans in 15 countries (including the U.S.) on four continents.

When the grosses were tallied, the tour had taken in $40 million but would end up costing Michael money. Throughout the tour, millions of dollars had been spent on an ultra-deluxe lifestyle, including the simultaneous availability of a jet, a helicopter, and a bus. Millions had been expended on every desire, and the show itself was one of the costliest ever mounted for a singer.

As Michael launched his *Bad* tour, rumors were rampant. It was falsely announced that Michael was going to star in the lead role of *Phantom of the Opera*, to be directed by Steven Spielberg. Around the same time, rumors circulated that Michael was planning to buy Motown Records. Adding fuel to the speculative fire was Michael's appearance, at the American Cinema Awards, with Sylvester Stallone and Sophia Loren.

Michael's so-called romance with a blonde, 25-year-old woman, Karen Faye, was just another attempt to give Michael a straight image. Faye, who was in love with another man at the time, had worked as Michael's makeup artist on the *Captain EO* video—nothing more. It turned out that Michael himself had ordered an aide to feed the story of the fake romance with Faye to the *National Enquirer*.

Faye herself was very defensive and supportive of Michael. "There is one special person who has given me more in my life than anyone. His name is Michael Jackson. It was the luckiest day in my life when this magical man sat in the makeup chair before me."

"If you believe that Karen Faye and Michael were lovers, then you'd surely believe

Karen Faye

that Rocky and Michael were lovers," said a Hollywood publicist. "Friends, yes. Lovers, no way, José."

Again, in another attempt to deceive his fans, a *faux* romance was promoted between Michael and Sheryl Crow, who had joined the *Bad* tour. Born in Kennett, Missouri, Sheryl was four years younger than Michael. In time she would emerge as more than a mere backup singer for Michael, and would enjoy a successful career on her own. Between 1994 and 2002, she would win nine Grammy Awards, including Best New Artist and Best Female Rock Vocalist, earning a place at Number 44 on VH1's 100 Greatest Women of Rock 'n' Roll.

Michael got on harmoniously with the singer, even enjoying Krispy Kreme doughnuts with her after the show. But as one stage manager said, "That was all the sugar that romance ever fueled."

One of the most glamorous women ever to play the guitar, Sheryl went from backup singer to international star, and Michael was said to resent her success. With her blonde hair and flowing locks, she exuded sex appeal. Michael was said to envy Sheryl's glammed out red-carpet outfits, and her to-die-for body, as the entertainer arrived to receive Grammy after Grammy.

During her two-year *Bad* tour, Sheryl remained silent as rumors spun out of control about a torrid romance between her and "The Gloved One." Later, when she became a staple in the music industry herself, she squashed all that gossip. "He never took off that glove for me," she reportedly said. In time to come, with artists such as Celine Dion and Wynonna Judd singing songs she'd written, Sheryl no longer needed to publicize her link to Michael. If anything, she seemed to want to distance herself from him.

More convincing were reports that Brad Pitt and Sheryl had shared a romantic involvement when they were students at the University of Missouri, but this gossip was never confirmed.

The pretend romance was carried out in public when Michael duetted with Sheryl in the song, "I Just Can't Stop Loving You." He actually caressed her thigh in what was called "the most heterosexual performance of his career."

Sheryl Crow

Instead of promoting a romance with him, Sheryl was instructed by Michael's manager "not to make eye contact with him unless performing with him." There would be no more kissing scandals, as in the case with the Florida dancer, Tatiana Thumbtzen. Since Sheryl had no romantic interest in gazing into Michael's eyes, she could easily comply with this draconian ruling.

One member of the *Bad* troupe claimed that,

"I just couldn't believe how far Jackson's contempt for women had gone. Not only was he horrified at the idea of fucking a woman, he didn't want what he called 'one of those heifers' even looking into his eyes unless it was officially mandated. What a guy!"

Sheryl would also work with Texas-born Don Henley, the American rock musician who is the drummer and one of the lead singers and songwriters of the band The Eagles. She once spoke about the difference between working with Don Henley and Michael. "The difference between Michael Jackson and Don Henley is quite obvious, in that Michael is very reclusive and Don is the type of person that makes you part of his family. He takes care of you and spends time with you. You are an equal with him, whereas with Michael, he didn't even know our names."

The *Bad* tour opened in Kansas City and was a smash hit. Michael was entertaining crowds within the same arena where he and his brothers had played during their famous "Victory" tour four years earlier, but now Michael was performing solo.

Bob Jones recalled visiting one of Michael's hotel suites during the tour. "I had never seen a suite that had been so destroyed. Lamps, tables, and chairs were thrown about. Food wrappers and all sorts of other garbage covered the floors, tables, and bed. The housekeeper had been paid off not to tell."

For three nights in March of 1988 Michael performed at Madison Square Garden, an event attended by Elizabeth Taylor. A benefit concert was performed for the United Negro College Fund, and Michael was presented with an honorary degree in front of, among many others, Yoko Ono and Liza Minnelli.

Even though the benefit was to aid young African-Americans, Michael was criticized in some black magazines for devoting all his attention to "certifiably white" stars such as Taylor and Minnelli and virtually snubbing such black entertainers as Whitney Houston.

Still miffed at Michael, Diana Ross did not respond to his invitation to the benefit. President Ronald Reagan found time to send a videotaped message. With the usual Reagan brand of humor, the President said, "Let me be the first to call you the new Dr. J." This was the benefit concert in which Tatiana Thumbtzen kissed Michael on the lips, feeling his entire body stiffen except in his groin.

Michael often didn't accept invitations, especially personal ones, such as the christening of Diana Ross's second son, Evan, with the Norwegian millionaire, Arne Naess. But along with Little Richard, he showed up at the 1988 wedding of his attorney, John Branca, to Julie McArthur. Bubbles came dressed in a hand-tailored tuxedo, and immediately "fell in love" with the handsome hot stud, Don Johnson, of *Miami Vice*.

Caught up in the hysteria surrounding his *Bad* tour, Michael still had time for two of the most significant events in his life: his move out of the family compound in Encino and the publication of his long-awaited and ultimately disappointing autobiography, *Moonwalk*.

Michael's move from Hayvenhurst in Encino to Neverland was long overdue. His family was seeing "too much" of his private life and interfering with his intimate time, especially when he wanted to be alone with his young friends. The 2,700-acre ranch in California's Santa Ynez Valley is located at 5225 Figueroa Mountain Rd., 5 miles north of the town of Los Olivos, about a two-hour drive north of Los Angeles.

Michael had fallen in love with the property when he'd visited Paul McCartney and his wife, Linda, here. They too were considering buying the property, but it wasn't for sale at the time.

When the ranch came on the market in the spring of 1988, Michael went for it, but he was a tough negotiator, acquiring the property for $17 million, even though the asking price was $35 million. Along with the budget purchase price came an array of European antiques. TV and radio media, not knowing the actual purchase price, reported that Michael paid $28 million for the ranch. He immediately changed the name from Sycamore Ranch to Neverland, in honor of the fictional island in the story *Peter Pan*.

One of Michael's former publicists (not Bob Jones), who had been dismissed from the star's staff, privately told reporters, "I'm sure Jackson selected the location because it's across from a nursery school. If the tots there were too young for his blood, there's also a prep school nearby filled with good-looking young boys, who have never had an older man 'Beat It' for them."

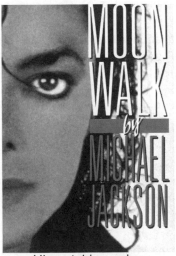

His autobiography, from Doubleday

Michael immediately set about securing the property from fans who might learn of his new address. Soon Neverland had a police force and was entered by an iron and steel gate which was topped by a mammoth gilded crown, symbol of the King of Pop.

After Neverland was renovated to his specifications, Michael threw a "warming bash," inviting friends and associates, but deliberately ignoring Papa Joe and Katherine. "I found out about Michael's new home by watching the TV news," Papa Joe said. However, Michael did invite his brothers and sisters, including Janet and Randy, to the housewarming.

Michael assured such friends as Elizabeth Taylor and Jane Fonda that, "You can come to visit me at any time. I'm less than a thirty-minute helicopter ride from Los Angeles."

Attending the housewarming were some of Michael's new celebrity neighbors, including Steven Seagal. Handsome actor John Derek, known for marrying some of the most beautiful women in show business, showed up with his voluptuous wife, Bo Derek, who'd enjoyed such success in the 1979 comedy, *10*. "He is my Svengali-like mentor," she told Michael. She later was surprised when she was asked to sign a release, swearing that she'd never divulge to the press anything she'd learned during her visit to Neverland.

Michael also had another seductive neighbor, Cheryl Ladd, a staple of 1970s pop culture and the actress who replaced Farrah Fawcett on the hit TV series, *Charlie's Angels*.

Even during the *Bad* tour, when Michael was performing around the world, he flew back to California for visits to Neverland as often as he could.

When *Moonwalk* was released on April 20, 1988, following four years of ghost-writing, Michael was in Liverpool, appearing in the hometown of The Beatles on his *Bad* tour.

He called home to apologize to Joe for his revelations in the book. His father had already gone on television in April of 1988 denying Michael's allegations. Joe called his discipline of his boys "little spankings." Also interviewed, Marlon Jackson claimed that Michael was accurate in his revelations of the beatings. "We were hit—and hit often," Marlon charged.

The prediction of Michael's editor at Doubleday came true, as the former First Lady, Jackie Kennedy Onassis, watched *Moonwalk* sell nearly half-a-million copies in 14 countries, topping the bestseller list of *The New York Times*.

Michael dedicated the book to Fred Astaire, and it carried an appreciation signed by Jackie. "To many people, Michael Jackson seems an elusive personality," she wrote. "But to those who work with him, he is not. This talented artist is a sensitive man, warm, funny, and full of insight. Michael's book, *Moonwalk*, provides a startling glimpse of the artist at work and the artist in reflection."

That was the public face she put on the book. In private she expressed her disappointment, revealing that Doubleday had turned down the first version—"not juicy enough. The second version wasn't a whole lot better. As juicy as a dried-up turnip."

Jackie oversaw much of the promotion for the book, including full-size cutouts of Michael in stores. A hand-

Bo Derek

written note by Michael claimed, "one of the reasons I haven't given interviews over the years is because I've been saving what I have to say for my book. Love, Michael." In spite of that claim, he had almost nothing to say in the book that his fans hadn't already heard or read elsewhere.

The reaction of his fans was as diverse as those fans themselves. One reader got carried away claiming *Moonwalk* was "the single greatest autobiography I have ever read in my life." This statement could be true, if we knew how many autobiographies, if any, this rabid fan had read. Other more realistic reviewers, such as Terry Callen, of Gloucester City, New Jersey, found the book, "A total whitewash. . . . The world as Michael Jackson thinks it should be." Another savvy reader, also from New Jersey, found *Moonwalk* "the most blatantly bogus and self-serving autobiography since Joan Crawford wrote her self-tome in the 60s."

The Jackson family was uniformly negative about *Moonwalk*, especially Michael's brother Marlon, who found three-fourths of the book "a lie." La Toya also expressed her disappointment. "Cold and impersonal. What did he leave out? The beginning. The middle. And the end."

At the same time Katherine was also shopping her version of life with the Jacksons. She called it *The Jacksons: My Family*, and sent a draft of her autobiography to Jackie at Doubleday. "All vanilla with no chocolate sauce," Jackie wrote to her publisher. The book was filled with such fairytale revelations as Michael telling his second-grade teacher, "Someday I'm going to live in a castle."

In spite of her troubled, often violent marriage to Joe, she wrote, "Occasionally when Joe and I are lying in bed at night, one of us will become nostalgic: 'Remember when. . .?' Before we know it, we're reliving one of the countless special moments in our family's past: Our kids' living room sock hops, The Jackson Five's public debut at a department store in Glen Park, Illinois. Joe will never admit publicly that he can be just as sentimental as I,

John Derek

so I just did it for him." She ends on an upbeat note, visualizing herself "watching the grandkids perform as professionals someday." Her book was eventually published by St. Martin's Paperbacks and released in 1990.

Flying into Narita Airport in Japan on September 9, 1987, Michael was besieged by fans, as police struggled valiantly to keep him from being mobbed. He was angered when 300 photographers arrived to take pictures of Bubbles, who had flown into Tokyo on a separate flight. "Just who in the hell does this chimp think he is?" Michael asked. "Once again forgetting who the real star is. *Me*!" He also seemed resentful that Japanese

Prime Minister Nakasone presented a ceremonial sword to Bubbles—and not to Michael.

When he was installed in grandeur on the 10th floor of Tokyo's Capitol Hotel, Michael was informed that the rooms would henceforth be known as The Michael Jackson Suites.

After Michael launched a total of fourteen sold-out performances at Korakuen Stadium in Yokohama, he was told that the Japanese had dubbed him "Typhoon Michael." In less than a month, he played to nearly half a million fans at fourteen concerts in three Japanese cities. The world press, covering the Japan tour, seemed to go wacko over Jacko, *Today* proclaiming—"No pets, no plastic—just raw sex." *News of the World*, using a politically incorrect term, proclaimed "Japs Go Whacko (sic) over Raunchy Jacko."

On the *Bad* tour, journalist Paul Voth accurately summed up media reaction to Michael. "Even as he triumphed on his world tour, the papers at home and abroad began an assault on Michael that would last for years. Speculation about his nose, his skin, his sexuality—slowly but surely a trend developed. The media concentrated less and less on Michael's musical contributions in favor of the much more profitable stature of portraying him as a weirdo with strange habits and ideas."

On September 14, Michael's manager, Frank DiLeo, informed the world press, including ten journalists flown in from London, that stories that Michael purposely lightens his skin "are preposterous."

In Australia, the press was not so kind. Michael was routinely labeled "Wacko Jacko." One Aussie journalist proclaimed, "In a word, Michael Jackson is a nut case."

Michael responded by writing a letter to *People* magazine that would have gotten an eighth grader an F in English: "Do not judge a man until you've walked 2 moons in his mocassins (sic). Most people don't know me, that is why they write such things in wich (sic) most is not true. I cry very often because it hurts and I wory (sic) about the children." The letter didn't turn the tide against the lingering wisecracks about him. It did, however, prove to the world that Michael couldn't spell.

Even late-night TV comedians began to suggest that there was "something queer" going on between Michael and Bubbles. "The question is," one raunchy comedian said in a Las Vegas night club, "Is Bubbles the top or the bottom?"

Privately Michael didn't turn such a kind face to the world as suggested by his child-like letter. Hearing of lagging ticket sales among the Aussies, he threatened to fire his entire managerial staff, including DiLeo, if the *Bad* album didn't top the sales of *Thriller*. Sales were so poor in Perth and Adelaide that concerts were cancelled. Comments in the local bars, particularly among cricket players, were nasty, some claiming they weren't going to pay eighty dollars "to see some dancing nigger faggot. If we want to see dancing, we've got our own aborigines."

Some of the press in Australia was more favorable, reporters labeling Michael "Crocodile Jackson." But for what reason, as that was hardly his image? British journalists wrote about "The Peter Pan of Pop." But some London reporters were fascinated by the stories that kept popping up that Michael was interested in young boys and that he preferred their company to that of a beautiful young woman. Many of his female fans continued to make themselves available to Michael, but he showed no interest. One journalist wrote, "Instead of the Peter Pan of Pop, I'd call him The Pied Piper, luring young boys to God knows what fate." Michael was furious when he heard that and threatened to sue.

One Australian journalist noted, "Jacko is grabbing his crotch more frequently. He really should masturbate in his dressing room before 'coming' on stage. His disgusting performance isn't suitable for children. Actually he doesn't seem to show any crotch at all—rather a concave. Maybe those rumors are true—that he had his pecker cut off."

"Now they're attacking my manhood," Michael lamented. "Who do these jackals think they are, Madonna?"

In January of 1988, Michael turned up in Las Vegas, watching a performance of "Siegfried & Roy" at the Frontier. Meeting the performers backstage, Michael was invited to spend the following day with them at their plush home in the desert. "A gay time was had by all," wrote a cynical Las Vegas reporter.

Siegfried and Roy worked with Michael on creating illusions for his show. To show his gratitude, he wrote their theme song, "The Might in the Magic." A tape of Michael performing the song opened the duo's future shows.

Flying to Pensacola, Florida, for rehearsals for an all-new show, Michael also brought his chef with him. It was reported that Michael existed for several days on a diet of fresh flowers.

He wanted to open the new show in Atlanta but Pepsi, his sponsor, objected. "Not in the home of Coca Cola," Michael was told by Pepsi executives.

Instead, Michael and his troupe opened his U.S. tour in Kansas City. It was reported that backstage before he went on, Michael assembled his troupe together to pray to God to "make us funky!" To judge from the show itself, God granted their request.

Right before leaving Kansas City, Michael

was told that his Standing Room Only performances there had brought in $750,000, topping the previous record set by Elvis Presley.

Michael danced a jig of joy. "Who's The King now?" he asked.

It was on to New York and Madison Square Garden. Michael was delighted when a *Newsweek* reviewer compared his Moonwalk as equivalent in fame to Charlie Chaplin's wobble. The Little Tramp still remained his favorite performer.

Back in the Midwest, Michael landed in St. Louis. To the extreme disappointment of his fans, Michael almost immediately came down with the flu and laryngitis. The culprit who exposed Michael to the infection was reportedly a thirteen-year-old boy introduced as "Peter." Somehow Michael had met this handsome child in New York and had invited him, along with his parents, to tour with them, even on future dates in Europe.

Michael had been seen with Peter so frequently that he touched off tabloid speculation. One journalist even claimed that Michael "bought the kid by giving the parents a Rolls Royce." It was later revealed by Steve Chabre, former head of MJJ Enterprises, that Michael did indeed purchase a Rolls for Peter's parents, as well as a luxurious house in California's San Fernando Valley.

A former garbage collector, Peter's father was hired to go on the road with the *Bad* troupe. As publicist Bob Jones noted, "On every stop of the tour, Michael and Peter stayed locked in Michael's suite."

While Michael was occupied with Peter, Bob and Michael's chief of security, Bill Bray, had to keep the boy's parents distracted with shopping jaunts. Michael placed no limit on the amount of purchases the parents could charge.

Recovering from "Peter's flu," Michael flew to his home state of Indiana to appear at the Market Square Arena in Indianapolis on March 18, 1988. Although publicly he remained smiling, Michael was overheard saying, "Indiana is a great state . . ." He paused. "To leave."

Siegfried and Roy

With Peter by his side, Michael speeded up his tour, playing in Denver, Hartford, and Houston, where he invited Vice President George Bush to attend. The offer was spurned. Next on the tour was Atlanta, where Pepsi, in a reversal of a previous decision, decided to take on the Coca-Cola giant on its home turf, slathering the town with Pepsi advertising.

Arriving in Chicago, Michael received the Key to the City from its mayor, Eugene Sawyer.

The leader of the Nation of Islam,

minister Louis Farrakhan had denounced Michael's "Victory" tour and had urged a boycott because of Michael's "Jheri-curl, female acting—he's a bad role model for our young boys." But in a grand gesture, Bob Jones invited Farrakhan to a performance. At Michael's request, Eddie Murphy had already given him tapes of Farrakhan's orations.

That night the controversial minister was won over, proclaiming Michael "A Special Messenger of Entertainment." In subsequent speeches, Farrakhan would praise Michael, who would later contribute $25,000 to Farrakhan's "Million Man March" on Washington, DC, on October 16, 1995.

Bob Jones delivered the money in his own name, as Michael didn't want his name used. "This is how Michael operated: Always willing to hang someone else out to dry and cover his own ass," Bob charged. "You see, if the media and public found out that Michael Jackson donated anything to an event sponsored by the Nation of Islam, he'd lose his Jewish friends and a lot of his fan base would turn against him."

After playing in Dallas and Minneapolis, the troupe flew to Europe, landing at Rome's international airport on May 23, 1988. It was time for a reunion with his new friend, Sophia Loren. He escorted her to a party thrown by Franco Zeffirelli, the movie director, at his elegant Rome villa, but Michael spent all the time playing with a gaggle of pajama-clad children and refusing to mingle with *tout Roma*.

The U.S. Ambassador to Rome, Maxwell Rabb, personally escorted Michael on a private visit to the Sistine Chapel. "Diana Ross taught me to love art," he told the ambassador.

Frank DiLeo had tried to arrange for a private meeting between Pope John Paul II and Michael, but the pontiff canceled at the last minute. Privately he let it be known that, "I don't want to become part of the Michael Jackson publicity machine."

In October of 1996, Michael decided that if he could not get an audience with the Pope, he wanted to own a piece of him. Reading that the Pope in Rome had successfully undergone surgery for an inflamed appendix, Michael sent an offer to the Vatican to purchase that appendix for a million dollars, noting that such a bequest could be most useful to aid Catholic charities. The private secretary to the Pope did not respond to the offer.

Suffering from laryngitis, Michael played to audiences of 75,000 at concerts at Flaminio Stadio in Rome. Attending were two celebrity guests, Sophia Loren and her rival, Gina Lollobrigida.

Louis Farrakhan

275

Lollobrigida confided to Michael, "I haven't spoken to the *bee-tch* in twenty years until you brought us together for the paparazzi."

Michael had been booked in Rome's deluxe Lord Byron Hotel. With time on his hands, he drew pictures in ink on the white, stiffly starched bed linens, including a self-portrait. After Michael had checked out, a maid at the hotel auctioned the doodles, getting $5,000 for Michael's profile.

Later, Michael was furious to learn that his concerts in Rome and also in the city of Turin in Italy's Piedmont had been illegally taped. These unauthorized tapes eventually made their way into the United States and Britain, although they had to be hawked underground.

Among the 55,000 fans who attended Michael's concert in Basel, Switzerland, was Elizabeth Taylor. It was during their time together in Switzerland that Michael astonished Elizabeth by proposing marriage to her. Both the glamorous mega-star and Michael would later deny the proposal of marriage, but intimates of both parties have insisted over the years that it happened.

To Michael, a May-December marriage to the aging star made a lot of sense. Before flying to Switzerland, he'd even discussed his proposal with Katharine Hepburn, who'd appeared opposite Elizabeth in Tennessee Williams's *Suddenly, Last Summer*, released in 1959.

"Would she expect sex?" Katharine reportedly asked, obviously being facetious.

"No, not at all!" Michael said, taking the question seriously. "It wouldn't be that kind of relationship."

A gossipy friend of Hepburn's was seated with her when Michael visited the star at her Turtle Bay townhouse in New York City.

"Then go for it if Elizabeth's willing," Hepburn advised. "I was married once. I made it clear from the beginning that there would be no sex after I said 'I do.' Since my groom wasn't particularly keen on the opposite sex, that proved no hardship for him at all. I invited his boyfriend along on our honeymoon to Bermuda."

Hepburn told Michael that reporters would stop calling attention to the fact he was not dating if he were married. "You don't ask married men what young girls they're taking out," Hepburn said. "It's not done."

Elizabeth turned Michael down ever so politely, her confidante, Roddy McDowall later said.

Pope John Paul II

"Marriage was proposed to Elizabeth by some of the most important men in the world, including a former president of the United States who offered to divorce his wife for her."

Michael, according to McDowall, made a counter-offer, promising to donate $5 million a year in AIDS research if she'd give him her hand in marriage. Still, she said no.

"As my personal history has shown, I'd make a terrible wife but a great friend," she said. "Let's be friends for always. If you need me, wherever you need me, I'll be there."

"That sounds very much like Diana Ross," he said.

"Did you ever propose marriage to her?" she asked. "I think I read that someplace."

"You are the only person in the world I'll ever ask to marry me," he said. "You could lead a life of luxury. Everything you want, all the jewelry you could ever wear."

"But Michael, I already lead a life of luxury. I have more gems than is good for me, with more on the way."

"Rock Hudson, Montgomery Clift, and even James Dean proposed marriage to me, but I told each of them it wouldn't work," she claimed. "It wouldn't have, you know? The same with us. It wouldn't work."

"But you'd be free to have lovers on the side," he said.

"That's a right all my husbands have retained in marriage," she claimed, "and a privilege I've always reserved for myself as well."

"Is your decision final?" he asked.

"Final and forever more," she said. "Now, let's not speak of this again. However, as compensation, I have a few stray children I'll let you adopt."

Before he flew out of Switzerland, Elizabeth promised him that even though she wouldn't marry him, she'd let him host her next wedding.

Before leaving Elizabeth and Switzerland behind him, Michael had one more "house call" to make. He'd solicited and received an invitation to visit Oona Chaplin, the widow of his all-time film hero, Charlie Chaplin, whom Michael always referred to as "The Little Tramp." Chaplin had died in 1977, and Michael wanted to bring flowers to his gravesite near her home in Vevey, Switzerland.

The Oona Chaplin Michael encountered was not what he expected from the famous widow. Her appearance shocked him. She came into her living room wearing tight-fitting clothes more suited to Tatum O'Neal or Brooke Shields. Her appearance was rather unkempt, and she wore too much makeup, as if trying to erase twenty years from her face.

She spoke of the "lonely years after Charlie died" and told Michael that The Little Tramp ended his life in a wheelchair. "I was his watchdog and nurse day and night, waiting on him hand and foot. He fired all the nurses I hired for him."

Oona joined Michael for the pilgrimage to Chaplin's gravesite. She spoke with a certain pain about her previous life and how she'd been dominated by two powerful men, both her famous playwright father, Eugene O'Neill, and Chaplin, whom she'd married in 1943 when she was just seventeen and he was fifty-four. "My father cut off communication with me when I married Charlie," she said.

She was surprised that Michael did not know who Eugene O'Neill was, but she patiently explained to him the significant role he'd played in the American theater.

Back at the Chaplin house, she led Michael into the bathroom. At first he protested, "I like to do my business in private."

"No, no, you silly boy." In the bathroom she removed a bottle labeled "shampoo." Drinking half of it, she offered him the bottle. "Want some?" she asked. He declined. "It's not shampoo, ducky. But liquor. My family hides my bottles from me, but I outsmart them."

Oona was living up to her reputation. Before meeting her, Michael had heard stories about her wandering the streets of Vevey at night in her bare feet, dressed in a nightgown. She'd shout obscenities to passersby. The tolerant policemen never arrested her, but drove her back to the safety of her home, where they would put her to bed.

Bizarrely, Michael wanted to know about the body-snatching caper that occurred one rainy night on March 1, 1978, at the Vevey cemetery where Chaplin was buried. A Bulgarian and a Pole had stolen her husband's coffin and had held it for ransom, demanding 600,000 Swiss francs. Eventually they were arrested, and Chaplin's body returned to Oona, who arranged for its second burial.

Oona Chaplin

"Imagine what grave-robbers would ask for my body if they ever snatched it when I die?" Michael asked, inserting himself into the drama.

"They're not going to get my body," she told Michael. "In my will I've demanded that my coffin be encased in a solid block of concrete two feet thick."

"But what if you're buried alive," he asked. "You'll never escape if you wake up in a coffin like that."

"That's something you need not worry your pretty head about," she said.

Before leaving, Oona startled Michael by making a request. "More than anything in the world I want to meet the divine Mel Gibson. Do you know him? If so, please introduce us. I'll fly to Los Angeles. If you don't know Mel, maybe some other handsome hunk in Hollywood. You won't believe the checks I've written to handsome men after Charlie died. I bought a luxury apartment in New York for one of my favorites. Like Charlie, he was very well endowed."

Whether Oona knew it or not, she was preaching to the choir. Michael himself had written many a check, but to males who were slightly younger than those Oona so desperately desired. And much larger checks awaited Michael's penmanship in his future.

Because she was trembling, he took her hand. "Aging courtesans in Europe used to give sound advice to young girls. Spend your youth with a rich old man so that you can enjoy old age in the company of a handsome hunk."

On June 27, Michael launched his concerts at the Parc des Princes in Paris. In attendance were Grace Jones and the designer Patrick Kelly. The mayor of Paris, Jacques Chirac, presented Michael with *La Grande Médaille de la Ville de Paris*, an honor usually given only to visiting heads of state. Michael accepted the honor but turned down the invitation to a formal state dinner. He had other plans.

Bob Jones later claimed that those other plans concerned "Peter," who had suddenly reappeared. Michael was staying at the grand *luxe* Hotel Crillon in the heart of Paris. Later, Jolie Levine, an aide to Michael, discovered a mysterious sheet in the star's bedroom where he'd been sleeping with Peter. Evocative of the incident at the Lord Byron in Rome, Michael had drawn a picture in ink of himself and Peter on the sheet.

"Also written on the sheet was what amounted to a love note to the boy," Jones claimed. "The sheet was my first tangible clue that Michael Jackson, the King of Pop, was up to no good with this young kid." Jones and Levine smuggled the sheet out of the hotel to prevent it from falling into the hands of the tabloids.

Bob told Frank DiLeo of his discovery. Michael's manager, according to Bob, topped him with a story of his own about an incident that occurred during Michael's trip with Peter to the Côte d'Azur. In Nice, DiLeo "found a sheet painted with human feces." Bob claimed that one of Michael's favorite words was "doo-doo." Now he knew why.

Michael had succeeded in making friends with two of the most famous women on the planet, Elizabeth Taylor and Jackie Kennedy Onassis. He had only one more conquest to make it a triumvirate. He wanted to befriend Princess Diana, the third woman he most admired in the world.

Michael's dream was realized on July 16, 1988, at the third concert of the *Bad* tour at Wembley Stadium. He'd flown into Heathrow Airport on July 11 with his personal doctor, dentist, throat specialist, and chiropodist. In addition, he brought with him a masseur, a manicurist, a hair dresser, a personal chef, two secretaries, and eight "minders."

Backstage he met the lady of his dreams, Diana, the Princess of Wales, for the first time. She seemed somewhat awed by Michael, later telling friends, "He is the most famous man I've ever met."

Another famous man, Prince Charles, stood at her side. Although formally polite, he was hardly in awe of Michael, who did not make his kind of music. As a student at Cambridge, the Prince of Wales had played Barbra Streisand recordings night after night. With that great diva, the Prince would have an on-again, off-again affair.

Michael seemed greatly disappointed that the Prince and Princess of Wales did not bring Prince William and Prince Harry to this special presentation. He'd had *Bad* tour jackets specially made for the boys. Recovering from his disappointment, Michael presented the royal pair with two checks—one for 100,000 pounds for the Great Ormond Street Children's Hospital, another for 150,000 pounds for the Prince's Trust for disadvantaged children.

Not only that, Michael presented them with a framed set of cassettes and compact discs of *Off the Wall*, his mega-selling *Thriller*, and *Bad*. He'd heard that he was the favorite pop star of the Princess.

Embarrassing the Prince, Michael asked him why he didn't bring his sons to the concert. "William is only six years old, Harry just three," Charles said. "There's a thing called bedtime."

Michael made a special request to the Prince, telling him that his pet chimp, Bubbles, had been denied entry into England. He asked the Prince to intervene so that he could be reunited with his pet. Charles smiled politely, saying nothing.

In parting, Charles astonished Michael by saying, "I hear you dance very well. The next time you're in London, you must come by and teach me how to dance. I'm a bit awkward on the ballroom floor."

French President
Jacques Chirac

Even before flying into London, Michael had debated removing the song, "Dirty Diana," from the evening's performance. He felt that it might offend the Princess, although it was not about her. At the last minute, Michael changed his mind and decided to perform "Dirty Diana" after all. The reaction of the Princess was carefully recorded. She seemed to like the song. Standing up from her seat, she danced with the music. Seated beside her, Charles sat in obvious discomfort. At the song's end, Diana applauded wildly, as Charles remained motionless, looking like he'd rather be somewhere else.

MJ, Princess Di, and Prince Charles

Michael later told the press, "I was so excited at meeting the royal couple. I'm very, very happy that they came to watch me perform. I thought the Princess was just wonderful." He made no mention of Charles.

After the concert, Michael was told that the royal couple had left the stadium in a limousine to avoid the crowds. Two other famous guests, he was told, were waiting backstage to greet him: Joan Collins and Ava Gardner.

He received the glamorously dressed Collins first for a very brief meeting. He'd met her once before. In front of people, she said, perhaps facetiously, "If you ever want to switch, darling, and try a woman for a change, you're welcome to lose your virginity to me. Countless other men have made such a sacrifice for me." Michael seemed embarrassed.

A more modestly gowned Ava Gardner followed, her great beauty of the late 1940s and early 50s a memory long faded but forever immortalized on film.

"Sugartit!, I loved your performance. I hear Ol' Blue Eyes himself is jealous of you—not for your singing, but for how much money you make."

"Weren't you the actress that married Frank Sinatra?"

"One and the same, honeychild."

"What was it like being married to a man like that?" he asked.

"I could write a book," she said. "He was great in the sack. Our troubles began while I was on my way to the bidet."

"I don't understand what that means," he said, looking puzzled.

"I'll explain it to you, but in the next lifetime, love," she said, air-kissing him on both cheeks. "You put on quite a show, child. If I ever do another musical like *Showboat*, I'll ask the studio to use your

Prince William
in uniform

281

voice to dub for me." She turned and walked away.

When she'd gone, Michael told an aide, "I can see why Sinatra divorced her. She's not gentle like Elizabeth. Or as kind as Sophia. She seems like a very brittle woman. Maybe she's mad because she's lost her beauty. With the breakthroughs in plastic surgery these days, stars don't have any more excuses to look old."

After Michael flew back to the United States, he began to call the Princess at least once a week. Since he was such an international star, she accepted the calls, at least at first. Most often they talked about

Ava Gardner

children. "I live for my children," she confided to him. "They are my joy, the reason I get up in the morning."

Both of them talked openly about the increasingly invasive and aggressive paparazzi and how difficult it was to live while stalked constantly the moment one left one's door.

Michael told the Princess that he admired her sense of style and grace so much that he'd dressed up one of his mannequins to resemble her, complete with a blonde wig and a diamond-studded tiara. He had seen Diana photographed in what she called "my Elvis dress." White and sequin-studded, the dress had a matching jacket with a turned-up collar. Diana told friends that she "felt both funky and feminine" when wearing the dress, "which I probably do too often, but I can't stand the idea of giving it up—it's my favorite."

Michael informed the Princess that he talked with her plastic version for hours.

"What do you talk about?" she asked.

"Mostly children," he said. "Our mutual love for them. How difficult it is to be shy and yet a public person. How to deal with the media. Our fears that it might one day destroy both of us."

Whether Michael deliberately promoted these stories or not, his so-called romantic link to Princess Di began to appear in the tabloids. *The Star* reported that Michael "at long last" had fallen for a woman, the object of his affection being Princess Diana herself. Not only that, but Diana, according to reports, wanted to star in Michael's next musical video in which she would dance with him. These reports were ridiculous, of course.

A student of media, Donald Tracy, said, "More lies have been printed in the tabloids about Michael Jackson than any celebrity in history. Why? I ask myself. Because the truth—at least until the child molestation charges became public domain—would be devastating. From the very beginning, I think reporters were too savvy to believe all that hype about Michael and women.

But they printed the stories anyway because Michael was hot copy, and they had to write something about him."

Michael sent lavish gifts to Prince William in London, but not to Prince Harry, who was a bit young, even for Michael's taste in special friends. These presents were always carefully rewrapped and returned to Neverland, with the same suggestion, written endlessly. "The Princess thanks you for such marvelous gifts, but William is already blessed with so many things given to him by his parents. He does receive gifts from well-wishers around the world. It is our policy to return these gifts with the suggestion that they be given to other children in need. Think of the joy that would bring."

Michael was said to be offended by this rejection, but that didn't stop him from sending even more expensive presents. He also kept beseeching the Princess to allow William to fly to Neverland. The more rejections he received, the more passionate he became in his campaign to entertain William for a sleepover.

While she was still speaking to him, Diana told Michael that she'd nicknamed William "Billy the Basher," because he liked to play rowdy sports. She said, "Like us, he has the paparazzi following him everywhere. Even if he rides his bike across the palace yard, it's a front page tabloid event."

One night the Princess told Michael that William had at long last chosen his desired profession. "I want to be a policeman," the boy said.

She claimed, "I informed him that his future role had already been determined at birth. 'You're going to be King!' I told him."

Michael hastily added, "I'm a king too. The King of Pop."

"I think I heard that somewhere," Diana said jokingly.

Prince William became an obsession of Michael's. He'd framed a blow-up of the young Prince taken on his first day at Wetherby School in 1987, wearing his regulation red shorts, which were mandatory even in the middle of winter. Under a hat and smiling, the Prince was seen dressed in a red tie

with red-trimmed stockings and waving at the crowds. He carried a Postman Pat lunchbox. Michael ordered his staff to send William a Michael Jackson lunchbox.

During his brief marriage to Lisa Marie Presley, Michael taunted her, claiming he had this ongoing affair with Princess Di. It was reported that Lisa Marie was jealous, although for what reason is not known. Certainly she had no sexual interest in her husband. It must have been for some other reason, perhaps resenting that Michael had such a world-famous friend.

Princess Di, 1985

When Bob Jones heard that Michael was creating some imaginary affair with Princess Di, he said, "Give me a break! The King (i.e., Michael) didn't have a relationship with Princess Diana. He admired her, and a number of calls were put into Diana's people on behalf of Michael. He badly wanted to be friends with her, but apparently she wasn't the least bit interested."

Bob claimed that he personally made calls to Kensington Palace. Instead of getting Diana on the phone, "a polite gentleman" answered. "I told him that Michael had matters he wished to discuss with the Princess," Bob said. "I was told to write down the subject matter in detail, send it along, and they'd get back to me. To my knowledge, none of those calls was ever returned."

Finally, through this "polite gentleman," Michael was told in rather harsh terms that no more presents for William would be accepted but would be returned unwrapped to Neverland. Michael was also told that because of prior commitments, William would not be available to be Michael's guest at Neverland—"not at the present time, not in the near or even distant future." At the bottom of the carefully written note, the Princess had scrawled in her own handwriting:

"Michael,

Please stop sending gifts! They aren't wanted. And please stop calling. Your calls will not be returned. Best wishes in your future career."

It was reported that Michael, after receiving this note, stayed in his bedroom at Neverland, crying for three days and refusing to eat except for a cup of vegetable broth a day.

Princess Di wasn't the only dilemma facing Bob Jones as Michael's publicist. Within a few months after signing on, Bob came to believe that his new employer was a racist.

In his book, *The Man Behind the Mask*, Bob writes: "Michael Jackson—beneath the bleached skin that has made him a grotesque caricature of a female alien—was black too. He was also the weirdest and most inexplicable of racists. His favorite word to describe blacks, his original race, was Splaboo. Yep, Splaboo. It was a word he used a lot, a word he used around people such as Macaulay Culkin."

Bob also noted in his memoirs that Papa Joe always "favored light-skinned black folks" and that "Tito, Jackie, Janet, and many of the younger generations have selected white or non-blacks as their mates."

Michael was never known as a public champion of black people, as was his close friend, Marlon Brando, or many other stars such as Harry Belafonte. As Bob and the rest of the world were observing in the late 1980s, Michael's skin color became a source of endless tabloid speculation. He was in denial of his own pigmentation, which was changing before the eyes of his fans.

In his role as a spokesman for Michael, Bob was constantly asked what

Michael was doing to change his original skin color. Through it all, Michael continued to deny skin bleaching and plastic surgery on his nose. "I guess he didn't want to look like a Splaboo," a security guard at Neverland said sarcastically.

To make himself even whiter, Michael smeared his already-bleached skin with white makeup, creating a freakish aura. Bob noted that Michael, between 1972 and 1998, had so much plastic surgery that "he went from being a really handsome African-American kid to an awful facsimile of a Caucasian woman."

Skin pigmentation wasn't all that was on Michael's mind during the late 80s as he installed himself at Neverland.

The tabloids followed his every move, reporting on one scandal after another whether true or not. One astonishing report may have had some authenticity to it. Michael was terrified of being recognized by his fans when he ventured out of his house. To prevent that, he adopted many disguises. One day he heard that some Swiss scientists were close to developing a potion that would make people invisible—movies, of course, have been made with that theme. Michael seemed willing to invest $1 million in that potion if it could make him invisible. He told some of his staff at Neverland that, if invisible, he could give some of the potion to Bubbles too. That way, both of them could go shopping at various malls, including toy stores, and not be molested by the public. How an invisible man could go into a toy store and buy merchandise without attracting attention was never explained.

After several futile attempts, Michael realized that the invisible potion, if such an elixir existed, was only in the early planning stages, far too soon in its development to make him disappear any time soon.

Far more obtainable—or so he reportedly felt at the time—was a desire to acquire another skeleton. He'd failed to secure the bones of the Elephant Man. But out there in a Los Angeles cemetery, with the traffic whizzing by, rested the bones of the world's most enduring sex symbol, Marilyn Monroe.

He'd heard that the heirs to her estate were "one greedy bunch," as his friend Marlon Brando had charged. Brando later reported that Michael had talked seriously of making an offer of $5 million to secure MM's skeleton. "I just went along with Michael for the ride," Brando claimed. "I thought, of course, it was just a joke. My mistake was in not realizing that Michael's doesn't joke. I like to play practical jokes on people all the time, especially if they are close friends."

As a great actor, Brando maintained a serious face when he told Michael what he might do with Marilyn's bones. "Marilyn and I were lovers," Brando said. "Our affair began right after the war when I picked her up at a sleazy bar in New York. It continued on and off right up until her murder. In fact, hours

Marilyn's fate?

before she was killed, we had a date to get together for dinner."

Brando's suggestion, if Michael could have her corpse removed from the Mausoleum of Memories at Westwood Memorial Park, was not to keep Marilyn's bones hidden away at Neverland. "First, I'd have a designer put Marilyn's bones in a bikini," Brando said. "She loved diamonds—even sang about them. Definitely a diamond tiara and a diamond necklace are in order. The costlier the better. I'd install her as an attraction on Hollywood Boulevard, charging fifteen dollars a ticket. People would gladly pay that. But it can't be just a stack of bones. I'd lay her out in the center like a funeral parlor. An open casket. But all around I'd have wide screens showing some of her famous moments. That walk in *Niagara*. That satiny pink gown she wore when she sang 'Diamonds are a Girl's Best Friend' in *Gentlemen Prefer Blondes*. Her walk at the rail station in Chicago in *Some Like It Hot*. Her singing 'Heat Wave' in *There's No Business Like Show Business*. Newsreels of Marilyn and Joe DiMaggio. Her standing on that subway grate in *The Seven Year Itch* as a blast of hot air blows her skirt up to her panties. Definitely pictures of her in New York, in that skin-tight gown singing 'Happy Birthday' to President Kennedy."

Michael told Brando that he thought "all your ideas are just great."

After Michael had left his house, Brando called one of his friends. "The kid actually thought I was serious. I was just talking shit like I like to do for fun. He really believed me. I must be a better actor than I thought I was."

Like Prince William, the bones of Marilyn Monroe eluded Michael. But he still wanted to live in a fantasy world, one he could create at Neverland. After recovering from several setbacks, he pulled himself up out of his bed to oversee construction, on the grounds of Neverland, of "another Disneyland," one far greater than he'd created at Hayvenhurst. "I don't have to dream, but can live in my dream," he told staff members.

At Neverland, Michael experienced the first real freedom he'd ever known in his life. At long last he was free of his smothering mother, Katherine, and dictatorial Papa Joe. He also did-

Goddess

n't have his siblings, especially their mates, interfering or, worse, judging his lifestyle.

Michael's freedom didn't extend to his employees, each of whom was forced to sign a confidentiality agreement. "He ran Neverland like Himmler might direct a concentration camp," said one disgruntled employee who had been fired because he'd violated a cardinal rule. "I talked to one of the other employees. We were not supposed to talk to each other. We were also told to look down at our navels when Michael walked by." As an afterthought, he added, "It was Jackson who should have bowed his head in shame."

In the years ahead, employees—most of whom were no longer working at Neverland—reported that dozens of young boys were dropped off at the guarded front gate and handed over to Michael's "security force." One of Michael's special policemen would then assist the boy into a fanciful carriage pulled by a Clydesdale.

After he had been escorted to the main hall of Neverland, the *boy du jour* was taken to Michael's bedroom. After securing clearance, the boy was allowed to enter the room. At such times, Michael himself would be lurking behind the door but would not appear within its frame. The aide would not see him in the flesh. Presumably the boy wouldn't get to feast his eyes on Michael until after he entered the darkened room.

When staff members did see Michael in his room, as when making a delivery, he was often in tight white briefs, but always in full makeup. Sometimes he'd be discovered in bed with a young boy, each nude from the waist up, a sheet covering their lower bodies.

Later, one employee told the police, "I don't know how Michael contact-ed the parents of these young boys and gained their consent to deliver a ten-year-old, or even a twelve-year-old, to Michael's den. How did he make contact with them and get their permission? I know he did that because it was the parents, sometimes just a mother, who would deliver her son to Neverland. Sometimes a boy would stay only a night, with his mother waiting to pick him up the next morning. In one case an especially beautiful wide-eyed boy, probably the best-look-ing kid I've ever seen in my life, was delivered to Michael's room where he stayed nearly a month. Michael must have really dug that kid."

Two courses of introductions have been sug-gested. Michael often invited young boys, including some young girls, to Neverland to

There are just some things
MJ can't have

287

enjoy its Disney-like attractions. Once the children were at play, he would select those boys whom he'd like to get to know better. Often he made his selection when they were playing shirtless or else wearing a swim suit to jump into his pool.

Another method of contact was through dozens of model agencies in Los Angeles, many of whom specialized in child models for both TV and print advertising. Michael would order publicity photographs of these boys sent to Neverland. Staff members reported that he would spend the good part of many a day studying each photograph carefully and evaluating it. His excuse to the agencies was that he was planning to make musical videos involving child actors, as he'd done in the past. It was reported that Michael seemed especially interested in the lips on a young boy.

Johnny Ciao was employed as a chef at Neverland during the greater part of 1988. During that time, he witnessed a parade of boys being entertained by Michael. One boy, who "looked like an angel," was estimated to be only eight years old. Staff members felt that the oldest boys Michael entertained were thirteen years of age—rarely sixteen or seventeen.

In a move he'd later regret, Michael hired Mark and Faye Quindoy, a Filipino couple, to manage his Neverland estate. They would later spill many of Michael's secrets to the world, appearing on such shows as Geraldo Rivera's *Now It Can Be Told*. When child molestation charges first appeared, and the Quindoys were questioned by California police, the couple agreed to testify against Michael. They would later sue Michael for $300,000 back pay and also sue his envoy, Anthony Pellicano, who denounced them as "cockroaches and failed extortionists."

Having replaced Johnny Ciao, Faye Quindoy became Michael's personal cook, preparing such treats as a Mickey Mouse Cake and the Seven Dwarfs Pizza. Her husband presided over Michael's small army of 15 armed guards, 32 groundskeepers, and two animal keepers, even a fire "brigade" of one firefighter.

When Michael and his special friend of the moment tired of his own Disneyland at the ranch, he'd asked Mark Quindoy to drive them to Solvang, which, like Neverland, lay in the Santa Ynez Valley. Because of its association with early Danish settlers, the town offers a taste of Scandinavia in California, with much of its architecture in the traditional Danish style. There is even a copy of the most famous statue in Copenhagen, the Little Mermaid, as inspired by the tale of Hans Christian Andersen.

One day Mark drove Michael to Solvang, accompanied by a seven-year-old boy who was spending his nights in Michael's bed.

After pulling a four-wheel-drive Chevrolet Blazer into Solvang, Mark accompanied Michael and the boy as they explored the town, stopping at a

288

mammoth dollhouse Michael was considering duplicating at Neverland.

On the way back to the ranch, Mark later reported that he was astonished to witness Michael in an embrace with the boy—"like a lover, kissing him passionately. It was just like a boy kissing a girl in the backseat," he later testified. He claimed that the boy put up no protest but just sat there quietly tolerating it even when Michael wet-kissed him on the lips. "Michael began kissing him everywhere—his neck, head, arms, shoulders, and body. I was utterly stunned—appalled that he could do that to a seven-year-old boy. The kid stayed for another three weeks at Neverland before departing with his mother, who had been staying in Michael's guest house. The next day a nine-year-old boy showed up and began his sleepovers in Michael's bedroom."

Years later, when contacted by investigative reporters while living in Manila, the Quindoys admitted that "Jackson chose one boy at a time. The kids were assaulted with sounds and lights. Lewd things went on right under the noses of the parents." The couple claimed that they did not go to the police because "we were just witnesses, not victims."

One big question has been raised—but never quite answered: Why did mothers allow their kids to be alone all night with an adult male in his bedroom? Rabbi Shmuley Boteach said, "No one has suggested that women have sunk so low that they would prostitute their own children in order to benefit from proximity to a superstar." He cited the case of Michael Jackson as "a frightening new sickness in the American soul. The pursuit of money and celebrity has driven some Americans to use their own children as the means by which to obtain rewards. Just when you thought that respect for women in our popular culture had reached its nadir, along comes a new stereotype: the mother as pimp."

Michael's bedroom was on the second floor of Neverland's main residence, a manor-style building with nearly a dozen additional bedrooms. There were an extra four bedrooms within an elegant and rather tastefully decorated guest house in back.

He had ordered that a secret playroom be constructed next to the manor. Like Michael's perpetually darkened bedroom, this playroom was strictly off-limits to other employees. Sometimes Michael would spend all day in this playroom with his special friend of the moment.

Michael not only maintained a shrine to Elizabeth Taylor, but he created the Shirley Temple Room. He'd seen all of her films, including *Wee Willie Winkie* and *The*

The Quindoy witnesses

289

Little Colonel, many of them countless times, and had decorated the room with film posters of his favorite Shirley Temple flicks. He'd also collected lots of Temple memorabilia, including a pair of patent-leather Mary Jane shoes that she'd worn in one of her movies. He'd also purchased curly haired wigs sold in the 30s to young girls whose mothers wanted them to look like the chubby-cheeked toddler.

Michael was especially intrigued with a series of shorts Temple had made in the early 1930s. Called *Baby Burlesks*, these films starring young kids spoofed movies and stars of the early Talkies. Viewed today, these seemingly innocent films have been called "baby porn," attracting every pedophile in America—that is, those who desired young girls instead of young boys.

To more mature and cynical audiences in the decades to come, Temple became a joke and was endlessly spoofed. One critic wrote, "She was precocious to the point of nausea, overemphasizing every goody-goody line, pouring on each inflection of cheer and wringing forth every tear in a manner that had nothing whatsoever to do with real acting." But Michael didn't agree with that. He was a self-admitted "sucker" for a Temple movie any time she wanted to take a ride on the Good Ship *Lollipop*. He even ordered a Shirley Temple mannequin, dressing it in baby pink with a pink bow holding up her curly coiffure.

One day he invited Mrs. Shirley Temple Black to visit Neverland, and she accepted his invitation. In her 60s and rather matronly, Temple had hesitated before accepting the invitation. Her nervousness was evident when Michael greeted her in the foyer of Neverland. "Are you disappointed in me?" she asked.

"Of course not," he said. "I'm honored."

"I'm always embarrassed to meet fans of my pictures from the 30s," she said. "I feel I've betrayed them by growing up. Even worse, growing old."

"You are not old," he assured her. "You'll be forever young in your films which will also live forever. The world will always remember you as young."

Michael appeared before Temple in full makeup, including mascara, eyeliner, and Honey Glow.

Not missing a beat, nor even appearing startled that she was greeting a man in heavy makeup, Temple studied Michael's face momentarily and said, "I like Honey Glow myself."

As he ushered her into the Shirley Temple Room, she took his hand and searched for his eyes behind his sunglasses. "Like you, I sacrificed my youth to entertain others," she confessed. "But by 1949 the studios told me I can't be a cute little girl forever. Now let's look around this Shirley Temple Room. I'm sure it'll bring back so many memories."

Mrs. Temple Black became the U.S. Ambassador to Ghana and later

Czechoslovakia. At the time of her meeting with Michael, the two stars exchanged autobiographies, he giving her a copy of *Moonwalk* and she presenting him with her tome, *Child Star*.

Mrs. Temple Black grew up. Michael never did.

For his master bedroom at Neverland, Michael purchased an oversized red velvet and gold throne, "fit for a queen," as a member of the Neverland staff jokingly suggested. He also had a four-poster bed. But for extreme privacy, he ordered the construction of a Secret Room. It was entered through a ten-foot walk-in closet packed with childish novelties and other bizarre artifacts. A door was hidden at the rear of the closet behind an array of Michael's favorite military costumes.

A narrow, carpeted stairwell, lined with rag dolls, led to the windowless, eight-by-seven-foot secret chamber.

In the 90s when the police searched Neverland, trying to find evidence to prove a case of child molestation against Michael, they accidentally stumbled upon this private hideaway. The room, police discovered, was sparsely furnished, containing an oversized sofa, upholstered in a satiny pink, a Trinitron TV, and a bed covered with pillows depicting Peter Pan and Tinkerbell. A bug-eyed, red-headed Troll Doll was placed in the center of the bed. There was also a Mickey Mouse phone. For art, pictures of smiling babies in diapers lined the walls.

When the existence of the secret room became known to the public, reporters labeled it Michael's "creepy lair." When Michael was not entertaining a boy in his bedroom, he would take the child out to enjoy the grounds at Neverland, which included Michael's Disney-esque attractions and his animal menagerie.

His private zoo was complete with tigers, lions, and giraffes. There were also two elephants, the baby elephant a gift from Elizabeth Taylor. Michael ordered that the animal be painted in his favorite shade of pink.

A "Lawrence of Arabia" camel was part of the menagerie, as was a baby llama called "Puddin' Pie." There were enough pink flamingos to rival their nesting ground on Inagua Island, in The Bahamas. Michael also had a cage of chimps, supplying them with papayas, mangoes, and boxed fruit juices.

Throughout the park were waterproof pictures of Michael holding hands with children. Both parents and children, even such famous guests as Elizabeth Taylor and Gregory Peck, were invited to enjoy Michael's fantasy park.

Security guards from the Nation of Islam required each guest to sign a waiver agreeing not to carry cameras. Later cell phones were added to the forbidden list. If a visitor violated the mandate, he or she might be escorted from the grounds of Neverland by a guard.

One of those guards reported that Michael threw rocks at his lion to make him roar. He could often be seen riding his Ferris wheel with a series of boys.

One guard claimed, "I can't count the number of young boys who rode with Michael on that Ferris wheel, his arm locked possessively around them. All the young kids were instructed to call Michael 'Daddy.'"

Sometimes he would simultaneously hold the hands of two boys as he escorted them around his amusement park, whose white-painted Victorian gazebos and ornate street lamps evoked *fin de siè-*

Shirley all grown up

cle Paris. He even had treehouses built on the property. He'd climb up to one of these getaways in the sky with his favorite of the moment.

After Michael adopted child star Macaulay Culkin as his favorite, he installed a water pistol range, "Mac and Mike's Waterforts," for some epic water pistol battles. Ice cream flavors came in an astonishing array, including one Michael himself created—kiwi fruit and peanut butter. One arcade played rap music all day, although Michael had ordered a sound engineer to edit out "the curse words."

He told his adult visitors that his flowerbeds cost him $300,000 a year to maintain. "I can't stand to see a flower die," he said. "When a flower withers, I order one of my gardeners to dig up the bulb and replace it immediately with one that will bloom again."

Lunch was always provided for the kids invited to Neverland. "The kids skipped the vegetables and main courses and went immediately for the desserts," said a former cook. "After a big lunch, they'd spend the rest of the day eating pink cotton candy or devouring bags of popcorn. All of them went home with a belly ache."

When the builders of Neverland thought they were finished with the project, Michael demanded more—his own steam railway, a fun fair, a cinema, and a make-believe Indian village. When everything was finished, Michael hired a Charlie Chaplin impersonator to wander the grounds, amusing the children, who usually didn't know anything about the silent screen star.

After Michael's guests had departed, he often retreated to "The Giving Tree" overlooking a lake. Here he would write lyrics, including the song, "Childhood":

> *People say I'm not OK*
> *'cause I love such elementary things.*

292

Trolls and Peter Pans
found in secret room

It's been my fate to compensate for the childhood I've never known.

For truly private getaways, Michael rented a so-called bachelor pad in the summer of 1989, calling it "The Hideout." Actually it was a condo on the 14th floor of The Westford, a luxury housing unit at 10750 Wilshire Boulevard. When the police, in years to come, raided the condo, it was discovered that it didn't have a bed, only a sleeping bag and a large-screen TV.

Many of Michael's special friends were taken surreptitiously to The Hideout. Often parents, usually a mother, delivered her son to Neverland. Michael sometimes, later in the dark of the night, took the boy to the condo.

When it was later revealed that Michael had a "secret address," one story was headlined: AT LONG LAST MICHAEL JACKSON DISCOVERS GIRLS.

Perhaps not believing what he wrote, one journalist claimed that Michael—"rather belatedly"—was discovering girls and now had a rendezvous condo for his private assignations.

"This was all a big joke, and the reporters writing such shit probably didn't believe it themselves," said Robert Estelle. "The story about the fuck pad turned out to be true. Only the reporters at the time got the genders confused."

Life was not all fun and games with young boys at Neverland. Michael worked on a 93-minute music video cassette *Moonwalker*, which included a montage of live footage of himself in concert. With Michael, of course, cast as the main character, *Moonwalker* also contained a series of fantasy pieces. Even fat boy Frank DiLeo, Michael's manager, appeared in the video, along with familiar faces such as Mick Jagger or Sean Lennon playing themselves. One of the dancers was Michael's nephew, Jermaine Jackson Jr.

Elizabeth Taylor as "Herself" appeared uncredited in archive footage. Michael originally wanted to release *Moonwalker* in theaters but budget restraints forced him to take it straight to video release.

The most disturbing part of *Moonwalker* wasn't associated with its view of the shrine to Ms. Taylor, but

Peter Pan pillows for the kids

293

Darkest corners of secret room

Michael dancing with what supposedly was the Elephant Man's skeleton.

Upon its release, *Moonwalker* was a hit, even outselling the former number one best-selling music video of all time, "The Making of Michael Jackson's 'Thriller.'" For twenty-two weeks *Moonwalker* held its position as *Billboard's* Number One video cassette. After that, it was knocked down to number two by the release of *Michael Jackson: The Legend Continues*.

The video racked up sales of $30 million. But Michael had invested $27 million, making his cut less than $3 million, even less when final expenses were deducted.

"He blamed everybody," an aide said confidentially. "He even threatened to fire DiLeo. Jackson shouted, screamed, and raged, placing responsibility on everybody but the one person responsible for the low return—Michael Jackson himself. When he wasn't screaming about *Moonwalker*, he was screaming about the final tallies coming in on the *Bad* album, even though it was the second best-selling album of all time. Jackson wanted one hundred million copies sold, not the fifth of that he actually got. We felt he was so unrealistic in the big sales he demanded that he'd become delusional."

After five years of being "inseparable," Michael, for reasons of his own, fired his Uncle Tookie, Frank DiLeo. From all reports, DiLeo had been a successful manager for Michael, the most temperamental star in Hollywood. His manager had stood by Michael through many a disaster.

He had his attorney, John Branca, do the dirty deed. Getting DiLeo on the phone, Branca told him, "Michael called this morning. He's decided he doesn't want to work with you any more."

Putting up a brave front, DiLeo said, "If the kid has mandated that, it's okay with me." That very day he set about trying to find another job. Ironically, he succeeded where Michael hadn't—in the movies. He was cast in Martin Scorsese's *Goodfellas*, appearing with Robert De Niro, and in both the *Wayne's World* movies with Mike Myers and Dana Carvey.

The Westford

There was much speculation about why Michael fired DiLeo, but only the impulsive star himself knows for sure. At times Michael blamed DiLeo for the tabloid "Wacko Jacko" image. He also blamed him that the album, *Bad*, didn't top *Thriller* in sales. He also felt that DiLeo was taking far too much credit for Michael's own achievements. Because Michael would not face the press, and DiLeo had to go on for him in front of TV cameras and microphones, he was becoming increasingly well known. Michael also claimed that DiLeo was getting "too bossy and possessive."

One member of the *Bad* troupe claimed that "Michael Jackson was seriously pissed about everything. DiLeo, a real sweet, good guy, who lived, breathed, and slept the advancement of the career of Michael Jackson, became the fall guy."

To friends, DiLeo expressed his hurt feelings, "It was cowardly not to call me personally and tell me I was out the door. I treated him like my own son."

Michael didn't want to meet DiLeo's demand for $5 million in severance pay. But when the man Michael once called "my shield of armor, my other half" threatened to go public with "secrets to make the tabloids blush," DiLeo got his $5 million check.

On Diane Sawyer's *Good Morning America* TV show in 2004, DiLeo gave a somewhat enigmatic answer to a question about why Michael fired him. "I think it was, he fired me because it was politically asked of him. There was an outside record executive with a big-time lawyer and one executive at Sony that would like to see Michael's power cut in half. And getting rid of me was half the power."

DiLeo's final word on Michael: "He's part Howard Hughes, part E.T. Michael Jackson begs description." Like Howard Hughes, who employed a so-called press agent, Johnny Meyer (actually his pimp) to handle many of his least pleasant tasks, the reclusive Michael hid behind DiLeo for a good part of the 80s.

Kenny Rogers, the country music star, was in the unique position of knowing both the King of Pop and the King of Rock and Roll. "Michael is the Elvis of his generation," Kenny said. "Like Elvis, Michael too is locking himself away from the real world. That's an extremely unhealthy way to live. I know what it's like to be mobbed by fans every time you go out. It can be terrifying. But, he's seen out so rarely that when he's spotted, it's a major event—and he gets mobbed. Even so, he's got to learn to get out more."

At Neverland, Michael ventured out very rarely and always in disguise. In spite of invitations from Katherine, he avoided a return visit to Hayvenhurst.

"There were weird things going on at Neverland, but unlike life at Encino, no violence," said a former maid who'd worked at both estates. "The difference between Neverland and Hayvenhurst is that family fights often occurred at Hayvenhurst. Except for Michael, the acorns didn't fall far from the tree."

She was referring to the sons of Papa Joe. In many ways, at least in their domestic lives, they emulated their father's own behavior and unhappy marriage.

A good example of this involved Michael's brother Jackie: Even though Enid Spann's marriage to Michael's brother, Jackie, had ended in August of 1987, Jackie was later arrested on a charge of harassing his former wife. Arriving at her home, where she was entertaining, Jackie kicked in her French doors, sending shards of glass flying. She called the police, who later charged Jackie with violating a restraining order issued by a judge.

Jermaine's marital problems seemed even more dramatic than those of Jackie. After a tumultuous marriage to Hazel Gordy, during which Jermaine frequently cheated on his wife, the marriage had wound down by 1988, and would eventually end in divorce. But before it did, Jermaine would start another family with Margaret Maldonado, eventually fathering two children with her—Jeremy and Jourdynn. At one point both Margaret and Hazel were pregnant with Jermaine's babies. As Enid Spann once claimed, Jermaine showed up with his three-month-old son at Marlon Jackson's birthday party in December of 1986, with a pregnant Hazel at his side. In August of 1988, Jermaine, while visiting his ex-wife, Hazel, attempted to rape her. She screamed as he forcefully held her down, but managed to escape by biting his arm.

Randy's romantic life would grow even more complicated than those of his brothers. After reportedly having as many affairs on the side as his older brother, Jermaine, Randy married Eliza Shaffe in May of 1989, an ill-fated union that would produce one child and end in divorce in 1991. The divorce was acrimonious, and Eliza later filed a criminal complaint against Randy, charging that he beat her during her pregnancy. He pleaded no contest to the wife-beating charge and in November of 1991, he was sentenced to a two-year period of probation. When he violated that probation, a judge sentenced him to one month in jail. Katherine appeared in court to plead her son's case. She was successful in getting the judge to change his decision. He agreed to commit Randy for 30 days to the Pine Grove Mental Hospital where he underwent domestic violence counseling.

Eliza was photographed by the press in front of Randy's Wilshire Boulevard condo carrying a sign that accused him of being a "Dead Beat Dad." She needed money to support their daughter, Steveanna, and Randy wasn't making the payments a judge had ordered. In the midst of all this turmoil, according to Margaret Maldonado, Randy launched an affair with the beautiful model, Paula Barbieri.

This Florida-born woman, who like La Toya

Margaret Maldonado

herself, would pose for *Playboy* magazine, later became famous because of a romance she conducted with another black man. Paula broke up with O.J. Simpson on June 12, 1994, the day that Nicole Brown, the athlete's ex-wife was murdered. Nonetheless, Paula stood by Simpson through his fifteen months in jail, and she later wrote a confessional, *The Other Woman: My Years with O.J. Simpson—A Story of Love, Trust, and Betrayal.*

It is not known whether Michael was even aware of Randy's involvement with Paula, but he avidly watched Simpson's televised court case. Later, when news of his own trial was broadcast on TV, he remarked, "O.J. drew better ratings than I did."

Randy's affair with Paula would not last long. But his affair with Alejandra Loaiza, a Colombian, would have far-reaching implications for the Jackson family. The attractive young woman had already had a traumatic life before arriving at the Jackson compound. Her mother had served time in a California penitentiary as a convicted cocaine dealer.

One day Alejandra confessed to Margaret Maldonado that she'd already had "several abortions" at Randy's request. Apparently, he preferred unprotected sex but didn't want to have a "bunch of babies" running all over Hayvenhurst. "My brothers have already brought enough kids into the world," he said. After an on-again, off-again affair, Randy finally married Alejandra in 1992 and would eventually sire three children with her.

To complicate matters even more for America's most dysfunctional black family, Jermaine would later marry Alejandra following her divorce from Randy on March 18, 1995. Jermaine and Alejandra were married in a secret ceremony at the Hotel Bel-Air. Della Reese administered the vows.

Diane Sawyer

Reese, who toured as a teenager with gospel great, Mahalia Jackson, is an ordained minister of the Church of Understanding Principals for a Better Living in Los Angeles. Katherine could only have been horrified at the choice of Reese as the presiding minister at her son's wedding. Reese's church has come under fire from the Christian Right, since it refers to itself as "Christian," but does not accept the divinity of Jesus Christ.

Margaret later said, "I tried to figure out how I was going to explain to my children that their Aunt Alejandra was now their stepmother, and their cousins, Randy Jr. and Genevieve, were now their stepbrother and stepsister. And that their Uncle Randy's girlfriend was now sleeping with their father. Talk about family values run amuck." Reporter Diane Dimond, on *Court TV*, raised a provocative question, "Do the children call Jermaine Uncle or Daddy or what?"

Even Tito wasn't immune from marital discord. His 1972 marriage to Delores V. Martes ("DeeDee") would also end in divorce in 1990. DeeDee discovered that Tito, following the Jackson pattern, had been unfaithful to her. He had three sons with DeeDee. As they grew older, they formed a group called "3T," releasing two

Alejandra Loaiza and her children

albums, *Brotherhood* in 1995 and *Identity* in 2004. The first album included the hit, "Anything and Why" which they performed with their uncle, Michael himself.

Many of the Jackson family's domestic dramas unfolded without making headlines in the tabloids. Instead, the media continued to focus on Michael, who could always provide some kind of hot, sensational story. He rarely spoke to his associates about his family problems. Weeks before he fired Frank DiLeo, Michael told his manager, "I hate confrontations, and I abhor violence."

Obviously the private lives of the Jackson family members weren't going well. And for the most part, their professional careers weren't going anywhere either.

From Neverland, Michael told his siblings they had to "go it alone" with their album, *2300 Jackson Street*, named after their small bungalow in Gary, Indiana. Janet and Rebbie joined their brothers—all except Marlon—in the album. Like Michael, La Toya also refused to join the group. Released in 1989, the album fared poorly, reaching only 59 on *Billboard's* charts. "I always told my brothers that without me, they're headed for oblivion," Michael once told Frank DiLeo.

Some of Michael's brothers, notably Jermaine, blamed him for "sabotaging" sales of the album, although how Michael did that was never made clear.

With the release of *2300 Jackson St.*, the Jackson brothers' contract with Epic Records was fulfilled. It would not be renewed. No

Della Reese

Paula Barbieri

record company seemed interested in committing themselves to an expensive contract with the Jackson brothers unless Michael was part of the deal.

In distinct contrast to the failure of his brothers, *Forbes Magazine* in September of 1989 listed Michael as the number one highest-paid entertainer for the second consecutive year, with a two-year estimated earnings of $125 million. By December of that year, *Entertainment Tonight* had named Michael "The Most Important Entertainer of the Year." *Rolling Stone* proclaimed *Thriller* the number one album of the 80s, and the best-selling record album in the history of the music industry.

Michael Jackson would go down in music history as the undisputed star of the 1980s. His triumphs, both artistically and financially, stunned the industry. He had become the 1980s' most enigmatic entertainer, a man of mystery.

The Pulitzer Prize-winning author, Margo Jefferson, stated it this way: "Was he man, boy, man-boy, or boy-woman? Mannequin or postmodern zombie? Here was a black person who had once looked unmistakably black, and now looked white or at least un-black. He was, at the very least, a new kind of mulatto, one created by science and medicine and cosmetology. Biology defines a mulatto as the sterile offspring of an animal or plant species. Michael Jackson's sperm count, I'm relieved to say, is one of the few things we know nothing about. We are reasonably certain he chose not to produce offspring by traditional means: here again, science joined nature to do his bidding."

The 80s were drawing to a close. Michael would never again experience such heady days of glory. The 90s were coming, a decade so dreadful for Michael that he would on several occasions contemplate suicide.

Diana Ross's early prophecy was about to come true for him in a very personal way: "The world likes to build a star up to tear him down," she said.

"Michael Jackson loves children—but mainly if they're drop-dead gorgeous, and in some cases even ready to drop dead. If Michael Jackson would just agree to be a pedophile, we could have our kook and eat him too."

--Michael Musto

"Forget about the superstar, forget about the icon. If he was any other thirty-five-year old man who was sleeping with little boys, you wouldn't like this guy."

--La Toya Jackson

"It was a child's dream, with every kind of soda in the world there, every kind of candy. A two-floor arcade, a carnival and a movie theater."

--Macaulay Culkin, on Neverland

"He never had a childhood. He is having one now. His buddies are twelve-year-old kids. They have pillow fights and food fights."

--Bert Fields, a former attorney of Michael Jackson

"We had very similar experiences in childhood. We're both going to be eight years old forever in some place because we never had a chance to be eight when we actually were."

--Macaulay Culkin

"Michael Jackson is just a successful pop singer, after all. Maybe this particular American life is just too strange to stand as anything other than its once-glorious, now-pathetic self. But in the end we walk away, shaking our heads in befuddlement. Maybe it's better to just put on 'I Want You Back,' smile sadly and leave it at that."

--Martha Southgate

Chapter Ten

In his mind at least, Michael's "affair" with Princess Di lasted until her tragic death in the summer of 1997.

"I had a concert on the day the news broke," Michael said. "My doctor woke me up to tell me Diana was dead. I collapsed. I fainted. He had to give me smelling salts to revive me, and I cancelled my show because I simply could not perform. I just broke down. I wept and wept for weeks afterward."

He spent all the day watching news reports of the death of the princess with her lover, Dodi Fayed, his other friend, in a car crash in a Paris tunnel while they were being chased by paparazzi on motorcycles.

"She used to confide in me," Michael told his friends. "She'd just call me on the phone, and we would talk about everything that was happening in her life. The press was hard on her in the same way they were hard on me, and she needed to talk to someone who knew exactly what she was going through. She felt hunted the way I feel hunted. Trapped!"

Dr. Steven Hoefflin

When he was interviewed by Barbara Walters on TV, Michael admitted, "I fell back in grief and started to cry, upon learning of Diana's death. I said there's another one real soon. I feel it coming. There's another one, and I pray it's not me. Please don't let it be me. And Mother Teresa came."

When Walters asked Michael if he were psychic, he said, "I don't want to say that but I've done it before." Michael's claims about his link to Princess Di contradicted reports made by staff members, such as Bob Jones. "Diana had desperately wanted me to meet her children," Michael said, "and we talked about it many times, but I never got the chance. Dodi talked very

301

highly of the boys. He says they are wonderful, and he had some good times on holiday with the boys and Diana."

In séances during the months that followed, Michael reportedly spoke to the spirit of the since-departed Princess Di. According to Michael, she assured him that she was "in good spirits," and asked him to intervene in the parenting of Prince William. According to Michael, the Princess told him, "William should be brought up by you—not Charles."

It is believed that Michael met Dodi in 1987 in the office of their mutual plastic surgeon, Dr. Steven Hoefflin. Michael was trying to erase the final traces of his "Negroid nose," whereas Dodi didn't like "my Arabic beak."

Born in Alexandria, Egypt, three years before Michael, Dodi was the son of billionaire Mohamed Al-Fayed.

Even before they met, Michael was impressed with Dodi's achievements in the movie industry, especially as they related to the 1981 Oscar-winning hit, *Chariots of Fire*. Michael was also impressed that Dodi's father owned Harrods in London, the world's most famous department store, and the Ritz in Paris, the world's most famous hotel.

Dodi's father had made a fortune by working for Saudi arms dealer Adnan Khashoggi. It is said that Khashoggi had been involved in almost every single conspiracy theory in the latter part of the 20th century, ranging from Watergate to the Iran-Contra affair.

Michael met Dodi as his eight-month marriage to the American model, Suzanne Gregard, was coming to an end. Dodi grew up in a world of privilege, dividing his time between family homes in Egypt and France. He also had homes in New York, Paris, London, Los Angeles, and Switzerland. An avid night-clubber, he was addicted to fast cars and even faster women.

Long before Diana, there were so many other women. Critics of Dodi called them his "trophy women" and suggested he was a Middle Eastern social climber.

Like Michael, Dodi had also dated Brooke Shields, but his dating with her was for real. Dodi, to make Michael jealous, would speak of his conquests of famous or infamous women, including Winona Ryder, Cathy Lee Crosby, Mimi Rogers, and the notorious Koo Stark who in 1982 had launched a scandalous affair with Britain's Prince Andrew. "I was far superior in bed," Dodi bragged.

Dodi's romance with Barbra Streisand had ended long before he met Michael. Again, Dodi liked to bring up the name of the diva to "send Michael into a jealous rage."

Dodi Al-Fayed

A gossip columnist reported, whether accurately or not, that Streisand once said, "Tina Sinatra and Michael Jackson may find the fire in Dodi. I never did."

In addition to bonding with Dodi, Michael had another reason for wanting to know him. At the time of their introduction, Dodi was contemplating his role as an executive producer of the Peter Pan story, and, of course, Michael still dreamed of playing "the boy who wouldn't grow up." The picture, after it was abandoned by Spielberg, later resurfaced as *Hook*. Michael lost the role.

He also claimed that he and Dodi discussed "night after night" the launching of other films starring Michael, with Dodi being the executive producer. "We laughed and joked about the mischief and mayhem we'd create in Hollywood," Michael said. "Dodi has taken a lot of flak in this country, which is so unfair. He is one of the sweetest, kindest men you could ever know. The problem is that people judge people before they even know them. To me, he is like a big Santa Claus. He loves giving, he's very wise, creative, talented, and kind-hearted."

Apparantly, Dodi loved fast cars. Long before his death in Paris, Dodi, once or twice with Michael positioned beside him in the back seat, sometimes ordered his chauffeur to "hit the floor" with the gas pedal. Michael was often shaken by the danger but apparently never objected. Months after the death of Dodi and Princess Di, Michael said, "There but for the grace of God go I."

One night when Michael was engaged in a private rendezvous at Dodi's house, two men arrived to evict Dodi. His house was one of the most expensive rentals in Hollywood, but Dodi had written a bad check to his landlord who wanted him evicted. In the film industry, Dodi had a reputation for writing bad checks. A producer who refused to be named claimed that "Dodi was a deadbeat, a bad guy."

Was Dodi's relationship with Michael sexual? That was the question at Hollywood parties for several months late in the 1980s. The answer might never be known. Dodi is dead, and Michael doesn't speak of such things. Michael's detractors claim that there was definitely "something there, more than a friendship, but we couldn't call it love." Even so, the two men seemed very devoted to each other.

Although Michael and Dodi had enjoyed a close bond, Michael didn't seem jealous when his friend launched an affair with Diana. "They were a match made in heaven," Michael claimed. "I thought they were beautiful together. It was lovely to see them like that. Diana was a wonderful person with a good heart. She went around the world as a philanthropist just like Mother Teresa. Diana proved that she really, really cared about people, children especially. The way I do."

Michael later confided to friends that he understood why Jackie Kennedy "married that beast, Onassis. There was this extraordinary circus going on around Jackie. Onassis offered her a chance to escape from that. For that same reason, I think Diana will marry Dodi. But there's a big difference. Jackie did not love Onassis. Diana loves Dodi. Of course, I love both of them."

The gay rumors linking Michael with Dodi remained confined mainly to insider Hollywood. But after a brief lull, the gay rumors about Michael resurfaced once again in the media during the late 80s and early 1990s. This time they would never go away.

Katherine Jackson's memoirs were released in 1990 and in her book this member of the homophobic Jehovah's Witness cult denied the rumors about her son. Either naïvely or with calculation, she claimed, "Michael is not gay." One of her reasons she cited for her son not being gay is that the "Bible speaks against homosexuality and he's very religious." By now, however, this absurd defense had become a tired cliché. In her memoirs, she claimed that Michael "wants to settle down and get married one day. We've talked about it. And he will." In this case, mama knew best. Her son would eventually "marry" not only once, but twice.

For her book, Katherine engaged Rebbie, her oldest daughter, in the cultural war raging around her younger brother. Even though Rebbie was far removed from what was actually going on at Neverland, she provided a quotation for her mother's book: "If Michael were married, the gay rumors would stop immediately."

Within Katharine's memoirs, Rebbie concluded with a statement that was particularly unconvincing to an America growing more hip, more cynical, and more skeptical than ever about her brother. "Just being around him and hearing the little things that he says about women tell me he's definitely heterosexual." That remark brought guffaws to some reviewers of Katherine's tome.

Michael's purported homosexuality was not the only angle pursued by the media. Because of the extraordinary changes in his physical appearance, they began to speculate even more daringly. One tabloid raised the question, IS MICHAEL JACKSON DEAD?

The journalist speculated that Michael might have died and that the "money men" behind him had substituted another singer and dancer to fill his shoes. As wild as this seemed, precedents for such scenarios aren't unknown. Some writers, for example, have died, but their estates have kept churning out novels in their name.

Tabloids not only focused on Michael but began to tear away at the public relations hype associated with the so-called loving Jacksons themselves. Papa Joe helped fuel that speculation by telling *People* magazine: "We wonder why things have changed like they have, why Michael doesn't seem to care about his family. The few times we've spoken to him, he seems glad to hear from us. But when you talk to other people, they say Michael doesn't want to be involved with his family."

Caught up in personal matters and spending days, even weeks, in his private quarters at Neverland with his boy of the moment, Michael often neglected business. But on September 13, 1989, he showed up for a press conference in Los Angeles. Officials of LA Gear announced that they had just signed Michael to a multi-million dollar two-year endorsement deal.

A lot of the journalists at the conference suggested that LA Gear had hired the wrong Michael—"perhaps they meant to hire Michael Jordan, not Michael Jackson," one reporter facetiously suggested.

For the $20 million he was being paid, Michael made a major concession to the sportswear company. He discarded his black loafers and white socks and showed up wearing a pair of LA Gear tennis shoes in black with silver streaks. LA Gear was retiring its spokesperson, Kareem Abdul-Jabbar, the basketball star. With its elaborate Hollywood-style palm trees and fog machine, the press conference cost LA Gear $50,000.

Michael's comments before reporters were very brief: "I am very happy to be part of the LA Gear magic, and I hope we have a very rewarding, successful career. Thank you."

Reporters noted that Michael appeared nervous and anxious, and he seemed like he wanted to flee from the press conference. One writer described Michael "in a panic to escape, like one of his pet rats if cornered menacingly." That reporter was right in his assessment. Regrettably for Michael and LA Gear, a concealed microphone picked up Michael's desperate plea to one of the company executives. "You've got to help me!" Michael said in a whimpering voice that verged on tears. "Get me out of here or I'll faint. Don't let them ask me questions!"

After Michael had fled into the fake fog being generated as part of the special effects, reporters openly jeered. "It was a total disaster," said Ronald Bank from a newspaper in Sacramento. "To think I drove all the way to Los Angeles to see Jackson run out of the room while blowing an insincere kiss. That lady's not to be believed! I'm convinced that Jackson not only thinks he's Marie Antoinette, he's become the Queen reincarnate!"

When reporters heard this, especially Michael's whimpering, they popped questions at Robert Greenberg, the company CEO. "Why have you hired a spokesman who can't—or won't—speak?"

The chairman was obviously embarrassed but tried to put a good spin on Michael's disastrous performance. "Pepsi couldn't get Michael to drink that soft drink," he said. "But at least we got Michael to show up at the press conference in our shoes—not bad."

Even though his days as Michael's attorney were numbered, John Branca had pulled off this amazing deal between Michael and LA Gear. Word got out that Branca, in the interests of his client, had "walked off with the company store."

When terms of Michael's deal leaked out, many of his fans were horrified. "With that kind of money at stake, he had to become a cry baby at that press conference," said Terri Carroll. "What a baby! What a wimp! That kind of money equaled the net income of some struggling Third World countries, and he's whimpering. I resign from the Michael Jackson Fan Club. I can only conclude that in a starving world, he's collecting millions for doing practically nothing—and behaving like a jerk!"

The Michael Jackson sneakers released by LA Gear

The deal with LA Gear was the sweetest ever made with a celebrity. It entitled Michael to a royalty on every pair of shoes sold, plus stock options. At the time of their ill-fated deal with Michael, the company was hauling in $800 million a year. If, after Michael's involvement, sales of the product increased, Michael would be entitled to a percentage of all annual sales in excess of $1 billion.

As part of the LA Gear package, Michael had promised to release an album—its working title was *Decade*, which would include some new songs, as well as cuts from three of his earlier albums, *Off the Wall*, *Thriller*, and *Bad*. For this album, Michael was offered upfront money of nearly $20 million. To everyone's embarrassment, Michael defaulted and *Decade* was delayed, postponed, and eventually abandoned altogether.

There were the inevitable lawsuits, LA Gear filing a $10 million lawsuit against Michael, charging him with fraud and breach of contract. Michael's lawyers shot back with a $44 million countersuit against LA Gear, making similar charges against them. The case was eventually resolved out of court, and the LA Gear campaign with Michael fizzled to an embarrassing death. Based on Michael's previous litigation with Pepsi and LA Gear, word spread through the business world that Michael, with his lawsuits, was a dangerous entertainer to sign contracts with.

"Michael simply didn't get his act together," Papa Joe later said. "If he had, he could have made millions and millions, not only from LA Gear, but from the album itself."

That wasn't the only business deal falling flat for Michael. Inspired by his ownership of copyrights to The Beatles' songs, he also tried to acquire Motown's catalogue from Berry Gordy Jr. The catalogue, known as "Jobete," was for sale for $200 million, but Michael was willing to pay only $135 million.

Michael had dreamed of acquiring the Motown hits of The Supremes which had starred his sometime friend, Diana Ross. If he could acquire the catalogue, he'd also control the music of, among others, Stevie Wonder, Marvin Gaye, The Temptations, and Smokey Robinson.

A smart musical entrepreneur like Gordy knew the exact value of his treasure trove, and he said no to Michael unless he was willing to come up with the full $200 million. When Gordy wouldn't budge, Branca called Michael and asked if he could increase his offer. Michael slammed down the phone, and the potential deal collapsed.

Business deals weren't working out, but by 1990 it seemed that everybody in the world was honoring Michael Jackson and his gravity-defying dance moves on music videos.

Even President George Bush wanted to get in on the act, following in the footsteps of the Reagans. In April of 1990, Bush invited Michael for a return visit to the White House where he was formally proclaimed "Entertainer of the Decade."

In the Rose Garden, the ceremony was sponsored by Washington's Capital Children's Museum, and Michael was being honored for his work with children's welfare.

Lacking Reagan's smoothness and charm, Bush had little to say to Michael, who showed up in military garb with wide red sashes. Barbara was more relaxed with the singer, introducing him to her dog Millie and telling him she wore red shoes for the occasion when her spies told her he'd arrived at the White House "all trimmed in red." She may have been aiming her sardonic wit at Michael, but he took everything she said at face value. Later, after Michael's departure from the White House with his entourage and three limousines, Barbara said, "I am underwhelmed."

In their wake, reporters crowded around the President in his pin-striped suit. One journalist asked Bush if he'd ever heard a Michael Jackson song. The President did not answer, but asked the reporter a question instead. "Why does he wear that red arm band and those red stripes on his pants? Was he in some school marching band?"

Between business endorsements and award ceremonies, Michael took plenty of time out for pleasure with his "special friends." Peter, the boy who had figured so prominently into the *Bad* tour, was replaced by another young white boy that Michael's publicist, Bob Jones, identified as Damon Patrick.

Instead of thinking that Michael was asexual—perhaps an early opinion—the publicist concluded in his book that "Michael did indeed have some sort of sexual drive, and it wasn't the least bit natural."

During her son's sojourn at Neverland, Damon's mother complained that the security guard often prevented her from seeing him. And although Michael hired a tutor for the young boy, Damon reportedly learned very few lessons. Throughout much of his stay, he was locked away in Michael's bedroom.

According to Bob Jones, the relationship with Damon was short-lived. But it was rumored that Michael paid out four million dollars when his involvement with Damon came to an end.

Michael still dreamed of a career in the movies. In this ambition, he was goaded on by David Geffen, who had a dream of producing a big-budget musical for the pop superstar.

In many ways, this movie agent and record industry mogul pursued power, money, and fame even more than Michael himself. Since Geffen had launched his own record company in 1980, selling Geffen Records for a huge profit ten years later, Michael had eagerly followed its progress. Geffen began spectacularly, signing John Lennon in 1980 in what would become the ex-Beatle's last recording contract.

Geffen's other achievements included producing *Risky Business,* the vehicle that made Tom Cruise a star. He was also the man who bankrolled Andrew Lloyd Webber's *Cats.*

Over the years Michael had known him casually and was thrilled when Geffen, along with Steven Spielberg and Jeffrey Katzenberg, founded DreamWorks SKG, the first all-new Hollywood studio to be established in more than half a century.

Michael envied Geffen's success and wanted to hook up with him, each man vying to become the biggest mogul in the entertainment industry. "If my role model, Howard Hughes, can do it, so can I," Michael told Geffen among others.

Geffen flattered Michael, telling him that, "Quincy Jones has taken too much credit for your own genius. It's time to move on from him."

Michael predicted to Geffen that the 1990s "belong to me. If people thought I was the most successful artist of all time in the 80s, they ain't seen nothing' yet. I'll double my success in the 90s, and I'm starting the decade as the highest-paid artist in the history of the music industry. Not bad."

At the time Michael met Geffen, the entrepreneur was still in the closet, leading a somewhat heterosexual life. He almost married Cher. Unlike Michael, however, Geffen would consensually "come out," which he did in 1992, albeit under some degree of pressure.

308

"I like men, I like women," Geffen declared. "I'm an equal opportunity seducer." After that announcement, it is estimated that a goodly percentage of the handsomest actors in Los Angeles sent Geffen their résumés, hoping to become his next toy boy. Along with another friend of Michael's, Elizabeth Taylor, Geffen became a champion warrior in the battle against AIDS.

Much of Hollywood thought Geffen already had a toy boy in Michael himself.

The world in the early 90s wasn't that familiar with Michael's sexual pattern, so rumors swirled through Hollywood parties that the ruthless producer "who would stop at nothing to get what he wanted" was having an affair with the ruthless singer/dancer "who would stop at nothing to get what he wanted."

"They should be lovers even if they're not," one producer said. "Even man and wife, David being the man, of course. Together, this dynamic duo, wearing Batman and Robin tights, could take over not only Hollywood, but lay America itself at their feet."

"If David Geffen is not actually plugging Jackson in the ass, he's doing it spiritually," said an executive at CBS Records who didn't want to be named. "Before Jackson takes a crap, he calls Geffen to get his OK. Geffen has total power over Jackson's career. In that little girl voice of his, Jackson calls Geffen two or three times a day. Jackson wants Geffen's advice on everything. I hear all the time that Geffen and Jackson are having sex. But Geffen is not the type of man Jackson would be attracted to. Perhaps if Geffen had been born in 1980, we could get some action here. Of course, there is the Jewish question, but I don't want to go into that."

Finding the right script for Michael proved a daunting challenge, even for Geffen. As head of Geffen Pictures, he offered Michael the script of *Streetdandy*, which had been written by Tom Hedley, co-writer of *Flashdance*. Michael read the script "but is giving me all this reluctant debutante shit," Geffen claimed.

He ultimately despaired of finding a proper script for Michael, telling his partners, "It's got to be Busby Berkeley meets *E.T.*, with *Stars Wars* as a backdrop."

As Christmas of 1990 rolled around, Michael could only note that Geffen, at the age of 47, had risen from a job in the mailroom of the William Morris Agency to become "the richest man in Hollywood," according to *Forbes* magazine.

Geffen's good will temporarily soured when Michael failed to show up in Florida for the opening of the spanking new Universal Studios Theme Park in Orlando, as Michael had agreed. It was said at the time that Michael Eisner, the CEO and chairman at Disney, had asked Michael not to appear at the opening of a competing theme park, claiming that if he did, it would "damage the

wonderful friendship you have with Disney—
threaten it even."

Michael, as he admitted himself, was "caught
between a rock and a hard place." There was a
way out. On June 3, 1990, Michael suffered what
was originally announced in the press as a mild
heart attack. An ambulance rushed him to Saint
John's Hospital in Santa Monica, where he was
booked into a room across the hall from Elizabeth
Taylor. Ironically, she'd been rushed to that same
hospital, suffering respiratory problems.
Although her illness was real, Michael's might
have been faked.

The next morning Elizabeth wheeled herself
into Michael's room carrying a white lily which
Michael added to a vase of black roses ordered

David Geffen

by La Toya from her hotel in London. When Elizabeth left, he spent the day
receiving phone calls from well-wishers. He expected Liza Minnelli to call,
but President Bush?

While in the hospital, and for reasons known only to Michael, he asked
the staff to perform an HIV test on him. These tests are always highly confidential, but someone on staff leaked the results to the press. The test came out
negative. One doctor asked, "If he's the virgin he publicly claims to be—you
know, saving it for marriage—why does he want to be tested for AIDS?"

Except for a young man who was evicted after sneaking into the hospital
with a plan to assassinate Michael, he rested well in his room and miraculously recovered after a week of rest.

Geffen wanted Michael to sever his ties with Branca, his faithful and
sometimes spectacularly successful long-time attorney. Somehow Geffen
managed to convince Michael that the attorney was getting "too much pork,
leaving you with the bone." That wasn't true, of course. To pry Michael away,
Geffen fanned the fires of Michael's jealousy. Geffen reminded him that
Branca's law firm represented not only Mick Jagger and the Rolling Stones
but the dreaded Prince, who was still Michael's nemesis.

"Not just Jagger," Michael said. "What about George Michael? The New
Kids on the Block? Branca even represents the Jim Morrison estate. One thing
is for sure: He won't be representing my estate when I die."

"Correction," Geffen said. "*If* you die. You're going to live forever."

Michael became furious when he learned that the "Steel Wheels" tour of
Jagger and his Stones broke the record set by *Bad* to become the most successful rock tour in the history of music.

310

Within days of his release from the hospital, Michael sent Branca word, "Your services are no longer required." Michael didn't want to face the attorney directly, so he had Richard Sherman, his accountant, deliver the bad news.

Michael fired Branca at the wrong moment, just as the attorney was ready to consummate a deal with Warner-Chappell for the acquisition of the James Brown catalogue. "It would be a great triumph for Michael to own the songs of James Brown," Frank DiLeo once told associates. "Imagine it. Michael had stood in the wings watching James Brown, his idol, perform at the Apollo Theater in Harlem. Then, presto, one day he ends up owning the fucker's catalogue. As for those people spreading rumors that Michael is gay, that's bullshit! They don't know what they're talking about. Michael Jackson is definitely not gay!"

In the beginning Geffen not only wanted to make Michael "the biggest of movie stars," but he wanted to sign him for Geffen Records. Regrettably for the promoter, Michael was locked into a firm contract with CBS Records. Geffen learned that the price of freeing Michael from CBS would have been costlier "than the gross national product of Uganda."

As head of CBS Records, Walter Yetnikoff stood in Geffen's way.

Geffen was producing the new Tom Cruise movie, which would be released in 1990. It was called *Days of Thunder*, and Geffen wanted Michael to supply a song for the soundtrack. Michael agreed but called Yetnikoff and told him that he wasn't going to allow Geffen to have the song.

Yetnikoff nixed the deal on *Days of Thunder* "at Michael Jackson's whining insistence," Yetnikoff claimed. In his memoirs the intensely competitive and sometimes abrasive Yetnikoff admitted that he taunted Geffen over his "sexual bent—I'd chase after him into gay clubs and demand his hand in marriage."

When Yetnikoff sent word that he'd like Geffen to give his new girlfriend lessons in how to give a blow-job, Geffen exploded. A new feud between Yetnikoff and Geffen was born.

Geffen wanted revenge, and he began to undermine Yetnikoff to Michael, hoping to get him out of his contract so that he could sign with Geffen Records. Michael owed CBS four more albums.

But unknown to either Michael or Geffen, Yetnikoff's reign at CBS was already drawing to a close. Within months he'd be out the door. By September 4, 1990, Yetnikoff was ousted as CEO of CBS Records. One of the reasons for his demise was his deteriorating relationship with the label's mega-seller, Michael himself.

"What the hell!" Yetnikoff said on the way out the door. "Sex, booze, power, prestige, money, glory. I tasted it all!"

When Michael was informed of Yetnikoff's departure, he said, "You're talking history. Yetnikoff is yesterday. I'm here today. What about me? What does this mean for my career?"

When Geffen heard of Yetnikoff's demise, he said, "Ding dong, the witch is dead!"

With Frank DiLeo, John Branca, and Walter Yetnikoff out of Michael's life, he needed a new manager. Geffen had a best friend, Sandy Gallin: Enter Gallin into Michael's life.

During the period he remained friends with Michael, Geffen helped him set up both a new legal staff and a managerial team to replace Yetnikoff, Branca, and DiLeo, who had guided Michael through his great triumphs, including *Thriller*. Under a new team, Michael would never achieve the worldwide sales he'd done in the past, although his notoriety would grow. Instead of millions flowing in, millions would flow out.

Previously, Gallin had worked with, among others, Dolly Parton and Neil Diamond. As a producer, Gallin had been a personal manager or agent to stars, including Cher and Whoopi Goldberg. He also went on to produce feature films such as *Father of the Bride* and the Oscar-winning documentary, *Quilt*.

When trouble loomed in Michael's future over child molestation charges, Gallin rose to his defense. He said, "Michael's innocent, open, child-like relationships with children may appear bizarre and strange to adults in our society who cannot conceive of any relationship without sexual connotations. This is not a reflection of Michael's character; rather it is a symptom of the sexual phobias of our society."

For his trouble, the movie editor of the *Los Angeles Times*, Claudia Eller, "outed" Gallin as a homosexual in a major cover story.

Michael also hired Bert Fields and Lee Phillips, who were attorneys for Geffen, and later, Allen Gruman. As his management team fell into place, Michael paraded through Neverland in "Windsor red robes, imitating a king.

He even wore a gold crown," his housekeeper, Blanca Francia, would later claim. That was not all Francia would claim in the years ahead, based on her having introduced Michael to her son, Jason. But before that happened, she witnessed the arrival of young Wade Robson at Neverland where he became one of Michael's all-time special friends. This eight-year-old Australian from Brisbane, with his platinum blond crew-cut, was exceedingly handsome with a certain macho air about him. Wade had been born in 1982, Michael in 1958, but they quickly became "great pals" in spite of the age difference.

Sandy Gallin

Wade later claimed that, like Michael, he'd shown an affinity for dancing "even before I was out of diapers." Michael had met him in 1987 when he was only five years old. Wade had recently won a dance contest. At one of his Australian concerts, Michael had invited him up on the stage. Later, Michael said that "Wade showed off moves dancers ten years his senior couldn't have pulled off." The young boy had learned to dance by watching Michael's music videos, especially "Thriller."

Michael invited the Robsons and their son to California. After a short stay, Wade's father seemed none too happy with the arrangement and returned to Australia. But Wade's mother, Joy, found Neverland "the happiest place on earth." She was soon on Michael's payroll and given a shiny new Rolls-Royce.

Joy roomed in the guest cottage, and Wade was invited for nightly sleep-overs in Michael's bedroom. Soon Michael had nicknamed him "The Little One," and was very affectionate with the boy.

Michael and Wade often danced together, and Michael became so impressed with Wade that he cast him in such videos as "Black or White," "Jam," and "Heal the World." Some of Michael's casting demands stirred up a lot of unfavorable press. Michael strong-armed Pepsi into hiring Wade for a commercial, even though the role should have gone to an African American—not a blond-haired white boy.

In the commercial, Michael sat at a piano, singing "I'll Be There." Ten-year-old Wade played a young Michael, his blond crew-cut concealed by an Afro wig and his porcelain white skin darkened by computerized colorization. Having a white child play young Michael was soundly condemned by African-American publications.

As Wade grew older and Michael moved on to other special friends, Wade became successful on his own, directing stage shows and videos for such stars as Usher and Britney Spears. He would later spearhead the *Wade Robson Project* on MTV, a dance version of *American Idol*.

In 2005 when Michael went on trial on charges of child molestation, both

Bert Fields

Wade and his mother, Joy, came back into Michael's life. Prosecutors wanted to know exactly what happened between Wade and Michael during his sleepovers at Neverland in the early 90s.

On the witness stand, Wade admitted to sleeping in the same bed with Michael but claimed that nothing sexual ever took place. "We slept in the same bed, but we both were fully dressed in pajamas. It's a huge bed. He sleeps on one side, and I sleep on the other."

Under severe cross-examination by prosecutor Ron Zonen, Wade admitted to other sleepovers, not only at Neverland, but at his mother's apartment in Hollywood, at Michael's secret condo hideaway at Century City, and even in a hotel suite in Las Vegas.

Wade refuted another eyewitness, Blanca Francia, Michael's maid. In front of the world, she claimed that she once found Michael and

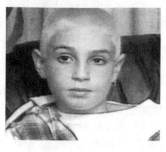

Wade Robson

Wade in bed together—"and they were naked from the waist up." Whether true or not, she also claimed that she walked into Michael's bathroom, finding Wade and Michael laughing and showering together. On the tiled floor she spotted Michael's white BVDs and the boy's "neon green Spiderman briefs," which she often laundered. On the stand, she claimed she slipped out of the bathroom without either Michael or Wade noticing her.

When asked to confirm or deny the maid's testimony, Wade said, "It simply never happened."

The prosecutor zeroed in on Wade. "If you knew that the person, the thirty-five-year-old man who was sleeping with an eight-year-old boy, possessed a great quantity of sexually explicit material, would that cause you concern about that person's motivations while he was in bed with a boy?"

Wade looked uncomfortable and paused a long time before answering. "Yes," he said in what amounted to a whisper.

Zonen forced Wade to look at a book seized at Neverland. Called *Boys Will Be Boys*, it featured naked pictures of young boys aged 10 to 13. His face growing stern, his shoulders drooping, Wade was also forced to look at another book, *A Sexual Study of Man*, in which masturbation, oral sex, and sodomy were depicted.

"Would you be concerned about a person who possesses that book crawling into bed with a ten-year-old boy?" Zonen asked.

"Yes, I guess so," Wade said in a soft voice.

It is believed that Wade's testimony about his long-ago sleepovers at Neverland went a long way in helping Michael retain his freedom.

As charismatic as Wade was, an even more charismatic blond-haired boy entered Michael's life after Michael saw the box office hit, *Home Alone*: Macaulay Culkin.

At Neverland, Michael watched the film repeatedly. One day he saw it three times. His staff felt that he had become obsessed with Macaulay, at least with what he saw on the screen. He hastily invited the beautiful young boy to Neverland, and Macaulay called with his acceptance. The first time he spoke

314

with the *Home Alone* child, Michael must have stayed on the phone for at least three hours.

He seemed mesmerized by the sound of Macaulay's voice and eagerly awaited his arrival at Neverland. "I never knew him to show so much excitement in his life," a security guard claimed.

Michael immediately ordered posters from the movie, depicting Macaulay with his hands on his face screaming. The concept was based on the famous painting, *The Scream*, by Edvard Munch.

Macaulay Culkin, the most famous and the richest child star of his time, was born in New York on August 26, 1980. By 2005 he would play himself in archival footage appropriately titled "Michael Jackson's Boys" for TV.

Wade all grown up

"Mack," as he's known to his intimates, broke into show business at the age of four, appearing in a bevy of off-Broadway shows.

After writer John Hughes recommended that director Chris Columbus cast Macaulay in his script, *Home Alone*, released in 1990, the rest is movie history. The movie went on to earn $285 million in the U.S. alone, making it one of the highest grossing movies in the history of the cinema. Internationally, *Home Alone* would gross $550 million.

His next film, *My Girl* (1991), was another hit for Macaulay and featured his very first screen kiss. In 1992 he filmed *Home Alone 2: Lost in New York*, and it was another hit. In 1993 Macaulay earned $5 million for appearing in *The Good Son* playing a murderous little demon. In contrast, his salary for the first version of *Home Alone* was $100,000.

The child star's luck changed in 1994 when he turned 14 and appeared in a series of duds, including *The Pagemaster*, *Getting Even with Dad*, and *Richie Rich*. For the last two films, he was paid $8 million, the highest fee ever for a child star. When the most famous child star of all time, Shirley Temple Black, heard this, she said, "I worked for peanuts—perhaps a banana or two—in the 1930s."

After his early success, it was a long road downhill, although Macaulay was considered for the male lead in *Titanic* in 1997. He lost the role, of course, to Leonardo DiCaprio.

Macaulay and Michael, after they first met, bonded on the issue of show business fathers. "Michael and I had an understanding about my difficulties with my father. He knew what that was all about. He'd lived some of my shit with his own father. It's not like I can just bump into people on the street and

315

say, 'Oh, you too!' It doesn't happen that often. Michael's still a kid. I'm still a kid. We're both going to be about eight years old forever in some place because we never had a chance to be eight when we actually were. That's the beautiful and the cursed part of our lives."

A former stage and child actor, Christopher (Kit) Culkin was his son's manager for a while. There were many disagreements. At one point Macaulay claimed that his father "was overbearing—very controlling."

When the cheeky ingénue with the impish grin arrived at Neverland, Michael was captivated.

Macaulay Culkin and MJ

Macaulay found Neverland "a child's dream—every kind of soda in the world there, every kind of candy. A two-floor arcade, a carnival, and a movie theater. Neverland is still the only place on earth where I feel absolutely, one-hundred percent comfortable."

When not playing video games at Neverland, Macaulay and Michael were often spotted at various California malls, shopping for toys. Their shopping carts would overflow with talking robots, water blasters, and battery-powered laser guns. On one occasion, Michael bought Macaulay a twelve-inch doll bearing the likes of Kevin McCallister, the suburban imp the child star portrayed in *Home Alone*.

One salesclerk told the press that "the two giggled their way up the aisle— okay for Culkin since he was only a kid, but a bit suspicious for a thirty-four-year-old man."

At one of the shopping malls, both Michael and Macaulay were recognized. "I think Jackson became really jealous of the Culkin kid," said the owner of a local store. "These girls were so young that Jackson seemed old enough to be their father. They were screaming for Culkin like he was all four Beatles in one little boy. Jackson stood by and watched the adulation of these pre-teen fans. It must have brought back memories of when he was a child star."

Michael's younger brother, Kieran Culkin, born in 1982, was also invited for sleepovers at Neverland. Like Macaulay, Kieran was an actor, appearing in the remake of *Father of the Bride* in 1991 and *Nowhere to Run* in 1993. Kieran had made his debut playing Macaulay's cousin in the 1990 *Home Alone*. He would later go on to bigger movies such as the *The Cider House*

Rules, released in 1999.

"Kit" Culkin, Macaulay's father, maintained that no abuse of his children ever took place during their visits to Neverland. He did, however, discover Rory, Macaulay's two-year-old brother, sitting on the floor with Michael, both drinking from baby bottles.

In June of 1991 Michael invited Macaulay and his parents for a vacation in Bermuda, and they accepted. The most cynical members of the press hinted that the King of Pop and the beautiful blond-haired child actor were actually "on a honeymoon."

Macaulay and Michael stayed at the Hamilton Princess in the penthouse suite, with the Culkin parents located in less spectacular digs on the sixth floor. On the island, Michael and Macaulay played games, shopped, and went swimming or diving. When devilish, they dropped water-filled balloons on passing tourists seven floors below.

In Bermuda, Michael did not endear himself to the local populace. When a taxi driver told him there were fewer than 60,000 people who lived on the island, Michael shot back: "I draw more fans than that at one of my concerts."

At one point in their Bermuda vacation, Michael and Macaulay were seen riding the waves in a speedboat. Their captain was H. Ross Perot, who maintained a lavish summer home on island. He'd failed in his bid for the presidency, losing to Bill Clinton.

In Bermuda, Macaulay told a journalist, "Michael is fantastic, he's not weird."

Bored with the entertainment possibilities on Bermuda, Michael, on June 21, 1991, paid for the private performance of a musical to be presented at his hotel for Macaulay and his parents.

After Bermuda, Macaulay and Michael flew to Disney World in Florida, enjoying the amusements there for a few days before winging their way back

Kieran Culkin

to Los Angeles in a private jet. The rest of Michael's staff returned to California aboard conventional commercial flights..

The intense bonding between the child star and Michael continued. On August 26, Macaulay arrived at Neverland to celebrate his 11th birthday.

So enchanted was Michael with Macaulay that he couldn't wait for him to finish his location shoot on the set of *Home Alone 2.* Michael flew to Winnetka, Illinois, to visit with his special friend.

Reportedly, Michael was disappointed when Macaulay told him he was marrying Rachel Miner in June of 1998. Both the bride and groom were only seventeen, Michael predicted the marriage wouldn't last. And it didn't. Rachel and Macaulay were divorced in August of 2000.

When Michael, by whatever means, became the father of "Prince Michael I," he asked Macaulay to be the godfather of his infant son, and the former child star eagerly accepted.

Once a picture materialized of Michael's first child, a baby with blond hair and a cherubic face, bloggers went to work, claiming that Macaulay was not only the godfather of Prince Michael I but had supplied the semen for the artificial insemination. This report cannot be confirmed.

Michael reportedly urged Macaulay not to sign on for the role of a gay club kid who kills a drug dealer in the edgy drama, *Party Monster*, released in 2003. The co-director of *Party Monster*, Fenton Bailey, said, "It doesn't matter how good Macaulay is in the film. The question is, Will people allow him to re-invent himself after a time in the wilderness?" He was referring to Macaulay's "retirement" from the screen. Apparently, the answer was no. Millions of *Home Alone* fans stayed away from *Party Monster*.

Most of Michael's special friends ended their relationship with the superstar when one of them turned fourteen. Not so with Macaulay. The friendship endured the turn of the millennium. "I love him," Macaulay once said. "He's a good friend of mine. He's affectionate but he never touched me or interfered with me."

Michael stood by Macaulay's side as the child actor suffered through intense agoraphobia and panic attacks, which sometimes made it impossible for him to leave his bedroom. From the first, Michael was sympathetic to Macaulay's plights, as he too had suffered these same panic attacks. He noticed that Macaulay fidgeted constantly. He'd run his hands through his beautiful blond hair, and he was also in the habit of playing with the rubber bands he frequently wore like bracelets on his wrists.

Like Michael, Macaulay had a horror of being recognized by fans who still remembered him from his *Home Alone* days. To disguise his blond looks, he sometimes dyed his hair a rainbow of shades. He admitted to Michael that he frequently spent eight hours a day in his bathroom, regarding it as a "sanctuary." He even installed a TV and DVD system there to keep him amused. "It's a rather tortured existence," he admitted.

To calm his nerves, Macaulay was taking the anti-anxiety drug, Xanax, along with Clonazepam, an addictive sedative used to treat chronic nervousness and seizures. These drugs, along with marijuana, were discovered in his car during his arrest in

Macaulay, all grown up.

Oklahoma on September 17, 2005, on a charge of speeding. When police discovered the pot and the medication without prescriptions, he was arrested, later pleading guilty to misdemeanor drug charges.

At the time of Michael's child sex trial in 2005, Macaulay had turned twenty-four. Consistently, he admitted having shared Michael's bed at Neverland, but staunchly denied that "anything untoward happened."

Staff members at Neverland contradicted Macaulay's defense of Michael. Philippe LeMarque who served as majordomo at Neverland for about ten months after the departure of Mark Quindoy, testified in court about Macaulay and Michael.

On the stand, LeMarque claimed that Michael called him at two o'clock one morning, demanding French fries for Macaulay and himself. When he called security and asked the whereabouts of "Silver Fox" (Michael's code name), a guard claimed he was in the video arcade. Entering from the more obscure second door, LeMarque claimed that as he came in, "I saw Michael groping the kid," meaning Macaulay. "He did not see me, so I stopped and quietly tiptoed back and re-entered through the other door."

Adrian Marie McManus, a former maid at Neverland, also took the stand, claiming that Michael groped Macaulay in a "smooch session" in the library at Neverland. She told jurors that she spied Michael planting "his razor-thin lips all over the young *Home Alone* star's face—and rubbing his hands on his body. I was coming out of the bathroom by his bedroom where I was cleaning up the area. I could see Mr. Jackson in the library. He was kissing him on his cheek. His hand was by his leg at his rear end." She also testified that the child star lived up to his reputation as a trouble maker.

McManus had replaced Blanca Francia as Jackson's personal chambermaid. A middle-aged Latina, McManus worked at Neverland from August 1990 to July of 1994 which was the "peak" of the bizarre friendship between Michael and Macaulay.

On May 11, 2005, Macaulay took the stand in Michael's trial, calling accusations that he was molested "absolutely ridiculous." Macaulay bridled at prosecutor Ron Zonen's suggestion that Michael might have molested him without his knowledge while he was sound asleep. "I find that unlikely," Macaulay told the court.

He was even questioned about the pornography police seized from Michael's bedroom. "Overall, he's still a human being," Macaulay said. "I don't find it inappropriate." He added that at the age of twelve he kept a copy of *Playboy* under his bed.

Macaulay's 45-minute appearance on the witness stand was viewed by legal analysts as a brilliant performance. Former prosecutor Ann Bremner, said, "He's a great witness. Unflappable. Jurors are well aware that Culkin is a trained actor."

Macaulay is so rich today he doesn't have to work unless he wants to. Just how rich is he? He once said, "I could sit around with my thumb up my butt watching TV and my kids would still go to college."

In the post millennium, the sweet-faced young boy, who became filmdom's most unexpected superstar, said, "I've had all the fame anyone could want, and I ran away from it. Maybe Michael will do the same thing one day."

At the time Michael was involved with Macaulay, he launched a *faux* affair with Madonna, each hoping for—and getting—maximum tabloid exposure.

Representatives of both Madonna and Michael each alerted the press and the paparazzi that they'd be dining together at the chic Ivy Restaurant in Los Angeles. Madonna arrived dressed in vampiric black, and Michael was attired in angelic white satin. Although the meeting had been touted as a romantic rendezvous, each of the two rivals left in separate limousines. It was almost impossible for two such widely diverse personalities to overcome their jealousies and actually like each other, but once it was launched, the show had to be played out.

"You might have been the hottest pop artist of the 80s," Madonna said to

Material Girl

Michael. "But Prince, George Michael, and Whitney Houston—and *moi*—certainly gave you a run for your money in the second half of that decade."

"All of you are very good," Michael said in a voice so low it was almost a whisper.

Not getting the response she obviously wanted, Madonna ribbed Michael. "So you made one big album and a Pepsi commercial where you caught your coiffure on fire."

Michael became defensive. "The world has recognized me as its greatest entertainer. *I'm* the biggest."

Madonna reminded him that newspapers and magazines polled in 1989 had named her "Artist of the Decade." Michael had nothing to say to that. Nor did he need to be reminded. When that news had been announced, an enraged Michael had called his manager at the time, Frank DiLeo. "Was it Madonna who recorded *Thriller*?" Michael screamed into the telephone. "Madonna who produced the best-selling album of all time? I think not!"

Madonna didn't stop there. "Honeychild, at the end of the 90s, I'll also be voted Number One Artist of the Decade. Not Prince. Not Whitney Houston. Not Bruce Springsteen. Not George Michael, and you can forget Phil Collins." She deliberately left Michael off the list. "Madonna will be the Mamma Mia of that decade too."

"How do I fit into this picture?" Michael asked, obviously peeved at her provocation.

Madonna answered, but it wasn't what he expected. "When I'm tired of one of my toy boys, I'll pass him on to you."

Michael requested carrot juice blended with spinach when the waiter approached, Madonna preferring a stronger libation. After the waiter left, she looked at Michael skeptically, as if annoyed. "The restaurant is candlelit," she said. "You don't need sunglasses." She reached for his glasses, jerked them off, and threw them to the floor, stomping them with her stiletto heel.

"Don't try to hide from the world behind sunglasses," Madonna warned him. "Be comfortable with yourself whether it's with a boy—even a woman, God forbid—or perhaps a *ménage à trois*." Her outrageous talk shocked him. "I lost my virginity to a woman," she claimed. "Moira McPharlin. She finger-fucked me."

At one point during dinner, she turned to him. "I don't like blow jobs. But I do like getting head—but only nonstop for a day and a half. What about you?"

"Oh, Madonna," Michael said, giggling into his napkin.

To blow Michael's mind, at least according to one of Madonna's gay dancers, she told Michael, "Of all the people I've bedded, do you know who's the best hung in Hollywood? Sandra Bernhard."

The staff at the Ivy did what it could to keep the paparazzi away from Madonna and Michael, not knowing that the two mega-stars wanted to be photographed and have their pictures in the tabloids.

Later that night, Michael was heard saying, "Madonna sure knows how to market herself. If only she could sing and dance." This was just one of many digs at his rival—all in a similar vein—that he would make over the course of her career.

When Cher heard about the outrageous publicity Madonna was getting by exploiting Michael, she said, "Madonna could afford to be a little more magnanimous and a little less of a cunt!"

Madonna agreed to be Michael's "date" for the 63rd annual Academy Awards ceremony. As the paparazzi went wild, Madonna arrived in a white sequined Bob Mackie gown wearing $20 million dollars worth of diamonds on loan. Her dress was cut so low she almost had a wardrobe malfunction.

People Weekly wrote that "Michael Jackson looked positively legendary in gold-tipped cowboy boots, a blinding diamond brooch and—in a dramatic sartorial departure—two gloves."

Barbara Walters, speaking on TV, said, "They looked like caricatures, they seemed untouched, larger than life." Privately, Walters (and this rumor cannot be confirmed) claimed that she felt Madonna was exhibiting Michael "the way a Bearded Lady might be put in a circus of long ago."

Before millions of fans around the world, Madonna sang Stephen Sondheim's "Sooner or Later," which had been nominated for Best Song from the film, *Dick Tracy*, in which she'd co-starred with her lover of the moment, Warren Beatty. Much to Michael's obvious discomfort, the song won the Oscar.

After the ceremony ended, Michael escorted Madonna to the über-trendy Spago's for an Oscar bash. Michael greeted many stars he knew casually, including Anjelica Huston, with whom he'd appeared in *Captain EO*. After their entrance, once Madonna and Michael had their pictures taken, they split up. Michael was seen chatting with Diana Ross, with whom he still maintained an uneasy relationship.

He reacted in horror as Madonna spotted Beatty. "Hey, Warren," she shouted. "Some guys in the press are asking me how big your dick is. I told them I never measured it. I hope that was the right answer."

Actually, Madonna, or so it was reported, wanted to seduce Michael as one of her rapidly growing corps of high-profile conquests. "I've had Prince," she told her bevy of gay dancers. "Why not Michael? Of course, there's a downside. After the mighty sword of Sean Penn, I'm not used to pinpricks." At Michael's expense, the dancers laughed.

A former friend claimed that Madonna was speaking the truth. "It's no joke, size matters to her. She's not interested in somebody who's not above average. That's why she sought out Mick Jagger, John F. Kennedy Jr., Jack Nicholson, Bob Riley, and toy boy Tony Ward."

Author Andrew Morton, in his biography, *Madonna*, wrote that Madonna "later told one of her lovers that she indeed tried to seduce Jackson shortly after the Oscars—but confessed that her bedside manner failed to arouse his interest. The same lover recalled her description of the scene: 'They were on the couch at his place and she would put the moves on him and he would stick out his tongue for a second. When they touched he would start giggling like a little boy. Nothing happened because he was giggling too much. That was one man she was not able to conquer.'"

In spite of their lack of chemistry, some time later Michael and Madonna were seen once again together at Spago's. As rumor had it, they were going to perform a duet on Michael's upcoming album, *Dangerous*. But nothing came of it. The two artists were simply incompatible.

At dinner, Michael preferred unseasoned boiled carrots, while Madonna ordering more sophisticated fare. The meal lasted three hours, and the couple was seen leaving the restaurant arm-in arm, then went their separate ways in separate limousines.

The press continued with its media buzz about the two superstars. It must be assumed that journalists who wrote these romantic fantasies didn't actually believe them, even for a moment. On April 15, 1991, Madonna and Michael shared the cover of *People* magazine, but staff members hardly predicted the sound of wedding bells in their future.

The press queried Madonna about those rumors of a romance. She didn't really answer the question but proposed something else. "I have this whole vision about Michael. We're considering working on a song together. I would like to completely re-do his whole image. Give him a Caesar. You know, that really short haircut, and I want to get him out of those buckly boots and all that stuff. What I want him to do is to go to New York and hang out for a week with the House of Extravaganza, a group of vogue-ers. They could give him a new style. I said, 'Could you give this guy a make-over for me?' because I think that's really what he needs."

Madonna stealing MJ's "crotch" move

Daringly, she made it clear to the press that she felt Michael "was in the closet." As depicted in her film, *Truth or Dare*, she was one of the most gay-friendly artists in the business, surrounding herself with gay dancers. Jokingly, but with a dash of conviction, she suggested that her dancing entourage of boys could help Michael "come out."

She even described what an evening with Michael was like. "First I beg him not to wear his sunglasses and of course he complies, because I'm stronger than he is. Then we exchange powder puffs—we both powder our noses—and we compare bank accounts."

Reportedly, Michael raged for days when *Forbes* magazine in September of 1991 published its list of the highest-paid entertainers. Madonna ranked number four with a two-year earning streak of $63 million. Michael had fallen to number five with a combined two-year gross of $60 million. Madonna sent him an autographed picture of herself. On it she scrawled: "Eat your heart out, Michael! I've got bigger tits too."

Again, Michael went into a rage at Neverland, firing three employees that day who got on his nerves. "That heifer! Damn her!"

When Madonna learned that Michael was referring to her as a heifer, she shot back, "I'd rather be a cow than a drag queen from outer space."

Madonna wasn't the only one casting an envious eye toward Michael. Sibling rivalry was rampant within his own family, as Janet competed furiously with Michael on the charts. June of 1991 found older brother Jermaine not exactly concealing his jealousy of Michael from the tabloids. "I could have been Michael," Jermaine claimed. "It's all a matter of timing, a matter of luck."

That same month, Jermaine released "Word to the Badd" to the world at large. The song was highly critical of Michael, attacking his bleaching creams and his endless plastic surgery.

Reconstructed. Been abducted. Don't know who you are. Once you were made. You changed your shade. Was your color wrong? Could not turn back. It's a known fact. You were too far gone.

When he heard the recording, a furious Michael called his mother, Katherine, ordering Jermaine to be evicted from Hayvenhurst, the Encino compound. Michael owned most of the property.

Since he also paid the bills on the compound, he had that right. Only the intervention of the matriarch of the family pleading with Michael kept Jermaine from getting the boot. "Your brother's got no place to go," Katherine pleaded. Eventually she won a reprieve for Jermaine. Michael visited Hayvenhurst only rarely. When he did, Jermaine was ordered to keep out of his sight.

"Word to the Badd" was released during the same week as "Black or White," Michael's hit single. The two brothers battled on the public air waves, with Michael emerging the victor, of course.

Appearing in London on the BBC, Jermaine attempted to explain why he wrote a song so highly critical of his brother, an almost unprecedented event in the music industry.

"I tried to put some phone calls to him and I didn't get a reply. It's a number of things but it's nothing that we couldn't have worked out had we spoken. But I wasn't granted an opportunity. The overall message is an older brother telling a younger brother to get back to reality."

Michael was irked at the snide comments made by both Jermaine and Madonna. But he flew into a rage when he heard reports claiming he had an "unnatural relationship" with Macaulay Culkin. He decided that a counterattack was needed to fight against press reports, some of which left the clear suggestion that he was a pedophile, long before such accusations were officially charged.

Michael wanted his publicists to spread stories that he was having a series of involvements with beautiful young women. Shoshana Hawley, a Las Vegas showgirl, was singled out as a suitable "date" for Michael.

They were spotted four times attending a pageant at the Excalibur Hotel in Las Vegas. One newspaper wrote a completely misleading story about Hawley and Michael, headlining it, SPARKS FLY BETWEEN DANGEROUS DUDE AND CASINO CUTIE. There were even reports that Michael and Hawley were spending days at a time in his hotel suite in Vegas.

The press got it all wrong. Michael was spending his nights in a sleepover with Brett Barnes, a ten-year-old, good-looking boy from Australia, where Wade Robson had originated. Brett, like Macaulay, was destined to become one of Michael's all-time "special friends."

Only two years behind schedule, "Black or White" was the first single released from Michael's upcoming album, *Dangerous*. On its first day of release, Michael triumphed over Madonna playing on 96% of 237 of the nation's Top Forty radio stations. With her "Like a Prayer," Madonna had set a previous record of 94%.

Before Christmas of 1991, "Black or White" was the number one single in the country on *Billboard's* top Pop Singles Chart, making it the fastest rising single since The Beatles released "Let It Be." Through Christmas and into the first of the year, 1992, "Black or White" held strong. In music history, Michael became the first performer to have number one pop hits in the 1970s, 80s, and 90s. Before sales died down, Michael eventually sold one million copies of "Black or White."

Production costs associated with the "Black or White" video rose to an astonishing $7 million. Michael brought back John Landis who had done such a brilliant job in directing the "Thriller" video. This time around, Michael and Landis often bitterly disagreed on how to film the video. At one point, Michael shut down production and retreated to his trailer, where he refused to come out for the rest of the afternoon. Thanks partly to this extravagant diva behavior, costs soared.

The eleven-minute video, or so the PR hype would have us believe, was designed to promote racial harmony throughout the world. Michael appeared in the video with Balinese dancers, American Indians, a tribesman from the

Sudan, *and* Macaulay Culkin. Still enchanted with Macaulay, Michael had cast the young boy in the video. The *Home Alone* star was one of a group of children surrounding Michael.

Many of the fast-escalating costs of the video were associated with having Macaulay on the set. With Michael, he fired squirt guns and tossed water-filled balloons at the crew. Tiring of that, the child star and Michael set off stink bombs, testing the patience of Landis. As a further insult to the director, he had to endure a custard pie in the face, a gift from Michael that was hurled in imitation of a gag from the silent screen.

"We had to put up with unbelievable shit," said one of the crew members. "It was disgusting. We could forgive this *Home Alone* kid. He was just a devilish imp. But Michael Jackson! What the hell! This silly little turd is pushing forty and acting like an eight-year-old on drugs."

Another crew member claimed that Michael "was completely infatuated with the boy and would let him do anything. When I got a lemon meringue pie in my face, I wanted to plow my fist into both of them. But, then, I would never work another day in Hollywood, and I have a wife and kids to support. I find both Jackson and Culkin arrogant little pricks. They seemed to think they own the world, and, I guess, at that point in their lives they did. We had to take their shit and smile. Incidentally, I hate lemon meringue pie. If it'd been chocolate fudge, I might have forgiven them."

When the video for "Black or White" was released, it is estimated that some 550 million fans around the world saw it, watching in fascination as a panther on screen was transformed, through a skilful use of computer graphics, into Michael.

In no previous video had Michael been so sexually explicit. He not only caressed and grabbed at his crotch, but was seen zipping up his fly. Thousands upon thousands of protests came in to the Fox network, which had exclusive rights to air the video. Fans objected to both the blatant sex and also to the depictions of crime and violence. Michael is seen smashing the windows of a parked car and tossing the steering wheel through a shop window.

After meeting with Fox executives, Michael agreed to cut the last four minutes of the "Black or White" video. He issued a statement to the press:

"It upsets me to think that 'Black or White' could influence any child or adult to destructive behavior, either sexual or violent. I've always tried to be a good role model and therefore have made these changes to avoid any possibility of adversely affecting any individual's behavior. I deeply regret any pain or hurt that the final segment of 'Black of White' has caused children, their parents or other viewers."

Controversy over the video launched a media blitz. One newspaper suggested that "Jackson has really gone insane with this one." The furor only goaded the public's interest, which was a good omen for the eventual release of the album, *Dangerous*.

Michael wasn't the only Jackson sibling generating comment in the press. Stories were rampant that La Toya was writing a tell-all memoir and shopping it to New York publishers.

La Toya, born in 1956, never obtained the fame as a singer that Michael and Janet did. What resentment she has about that is best left to her private thoughts. She'd had such minor achievements as hitting #17 on the *Billboard* Singles Charts in 1980 with her recording of "If You Feel the Funk." The first Jackson woman to have a solo career, she released her first album in 1980 and went on to record six albums, four in the 90s. Her biggest hits were "You're Gonna Get Rocked," "Heart Don't Lie," and "Bet'cha Gonna Need My Lovin'."

La Toya didn't have the voice, the charisma, or the dancing skills of either Michael or Janet, and her career eventually fizzled. Even abandoning Polydor Records for RCA produced only lukewarm results among the record-buying public.

As he worked on his own *Dangerous* album, and pursued his own diversions, Michael grew increasingly disturbed about what La Toya might write about him in her memoirs. He'd already been embarrassed by the publication of Katherine's book, even though his mother, predictably, was kind to him. But he feared La Toya's recollections, especially if she printed stories about his being molested as a child. For some reason, he seemed to dread this type of revelation more than anything else she might tell a world audience. He ordered John Branca, who was his attorney at the time, to write La Toya a letter, threatening a lawsuit if such revelations were made.

Dominated by her parents for years, La Toya was demonstrating independence for the first time in her life. Papa Joe himself had picked a shadowy figure, Jack Gordon, to help manage La Toya's career. For four years, he'd run a Nevada whorehouse. He'd also spent some time in prison.

Gordon had once tried to bribe Harry Reid during his tenure, in 1978, as chairman of Nevada's Gaming Control Board. For $12,000, Gordon wanted Reid to approve two new, carnival-like gaming devices for casino use. Reid allowed the FBI to videotape the attempted bribe. At one point, as registered on the videotape, Reid put his hands around Gordon's neck and said, "You son of a bitch, you tried to bribe me." Gordon was subsequently arrested, convicted in federal court in 1979, and sentenced to six months in prison.

Reid eventually went on to greater glory, becoming the senior United States Senator from Nevada and the Senate Majority Leader during the administration of "the second Bush."

In 1988, La Toya, to the surprise and horror of her family, fled from Hayvenhurst with Gordon. In September of 1989, La Toya, age thirty-three, married Gordon, provoking yet another violent reaction from her family. After her marriage, La Toya telephone Katherine. "I've disowned you," La Toya shouted into the phone. "All of you."

Hoping to make a fast buck, it was Gordon who was urging La Toya to write the tell-all. Gordon claimed, accurately or not, that Michael called one night to offer his sister $12 million if she'd drop plans to publish her memoirs. La Toya has never confirmed that.

Gordon himself had once confronted Papa Joe and Katherine with a proposal. For $5 million, he claimed that he could get La Toya to stop writing. Although Gordon may have exaggerated the millions, it is believed that there were behind-the-scenes offers to get La Toya to dispense with her book.

In 1991 the respected writer, J. Randy Taraborrelli, was set to publish his unauthorized biography, *Michael Jackson: The Magic and the Madness*. The author's literary agent, Bart Andrew, revealed to the media that agents on Michael's behalf had offered $2 million not to publish the book. Taraborrelli allegedly refused, claiming that he could not be bought off.

La Toya and Gordon found interest in her memoirs at Putnam. When he heard this, Michael threatened to purchase the publishing firm for $85 million and suppress the memoirs. It was the editors at Putnam themselves who turned down La Toya's memoirs after reading the first draft—"not enough juice." She eventually found a willing publisher at Dutton, which issued her memoirs in 1991.

For her book, a gleeful La Toya was paid $500,000, and she could only note that that was $200,000 more than Jackie Onassis at Doubleday had paid for *Moonwalk*.

La Toya's memoirs hit *The New York Times* bestseller list and remained there for several weeks, eventually selling more than one million copies.

Michael escaped condemnation in her memoirs, but La Toya didn't spare either Papa Joe or Katherine. She wrote of her father's brutality not only to her but to her brothers and sisters. She claimed that Joe once beat her and left her bleeding on the bathroom floor of their Gary, Indiana, bungalow. She said that her brothers just stepped over her when they wanted to use the bathroom, as they feared getting involved.

At the last minute, La Toya pulled the plug on an allegation of sexual abuse at the hands of her father, although in media interviews, she suggested that she had been a victim of incest.

La Toya and Katherine had once been "best friends," but in her book, La Toya turned on her mother, revealing her not as a kindly matriarch, but as a

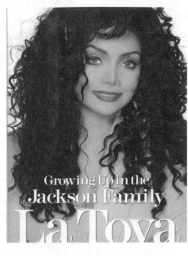

La Toya's autobiography

Dr. Jekyll and Ms. Hyde. She went on to assert that at one point her mother offered her medication that she knew could kill her if she took it.

One startling statement in La Toya's memoirs, perhaps engineered to cause maximum embarrassment to Katherine, claimed that her mother said that "Hitler's one mistake—he didn't kill all those Jews. He left too many damn Jews on this earth, and they multiplied."

The talk-show/tabloid circuit went for La Toya big-time, as interviewers goaded her to reveal even more shocking allegations about her family than she already had in print. She did detail the physical and psychological abuse she and her eight brothers and sisters had endured at the hands of Papa Joe. She even claimed that Joe and Katherine once tried to kidnap her and bring her back to Hayvenhurst to break her emotional involvement with her manager, Jack Gordon.

Like Michael, La Toya had been raised as a Jehovah's Witness. She asserted that the elders of the church had ordered Michael never to speak to her again because she had "missed too many meetings." She found him sobbing on Janet's bed. He couldn't go through with the harsh dictates of his cruel church, and they maintained their friendship until Michael freed himself from the dictates of this cult.

Although a darling of the media, because she made "hot copy," La Toya came in for her share of attacks. One reporter wrote, "Michael may have earned the moniker 'Wacko Jacko,' but La Toya is as crazy as any of her siblings. With a modicum of talent and a lot of nerve, she has parlayed her name into a career. She has received more publicity for her antics than for any of her recordings."

In 1987 La Toya had electrified her fans by posing nude for *Playboy*. Some eight million copies of the magazine sold within one month. It was the most sensational issue since nude pictures of Marilyn Monroe were published. When *Playboy* came out, La Toya's brothers responded in horror, Jermaine calling to denounce her as "a piece of shit."

Michael was more sympathetic, telling her that

Harry Reid

329

Sexy Janet

he knew why she'd posed: To strike back at her parents and at the Jehovah's Witnesses who had brainwashed her for years. He claimed that he grabbed his crotch on the stage for the same reason. "I want them to know I'll do what I want to do. They no longer control who I am."

As two-faced as ever, Michael called Katherine and expressed his "moral disgust and total outrage" at La Toya's photographs in *Playboy*. He informed Katherine that he'd changed his private phone number and vowed never to speak to La Toya again.

Michael had visited Hugh Hefner's Playboy mansion and had seen the photographs that La Toya had posed for—"that ruins the family image. That's it! There's nothing left."

The magazine came out with eleven pictures of La Toya. In one she posed naked with a sixty-two pound boa constrictor—not "Muscles"—slithering between her shapely legs, suggesting a massive phallus. La Toya received $1 million from *Playboy* for the photo session.

Madonna, who was also fond of her own big breasts, seemed jealous of La Toya when Madonna appeared on *The Arsenio Hall Show*. She claimed that La Toya had undergone breast implants. "I know because people have told me," Madonna charged. "It's obvious that La Toya's bosom has grown in just a week."

La Toya countered, "Madonna is the one who's undergone breast surgery. It was her only chance to look anything like a woman. I saw a photograph of her where she showed one of her new breasts. I've gotta tell you, they're still not as good as mine."

Gordon called Arsenio Hall and offered "my wife for a night," so that the talk show host could determine for himself if La Toya's breasts were real.

Jack Gordon, throughout most of the 1990s, managed not only La Toya but John Wayne Bobbitt, Paula Jones, and even the so-called illegitimate son of Elvis Presley.

On the night of June 23, 1993, Lorena Bobbitt, a manicurist from Ecuador, cut off the penis of her husband, John Wayne Bobbitt, as he lay sleeping in their Manassas, Virginia, home. Realizing that her husband's penis might be surgically re-attached, she grabbed the severed appendage and raced off in the family car, flinging it out the window. After a diligent search, the local police located the part and Bobbitt had his manhood restored, after grueling surgery

330

He later had his name legally changed to Elvis Presley Jr., claiming that his birth mother was Angelique Delores Pettyjohn, a walk-on for Elvis in his movie *Blue Hawaii*.

Elvis Jr. was short and stocky. He is not handsome and bears little resemblance to the King, but he learned the Elvis moves and transformed himself. In the words of one critic, "He got the look down pat."

Gordon promoted Elvis Jr. as a singer in night clubs, proposing a multi-million dollar deal for Michael to sign a contract for an extravaganza in Vegas, with Elvis Jr. as his opening act. Elvis Jr. said he believed that "my father gave me up for adoption because having a child out of wedlock in that era could have had an adverse affect on his career."

Although Michael refused Gordon's offer, he was intrigued by Elvis Presley Jr. and wanted Gordon to provide him with all the details about the young man's life. Michael was especially intrigued to learn that Elvis Jr. started his career as a clown in the circus at the age of five. By the time he was twelve years old, he was training lions, tigers, and other animals. When only sixteen, he began singing in the lesser-known lounges in Vegas.

Gordon claimed that Michael, in disguise and at his invitation, slipped in to a lounge one night to hear Elvis Jr. sing. "He is not the son of Elvis Presley!" Michael later told Gordon.

Gordon wanted to keep Elvis Jr. impersonating Elvis Sr. as he was in his "Hound Dog" years, complete with jumpsuits and sideburns. But eventually Elvis Jr. pulled the plug. "It wasn't me," he said. "I can't live my life as *him*."

Unlike Lorena Bobbitt, La Toya didn't cut off Gordon's penis, but their marriage was frequently violent.

On one occasion, in their luxurious New York apartment, Gordon plowed his fist into La Toya's face. Blood splattered on the white marble floor of the couple's bathroom. Before she could escape from his attack, he picked up a heavy oak dining room chair and crashed it into her back. An ambulance carried her to Lenox Hill Hospital where Michael called her the next day, urging her to "dump him." Although she told her brother that she would, she was back with Gordon a few days later.

La Toya wrote of physical and emotional abuse from Gordon for ten years. "He grabbed me and said 'I own you,'" she claimed in an interview in 2005 on *20/20*.

Earlier she had revealed that her husband had booked her into strip clubs and had falsely advertised that she would appear in the nude. Not only that, but he tried to coerce her into making hard-core porn films.

To Michael's relief, La Toya finally divorced Gordon

John Wayne Bobbitt

333

in 1997. "I had to get rid of all the cancer in my life, beginning with my husband." She placed the entire blame on her former husband for causing an alienation between Michael and herself and other family members, especially Katherine. The family seemed to accept that explanation, Papa Joe claiming that his daughter had been "brainwashed."

In the spring of 1992, La Toya signed a $5 million year-long deal with the landmark Moulin Rouge in Paris. She was the single greatest attraction ever booked in this world famous theater. "Just think about it," Gordon told her. "You'll appear on the same stage that made Josephine Baker a legend in the 20s."

On that same stage, other acts included an assortment of French comedians, acrobats, jugglers, and one performer who wrestled three live crocodiles plus a topless snake charmer who danced with a six-foot boa constrictor evocative of Michael's "Muscles."

During this time La Toya was also honored as one of the ten best-dressed women in the world by the designers of Milan and Paris.

Fortunately, in ways that perhaps reflected a growing maturity and wisdom, she eventually toured with Bob Hope and the USO in support of the servicemen and women fighting the first Gulf War, and she also worked with Nancy Reagan in her "Just Say No" anti-drug campaign.

The following year, in 1993, when charges of child molestation against Michael were first aired, La Toya, standing alone among the Jacksons, led the attack against him. She accused Michael of paying hush money to the parents of his accusers. "He would stay in his room at Hayvenhurst for days on end with young boys."

At the Wailing Wall in Tel Aviv, Israel, and while accompanied by Gordon, La Toya delivered a statement heard around the world: "I love him a great deal. But I cannot and I will not be a silent collaborator to his crimes against small, innocent children." This was viewed by the media as the harshest and most damning statement one sibling had ever uttered against another in the history of the entertainment industry.

She also renewed charges that her own mother, Katherine, had once again denounced Michael— "That damn faggot, I can't stand him."

Gordon jumped into the fray, charging that "Michael used to have the LAPD in his back pocket—but no more." He also leveled more charges against Michael, claiming that he'd learned that her brother "had paid hit men to assassinate La Toya if she ever returned to America."

Paula Jones

334

Londoners woke up to read *The Sun* and its screaming headlines: LA TOYA TO BROTHER: CUT OUT THE BOYS! In the story, La Toya claimed that she'd warned Michael five months previously to "stop spending so much time with young boys."

After their divorce, Gordon continued to call La Toya, making threats against her, even death threats. And, post-millennium, he announced plans to "write the tell-all book of tell-alls about La Toya, Michael, and the Jackson family."

He called it *Never Neverland: The True Story of the Most Powerful Family in the Music Industry.* The slippery Svengali began to release revelations to the press, hoping to interest a publisher in his startling exposé.

During his time with La Toya, Gordon claimed that he witnessed Michael "injecting himself with some kind of fluid to whiten his skin. He would look in the mirror and say, 'I'm getting lighter, I'm getting lighter.' I don't know what the fluid was, but Jackson *was* getting lighter. I saw him do it in 1985. Boxes containing this mysterious fluid were delivered to Jackson's house every day."

One night at the Jackson compound in Encino the following year, Gordon claimed that "I saw a monkey set ablaze as part of a voodoo ritual in the Jackson backyard at Hayvenhurst. They asked me to leave and never talk about it again." Other writers, with credentials more impressive than Gordon's, would also link Michael with voodoo rituals.

In another monkey story—in this case, a tale about a pet chimpanzee— Gordon charged that he'd witnessed Michael "abusing his pet chimpanzee, Bubbles. He beat him a lot. I saw him punch him, kick him in the stomach. The chimp was on the ground crying. Jackson used to say 'he doesn't feel it. He's just a chimpanzee. I have to discipline him.'" The first of the beatings that Gordon claimed he witnessed occurred in Encino in 1985.

Branca, Michael's attorney at the time, denounced the accusations of Michael's former brother-in-law. "These are all absurd, made-up, outrageous allegations. Consider the source. It's a joke. I don't believe that anyone will believe anything that comes out of Jack Gordon's mouth."

"Elvis Jr."

Nearing the end of his life, Gordon told a reporter, "I've had cancer four times. I feel like the book should have been written a long time ago. It's about time the world learns what the Jackson family, especially Michael, is all about. All that family does is tell one lie after another. Of course, they'll denounce anything I say about them. But I was around them for a long time, and I saw plenty. I've lived long enough to see much of the truth about Michael made public. There's a lot more here that's going on. They want to conceal the truth and claim everybody's a liar. You want the truth? Michael Jackson and all his family have engaged in a deliberate campaign to conceal the truth from their public. With good reason, I might add."

In a November 25, 2003 interview with Rita Cosby, Gordon gave other damaging testimony against Michael.

GORDON: I saw him take children into his bedroom and the children would stay there three or four days and they would come out and there would be a noticeable change in their behavior from a happy child to a very despondent—you know, unhappy child.
COSBY: What do you believe?
GORDON: What do I believe? Well, I believe he's a pedophile.
COSBY: You do?
GORDON: In every sense of the word.

On April 19, 2005, at the age of 66, after a drawn-out battle with cancer, Gordon died in a Las Vegas hospital.

Reportedly, La Toya sent a security expert to eyewitness his burial, wanting to make sure his death was for real. "I was fearful of his lies and death threats," she said.

Upon hearing the news, Michael reportedly said, "The world is now a better place."

After her divorce, La Toya "disappeared" for a number of years. "I didn't know what to do with my life." At one point she started going out again, disguising herself in a suit, mustache, and goatee. "Everyone thought I was a guy," she said. "Actually everybody thought I was Michael. They didn't know if I was a girl or guy."

Her appearance led to media speculation, and rumors spread among the Los Angeles underground that La Toya was a lesbian. The same charges had been leveled against her younger sister, Janet. These charges appeared in a June, 2005, interview that La Toya granted to journalist Paul E. Pratt.

PRATT: In the song's lyrics, 'Just Wanna Dance,' you mention kissing a woman on the neck and dancing chest to chest. Have you had sexual interaction with a woman?
LA TOYA: It's a question I prefer not to answer.
PRATT: What would you like your fans, in particular, your gay fans, to know about La Toya Jackson?
LA TOYA: I want to say that it's because of my fans, in particular my gay fans, because they tend to be a little more outspoken about their feelings,

that I have gotten the inspiration to do this. It's because of them I'm 'Startin' Over.'

Her album with the same name was released in 2005.

After years of being sheltered by her parents and under the domination of her husband, La Toya, along with Janet, has emerged as the most sophisticated of the Jackson family. Michael's comments on homosexuality were offensive to the gay community and cost him thousands upon thousands of fans. La Toya proved the more tolerant one. On gay marriage, she said, "It is so difficult in the world for people to find love, true love. When people are in love, I don't see anything wrong with it in the world. If they choose to live their lives and get married, why should we interfere? A lot of people don't agree with me, but that's how I feel."

Imagine Michael making such a socially advanced statement.

Post-millennium, La Toya's views about her brother changed markedly during his renewed charges of child molestation. "We're all behind him 1,000 percent," she said. "The public hears so much that's not true."

She said, "Michael knows my heart. I have always been with him in my heart. He knows the influence of somebody else who made me do something against my will." She was clearly referring to Gordon. "My family knew I didn't want to do what I did, but I couldn't say no."

On *20/20* in 2005, she also said, "I love my brother. Michael is one of the sweetest persons on this earth. You have no idea. He is so misunderstood."

Another woman who loved Michael was Elizabeth Taylor, but not enough to marry him. On his "red hotline," with a direct link to Elizabeth Taylor's Bel Air mansion on 700 Nimes Rd., a call came in for him at midnight. Michael was engaged in a sleepover with Macaulay Culkin.

"Guess what?" said Elizabeth (or so Michael later claimed). "I've gone and done it. I got down on bended nylon and popped the question to Larry." It was a hot night in June of 1991 when Elizabeth placed the call to Michael, her confidant.

On that very same night, he agreed to host their wedding at Neverland. By July of 1991, Elizabeth was about to enter into her eighth and final marriage, this time to a husky, thirty-six-year-old truck driver, Larry Fortensky, who boasted a six-inch penis, according to a former wife. Elizabeth had met him when both of them were in rehab at the Betty Ford Clinic in 1988.

She told Michael, "I have the hots for him." She also claimed that he planned to continue working even after they were married "because he doesn't want to be a kept man. It's his way of maintaining his balls."

When she met Larry at the rehab center, he'd been driving an off-road Caterpillar dirt compactor. But he'd become a self-described "walking nightmare," with his consumption of hard liquor, pills, and pot, and had voluntarily checked himself in.

He soon bonded with Elizabeth. Fellow inmates watched the romance blossom as he hauled her around the grounds in a wheelchair. Outside the clinic, he took her out on their first date together, dropping into McDonald's for their supper. Elizabeth, who had dined in some of the world's greatest palaces, liked the taste of the Big Mac and became addicted to the burgers, which only increased her waistline.

"There's only a twenty-one year age difference between us," Elizabeth told Michael, "but Larry just loves my not-altogether-fallen breasts. We have passionate sex."

When he'd first introduced himself to Elizabeth, Larry had said, "I'm from Stanton, California. Born there 100,000 Heinekens ago." He'd been born in 1952 in the wake of Elizabeth's big success with *A Place in the Sun* opposite Montgomery Clift.

He also told her that he'd gone to Pacifica High School but had dropped out, so he warned her that he wasn't very well educated and dreaded "meeting all your fancy friends."

One of those friends Elizabeth wanted Larry to meet was Michael. Before his association with Elizabeth, Larry had the typical hard-cut prejudice against gay people. From what he'd read, Larry just assumed that Michael was gay.

But they did meet and, in spite of their widely different backgrounds, became friends of a sort. "I don't give a shit if people in the tabloids are making fun of me for marrying a woman so much older," Larry said. "You like to hang out with younger companions. I like to hang out with and make love to an older woman."

Michael said that he didn't see anything wrong with that. "I'm happy if Elizabeth is happy, and she seems to be. But does she really have to pose for that magazine cover holding a condom? Naughty, naughty."

In time, Larry would meet many of Elizabeth's other gay friends, including Roddy McDowall and millionaire Malcolm Forbes.

The "wedding of the year" took place in October of 1991 at Neverland, Michael picking up the tab of $1.5 million. Two American presidents attended, Ronald Reagan with his wife, Nancy, and Gerald Ford. There were 160 other guests.

Larry invited members of his family, except his father with whom he was on the outs, and Elizabeth invited both children and grandchildren. Michael invited his Hollywood Golden Age friends such as Gregory Peck. Merv Griffin arrived with "arm candy," Eva Gabor, and even Diane von Furstenberg put in an appearance and was seen talking to—of all people—Phyllis Diller.

In return for his generous hosting of their wedding, the Fortenskys presented Michael with a rare albino bird from the Amazon. It was rumored to have cost Elizabeth $25,000.

After the wedding, Jack Gordon called with another one of the many get-rich-schemes he had come up with for Michael. So far, Michael had rejected all of Gordon's "deals," but Gordon never stopped trying until the two men discontinued their association.

Gordon later recalled Michael as saying, "I wanted to marry Elizabeth myself. But I understand why she chose Larry over me. But her marriage has given me an idea. I'm going to get married myself. My new bride is not as famous as Elizabeth but her father was."

"Just who might that be?" Gordon asked. "I'm all ears, and I want the rights to the photographic coverage."

"I'm not telling," Michael said. "I haven't even dated her yet."

"What makes you so cocky?" Gordon asked. "Maybe the bitch won't even be attracted to you."

"Sexual attraction is *not* part of the deal," Michael said adamantly. "There are other things."

"Yeah, money," Gordon snapped.

"That too, to the tune of $15 million dollars."

"For $15 million, I'll marry you myself—and I'm a straight arrow."

"There will be more than money on the table," Michael said. "I'll agree to spend millions more on launching her singing career."

"Oh, my God," Gordon said. "You're going to propose marriage to a singer. I want her management contract."

"You're always wanting something." Michael said, slamming down the phone.

"It's being offstage that's difficult for me."

--Michael Jackson

"Thank God for Michael Jackson. He has helped me so much. These songs on Dangerous *will determine how my career will be. I was worried that people were getting tired of my music. I don't know what the future holds, but whatever happens I'll always have this."*

--Teddy Riley

"Michael Jackson is the least weird man I know. My childhood and Michael's childhood are so similar and so strange."

--Elizabeth Taylor

"Whatever we do whatever we say now we'll make a vow to keep it in the closet."

--Michael Jackson
"Keep It in the Closet"

"Michael's vision is to present the most spectacular, most state-of-the-art show to the world that it has ever seen, and that's the goal we're moving toward."

--Benny Collins
On the "Dangerous" tour

"I was glad to pose nude for Playboy. It forever squelched the rumor that Michael and I are the same person."

--La Toya Jackson

"Because with time my skin condition has gotten worse. I have vitiligo and I'm totally allergic to the sun. I'm not even supposed to be outside actually. Even if I'm in the shade, the sun rays can destroy my skin."

--Michael Jackson

340

Chapter Eleven

At the dawn of the 1990s, Michael seemed to be making a career out of receiving awards. Most often, he didn't show up to accept these honors. When he did, he became notorious for giving a brief and predictable speech, always of the "thank you very much, I love all of you" variety.

On ABC's *Good Morning America*, host Charlie Gibson referred to Michael Jackson as "a guy who made one big album and a Pepsi commercial where his hair caught on fire." Appearing with him, Tina Brown, then editor-in-chief of *Vanity Fair*, defended her choice of Michael on the cover of one of that magazine's recent editions. He was pictured with his long hair blowing back in an unseen wind. "We chose Michael Jackson because he is the premier entertainer of our time," Brown said. "He's the biggest!"

Michael did put in an appearance at the Beverly Hilton Hotel for the unveiling of a portrait that he had commissioned of himself. Called "The Book," it depicted Michael in a chair holding a book on his lap. In the background was a statue of Peter Pan. A Japanese businessman paid $2.1 million for the painting. This was the highest amount ever paid for a portrait of a living person. When Whoopi Goldberg heard of this, she remarked sarcastically: "You've got to be kidding!"

With the collaboration of his new manager, Sandy Gallin, Michael took more of a hands-on approach to his own career, leaving Gallin free to pursue his other clients, who included not only Whoopi, but also Dolly Parton and Neil Diamond. When Dolly heard that she and Michael were being managed by the same agent, she was reported to have said, "Don't forget! I have bigger tits than Michael Jackson unless he goes back for plastic surgery again."

Michael refused to attend the 1990 Grammy Awards. It was just as well. If he'd gone, he would have seen Janet Jackson's "Rhythm Nation 1814" edge out "Moonwalker" for Best Long Form Video of the year.

One award Michael received was later to cause ridicule and embarrassment. The homophobic Los Angeles Council of the Boy Scouts of America created an award and named it in honor of Michael, its first recipient. On September 14, 1990, he accepted the Michael Jackson Good Scout Humanitarian Award for his "humanitarian efforts" and fund-raising.

Michael Eisner, CEO of the Walt Disney Company, presented the award to Michael, who appeared in a black and gold military costume with sunglasses. In a brief acceptance speech, Michael said, "On behalf of the millions of past, present, and future Boy Scouts, I will try to abide by your motto of being prepared and always extending a hand to others."

Joan Rivers ridiculed his short speech. "I bet he'd like to extend a hand to a cute little boy scout. Why? To 'Beat It,' of course!"

Michael slowly moved ahead with his long-delayed new album, *Dangerous*. He set unrealistic goals for himself, demanding of his back-up musicians that they produce an album that would top the sale of *Thriller*. Privately, Sandy Gallin had his doubts that Michael would ever top the sale of *Thriller*. *Dangerous* would eventually sell thirty million copies worldwide. Michael had an even loftier goal. He said, "I want to create something like Beethoven did so that people would still listen to it in a thousand years from now."

When *Forbes* magazine published its list of highest paid entertainers for 1990, two black men ranked as number one and two. Michael was furious that he came in after Bill Cosby. "Cosby does a little dance to open the show," Michael said. "But he can't dance. I mean, not a step! And for not being able to dance, he earns $100 million in two years as opposed to me."

With Walter Yetnikoff and John Branca out of the picture, Michael proved a hard-assed negotiator when it came time in 1991 to talk turkey with Sony, the new owner of CBS Records. Tommy Mottola, who would later be denounced by Michael, took over for Yetnikoff.

Up front, Michael demanded an $18 million advance for each album. Not only that, he wanted to split expenses and profits fifty-fifty with Sony, an unheard-of request in the industry. He also wanted to start his own record label. "What next" Mottola asked. "Pay for his flight to the moon?"

The staff at Neverland reported that Michael shouted and ranted for three days and nights, even firing five of his team, when he learned that sister Janet had signed with Virgin Records for a contract estimated to be as high as $50 million, the largest recording deal in the history of the industry.

Michael struck back, signing a deal with Sony that might bring him up to $1 billion, at least in potential earnings. Not only was the amount unprecedented, but so was the deal, which included film, record, and TV options. The fifteen-year contract, after much bickering, finally granted Michael the right to start his own record label, Nation Records. For being CEO of the company,

Michael would be paid $1 million a year.

He also got Sony, again after much bickering, to grant him a seventy per-cent profit on all video rights. Since Sony owned Columbia Pictures, it was announced that Michael would also be making his first film for that company.

In rebuttal, Janet's people, as they are called in Hollywood, announced that her deal with Virgin Records did in fact exceed "the record segment of the contract" signed by her brother with Sony. But the *Wall Street Journal* soon shot down Janet's claims, estimating that the record portion of Michael's Sony deal would be "worth at least $60 million," a good $10 million more than the terms defined by his younger sister's contract. Michael's rivalry with his older brother, Jermaine, receded into the background as he seemed to an increasing degree to be pitted against Janet. A fan in Chicago, Laraine Maven, said, "I don't have much allowance to spend in a record store. If it was a question of buying Janet or buying Michael, I'd go for her, since she sings better."

In 1992 the *Guinness Book of World Records* asserted that Michael's Sony deal was indeed the largest contract ever signed in the music industry.

For his first movie role at Columbia, Michael wanted to depict Little Richard, but so did Eddie Murphy. "Eddie wouldn't be believable as a *Tutti Frutti*," Michael shouted at Gallin. "I practically own Little Richard. Get the role for me. Tell Eddie to star in . . . dare I say the title, *Mother Fucker!* "

Back at Encino during this time in 1992, Margaret Maldonado Jackson, now living with Jermaine, was in the process of producing a mini-series called *The Jacksons: An American Dream*. Her problems were detailed in her memoir, *Jackson Family Values: Memories of Madness*, ghost-written by Richard Hack and published in 1995.

Among Margaret's travails, La Toya threatened legal action if her likeness was used in the mini-series. In January of 1992, a nationwide search that rivaled the hunt for an actress to play Scarlett O'Hara in *Gone With the Wind* was launched. More than three dozen young actors were needed to portray the Jackson family at three different stages in their lives. Margaret not only had La Toya to deal with, but Michael himself. Reports surfaced, but were later denied, that Michael demanded actors playing him to be white.

Margaret finally got Michael to agree on the cast, and made some intriguing choices of her own. In the end, a talented actor, Jason

December, 1989 edition of
Vanity Fair

343

Weaver, played young Michael, with Alex Burrall and Wylie Draper starring at later stages of his life.

Margaret cast Holly Robinson, familiar to audiences for her appearances on *21 Jump Street*, as Diana Ross. For her lover, Berry Gordy Jr., Margaret cast Billy Dee Williams. The first black Miss America (later dethroned), Vanessa Williams, was cast as Suzanne de Passe, who, as a Motown executive, played an instrumental role in launching The Jackson 5.

Margaret recalled, "Seeing the actors re-enact segments of their lives brought back all the love, the pain, the anticipation, the heartache, and, in several cases, the anguish as memories came flooding back."

As the head of his own record company, Michael signed up some other family members to his label. But his motives may have been suspect. Some executives at Sony privately claimed that there was a feeling that the King of Pop wanted only one Jackson in the recording studio, Michael himself. Of course, there was nothing he could do about Janet. At this point, she was beyond his financial control.

"I think Michael secretly wanted to sign the other Jacksons as a means of suppressing them instead of promoting them," said a Sony official, speaking confidentially. Michael did release a recording by his older sister, Rebbie, and one by Tito Jackson Jr., both of which showed a great deal of promise, but reportedly he then went on to sabotage the promotion of both of these recordings.

Michael had begun what was for him a long, arduous, and costly project, his long-awaited *Dangerous* album. In a surprise move, he did not use Quincy Jones as the producer, even though the very talented Jones had brought Michael his greatest success.

He decided to go with Harlem-born Teddy Riley as producer. Riley was famous for a new musical genre, called "New Jack Swing"—or "Swingbeat" in Britain—and had pioneered the sound with such R&B performers as Keith Sweat.

New Jack Swing eventually translated into hip-hop soul. Riley had also worked with Boy George. By 2006, Riley was at work with a New Jack Swing revival.

The album, *Dangerous*, premiered on *Billboard's* top album chart at Number One in 1991, as Michael himself had predicted. It had been produced at an estimated cost of more than $12 million, an industry record. CBS Records shipped out four million copies.

In addition to the title song, "Dangerous," the album featured such songs as "In the Closet" and

Teddy Riley

"Remember the Time," the latter dedicated to Diana Ross. Michael was feeling better about her again. As a political message, he recorded "Heal the World."

Internationally, *Dangerous* would eclipse the sales of *Bad*, as 32 million albums disappeared around the world, even in East Germany. Not all of these were legitimate sales. On November 20, 1991, a group of armed men stole 30,000 copies of *Dangerous* from an air freight terminal at the Los Angeles airport.

In spite of strong sales, critical response to the album was for the most part unfavorable. *The Los Angeles Times* asked: "How dangerous can a man be who literally wants to please everyone?" The reviewer called the album "a messy grab-bag of ideas and high-tech *non sequiturs*, with something for everyone from the man who has everything—relatively tame, wildly unfocused." Another critic asserted, "Michael Jackson desperately wants to be a classic star like his good friends Elizabeth Taylor and Katharine Hepburn."

Teddy Riley, the producer of the *Dangerous* album, said that Michael talked a lot about what he'd done to his face and skin during their production work. "I'm quite sure if Michael could have done it all over again, he would not have done what he did," Riley said. "But there's no turning back. Once you change your description, you're stuck with it. You can't get your own face and your own skin back. But he is still Michael Jackson, still the talented man that everybody grew up on."

Although at least three music videos were generated by the *Dangerous* album, the video associated with the single "Remember the Time" generated more than its share of strife.

John Singleton, director of *Boyz N the Hood,* was hired to direct it, opting for, in full cooperation with Michael, a setting in ancient Egypt.

In a surprise move, Michael decided to cast Eddie Murphy in the video, despite the fact that it was widely assumed that the two men detested each

John Singleton

other. Throughout the 80s Murphy had made a career in stand-up comedy routines which sometimes viciously ridiculed gays and their vulnerability to AIDS. Even Richard Pryor found Murphy "a little too mean," and Michael was frequently the butt of Murphy's jokes.

Michael, of course, was aware that Murphy had mocked him on nationwide television and made fun of him in club acts, but despite all that, the two men worked harmoniously together, concealing whatever private feelings they might have had about each other. Murphy was cast as the

Pharaoh Ramses, playing opposite the glamorous actress and supermodel, Iman, who played his wife, Queen Nefertiti. Before signing on, Murphy, joking or not, said, "There ain't gonna be no scene with me kissin' no faggot!"

Born in Somalia, the exotic Iman became the wife of David Bowie on April 24, 1992. Channel 5 ranked her #29 in their roster of "The World's Greatest Supermodels." Iman later proclaimed, "I had breast enlargement to quiet that noise in my head and fill the gaping hole in my self-esteem."

Iman confided that she would not be able to show the video to her father, a strict Muslim. Her father was the Somalian ambassador to Saudi Arabia. "Nudity and erotic video are against his religion, and has been a major conflict in our family. Even my being a model goes against my father's religion. At the end of the day, I'm my father's daughter. If there are any naked pictures up when he comes around, I hide them."

She'd posed topless for the 1985 edition of the popular *Pirelli Calendar*. She had also performed in a music video for Jermaine Jackson, "Do What You Do."

In Michael's video, Eddie Murphy, as the Egyptian pharaoh, sends his guards chasing after Michael, who manages to elude them and ends up with an embrace and a kiss from Iman.

Michael seemed to freeze during his kiss with the delectable Iman. "I wouldn't freeze, man," Murphy said. "That would sure get a rise out of me."

Later, reviewers attacked the kiss as "the most unconvincing in the history of the movies." One critic wrote, "if Michael Jackson was trying to assert his heterosexual credentials in this video, he failed miserably. If Sir Winston Churchill had ever been forced to kiss Adolf Hitler, I think the British prime minister would have pulled it off with more fervor." Singleton begged Michael to film the scene over again, but Michael retreated to his dressing room for the rest of the day. Sobbing, he was found watching *The Little Mermaid*.

Magic Johnson was also cast in the video. Privately, Michael told his producer that he wanted to limit his contact with the athlete. He'd heard that he had HIV, and Michael, perhaps unaware of how the disease is transmitted, was overly sensitive.

The director wanted his actors in Egyptian dress, which meant showing some leg. But Michael refused, allegedly because his legs were still "as brown as an acorn," whereas his upper torso had turned white. To the horror of the wardrobe department, Michael insisted on wearing black pants underneath his Egyptian dress.

Later, Michael agreed to a minor participation in Murphy's 1992 album, *Love's Alright*. In the video of the song, "WhatZupWitu," Michael and Murphy appear in a Technicolor-like dream together. The Boys Choir of

Harlem also makes an appearance. The video was so horrid that it was at first released only in Japan. Later when it reached the United States in 1999, MTV voted it as "one of the 25 worst music videos" in history.

For yet another video from the *Dangerous* album, Michael filmed "In the Closet," as if dangerously courting more ridicule from Joan Rivers. "In the Closet?" she shrieked. "Michael, tell us something we don't know."

If his kiss with Iman was a bomb, he hoped to right that wrong by hiring another supermodel, the ravishingly attractive Naomi Campbell.who had been chosen by *People* magazine as one of the 50 Most Beautiful People in the World.

A Californian, Herb Ritts, who had directed videos for both Janet Jackson and for Madonna, signed on as the director of "In the Closet."

As a director of music videos, Ritts was an odd choice. He was mainly known for celebrity photography, taking pictures of everyone from Jack Nicholson to Mick Jagger. His photos had graced album covers, including Madonna's *True Blue* in 1986. He'd photographed Cindy Crawford for both the July 1988 and the October 1998 issues of *Playboy*. As a respected photographer, Ritts gained unprecedented access to many of his subjects, including a paralyzed Christopher Reeve and a post-brain surgery Elizabeth Taylor.

During the publicity associated with "In the Closet," Ritts proposed a daring concept: Michael would pose nude for a centerfold for publication in either *Vogue, Elle, Harper's Bazaar, Vanity Fair*, or *Rolling Stone*.

When he saw the horror of Michael's face, Ritts assured him that in his photo shop he could make a penis look bigger. Ritts later claimed that Michael burst into tears at the suggestion and ran away from him. Ironically, despite his horrified reaction to Ritts' proposal, within just a few short months, Michael would be posing nude for a Santa Barbara police photographer—definitely against his wishes.

For six weeks prior to the filming of a third video, Michael hired a personal trainer "who looked like Arnold Schwarzenegger." Since he didn't plan to show his legs, they worked mostly to build up his upper torso.

In spite of all his efforts, Michael still emerged, in the words of one critic, "as the 97-pound weakling in all those old Charles Atlas ads where bullies on the beach kick sand in his face, embarrassing him in front of his girl."

On location in Palm Springs, Michael and the artfully underclad Naomi executed their videotaped maneuvers together. Naomi comes on strong, provocatively wrapping her bare legs around Michael's waist.

In the video, she reveals that she should have been a film star—not just a "supermodel." In contrast, in the words of one critic, "He absolutely froze as Naomi comes at him like a tigress. Michael was out of his element with a hottie like Naomi."

On a trivial note, Princess Stéphanie of Monaco was credited with supplying the female vocal. The final track also included a brief appearance by rapper Heavy D, and an appearance by superstar Michael Jordan. In the video, he dances and plays basketball with Jordan. Michael, even at this late date, was still confusing Magic Johnson with Michael Jordan. To resolve the confusion, he developed a somewhat insensitive way of differentiating the two athletes: "Oh, Jordan is the one who's not HIV positive."

Some TV stations, perhaps because of Naomi's sexy dance, refused to air the video. But despite their lack of cooperation, and despite Michael's frigidity, "In the Closet" emerged as the third consecutive number one hit from the *Dangerous* album.

Back at Neverland the staff was being supervised by Bill Bray, Michael's grizzled chief of security. Michael once referred to him as, "The father I never had." But Bray needed help, and Michael hired Norma Staikos, a stocky, middle-aged immigrant from Greece. According to a staff member at Neverland, "She wore a frown set in stone."

"Michael had his father in Bray," said a disgruntled staff member. "Now he found another mother in Staikos. She soon became the virtual chatelaine of Neverland." The same staff member claimed that Staikos operated Neverland "like the Gestapo—we were terrified of her. Firings were frequent. You never knew from day to day whether you had a job or not."

After a few weeks, Staikos issued orders that the security guards at the gate were not to record the arrivals of "the little boyfriends," some of whom began appearing at three o'clock in the morning. As increasing numbers of young boys arrived at Neverland, Staikos became vigilant in her efforts to blot out evidence of that, as if sensing some future trouble for her employer.

Hired as an assistant to Staikos was Orietta Murdock of Costa Rica. Apparently, Murdock was hired because Staikos thought she was a Latina. But when Staikos met Murdock's sister, whose skin was much darker, both Staikos and Michael learned that Murdock was black. Michael said, "I prefer to think of her as Latina instead of black."

Murdock was assigned to organize letters and photographs from Michael's young fans. "I felt bad seeing Michael separate the photos and reading the letters he saw with children's handwriting," Murdock later said. "Black kids and kids older than thirteen didn't interest him. And when he was reading a letter and realized that it was from a little girl, he threw it in the trash. He

Herb Ritts

348

kept and took to his room only the photos and letters from white, Latin, and Asian children. As for the rest, he told us it was useless to answer them, so we had to fake his signature. It was a shame that those children didn't fit into his racial tastes."

After Murdock was fired, she filed a complaint on January 29, 1991 with the Equal Employment Department of California. "I was fired and intimidated for being black. Michael doesn't like black

MJ and Naomi Campbell in "In the Closet"

people. He would say that he wasn't black, but a chameleon. He used creams and white make-up like they use in the theater since he didn't like to look black. He called his black guards Big Gorillas." In addition to accusing the singer of being racist, Murdock also charged that he was a child molester.

At least one of Michael's "special friends" would disagree with Murdock. He was Brett Barnes, a 23-year-old, out-of-work roulette dealer when he took the witness stand to testify in Michael's behalf during his trial in 2005 on charges of child molestation. Like another one of Michael's special friends, Wade Robson, Brett too was from Down Under.

He claimed that Michael "did not have wandering hands," refuting the testimony of an ex-Neverland maid. "And I can tell you that if he did, I wouldn't be here right now . . . I wouldn't stand for it," Brett said. He also expressed his anger that he'd been referenced at the trial as one of Michael's alleged victims. "It's untrue, and they're putting my name through the dirt," he testified.

Marie Lisbeth Barnes, Brett's mother, testified that her son had slept with Michael "just on occasion." Brett's older sister, Karlee Barnes, recalled that her brother and Michael spent about 365 nights alone in his bedroom.

When the police made a search of Neverland in 1993, they discovered Brett living at the ranch. At the time, he was eleven years old. While Michael was on the *Dangerous* tour in Europe, Brett stayed behind at Neverland with his mother and sister. The police raid reportedly left the boy trembling and insecure.

He was questioned by the police, and vehemently denied that any improper behavior ever took place between the star and himself. He did admit that Michael was affectionate—"more like a big brother. He's a best friend, except he's big." Under more intense questioning, he also admitted that he'd slept in Michael's bedroom at night. "He slept on one side, and I slept on the other," the boy said. He added, "It was a big bed." He later defended Michael on KNBC, a television station based in Los Angeles.

After the raid, Michael called Brett at Neverland to reassure him that "this is all a big mistake—it'll blow over."

A rabid Jackson fan, Brett was actually five years old and in Australia when he first tried to approach Michael, who was on tour there at the time. In the late 80s, Brett, with his older sister, had come to the airport to greet his idol. With him, Brett carried a handwritten letter with his telephone number.

He didn't actually meet Michael that day, but his letter obviously reached the star. In a few days, Michael called Brett. It was the beginning of several long phone dialogues.

In 1991 an invitation arrived with airplane tickets for Brett, his mother, and sister. Off they went to California to visit Michael at Neverland. Many such visits would follow in the future.

In the wake of the raid on Neverland, the press began a search, reporters hoping to find pictures of Michael photographed with young boys. Literally hundreds of such pictures turned up in newspaper and magazine files. After the raid, these pictures took on a more ominous aura.

Photos were found of Michael with a young Australian boy—not Brett Barnes but a child identified as "Brett Jackson." Michael had introduced Brett as "my cousin," erroneously passing him off as one of the Jackson family members.

The most unusual photo depicted Michael taking time out from his *Dangerous* tour in 1992 to escort two young boys to Euro Disney, south of Paris. In the picture Brett stands between Michael on his right and a mysterious young boy on his left.

The world had never seen such a plastic face on Michael Jackson before, the result of endless surgeries. His nose had shrunk to the size of that of the mysterious nine-year-old in the picture. Michael flashes Chiclet-white teeth and has an unreal aura about him.

Brett's face is partially hidden, because he is sucking his thumb. But, finally, the mystery boy was identified by some eagle-eyed editor. It was the face of the Bavarian prince, Albert von Thurn und Taxis.

Born on June 24, 1983, Prince Albert was the world's youngest billionaire, with an estimated net worth of $2.1 billion, according to the *Forbes Rich List*. His 30,000 hectares (74,132 acres) of woodland in Germany is one of the largest forestry holdings in Europe. He grew up in one of the family castles, Schloss Emmeram in Regensburg, but also had other residences in Germany and throughout Europe, including Russia. How Michael linked himself with such aristocracy and was allowed to travel with this rich and unusual child is not known.

Brett Barnes

Michael certainly could not wow Prince Albert with money and toys, as the young Bavarian was obviously very wealthy in his own right.

In the wake of the Euro Disney photograph, pictures of Michael and Brett traveling together began popping up in dozens of archives. Wearing a baseball cap and a jacket far too large for him, Brett was photographed arriving in London with Michael in March of 1992.

In London, Michael and Brett paid a call on the dying comic, Benny Hill, who was in a hospital suffering from having had a heart attack. Other than Charlie Chaplin, the English comedian was the artist Michael most admired. Michael loved Hill's cheeky humor, songs, and impressions. As a fan of Benny Hill, Michael was in good company. Greta Garbo and Walter Cronkite were also devoted to Hill's humor. After Hill's death, Michael, through his agents, tried to acquire the artist's memorabilia, hoping to make a shrine to him at Neverland.

It's estimated—there is no way of knowing the exact amount—that Michael spent a quarter of a million dollars entertaining young Brett on their five-day swing through London. They stayed at the swanky Dorchester Hotel where hysterical fans gathered outside to wait for Michael.

Both the man and the boy were housed in the hotel's most luxurious suite on the ninth floor. Michael had arrived in London with two dozen staff members, who occupied the entire eighth floor of the Dorchester. The entourage consisted of, among others, a manicurist and a full-time doctor.

While at the Dorchester, Michael and Brett purchased some $10,000 worth of toys, which they played with at the hotel, abandoning the items when they checked out for a flight aboard the Concorde.

Young Brett traveled and slept with Michael during a twelve-day tour that carried them to four continents, including five African nations.

On one lap of the journey through Europe, Michael and Brett reserved the entire *Orient Express* just for themselves. "Talk about luxury," said one of the staff members aboard the train. "No potentate in history ever traveled in such style."

It was during this tour that Brett came to realize that he was about to be replaced as

Brett all grown up

351

Michael's special friend. As he and Michael raced through more than a dozen countries, Michael was on the phone at night—sometimes talking for as much as three hours—with a young boy in California called Jordie Chandler.

Brett and Michael were next seen in Las Vegas where they were photographed as they viewed the magical act of Michael's friends, Siegfried and Roy. Later Brett shared Michael's suite at the Mirage Hotel & Casino.

Albert von Thurn und Taxis

Invitations had gone out to Brett and Michael to attend Elizabeth Taylor's much-hyped birthday party, for the celebration of her "Big 6-0." It was staged at, of all places, Anaheim's Disneyland. The star was said to be "bitterly disappointed" when Michael didn't show up.

Publicist Bob Jones believed that the Disneyland bash would be a "sure bet" for Michael to attend. But it was later revealed that Michael and Brett were locked away in the most luxurious suite at the deluxe Helmsley Palace in New York. "The Queen of Mean," Leona Helmsley herself, had personally greeted Michael and Brett, welcoming them to her hotel.

Michael seemingly would do everything for Brett, even calling the manager of the Sportsworld in Paramus, New Jersey. For an undisclosed price, Michael got him to empty the park at 9:30pm, giving patrons their money back so that he and Brett could enjoy Sportsworld and its 175 video games by themselves. The couple stayed until two o'clock in the morning, and Brett later said he had "one of the best times of my life."

In 1993, Jordie Chandler, about to become Brett's replacement, met his rival, Brett. In Los Angeles, Michael had come to pick up Jordie in a limousine. In the back seat, Jordie noted Brett with his big eyes, sitting on Michael's lap. There was a slight resemblance between the two boys. Jordie may have been jealous at the open affection displayed between Brett and Michael. He later told his father that the experience had made him "a bit uncomfortable."

Dr. Richard A. Gardner, the leading authority in California on false claims of child abuse, conducted a series of psychological tests on Jordie on October 6, 1993. In this interrogation, the name of Brett cropped up. Jordie refuted Brett's claim that Michael had never violated him sexually.

According to Jordie, "if he [meaning Michael] wanted me to do something with him, he would say that Brett did that with him, so that I would do it. And, like, if I didn't do it, then I didn't love him as much as Brett did."

That Michael could juggle far more than one "special friend" in his life became evident in testimony provided by El Salvador-born Blanca Francia, who was the star's personal maid from 1986 to 1991. Her testimony became vitally important because she had been granted access to the inner sanctum of Michael's bedroom, where she'd discovered—long before the police—pornographic materials. Blanca had seen the pictures and books first. She later claimed that she'd also seen "inappropriate touching" between Michael and young boys.

Blanca was not adverse to making money off what she'd witnessed. Television's *Hard Copy* paid her $20,000 for an interview. But she won lotto when Michael paid her $2.4 million when she threatened legal action against him for fondling her handsome young son, Jason Francia.

At Michael's jury trial in 2005, Jason was the only witness who came forward and claimed that Michael had molested him, beginning when he was only seven years old. After five years of therapy, he had become an evangelical Christian, devoting part of his life to working with troubled young people when he wasn't selling auto parts.

Before the world, Jason testified that Michael had taken him twice to his hideout condo. In his testimony, he claimed that Michael and he had played "tickling games" in which the star would move his hands over Jason's genitalia on the outside of his shorts. "Pretty much at every tickle thing there was money," he said. Allegedly, two of these molestations took place at the hideout and the third molestation occurred at Neverland when Jason had turned ten.

This time, according to Jason, Michael's hands went inside his pants. But when tears welled in the boy's eyes, Michael stopped.

During the investigation of Michael in 1993, Jason was questioned by the police in the Jordie Chandler case. At the time, Jason was thirteen. He denied that he'd been molested. Later, however, he changed his testimony and asserted that he had been molested after all.

Lawyers for Michael intensely grilled Jason over why he'd changed his story when first interviewed by police investigators. "In the beginning, I thought I could hold them off and make them go away. I didn't want to tell anybody I had been molested." The implication was that he was ashamed and embarrassed by the incidents

When defense lawyer Tom Mesereau confronted Jason with his conflicting statements made during a series of interviews with police and prosecutors over the years, Jason uttered a tearful response.

"In the fifth grade, I told my friends I knew Michael Jackson and it was cool. They didn't believe me but it was cool. In junior high, it was no longer cool to know somebody who had issues with kids."

Before the trial, Blanca had given interviews, shedding light on what was going on behind the closed doors of Neverland. One of those interviews was with Diane Dimond, an investigative reporter for TV's *Hard Copy*. In that session, Blanca made it clear that she had not wanted her son to become another one of Michael's "special friends."

The former maid also made the claim that she once entered a room and caught her son on Michael's lap. She also claimed that she once found her son "so close" to Michael in a sleeping bag at his hideout. Later, when she was taking him home, Jason confessed that Michael had given him three hundred dollars. "Three hundred dollars for a seven-year-old?" Dimond asked in astonishment.

Jason wasn't the only young boy Michael had tempted with money. A maid at Neverland claimed that one twelve-year-old boy risked killing himself when trying to retrieve an Easter egg hidden in a crystal chandelier by jumping off a balustrade. The eggs were filled with one-thousand dollar bills. "Why would you do that?" the maid asked the boy. "I'd do anything for money," he replied.

Blanca claimed that she was not fired, but that she quit her job. "I got tired of what was going on—Michael sleeping with boys and taking showers together. I think I saw too much."

In an interview with reporter Dimond, Blanca claimed that the string of boys who visited Neverland were always prepubescent, ranging in age from seven to twelve years old. Other witnesses' accounts differed with Blanca's testimony, claiming that some of the boys were thirteen or fourteen. No one stepped forward to claim that any boy was six years old or younger.

She also claimed that Michael preferred to pick boys who came from split families . . . "a divorced mother or single mother." Apparently, such parents were easier to manipulate than a mother and a father within a more traditional marriage.

Several witnesses, including Blanca, have suggested that Michael was intrigued by the mouths of young boys, especially the lips of Macaulay Culkin. Blanca once found Polaroid snapshots Michael had taken just of close-ups of the lips of his "special friends."

All the boys were nicknamed "Rubba" by Michael. Rubba may have meant that boys sat on his lap and rubbed up against his privates—hence, the name.

Blanca said she was never tempted to go to the police, and that she was manipulated by Michael with money and gifts. "I didn't want to lose my job," she said.

Blanca was grilled as to why parents— even those who stayed in Michael's guest-

Jason Francia

354

house while their sons slept in his bedroom in the main house—allowed such activity. "I think they just looked the other way as long as they were getting money or expensive gifts like jewelry."

A mystery still surrounds Blanca after she gave a sworn deposition in the case of Jordie Chandler. Even though she had enough money to retire after her settlement with Michael, she, for reasons of her own, continued to work at menial jobs. She obtained a job working for a senior citizen.

Still living in Santa Barbara County, she bicycled to work every morning. On the way to work, she was struck by a car. This caused rampant speculation and a flurry of rumors that a hit man had been hired to kill her but had not succeeded. The police investigated but no charges were ever filed.

Throughout all of Michael's involvements with these young boys, and his subsequent legal troubles, Elizabeth Taylor remained a steadfast friend.

Over the years, this friendship has caused much speculation in the press. Elizabeth always had an answer to reporters who questioned her about her involvement with Michael. "We love each other," said Elizabeth. "Michael and I. If nobody understands that—or doesn't dig it—then tough shit!"

Gloria Berlin, the real estate agent who sold Michael Neverland, asked him why he wanted a place so big for just one person. She quoted him as saying, "I plan to adopt twenty-nine children and marry Elizabeth Taylor."

"But she's old enough to be your grandmother," Berlin said.

"But I love her. I just love her. I love her. *I love her.*"

Of course, these remarks reportedly were said before Elizabeth's marriage to Larry Fortensky.

Michael's relationship with Elizabeth was viewed very differently by others, opinions often in total conflict. One of Michael's former publicists at Epic completely dismissed the friendship. "The relationship is this," she said. "He brought her just as much publicity as she brought to him. He also bought her a lot of jewelry in appreciation for her 'friendship.' They used each other."

The press often put yet another spin on the relationship. "They're just two former child stars being kids again," wrote Cynthia Lambert. "Food fights. Cotton candy. Taylor's a grandmother but she can still revert to being a kid again."

One of the most far-fetched tabloid rumors was that Elizabeth visited Neverland for "treatments in Michael Jackson's hyperbaric chamber." One headline claimed: TAYLOR PLANS TO STAY FOREVER YOUNG.

It is true that this unlikely pair of Elizabeth and Michael has stood by each other through "Thick and Thin," a song Michael attempted to write about their friendship but which was never finished.

"Elizabeth was always there for Michael and Michael for Elizabeth," Frank DiLeo once said, forgetting that Michael had skipped out on her 60th birthday bash at Disneyland.

It is not known how many presents Michael gave Elizabeth over the years, but it was rumored to have been more than $5 million worth of jewelry alone. Michael generated millions more in publicity for her.

"Let's face it," said publicist Howard Brackett. "Taylor hadn't made a movie since dinosaurs walked the Earth. By hanging onto the arm of Michael, she generated untold press. All that notoriety helps her sell that Goddamn perfume and the jewelry she designs. Anyone would want to be a friend of Michael if he gets all that publicity for her. What I don't understand is this: exactly what does Michael Jackson get in hanging out with Elizabeth Taylor?"

Another publicist, who refused to be named, said "Michael basks in the glow of having a fabulous friend like Elizabeth. I've heard that he even tells tricks, 'I'll introduce you to Elizabeth Taylor.' Even that story doesn't make sense to me. Why would a nine-year-old boy want to meet Elizabeth Taylor? Superman, maybe. Even Tom Cruise, though I doubt that. But *Elizabeth Taylor*, who became a star back in the days of a kid's grandparents?"

To Michael's credit, he did respond to Elizabeth's call for help in the plight of AIDS. He contributed freely of his time and money, as when he showed up for a benefit she wanted him to attend in September of 1985. Elizabeth had called major stars such as her former lover, Frank Sinatra. He told her, "This is just another of your lame duck causes—back away from it! It's going to hurt you."

Fortunately, along with Michael, Elizabeth got Betty Ford and Barry Manilow to show up and lend their names to the cause.

Michael also generated a lot of good publicity for himself, portraying both Elizabeth and himself as two crazy kids who didn't grow up. Reportedly, they engaged in food fights and tried to "tickle each other to death" until one of them cried uncle. At Neverland one staff member reported seeing Elizabeth sneak up on Michael and burst a red water balloon over his unsuspecting head.

Blanca Francia, Michael's maid, painted a different portrait, suggesting that this "odd couple" had more of a business relationship than a friendship. At one point she referred to Elizabeth as "Poor Lady," because Michael neglected her for the most part when she came to visit Neverland.

"Michael was just playing with her," Francia charged. "Everyone knows they're not close." She claimed that during one two-week visit, Michael saw Elizabeth only once for dinner. Reportedly, when Elizabeth went looking for Michael to talk to him, he made himself unavailable, instructing Francia to tell the star that he was sleeping.

"I feel so bad for her," Blanca said. "She goes to Neverland and wants to talk to someone. The staff is not allowed to talk to guests, so she's by herself. Michael just wanted to stay away from her."

Mark Quindoy, the majordomo, more or less agreed with the maid's assessment. "Michael's relationship with Ms. Taylor is pure farce. They just use each other to promote their own images." He too agreed that during a two-week visit to Neverland, Michael had dinner only once with Elizabeth. "In contrast, he not only had breakfast, lunch, and dinner with Macaulay Culkin, he slept in the same bed with him."

It was February 4, 1992, and Michael had just put down the phone, after receiving a "good luck" call from Elizabeth. Dressed in black leather with a red armband, he went from his dressing room down the Art Deco staircase of Radio City Music Hall in New York to appear at a press conference. In the background, reporters heard the sound of "Black or White."

For some $20 million from Pepsi—maybe a lot more—Michael announced a worldwide *Dangerous* tour. It was to be publicized as "The Greatest Show on Earth." He claimed that with the success of the tour, he might raise as much as $100 million for children's charities. Since he didn't need the money, Michael—falsely or otherwise—said that his aim was to "spread global love" among the children of the world.

He had formed The Heal the World Foundation in 1992, hoping to bring aid to underprivileged children. Even though he was doing it for charity, his critics were unrelenting. On the *Dangerous* album, Michael had inserted his version of the foundation's theme song. One music critic called it "a Hallmark card knockoff of 'We Are the World.'"

With interruptions, cancellations, and much dreaded headlines, the *Dangerous* world music tour would be launched by Michael on June 27, 1992, grinding to a crashing end on November 11, 1993. Some 3.5 million fans would hear him in 69 different concerts, the biggest tour any performer had ever done until Michael broke his own record with his *HIStory* follow-up in the years ahead.

Germany, Britain, France, even Romania, lay before him. However, because of medical problems with his vocal cords, he had to cut short the tour, resuming it in December of 1992 in Japan.

In another record-breaking deal, Michael sold the film rights to his *Dangerous* tour for $21 million, the highest deal ever scored for a live concert. The footage was shot in Bucharest. When HBO aired the film in October of 1992, it played to fans in 61 countries, receiving the highest TV ratings in history.

Some of the countries Michael—accompanied by Brett Barnes—visited were on the continent of Africa, which he hadn't seen in nearly two decades. Wherever his plane touched down, he drew bigger crowds than either Nelson Mandela or the Pope.

Before arriving in Africa, Michael made certain that his own frozen blood was flown in. Associates reported that he was terrified of contracting AIDS. He feared that if he became ill during the tour and needed blood transfusions, he might be injected with tainted blood. "The only blood I trust is my own," he told his aides. "See that it's shipped wherever I go."

Like his role model, billionaire Howard Hughes, Michael was almost paranoicly germ-conscious, once suggesting that he wanted a Plexiglas shield erected between him and his fans. But he was warned that there would be an outcry against this. Bob Jones himself felt that such a move would be a public relations disaster. Nonetheless, word of the Plexiglas shield made it into the press. Eventually Michael abandoned the plan.

Even before his plane touched down in the Republic of Gabon, the local press was raising provocative questions. One headline read: IS MICHAEL JACKSON REALLY BLACK? Articles about his changing skin color were appearing not only in Africa, but in newspapers around the world. Prior to the example set by Michael, most of the world didn't believe that it was possible for a black man to change his skin color to white.

Doctors, presumably experts, were interviewed on the subject. From Europe, Dr. Hans Geiler (country of origin unknown) issued a statement that a black skin could be turned much lighter by the use of "certain bleaching agents." A group of compounds known as "Hydroquinones," or so it was claimed, could make dark skin much lighter—"but not quite white."

Obviously bleaching agents worked better on a light-skinned black or a mulatto than on persons whose skin was extremely dark or "blue black," claimed one doctor, a plastic surgeon, who didn't want to give his name, fearing a "backlash from people of color." As if the world didn't already know this, the doctor warned, "Race is a delicate issue to discuss."

Thousands of people use Porcelana's Skin Lightening Serum with Hydroquinone, the only FDA-approved ingredient to effectively lighten skin discolorations.

Michael was said to travel with tubes of Hydroquinone. In the past it had been noted that he used Porcelana, a bleaching cream. La Toya was also rumored to have used Porcelana on her beautiful face.

It was alleged that Michael had studied the makeup techniques of George Masters, which he perfected with Marilyn Monroe in years immediately prior to her death. It was called the "white-on-white look." Makeup expert Mitchell Geller claimed that Masters "transformed Marilyn from Technicolor to 'frosted' way before that became the fashion."

As his skin grew whiter and whiter, Michael developed an aversion to the sun. The hot sun of Africa held a particular terror for him. "The direct sun must never touch my face," he warned aides. One way to conceal his face was to wear large hats. In time, he began to travel with an aide who held a large

MJ crowned King of Sani

umbrella, most often black, over his whitening head.

It was believed that much of Michael's look came from heavy applications of pancake makeup. He really coated it on. When any aide delicately suggested that he might be using too much, Michael quoted a statement by Masters, who was acclaimed as the leading makeup artist of Hollywood. Masters once claimed that upon Elvis Presley's return from a tour of duty with the Army in Germany, "he was wearing more pancake makeup and more mascara than Marlene Dietrich and Joan Crawford would ever dare."

Attracting thousands of hysterical fans, many of whom were later injured, Michael touched down in Libreville, the capital of Gabon, a port on the Gabon River near the Gulf of Guinea. He was there as the guest of Omar Bongo, the country's president. Although advertised as a good will tour, Michael's trip was financed by the government ministry, it was later revealed.

Omar Bongo was one of the most controversial of all African leaders, having assumed the presidency of Gabon in 1967 at the age of 32, the world's youngest president at the time. Still in office in 2007, he is the world's seventh longest serving ruler. If he picked up the tab for Michael, he could well afford it, as Bongo is one of the globe's wealthiest heads of state, an empire attributed mainly to oil revenue and alleged corruption.

Bongo emerged in headlines again in 2005, when a Senate investigation revealed that lobbyist Jack Abramoff had offered Bongo a chance to meet with President George W. Bush in exchange for $9 million. Ten months later, on May 26, 2004, Bongo was photographed talking head to head with Bush himself.

In Gabon, grade school children turned out to greet Michael, carrying a banner that proclaimed: WELCOME HOME MICHAEL. The sounds of drums filled the air. One nine-year-old boy cried out, "Michael is love, love, love! I want to be like him."

A British journalist, Peter Hodges, was at the Gabon airport to witness the arrival of Michael and his entourage. He later wrote provocative copy. "Michael Jackson often flaunts his arrival at airports with handsome young boys. Not so in Africa. The word was out that he wanted his companion, Brett Barnes, to be kept away from the lens of carnivorous paparazzi. Even so, I got to see the kid get off the plane after the paparazzi went chasing after Michael. In London, Jackson had passed the boy off as 'Brett Jackson,' his cousin. I later learned that Brett hails from Sydney, Australia. He was one charismatic and gorgeous boy, fit competition for Tadzio." The journalist was referring, of course, to the young boy beauty in the Thomas Mann novel, *Death in Venice*.

In Gabon, President Bongo presented Michael with the Medal of Honor, an award often reserved for visiting Heads of State such as Nelson Mandela.

Before the good will tour of Africa was over, Michael would visit not only Gabon, but the Ivory Coast, Tanzania, and Egypt, discovering "Michael-mania" wherever he landed. He logged 30,000 miles in 11 days. His 26-person entourage was flown on a Boeing 707 executive plane. It came complete with a stateroom, a private bathroom, an open bar, lounges and dining areas, and lots and lots of video and audio equipment.

One picture of Michael, with his arms outstretched, his hat removed, was published around the world. Said to be "deeply moved," he was photographed in front of the world's largest church, the Basilica of Our Lady of Peace, in Yamoussoakra, capital of the Ivory Coast.

The highlight of the African safari for Michael came in the Côte d'Ivoire, a little country that had declared itself independent of French colonial rule back in 1960. Even so, by as late as 1969, the Sanwis of Krinjabo wanted to break away and form an independent kingdom. Michael was taken to the Ivory Coast village of Krinjabo, not far from the border with Ghana. The Sanwis had invited Michael for a coronation ceremony to crown him King.

A little boy born into near poverty in Indiana was welcomed to Africa like a ruling dignitary and long-lost son. But it wasn't long before sentiment began to shift against him.

Attired in black trousers and a "flaming" orange shirt, Michael was fanned by four teenage, bare-breasted girls during his coronation. "Kings" and chiefs from nearby villages came to town to watch Michael's crowning. Medicine men chanted incantations as they poured precious gin on the dry parched earth in honor of the memory of their Krinjabo ancestors.

The traditional tribal chief of Krinjabo, Amon N'Djafolk, placed a crown of gold on Michael's head and pronounced him "King of Sani." In a whispery voice, Michael said, "*Merci beaucoup.* Thank you very much."

He was draped in a traditional gold and orange robe. When he was crowned, he accepted a long golden chain, a symbol of authority. Placed on a golden throne and decked out in tribal drag, Michael, in the words of one reporter, "looked more like a Queen than a King."

Regrettably, Michael insulted the villagers by removing his royal robe immediately after the ceremony. In the local newspaper, a reporter wrote that "Michael Jackson's communication talents are lacking." It was later noted that this was "only one of a series of gaffes and other troubles that caused Michael to abandon his African trip after a week. Originally he had wanted to visit the continent to film scenes for a "Return to Africa" video.

360

Omar Bongo

Not all was a disaster. During his visit, Michael went to schools, churches, and institutions for mentally retarded children. In his child-like way he bonded successfully with these children born into a world that was radically different from the glitzy life that Michael knew in America.

Without his surgical mask, he hugged and kissed children, some of whom had AIDS. The tour organizer, Charles Bobbit, said, "I was impressed with the interaction between Michael and the children. He sat on the bed with children who were deformed and children who were ill. He sat there and talked to them, hugged them, cuddled them."

His feelings were expressed in the song, "Why You Wanna Trip on Me," part of the *Dangerous* album.

They say I'm different
They don't understand
But there's a bigger problem
That's much more in demand
You got world hunger
Not enough to eat
So there's really no time
To be trippin' on me . . .

Throughout the tour, Michael kept touching his nose. Noting this, Africans were offended. It appeared that Michael was holding his nose to avoid the raw smells of Africa. He was said to object in particular to hunks of meat rotting in the sun and attracting flies.

The editor of Gabon's leading newspaper was direct in his attack. He called Michael "the sacred beast of America. Holding his nose, he reminds us that we are undeveloped and that our sewer system doesn't equal that of California. When he comes into contact with us, he reminds us that we don't have the luxurious marble bathrooms of rich movie stars in Hollywood. As he passes our markets, he seems horrified at our rotting foodstuff, noting that we lack refrigeration. What are we to make of this strange creature among us? He's not a black man. But not quite white either. He's neither man nor woman but some androgynous thing caught between the sexes. That might be all right in a frail little boy. In a grown man, such an effeminate character, who speaks with the voice of a little girl, is frightening. Maybe it is up to the people of

Gabon to turn up their noses at Michael Jackson—not the other way around!" The scalding editorial didn't diminish the crowds who turned out not to greet Michael, but to worship him.

The ever-sharp publicist, Bob Jones, rushed to Michael's defense. "We would not be here if we thought your country smelled," Jones announced in Gabon. "You are our roots. The air here is fresher than anywhere else." The publicist dismissed the nose touching as "just a nervous tick Michael has." But there may have been more to the nose touching than Jones had suggested.

Reports began appearing in America and London that Michael's nose was in danger of collapsing. Before the debut of his Africa tour, he may have endured a total of six rhinoplasties. The suggestion was that during his sixth operation, a hole had appeared in his right nostril that had to be "packed" and stitched. These stitches may have caused the itching and nose scratching he experienced in Africa. In London a plastic surgeon speculated that Michael might one day have to wear a plastic nose.

Back in Africa, Michael told Bob Jones that the African tour was evolving into a disaster. He cancelled a safari—"I wanted to see the wild animals"—and also sent his regrets to Kenya. Instead, he and Brett flew back to London.

Even though Michael fled Africa, Amon N'Djafolk, who'd crowned him King of the Sanwis, paid a surprise visit to Michael to Los Angeles three years later at the time of his marriage to Lisa Marie Presley. The exalted ruler had called Michael the "prodigal child of the Bible" before placing a crown of gold upon his head.

"King N'Djafolk is more than a symbol," Michael said in Los Angeles. "He is the spirit of his people and the father of his subjects. His person is sacred and inviolate."

For some reason, Michael arranged a meeting between the King and attorney Johnnie Cochran, who had not only represented Michael during charges of child molestation, but achieved world fame as the chief defense attorney for O.J. Simpson. The purpose of the Cochran/N'Djafolk meeting was never revealed, but it may have been an attempt to get the attorney to convince Michael to invest his millions into the economy of the emerging nation.

En route to London after the 1992 African trip, Michael received a disturbing report. For every legitimate sale—say, 30,000 copies—of his album *Dangerous*, piracy sales amounted to 800,000 copies. In Thailand alone, piracy sales comprised 98 percent of his record market.

Once in London, speculation about Michael's nose reached a crescendo. In addition to those six rhinoplasties, plus the chin cleft, a virtual laundry list of Michael's other surgeries was being published in the press. He was rumored to have had his upper lip "thinned." Before-and-after pictures of Michael were run, more or less confirming that this was true.

He also was said to have had several face-lifts, although "God only knows why" Joan Rivers said on TV. "It's yours truly who needed the massive face-lift—not Michael Jackson."

He was thought to be trying to replicate the image of Marlene Dietrich in the reconstruction of the contours of his face, which included everything from a "lifting" of the skin covering his forehead to bone grafts on his cheeks and jaw.

He was even rumored to have had several surgeries to remove crow's feet and bags from around his eyes. Why at this relatively young age he needed such massive surgery—more suited to a seventy-year-old—was not reported.

Even though it was believed that he'd gone under the knife any number of times, the press might have grossly exaggerated the extent of the work done on his face.

Michael became particularly outraged when he played to nearly 375,000 fans at London's Wembley Stadium. *The Daily Mirror* was delivered to him at his suite at the Dorchester. The more he read about himself, the more enraged he became. In an article by Rich Syke, Michael was called "Scarface" and a "cruelly disfigured phantom." The article also made the claim of a hole in Michael's nose—"like an extra nostril"—and asserted that one of Michael's cheeks was higher than the other. "Michael now looks like a grotesque burn victim," the article said. "His nose is so deformed it looks like misshapen plastic." Michael ordered his new attorney, the hotshot legal ace Bert Fields, to sue for libel.

In addition to the conventional press, several highly visible websites distributed trenchant comments about the rapidly evolving saga of Michael's fast-changing face. Anomalies-unlimited.com posted the most authentic history of Michael's face. Their "blithering, yet witty commentary" (their description) suggested that in 1987 Michael's face had "gone from a beautiful cocoa bronze to fish belly white—on his nose he now sports little teeny triangles for nostrils and a sharp razor ridge you could grate cheese on." The website suggested that by 1993 Michael's current color —subject to change, of course— was "toilet paper pink" and that his massive plastic surgery could be interpreted as "self-mutilation."

Fans took notice that by 1997 Michael's Kirk Douglas cleft chin had disappeared to be replaced with a fake chin implant. "The sides of his face are stretched taut, his nose isn't pointing north any more, and it's anyone's guess what the hell he did to his skin this time. He's getting his face done at the local morgue. He's a ghoul and seems to be a sick puppy with all this stuff he's done to himself."

By 1999, as Michael turned 41, his fans once again noted a dramatic change in his appearance. Anomalites-unlimited.com now compared Michael to "The Joker," Batman's arch-enemy. "New chin again. Nose again. New cheeks. Smaller jaw. The gaunt look is replaced by rounder fluff. Rumor has it he transplanted some pubic hair to make a goatee in an attempt to butch up, but the thought is too repulsive to dwell on."

At the turn of the millennium, Michael had yet another face, again duly noted on the web. "Oh, this isn't looking good . . . a goatee! Ack! Is that pubic hair? Suddenly, his jaw is an inch longer. He got his eyes pulled so tight he looks

Sporting the Kirk Douglas cleft

Oriental, and they've ceased to line up properly. His lips have a hint of that lizard-lock smile you see on people who have overdone the facelifts. Good thing Japanese Anime cartoons are taking America by storm, so this is kind of fashionable."

By the time Michael turned 42, former admirers were posting on the web news of his "wrecked face." Anomalies-unlimited.com described a "fake-nose-tip prosthesis hanging off as well as scars. The pink little beak nose of 1997 seems to have expanded once again."

The shocking photographs the world saw of Michael, appearing without makeup (could that have been true?) gave him eyes as wide as Joan Crawford. But it wasn't Crawford that Michael was compared to, but her nemesis, Bette Davis, as she looked in *Whatever Happened to Baby Jane?*

Finally, in 2004, a year before his trial on a charge of child molestation, Anomalies-unlimited.com concluded that Michael had gotten a new nose, thanks to the brilliant carving technique of a German plastic surgeon, Dr. Werner Mang. Michael was alleged to have gotten a new nose constructed from cartilage from his ear.

A former publicist, refusing to be named, said, "For a while, Michael didn't really have a nose. It was in 1999 that Dr. Steve Hoefflin, who had done Michael's earlier plastic surgeries, refused to touch up his nose again. In true Jackson style, Michael refused to take no for an answer and went to Europe to get his nose jobs there. Eventually with all of the cauterizing of the blood vessels, there was no circulation to the tip. The tip of the nose eventually turned sort of a black color and began to fall off. He later had a waxy kind of prosthesis made that attached on the end. However, he eventually found a doctor who was able to take some cartilage from his ear and re-sculpt his nose. Some

364

people still believe he has a prosthetic tip, but it's all sculpted now."

As late as Michael's trial in 2005, plastic surgeons around the world were still giving their opinions to the press about the ethics of too much plastic surgery.

While testifying in his defense during a court trial in Santa Monica, Michael removed the surgical mask he routinely wore. He revealed that the tip of nose was scarred and discolored, the skin tissue dangling from it.

"It appears to me that he's had numerous surgeries on his nose, and it appears he's had something to widen his chin, perhaps a chin implant," a leading New York plastic surgeon, Thomas Loeb, told UPI. Dr. Loeb had performed reconstructive surgery on many celebrities, even notorious ones, such as Paula Jones.

On the question of "When is there too much plastic surgery?" both the American Society of Plastic Surgeons and the American Society of Aesthetic Plastic Surgery have refused to discuss the ethics of cosmetic procedures. "The position of the medical profession has been that everything the customer agrees to is fair game so long as the risks are fairly presented," said Steve Miles, a professor of medicine at the University of Minnesota's Center for Bioethics.

Dr. Robert Kotler, who at 61 had performed more than 5,000 procedures during 27 years of practice, wrote a book called "Secrets of a Beverly Hills Cosmetic Surgeon." He was the most outspoken critic of Michael's nasal cosmetic surgery. He boldly stated that, "You can't take a black person and make him white." He went on, "there was a point with Michael where the work looked great. After the second operation it looked good, a marvelous result. If he, in his mind, was unhappy and wanted to continue, no doctor had to go along with a misguided adventure. Jackson was in the wrong in wanting to go beyond what was reasonable, and the doctors who went along with his request, I think didn't exercise their best judgment."

The original Kirk Douglas cleft

Dr. Kotler not only claimed that Michael Jackson "has gone way too far, but Marie Osmond looks perpetually surprised, her eyebrows are a bit high. I think Joan Rivers has reached the limit as to what is reasonable or has gone just a step beyond."

In spite of overwhelming evidence to the contrary and the posting of pictures of Michael's changing face over the years, he was still maintaining, post-millennium, that "I've had two procedures done on my nose—nothing more, nothing less."

Many members of the press were calling Michael's new appearance the "wet shaggy dog look." Strings of wet-looking black hair hung down over his eyes. "In those WWII movies, Veronica Lake adopted the peek-a-boo look with a bang covering her eyes," wrote Betty Fielding. "Michael wouldn't set-

Joan Crawford and Bette Davis in *Whatever Happened to Baby Jane?*

tle for that. He must spend an hour before the mirror each morning getting all that gel just right to make those strings of hair hang just so. His new hair design must have been the creation in Los Angeles of the Queen of All Hairdressers. Or could the stylist have been Michael himself? Bizarre. What's next for Michael? He bleaches his face. Why not go all the way and bleach his hair as well?"

His new look was the most obvious when he showed up at the 1993 Soul Train Awards in Los Angeles to accept three awards. Eddie Murphy greeted him backstage and was astonished to see him in a wheelchair. He told Murphy that he had sprained his ankle while dancing but was going on anyway. On stage he performed his "Remember the Time" song as dancers pranced around him.

Michael walked away with three awards, which he accepted to thunderous applause. "At least he didn't show up in a surgical mask," Murphy told reporters backstage. One journalist claimed that after the ceremony he saw Michael, in the back of the theater, get up out of his wheelchair and walk without a limp to a waiting limousine. That sighting could not be confirmed by other reporters.

Since his face wasn't being worked over and in the process of healing, Michael began to make more appearances, showing up at the Grammy Awards in 1993 to accept a Lifetime Achievement Award. The honor was presented to him by Janet Jackson. Plastic surgery had made her look more and more like her brother. Aware of this, Michael moved in close to her and announced to the audience, "See, me and Janet are really two different people."

The statement was confusing to those who hadn't read the press speculation that Michael had two identities—one when he appeared as a Jackson sister and the other as himself. But it wasn't Janet the speculation whirled around but La Toya. One reporter provocatively asked, "Have you ever seen a picture of Michael and La Toya together?"

Of course, they were two different people, but it was alleged that La Toya had had plastic surgery done to make herself look more like her brother. The resemblance between Michael and La Toya was even greater than the look-alike appearances of Janet and Michael.

Fans were wondering why Michael was popping up everywhere after leading a life as a recluse when not performing. Inquiring minds wanted to know, and an answer emerged.

In the decade since the release of *Thriller*, his popularity had slumped. In a California-based survey of music industry honchos, Michael was placed #14 on a list of stars, far behind such rivals as Madonna or even Janet Jackson herself.

"Michael, by his own hand, had transformed himself into a freak," said one music executive who refused to be named. "Skin bleaching, hyperbaric chambers, the Elephant Man, the fantasy world of Neverland, and the persistent gay issue that was about to explode in his face—it had all become too much. And, to make matters worse, it wasn't just the gay thing. Parts of the world have grown more accepting of gays, and certainly all media attracts thousands of gays. But there were rumors of child molestation that were making the rounds even before the Jordie Chandler press explosion. That was too much. Some of the world—not all—might forgive gay. On the other hand, the suggestion that an artist is a pedophile will make some people go ballistic. But Michael had become such a famous artist, with so many fans around the world, that he'd retain a certain fan base through it all."

Michael also popped up at the NAACP Image Awards. Reporters from black newspapers cornered him, asking him if he had tried to cast a white boy to play himself as a young child in a Pepsi commercial. He'd denied this persistent rumor before, and he would deny it again on that night of the NAACP ceremony. "I'm a black American, and I'm proud of my race. I'm proud of who I am." He would more or less repeat this same statement when cornered by Oprah Winfrey on television.

He also accepted an invitation from the Clintons to attend one of their inaugural balls on January 19, 1993 in Washington. The first daughter, Chelsea, or so it was said, was "ecstatic" upon meeting the King of Pop. Pictures taken of the two of them together have her looking on adoringly.

As part of the event, Michael led an all-star chorus of "We Are the World." Later, he shook hands with the new president, Bill Clinton. Unknown to each of them, both Michael and Clinton would face charges of sexual harassment before the 90s came to an end.

In Washington, Michael checked into the Madison Hotel. Along with him was a young boy (unidentified), one of his "special friends." All that the staff remembered about the visit were requests for the pressing of military costumes and several orders for strawberry ice cream to be delivered to Michael's darkened suite.

The press reported that prior to the Inaugural festivities, Michael had agreed to perform before the newly elected President, but had demanded that the other dozen scheduled balls be cancelled so that "I can be the sole performer." This rumor gained such vogue that Bert Fields, Michael's attorney, had to hold a press conference to deny them. Even so, rumors didn't go away. Oprah Winfrey pointedly asked Michael on TV: "Did you tell President Clinton that you had to be the only person there singing?"

"That's the stupidest, craziest story that I have ever heard," Michael said, barely concealing his anger. "That's not even in my heart. I would never say anything like that."

In spite of all these denials, aides to President Clinton, speaking off the record, said that such a request did arrive "from Michael's people." At this point, the truth can't be confirmed.

Michael's appearances at The Soul Train and Grammy Awards were dwarfed by the audiences who tuned in to watch a televised appearance, at Neverland, with Oprah Winfrey on February 10, 1993. His appearance on this show has become legendary. But in reviewing a transcript years later, it is much tamer than the reports written about it at the time.

Oprah did move in on some delicate topics, but surely this skilled interviewer didn't expect Michael to answer any of her questions truthfully. Among other untruths, he made up love affairs with women, including Brooke Shields, which did not exist, and denied bleaching his skin.

As the world tuned in, Oprah was allowed to ask Michael whatever questions she chose, although she showed remarkable restraint.

Before air time, Oprah was introduced to Jordie

President Bill Clinton and MJ

Chandler, Michael's new "special friend" who would soon file charges of sexual molestation against the King of Pop.

It was estimated that 90 million people around the world watched Oprah fire questions at Michael, making it the fourth most watched show in television history, top place going to the final episode of *M*A*S*H*.

On her show, Michael blamed the press for the stories about the hyperbaric chamber ("it is a lie") and of his attempt to buy the bones of the Elephant Man ("and why would I want some bones?"). What he didn't tell was that he was behind the planting of those stories.

Michael had only good things to say about his family, with one exception. Papa Joe was singled out for condemnation.

"I love my father," he said. "but I don't know him. To me, my mother's just wonderful. She's perfection. I just wish I could understand my father. There were times when he would come to see me and I would get sick both as a child and as an adult."

In a blatant attempt to deceive the public, Michael claimed that his use of plastic surgery "was only two things," admitting to a nose job. He later said, "I've never had my cheekbones done, never had my eyes done, never had my lips done and all this stuff."

When asked if he bleached his skin, Michael pretended that "as far as I know of there is no such thing as skin bleaching. I have never seen it. I don't know what it is. I have a skin disorder that destroys the pigmentation of my skin; it's something that I cannot help. It's in my family. My father said it's on his side."

He may have been suggesting that he had vitiligo, a genetic skin disease. The disease is closely related to albinism. Those who have vitiligo experience the loss of pigmentation in small oval-shaped patches of their skin. That is because skin cells, known as melanocytes, fail to produce and store melanin, which is largely responsible for the uniform pigmentation of the skin.

In the aftermath of the Oprah broadcast, La Toya among others, asserted that Michael had been using bleaching creams for years. Michael's claim that vitiligo runs in his family has never been confirmed.

Oprah even asked him why he grabbed his crotch while performing.

In his reply, Michael wandered. "I think it happens subliminally. If I'm doing a movement and I go 'bam,' and I grab myself . . . it's the music that compels me to do it. You don't think about it . . . it just happens. Sometimes I'll look back at the footage and I go, 'Did I do that?', so I'm a slave to the rhythm."

When asked if he dated, Michael introduced the name of Brooke Shields. He even claimed, as he had before, that he was in love with her. Watching TV with her mother, Brooke reportedly burst into laughter at this revelation.

Michael also admitted that he'd been in love with "another girl," but refused to name her.

Oprah even asked him, "Are you a virgin?" Michael answered, "I'm a gentleman," and therefore was not willing to discuss "something that is private." When pressed for more details, Michael admitted that he was too "embarrassed" to answer the question.

MJ on *The Oprah Winfrey Show*

At one point Elizabeth Taylor appeared from out of the wings, making a surprise visit to the set. In front of the camera, she denied that Michael ever proposed to her. "And I never proposed to him." It was in front of Oprah that Elizabeth delivered her famous and often repeated line: "He is the least weird man I have ever known." She had such bubbling praise about Michael that after the telecast, rumors circulated that she had been paid two million dollars by MJJ Productions for her worldwide endorsement. Again, like so many aspects in the life of Michael Jackson, this rumor cannot be confirmed.

The broadcast ended with Michael taking Oprah on a royal tour of his own Magic Kingdom.

His appearance did not exactly convince the world he was not weird in spite of Elizabeth's glowing enthusiasm. On late-night TV, Jay Leno quipped that "the Elephant Man called and wanted to buy Michael's bones." In a cover story, *Entertainment Weekly* asked a provocative question: CAN YOU BELIEVE THIS GUY?

One scalding critic, on reviewing Michael's performance with Oprah, wrote: "He was obviously lying on camera, but the evidence was right before millions of viewers. No longer a so-called 'Negro,' he was all aglow in an albino whiteness, the ghost-like effect only heightened by the unfortunate choice of a coral-colored lipstick best reserved for an aging Joan Crawford in Technicolor as when she appeared in *Torch Song*."

Special friends such as Jordie Chandler, who had watched Michael's interview with Oprah Winfrey, had to go to school during the day. That often left Michael alone. Sometimes he was photographed with adults, especially his friend of many years, Michael Milken, the notorious "junk bond king" of the 1980s. Milken was another "odd couple" relationship for Michael.

At the peak of his career, Milken earned between $200 and $550 million annually. A United States attorney aspiring to higher office, Rudy Giuliani, went after Milken, charging him with 98 counts of racketeering and fraud. Milken was indicted by a federal grand jury. Entering into a plea bargain, Milken pled guilty to six lesser securities and reporting violations. He was forced to pay $900 million in fines and served only 22 months in prison between 1991 and 1993. Even after his release, he still had one billion dollars of his personal fortune intact.

This impressed Michael. The two men began to hang out together, ostensibly talking about launching an entertainment cable TV network aimed at children.

When criticized for hanging out with Milken, Michael defended him. "Michael Milken is my friend because he has been through the fire, as I have, and emerged better for the process. He has been misunderstood, as I have been, and harshly judged by those who had no right to assume they knew this man without ever spending an hour in his company."

Michael often flew with one of his special friends to Las Vegas where he was seen with not only Milken but with Steve Wynn, the Mirage Casino owner. Michael later said that he liked Las Vegas because "people here don't judge you as they do elsewhere." He could also spend hours at a time playing video games with young boys he flew in, later retreating with these special friends to the privacy of a hotel suite where, in Michael's words, "you can order anything you want, even a pink elephant delivered to the parking lot if that is your desire."

Michael was photographed with Milken and Wynn on a pirate ship during the grand opening of the Treasure Island Hotel. Steve Miller, a former Las Vegas City Councilman, once wrote that his hometown was a perfect place for both Milken and Michael Jackson to use as a haven from the world.

Winfrey "embarrassing" MJ

Even after Michael's trial on a charge of child molestation in 2005, Miller said, "I realize Jackson was found not guilty, but I still like to use the Milken example to show the forgiveness of Nevadans when it comes to prominent people who have had run-ins with the law. After the six-week trial revealed so much about his personal life, it's no doubt Jackson will need a lot of forgiving if he wants to continue his career. But, if he chooses to seek social acceptance in Sin City, he'll be making the right choice!"

That piece of civic boosterism, however, seemed rather fragile after the first charges of child molestation were aired against Michael by Jordie Chandler. As Michael made his way through the casino of the MGM Grand on New Year's Eve in 1993, a drunken crowd greeted him, many with angry shouts. CHILD MOLESTER! PERVERT! SUCK ON THIS, FAGGOT! Yet earlier in the day, he'd signed autographs for several kids.

In a black chador, looking like a repressed Arab woman, a disguise he'd don in the future, Michael toured the MGM Grand Theme Park with Milken. In the evening he was in his braided Sgt. Pepper drag when he showed up at the MGM Grand again to hear Barbra Streisand in concert. Introduced by the great diva, Michael received a thunderous applause, so maybe Steve Miller was right in his assessment of Vegas as "a second chance town."

Although Michael occasionally toured amusement parks with adults who in the past had included not only Milken but also Jackie Onassis, he much preferred to enjoy these attractions with children, whose ranks now included Frank and Eddie Cascio.

Michael, even back in the 80s, had a sharp eye for beautiful boys. Once, when visiting New York, he was introduced to the concierge of New York's Helmsley Palace Hotel, Dominic Cascio. Cascio greeted Michael warmly. During a discussion of the star's needs at the hotel, Michael spotted a picture of Cascio's two sons, Frank and Eddie. They were just babies at the time, but Michael stayed in touch with Dominic and his interest in the boys continued over the years. A meeting was arranged. Michael sent occasional presents to the boys as they grew older. By the time Eddie turned nine and Frank a robust thirteen, they were entertained at Neverland where, it was reported, "they played day and night."

Michael continued his kindnesses to the Cascio brothers while still entertaining Brett Barnes and his new young friend, Jordie Chandler.

The year was 1993, the very same year that Michael would take the young Cascio brothers on a world tour—with their parents' permission, of course. This was a blatant act on Michael's part, as charges of child molestation against him were being aired at that time around the world. But instead of at least trying to be discreet, he openly traveled with these two underage boys and allowed himself to be photographed with them, which only caused more speculation about what he was up to.

Michael Milken

As headlines about Michael and child molestation blazed, he traveled with the two young boys in August, September, and October of 1993. Diane Dimond, the investigative reporter, stated the obvious. "It seemed odd that a man accused of molesting a prepubescent boy would continue to travel with two of them."

She even traced the parents to their home in Franklin Lakes, New Jersey, where they ran Aldo's Restaurant. Both parents, according to the reporter, asserted that "we trust Michael Jackson with our sons."

Michael's main interest was in Frank Cascio, who would later change his name to Frank Tyson. He slept with Michael in his suite whenever they traveled together. In the words of publicist Bob Jones, Michael "adored the young fellow. Michael even had clothes made for Cascio so that the youngster would look just like him. Michael Jackson would even cancel business meetings if Frank instead wanted to go to Disneyland or just play with water guns or just sleep."

Dominic Cascio and his wife, Connie, often traveled on the road with Michael, serving as "advisors" to him. Once, when Bob Jones confronted Michael about the "impropriety" of having the Cascio brothers in his suite, Michael exploded in anger, sending his publicist back to the States from Romania.

The Cascio brothers were a pleasant diversion for Michael, although a life-long friendship would develop with Frank, who would become Michael's trusted aide. But in 1992 and 1993, the one boy who occupied Michael's thoughts both day and night was Jordie Chandler. How could things have gone so wrong between them?

When they had first come together one bright May day in 1992, Michael's world was so very different. Elvis was no longer "The King" since Michael had replaced him on the throne. He presided over his fans as the king of music and was, indeed, a crowned king of a tribe in West Africa. Those were heady times.

When he first gazed into the beautiful face of Jordie, with his dark skin, beautiful hair, delicate eyes, and fine bone structure, the boy looked so innocent and trusting.

Michael, of course, would have no way of knowing that Jordie would have the power to bring Michael's carefully structured kingdom to an end, a drama that would be played out before the world.

"With Michael you can establish in a few days the kind of good friend relationship it takes years to develop with most people. Or at least that's what you believe. He's the opposite of intimidating. He's accessible and vulnerable. You get the feeling that not only would he never hurt you, but also that he's incapable of hurting you.

It's like finding a bird with a broken wing. In some ways Michael's a little broken. You become protective of him. You want to nurse him back to health. You want to make him happy. But deep down a strange phenomenon is taking place.

In believing that you're safe and in control, you let your guard down and become vulnerable to manipulation without realizing it. His ability to sense who you are and how you can be manipulated is highly refined. By the time you figure out that the helpless sparrow is actually a vulture that can rip the meat off your bones, it's too late.

He goes to great lengths to make you believe he's giving and generous. But he's smart and cunning, like a fox on the hunt. You must remain emotionally remote with Michael to be safe. He means business. He's all business.

Nobody controls Michael Jackson. Nobody! He either controls you by manipulating you emotionally or by paying you obscene amounts of money. Either way, you are going to be controlled."

--Evan Chandler

"Unfortunately for Michael, when you reach his level of stardom, there is not much you can do...You are up there alone setting a precedent, making history—a living legend. Many people hate to look up and so they must try to bring him down. It's been the same throughout history, from Mozart to Lennon."

--Adrian Grant from *Michael Jackson: Live and Dangerous*

"He hums things. He can convey it with his voice like nobody. Not just the lyrics, but he can convey the feeling in a drum part or a synthesizer part."

--Bill Bottrell, co-producer of *Dangerous*

374

Chapter Twelve

Driving incognito down Wilshire Boulevard in Los Angeles, Michael's Rolls-Royce broke down. The nearest auto repair shop and car-rental firm was called Rent-a-Wreck. Its owner, David Schwartz, came to offer assistance and was startled to encounter the pop star. Schwartz picked Michael up in his own van and drove him back to his shop, after calling a tow truck to haul the vehicle in for repairs.

In his office, Schwartz called his wife, June. Within minutes she'd arrived at Rent-a-Wreck with her daughter, Lily, age 5, and her 12-year-old son, Jordie Chandler. The startlingly handsome young boy caught Michael's eye. He was instantly smitten.

It was not the first time the man and boy had made contact with each other. After Michael's hair was set aflame in the Pepsi commercial, Jordie had written him a fan letter and Michael had called, thanking Jordie personally for his concern. Jordie also had a younger half-brother, Nikki, the product of his father's marriage to his new wife, Nathalie Chandler.

For most of his young life, Jordie had worshipped Michael Jackson. The boy knew how to moonwalk to the sound of "The Way You Make Me Feel," and the child's grandmother had even knitted him a sequined glove.

Jordie Chandler

At the shop, Michael presented Jordie with a copy of *Dancing the Dream*, a coffee table book published by Doubleday under the supervision of Jackie Onassis in 1992. It was a sappy tome for aficionados only. Elizabeth Taylor wrote the purple introduction, claiming that when she heard the name of Michael Jackson, she thought of "brilliance, of dazzling stars, lasers, and deep emotions." The words didn't sound like the gutsy and irreverent broad we all know and love, the woman who on a winter's night in Gstaad would call Peter Lawford a "cocksucker" for bringing Richard Burton back drunk to her chalet.

After giving Michael his telephone number, Jordie took the book home with him that night and read every word, studying the pictures carefully.

Astonishingly, full-page color photographs appeared of Michael as Julius Caesar (Marc Anthony would have laughed); Henry VIII (Charles Laughton would turn over in his grave); Napoléon (Josephine would have said, "Not tonight!"), and as Romeo (without his Juliet).

In this vanity book, Michael revealed to all the world that, in spite of his pretensions, he was not a poet:

> *Who am I?*
> *Who are you?*
> *Where did we come from?*
> *Where are we going?*
> *What's it all about?*
> *Do you have the answers?*

Jordie Chandler (also known as Jordy or Jordan) was born in January of 1980, making him twenty-two years younger than Michael. His father, Evan Chandler, was a Jewish dentist and aspirant screenwriter in Los Angeles, and his mother, June, came from the Caribbean island nation of St. Vincent and the Grenadines, from black and Chinese ancestors. Their multi-racial son had an extraordinary beauty, as has been frequently reported in the press.

The next day Michael telephoned Jordie and "we talked for hours," the boy would later testify. It was the beginning of a phone romance that would last for weeks, preceding Jordie's actual visit to Neverland.

Beginning with Michael appearing at Rent-a-Wreck, he placed daily phone calls, some lasting three hours, to Jordie. As was later revealed in the police investigation of Michael, these calls began in May of 1992 and lasted until February of 1993, the latter marking the end of the first leg of the *Dangerous* tour.

When not phoning, Michael sent notes: "I have such golden dreams for you. You are my new inspiration."

In late February, Jordie, along with his half sister, Lily, and his mother, June, was invited to Neverland. They would return to Neverland nearly every weekend (Jordie had school during the week). During those early visits, all the Chandlers stayed in the guest house. Invited earlier for a sleepover, and occupying Michael's bedroom in the main house, was Brett Barnes.

Michael began to woo Jordie, Lily, and June with expensive presents. One night at the local branch of Toys "R" Us , which had opened after hours just for them, Michael spent $12,000 on gifts for Jordie and Lily.

During Michael's initial courting of Jordie, it's estimated that he spent

$250,000 on gifts for the family, showering June with such elegant presents as $25,000 in jewelry and Jordie with $20,000 worth of computer equipment.

Michael was obviously buying their friendship and, in the case of Jordie, perhaps his love. One night in FAO Schwarz, the famous toy store of New York, Michael spent more than $75,000 on toys for his friend, although earlier, he'd refused to buy a million-dollar solid gold Monopoly set.

In the civil lawsuit Jordie later filed against Michael, he claimed that it was because of these expensive and lavish gifts that the pop star was "able to seduce the plaintiff and thereby defendant Michael Jackson was able to satisfy his lust, passions, and sexual desires."

June's first concern about Michael was raised in February of 1993 when Jordie and she took a two-hour limo drive to Santa Barbara. A young boy sat in the front seat with Michael. June later reported that Michael hugged and caressed the boy, kissing him often on the ear and cheek—soft, lingering kisses.

She reported that this blatant display ensued during the following day on a three-and-a-half hour drive to Disneyland.

On a spectacular outing on April 9, 1993, Michael flew the Chandlers to Las Vegas, checking them into a lavish $3,500-a-night suite at the swanky Mirage Hotel. After Lily and June had retired for the night, Michael invited Jordie to join him in bed to watch *The Exorcist*. Jordie was horribly frightened by the movie, particularly when the demon-possessed nine-year-old Linda Blair violated herself with a crucifix. Michael cuddled the boy to comfort him and asked him to sleep over with him that night.

Sharing the same three-bedroom suite occupied by Michael and Jordie, June discovered the sleepover arrangement the following morning when she found that Jordie's bed had not been slept in. She went searching and found Michael in red silk pajamas and Jordie in sweatpants sleeping in each other's arms in the pop star's bedroom. Immediately she protested such an arrangement.

According to Jordie's testimony, Michael, in tears, seemed shocked and extremely hurt by her suspicions. He claimed, "We are a loving family. There's nothing wrong with my sleeping with Jordie. You should allow it because it's simple and fun—and you shouldn't set up barricades. You don't trust me? Why can't he sleep in my bed? There's nothing wrong. There's

Nikki and Jordan Chandler

nothing going on."

That night June received an $18,000 diamond-and-ruby bracelet personally delivered by a representative of Cartier's.

Michael's seduction of Jordie began gradually with slight protests. He didn't want Jordie to close the bathroom door when showering. "It's okay for us to be naked with each other," Michael assured the boy. These maneuvers graduated to hugs and long, lingering kisses on the cheek.

Author Victor Gutierrez

Beginning with the incident that occurred with the screening of *The Exorcist*, Michael and Jordie would sleep together in beds from Monte Carlo to Orlando until their intimate relationship came crashing down in flames in July of 1993.

Soon, according to testimony later delivered by Jordie, it was mouth-to-mouth kissing with tongue insertions. At first Jordie's protests brought tears to Michael. "Just because most people believe something is wrong with it doesn't make it so," Michael told the boy. In the nights to follow, again according to Jordie's testimony, both the man and boy took turns lying on top of each other with erections.

Jordie would later reveal some of Michael's private vocabulary—erection was "lights," cum was "duck butter."

In April of 1993 Michael stayed for one month at June's modest home in Santa Monica, sleeping in a bed with her son. Journalists who got news of Michael's relationships with June and Jordie at first misinterpreted it, speculating that Michael was trying to create a ready-made family by marrying June and adopting Jordie as his son. The *National Enquirer* even managed to run a picture of Michael with June, Lily, and Jordie under the banner: JACKO'S NEW FAMILY.

When Evan Chandler dropped by to call on his ex-wife and visit with his son, he was surprised to find Michael in residence. During his visit, Evan snapped a now infamous picture of Michael sitting in Jordie's bedroom. In striped silk pajamas, Michael with stringy black hair is

The infamous exposé

378

wearing a black hat. He'd coated his lips with a very bright ruby-red lipstick, and is in full pancake makeup with a Band-Aid on his nose. He'd applied a thick black eyeliner. The picture was later used as the cover photo on a notorious book, *Michael Jackson Was My Lover: The Secret Diary of Jordie Chandler*, written by Victor M. Gutierrez, an investigative journalist. Instead of white socks that day, Michael wore one sunflower yellow, the other as bright as a Christmas orange.

A bright, well-educated, and concerned parent, Evan was initially suspicious of Michael and the obsessive attention he was showing Jordie. In spite of that, Michael overcame Evan's doubts and for a very brief time the two men bonded. But the relationship almost ended before it had begun. The first time Evan was alone with Michael, the dentist bluntly asked the pop star: "Are you fucking my son up the ass?"

Raymond Chandler, Evan's brother, claimed that "Michael giggled like a schoolgirl, but never batted a false eyelash. 'I never use that word,' he responded."

Michael bragged to Jordie about all the powerful people he knew and promised to introduce the boy to many of them, including Elizabeth Taylor. When he learned that Ronald Reagan was operating out of an office near his Century City condo, he called Reagan's office and solicited an invitation to come by. Ostensibly Michael wanted to welcome the former president to California and to thank him for the hospitality that Nancy and the President had shown to him during his visit to the White House in the 80s.

Surprisingly, Michael's request for a meeting was granted, although Reagan's aide warned Michael to "make the visit short."

Michael arrived at Reagan's office accompanied by Jordie, who sat close to him in the back of a limousine. After a security search by Reagan's Secret Service staff, Michael and Jordie were ushered into the office of the former leader of the Free World.

President Reagan

Jordie had expected to meet an old man and therefore wasn't surprised by Reagan's appearance. But Michael later claimed that, "I was devastated." This was not the leader of charm and grace that Michael had encountered on the White House lawn. Reagan seemed to have aged twenty years, not ten, and Michael was not at all certain that the former president knew who he was.

Reagan knew enough to realize that Michael was a singer, and he seemed to assume that Jordie was the star's son. "I have a son of my own," he informed Michael as if it was a revelation and not a fact known around the world. "He dances in the ballet, or at least I think he does. Maybe not."

The president spoke nostalgically of how Nancy and he would drive along the California coast listening to Michael's music. He claimed that he particularly liked "Surfin' U.S.A." and "Sweet Little Sixteen." Suddenly, Michael realized that Reagan was not talking about him, but The Beach Boys.

To avoid embarrassment, Michael tried to change the subject. He noted a photograph of the White House placed on a shelf near Reagan. Michael picked it up and began to comment on his visit there, perhaps in the belief that it would refresh the president's memory.

Raymond Chandler

Reagan asked to see the picture, staring at it for a long moment. "This house looks familiar," he said. "But I don't think Nancy and I would like to live there. It's too big, too impersonal."

Reagan's mind seemed to wander. To Michael's utter astonishment, he was left with the impression, as he'd later report to friends, that he felt that Reagan did not recognize the White House or even know that he had for eight years been the President of the United States.

After thanking Reagan, Michael retreated, holding the boy's hand as he made his way out of the building. When Michael later learned that Reagan suffered from Alzheimer's disease, he was not surprised.

The most spectacular trip that Michael ever took with Jordie and June, and one that attracted world attention, occurred in Monaco when Michael accepted an invitation to attend the World Music Awards, where he was to be honored as the "World's Best-selling Record Artist of the Era."

Michael's publicist, Bob Jones, related that on the plane from Los Angeles to Paris, "Michael and the young boy were hugging and very close. They held hands and Michael lovingly gazed into the boy's eyes much like a man would gaze into the eyes of a woman he's in love with. He'd kiss him on the cheek, rub his arms, pet him and inexplicably lick the boy's head."

After the plane landed in Nice, the Jackson party flew by helicopter to Monaco where a stretch limousine took them to their $2,500-a-night suite at the Hotel de Paris. Jordie was installed in Michael's quarters, called the Sir Winston Churchill Suite. The next day Michael took Jordie to meet Prince Albert at the palace, with its memories of Grace Kelly. A French newspaper tabloid, perhaps falsely, speculated that Michael asked to purchase some of the wardrobe left by the prince's mother, the late Grace Kelly who'd died in an auto accident in 1982. His offer was politely refused.

380

The royals of Monaco:
Caroline, Albert, and Stéphanie

Throughout most of the trip, Michael stayed locked away in his hotel suite with Jordie. The staff at the Hotel de Paris referred to Michael and Jordie as "the honeymoon couple." Michael instructed his aides to take June on as many *carte blanche* shopping expeditions as she wanted.

At the actual awards ceremony, Michael was to be seated between Prince Albert and the actress Linda Evans. At the last moment, Michael insisted that Linda be moved and Jordie given her seat. Actually Jordie didn't need a seat, as he spent most of the ceremony sitting on Michael's lap in front of 500 million TV viewers around the world. Michael planted frequent kisses on the boy's head. Bob Jones reported that at the actual awards ceremony he heard guests saying, "Did we miss the wedding?"

Reporters in Monaco claimed that Michael, even though in public view, could hardly keep his hands off young Jordan, even running his right hand up and down the boy's leg. An aide to Prince Albert found the "spectacle disgusting!" But Grace Kelly's son had seen it all and didn't indicate the least surprise, at least not publicly.

Princess Stéphanie was overheard saying, "Jackson is out of his mind." As the world looked on, Michael and Jordie giggled; they nuzzled each other's noses, and Michael stroked the boy's hand. At one point Michael's hand moved dangerously close to the boy's crotch.

They were attired in matching outfits, both of them in Johnny Cash black with red armbands like Chinese soldiers. Not only that, but both of them wore mirrored sunglasses.

Jordie was thirteen at the time but looked no more than ten years old. If fans had been aware the boy was actually thirteen, and that he had at least a six-inch penis, Michael's behavior would have been beyond outrageous.

Princess Caroline invited Michael as the guest of honor at a banquet at the palace. Michael did not show up for the dinner, which infuriated her Royal Highness. The daughter of the late Princess Grace was not used to being treated with such lack of respect. At her royal banquet, Caroline vowed that "Michael Jackson is off my guest list forever!" She settled for entertaining Luciano Pavarotti, instead.

While this dinner was taking place, Michael and Jordie remained within their hotel suite. It was later learned that Michael bathed naked with Jordie. This was the first time that either of them had seen the other nude. "Michael

Jordie

Jackson named certain of his young friends who masturbated in front of him," Jordie later testified. "Michael Jackson then masturbated in front of me. He told me that when I was ready, he would do it for me. While we were in bed, Michael Jackson put his hand underneath my underpants. He then masturbated me to climax. After that, Michael Jackson masturbated me many times both with his hand and with his mouth. Michael Jackson told me that I should not tell anyone what had happened. He said this was a secret."

According to Jordie's later testimony, Michael would orally copulate the boy. Or, in Jordie's words, "Michael masturbated me with his mouth." He also testified that Michael "ate my semen."

After Monaco, Michael and the Chandlers flew to Paris for a visit to Euro Disney. Not getting enough of Disney in France, they flew to Orlando, visiting The Magic Kingdom. Later Jordie reported that Michael asked him to "suck on one of his nipples and twist the other one while he masturbated."

In his later testimony, Jordie also claimed that Michael tried "to make me hate my mom and dad." Gradually Michael began to say to Jordie, "I love you." He got Jordie to reply, "I love you, too."

He also got the boy to recite vows such as "Live at Neverland with me forever." Another very revelatory "wish" that Michael got Jordie to recite was "never grow up."

Following June's divorce of Evan in 1985, she received custody of Jordie. Both June and Evan later remarried, not successfully. When Evan began hearing reports of Michael befriending his son, he at first was flattered. There were rumors that he "wanted in on the action," meaning he hoped to benefit financially from Jordie's involvement with Michael. Evan also had a secret wish that Michael, with his MJJ Productions, might help him in his fledgling screen career. Instead of extracting teeth, Evan wanted to write screenplays, as did many other people in Hollywood.

He'd already sold one script to Mel Brooks, the comedy director. Jordie had given his father the idea for *Robin Hood: Men in Tights*, which was filmed as a spoof of Errol Flynn's successful 1938 version of *The Adventures of Robin Hood*. The film that Evan wrote bombed at the box office, but nonetheless, the dentist still clung to his dream.

As stipulated within his custody arrangement with June, Jordie eventually showed up to spend a week with his father. To Evan's surprise, his son was accompanied by Michael.

Evan was shocked when Michael announced that he was going to share Jordie's bed. Against his better judgment, and although he found it troubling, the father did not object to this. He later said, "What father in his right mind wouldn't suspect something?"

During his visit, Evan quizzed his son when Michael went to take a shower, asking him if there had been any intimate contact between Michael and himself. Jordie denied that his relationship with the star was sexual, but Evan suspected that his son was concealing the truth.

On the morning of the third sleepover, Evan discovered his clothed son sleeping with a pajama-clad Michael whose left hand rested on his son's covered crotch.

That day Jordie and Michael, even in the presence of Evan, showed extreme familiarity with each other. Jordie had never been that affectionate with his own father. But Evan wondered if it were more than affection as he watched the man and boy play together like children. Evan asked himself a painful question: "Is Jordie in love with Michael?"

Even so, Evan did not move to put an end to the relationship, as he allegedly viewed Michael as a "cash cow." He even asked Michael to build an extension onto his home. When the zoning board would not allow that, Evan asked Michael to buy him a larger house. Michael indicated that he might do that.

But in the days and weeks that followed, Michael stopped showing up at Evan's house with Jordie. In fact, an entire month went by that Jordie did not even call his father.

Evan was growing despondent and troubled over Michael's intimate relationship with his son. In his diary he wrote that he felt "alienated, sad and frightened" about his son, especially when he learned that Jordie had made several unsupervised visits to Neverland.

Disturbing news reached Evan that June was going to withdraw Jordie from St. Matthew's School and allow him to accompany Michael on the second lap of the *Dangerous* tour that autumn. Feeling cut off from Michael, who had ceased to visit and call, as well as from Jordie, Evan decided to battle June for custody rights. Perhaps he hoped that would get Michael to pay him some attention and listen more attentively to his requests, especially about his screenwriting career.

Evan called a famous attorney in Century City, Los Angeles, Barry Rothman, who did not specialize in custody issues. A well-known entertainment lawyer, Rothman specialized in making deals for

Geraldine Hughes

rock groups or even rock stars. His legal secretary, Geraldine Hughes, later wrote a pro-Michael Jackson book called *Redemption*, published in 1997. In her revelations, she was highly critical of her former boss. "Although I have never met a real-life demon straight out of the pits of hell," she wrote, "after encountering Mr. Rothman I knew what it would feel like."

In *Redemption*, Geraldine claims that Evan "admitted to hiring Mr. Rothman because of his unethical business dealings. He [meaning Dr. Chandler] needed someone that did not mind bending and/or breaking the rules."

Somehow Michael learned that Evan was consulting a lawyer. Michael knew of Rothman's reputation in the music industry, and feared having to deal with him on a confrontational basis.

Michael called his lawyer, Bert Fields, to alert him that there might be trouble ahead and to warn him to stand by "to put out brush fires." To an increasing degree, Michael was relying on this Harvard-educated celebrity attorney who had represented many stars, including The Beatles, Warren Beatty, Dustin Hoffman, John Travolta, and Tom Cruise.

After the warning, Fields did what many a movie star did when he or she gets into trouble. He hired the notorious Anthony Pellicano.

Pellicano had been L.A.'s favorite celebrity detective for years. "When the stars need a wise-guy to leave a dead fish and a rose on somebody's windshield, *allegedly*, they know who to call," wrote Bob Sheffield in *L.A. Confidential*. As a Sunset Boulevard gumshoe, no one came near topping the behind-the-scenes chicanery of Pellicano.

Michael viewed him as "just the man" to deal with Evan. Over the years Tom Cruise would call Pellicano for his services, as would Sylvester Stallone, Rosanne Barr, Kevin Costner, and Farrah Fawcett. Other clients would include "bloody glove" cop Mark Fuhrman of the O.J. Simpson murder case and Michael's future mother-in-law, Priscilla Presley.

Pellicano had been involved in everything from the investigation of the JFK assassination to Steven Seagal's alleged mob ties. He made a reputation for himself as one of Richard Nixon's tape experts during the Watergate trials. If someone in Hollywood threatened to sue a star, Pellicano was called in to dig up dirt on the accuser.

The son of Sicilian immigrants, he grew up in the seedy, criminal-laden Chicago suburb of Cicero in the 1950s.

Elizabeth Taylor had already endorsed Pellicano. In 1977, grave robbers dug up the body of Taylor's third

Anthony Pellicano

Elizabeth Taylor, Mike Todd

husband, Mike Todd, ostensibly looking for a 10- carat diamond ring that was widely believed to have been buried with him. After a well-publicized search, Pellicano discovered the missing body in the Forest Park cemetery in Illinois, where it lay hidden under a canopy of dead leaves. After that, Elizabeth sang the praises of Pellicano and helped launch his career as a private investigator. In time, Pellicano's clients even included the *National Enquirer*.

When Michael and Pellicano came together, both were at the peak of their careers.

But in February of 2006, Pellicano would make national headlines when he, along with six others, was indicted on a charge of conspiring to wiretap, blackmail, and intimidate dozens of celebrities, including Sylvester Stallone. The 220-count federal indictment outlined a web of payoffs to police, high-tech eavesdropping, and other skullduggery.

Before that, on November 21, 2002, FBI agents in Los Angeles raided Pellicano's offices, finding two practice grenades modified to function as homemade bombs as well as enough military grade C-4 plastic explosives to take down a passenger jet.

After his arrest, Pellicano pleaded guilty to illegal possession of danger-ous materials and was sentenced to thirty months in federal prison. Theoretically, his release had been scheduled for February 4, 2006, but on February 3, based on a new indictment of charges of wiretapping and racket-eering, he was transferred to the Los Angeles County Jail.

Meanwhile, during ongoing negotiations with Fields, Evan regained cus-tody of his son for one week, beginning on July 12, 1993.

Fields had worked out this agreement, and it was endorsed by Michael. But, unknown to Michael, Evan wanted private time with his son to gather more information about his relationship with the pop star.

During the week Jordie lodged with his father, one of his teeth was extracted on July 16.

A pivotal moment in the drama came when Jordie sat in his dental chair. If later testimony is to be believed, Jordie revealed to Evan that Michael had touched his penis. Later Evan would be accused of "planting" the idea of molestation in Jordie's head while the boy was under anesthesia. Evan consis-tently denied this accusation.

"I know everything," Evan said, lying to his son. "I know about the kiss-ing, the jerking off—and the blow jobs." He claimed that he'd bugged Jordie's bedroom on those nights he'd spent with Michael in Evan's house. Threatening his son, he warned him, "If you lie to me, I'm going to take Jackson down." Looking frightened, Jordie burst into tears. Between sobs, he admitted to having had sex with Michael.

When the charges against Michael were later made public, Jordie's visit to his dentist father became a media event. Writing in *GQ* magazine in October of 1995, Mary Fischer claimed, "In the presence of Dr. Chandler and Mark Torbiner, a dental anesthesiologist, the boy was administered the controversial drug, Sodium Amytal. It was after this session that the boy first made his charges against Jackson."

Doctors have claimed that patients are very liable to emotional manipulation after taking Sodium Amytal. Ray Chandler, Jordie's uncle, would later claim that his nephew was not given Sodium Amytal that day. A search of Dr. Torbiner's records show that Jordie was administered doses of Robinul and Vistaril instead.

Since Jordie had been taken from him, Michael was seen once again with Brett Barnes, shopping the real estate market in Beverly Hills. In addition to Neverland, Michael said he wanted a "real house—not just a condo"—closer to his business interests in Los Angeles.

The real estate agent later reported that she had no idea at the time that Michael was in any kind of legal trouble. "He chased the young boy through the house and at one point they collapsed on each other in a pile on the floor, giggling and tickling each other's ribs. They seemed to be having a romp. But within days I heard of the child molestation charges. I just naturally assumed that the boy house-hunting with Michael was Jordie Chandler, only to learn later it was the Brett Barnes kid."

In spite of Michael's obsession with Jordie, which consumed his nights and most of his waking hours, his career continued. *Free Willy* was released into movie houses, depicting a boy's effort to free a whale from a theme park. This was the first release for Michael on his new MJJ Records label, featuring "Will You Be There," the film's theme song.

The song rose rapidly on *Billboard's* charts, the film becoming a sleeper hit. Michael showed it to Jordie a dozen times, neither man nor boy tiring of it. Each night before Jordie fell asleep, Michael inserted his tongue into Jordie's ear, then sang the lyrics of the song to him.

In our darkest hour
In my deepest despair
Will you still care?
Will you be there?

Michael had decided to change the name of his record company from Nation Records to MJJ Records. He was furious when his sister released *Janet Jackson's Rhythm Nation 1814*, feeling Janet had "taken the word nation for herself."

Evan did not return Jordie to the care of his mother at the appointed time, and, through Rothman, demanded that June sign a stipulation which would forbid Jordie from any further communication with Michael. June signed the agreement. Even so, Evan refused to return the boy once he had June's signature on the agreement. Later, June claimed that she was cajoled and manipulated into signing.

Geraldine, Rothman's legal secretary, revealed that since August 16, 1993, Evan had been negotiating with Michael "for money in exchange for not going public with the suspicion of child molestation."

In court, June prevailed, and Evan was ordered to return Jordie to his mother. Increasingly desperate, Evan played a dangerous card, at least from Michael's point of view. Evan took the child not back home to his former wife but to see a psychiatrist, Dr. Mantis Abrams.

For Michael, as events subsequently revealed, this would become a fatal blow to his reputation.

Dr. Abrams became Jordie's psychiatrist. Their first session together on August 17, 1993 lasted for more than three hours. Under intensive questioning, Jordie admitted that Michael, in the words of the psychiatrist, "orally copulated" Jordie but "he did nothing oral to MJ and nothing anal happened."

In Florida, Jordie alleged that he protested sexual contact with Michael, but was threatened that if he ever told anyone "about what we did, you'll be sent to a juvenile hall for punishment." According to the psychiatrist's report, Michael revealed to Jordie the names of "other boys I've done this with."

After hearing Jordie's testimony, Abrams was bound by California law to report the boy's charges to the Los Angeles Department of Children's Services. Jordie was called in for intensive interviewing by staff member Ann T. Rosato. After grilling him, Rosato was convinced that he was telling the truth, that Michael was committing sex acts with the boy.

The Los Angeles police were also called into the investigation. Officers known only as "E. Cateriano" and "J. Calams" arranged for Jordie to be interviewed by them as well. In their report to their superiors, the two officers concluded, "The boy is telling the truth."

Police and prosecutors in Santa Barbara began an investigation of Michael to determine if he were indeed a pedophile and had engaged in sexual activities with minors. If convicted of such charges, of course, a man could go to jail.

June's husband, David Schwartz, and Evan were on friendly terms, even though both men had married the same woman. Evan learned from Schwartz that his marriage to June was unraveling. "I rarely see her," Schwartz claimed. "She spends all her time with Michael."

In a conversation taped by Schwartz, Evan is heard telling him, "Jackson is an evil guy. If I go through with this and blow the whole thing wide open, I win big time. I will get everything I want. She [meaning June] is going to lose Jordie, and Michael's career will be over. He has June in his pocket. She likes the glitzy life that he can provide for her too much to give it up. I'm convinced she'll allow Jackson sexual access to our son again. I will be granted custody and June will have no rights whatsoever."

Howard Weitzman
and Anthony Pellicano

In a further comment, Evan claimed that "Jackson is going to be humiliated beyond belief. He will not believe what will happen to him. It'll be beyond his worst nightmare. He will not sell one more record. The facts are so overwhelming. Everyone will be destroyed in the process."

Fields, Michael's attorney, helped June obtain a court order that demanded the return of her son.

But through his attorney, Evan countered with a court order of his own, forbidding June to allow Jordie to accompany Michael on the *Dangerous* tour. With Michael hovering in the background, the battle lines over Jordie were forming.

On August 4, 1993, Evan, with Jordie at his side, met Michael and Pellicano in a suite at the deluxe Westwood Marquis Hotel in Los Angeles. Evan later wrote, "Michael looked Jordie straight in the eyes, smiled, and denied charges of sexual molestation. It was a chilling smile—like the smile you see on a convicted serial killer who perpetually declares his innocence despite the mountains of evidence against him. I knew it right then. Michael Jackson had not only molested my son but he was a criminal! It was suddenly all so obvious—June had been fooled, Jordie had been fooled, I had been fooled—the ENTIRE WORLD has been fooled by this fragile, pitiful creature with an absolutely brilliant criminal mind."

For some mysterious reason, Evan's attorney, Rothman, did not attend the meeting, which lasted five minutes. But Evan reported to Rothman later, and, from all reports, the two men agreed to seek $20 million in punitive damages from Michael. Hearing of this offer, Pellicano presented a counter-offer: to purchase three of Evan's screenplays over a three-year period for $350,000 each. Evan rejected the offer as too little. When he delivered additional demands to Pellicano, the detective was astonished—"and I've seen it all."

Evan wanted a trust fund set up for Jordie for $20 million. But that wasn't all. He also demanded that Michael purchase four of his screenplays for $5 million each.

Michael told Pellicano that "I don't want to pay one cent to the Chandlers. If anybody pays, let it be my insurance company."

Based on his perception that Fields needed a back-up attorney, Michael hired Santa Monica lawyer Howard Weitzman, one of the most influential attorneys in America, to work with Fields. His list of celebrity clients included Marlon Brando, Magic Johnson, O.J. Simpson, and Arnold Schwarzenegger.

On August 20, 1993, at the debut of the most disastrous trip of his life, Michael flew to Bangkok for the second part of his *Dangerous* globetrotting. This time there would be no Jordie flying with him.

Two and a half weeks after the Westwood Marquis confrontation, Michael checked into a luxurious suite at the Hotel Oriental in Bangkok.

News of the child molestation allegations first reached the world when KNBS in Los Angeles broadcast the revelation of the police raids on Neverland and on Michael's Century City condo.

"Pop star Michael Jackson is the subject of a criminal investigation by the Los Angeles Police Department," came the startling news over the radio. At first listeners didn't know that the investigation was based on a charge of sexual molestation from a young boy. That tantalizing piece of news was actually revealed by Pellicano himself.

The detective went before television floodlights to deny all charges. He suggested it was part of an extortion attempt. He also noted that this was but one of some three dozen attempts that cropped up every year to extort money from Michael. He also claimed that the family of the young boy was attempting to milk $20 million from Michael.

Evan was furious, angrily denying he was a blackmailer. Instead he portrayed himself as a "morally offended parent" who wanted to protect his son from further sexual advances from Michael.

IS PETER PAN THE PIED PIPER IN DISGUISE? asked one headline. *Newsweek* raised another provocative question, IS HE DANGEROUS OR JUST OFF THE WALL?

Only hours before, the police had raided both Neverland and Michael's lavish condo in Century City. Armed with search warrants, the police were looking for evidence that he was a child molester. Accompanying the officers was a locksmith with instructions to break into Michael's secret playroom at Neverland where in most cases only his special friends—usually young white boys—were permitted to go.

Police seized evidence, including boxes of photographs and video tapes. Among the possessions the police hauled away was a picture book, *The Boy: A Photographic Essay*, featuring prepubescent boys with their undeveloped penises exposed.

Within his Bangkok suite, Michael's telephone was urgently ringing. It was his criminal attorney, Howard Weitzman, calling from Los Angeles with some very disturbing news.

Michael listened intently in stunned disbelief to the details of the raids on Neverland and his condo.

"I love children," Michael shouted into the phone at Weitzman. "The whole world knows that. How could they do this to me?"

After his discussion with Weitzman, Michael went on a rampage, breaking chandeliers and upturning and smashing furniture in his suite, even tossing vases of fresh flowers out the window.

"He came unglued," reported a staff member at the hotel. "When I was delivering a tray to the room, I spotted the American entertainer running screaming from room to room. He looked like a crazy man. I put down the tray and fled from the room. The entire suite was a wreck. I reported it to the manager so he could assess damages."

At first, reporters in Los Angeles rallied to Michael's defense when polls showed that only twelve percent of the public believed the accusations against Michael. Most TV viewers felt that he was the victim of extortion.

Shortly thereafter, a staff member of the television show *Hard Copy* claimed that a representative of Papa Joe, Michael's father, had approached the show and asked $150,000 for him to appear before the camera to talk about Michael's legal troubles. When *Hard Copy* turned that down, Papa Joe's staff made a counteroffer of $50,000. But negotiations broke down because the TV studio wanted Katherine to appear with her husband, and Papa Joe could not produce his wife.

One staff member said, "Maybe old Joe could come on and tell how he used to frighten little Michael by telling him there were bad men in the audience with guns who would shoot him onstage if he didn't make the right moves. I don't know why my boss insisted on Katherine, who was known for sweeping everything under the rug and prevaricating."

Jordie's name was initially withheld from the media because he was a minor.

Even so, everybody who knew Michael

Eddie Reynoza

390

Corey Feldman

Jackson, and many who didn't, seemed to take to the air waves to deliver their opinions on radio and TV about Jordie's accusations. The most sensational charges emerged from Eddie Reynoza, who charged that "Michael Jackson raped me when I was 16 years old." The boy claimed that he was auditioning for a music video when Michael spotted him. In his 1993 charges, Eddie claimed that he was "drugged, dumbed down with alcohol, and sexually assaulted."

Eddie went to the police and the press with charges of his rape, but some journalists attacked his credibility. Today, Eddie, an actor, is hoping to see a television movie made of his story, with his alleged rape by Michael being the centerpiece of the plot.

As a rising young child actor, Corey Feldman, who has appeared in more than 100 feature films, said that Michael befriended him when he was a young boy. Feldman claimed that the pop star never molested him or touched him inappropriately.

But he did reveal in an interview on *20/20* that he felt some of Michael's actions were questionable. He charged that Michael tried to persuade him to look at nude magazines.

In a sensational interview, Feldman revealed that he had been one of a group of child actors in Hollywood who were preyed upon and "molested by a gang of Hollywood pedophiles." He did not name Michael as part of that group. The former child star did admit to sleepovers with Michael, including one in a hotel room when Michael slept on a cot, giving Feldman the bed. "I was molested as a child but not by Jackson," Feldman said.

Known for his roles in such movies as *Gremlins*, Feldman ended his friendship with Michael in 2001. Later he released "Megalo-Man," a song highly critical of the pop star.

On the verge of a nervous breakdown, Michael managed to get through his first performance in Bangkok, but he had to lip-sync his way through the show, much to the disappointment of dozens of fans who realized what he was doing. "I could have stayed home and listened to my CD instead of seeing him live," said one disgruntled fan, who demanded that the box office return the hefty price he'd paid for a ticket.

Just hours before his scheduled second appearance on stage in Bangkok, Michael canceled the show. A doctor reported that Michael had succumbed to the heat and humidity prevalent in Thailand. The singer reportedly had become dehydrated. The doctor ignored the fact that Bangkok was experiencing unseasonably cool weather, and that the auditorium where Michael was scheduled to appear was climate controlled.

Within his Thai hotel suite, Michael ingested inordinate amounts of Valium and Percodan, which were mixed with his regular painkillers. A maid reported to the press that she'd come upon the star in his bedroom. "He was crouched in a fetal position," she claimed. "He was actually sucking on his thumb like a little baby."

In a call to his mother, Katherine, Michael warned her that he'd commit suicide rather than face arrest. Michael's chief of security in Thailand, retired police officer, Bill Bray, placed a 24-hour suicide watch on Michael, taking his threat to kill himself very seriously.

On August 25, 1993, Michael placed a call to Elizabeth Taylor, pleading for her help. The star told him that she believed he was innocent and begged him to be strong and not harm himself. She promised to fly to his side. Significantly, Michael turned to Elizabeth instead of Katherine, his mother.

Having survived an emotionally turbulent relationship with actor Montgomery Clift, among countless others, Taylor was an old hand at playing Fairy Godmother and Maternal Savior, taking troubled young men, often homosexually oriented, and pressing them into the warmth of her ample and much-photographed bosom.

From Bangkok, Michael flew to Singapore for the continuation of his concert tour, arriving there in a fragile state.

Meanwhile, dressed in a white sweat suit, Larry Fortensky stood by the side of his bride, Elizabeth, as she spoke to journalists during her long flight to Singapore. Clad in a sweat suit herself—only hers was baby pink—Elizabeth said, "This is the most awful thing that could happen to a man like Michael who loves children and would never harm one of them. I believe that Michael will be vindicated." She went on to claim that Michael was "the victim of extortion."

At the Singapore airport, at 2am, Larry and Elizabeth, "with a ton of luggage," were seen getting into a limousine which took them to a penthouse suite at the Raffles Hotel, one of the ten most famous in the world. Leaving Larry to sleep off the flight, Elizabeth went at once to see Michael across the hall.

Elizabeth arrived in Michael's suite at 3:30 that morning. She found him sucking his thumb "and curled up like a two-year-old boy in his bed."

She dismissed the guards, telling them that "the suicide watch is over. I'll take charge." She surmised that Michael had taken an overdose of painkillers, which had caused him to go berserk. He would not be the only friend of this Golden Age Hollywood star who had done that.

She urged him to fly to the Betty Ford Clinic, where she'd met her present husband, Larry, then an inmate there, too. But Michael told her, "I have no intention of ever setting foot in Los Angeles again."

He seemed revitalized the following day, his birthday (August 29), when Elizabeth gave him a party to celebrate his turning thirty-five. She even got him to eat a piece of birthday cake, as he'd suffered a dramatic weight loss and was living on cups of vegetable broth.

That night, in front of his Singapore fans at the National Stadium, all 45,000 of them sang "Happy Birthday, Michael." His only reaction was to turn to one of his managers, "Isn't that song copyrighted? Will I have to pay royalties?"

The following night, he could not go on. Sobbing hysterically and threatening suicide, he fainted and the performance was canceled. In a local hospital, Michael underwent a brain scan to try to determine why he was suffering "from history's worst case of migraines." No physical cause could be determined by the presiding physicians.

After Singapore, Michael, along with Larry and Elizabeth, flew to Taiwan. Papa Joe and Katherine, along with Michael's brothers, each having flown in as a gesture of support for Michael, were waiting to greet their errant son.

Katherine hosted a family luncheon for Michael, to which she pointedly did not invite Elizabeth and Larry.

Perhaps feeling rebuffed, the Fortenskys flew back to Los Angeles. Elizabeth had been angered by remarks that Katherine allegedly told a reporter when boarding a plane in Los Angeles. "I'm his mother—not Elizabeth Taylor—and I'm flying to the side of my son, even though I'm not *Cleopatra* reincarnate."

Much of *tout* Hollywood continued to rally behind Michael, including Sharon Stone speaking at the MTV Awards in Los Angeles. "I firmly believe

Frank Cascio and MJ

that if this family has—or ever had—evidence of abuse, it would have surfaced by now. All I know is that if a child of mine had been abused, I would not have been making deals."

Back in Los Angeles, Evan Chandler was working day and night to bring down Michael. Evan had obtained a high profile lawyer, the "fighting attorney," Gloria Allred, to represent Jordie. She immediately called a press conference, announcing that her thirteen-year-old client was "more than ready, more than willing, and more than able to confront his molester in court."

This ballsy attorney perhaps was too aggressive for the Chandlers. She really wanted a criminal suit against Michael, whereas the Chandlers preferred civil action so that damages could be claimed. The attorney charged that such a strategy would make the parents look too "money grubbing." Allred was removed from the case, and a more modest but also competent attorney, Larry Feldman, was hired instead.

On September 14, 1993, Feldman filed a civil suit for Jordie. He was in the eighth grade, aged thirteen.

In Jordie's civil complaint, Michael was charged with:

(1) sexual battery
(2) battery
(3) seduction
(4) willful misconduct
(5) intentional infliction of emotional distress
(6) fraud
(7) negligence

As this suit was being filed, Michael, in another part of the world, confronted soaking rain and large crowds as he marched with Russian soldiers in Red Square with the Kremlin in the background. A large banner (in English) was unfolded for his benefit: MICHAEL, RUSSIA LOVES YOU!

Flying to Tel Aviv, Michael met a different set of people. Although many citizens of Israel are as liberal as some of their counterparts in New York, others are staunchly conservative and almost violently anti-homosexual.

Flaunting convention, and under indictment on charges of child molestation, Michael landed in Israel with the Cascio brothers, Eddie, 9, and Frank, 13, in tow. When they went to visit the Wailing Wall in Jerusalem, angry protesters threw stones at them. The trio fled into a waiting limousine which was also pelted with stones as it made its get-away. En route to their hotel, signs greeted Michael: GO HOME, PERVERT. YOU'RE AN ABOMINATION!

Under pressure, the American Friends of the Hebrew University, originally planning to give Michael the Scopus Award for his humanitarian activities around the world, abruptly withdrew the honor they were about to bestow on him.

Not all the people of Israel agreed with these arch conservatives. It was estimated that some 85,000 fans filled a local auditorium at two sold-out concerts. One student outrageously proclaimed Michael as "our new Messiah. He's come back to Earth to save us!"

In Los Angeles, Michael's attorneys, Fields and Weitzman, denied that he was "in hiding" in the French Alps to avoid arrest in California. Actually, he was.

Desperately needing a rest, Michael, in a break on the *Dangerous* tour, accepted an invitation to fly to Geneva, where he was driven with the Cascio brothers to the chic enclave of Gstaad and Elizabeth Taylor's luxurious villa where she'd previously romped with Richard Burton, other husbands, and lovers.

Michael, Frank, and Eddie were guarded by Elizabeth's security force, each of whom earned one hundred dollars a day. At this point, Michael's addiction to painkillers reached dangerous levels. "He was a ticking time bomb," one of Elizabeth's security guards leaked to the press. "A male version of Marilyn Monroe flirting dangerously with death, almost inviting it."

In Gstaad, Michael was informed that his trusted aide, Norma Staikos, was being sought by the police for questioning. He demanded that she be given tickets to her native Greece. Staikos flew there and into exile, far from the authorities in Santa Barbara.

When queried about why a key witness, Norma Staikos, the duenna of Neverland, had flown away, Howard Weitzman said, "I know she's coming back, and I've told this to the police. To use the word 'flee' is egregious."

The *National Enquirer* managed to obtain an exclusive interview with Jordie. The boy was quoted as saying, "I imagine Michael Jackson is pretty scared right now, really scared. And he should be, because what he did to me is a really bad thing."

When Michael left Elizabeth's villa in Gstaad, he was confronted with about a dozen angry mothers holding up signs. One read: SAVE OUR CHIL-

DREN. Another in bold red letters demanded: PIED PIPER, LEAVE OUR BOYS ALONE! Yet another merely requested that Michael: GO HOME!

Abandoning Gstaad, Michael and the Cascio boys flew to Buenos Aires aboard a red-winged 747, a private jet, to continue the course of the *Dangerous* tour. They checked into a marble-clad mansion which Michael had rented for $12,000 a day. The villa, administered by the nearby Park Hyatt Hotel, was often reserved for visiting heads of state.

Daringly and provocatively, as if flaunting the charges against him, Michael

MJ and Norma Staikos

395

appeared on the balcony of the mansion, in his pajama top, with Frank and Eddie. The brothers, "looking cuter than any two boys have the right to," in the words of one woman journalist, waved to the crowds.

A few moments later, after they'd retreated inside, Michael reappeared. At least his arm, still clad in pajamas, reappeared. He waved a copy of *Child*, a magazine for parents, at reporters who seemed shocked at such outrage.

Johnnie Cochran

Back in Los Angeles, because of the hysteria generated by his case, Jordie temporarily dropped out of school. He was grilled by psychiatrists, questioned by prosecutors, and "trial rehearsed" by his attorneys. Later, Evan discovered a picture that his son had drawn of himself. It depicted Jordie on the roof of a tall building ready to jump to his death. It was later reported that this was not necessarily a suicide drawing but an expression of fear on Jordie's part at being forced to testify against his formerly close sleepover buddy.

Michael's attorney, Bert Fields, antagonized authorities by firing off a letter to the police commission. He charged the police with using "scare tactics and intimidation" in the young boys they questioned. Not only Jordie, but Brett Barnes, Wade Robson, and Macaulay Culkin. The press reacted with astonishment to Fields' next move: He filed a motion in Santa Barbara, asking that the case against Michael Jackson be postponed for six years. At that time the statute of limitations would have run out, and the Chandlers would have no case, not even a criminal one.

Meanwhile, Michael's lawyers were concerned with more than just "little boys coming out from under rocks to tell nasty tales about Michael," as one member of Michael's legal team claimed. A business deal was concluded with EMI, which announced a five-year agreement to administer Michael's rich ATV publishing catalogue, which included all of those Beatles hits. The deal called for Michael to get $40 million upon signing what potentially could be a $100 million—*plus*—transaction.

Both Fields and Weitzman advised Michael to fly to Los Angeles to face charges. Michael reportedly "threw a fit" when neither Fields nor Weitzman could assure him that he would not be arrested if he set foot on American soil. Michael's trusted security aide, Bill Bray, denounced Fields for hiring Pellicano, who, according to Bray, "is far too notorious to put on this case." Bray urged Michael to hire Johnnie L. Cochran, "the best black lawyer in America when it comes to something criminal."

396

The next stop on the tour was Puerto Rico, a U.S. territory, of course, and there were genuine fears that Federal agents might come aboard the plane and remove Michael in handcuffs to be photographed before the world's paparazzi. "Even the *New York Times* would run that picture on its front page," Michael predicted.

Michael, deeply addicted to Codeine, Percodan, and Demerol, continued to call Fields daily with the same question: "Will I be arrested if I fly back to America?"

Instead of Puerto Rico, Michael opted instead to fly into Mexico City on October 24, ordering his attorneys, Fields and Weitzman, to join him there to plot strategy. Michael also requested that his dermatologist, Dr. Arnold Klein, join him in Mexico City as well.

As part of a tantalizing detail whose implications would extend deep into Michael's future, he also invited Dr. Klein's assistant to fly to Mexico too. A tough woman, known as a "biker babe" or "motorcycle mama," Debbie Rowe would become Michael's second wife and the bearer of two of his children.

Dr. Klein is an internationally renowned dermatologist. Michael could find no greater expert on skin disorders in America. In the early days of the AIDS crisis, Dr. Klein was the first physician to diagnose a case of Kaposi's sarcoma in Southern California, which marked the beginning of a life-long commitment to fighting the disease. This commitment established a dialogue with Dame Elizabeth. Klein eventually helped establish the Elizabeth Taylor Center for AIDS Research, Treatment and Education at UCLA.

Word was spreading that Jordie had identified "marks" on Michael's genitalia, and that the pop star wanted Klein to "disguise the evidence." Reportedly, Michael went into a "screaming rage" when he learned that the Santa Barbara police could force him to undergo a strip search.

Dermatologist
Dr. Arnold Klein

On November 8, 1993, while the Jacksons were attending Samuel Jackson's funeral—he was Michael's grandfather—police raided Hayvenhurst in Encino. With a search warrant, more than a dozen officers fanned out through the premises, including Katherine's bedroom. But mainly their attention focused on Michael's bedroom which he no longer used, having more or less abandoned it and many of its contents.

All the dolls, fancily dressed mannequins, and expensive toys were left just as they were the day Michael moved to Neverland. Katherine had insisted on this. Before the raid ended, the police had rounded up seventy-five boxes of evidence, including videotapes, magazines, and photographs belonging to Michael.

Distraught and suicidal once again, Michael called Elizabeth at her home in Los Angeles, pleading with her to come to Mexico City "to rescue me." Within eleven hours, Elizabeth and her construction worker hunk, Larry Fortensky, were flying south. In Mexico, the Fortenskys discovered that Michael was suffering a complete nervous breakdown. The night before, Michael had overdosed on Percodan.

Sleeping in the room next to him, Elizabeth maintained a 24-hour suicide watch until Michael pulled through this latest crisis. Once again, she urged him to admit himself to the Betty Ford Clinic.

The hotel manager later told the press that he had to send three of the hotel's security guards to Michael's suite to subdue him. "He was threatening to jump out the window. He was butting his head against the stucco walls. There was blood on the walls. He'd vomited on the expensive Oriental rugs. The guards managed to hold him down as he struggled. 'Let me kill myself,' he shouted. 'I want to die!'"

Later, when he seemed under reasonable control, Michael took magic markers and began to write his initials, MJ, over all the walls and on every surface. One of the security guards called the manager, who said Michael should be allowed to continue. "If that will subdue him, let him go for it. I'll bill him—and bill him good—when he checks out of this hotel to the relief of everybody."

Somehow by November 12, Michael was able to perform at his final concert in Mexico City, delivering a lackluster performance and acknowledging the Fortenskys as his special guests of honor. But instead of going on to San Juan, which his hectic schedule called for, Michael greeted Elizabeth backstage. Then, in the dark of night and concealed in a blanket in a limousine, he was driven to the Mexico City airport. There, an MGM Grand 727 (a chartered jet) waited to take him to London.

Afraid of Heathrow and its paparazzi, the private charter landed at Luton Airport on the outskirts of London. After disembarking, Michael, along with the Fortenskys, was taken to the Charter Nightingale Clinic, an establishment originally founded by Florence Nightingale.

As the world asked, "Where's Michael?" an audio-taped message was released to the media:

"As I left on this tour, I had been the target of an extortion attempt, and shortly thereafter was accused of horrifying and outrageous conduct. I was humiliated, embarrassed, hurt and suffering great pain in my heart. The pressure resulting from these false allegations coupled with the incredible energy necessary for me to perform caused so much distress that it left me physically and

emotionally exhausted. I became increasingly more dependent on the painkillers to get me through the days of the tour. My friends and doctors advised me to seek professional guidance immediately in order to eliminate what has become an addiction. It is time for me to acknowledge my need for treatment in order to regain my health. I realize that completing the tour is no longer possible and I must cancel the remaining dates. I know I can overcome the problem and will be stronger from the experience."

Later that night, Elizabeth and Larry, with a Michael Jackson look-alike, flew to Switzerland in a deliberate campaign to trick the media.

Meanwhile, federal marshals waited in vain at the San Juan airport for Michael's arrival. The plan was to hold him for questioning about the child molestation charges. When a plane arrived from Mexico City, Michael was not aboard, of course.

On the morning of November 12, Michael's publicist announced that the remainder of the *Dangerous* tour had been canceled, and that Michael's addiction to painkillers began when his hair caught fire in 1984 during the taping of a Pepsi-Cola commercial.

When confronted with the cancellation of the remainder of the tour, executives at Pepsi breathed a sign of relief. Some youth organizations were threatening a boycott of the soft drink. "When Michael canceled the tour we were sponsoring, we were off the hook," said an executive off the record. "There's no way that Pepsi wants a spokesman who's implicated as a child molester."

In contrast, at least publicly, executives at Sony stood by Michael, affirming their "unconditional and unwavering support."

Weitzman then called Michael with horrific news. The police had obtained a warrant for a strip search, although there was a fear that Michael had been out of the country long enough to "alter" the identifying markings on his genitals. "There is no way in hell I'm going through with a strip search," Michael shouted. "Get me out of this, or else find new employment. I'll hire a lawyer who can get me out of this. I've never heard of anything so humiliating!"

During all this turmoil, Michael had five bodyguards he trusted—Leroy Thomas, Donald Starks, Aaron White, Morris Williams, and Fred Hammond. However, by 1995 he turned on them and fired them. The men sued Michael for wrongful dismissal, claiming that the only reason they were fired was "because we knew too much." One security guard reported that Michael had called him, asking him to destroy a photograph of a nude boy, perhaps ten years old, that was in a bathroom in the family home at Encino. The bodyguards' case was thrown out of court in July of 1995.

Michael had been slated to perform the theme song and appear in a video for the film *Addams Family Values*. But he dropped out. Nevertheless, his image appeared in the final release. A kid sees a Michael Jackson poster and recoils in horror.

The November 29, 1993 cover of *People* magazine blared the headline: MICHAEL JACKSON CRACKS UP.

As part of a separate development, Fields made some indiscreet statements to Judge David Rothman of Santa Barbara County on November 23, 1993 when he was fighting for a delay in the trial. "You have a DA sitting up in Santa Barbara County about to indict, and if they do, we are going to have a criminal trial very soon." Judge Rothman rejected Fields' request for a delay, scheduling the trial for March 21, 1994.

Michael was infuriated that his attorney was even daring to suggest that a trial was imminent. Weitzman, recognizing potential damage, claimed that Fields had "misspoke." Hearing of this, it was reported that Elizabeth Taylor, working through her own lawyer, was behind the move to oust Fields. Michael abruptly fired him. With Fields removed from the case, so went the investigative skills of Pellicano.

Michael sensed that he needed a powerful figure on his legal team. As his security guard, Bill Bray, had recommended, Michael hired the high-profile lawyer, Johnnie Cochran, who would later be immortalized in 1995 for his role in the O.J. Simpson trial, "that great trash novel come to life." During the Simpson trial, even Margaret Thatcher and Boris Yeltsin dropped their busy schedules to watch its televised proceedings, especially the skill of Cochran in evading overwhelming evidence against Simpson.

Cochran's first assignment from Michael involved a confrontation with the insurance company, Transamerica. Michael wanted the company to pay for any cash that flowed to Jordie. When the executives there received Michael's outlandish demand, they went into an emergency huddle. Before the day was over, they had rejected Michael's claim. To retaliate, Cochran began to fire off threatening letters.

He warned the company that if they did not participate in the settlement, "Mr. Jackson will pursue all civil remedies available to him against Transamerica for a host of claims, including failure to pay defense costs, failure to contribute toward settlement costs, and/or for punitive damages for bad faith."

Russ Wardrip, a claims analyst at Transamerica, shot back that Michael Jackson's policy covered injuries in an accident—"not acts of sexual activity."

Although Transamerica officials had valued Michael as a client, executives privately expressed astonishment that any celebrity could possibly think that an insurance policy would cover a client's criminal child molestation. Cochran admitted privately to friends that he hated writing such a letter to

Transamerica, knowing how spurious the claim was.

In his dossier, Wardrip also asserted that acts of child molestation are "inherently intentional, wrongful, and harmful,"—and hardly accidental.

In one of the most amazing stories ever recorded in the insurance industry, Transamerica under "heavy beating up" by Cochran agreed to pay an undisclosed amount. Even more amazingly, Michael rejected the offer. "I want them to pay every penny—not just part of the settlement to the kid."

Under Cochran's direction, Michael's camp upped the ante to nearly a million dollars, but that is only a fraction of what Evan was willing to settle for now, as he saw a vast fortune possible for Jordie and money for himself.

In addition to Cochran, Michael wanted John Branca back on his legal team, not for his defense in the child molestation case, but to handle his increasingly complicated business affairs. After three years in exile, Branca was back. Michael immediately demanded that the attorney ask for an even higher royalty rate from Sony than that which had previously been agreed upon.

Under the urging of his new attorney, Cochran, Michael agreed to return to Los Angeles. Shortly before dawn, he was smuggled out of the Charter Nightingale Clinic where he was driven in a "hearse-like" ambulance to Heathrow. There he boarded a 727, the property of one of his greatest admirers, the Sultan of Brunei, who was also the owner of London's very posh Dorchester Hotel, an address that Michael often used during stays in that city. As the richest man on the planet, the sultan could afford such indulgences. On the plane, Michael was accompanied by Frank and Eddie Cascio.

The jet set down in Boston for refueling before flying on to Billings, Montana. Fearing arrest on the ground, Michael refused to disembark to clear Customs. Consequently, a U.S. Customs official boarded the plane to check Michael's passport.

With the young boys, Michael landed at Santa Barbara where he concealed himself within a stretch limo that had been waiting to take him and his young charges to what he thought was the safety of Neverland. Outside the gates of the estate, reporters from magazines, newspapers, and TV waited feverishly.

On January 16, 1994, against the advice of both his attorneys and his mother, Katherine, Michael hosted his annual party for 250 underprivileged children at Neverland. *Black Entertainment TV* covered the event. But one newspaper asked, "Has Peter Pan become the Pied Piper?"

After the event, the Northridge earthquake struck across California, causing billions of dollars in property damage and even the loss of life.

The earthquake became oddly symbolic for Michael, as his Trophy Room at Encino, with all his platinum records, was severely shaken. And at the

Hollywood Wax Museum, the head fell off the Michael Jackson effigy.

Within three days of his secret return, news people accurately surmised that Michael was once again in residence at Neverland. The circus lights were switched on within his own private theme park, and the carousel began grinding out the sounds of "Like a Virgin" once again. The song became oddly symbolic, since Michael had hired a team of psychiatrists to maintain—in court if necessary—that he was a virgin in spite of all the crotch-grabbing and simulated masturbation on stage.

Appearing on both *Hard Copy* and CNN, Katherine still continued her increasingly tired defense of her son as a straight shooter. "Sometimes you look at a person's face and you can say, 'Oh, my God, that guy is gay.' Michael is not gay."

Such appearances inflamed the gay community. "Every time Katherine Jackson opens her mouth, she costs Michael thousands and thousands of gay fans," said an activist in Los Angeles.

In references to Michael's attackers, brother Jermaine claimed that "Michael is ready to kick some butt!"

Eventually, Michael met privately with Cochran. There were no minutes made of their confidential chat, but the end result was the ordering of Cochran "to buy Jordie Chandler's silence no matter what the cost." Cochran went on to inform Michael that all appeals had been exhausted. He would have to agree to be photographed in a strip search at Neverland on the morning of December 20, 1993.

Jordie later told police where "mottled pink spots" on Michael's scrotum and buttocks were, although mottled seems an odd word for a thirteen-year-old to use. Apparently, he also testified that there was "a dark splotch" at the base of Michael's penis, but it was underneath, where it was not immediately visible.

Jordie testified that the first time he saw Michael in the nude and noticed the spots, he mocked the star. "You look like a cow!" Michael was furious. Jordie had also drawn a detailed picture of a nude Michael.

The prosecutors in California threat-

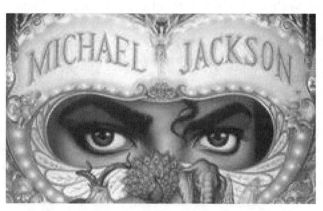

Detail from the cover of the *Dangerous* album

ened to handcuff and arrest Michael and haul him to jail if he didn't agree to strip and have his nude body photographed. As Cochran told him, "You don't have much choice. In jail, they could strip you and photograph you any time they wanted."

Tom Sneddon, the Santa Barbara District Attorney who would become Michael's nemesis, was part of the entourage who descended on Neverland at 4:45 in the afternoon. Gary Spiegel was the office photographer for the sheriff's department.

Michael was forced to strip and have his genitals photographed. During the ordeal, Michael, in the nude, stood helplessly by, looking at a picture of Elizabeth Taylor at her most beautiful from the 1951 release of *A Place in the Sun.*

Also present was Michael's Beverly Hills dermatologist, Dr. Klein, as well as a personal doctor, David Forecast, who practiced medicine in London.

Although calling two detectives "assholes," Michael cooperated to a degree but only to a degree, refusing to submit to all the photographs authorized by the court. Later Michael issued a statement to the press:

It was the most humiliating ordeal of my life—one that no person should ever have to suffer. It was a nightmare, a horrifying nightmare. But if this is what I have to endure to prove my innocence, my complete innocence, then so be it. I shall not in this statement respond to all the false allegations being made against me, since my lawyers have advised me that this is not the proper forum in which to do that. I will say that I am particularly upset by the handling of this matter by the incredible and terrible mass media. At every opportunity, the media has dissected and manipulated these allegations to reach their own conclusions. I ask all of you to wait to hear the truth before you label or condemn me. Don't treat me like a criminal, because I am innocent.

His statement was met with skepticism in the press, and voice stress experts denounced the tape as "a pack of Jackson lies."

"The stress in his voice clearly goes off the chart," claimed Dr. Martin Markowitz from his offices in Atlanta.

Too many persons witnessed Michael posing nude to keep their mouths shut. An assistant in the photo lab where the films were processed claimed, "It's of normal size. There is very little pubic hair. It's light brown, not jet black. His penis is white but with a brown blotch or two. There are pink and brown patches on his testicles, which are not large."

Bob Jones later claimed, "The boy turned out to have an unerring eye for accuracy."

On the dawn of a civil trial, life wasn't going smoothly for the Chandlers either. Threats arrived daily, including a dead rat in a box. Evan Chandler's dental office was ransacked and subjected to bomb threats. After death threats came in for the Chandler attorney, Larry Feldman, a security force from the U.S. Justice Department was assigned to protect him.

After violent arguments from both parties, a settlement was agreed upon with the Chandlers, a sum so high it would have devastated the fortunes of most rich people.

According to the agreement, Michael pledged to place $15,331,250 to be held in trust by the minor's attorneys, plus another $2 million as an extra signing bonus. Both June and Evan were to receive an additional $1.5 million each, up front. There was more. Larry Feldman and his legal team were to be paid an extra $10 million. In all, financial advisers estimated that Michael's total cost from the case, including his own legal fees and lost revenues from *Dangerous*, amounted to more than $100 million, maybe a lot more.

Based on prevailing interest rates and if the funds in the trust were invested wisely, Jordie could make "multiple millions of dollars more as long as he and his parents and his attorneys kept their mouths shut," according to reporter Diane Dimond.

The final agreement was signed on January 25, 1994.

Both Larry Feldman, representing Jordie, and Cochran, representing Michael, spoke to the press. Feldman, referring to Jordie as "the boy," claimed that he "is very happy with the resolution of this matter." Still maintaining Michael's innocence, in spite of the huge pay-off, Cochran claimed, "The time has come for Michael Jackson to get on with his life." Privately he told colleagues that he detested child molesters and "despised" working on the case. He also told associates that "I feel Michael was completely in the wrong. The way he was carrying on, he was headed for big trouble." Cochran accurately predicted that there would be additional "Jordie Chandler cases in the future if Michael didn't reform. Personally, the way he was cavorting with those Cascio brothers, even as child molestation charges against him raged, I don't think he's learned his lesson . . . even now!"

Michael waited months for the media circus to die down before speaking out about the settlement:

I asked my lawyer if he could guarantee me that justice would prevail. He said that he could not guarantee what a judge or jury would do. So I said that I have got to do something to get out of this nightmare . . . all these people were coming forward to get paid on these tabloid TV shows. And it's lies, lies, lies. So I got together with my advisors and they advised me in an unanimous decision to resolve the case. It could go on for seven years.

Although prosecutors in Santa Barbara didn't want Michael to escape from their clutches, their criminal investigation into Michael's alleged child molestation began to wind down.

When word reached the prosecutors that the Chandlers were "making a deal" with Michael, they knew their criminal case against him was collapsing. At the time of the Chandler case, California law stated that a child could not be made to testify to confirm molestation charges. "Without Jordie, we've got no real case to present to a jury," a police officer said, "and then there's

Janet Reno

the question of Jackson's fame. What if everybody on the jury loved *Thriller*?"

Feldman denied that there had ever been a private understanding that Jordie would not testify in the event that criminal charges against Michael would be filed anytime in the future. But despite those denials, prosecutors suspected that an agreement *had* been established between Michael and Jordie's father. "Because Jordie has removed himself from the picture, our case has been shot full of holes," a staff member of the district attorney's office, who refused to allow his name to be printed, told a reporter in Los Angeles

Appearing on *Nightline*, a New York attorney, Raoul Felder, told America that "If people believe that Michael Jackson paid millions of dollars and didn't get a promise that the boy wouldn't testify, then they also believe in the tooth fairy. The settlement sends a terrible message. That statue on the courthouse should hang its head in shame that this could happen. If you're rich, you can buy justice—pure and simple."

Allegedly, Michael threatened a lawsuit, but most lawyers agreed that Felder was allowed to speak his mind under fair comment and criticism of a very public event.

The matter even went to the White House, where Bill and Hillary Clinton were now in residence. Within the very recent past, they had warmly welcomed Michael to Washington and considered him a friend. Attorney General Janet Reno met privately with both Bill and Hillary, reviewing the evidence that Michael had transported Jordie across state lines (Nevada and Florida, for example) and had even taken him abroad to such countries as Monaco and France. It was alleged that President Clinton was reluctant to intervene in a high-profile case against a black person, particularly in the wake of the 1992 L.A. riots over the arrest of Rodney King. "Leave it to those guys in Santa Barbara," Clinton told Reno. "We're not getting involved with this one. I have enough problems as it is without alienating the black community."

Michael was never forced to go into court. Neither was Jordie. In January of 1994, LAPD prosecutors announced that they were not moving forward with the case because of lack of evidence. They also announced, on January 24, that there wasn't enough evidence to charge Evan Chandler with extortion. Jordie dropped the charges against Michael.

Right at this time, Reuters News Service dropped a bombshell. A bulletin went out that the photographs of Michael's genitalia did not match Jordie's description of them. This was in total contradiction to other reports, including those made by police investigators who had minutely examined photographs of Michael's private parts.

"Money talks," said a police investigator who didn't want to be named. "Or, should I say, money silences. Millions can silence even the most talkative witness."

Terry White, once the Santa Clara, California, District Attorney, in his review of the evidence, claimed that there was "more than enough evidence" to indict Michael and probably convict him on charges of child molestation.

"Although it is hard to put a price on the emotional suffering of child abuse victims," one reporter wrote, "at least the young boy will not have to work another day of his life, and can live in the lap of luxury that he'd enjoyed as a twelve-year-old at Neverland."

Years later, Maureen Orth, writing in *Vanity Fair*, had a different spin. "Jordie Chandler's life has been completely broken by his association with Michael Jackson. He went to college, he manages his own money. He's a very attractive, bright kid but I don't think he really is able to have a normal life. He can't go anywhere without being identified as the Michael Jackson boy. People want to know all about Michael and how much money did Jordie get."

Many celeb friends, such as Elton John, wondered in public why Michael settled out of court if he were indeed not guilty. But the ever-steadfast Elizabeth Taylor, in a press release, stood by him. "As one of Michael's closest friends, who is convinced of his innocence, I agonized over the daily avalanche of lies, innuendos, and slurs, none of which Michael deserved. Michael's love of children is one of the purest things I have ever seen; it shines like an extra sun. In spite of the media's distorted lens, I was repeatedly touched by the faith that so many of Michael's friends and fans had in his complete innocence."

In the closing weeks of World War II, some Neapolitan women painted lipstick on the mouths of their young teenage sons and offered them for sale to U.S. servicemen for purposes of sodomy. "If that sounds amazing," said Lieutenant Jerry Grayson, "maybe you don't know what hunger tastes like in your gut."

After word leaked out to the world that Michael had paid millions to

Jordie, dozens of women from around the world sent letters to Michael, including nude pictures of their young sons, offering their offspring "as a companion." Some of the letters were so explicit that authorities considered filing charges against the mothers.

Michael had been warned that prosecutors in California "were still watching him like Big Brother."

"But his habits didn't change," Bob Jones said. "He still paraded around the globe with little boys. These little boys were costing the King millions upon millions."

James Hahn, who was a city attorney (later mayor) of Los Angeles, privately said that "Michael Jackson had better be very, very careful because authorities are watching him."

Publicity about the Jordie Chandler case died down except for a scandalous book in 1995, but it forever tarnished Michael's image, in spite of the settlement or because of it.

Jordie was back in the news again in 2005 when Michael actually did go on trial, this time in a criminal case alleging child molestation of another young boy.

At the time of that trial, Jordie refused to testify against Michael. It was learned that he hadn't seen his mother, June, for the past eleven years.

Jordie, at the age of 26, was back in the news again in 2006 when he charged his father, Evan, with "life threatening physical abuse."

The former dentist was charged with striking Jordie on the head from behind with a 12 ½ pound dumbbell. His father was also charged with "spraying my eyes with Mace and trying to choke me." The alleged incidents occurred in August of 2005, just two months after Michael's acquittal in another kiddie sex case. At the time of the alleged assault, Jordie was said to be living with his father "somewhere in New Jersey."

Jordie's uncle, Raymond Chandler, who practices law in Santa Barbara, wrote a shocking book, *All That Glitters: The Crime and the Cover-Up*, published in 2004. He was not bound by the confidentiality agreement signed by Michael and Evan Chandler on behalf of his son.

In this book, Raymond Chandler had this conclusion:

The difference between Michael Jackson and any ordinary pedophile is one of degree, not kind. Using his stardom and fantasy world he created at Neverland, Michael could entice a child in a way that no other pedophile could hope to match. But beneath the façade of fame and fortune lies a child molester no different from the one down the street. "Come to my house, I'll give you candy." It's as old as the hills.

"Just think, nobody ever thought this would last."

--Michael Jackson, 1994
On his marriage to Lisa Marie Presley

"In an insult to transvestite men everywhere—who can look pretty damn good in a dress and makeup and can project alluring female charm—when Mike does this, he doesn't even have the decency to stop grabbing his crotch every 1.0045 seconds and allowing that image for us."

--www.anomalies-unlimited.com

"All of Hollywood has plastic surgery! I don't know why the press points me out. It's just my nose, you know."

--Michael Jackson

"I've seen this. I've seen it a lot. I have seen him with children. They don't let him go to the bathroom without running in. They won't let him out of their sight. They even go to bed with him."

--Lisa Marie Presley, explaining
Michael's relationship with children

"He's not gay, I really feel certain of that. Many times, a good-looking girl would walk by and Mike would whisper, 'Hey, what do you think of her? She's somethin' else, isn't she?' His brothers are much more open in the way they pursue women, but Michael's discreet. He's a gentleman."

--Tim Whitehead (Michael's First Cousin)

"Michael continues to be completely fucking insane ill flipped crazy out of his gourd lost his shit incomprehensible what the fuck got in that boy do you even remember back when he used to be cute and talented and oh my god."

--www.AnilDash.com

Chapter Thirteen

After lengthy delays and postponements, the taping of the *Jackson Family Honors* took place on February 19, 1994 in Las Vegas. The setting was the luxurious MGM Grand Garden before a crowd of 15,000, some of whom had to be virtually pulled in off the street to fill the seats.

Promoters handed out WE LOVE MICHAEL signs to teenagers. There was speculation that Michael would not even show up, but he did. Celine Dion and Smokey Robinson performed, as did Michael's discoverer, Gladys Knight, but the highlight of the evening was Janet Jackson singing "Alright." But despite the presence of these other five-star entertainers, the audience was eager to hear and see Michael on stage.

To hysterically cheering fans, the King of Pop suddenly appeared, looking incredibly thin in a black military jacket with a gold-leaf pattern. He'd come out on the stage to present an award, one of the *Jackson Family Honors*, to Motown's Berry Gordy Jr., with whom he'd had a troubled relationship, one that had even involved lawsuits. Michael went into his usual kiss blowing and "I love you!" pronouncements. For once, he took Katharine Hepburn's advice and left the sunglasses in his dressing room. After a suck-up speech praising Gordy, Michael welcomed the Motown mogul onstage to receive his honor.

Later, Michael returned to the stage to present another Jackson honor to Elizabeth Taylor, claiming that she was "one of the most celebrated women of the 20th century." He thanked her for her "unwavering strength and support" in the middle of all his "trials and tribulations."

Elizabeth came on, blasting the tabloids for their constant attacks on Michael. She even asked the public to "stop buying the garbage." She called Michael "the brightest star in the universe." Later, critics without evidence claimed that Michael must have paid Elizabeth two-million dollars for her glowing tribute.

Suddenly, things began going wrong at the lovefest. Elizabeth announced, "I know you'd like to hear Michael sing, but he doesn't have any music prepared." Boos went up from the audience. "Don't boo," Elizabeth admonished the audience, "it's an ugly sound."

Michael did, however, join family members and other guests onstage for the song, "If Only You Believe." Janet was not to be seen. She'd left word with the stage manager, "Tell them Janet Jackson has left the building."

The following morning, *USA Today* headlined the event: JACKSONS NO THRILLER WITHOUT MICHAEL SOLO. Some fans had paid as much as $1,000 per ticket hoping to see Michael sing. Many other headlines also appeared expressing the disappointment of loyal fans, whose numbers would fade year by year as their faith in Michael waned.

Instead of watching the lackluster *Jackson Family Honors*, most viewers tuned in to the Olympics instead. Whitney Houston suggested that attacks on Michael might be because he was black, although at this point he didn't look black. Louis Farrakhan, head of the Nation of Islam, agreed with Houston. On *Arsenio Hall*, he claimed that the King of Pop was being "treated like a slave on a plantation because of a charge that has yet to lead to a criminal charge." The controversial Muslim had attended the taping of the *Jackson Family Honors*.

After the show, Katherine Jackson was subpoenaed to testify against her son. Michael's attorney, Howard Weitzman, shot back in anger, denouncing the DA's office for trying "to humiliate Michael Jackson and harass him. In all the years of my experience, I've never before seen the mother of the target of an investigation called before the grand jury. It's just done in real poor taste."

In the aftermath of the *Jackson Family Honors*, Gary Smith, its co-producer, sued the Jacksons for $2.2 million, alleging that cast and crew had not been paid, including his own fee of $400,000. In a damaging report, it was revealed that the show had taken in $4.5 million, only $100,000 of which went to charity, although it had been billed as a charity event.

La Toya appeared in Las Vegas. But when Katherine told La Toya she wouldn't be allowed onstage without signing a gag order, she slammed down the phone on her mother and boarded a plane that night for Nashville with her husband, Jack Gordon. Arriving in a pair of cowboy boots in Tennessee, La Toya announced she was in Nashville to record an album of country songs. Gordon predicted, "La Toya Jackson will be the next country/western heartthrob." A Nashville music critic had another prediction: "Dolly Parton and Loretta Lynn can sleep peacefully with their boots on. They need not fear La Toya Jackson."

The *Jackson Family Honors* was an attempt at image building and spin control, but it failed to impress "Walt's Boys." Officials at Walt Disney World met in secret February 25, 1994, and decided to yank *Captain EO* from its Orlando theme park. Although Michael had not even been charged with child molestation, the suspicions and the publicity were just too much for Disney officials. They pulled the plug. The film was replaced with a 3-D movie, *Honey, I Shrunk the Theater*.

After the *Jackson Family Honors*, Michael met privately with Elizabeth to share a secret with her. He told her that he was going to get married, only the bride-to-be didn't know it yet. He declared—no doubt falsely—that "I'm in love with Lisa Marie Presley."

Although Elizabeth had spurned Michael's offer of marriage, sources reported that she was clearly jealous of the much younger Lisa Marie. At one point the superstar was heard contemptuously referring to Lisa Marie as "a punk rocker." Elizabeth and Lisa Marie probably suspected that each of them had shouldered the responsibility of rescuing Michael from himself. Elizabeth was quoted as saying, "I've saved Michael countless times—and I can do it again. I will do just that!"

Privately, Lisa Marie agreed with members of the family that Katherine Jackson was mother enough for Michael. "He doesn't need another interfering mother image in his life," Lisa Marie is reported to have said, referring pointedly to Ms. Taylor. "He needs *me*. Someone young and vibrant, like he is. Someone who can cuss and get low. Like Michael, my future is ahead of me. His future is ahead of him. It's been a long time since Elizabeth had a hit with *Cat on a Hot Tin Roof*. And who is this Tennessee Williams anyway? I always thought his songs were pure cornpone. Elvis hated him."

No doubt Lisa Marie was confusing Tennessee Williams with the country singer, Tennessee Ernie Ford.

Prsicilla Presley, Lisa Marie (aged 3) and Elvis, circa 1971

Separated from her husband, Danny Keough, whom she'd married in 1988, Lisa Marie was in Las Vegas during the taping of the *Jackson Family Honors*. With her, she'd brought her children, Danielle Riley, born in 1989, and Benjamin, born in 1992.

She got a call from Michael inviting her for a date on February 2, 1994 at the Sheraton

411

Desert Inn where The Temptations were performing. Normally, Michael would have slipped into the concert after the lights had been darkened. But he wanted to parade one of America's most famous daughters through the front door with the regular customers. Lisa Marie looked stunning in a low-cut black gown. During the performance, they were seen holding hands in a section called "King's Row," appropriate seats for the King of Pop and the daughter of the King of Rock 'n' Roll. Many observers referred to it as "the romance that never was," but at least the Jackson/Presley alliance had more of a reality bite than Michael's earlier "love affair" with Princess Di.

The outspoken La Toya, when she heard about the date, denounced it as a sham, claiming that Michael was "just kidding the public. It's an obvious public relations exercise aimed at portraying Michael in a more manly, heterosexual light. But girls are not part of Michael's life. He's not interested in them."

Back in California, Michael entertained Lisa Marie and her children at Neverland. He later told the press, "One of the things that most attracted me to Lisa is that she gets along swell with the animals in my own zoo."

Reportedly, staff members at Neverland were surprised at Michael's interest in Lisa Marie. "In all the months I've worked here," said one member of the staff, "I always saw him with young boys—never a gal, particularly one who looked hot-to-trot like that Presley gal."

Regardless of what he might have thought personally, the very hip Donald Trump invited the couple to visit his luxurious estate, Mar-a-Lago, in Palm Beach. He later told the press, "They looked like any other lovey-dovey couple to me."

J. Randy Taraborrelli, in his *The Magic & the Madness*, reported that the first time Michael made love to Lisa Marie was at Mar-a-Lago. Taraborrelli quotes an unnamed source, identified only as "another one of Lisa's confidantes":

She [Lisa] said it was intense, it took her breath away. I have no idea what they were doing, or what he was doing to her, but since she gravitates to the unconventional, she was out of her mind over this guy. Maybe it's hard for some to believe, but true, just the same.

The unnamed source was right on at least one point—"it's hard for some to believe."

Taraborrelli later wrote that Lisa Marie's "sexual chemistry" was so intense with Michael that she "wasn't about to give it up." The author, who would later write a biography of Elizabeth Taylor, found himself standing virtually alone in the world with that point of view.

Years previously, close to Lake Tahoe, a seven-year-old Lisa Marie

Presley had first laid eyes on Michael Jackson during one of his performances with The Jackson 5.

She came back into Michael's life through the intervention of a mutual friend, an artist from Australia, Brett Livingston-Stone, who had painted a portrait of Michael that had sold for $2 million. Strong called Michael to ask him if he'd listen to a tape of Lisa Marie singing, hoping that he might produce an album for her. "Send it over," Michael said.

Lisa Marie did better than that. With her tape in hand, she showed up in person to see Michael. Accompanying her was her husband, Danny Keough.

After listening to the tape, Michael told Lisa Marie that she had "promise." During her meeting with Michael, the star is alleged to have told both Lisa Marie and her husband, "Listen, I'm not gay! Don't let these false eyelashes and red lipstick fool you."

Lisa Marie later admitted that she was impressed that "Michael could curse just as good as the rest of us cotton pickers." It has been alleged that Michael shared with her some indiscreet gossip he'd picked up when attending President Clinton's inaugural in Washington. They both acknowledged that the new president was a rabid Elvis fan. Clinton, or so it was rumored, once told some cronies that one of his greatest dreams in life "was to fuck Elvis's daughter."

"A lot of people have that fantasy," Lisa Marie was alleged to have said.

"Let them dream on," Danny interjected.

When Lisa Marie later confessed to Michael that her marriage to Danny was falling apart, Michael actively pursued her with flowers and presents. Privately she told friends that "even though Michael is a little bit cute, he's very immature compared to Danny. I still love Danny. I will always love Danny even though we might divorce."

Divorce Danny she did, rushing into a secret marriage to Michael Jackson. Far from the paparazzi and the ravenous tabloids, the wedding took place on May 26, 1994 in La Vega, an obscure village in the Dominican Republic. Two months would go by before the world learned of this bizarre marriage. None of the Jacksons had been invited.

Lisa Marie's divorce papers had arrived only on May 6. Seemingly she was rushing impulsively from one marriage into another.

Before flying to the Dominican Republic, Michael and Lisa Marie signed a prenuptial agreement.

Civil Judge Hugo Francisco Alvarez conducted the wedding in Spanish but with an interpreter.

Michael tried to use more flaming red lipstick than his bride, or so it was reported. His face was partially hidden under a wide-brimmed black hat, the type worn at *ferias* in Seville. His ponytail was slicked back, and his cowboy belt would have made John Wayne proud. Lisa Marie also wore a black hat evocative of a flamenco dancer.

"Michael looked like a little boy lost," said Judge Alvarez. "He stared at the floor throughout the ceremony."

Alvarez called the ceremony "surprisingly without any passion. When I asked him if he'd take Lisa Marie for his lawfully wedded wife, he turned to me and said, 'Why not?' When I pronounced him and Lisa Marie man and wife, he was reluctant to kiss her. She had to pull his face to hers to kiss him on the lips. There were no tears of happiness—no joy, no laughter. I felt I was presiding over a funeral—not a wedding."

The only enthusiasm Michael showed was for the judge's tie which depicted Fred Flintstone. "It's a great tie," Michael told him. "I love Fred Flintstone."

"Although he complimented my tie, I never heard him say he loved Lisa Marie," the judge claimed. Judge Alvarez was "loose-lipped" and informed a Dominican newspaper about details associated with the wedding. However, his observations were dismissed by the press at the time as "some of the most ridiculous rumors ever spread about Michael Jackson."

For their honeymoon, the couple retired to Casa de Campo in the south, a resort built by the now-defunct Gulf + Western. On their honeymoon night, Michael stayed in a villa on the grounds of the resort, with Lisa Marie occupying a less opulent lodging, known locally as a *casita*, some five miles away.

During the course of his wedding night, away from any potential interference from his bride, according to the staff, he placed a call to Elizabeth Taylor, informing her of the marriage.
For reasons known only to herself, Elizabeth was said to have broken into tears. Sobbing, she is alleged to have said, "Michael, how could you? *Her*, of all people. She'll ruin your life!"

When confronted by a reporter two days later in Los Angeles, Elizabeth snapped, "That's the most ridiculous rumor I've ever heard. Michael Jackson is a sane and reasonable man. Marrying Lisa Marie Presley would be an insane act. He is not crazy!"

After their "wedding night,"

MJ and Lisa Marie

414

Lisa Marie

Lisa Marie and her new groom were seen leaving the Punta Aguila airport (which was renamed in 2000 as La Romana International Airport) in a private jet. Their flight plan listed their final destination as Los Angeles.

But instead of California, they landed in Orlando where Michael, in a Fu Manchu disguise, was seen escorting his new bride around Disney World.

After that, they flew to New York where Donald Trump housed them in a luxurious twelve-room complex on the 65th floor of the Trump Tower. The apartment normally rented for $125,000 a month, but its occupancy was presented as a gift to the newly married Jacksons. Obviously, Trump knew about the secret marriage, but wasn't talking. "I know how to keep a secret," he later said.

At the Trump Tower, photographer Dick Zimmerman snapped pictures of the newlyweds. In his review of the body language of the two subjects, writer Nick Bishop said: "In the photos, Michael and Lisa Marie are draped all over each other, but Michael's eyes are always focused on the camera. He plays exclusively for the lens. He touches Lisa Marie when they're draped all over each other, but he does it lightly and tentatively. She, on the other hand, is obviously into it. She touches Michael with real enthusiasm. She throws herself toward him. He merely leans into her, holding back, watching the camera."

During their honeymoon in Budapest, Michael was working on shooting a video for his new album, *HIStory*. On many a night, Lisa Marie was said to have eaten Hungarian goulash on her own.

When asked months later to comment on her marriage, Lisa Marie ducked the question. "Elvis liked to wear uniforms, so does Michael. Elvis loved amusement parks. My Daddy used to rent out Memphis's Liberty Land. Michael has his own amusement park."

Back in Los Angeles, Lisa Marie began married life by going to her own plastic surgeon. Press reports claimed that her "breasts looked perkier" when she recovered. She may also have had her thighs trimmed. Earlier she'd complained that child birth had caused her breasts to sag. As for her thighs, she told friends that they "looked like two blobs of Jell-O that Elvis was so fond of eating." She may also have had some acne scars removed.

In the aftermath of the wedding, Elizabeth Taylor invited Lisa Marie and Michael to her lush home in Bel Air. While strolling with Lisa Marie through her luxuriant gardens, Elizabeth reportedly advised her "to go for the diamonds. I never turned down emeralds either." When Lisa Marie told her she didn't like expensive jewelry, the world-class gem collector informed her, "Then put the gems in your safe for your old age. As Marilyn sang, 'These rocks don't lose their shape.'" She also gave Lisa Marie a fashion tip. "Always find out what outfit Michael is wearing when he takes you out. Top him! Dress even more glamorously than he does."

Lisa Marie later reported Elizabeth's comments to Michael. "How retro this woman is. She belongs back in my daddy's heyday."

On August 1, 1994, Lisa Marie herself, through a press agent, announced that she had become "Lisa Marie Presley-Jackson." She promised to "dedicate my life to being the wife of Michael Jackson. We both look forward to raising a family and living a happy, healthy life together."

In her statement, she claimed that she was very much in love with Michael. She said that news of their marriage was kept a secret to avoid turning the "happy occasion into a media circus."

"People wouldn't think I was so crazy marrying Michael if they saw who the hell he really is," she said. "That he drinks and curses and is funny and doesn't have that high voice all the time. I once had this romantic idea that I could save him and we could save the world. But then I realized Michael was constantly at work, calculating, manipulating. He scared me like that."

From New York, Lisa Marie called her mother, Priscilla, in Los Angeles to tell her she'd married Michael. "Yup, I did it!" Lisa Marie said. Her mother's screams could be heard all the way from Los Angeles to the Trump Tower in New York. "Are you crazy?" It cannot be confirmed, but Priscilla was said to have called Michael a "black faggot." She was also alleged to have said, "Elvis will rise from his grave. In a life of making stupid decisions, you win the prize for this one. I can't believe you've made me the mother-in-law of Michael Jackson. Weirdo. *Wacko Jacko*. Just don't have any kids with him, not that I have to worry about that!"

When Lisa Marie slammed down the phone on Priscilla, she told her new husband, "I gave her the finger in marrying you."

Priscilla was distraught at the news. "Picture this, the former wife of Elvis Presley, and now today the mother-in-law of Michael Jackson. What a

Thriller!"

In the days and weeks to come, Michael and Lisa Marie would make even more headlines, including one within a tabloid that proclaimed: THE CENTURY'S ODD COUPLE MARRIAGE!

After charges of child molestation were leveled against Michael, and in the wake of his marriage to Lisa Marie, John Evans, a reporter, wrote: "Priscilla Presley should know all about child molestation from her own life. After all, she was only fourteen when Elvis became smitten with her when he was stationed in Germany. She should identify with her new son-in-law. She is reported to have regular chemical peels to get rid of wrinkles and unwanted brown spots. Maybe she can give Michael tips about how to get rid of that alleged brown spot on his dick."

The media responded in a frenzy of headlines, *The London Times* calling the secret wedding, "A Marriage from Mars!" TV talk show host David Letterman evoked riotous laughter when he told his audience, "If he comes home with lipstick on his collar, you can be pretty sure it's his own."

The astrologer for *The New York Daily News* told her readers that "according to the stars, the marriage has not been consummated."

Bulletins were flashed around the world: The King of Pop had taken as his bride the daughter of the King of Rock 'n' Roll. "It wasn't really an interracial marriage," said a TV commentator (in Spanish) in Santo Domingo. "By now, all of us know that Michael Jackson is white."

One journalist went even further. "It could happen only in America. Michael Jackson was born a black boy. Now he's become a white woman. Does that make Lisa Marie a lesbian for marrying him?"

Bob Jones, Michael's publicist, alleged that, "the poor girl seemed genuinely smitten with Michael before she realized that she had been the victim of a heartless scam." He alleged that Michael's real intent in marrying Lisa Marie involved not only adding a "testosterone boost" to his soiled image, but a desire to gain control of the Elvis Presley songbook, evocative of the way he had secured copyrights to The Beatles' songs.

Michael, of course, would never own the complete Presley catalogue. However, unknown to many of Elvis's fans, Michael did own several of the Presley songs as part of his Sony/ATV Music Publishing Company.

Jones faced a public relations nightmare. Even though the press was not fully aware of all of Michael's activities, as they became in the years ahead, reporters knew enough to realize that this bizarre wedding smacked of a publicity stunt. Jones, fending off the vultures, said privately that he knew that Michael "had no desire for a woman—not the natural desires that straight men have."

As the press inquired deeper into how the pop star came to marry Lisa

Marie, Michael said, "We were in my living room at Neverland having a glass of wine after we'd watched that old film *All About Eve*, with Bette Davis. We both love that movie. I just walked over to her, reached into my pocket, and pulled out a knock-you-dead diamond ring. 'You wanna?' I asked her. Other than that, I never popped the question or got down on my knees."

When Michael was asked about the interracial aspects of his marriage to Lisa Marie, he said, "Somehow it seems appropriate. When Elvis was first heard on radio, listeners initially thought he was black."

The marriage was greeted with cynicism in the press, some commentators even suggesting that it was a business move to unite the music houses of Graceland and Neverland. A lavender marriage was suggested: That is, a marriage of convenience wherein one or both of the parties is trying to conceal the fact that one or both of them is gay.

Journalist Nick Bishop claimed that Michael entered into a marriage to Lisa Marie to combat charges of homosexuality with young boys. "Because Michael Jackson settled with the Chandlers, the perception of him on the street among many people is that he is a compulsive pedophile, a sexual addict in a way that most people find repellent. People these days often turn up their noses at the mention of his name. He is reviled by many and seen as decadent and deeply troubled. He didn't take his own marriage seriously and neither did anyone else with an IQ in the double digits. This move was clearly the old wedding bells as the ultimate sexual bearding trick, and of course it didn't work."

A PR agent privately said, "Michael Jackson married Elvis's daughter just to publicize his greatest hits album." He was referring to *HIStory*. "He needs all the help he can get with that album. I think most of his fans will desert him."

Jack Gordon, La Toya's husband, said that Michael had promised Lisa Marie a music career as a condition of her marrying him. He would never deliver on that promise. Gordon had other comments to make. "It's one thing to get married, but to Elvis's daughter was totally absurd. Something went wrong in that marriage, and Lisa Marie will soon be telling all. Michael will be destroyed."

Graceland

Comedian Dennis Miller cited the wedding as conclusive evidence that Elvis was not alive. "If Elvis were alive, he would have put the kibosh on it."

Weeks after news of Michael's marriage was made public, fans sent letters to him claiming, "You married the wrong Lisa Marie Presley. The woman you married is an imposter."

Had only one such letter arrived, it would have been ignored. But hundreds of letters had to be reckoned with. Some of Michael's aides set out to discover what the fuss was about and came up with the startling news that a young Swedish girl, Lisa Johansen, was filing claims that she was the real daughter of Elvis and Priscilla Presley.

Not only that, she was detailing her story within an autobiography, *I, Lisa Marie: The True Story of Elvis Presley's Real Daughter*. Her so-called memoirs would eventually be published in 1998 in China. Perhaps fearing legal action from the Presley empire, copies were published underground but surreptitiously sold in the United States and Britain.

In her tome, Lisa Johansen makes it rather clear that the real Lisa Marie Presley would not have married Michael Jackson.

According to Johansen, after the untimely death of Elvis when she was nine years old, the aspirant Lisa Marie was "whisked from an idyllic life in America to the obscurity of a comfortable exile in Scandinavia." She claimed that family members arranged this exile for her own safety, because there had been reports of kidnapping attempts. In Sweden, she lived with a kindly family and assumed a new identity as Lisa Johansen. According to instructions, recited to her at Graceland, she was to live in Sweden until she came of age and could take her "rightful place as the sole heir of a huge estate."

After reaching maturity, the Lisa living in Sweden attempted to reach across the Atlantic to Tennessee to claim her legacy as Elvis's daughter. She naïvely states in her book that she expected to be received by "a loving mother and friends eagerly awaiting her return to Graceland."

It took no prophet to predict that such would not be the case. Lisa claimed that at every turn she was blocked by "powerful and sinister forces." Along the way, the Lisa living in Sweden reported that she had been shocked when pictures "began to appear of an imposter, a young woman claiming to be Lisa Marie."

"Her public high jinks and questionable antics, and a circus-like marriage to controversial entertainment legend and paparazzi favorite, Michael Jackson, led millions of loyal fans of the late Elvis to question whether this person could be his real daughter," she said.

It is not known if Lisa Johansen has ever submitted to a DNA test to prove that she is actually Elvis's biological daughter. The young woman's odyssey to reclaim what she views as "my estate" has taken her into the courts and even to Graceland. Once there, she charged that representatives at Graceland, including Priscilla, had tried "to vacuum up every photograph depicting me with my father."

In one of her more blatant accusations, she charged that as a young girl she had been forced to submit to plastic surgery, a procedure that left "scars behind my ears. No one had cut off my fingers; but instead, they surgically altered and disfigured me, to keep me from being identified."

Reportedly, the Lisa Marie in Sweden continues to fight to this day to reclaim what she feels is rightfully hers. She concludes, "It is really not important what has gone before, and no matter what else happens in the future, I am who I am. I am the *real* Lisa Marie."

Michael Jackson and Elvis's daughter remained hot copy in the tabloids for months, as former staff members came forward to reveal behind-the-scenes insights into the marriage. A former maid, Adrian McManus, even testified that she used a media broker to sell stories to the tabloids, including one which claimed inside knowledge of the star's sex life, or lack thereof, with Lisa Marie. Several staff members said Michael and his bride never slept in the same room, alleging that intercourse was not part of this marriage. McManus maintained that she never saw Lisa Marie enter her husband's bedroom.

Maids reported that Michael often left out expensive lingerie in his bedroom to make it appear that he was sleeping with Lisa Marie. It was also alleged that he'd bugged her bedroom and monitored her phone calls, the way his role model, Howard Hughes, used to do with Ava Gardner.

Another maid at Neverland said, "I have no doubt that Michael was still a virgin—at least with women—on the day he married Lisa Marie Presley. I am firmly convinced that he remained a virgin throughout his short marriage to her. I don't think they ever touched, except for one big kiss at a public event."

The marriage became fodder for late-night comedians. Jay Leno proclaimed that Michael and Lisa Marie stopped off in Austria after a trip to Budapest. With a smirk, Leno said, "Lisa Marie bought Michael a beautiful, beautiful wedding gift—the Vienna Boys' Choir."

An army of other sources—named or unnamed—could probably be summoned to claim that Michael never had sex with Lisa Marie during their entire marriage. The obvious conclusion is that no one really knows for sure—except Lisa Marie and Michael. But whatever evidence there is suggests that even though Lisa Marie may have been momentarily infatuated with Michael, sexual play wasn't part of the equation.

"His new bride inherited the famous Presley lip curl," said journalist Peter Godsend. "Perhaps when Michael kisses his new bride, if he ever does, he fantasizes that he's kissing a young and handsome Elvis before the bloat."

Unlike most of his extended family, whom he could control financially, Michael could not dominate Lisa Marie by tightening the purse strings. In time, she would have far more money than he did.

To make himself appear wealthier in front of his new bride, Michael had his publicists exaggerate the terms of his contracts. For example, one-million dollars on paper became fifteen or twenty million dollars when reported in the press.

If reports are to be believed, Michael might not have wanted Lisa Marie, but he wanted to adopt her children, Danielle Riley and Benjamin. It is alleged that he offered their father, Danny Keough, $1 million if he'd allow Michael to adopt the children, but the offer was rejected.

In fact, Danielle Riley didn't want Michael to adopt her. Shortly after she met him for the first time, she ran away, screaming. She later told Lisa Marie, "He's weird, mother. You warned me about men like him. You said they'd offer me candy to go with them. The first time I met Michael, he offered me candy. Just like you said."

Michael resented Lisa Marie driving over to Encino without him to introduce herself to her in-laws at the Jackson compound. Lisa Marie became friends with Rebbie, the older sister, and also bonded with Janet. Michael told his staff that he didn't want Lisa Marie associating with her in-laws.

She and Michael couldn't agree on much, including food. Like her father, Lisa Marie preferred such soul food as collard greens in bacon fat, corn bread, Southern fried chicken, and sweet potato pie. Apparently, Michael preferred not to be reminded of his own humble origins, preferring a plate of steamed fresh organic vegetables from his own gardens at the ranch.

Lisa Johansen: the real Lisa Marie Presley?

In one of their talks, according to a friend of Lisa Marie, Michael told her that "the ghost of Elvis haunts me. He's a white person with a black person's voice. I want to make films like he did—only good films, not bad films like he did. But I won't play Vegas. I'm offered millions but I won't perform in his old stamping ground. I'm bigger than Elvis. That's why I can't perform in Vegas."

On another occasion, he told his wife, "Nobody in the music business understands me because

I'm a genius. At least thousands of my fans understand that. But the people who control the industry don't give me my due because I'm black. So I decided to become white to get my due."

Their first official appearance as man and wife came on September 8, 1994 at New York's Radio City Music Hall on the occasion of the 11th Annual MTV Video Music Awards. Before the world, Michael said, "Just think, nobody thought this would last." Then he grabbed Lisa Marie and gave her a lingering kiss in front of 250 million viewers on television. The next morning, one headline proclaimed: LIP-LOCK PROVES MICHAEL JACKSON STRAIGHT SHOOTER.

Lisa Johansen, in a photo montage, trying to prove her status as the daughter of Elvis Presley

An authority on body language, Maxine Fiel, claimed that it was "the performance of a lifetime." However, Fiel felt that Lisa Marie pursed her lips "like you do when you kiss your uncle, not your husband."

Lisa Marie had her own reaction. Before the applause died down, she walked off the stage and was seen wiping her mouth with the back of her hand. She later said, "I thought the kiss was stupid. I hated it. I felt used. All of a sudden, I've become part of a public relations campaign for Michael. What am I? Just some prop?"

From all reports, she felt that she'd been "callously used" to help her husband's seriously damaged public image. Her belief that she was being used for promotional purposes was soon reinforced. "It would be 'come and meet me here,' and when I turned up there would be photographers everywhere."

Soon after, Michael asked Lisa Marie to join him in a video, entitled "You Are Not Alone" in which it would appear that Michael was genuinely attracted to women.

Within it appeared a provocative semi-nude scene of the two of them within a pink-and-lavender landscape inspired by the 1920s illustrator Maxfield Parrish. There have been many published reports that Michael showed his genitals in this video and that, prior to its release, a computer process blurred his privates.

That report was probably untrue. "There's no way that Michael's going to show his dick," said an employee of MTV who saw the original video.

"He's spent a few million trying to get those nude pictures of himself returned from the Santa Barbara DA's safe to Neverland. He's never going to show the full monty to the world. Who do you think he is? Richard Gere?"

Eventually, writers Sean Kelly and Chris Kelly released a satirical parody of the Jackson/Presley union, entitled *HERstory*. Referring to them as "The Oz Couple," and configured as a *faux* diary that had supposedly been penned by Lisa Marie, it asked "How could a simple country girl hope to find happiness as the wife of a wealthy and talented extraterrestrial?"

Within the context of this so-called "diary," the Kellys have Lisa Marie writing:

Dear Diary,

I had an early call and we were on the set all day shooting the video for a song, 'You Are Not Alone.' Here's a Polaroid." (Running immediately adjacent to the "diary entry" is a picture of the Jacksons semi-nude.) The contrived "diary" entry continues: *It's supposed to be real and all so both of us were actually NAKED for hours rolling around on this bed in front of the cameras under these lights which made me hot in more ways than one (get it?). Although he was careful that I never got a real look at his famous Spotted*

The famous kiss

Thing, I actually thought we might end up doing 'it.' But at six o'clock Michael said cut, and I got up and put on my clothes and left.

Security guards at Neverland reported that whenever Lisa Marie came to visit, she always left the property before midnight to drive her children back to their own $4 million home in Hidden Hills.

Even after the passage of many weeks, reporters continued to speculate about the state of the marriage. One particularly outrageous rumor making the rounds asserted that Michael wanted a child with Lisa Marie, and that he had a candidate in mind as the secret father. That candidate was Michael's long-time friend and traveling companion, Frank Cascio. Michael, according to the rumors, was committed to witnessing the moment of conception wherein Frank, without a condom, would penetrate Lisa Marie. Neither Lisa nor Michael ever commented on this outrageous rumor.

According to the staff member, Michael was "filled with anxiety and tension whenever Lisa Marie came to visit. He was particularly irritable on those days, and obviously didn't welcome her presence, especially when he was keeping boys in his room, which he continued to do even after the Jordie Chandler fiasco."

Occasionally they would talk, usually in the presence of others, as it seemed that Michael sometimes didn't want to be alone with his new wife.

He warned her that if she attempted a musical career, she would inevitably be compared to her father, perhaps unfavorably. "I think that there is that huge mountain to climb," she told him. "Oh, people always think about *him* when they think about me. There will always be some of that, and I must embrace it and understand it. I have to find a good balance between my own identity and the role of always being the daughter of Elvis Presley."

In one bizarre story that may have only the slimmest basis in truth, Michael was said to have promised Lisa Marie that he'd build a replica of Graceland in the greater Santa Barbara area. But then the pop star changed his mind. He came up with the idea of moving into the actual Graceland. To do that, however, he would have to get the approval of his mother-in-law, Priscilla, who runs the board that controls Graceland. "She would never have gone for that," reported a publicist.

When the married couple traveled to Memphis for a Pay-Per-View tribute concert to Elvis on October 8, 1994, they stayed at the Adam's Mark Hotel, but in separate suites. Michael even refused to visit Graceland, where he once said he wanted to live. When Priscilla asked him to perform as part of the evening's entertainment, reports say that he refused, declaring, "I'm not appearing on a bill with other singers, especially one called Dwight Yoakam." Priscilla later told friends in Memphis, "Lisa Marie is married to a jerk."

Within Michael's presence, Lisa Marie once spoke candidly about her role as one of the most famous offspring in music history. "I could capitalize off Elvis in a zillion cheesy ways. Just look at Natalie Cole for example. She raised daddy from the grave for a hit song. I might not be the greatest of singers, certainly no female Elvis, but I plan to bring a sense of my own identity to my music. I'm not going to go through life singing 'Hound Dog' to a bunch of drunks at a night club in Memphis."

She also revealed that she and Michael talked about how hard it had been "growing up in a fish bowl. I'm not someone who desires or wants attention, and that's why I'm different from you," she told him. "I became famous the day I was born. But I've never been one of those people who run around, you know, walking every red carpet and going to every opening of every envelope, touting Presley perfumes and singing Elvis cover songs. I don't want attention."

Michael and Lisa Marie agreed to a joint appearance on ABC Television just before the release of his *HIStory* album. The host was a very friendly

Diane Sawyer, who didn't ask the really tough questions. At the appointed time, Michael and Lisa Marie showed up at ABC with a phalanx of attendants, including attorney Johnnie Cochran.

Eventually aired on June 14, 1995, the Sawyer interview took place on the old MGM set on the Sony Pictures lot in Culver City.

The world was watching as Michael and Lisa Marie faced

"You Are Not Alone" video,
Lisa Marie, left, and MJ

Diana Sawyer on *Prime Time Live*. "I was seventeen," Michael said in a voice evocative of a little girl, "when I first met Lisa Marie. And she was seven."

It was obvious that they hadn't rehearsed their stories enough, since there were contradictions. Michael claimed that he'd kept in touch with her over the years. Lisa Marie said they had not been in contact.

At one point she said that children "won't leave him alone—they follow him into the bathroom." As claimed by some members of Michael's staff at Neverland, that even included young boys taking off their underwear and joining Michael in the shower. "Didn't it ever occur to Michael Jackson to lock the bathroom door if he wanted privacy from young kids?" a commentator asked after viewing the show.

Cynics had their tongue in their cheek when the couple discussed their dream of having children—something that would never happen. They even talked about leaving America, possibly moving to Switzerland. Lisa Marie denied that her marriage to Michael was one of convenience. "Why would I marry somebody I didn't love? I admire him, I respect him, and I love him. He's in the studio, I'm in the kitchen. We run around the same house and we're normal people. And we don't sleep in separate bedrooms." Actually, Lisa Marie was not being truthful. Michael's staff leaked news to the press that they not only slept in separate bedrooms, but in separate houses.

Michael also denied that the drawings made by Jordie Chandler matched police photographs of his genitalia. "There was nothing that matched me to those charges," Michael alleged. He was backed up by Lisa Marie, who said, "There was nothing."

When Michael told Sawyer that "The whole thing is a lie," he breached his confidential settlement with Jordie Chandler.

At one point the question-and-answer session went like this:

SAWYER: *What is a thirty-six-year-old man doing sleeping with a twelve-*

year-old boy or a series of them?

MICHAEL: *Okay, when you say "boy," it's not just boys. I never invite just boys to come in my room. That's ridiculous. And that's a ridiculous question.* (The question was not ridiculous but rather pertinent, and Michael's answer was an obvious lie.)

MICHAEL: *I guess you want to hear it, the answer. I'll be happy to answer it.* (He obviously was anything but happy.)

MICHAEL: *I have never invited anyone into my bed, ever. Children love me, I love them. They follow me, they want to be with me. But anyone can come in my bed—a child can come in my bed if they want."* (Critics, who mocked Jackson, later cracked, "I bet many a kid has cum in Michael's bed.")

Observers who had expected Sawyer to be confrontational later asserted that "she had all the fierceness of the Stay Puft Marshmallow Man."

A hesitant Sawyer was edging up to the big question of the night. "I didn't spend my life as a serious journalist to ask these kinds of questions, but I'm not oblivious to the fact that your fans have one question they most want . . ."

With defiance on her face and disgust in her voice, Lisa Marie interrupted, "Do we have sex? Okay. Go ahead. Is that what you were going to ask? Yes! YES! Yes!"

Sawyer was called a "wimp" by Brad Dilford, a journalist, who later said that "Sawyer did not challenge Michael on any of his more questionable claims." Sawyer was also accused of several misstatements, including that Michael had been cleared on child molestation charges. Actually, the DA was officially keeping the case open until the statute of limitations would take effect in 1999.

On the show, Michael denied that the police in their raid on Neverland and on his secret condo had seized books with pictures of nude boys. The police, however, maintained that they did confiscate such materials.

Actually, Michael left himself an out. When Sawyer asked if material depicting young, undressed boys had been found among his personal effects,

United they stood

426

Michael replied, "No, not that I know of, unless people sent me things that I haven't opened."

In a review of the show, journalist Julene Snyder said, "Putting the two on live TV may have seemed like a good idea at the time, but it's hard to say which came across worse on camera. Lisa Marie quickly established herself as a tough, if inarticulate, cookie, who'd fit right in at a rundown trailer park. She is not now, nor has she ever been, a brain surgeon. Her quote in the current issue of *Vibe* magazine, which sports a nearly life-size headshot of hubby on the cover, starts off sweetly enough but quickly degenerates into a convoluted hiss of rage: 'Michael is a true artist in every fact of his nature—extremely aesthetic and very, very romantic. This is who he truly is despite degrading comments made in the past by certain larva. I can't wait for the day when all the snakes who have tried to take him out get to eat their own lunch and crawl back in the holes from which they came. We know who they are and their bluff is about to be called.'"

After the interview was aired, Tom Sneddon, the Santa Barbara DA who had been involved in the Jordie Chandler controversy, claimed that Michael had lied. "His statement on TV is untrue and incorrect and not consistent with the evidence in the case."

An enraged Evan Chandler witnessed the interview in which his son was virtually called a liar. Michael also claimed that the settlement is "not about all this crazy, outlandish money. No, it's not at all." There was no suggestion that the settlement was in the millions.

In the aftermath of the airing of the interview, Evan Chandler filed a $60 million lawsuit against Michael. In the suit he named not only Michael, but Lisa Marie Presley, Diane Sawyer, and ABC News. Attorneys for Lisa Marie eventually got her dropped from the suit, claiming that she had never been a party to the Chandler settlement. And eventually, a judge dismissed charges against Sawyer and ABC.

Matters were settled privately between Evan and Michael's lawyers. The terms would never be made public, but as regards the Chandler affair, Michael would never again utter a statement such as "the whole thing was a lie."

During the Sawyer interview, Lisa Marie had burst into anger when questioned about whether her Church of Scientology may have urged her to marry Michael, perhaps as a means of gaining a rich convert. "This is crap," she said. "I'm sorry. It's, like ridiculous. It's the most ridiculous thing I've ever heard. I'm not going to marry somebody for any reasons other than the fact that I've fallen in love with them. Period. And they can eat it if they want to think anything different!"

She has admitted that she was expelled from boarding school because of illegal drug abuse, especially cocaine. She later claimed "I got off drugs because of my religious conversion." When she was ten years old, she had a crush on the actor John Travolta. When meeting him for the first time, they developed a friendship in spite of their age differences. The actor is credited with encouraging her membership in the Church of Scientology, an organization to which her mother was already devoted.

Lisa Marie did make an attempt to convert Michael to her cult religion, though he found some of her conspiracy theories bizarre, including the church's attempt to link Adolf Hitler to the psychiatric profession. Tom

Lisa Marie with her son, Benjamin, 2001

Cruise might have fallen for that, but not Michael.

Lisa Marie's attempts to convert Michael to Scientology failed miserably, in ways that reflected Priscilla's earlier (failed) attempts to involve Elvis. Lamar Fike, one of Elvis's cronies, claimed that he was with Elvis when he visited the Scientology Center in Los Angeles. Elvis went in and talked to church leaders. When he came out, Elvis said, "Fuck those people! There's no way I'll ever get involved with that son-of-a-bitchin' group. All they want is my money." According to Fike, "Elvis stayed away from Scientology like it was a cobra. He'd shit a brick to see how far Lisa Marie's gotten into it."

On the Sawyer show, Lisa Marie claimed she was sharing Michael's bed at Neverland. Actually, following the show, she left for Hawaii and a family vacation with her ex-husband Danny and her two children. They shared a suite on the Big Island. Her publicist maintained that Lisa Marie was involved in a "family reunion trip. They're the best of friends."

That was evident to guests of the 3,200-room Mauna Lani Bay Resort who saw her walking about the gardens, holding hands with Danny and kissing.

Whenever Lisa Marie came back to Neverland, she inevitably got into an argument with Michael. It became obvious that this surreal marriage was heading for the divorce courts. Michael went "ballistic" when little Benjamin accidentally pulled off his wig. In anger, Lisa Marie took her children and fled from Neverland, vowing never to return.

In August of 1995, when Lisa Marie was spilling her woes to Priscilla, her mother urged her to "Dump the jerk! You should never have married the selfish bastard in the first place. Come to your senses and kick this freak out before these allegations of child molestation taint you too." For a change, Lisa Marie decided to take her mother's advice, even though it would take her a few months.

It was obvious to the entire staff that Lisa Marie's days at Neverland were numbered. She was particularly incensed when she learned that Michael was planning to build a villa on the grounds of Neverland to house Macaulay Culkin. Her patience with Michael and his obsessions with boys was running out. Constantly she complained that she was living in a zoo, with screaming children racing about with no one to discipline them.

Michael confronted her with evidence from a private investigator he'd hired to tail her. The detective reported on "many liaisons with Danny" which had taken place throughout the course of her marriage to Michael. Lisa Marie allegedly screamed back at him, "I had to get it from somebody."

In anger, Michael deserted his "fairytale marriage" and flew to Europe— not with Lisa Marie but with his eternal favorites, Eddie Cascio, now 11, and Frank Cascio, a ripe 15. The trio was seen at Euro Disney.

Lisa Marie had also flown out of Los Angeles, heading for another reunion with Danny in Hawaii and another "family vacation." All she would say to reporters was, "I'm a chip off the old block. Elvis liked Hawaii too." Privately she told friends, "Danny and I are soul-mates who should never have split. He's the father of my children."

Holding hands with Danny once again right in the lobby of their hotel in front of other guests, they were talking about getting back together again, discussing Lisa Marie's upcoming divorce from her "non-husband." A plan was set into motion in Hawaii.

At the release of *HIStory*, Michael made a number of commitments, which for reasons of his own he decided not to honor. One involved an HBO special, *One Night Only*, that had promised to rope in a global audience of some two-hundred-fifty million viewers.

During rehearsals for the HBO event, Michael collapsed. By ambulance he was rushed to Beth-Israel Medical Center where doctors reportedly found an "irregular heartbeat and dehydration." A newspaper the next morning asked a provocative question—"Dehydration? Doesn't he drink enough Pepsi?" The answer to that was that he drank no soft drinks at all.

Michael, however, resisted his advisers when they urged him to allow Lisa Marie into his hospital room. He relented when told that his refusal to see her would be a disastrous public relations move. Among the other visitors rallying to his side was Diana Ross.

Consequently, Lisa Marie was allowed to call on Michael at the hospital to discuss the terms of their impending divorce. Michael agreed to a payment of $15 million, but in exchange for that, he wanted some sort of guarantee that Lisa Marie would not speak about their marriage. . .ever. He most definitely didn't want her writing a tell-all autobiography. "I'm far too young to record my life," she responded. In addition, she asked for ten percent of the royalties on Michael's *HIStory* album, which he conceded.

The actual terms of the divorce would be ridiculed across America. On the *Tonight Show*, host Jay Leno quipped, "This is going to get ugly. According to divorce lawyers, you know, Lisa Marie is entitled to half of all the noses Michael acquired."

According to a nurse, who overheard the famous pair fighting, part of their argument involved their continuing debate over Danny. Michael, apparently, still had his private investigator following them. Not only that, but having bugged her private quarters at Neverland, where she stayed only during daylight hours, he claimed that on several occasions he had heard her having "phone sex" with Danny. He confronted her with this, and she responded in fury, enraged not so much by the fact that Michael knew details associated with her involvement with her former husband, but because of the fact that her phone had been bugged.

Lisa Marie denounced Michael in his hospital bed, accusing him of having spent their marriage "locked up in his bedrooms with young boys," instead of trying to be a husband to her. Often when Lisa Marie had called Neverland, he refused to take her calls. But she learned from the maid, Adrian McManus, that if Frank Cascio called, he was to be connected immediately.

At some point during that dialogue at the hospital, Michael ordered Lisa Marie from his room. In the corridor, a nurse overheard her shouting, "I'm outta here. And I'm not coming back."

In the wake of her split from Michael, Lisa Marie began to get her life together again. She spent more time with her children and saw a lot more of Danny. There was talk of a remarriage after her divorce from Michael. Danielle and Benjamin were happy to have daddy back home again. But impulsively Lisa Marie fell for her tall, blond bodyguard, Luke Watson, and Danny was out the door once again.

Lisa Marie made an appearance at the 12th annual MTV Awards on September 7, 1995 at Radio City Music Hall, the setting of their infamous kiss a year before. This time she sat through her husband's appearance. She'd not seen him in two months. She watched him grab his crotch and seemed disgusted. "Elvis would never have been so tasteless," she later said. Before the curtain went down, she'd mysteriously exited the theater to avoid paparazzi and her husband.

Lisa Marie later said that "the last straw" in her marriage to Michael came when he gave an interview to *TV Guide*, claiming that she'd told him that Elvis had had a nose job. "This is bullshit!" his daughter charged. "And all this from a guy who claims he's had only two nose jobs."

On January 18, 1996, in Los Angeles Superior Court, citing "irreconcilable differences," Lisa Marie at the age of 27 filed for divorce from her husband, Michael, who had turned 37. In her petition, Lisa Marie Presley-Jackson also called for the restoration of her original name, dropping the Jackson from it. A sexless, loveless marriage of twenty troubled months was coming to a notoriously publicized ending.

"The divorce was more predictable than the marriage," said Memphis music critic Stanley Booth.

Journalist Karen Schoemer summed it up: "No more strangely unwarm hand-holdings, no more endless speculation over whether they did or whether they didn't. No more prime time TV interviews with the two of them sitting stiff and pretty as alabaster statues, trying to convince the world of their deep love for one another when they barely seemed able to make eye contact. It wasn't the romance of the century, but it was the kind of twisted royal wedding our celebrity-glutted minds deserved."

On January 19, *The New York Post* said it all: JACKO GETS THE SACKO!

When the news of the divorce was reported in the press, it was revealed that Lisa Marie's petition to the court was a "basic, boilerplate, bare-bones document that leaves virtually all options open," at least according to her Beverly Hills attorney, Douglas Bagby. "She reserved the right to address community property issues and other asset concerns at a later date, to ask that Jackson pay her attorney fees, and to state her assets at a later time," said journalist Janet Gilmore.

"The marriage was a mere publicity stunt," said a member of Michael's staff, who refused to be named. "On Michael's part, he was trying to distract attention from the child abuse allegation. As for Lisa Marie, what was she thinking? She must have been 'All Shook Up.'"

Lisa Marie, in calling it quits, admitted that her marriage to Michael occurred during "a moment of madness." The world agreed with her, especially Priscilla.

Staff members at Neverland reported that they had heard Michael screaming at Lisa Marie, "Your fame comes from DNA. I'm the genuine star."

In public, at least, Lisa Marie had steadfastly maintained Michael's innocence in child molestation. Yet Rick Stanley, the stepbrother of Elvis, claimed that she confessed to him that she'd come upon videotapes at Neverland that "caused me great distress." She refused to discuss the exact nature of those tapes, but Stanley alleged that she learned "the sick truth about Michael and did indeed know that her husband had an unusual interest in young boys."

Lisa Marie later told a friend, "I feel deep guilt over my marriage to Michael. I brought shame on my father. I suppose that's why I'm having these awful dreams."

The story of Lisa Marie's involvement with the Jackson family did not end with her divorce from Michael. Gossips began speculating about the intriguing possibilities when Lisa Marie in 1998 began "dating" Janet Jackson. They were spotted at such New York clubs as Life, allegedly embracing and even kissing. This does not necessarily prove a lesbian involvement. Janet, for years, has been known for what some have termed her excessive embracing and loving "fondling" of her friends, and Lisa Marie was no exception. A waiter at one club claimed that the famous pair had been spotted "with their tongues down each other's throats," but this is only heresay and can't be verified.

When asked about her emerging new friendship with Janet, Lisa Marie, according to some reports, claimed that she was helping Janet get back into shape for her *Velvet Rope* road tour. It's true that Janet's weight at the time had ballooned by forty-five pounds. Although on most occasions she has a "sex kitten" figure, she could, during bouts of depression, become bloated, much to the delight of the paparazzi who seemed to know whatever fast-food hamburger joint she happened to have patronized during the previous week.

On many occasions during their joint forays into the world at large, Lisa Marie and Janet wore disguises, but they were often recognized in spite of their efforts to conceal their identities. They were seen shopping on Rodeo Drive in Beverly Hills and on Fifth Avenue in New York. They went to off-Broadway plays together, and "like two ladies who lunch," according to a waiter, were seen together at a swank Manhattan eatery. Their club nights were much wilder, particularly as the evening moved toward the early morning hours.

Lisa Marie was the star guest at Janet's launch party for her seventh album, *The Velvet Rope.*

Elvis's daughter warmly embraced Janet when she seemed near tears after one of Michael's fans thrust a review at her. In the review, a music critic claimed, "Janet Jackson is a failed cloning experiment, with all of Michael's foibles and bizarre personal quirks but none of the musical or visual talent."

Lisa Marie not only consoled her former sister-in-law, but accepted her invitation to be her "date" at the upcoming MTV Awards.

When reports of this strange friendship reached Michael, he was furious, fearing that Lisa Marie was using these occasions to gossip about him to his sister. "Who knows the tales she'll tell about me," Michael was reported to have said.

Lisa Marie sent word to Michael, via Janet, that as a devotee of Scientology she had been taught "not to hold anger in my heart." In a card to her former husband, she scribbled, "All is forgiven." A friend of Lisa Marie's claimed that she once told her, "Who wouldn't want to hang out with Frank Cascio—that's one hot man." That alleged quote cannot be verified.

After their divorce, Michael tried to mend his broken friendship with Lisa Marie, and she eventually accepted an invitation to join him on his *HIStory* tour in both London and South Africa.

In Johannesburg, Lisa Marie told friends that she hoped to spend some quality time with Michael as a means of re-establishing a relationship with him—"strictly as friends," she hastened to add.

But in South Africa, she was disappointed to find Michael spending all his free time with a young boy from Norway, who appeared to be only thirteen years old if that. "All I remember about the kid is that he was cute and was never seen without a red baseball cap, a gift from Michael," Lisa Marie said. At the time the press was unaware of the identity of this boy. In time both photographs and his real name would be revealed. In South Africa, Michael—and only when forced to do so—introduced him as his "nephew."

Once again Lisa Marie allowed herself to become a "prop" in a photo opt for Michael when she accepted an invitation to be photographed with him, along with her two children, at a tribal ceremony that took place in the seedy town of Phokeng, some ninety miles to the north of Johannesburg. At the time he was deep into his second marriage, and Michael shocked the world when he appeared with Lisa Marie on his arm. That naturally led to press speculation that the ill-fated duo were getting back together.

Back in Los Angeles, Debbie Rowe, Michael's new wife, reportedly said, "If Michael Jackson [she always referred to him by his full name] wants to date his ex-wife, and I want to date my ex-boyfriend, that is nobody's business but our own."

Under the shade of a red-and-white umbrella at least five feet wide, Michael arrived at the tribal ceremony like a king for his induction into a tribe known as the Bafokeng Ka Bakwena ("People of the Crocodile"). With some 325,000 members, the tribe was not among the poor and needy of Africa, as they owned the second-largest platinum reserve on earth.

On hearing of Lisa Marie's adventures in South Africa with her ex-husband, one underground columnist in Hollywood wrote: "Lisa Marie is back with Michael while still dating Janet. The next thing you'll read in this column is that Elvis's daughter is having a three-way with Jermaine and La Toya. I wouldn't put it past this 'Hound Dog!'"

Even after her friendships with Janet and Michael had cooled, throughout the rest of her life Lisa Marie would be plagued with probing questions about her marriage to Michael.

On *The Howard Stern Show*, the host asked her to describe Michael's genitalia. She refused. She did answer Stern's question about whether she had "dabbled with chicks?"

"Just one," she said. "It's not like I haven't had an urge, but I just . . . I like to keep it at bay."

In a candid conversation with *Playboy*, she claimed that her preference in sex was "porn style—I am a little dark on the subject. I like it rough, the way they do things in porn movies."

In trying to explain her association with Michael to *Playboy*—of all magazines—Lisa Marie said, "Yes, there was a physical attraction. He's not sexually seductive, but there is something riveting about him."

If attorney Johnnie Cochran is to be believed—and after the O.J. Simpson trial there remains much doubt as to his veracity—Lisa Marie made an astonishing call to him one night. Reached in New York, he came to the phone to hear the distraught young woman pleading for his intervention in getting Michael back.

"I don't want him gone from my life," Cochran later quoted Lisa Marie as saying. "I know the marriage didn't work out. But we didn't give it a chance. I think I could make him love me. But to do that, you've got to prevent his marriage to that nurse."

Cochran promised to intervene on her behalf. But he told friends in New York that there was really nothing he could do. "Michael wanted someone to make babies for him, and Debbie Rowe seems willing. Lisa Marie wanted romance. Something, in my opinion, I believe she would never have gotten from Michael. I can't believe that after completely ignoring her during the marriage that she could even entertain the idea of wanting him back. She never had him in the first place. Personally, I think it was just one of those crazy ideas that occurs to young people in the middle of the night. Lisa Marie is smart enough to know that the marriage was doomed from the start. Or was she? I know why Michael married her. The reasons were selfish. The question remains, why did she marry him? She's got all the money in the world. Everyone who surrounded Michael wanted his money, Lisa Marie could buy and sell her husband. Surely she didn't want Michael for sex? Not that! Oh, please, never that!"

In 2003, six years after Lisa Marie filed for divorce, stories about the Jackson/Presley relationship were still generating headlines. It was reported that Michael was trying to reunite with Lisa Marie as a means of retaining custody of his three children.

After divorcing Michael, Lisa Marie drifted from relationship to relationship until she finally fell in love with actor Nicolas Cage, marrying him on August 10, 2002. Michael learned that their relationship was tempestuous, even though they would not finally divorce until May 26, 2004. In the months that preceded Lisa Marie's divorce from Cage, it was reported that Michael wanted to reactivate the Jackson/Presley alliance.

As reported in the press at the time: "Jackson reportedly wants to re-marry Lisa Marie, who divorced her husband, actor Nicolas Cage," one report stated. "Jackson apparently believes he has a better chance of evading an investigation into his suitability as a father—promoted by his dangling of baby Prince Michael II over the balcony of a German hotel last month—if he is in a stable relationship."

It is not known if Michael actually proposed to Lisa Marie again. But when hearing reports of this potential offer, she was alleged to have said, "I won't be used again!"

In March of 2003, during the course of a particularly candid interview , Lisa Marie—rather unconvincingly—maintained that she did have sex with the pop king. She said that "he was just a normal guy" underneath his eccentric exterior. Reporter Phil Blackman said that "surely Lisa Marie is putting us on with that comment."

She also said that she was "smitten with Michael until the relationship turned ugly at the end. I absolutely fell in love with him. He was just a typical man when I began to date him." Again Blackman found her statement difficult to swallow. "How, even on the darkest night, could she really believe that Michael Jackson by any stretch of the imagination was a typical man? Maybe after having Elvis for a father, Michael Jackson might have been typical but I doubt that."

When Lisa Marie eventually got around to releasing her debut album on April 8, 2003, on Capitol Records, she did it on her own without Michael's help. Bought mostly by Elvis fans, *To Whom It May Concern* reached number 5 on *Billboard's* Top 200 albums chart. When Michael first heard her album, he referred to it as having been sung by "a brawny collection of Sheryl Crowish pop rockers."

During her promotion of her album, in references to her previous marriage, Lisa Marie said that she felt "powerless." "I was part of a machine. I saw things going on that I couldn't do anything about. Don't ask me what sort of things, because I'm not going to answer. But just stuff."

In an interview with *Rolling Stone*, she claimed that "I never thought for a moment that someone like him could actually use me for a reason like that.

It never crossed my mind, and I don't know why—I'm sure it crossed everybody else's."

At the same time, she admitted that she was "terrified" when her husband kissed her on the mouth at the opening of the 1994 MTV Video Music Awards. "That was not my idea, by the way." When asked if Michael was trying to prove that he was straight by kissing her, she said, "Yeah, but again, I wasn't looking at it like that. See, if I had been, that wouldn't have happened."

When asked in 2004 how she felt about Michael, she claimed, "It's really bizarre. I feel nothing."

Her second album, *Now What?* in 2005 reached number 9 on *Billboard's* pop charts and was certified gold. Unlike her first album, *Now What?* included a parental advisory sticker.

In March of 2005, as a means of promoting her album, Lisa Marie appeared on *The Oprah Winfrey Show*. "Do you think that he loved you as much as he could?" the talk show diva asked Elvis's daughter in regards to Michael.

"Yes, as much as he was capable of loving somebody," she said. Oprah then asked if Lisa Marie felt that Michael had used her. "All signs point to yes on that. I can't answer for him." On the show she admitted that she felt uncomfortable talking about Michael. "This seat is hot!" she said. Later she told the Associated Press that Michael was the "most toxic" of her many relationships. "I don't want to bash him. I don't hate him. I don't have any of that going on."

No great fan of her former son-in-law, Priscilla also spoke to Oprah on camera, suggesting that Michael may have used her daughter in the hopes that Lisa Marie would have his children. "That would ensure his connection to Elvis's legacy," she claimed. "There's something very calculating and manipulative about how he does things."

For reasons known only to herself, Lisa Marie continued to issue bizarre statements about Michael that "the whole world knows aren't true," in the words of one reporter. He was referring to her comment about her ex-husband's second marriage to Debbie Rowe. "With me, Michael did redeem himself in the end and things are better between us now. It was not a fun time for either of us. He's happily married and has a baby coming now, which is great!" Lisa Marie's claims of Michael's "happy" second marriage brought ridicule in press offices around the country.

As Elvis's only recognized child, she inherited his entire estate when she turned thirty. In August of 2005, she sold 85 percent of the estate's business holdings to CKX, Inc., excluding Graceland itself.

Although long since divorced, Michael still followed the career and activities of Lisa Marie, learning that in February of 2006 she had married Michael

Lockwood in a ceremony in Kyoto, Japan. She was thirty-eight at the time. It was her fourth marriage. The best man was Lisa Marie's first husband, Danny Keough. Michael was not invited to the wedding.

Lisa Marie's final word on both her marriage to Michael and to "hothead" Nicolas Cage was, "I was really into this lioness thing with Michael and wanted to protect him," she claimed. "How could I be so naïve? One needs to protect oneself from Michael."

"As for Nick, we're both so dramatic and dynamic that when it was good, it was unbelievably good, and when it was bad, it was just a fucking bloody nightmare for everybody," she said. "If you lined up all the men I've been with in a row, you'd think that I was completely psychotic."

Neither Nicholas Cage nor Michael had any comment about Lisa Marie's remarks.

On the website, "NNDB: Tracking the Entire World," the sexual orientation of Lisa Marie is listed as "bisexual," her occupation, "relative."

During the course of his marriage to Lisa Marie, in the wake of the Jordie Chandler out-of-court settlement, Michael found himself embroiled in yet another lawsuit. In December of 1994, in a "wrongful termination" suit, five former employees, including Michael's maid, Adrian McManus, filed a lawsuit against the star and seven members of his staff. The suit charged that the employees were repeatedly subjected to retribution for their agreeing to help Santa Barbara authorities with the criminal investigation of Michael and for their testimony before a grand jury.

Joining McManus in the suit were security officers Kassim Abdool and his assistants, Ralph Chacon and Melanie Bagnall, one of the few women who worked in security. The final plaintiff was longtime office manager, Sandy Domz.

In Michael's opinion, his staff "had been only too willing to cooperate with the grand jury." For doing that, the former Neverland employees cited "a pattern of intentional, willful, and malicious conduct designed to threaten and intimidate" them. The plaintiffs also charged that they had been threatened with bodily injury, even subjected to death threats. It was also revealed that Neverland security forces had installed an elaborate "Gestapo-like" system of wiretapping, and that Michael himself often eavesdropped on the personal calls of his employees.

One Neverland employee charged that the "surveillance equipment at Neverland was so intricate, as was the telephone-tapping system, that the CIA should hire Jackson's OSS officers," a reference to the special force—known within Neverland as the Office of Special Services—that Bill Bray, Michael's most devoted employee, had brought to Neverland to "protect Michael from all harm."

All three of the female plaintiffs charged that the OSS officers had subjected them to sexual harassment. McManus also claimed that one of the officers "threatened to slice my throat if I ever revealed Michael's private life to the press."

The plaintiffs never revealed exactly what they told the grand jury, but their testimony was believed to have been devastating in the Chandler vs. Jackson case. Abdool said that he, along with his aide, Ralph Chacon, delivered a jar of Vaseline to Michael's suite. It was not explained why Abdool's assistant, Chacon, delivered that one jar of Vaseline. Chacon reported that he saw "two young boys" in the room with Michael, before he took the jar and slammed the door in their faces.

Sandy Domz had gone so far as to call the Santa Barbara County Sheriff's Department to reveal that "illegal wiretaps" were being carried out at Neverland. In September of 1994, the employees, claiming they could no longer tolerate the harassment and intimidation at the ranch, quit their jobs.

It wasn't until shortly before Christmas of 1994 that they found an attorney, Michael Ring, in Santa Barbara who would take their case. In the suit, Michael was charged along with his employees, specifically Bill Bray, but also James Van Norman, Jerome Johnson, Tony Coleman, Andrew Merritt, Bettye Bailey, and Marcus Johnson (no relation to Jerome).

In his defense of the Neverland employees, Ring faced a battery of the highest paid attorneys in California, the firm of Katten Muchin Zavis & Weitzman.

Their case may have been lost shortly after it began, when Judge Zel Canter ruled that any evidence from the Jordie Chandler civil case would not be permitted in court. Since the plaintiff's entire case depended on the harassment they were allegedly subjected to during the Chandler case, the die was cast. The trial, which was a disaster from the beginning, would slog onward from September 15, 1996 to March 17, 1997.

Michael's defense team suffered a near-mortal blow when Jerome Johnson, one of the co-defendants, seemingly switched sides during pre-trial hearings, claiming that he backed up the allegations of the former Neverland employees. As an elite member of the OSS, Johnson said that his sole job was to apply "pressure on the staff by harassing them." Johnson filed an official decla-

Lisa Marie on Oprah's infamous couch

ration with the court, backing up the allegations of the "Neverland Five," even though they were suing him. Privately, he told a reporter that he was deeply religious and "I can no longer participate in the lies of Michael Jackson. I can't sleep at night thinking about what I have done for Jackson."

In April of 1995, Jerome Johnson, for "his act of betrayal," was terminated at Neverland after seven years of employment there. In addition, Michael's lawyers cut Johnson loose from the case, leaving him with no lawyer until he hired the defense attorney, Charles Matthews.

On January 24, 1996, a blackmail note was delivered to Michael's business office, demanding that $7 million be wired to a bank account in San Francisco. Each plaintiff was quizzed to see if he or she had sent the note. All of them testified that they did not. Judge Zel Canter ordered that a DNA swab be taken from each participant in the case. According to court reporter Diane Dimond, a match came back. Apparently, the envelope that contained the note had been licked by the wife of Jerome Johnson.

In 1996, when Johnson appeared at the trial, something akin to despair showed on the faces of the plaintiffs. Apparently because of the incriminating note, Johnson pleaded the Fifth Amendment and refused to repeat or validate any of his earlier testimony—testimony that had verified the claims of the plaintiffs. After this setback, it became increasingly obvious that the plaintiffs' case against Michael Jackson was lost.

Even so, reporters were astonished at the verdict. Michael was found innocent of all charges. But in a countersuit the star had filed against these employees, they were ordered by the court to pay one and a half million dollars to Michael for various transgressions. McManus, for example, was charged with "stealing souvenirs from the ranch for resale to Jackson fans." Having no money to pay the judgment, the plaintiffs filed for bankruptcy.

After the case, one juror, who refused to give his name, said, "Most of us on the jury, with one notable exception, were very impressed with Michael's talent and his stardom. It was hard to throw the book against him. Some of us felt that he'd suffered enough humiliation—not to mention losing millions— in that Jordie Chandler case we'd all heard about. Most of the plaintiffs struck us as disgruntled former employees hoping to catch a free ride on the gravy train."

Disgruntled employees at Neverland were not the only ones hoping to catch a ride on the MJ gravy train. Victor M. Gutierrez, an investigative journalist living in Los Angeles in 1995, wrote the most sensational book ever written about Michael. It was called *Michael Jackson Was My Lover*, and it was reported to be *The Secret Diary of Jordie Chandler*.

The story came to the attention of America when Gutierrez appeared that year on *Hard Copy*, the TV show. On the air, he claimed that he knew of a

Nicolas Cage with Lisa Marie, circa 2001

videotape containing footage of Michael Jackson molesting a boy.

His source allegedly was "the mother" (unnamed) of the young boy. It was rumored that the child was Jason Francia, the son of Michael's former maid, Blanca Francia. Later Gutierrez reportedly told the *National Enquirer* that his source had been Margaret Maldonado, who had been married to Jermaine. On hearing of the rumor that her son, Jeremy, was filmed having sex with Michael, Maldonado threatened to bring a lawsuit against the *National Enquirer* if the paper ran the story. "I will end up owning the paper," she threatened.

Hard Copy correspondent Diane Dimond did report the allegations, though the *National Enquirer* never published the story. Gutierrez had told Dimond that he'd seen a "27-minute video of the King of Pop in a compromising position with a boy." The *Hard Copy* reporter later repeated those allegations on a Los Angeles TV station.

In retaliation, Michael issued a $100 million slander suit against both Gutierrez and *Hard Copy*. An investigation into the matter revealed no copy of the video to back up the journalist's claim.

At one point the writer claimed that Elizabeth Taylor and Gil Garcetti, the Los Angeles County District Attorney, could verify the existence of the videotape. Of course, they could not—and did not. On October 15, Judge Reginald Dunn ruled that the story was false and that Gutierrez had "acted with malice" and was therefore liable for presumed and punitive damages. On October 15, 1996, the jury awarded Michael $2.7 million in the slander suit, and Gutierrez filed for bankruptcy in October of 1997.

"Jurors told us that they not only wanted to compensate Mr. Jackson and punish Victor Gutierrez, but to send a message that they are tired of tabloids lying about celebrities for money," Michael's attorney, Zia Modabber, told the Associated Press.

In April 14, 1999, Modabber spoke to the press once again. "Unfortunately, anybody can walk into a courthouse with a couple of hundred dollars and file a lawsuit. It doesn't take any more than that. And if you happen to be suing Michael Jackson or any other celebrity for that matter, you are going to find yourself all over TV. You can tell the whole world about your scandalous accusations and people are going to listen to you."

Gutierrez fled to Chile and wrote his book *Michael Jackson Was My Lover*. It was published in Santiago, Chile, in March of 1996, with a subsequent second edition printed in January of 1997. It was subsequently banned from sale in the United States, and as such, the "tell all" has become a high-priced collector's item.

The book was illustrated with very intimate private photographs of young Jordie, even of the bed where Evan Chandler found his son sleeping with Michael in a sexual position. Candid photographs of Jordie's naked torso were also published under the caption, "Jackson's Taste." One photograph displays what are purported to be five pairs of underwear worn by Jordie, both boxer and jockey shorts. Gutierrez alleges that "the singer kept these in his room, including some with shit and urine stains."

In the book, private documents not previously available to the public were also published, even the drawing that Jordie drew during the sexual abuse scandal that depicted the boy committing suicide by jumping off a building. It is not known how Gutierrez obtained these documents, which included some of Evan Chandler's handwritten notes to his attorney, Barry Rothman. The authenticity of these documents has never been challenged.

The most controversial diagram is a sketch of Michael's penis which was drawn by Jordie and presented to his father on October 24, 1993 at 11:45pm. The boy, staying up late that night, even dated the time of submission. The following morning, after studying the sketch, which included notes about "spots and marks" on Michael's body, Evan Chandler turned his son's document over to the police. It is not known how this secret document became available to Gutierrez, but it did, and he subsequently published a replica of it in his book.

In his author's acknowledgements, Gutierrez thanks many people whom he alleges contributed to the book, including two of Michael's former maids, Blanca Francia and Adrian MacManus. He also thanks such formerly intimate friends of Michael as Wade Robson and even detectives of the Sheriff's Department of Santa Barbara and officials and detectives of the Child Abuse Unit of the LAPD.

Despite the controversy raging around them, Gutierrez's book and its illustrations are far too detailed and "insiderish" to be easily dismissed. It is obvious that Gutierrez had inside knowledge culled from many sources. It's also obvious that he secured documents and illustrations not available to other journalists and biographers.

In the book Gutierrez draws some shocking conclusions:

Jackson loved Jordie. The King of Pop had had sexual relations with many children, but Jordie was special. Jordie was his lover, his companion. He desired him physically and couldn't be separated from him. He was his top priority, his life, the only person he wanted close to him. That's why he told Jordie "I've never gone so far sexually with a boy as I have with you." Jordie felt the same. He was attracted to his friend, his idol, and lost his virginity, so to speak, with him. He enjoyed sex with his friend. He received his friend's attention, care and gifts.

As late as April of 2005, *Michael Jackson Was My Lover: The Secret Diary of Jordie Chandler* was still making news. Karina Longworth reported that Fenton Bailey and Randy Barbato of "World of Wonder," the production company behind films that included *Inside Deep Throat* and *The Eyes of Tammy Faye*, had optioned Gutierrez's book for the movies.

The Spanish language edition of the book, unlike the English version, contained a description of Michael's "alleged inappropriate dalliance with singer Ricky Martin," according to Longworth.

Months after the event, it was revealed that the raid on Neverland had turned up two trunks filled with pictures of young Ricky Martin.

In the Spanish language version appears a statement that was translated into English as follows: "Amongst the photographs confiscated by the police during the raid [a reference to the first raid on Neverland], the detectives found some of an unidentifiable Hispanic boy. Later they discovered that they were of Ricky Martin, the singer and ex-member of the band, Menudo, who is now an actor on the North American soap opera *General Hospital*. Even though the photographs of the now-actor were taken from magazines and promotional stills, they sufficiently indicate a liking towards the ex-member of Menudo."

There is no evidence that Ricky Martin, as a member of Menudo or as a successful solo singer of such hits as "Livin' La Vida Loca," ever had a relationship of any kind with Michael.

Rumors about Martin's sexual preference have appeared frequently in the press, but Martin has denied charges of homosexuality.

Martin joined the Latin boy group, Menudo, in 1984 at the tender age of twelve, when he first came to Michael's attention.

Ricky Martin

The police concluded that the then-minor, Martin, "never reached the point of knowing Jackson." In an interview, the singer was asked about the photographs found at Neverland. He indicated his surprise but admitted that he had always thought "that the King of Pop had a platonic liking towards me." At one point Michael invited the Menudo boys for some photographs but Martin claimed that he was not a member of the group yet. "When I did join the group, I was fully aware that Jackson liked Menudo. But I never would have thought that this man would have kept photographs of me when I was a young boy. The police never contacted me, because I never knew Jackson."

Although no one has successfully linked Martin sexually with Michael, the Puerto Rican singer did shock his fans in December of 2005 when he bluntly told *American Blender* magazine that he "loved giving the golden shower" to his partners. Martin later posted a message on his website, claiming that he "regretted his frankness and wished I had kept quiet."

As Michael's looks deteriorated after 2000, Martin was named by *People* magazine as one of the "Fifty Most Beautiful People in the World." In 2006 *People en Español* bestowed the same honor upon this handsome man.

One of his most ardent fans posted this message on a website: "Ricky baby, you can piss on me in the early morning, before lunch, twice in the afternoon, and all night long. But why waste it down the bathtub drain? It's my favorite cocktail. Better than *cerveza*."

In a startling report in *La Cuarta Diario*, under the head (translated into English) VICTOR GUTIERREZ PLANS HIS REVENGE, the journalist is quoted as saying, "This time, the Neverland ranch will be mine." It is not clear how Gutierrez planned to take over as the chatelain of Neverland. Perhaps by counter-suing Michael?

Despite these legal woes, Michael continued to plan public appearances, the release of a new album, and a major upheaval in his private life . . . and not one that revolved around a boy.

During the declining months of his relationship with Lisa Marie, Michael seemed less concerned with his wife than he was with his latest album.

Released in the summer of 1995, *HIStory: Past Present and Future*, was divided into two different segments—*HIStory Begins* and *HIStory Continues*. The first collection featured Michael's all-time hits such as "Billie Jean," "Beat It," "Bad," and "Black Or White." The songs on *HIStory Continues* were new, including "Scream," "Smile," and "Tabloid Junkie." Some of these songs were autobiographical, a musical and poetic record of what had overtaken him during the previous two years. Executives at Sony were clearly worried about sales during the week leading up to the release of the album.

Michael launched his *HIStory* world tour in Prague in the Czech Republic on September 7, 1996, ending it in Durham, South Africa, on October 15,

1997. He performed a total of 82 concerts to some four and a half million fans in 58 cities, 35 countries, and 5 continents. This was the first album in which Michael showcased his instrumental talent, playing keyboard and synthesizer, guitar, drums, and percussion on the album.

Fans who bought his *HIStory* album confronted a more aggressive Michael, especially in the single, "They Don't Care About Us." In the song, Michael laments, "I'm tired of being the victim of shame, you're throwing me in a class with a bad name, I can't believe this is the land from which I came."

One of his finest compositions, "Strangers in Moscow," was also on the album. The first single from the album, "Scream," was a duet with the other successful sibling in the family, Janet. In "Scream," Michael laments, "Stop pressuring me, stop pressuring me." Janet also made an award-winning video of the song with her by now-notorious brother.

The most controversial song from the album, "They Don't Care About Us," brought angry protests from the Anti-Defamation League because of its anti-Semitic lyrics. "Michael Jackson has an anti-Semitic streak," claimed Abraham Foxman, the director of the Anti-Defamation League. "It seems every time he has a problem in his life, he blames it on Jews."

"Jew me, sue me, everybody do me, kick me, kike me," Michael sang.

The reaction of Jews was so hostile that it forced Michael to apologize. He changed the lyrics, claiming most unconvincingly that "the song was intended to fight prejudice." Considering the original lyrics, virtually no one bought the defense. Michael would later solicit—but not receive—Louis Farrakhan's support following the outcry raised by his song.

Privately, Michael wanted the Islamic minister to launch a "holy war" against Jewish music executives in the industry.

Astonishingly, Michael claimed that Jews objecting to his anti-Semitic lyrics were, in fact, "persecuting me" for his tirades. This showed an amazing lack of sensitivity on his part. The Jewish community, of course, had a legitimate right to attack the anti-Semitic lyrics. But nonetheless, Michael seemed to want revenge for the Anti-Defamation League's attacks on his lyrics.

Farrakhan wisely opted to sit out this dispute. "If Jackson wants to take on the Jews, let him," the minister said. "I'll battle them in my own way, without getting involved in Jackson's music wars." On October 16, 1995, Farrakhan had denounced Jews as "financial bloodsuckers" at his "Million Man March."

With *HIStory*, Michael—at least in initial sales—showed that he could still "cut it" at the age of 40. The album sold 18 million copies before tumbling from the charts. It appeared that the mind-boggling sales associated with his *Thriller* days during the 1980s were over.

Much of the reaction from the press was unfavorable. Julene Snyder, a

San Francisco based freelance writer said. "Thus far, outrageously expensive promotion (a reported $30 million) for *HIStory: Past, Present and Future, Book I,*' has been characterized by remarkably poor judgment by people who really should know better. The deeply disturbing neo-fascist trailer for *HIStory*—rife with screaming children, fainting girls, marching soldiers, helicopters and explosions—climaxes with the unveiling of a huge statue of the singer, and a young blond boy's dewy look as he shouts, 'Michael, I love you!' As if that weren't peculiarly creepy enough, the next shot follows a helicopter as it flies through straddled-apart legs of the statue—fairly ambiguous imagery, given the circumstances. Jackson, who clearly craves adulation as much as any junkie needs a fix, has announced a tour of 40-foot statues of himself, starting with one floating down the Thames in London. Can you say overkill?"

Many other artists would have considered *HIStory* a smashing success, but Michael was bitterly disappointed in its sales, hoping again for another *Thriller*. Critics in the music industry said that Michael's most loyal fans already owned the hits on the album and didn't want to buy the same music twice. "Not only that, but the new songs weren't strong enough to offset the added cost of the album," or so wrote critic Bob Griffith.

Michael faced yet another disappointment when he learned that *Eagles: Their Greatest Hits 1971-1975* was threatening to catch up with *Thriller*'s record-breaking sales. The Eagles eventually topped *Thriller* in sales.

An American rock music group formed in Los Angeles in the early 70s, The Eagles, were among the most successful recording artists of that decade. Two of their albums, *Eagles: Their Greatest Hits 1971-1975* and *Hotel California*, rank among the ten best-selling albums of all time. On December 7, 1999, the Recording Industry of America honored the group with an award for the "Best Selling Album of the Century" for their Greatest Hits album, which chronicled the high-flying 70s with what they called "life in the fast lane" and the pursuit and unraveling of the American dream.

While touring with *HIStory*, Michael released a mini-movie, *Ghosts*, a horror story. In the plot, Michael is appropriately cast as a "weird man" who's living in a haunted house on the hill. Directed by Stan Winston, *Ghosts* had a mixed reaction. As one reviewer noted, "I think commercially his best days were behind him but this is still an excellent video and far exceeds a lot of crap put out there today."

In 1997 he also released a "remix" album, *Blood on the Dance Floor—HIStory in the Mix*, featuring five new songs, two of which had been featured in *Ghosts*. The other eight songs were remixes from the *HIStory* album. Ironically, even though many of its songs were re-releases from earlier albums, *Blood* became one of the biggest remix albums ever, selling seven million copies globally.

Michael's onstage behavior, meanwhile, had become increasingly imperial and in some cases, bizarre, so much so that Michael sometimes suffered from the outrage these acts seemed to catalyze in the minds of competitors. In 1996, in London at the Brit Awards, Michael selected "Earth Song," as his big number. At the end of "Earth Song," Michael in dazzling white was hoisted over the stage in a crucifixion pose and was then surrounded onstage by children and a rabbi yearning to touch him. As one former fan put it, "Jackson rose to Grace amidst the steaming pile of sub-Disney doo-doo."

Jarvis Cocker

The quasi-religious assumptions of the choreography proved to be too much for Jarvis Cocker, the outspoken lead singer of the British band, Pulp, who immediately raced onto the stage and in front of millions of onlookers, shook his ass derisively at Michael. Michael did not conceal the look of shock on his face when he registered that his "big number," in front of millions of onlookers, wasn't going off as had been previously planned. At no point did Cocker ever threaten Michael. But in a rock-hooligan kind of prank that was permeated with comic, or absurdist, relief, Cocker, who was joined at some point onstage by his friend, Peter Mansell, made it abundantly clear that he did not wholeheartedly approve of Michael's act. In quick reaction, Michael's security forces chased Cocker across the stage and eventually, out of the range of the cameras.

Cocker later admitted that the prank had been conceived as a protest against Michael's "quasi-religious pretensions." Cocker went on to say that because of the accusations of child abuse still swirling around Michael, he found Michael's inclusion of under-aged performers "distasteful."

Later, Michael's guards falsely asserted that Cocker had injured a child

Pulp

446

dancer during his on-camera escapade. Partly as a result of that, Cocker was hauled to a nearby police station where he was questioned in an hours-long interrogation that began at 1am. Subsequently, Cocker was released, and no charges were filed against him.

Michael later told the press that he felt "sickened, saddened, shocked, upset, cheated, and angry" at the caper, calling Cocker's behavior "disgusting and cowardly." On hearing that, Cocker countered, "My actions were a protest at the way Michael Jackson sees himself as some kind of Christ-like figure with the power of healing. The music industry allows him to indulge his fantasies because of his wealth and power. People go along with it even though they know it's a bit sick. I just couldn't go along with it anymore. It was a spur-of-the-moment decision brought on by boredom and frustration. But also, I find it very insulting to be accused of assaulting children."

Ironically, the protest generated headlines worldwide. Sales of Michael's single, "Earth Song," soared, as did the Cocker album, *Different Class*. And despite the somewhat childish way in which Cocker had protested Michael's self-portrayal as an object of religious veneration, Cocker had a point. A video later showed that in their denunciations of Cocker's protest, Michael's staff had lied. "It was the bouncer's arm, not Cocker's, that went up and accidentally thumped a child in the face," a report concluded. The March edition of *Melody Maker* even suggested that Cocker should be knighted.

Just when it seemed that Michael had run out of surprises for the press, a new woman, a "motorcycle mama" who was anything but demure, entered his life.

Michael had known her for some time, ever since as an assistant to Michael's dermatologist, she had applied Benoquin, a bleaching cream, to his scrotum, trying to make the pink spots on dark skin even out into a harmonious whole.

Michael evoking Christ.

"I go around the world dealing with running and hiding. I can't take a walk in the park. I can't go to the store. I have to hide in my room. You feel like in prison."

--Michael Jackson

"I would never do this for money, I did this because I love him. That's the only reason I did this."

--Debbie Rowe, wife #2

"How do you square Jackson's preoccupation with childhood innocence with the pseudomilitary iconography of his wardrobe and the flashes of violence in his videos? Or the business savvy that led him to purchase the lucrative song catalogs of The Beatles and Sly Stone with the gross financial mismanagement that may soon cost him those catalogs?"

--Touré

"See, we both like to write in private. And now we know why. 'Cause we talk to ourselves. Lines just come zinging out. You have to have someone who you respect hear you sound stupid."

--Lionel Richie on writing "We Are The World"

"My friendship with him is the most important thing to me, and if this marriage gets in the way of that friendship, then we'll put that marriage aside."

--Debbie Rowe

"I really screamed at him. Michael, you've got to change your behavior. Mainly with children, because again, although you know you are innocent and you are doing nothing to them, it just doesn't look good. It doesn't look right!"

--Uri Geller

Chapter Fourteen

"Who the hell is Debbie Rowe?" Madonna asked a roomful of her cohorts. One of her hairdressers responded that she was a "motorcycle mama" and that he'd dated one of her biker boyfriends.

Madonna wasn't alone in asking that question. If news of Michael's marriage to Lisa Marie had electrified the world, the pop star's second marriage came as a shock, catching the hound dogs of press and paparazzi unaware.

On November 15, 1996, about a year after his divorce from Lisa Marie, Michael took Debbie Rowe, a nurse, as his second bride. This time the bride didn't have fame, beauty, or money.

The zaftig blonde, thanks to her role as the assistant to Michael's dermatologist, Dr. Arnold Klein, is credited with "making Michael white."

She had known Michael for fifteen years, and reportedly is the only woman, other than his mother Katherine, who ever saw him completely undressed.

Rowe, accompanying Dr. Klein, had flown across the world to minister to Michael during his tours, and she had reportedly given him massages and rubdowns. "I'm familiar with his body, and I can identify any markings on his buttocks," she said, supporting a claim that a biopsy of Michael's scalp revealed that he was suffering from Discoid Lupus, an autoimmune disease causing hyper-pigmentation, which either darkened or lightened the skin. If he did indeed suffer from Discoid Lupus, as Dr. Klein was rumored to have diagnosed, Michael would have to avoid all exposure to the sun throughout the rest of his life. People suffering from Discoid Lupus, especially those with prolonged exposure to direct sunlight, often

Debbie Rowe

develop coin-sized red bumps upon the skin, the surface of these lesions looking "warty."

At the time of his marriage, Michael falsely claimed that "Debbie and I love each other. I fell for this beautiful, unpretentious, giving person that she is, and she fell for me."

Her first attempt at childbirth had miscarried, but Rowe was several months' pregnant when at the age of 37 she married Michael in his suite at the Sheraton on the Park Hotel in Sydney, Australia, where he was on the second lap of his *HIStory* tour. Rowe related stories about romantic evenings, wherein Michael filled her bedroom with exotic fragrances, but technically, those romantic interludes didn't occur on their wedding night. As the continuation of a pattern that Michael had established with his first wife, wife number 2 also spent her wedding night alone.

As part of the ceremony, her husband presented her with a 2½ carat diamond, set into platinum, but all she got from him physically was a peck on the cheek, not "the big kiss I'd been expecting." As she lay alone in a $3,000-a-night suite, she cried herself to sleep, or so she said. Later she told friends that "my honeymoon night was the most disappointing of my life."

Accompanying Michael during his honeymoon was an eight-year-old boy, his origin unknown, nicknamed "Tony." Michael claimed that the good-looking boy was his nephew, although that wasn't true. While Rowe was confined to her hotel suite, Michael and Tony were photographed attending the opening night of the film, *Ghosts*, and also paying a visit to Sydney's Taronga Zoo.

"The marriage and the entire setup with Debbie Rowe was nothing more than a sham," Michael's former publicist, Bob Jones, claimed. "Michael Jackson wasn't the least bit interested in Debbie Rowe. He was only interested in her churning out those blond-haired, blue-eyed babies." Jones added a provocative comment to the effect that Michael didn't want to have a "splaboo," the pop star's standard reference for a black child.

During their marriage, Michael and Rowe never lived together.

Nick Bishop, in The *National Enquirer*, reported that Rowe had been "passionately in love" with Michael for 15 years and was his most ardent fan, claim-

Debbie Rowe with MJ

ing that "he broke my heart when he married that Lisa Marie." She reported that he was distraught when he and Lisa Marie could not have a child and that she volunteered, "Let me try to get pregnant with you." She also said that Michael burst into tears of joy, as they went to his bedroom "and started to make love—he was fantastic, once he got started."

She reported that as a kind of foreplay to their lovemaking, Michael sometimes dressed up, once donning a suit of armor "so he could be a knight conquering a peasant girl. Another time he dressed as a pirate." It cannot be ascertained if these were mere fantasies on Rowe's part, the equivalent of stories of humans being abducted and then "violated" by aliens aboard space ships.

Bishop reported these fantasies, but as a good reporter he also wrote, "Few will believe this rigamarole when subsequent events are factored into the equation. Debbie sounds like an intelligent and well-paid shill, and yet another sexual beard, but this one was assigned the role of breeder as well."

Privately, associates of Michael said that he wanted to have children of his own, and that he was "shopping for a breeder," who would agree to be artificially inseminated. He found such a candidate right under his nose: Debbie Rowe, who originally came from Australia and had formerly been married to a so-called "computer wiz."

Rowe must have realized at the very beginning that her marriage to Michael would be a sham. In complaints to her friends back in California, she was already predicting divorce only weeks after her marriage. Perhaps she longed for the days when, as a biker chick—comfortable in the seat of a Harley-Davidson—she rode like a Hell's Angel.

She was said to "curse like a sailor and swill tequila like a Mexican bandit." In the media she's been portrayed as a dumb blonde. Yet others have called her "cool and calculating, a show-me-the-money type of woman with a womb for rent if one put millions of dollars on the table."

During her marriage to Michael, Rowe was said to have dated former biker boyfriends.

In 1996, the year he married Rowe, Michael launched another special friendship. Omar Bhatti, a young man from Norway but with a Pakistani background, lived intermittently at Neverland. Michael told the staff that Bhatti was his biological son, but absolutely no one believed him.

The world first heard of Bhatti in 1996 when the 12-year-old amazed Michael with his talents as an imitator outside his hotel in Tunis in Tunisia. Bhatti was invited into Michael's suite and a friendship emerged when Bhatti brought him a beautiful rose. Soon the young boy and Michael were traveling the world together, with Bhatti on stage performing as "The Mini-Jackson."

The relationship became so close that Bhatti and his family sold their home in Holmlia, outside Oslo, and moved to Neverland. During the months that followed, Bhatti lived with Michael, whom he proclaimed as "my idol."

The friendship would continue for years. Bhatti was even seen later in Colorado visiting with Michael and his children, Prince, 7, and Paris, 5. Bhatti is said to have remained extremely loyal to Michael, and supported him when he went into drug rehab. Ironically, in 2004, eight years after their initial meeting, the then-20-year-old Bhatti, by now a dance artist in his own right, was arrested in Oslo for possession of drugs. The arrest occurred only ten days before he was scheduled to perform at the anti-drug event, Norway Cup, the world's largest soccer tournament for young people.

Bhatti and two of his teenage friends were visiting Neverland at the time of its second police raid. In the aftermath of the raid, Bhatti refused to speak to the press after tabloids ran a front-page photo of Michael and him.

During the raid, Bhatti was questioned by police about Michael's activities. Jeffrey Ellis, a police investigator, later claimed that when he broached the subject of pornography to Bhatti, the boy "became nervous and seemed to have trouble forming a sentence. It was almost like a stutter." From Bhatti, prosecutors got no case. Ellis reported that when the boy was asked about the consumption of wine and alcohol, referring to Michael's now famous "Jesus Juice," Bhatti displayed "that same type of uneasiness that I noticed when I started talking to him about Michael's pornography."

With an unknown father donating the sperm, Prince Michael Jackson was born on February 13, 1997 at Cedars-Sinai Medical Center. After delivery, Michael took the baby from Rowe, because "I don't want you to become too attached to it." Obviously there had been some agreement between them for him to do that. Reportedly there was a contract, establishing "ownership" of the baby and also promising to award her with millions if she stayed married to him and bore him yet another child.

After the birth of her baby, Rowe was banished from Neverland, showing up soon thereafter on the streets of Phoenix.

Reports of artificial insemination were consistently denied by both Jacksons in spite of surface evidence to the contrary. Gordon Rowe, grandfather to the children, publicly stated that his daughter had privately told him that the birth was by artificial insemination. Rowe allegedly told friends that "I'm just the vehicle carrying Michael's babies."

Taken from his mother, the newborn was deposited into the back seat of a stretch limo and driven to Neverland, where a professional nurse

Omar Bhatti

452

Omar Bhatti with MJ

had been hired to care for the infant. In the weeks ahead, even though Michael would hire a bevy of nurses and nannies to look after the newborn, he insisted on overseeing most of the child's care himself.

One could almost imagine a derisive hoot coming from Madonna after she read Rowe's quote: "I have married and had a baby with a man I will always love. And I am on top of the world." Even if those sentiments had been true, Debbie was slated to slide off the top of that world very soon.

Michael often insisted on changing his son's diapers himself. And although Prince Michael's name was elegant and regal, he nonetheless had to endure the nickname his father bestowed upon him: Baby Doo-Doo.

"Being called Baby Doo Doo by Dada is the kind of thing that could scar a kid for life," said writer Marcus Errico in 1997. "We just hope Jacko isn't a literalist."

Most reports indicate that Michael designated Dr. Klein as the godfather of his son, with Elizabeth Taylor appointed as his godmother. Other reports relay that instead of Dr. Klein, Macaulay Culkin had been named as the godfather of Prince Michael.

After Michael named his first son Prince Michael, Jermaine responded more or less in kind by naming his own son, "Jermajesty."

In 1997, Rowe and Michael released a joint statement to the press that virtually no one believed. It read: "Deborah is adamant about setting the record straight that Michael is the father of the child [a reference to Prince Michael], the pregnancy is not the result of artificial means, that she has not been paid to have Michael's baby, and that she is not seeking or filing for divorce."

Whereas in the past Michael had faked illnesses to avoid unpleasantness, it now became obvious that he wasn't opposed to the use of Prince Michael as a means of avoiding an engagement. As its date approached, he decided that he did not want to fly to Modena, Italy, to perform with Luciano Pavarotti at a charity concert. In a press release that attempted to justify his non-appearance at the event, he claimed that his son "had suffered a seizure and nearly died." That later turned out to be completely untrue, although Rowe was said to have "gone into a frenzy" when she heard the news for the first time as it was broadcast over television.

As Michael was celebrating becoming a father, the press recalled that in the early 90s Jordie Chandler had been "the apple of Michael's eye."

Meanwhile, Jordie Chandler, having turned seventeen in 1997, was a rich young man worth millions of dollars in bonds and shares. Reportedly, he frequently dabbled in the stock market with the help of a financial guru, Jeffrey Hahn, vice president of the Santa Monica Bank. Jordie had even acquired a partial ownership of the Bank of New York. He'd instructed his financial aides to buy the Crossroads School when he noticed how much the annual fees were.

He was known to pop up at ski resorts in Tahoe and Vail, and to depart spontaneously on scuba-diving trips to The Bahamas and surfing excursions in Florida.

At the time of the birth of Michael's first child, Jordie was still awaiting the final installment of Michael's payments to him, due in June of 1999. As Michael's lawyers had cleverly planned it, that coincided with the date when Michael could no longer be prosecuted over sex abuse allegations.

Jordie, reportedly, was said to have abandoned watching TV broadcasts on the day Debbie gave birth to a son. "I can't bear to watch," he said. Instead he donned a pair of Armani pants and played roller hockey outside his home with his half-brother, Nikki.

In a surprise move, also in 1997, Michael fired his long-time personal managers, turning his career over instead to Prince Alwaleed, a member of the Saudi royal family. He'd met Michael in 1994 at Euro Disney in Paris. With the prince, Michael established Kingdom Entertainment as a development vehicle for film projects, theme parks, hotels, and restaurants. The prince would also be charged with the development and organization of Michael's future world tours. The union of the unlikely pair would be short lived and not meet its expectations.

MJ with Omar Bhatti

Again through the participation of an unknown father, another child, Paris-Michael Katherine Jackson, was born to Rowe on April 3, 1998 at the Spalding Medical Clinic in Beverly Hills. Ironically, when his son had been born, Michael had rented the VIP floor at Cedars-Sinai and

454

hired ten security guards to protect the security of his son. However, when Paris came along, she was assigned only one security guard and her room at Spalding was decidedly modest. Rumors began to circulate that Michael was "hurting financially," and these stories with specific details would mushroom in the months ahead.

According to reports at the time, Michael was so eager to take this child to Neverland that he went to the hospital and removed her at once, even with placenta still covering her body. He wrapped her in a towel and waited to give her a bath when he got her home.

One employee reported that when she brought the baby to Michael at Neverland, she had to pass under life-size mannequins of a Boy and a Girl Scout. Once inside the room, she saw a large painting of Jesus Christ, with blonde hair and blue eyes, complete with a Sacred Heart.

Even as late as the birth of his second child, the press was still publishing ridiculous headlines such as MICHAEL STILL PINES FOR LISA MARIE. That report may have originated when a maid saw a picture of a pre-school Lisa Marie with Elvis resting on the pop star's nightstand.

In 2004, J. Randy Taraborrelli, in a revised edition of his biography of Michael Jackson, *The Magic & the Madness*, wrote that even though Michael had remarried, Lisa Marie Presley was "still the one who had his heart."

In a review of the book in England, Howard Turner addressed that assertion. "Yeah, right! Anyone who believes that also believes that we have a fairy godmother, that Grace Kelly was a virgin, that John Grisham is the world's greatest writer, that Iraq possessed an arsenal of nuclear bombs, and that George W. Bush will go down in history as America's greatest president. And, finally, they also believe that Michael Jackson, unlike the rest of us, never had a homosexual desire in his life."

In the wake of the birth of two children, Michael was still plagued with financial difficulties. His family was even worse off.

In 1999 both Janet and Michael came in for unwanted headlines claiming that the two multi-millionaires were standing by as their own family faced financial ruin. In March, both Joe and Katherine filed for bankruptcy, claiming debts of nearly $35 million.

Neither Michael nor Janet, according to reports, offered financial assistance. To raise immediate cash, Katherine auctioned off a Rolls-Royce given to her by Michael. Katherine asked the court to exempt her two mink coats from being seized. Michael had bailed out his parents in the past, but seemed immune to helping them out of their latest difficulties. In 1995, he'd already written Joe and La Toya out of his will.

But as the century came to an end, Michael was reported to be avoiding bill collectors. He wanted to keep his children from view as well. When seen in public, they were veiled. But in the autumn of 2000, the children were play-ing in a limousine outside their hotel waiting for their "father" to appear. Prince Michael stuck his head out the window and was photographed by a paparazzo. "There's no way in hell that child could have been fathered by Michael," said a Los Angeles pediatrician off the record. "The kid has light blond hair and is whiter than the Queen of England. He looks exactly like Macaulay Culkin at that age."

In a rare statement about his children, Michael said, "I've never had so much fun in all my life. That's the truth. Because I'm this big kid, and now I get to see the world through the eyes of the really young ones. I learn more from them than they learn from me. Children are always the best judges to monitor something."

In the future, Michael would provide a devastating look into his private world and admit sleeping with young boys in Martin Bashir's now notorious TV documentary, aired in 2003. In that future exposé of his private life, he would claim that the two children born to Rowe were biologically his. Both children have white skin and light complexions. Michael's claim on TV would be met with derision in the press.

In legal papers filed later, Rowe claimed that she'd agreed to refrain from sex for six months to "avoid any possibility of semen being introduced into my body other than by way of surgical artificial insemination."

It was reported that Dr. Hal Danzer, a Beverly Hills specialist, performed the insemination which led to the births of both of the Rowe-Jackson children. Rowe claimed that for her services she received a payoff of $3 million from Michael.

After contradictory statements in the 1990s, Rowe in 2006 allegedly told an Irish newspaper that Michael was not the father of their two children, Prince Michael and Paris. She claimed that both children were conceived using anonymous semen purchased from a sperm bank. To the *Sunday World*, Rowe said, "Michael knows the truth—that he is not the natural father. He has to come clean. I have no information whatsoever about the identity of the donor for either child. There was an agreement of confidentiality with the sperm bank."

Then, to confuse matters even more, Rowe attacked the *Sunday World*, denying that she ever gave such an interview. In putting a spin on the situa-tion, her lawyer, Iris Finsilver, declared that Rowe would "never make a press deal that might risk her visitation rights—she never spoke to any newspaper." The *Sunday World*, however, stood by its story.

As could have been predicted, Debbie eventually asked for a divorce, and she got her wish on October 9, 1999.

In 2006 when Rowe took Michael to court in a custody battle, legal documents revealed details of their divorce settlement. According to these documents, Rowe was to be paid $900,000 a year in "hush money" after she split from Michael. The ex-Mrs. Michael Jackson also picked up a $2.5 million mansion in Beverly Hills and a lump sum of $4 million.

In her court filing, Rowe said, "I have just been advised by Michael's inner circle that he is abusing drugs, and I was even given the name of a physician that is prescribing all of Michael's medications, which I fear is dangerous not only to Michael but also to my children."

Having deserted her small apartment, Rowe had moved into a lavish million-dollar home in Beverly Hills. There was no question where she got the money to pay for this upgrade in lifestyle.

Despite the fact that her contract called for her to remain married to Michael for six years, Rowe told her friends, "I can't take it anymore. That's why I had to file for divorce."

Myung-Ho Lee, Michael's former business manager, claimed that Rowe had threatened that if Michael didn't pay $10 million as part of their divorce settlement that she would "spill the beans" on family secrets. Ironically, Rowe had surrendered her parental rights at the time of the divorce. And later, during Michael's trial for child molestation, Rowe revealed that she had never met her own children until they were three or four years old. She also revealed that during that period, she was never presented to her children as their mother, but as "a friend of your Daddy's." Michael later told a friend, "I bought all rights to my kids."

As the terms of the divorce were released to wire services around the world, weird speculation arose. The most outlandish rumor was that the former King of Pop had sought help from scientists in the hopes that he could clone both male and female versions of himself. Reporter Nick Bishop even speculated that "the two children could even be a kind of Victor/Victoria experiment in artificial breeding."

While Katherine and nannies minded the children, and while Rowe pined for "my lost love," videotapes revealed that Michael was entertaining three, and sometimes four, adolescent boys at Neverland. He filmed these videotapes himself, always asking the boys to remove their shirts as part of the filming process.

As a means of settling his divorce payments, and to meet mounting millions in other obligations, Michael borrowed $140 million in a loan from Union Finance and Investment Corporation.

Myung-Ho Lee arranged the loan, but later sued Michael, charging that the star failed to fulfill a number of commitments that Michael had made to him as a reward for having secured those millions. In June of 2003, Michael settled the lawsuit with Myung-Ho Lee, the terms of which were not divulged.

Lee's lawsuit was one of about a hundred such lawsuits filed over a two year period during the late 1990s. Marcel Avram, who handled details associated with Michael's tours during the 90s, also sued when the star cancelled "Millennium Concerts" in Honolulu and Sydney, respectively.

Avram sued for $25 million, winning his case, but subsequently receiving only $6 million to make up for lost profits. It was during Michael's testimony in this trial that photographs of his bandaged nose were splashed in media around the world. For perhaps the first time, Michael's fans and enemies alike could witness firsthand the disastrous results of "just one nose job too many."

At the debut of the 21st century, Michael continued a pattern of involvement in other lawsuits as well, both minor and major. Most of them weren't associated with charges of child molestation, but with demands from merchants who asserted that Michael had reneged on previous purchases. One of the more spectacular examples included Michael's alleged promise of $1.6 million to Sotheby's for the acquisition of two 19th-century paintings—one of a cupid and the other of a woman holding a boy and a sheep.

Although Rowe had been restrained by a gag order, she continued to issue statements about Michael, including one she revealed in February of 2003. She said that if "Michael called me tonight and said he wants to have five more, I'd do it in a heartbeat." Michael had enlisted Rowe's help, asking her to appear on a TV documentary to counter the damaging portrayal of British journalist Martin Bashir, who exposed Michael on the air in 2003.

Fox won the bidding war to air the two-hour TV special, *The Michael Jackson Interview: The Footage You Were Never Meant to See*, narrated by Maury Povich. In the special, Rowe said, "My kids don't call me mom because I don't want them to. They are Michael's children."

Within the televised tell-all, Rowe also claimed that it was her decision—not Michael's—to cover the faces of her two children with scarves whenever they appeared in public, citing a possible kidnapping threat. "I don't want a Lindbergh baby," Michael had previously said.

Although Rowe had formally relinquished her parental rights in 2001, she was pursuing a lawsuit late in 2005 that requested the immediate return of their children from the Middle East. In that lawsuit, she accused Michael of "abducting" Prince and Paris. In legal documents she filed with the court, Rowe went on to assert that she had seen the children only once since the summer of 2005, when she won limited visitation rights.

But as events unfolded, Rowe's lawsuit would face many hurdles. And in the interim, as lawyers for both sides wangled, Prince and Paris remained in the Middle East, held in check by the gloved clutches of Michael himself.

Attorney Raoul Felder claimed that "Even if Rowe got Jackson back into court, it could be opening a can of worms that would get them both into trouble. Maybe the law will do what it should have done in the first place and take custody away from both of these two."

A presupposition of the legal system of both Bahrain and Dubai, as endorsed by Islamic tradition and according to many legal experts, maintained that a court order originating in Los Angeles would not be enforceable.

Felder went on to say that if the case indeed ever came to court, a judge might justifiably confront Rowe with, "How did you ever allow your children to be with Michael Jackson in the first place? It's a tough Rowe to hoe."

In spite of the legal muddle and disagreement emanating from these issues, in 2005, a judge decided that proper court procedures had not been observed in 2001 when Rowe was denied custody rights, even though she had volunteered to give them up at the time.

Rowe apparently changed her mind about abandoning her rights as a parent after Michael was charged with child molestation and began associating with the Nation of Islam, which espouses anti-Semitic causes. Rowe, who is Jewish, was deeply offended by this association.

In 2005, Tom Sneddon, the Santa Barbara County District Attorney and a figure who would emerge as one of Michael's most aggressive nemeses, subpoenaed Rowe for an appearance in court. Sneddon's motivation involved his belief that her testimony would damage Michael in front of a Santa Barbara jury, where he was facing charges of child molestation in the Gavin Arvizo case.

On the stand, Rowe appeared to want to get back into Michael's good graces, despite that fact that she had, in a separate legal maneuver, inaugurated a lawsuit to reinstate her custody rights over her children.

The prosecution hoped that Rowe would depict Michael "as a coercive cad and lousy dad." To everyone's surprise, she did the opposite, presenting instead a lively defense of her former husband. During a full three hours on the stand, she praised Michael repeatedly. She ended her largely favorable testimony by blaming Michael's associates for the pop star's troubles and claiming, "I've always considered him a friend. . .generous to a fault and a brilliant businessman." She denounced the un-indicted co-conspirators as "opportunistic vultures."

Earlier sheriff's deputies had claimed that she'd called Michael a "sociopath" who referred to their children as "my possessions." But she didn't repeat or admit those charges on the witness stand.

Later, Detective Sergeant Steve Robel took the stand to repeat Rowe's original damning testimony. "But it was too little, too late," said a source on Michael's defense team.

At the end of the day, her favorable testimony about her ex-husband's character was defined as a startling setback for the prosecution. On the stand, however, Rowe did admit that "Michael's henchmen" had promised her visitation rights with her kids if she agreed to "gush" about the pop star in a video made to counter the damaging effect of the Bashir documentary.

In court documents filed in July of 2006, Rowe asserted that she was flat broke and that Michael owed her hundreds of thousands of dollars in attorney fees and other costs. She claimed that her legal fees and mortgage, plus other expenses, had left her with only $173,000 in the bank, all her other monies from Michael having been spent.

Five years after divorcing Michael, Rowe said, "If you fall in love once—and if you're lucky enough—it's forever. I'm not one of the lucky ones." At her Beverly Hills estate, she burst into tears three times during an exclusive interview with *Entertainment Tonight*. She claimed that she was studying to become a forensic psychologist and had been breeding prize-winning horses. "I don't know that it would be fair to me to have a relationship with anyone because I'm trying to figure out what I want," she said.

It was later revealed that Rowe was indeed owed $1 million in back alimony from Michael and that she had been forced to sell her 2½-carat diamond wedding ring on eBay. The star's attorneys countered with the charge that Rowe had "violated a confidentiality agreement by appearing on *Entertainment Tonight*."

After much bickering, a secret deal between Michael's lawyers and Rowe was concluded in late September of 2006. The terms were not announced. "We're still dealing with the details but it addresses all of the disputes between the parties," said Marta Almli, the lawyer who represented Rowe. The attorney refused to say what the settlement involved. It was rumored that Rowe received both a "large monetary payment" and was granted visitation rights with her two children, Prince Michael and Paris.

In spite of mounting financial difficulties, continuing lawsuits, and payouts to Debbie Rowe, Michael still seemed to think he had the funds to pursue whatever whim came into his head. In June of 1999, he spent $1.54 million to purchase the statuette associated with the Oscar Best Picture award that David O. Selznick had won for *Gone With the Wind* in 1939. The former King of Pop was spending far more money than he generated.

Debbie Rowe

Not since the days of Woolworth heiress Barbara Hutton, who seemed obsessed with spending herself into the poorhouse, has a media headliner wasted so much money or owed so much. His bestseller album, *Thriller*, for which he was paid $100 million, should have set him up for life.

Fans were asking, "Where did all the money go?" After all, Michael had made the most successful album of all time and had amassed a fabulous fortune. How could he end up in debt, his life in ruins?

To pay for his mounting debts, Michael went to Bank of America, initially taking out a loan for $70 million, which was followed by another loan for a staggering $200 million. These were in addition to loans from Union Finance and Investment Corporation. For collateral Michael put up his ATV catalogue, including dozens of Beatles' songs, which he owned jointly with Sony. His other assets included not only Neverland, but royalties from his own music, such as "Billie Jean" or "Beat It." His music is estimated to have a market value ranging from $75 to $90 million.

In reviewing Michael's assets, a former Bank of America official, who did not want his name used, said, "We were shocked to find out just how many songs Michael owned. Of course, everybody knew about The Beatles' catalogue. But I was unaware that he owned some of the songs of Elvis Presley, even Madonna. When we drew up an estimate of his publishing rights, it came to $450 million, which we thought would more than guarantee a loan in the millions. A singer who had earned at least half a billion in his lifetime was turning to the songs of other artists such as John Lennon and Elvis to save his financial hide."

In 2001, as a means of securing the loan from Bank of America, Michael offered as collateral his two most valuable assets—a fifty percent stake in his Sony partnership and the rights to his own music library.

Martin Bashir

This was not the first time Michael had used The Beatles' catalogue to raise much-needed cash. After the lukewarm reception of his *HIStory* album, he had set up a joint ownership of his ATV Music with Sony, for which he was paid an astonishing $95 million. "Hot damn and save the Queen," Paul McCartney reportedly said when hearing of this fabulous outflow of cash. There was a certain irony in this deal. Signing the agreement was Sony honcho Richard Rowe, the son of the late but not lamented Dick Rowe. Originally Dick Rowe, a senior Decca Records A&R executive, had turned down The Beatles, claiming "they just aren't commercial."

Michael had long been infamous for his choice of sometimes bizarre pals he hung out with. In December of 2003, he was linked with another in a long list of "strange bedfellows," in this case the flamboyant Alvin Malnik, no stranger to scandal himself. Michael later claimed that he was taken to Malnik's house in Miami Beach by Brett Ratner, the film director, who had promised to show him a "house so beautiful it will make you catatonic."

The multi-millionaire Malnik has been "fodder" for federal files since the 1960s and has been called the successor to mob moneyman Meyer Lansky.

In 1966, the U.S. attorney in New York indicted Malnik on charges of using the mail to defraud investors, but in 1971 prosecutors dropped the case.

In 1993, a New Jersey Gaming Commission linked Malnik to organized crime figures, a charge he has denied. The commission in its report concluded, "The evidence establishes that Mr. Malnik associated with persons engaged in organized criminal activities, and that he himself participated in transactions that were clearly illegitimate and illegal."

Malnik was the owner of The Forge, the trendy South Beach hot spot to which he took Michael on a "date" (no homosexual reference intended). It was reported that Michael and Malnik "bonded at the hip," becoming such fast friends that Malnik offered the pop star the use of his lavish mansion in Ocean Ridge, Florida. Later, from a base in Miami Beach, Michael even hosted a 70th birthday party for Malnik at The Forge, inviting such glitterati as Smokey Robinson, B.B. King, and even the famous attorney, F. Lee Bailey.

Rush & Malloy in the *New York Daily News* reported that guests "were surprised to see how openly affectionate the 44-year-old musician was toward several boys who appeared to be in their teens." A Miami headline asked the question: IS JACKO MARRIED TO THE MOB?

The Forge had actually opened in 1969, attracting everybody from Richard Nixon to his shady pal, financier Bebe Rebozo. In previous years, even Richard Burton and Frank Sinatra had patronized the club.

Malnik also owns Title Loans of America, a national chain lending money legally at high percentage rates, sometimes as much as 22%.

Michael was said to have turned to Malnik for help in paying off millions of dollars of debts. Malnik began giving Michael financial advice, something he also has supplied to the ruling family of Saudi Arabia. To reporters, Malnik denied that he lent Michael the $3 million needed for him to post bail when he was charged in 2003 with molesting a 12-year-old, cancer-ridden boy.

In February of 2004, a $70 million loan came due from the Bank of America, and Michael had no money to repay it. Through the aid of Malnik, Michael got the loan extended. Advisers to Michael told the press that the star's links to the Nation of Islam, the black separatist group, has "scared banks off and hurt Jackson's ability to make more money." Two groups of investors, each prepared to make business deals with Michael, had backed away when criminal charges were filed against him for child molestation.

Financial sources disclosed that in the late 90s and post-millennium, Michael was spending about $20 to $30 million annually—more than he earned. "The result is an ongoing cash crisis," Duross O'Bryan, a forensic accountant, testified at Michael's child molestation trial in 2005. The accountant also testified that Michael has long-term liabilities of about $415 million. According to that estimate, the $475 million (plus) value of his assets outweighs the value of his liabilities by at least $60 million.

After being fired by Michael, publicist Bob Jones later commented on Michael's financial woes. "Look, when you spend $2 million a month, you run into these problems. This guy has been unable to face the fact that he no longer brings in income to support his spending habits. Buying expensive gifts for Elizabeth Taylor, Marlon Brando, Liza Minnelli, and other so-called friends, along with the millions he's had to pay these boys, their attorneys, his lawyers, and others—all of this has caught up with him."

By now hundreds of incidents associated with Michael's reckless spending had seeped into press reports. On his way to visit Elizabeth Taylor at the Bellagio in Las Vegas, Michael made an impromptu stop to pick up a $10,000 bottle of perfume as a gift. Speaking privately, the store owner said, "I sure was glad to unload that bottle although I wondered what Elizabeth Taylor, of all people, needed with another bottle of expensive perfume. Surely she has enough scent."

At one point, faced with $10 million in legal fees on child molestation charges, Michael defaulted on his Bank of America repayment loans once again. Bank of America sold his debt to a New York company, Fortress Investment Group, which specializes in "distressed debt."

Over the next several months, Michael failed to make payments on the loan, giving Fortress the right to foreclose. In a last-ditch effort on the part of Michael's attorneys, the star won the right to extend the loan, allowing Michael more time to accumulate funds.

The refinancing saved Michael from bankruptcy but deprived him of part of his share of the music catalogue.

Fortress also held a $70 million loan on Neverland.

In October of 2005, Michael defaulted on loan payments to Fortress. Ominously December 20, 2005, was to have been the deadline for foreclosure on the assets Michael had posted as collateral when he'd secured loans.

In August of 2006, it was revealed how Michael may have bailed himself out of his massive debt. In papers filed in Manhattan, a financial group, Prescient Acquisition Group, claimed that it helped Michael refinance $272.5

million owed to Fortress and arranged a $537.5 million loan related to his ownership interest with Sony in The Beatles' song library.

The court statement contained the first news of how Michael had escaped—but only temporarily—a debt load deemed "almost impossible." But although Prescient had maneuvered adroitly to set up those remarkable loans, they now faced another problem, and that's why they were taking the singer to court. According to officials at Prescient, Michael owed them $48 million in administrative fees for their role in having arranged the refinancing.

At press time for this biography, Michael's finances remained in disarray. Some attorneys have claimed that even upon his death lawsuits would keep those finances in chaos long after his burial.

Taking time off from his financial woes, Michael flew to New York to attend a gala.

As Bill Clinton was leaving office, Michael agreed to attend the annual New York Charity Ball of his friend, Denise Rich, whose billionaire husband, Marc Rich, was pardoned in an 11th hour decision by Clinton. Denise had wanted Paul McCartney to be the headline act. But he cancelled for "private reasons." He was replaced by Michael himself, who welcomed the opportunity to sit alongside President Clinton and his first lady, Hillary.

Denise staged her annual Angel Ball for her G&P Charitable Foundation for Cancer Research in November of 2000. Michael showed up at the grand ballroom of the Marriott Marquis Hotel in New York, where he greeted, among others, Goldie Hawn and Kurt Russell, Stevie Wonder, Rod Stewart, Dionne Warwick, Natalie Cole, and Gladys Knight, who had been instrumental in her initial "discovery" of The Jackson 5. The gala went off without a hitch, allowing Michael to forget his troubles, at least momentarily. But once he returned to Los Angeles, he began the compilation of an enemies list evocative of Richard Nixon during his ill-fated final term. The pop star wanted revenge.

"I'd rather receive praise from my fans than think about the people on my enemy list," Michael said as he flew to New York in March of 2001 for his induction into the Rock 'n' Roll Hall of Fame, making him the youngest solo artist to achieve that coveted award. The ceremony was conducted in New York at the Waldorf Astoria.

Michael put in an appearance, but arrogantly refused to perform. To get away with that, he arrived on crutches, claiming a leg injury that was faked. Rumors were flying that night that the star was "too high" to perform even though those charges may have been unfounded. Nonetheless, he was inducted into the Hall of Fame before the evening ended, an honor he richly deserved, of course.

That same month he flew to England for one of his most bizarre public appearances. At the Oxford Union in Oxford, he broke down in front of the audience, sobbing for his lost youth.

He claimed that he had wanted to be a typical little boy, building tree houses and having water balloon fights. "But my father had it otherwise and all I could do was envy the laughter and playtime that seemed to be going on all around me." Still sobbing, he went on to say that he wanted "the weight of my past lifted from my shoulders."

He was in Oxford to launch his charity, "Heal the Kids," aimed at bringing parents closer to their children.

A reporter for *The Mirror* in London, Sue Carroll, was at the gathering and filed this report: "The one thing that Jackson did not look like last night was a dad. There was a distinct resemblance to Liz Taylor, perhaps a touch of Pinocchio, his sister Janet even . . . but an old-fashioned father, nope. He hobbled on stage with an injured right foot, bearing crutches but looking as though he had just stepped out of a Chanel boutique. His black hair was glossy and beautifully blow-dried, his lips were a fetching pink, and there was eyeliner to emphasize his dark eyes. From where I was sitting in the gallery, it was impossible not to be fascinated by that nose, which looked so small and manufactured. It was hard not to see this as some bizarre freak show."

"All of us are products of our childhoods," he told the audience. "But I am the product of a lack of childhood. An absence of that precious and wondrous age where we frolic playfully without a care in the world." In a very revealing statement, he claimed, "If you don't have the memory of being loved, you are condemned to search the world for something to fill you up."

At New York's Madison Square Garden, on September 7 and 10 in 2001, just prior to the terrorist attacks on the World Trade Center, two special concerts were staged by Michael in celebration of his 30-year career as a solo artist. Nearly fifty million viewers would later watch one of the concerts when it was broadcast on November 13, as a CBS Television special. Celebrities appeared onstage to pay tribute to Michael, including his rival, Ricky Martin. Liza Minnelli put in an appearance, as did Britney Spears, Gloria Estefan, and Ray Charles.

Michael also showcased songs from his new album, *Invincible*. The first single off the new album, "You Rock My World," was accompanied by a video that starred Marlon Brando and actor/comedian Chris Tucker.

Tucker and Michael were friends. Once they were seen together in Las Vegas, leaving their separate hotel suites to emerge onto the gaming floor. "People had to touch me," Michael told Tucker. "Everywhere I turned, I felt hands on me. Other than the Pope and the Queen of England, I'm the most recognizable man on the planet."

Justin Timberlake and 'N Sync also were billed on the 30th anniversary

TV special. The pop heartthrob's girlfriend at the time, Britney Spears, also appeared on the anniversary program, performing "The Way You Make Me Feel" with Michael. But that footage was later cut from the broadcast. "Too damn bad," said Spears. "Just too fucking damn bad!" her sometimes friend Paris Hilton echoed.

At Madison Square Garden, in one of the most bizarre appearances in a lifetime of bizarre appearances, Marlon Brando—who had been paid a million dollars for his involvement—came onstage to confront a mostly youthful audience, some of whom weren't necessarily aware of who he was. Gigantically overweight and aging, Brando took a seat and introduced himself, "You may be thinking, who is that old fat fart sitting there." He then removed his watch and informed the audience, "In the last minute, 100,000 children have been hacked to death with a machete." After rambling on for ten minutes, the 77-year-old Oscar winner was booed off the stage. "He played a madman in *Apocalypse Now*," said a witness. "Now I know Brando wasn't acting."

Brando's appearance was considered so boring that it had to be cut from the final televised show.

Following the Brando debacle, the show peaked when The Jackson 5 reunited with their performance of such bubblegum former hits as "ABC."

Bob Jones revealed that a reunion with Michael's brothers "was purely a money move on his part. The last thing in the world Michael wanted was to perform with his brothers. He made it clear to all who worked with and for him that his family was to be kept as far away as possible. This is a man whose dressing room was off limits to his parents. He would have only little boys in his dressing room."

During the historic early-morning events of September 11, 2001, Michael was still asleep. Most Americans learned of the attacks on the World Trade Center and The Pentagon by watching the dramas unfold on television. Michael was awakened by a mysterious call from a friend in Saudi Arabia, telling him of the attacks. He immediately panicked and wanted to flee New York. But he was also concerned for his friends, Elizabeth Taylor and Marlon Brando, who were still in New York at the time.

Immediately, Michael placed several emergency calls seeking an underground shelter for himself, for Elizabeth, and for Brando. He did not seem concerned about members of the Jackson family, who at the time were also in New York.

In an interview with *Vibe* magazine, Michael said that "Marlon Brando was on one end of the hotel, his security was on the other end, and Elizabeth Taylor was at another hotel." In the wake of the attacks, after vehicular traffic was once again allowed in and out of Manhattan, instead of heading for an

466

underground shelter, Elizabeth and Brando were hauled by Michael to a "secure location" somewhere in New Jersey.

It was sister Janet who eventually rescued those members of the Jackson clan remaining in New York. Since airplane transit in and out of the city had been disrupted, she rented Winnebagos to drive them back to California.

Later, Michael asked other major stars to join him in a post 9/11 tribute. Reporter Clay Risen revealed their reaction to Michael's request. He was turned down. "It couldn't have happened to a freakier guy," Risen wrote. "The King of Pop is a star pariah. Michael Jackson's invitation to sing on a September 11 tribute was turned down by a platoon of big-name stars."

Only weeks after the attack on the World Trade Center, Michael's lackluster *Invincible* album was released. He was hoping that income it generated would save him financially. But in eight months, it sold just six million copies worldwide, a poor return on the $40 million spent to produce it, and the $25 million Sony had spent to promote it.

By now, it appeared that Sony had lost its patience with Michael. As long as the pop star made money, they could overlook his eccentricities. When it appeared that he couldn't, one Sony executive confided, "Michael Jackson is a drain, a money pit."

"For a guy who sold *Thriller*, this can only be an indication of his diminishing popularity," said Tom Vickers, the music consultant. "Jackson is the last person to realize his fan base no longer exists," Vickers said. "For most people, he's the car wreck we slow down to rubber-neck. People have a ghoulish fascination that has little to do with his singing or dancing abilities and everything to do with his freakish looks and behavior. A shrinking core of devotees may continue to buy his music, but they can't sustain his lavish lifestyle. Mainstream interest in Michael Jackson as an artist is over!"

Invincible

Craig Marks, editor of *Blender*, the music magazine, echoed similar sentiments. "I don't think he has earning potential on the music side anymore. He has it on the TV side, on the rubber-necking freak-show side. People will tune in to watch him do anything, but they don't buy his records any more. It's almost impossible to hear his records and not conjure up that scary, weird guy."

One music executive said, "Our customers prefer the oldies—the darker complexion and the big nose."

Increasing numbers of critics were reappraising Michael's phenomenal music career. American writer and soul expert, Ben Edmonds, didn't see him as a fallen genius. "Everything about Michael Jackson's career has been so managed and produced that it's really hard to tell where his collaborators end and where he begins. In *Thriller* and *Off the Wall*, you don't really know how much of it is Michael and how much is Quincy Jones, the producer. We don't see him as a human being, but he might not see himself that way either. He may be like Andy Warhol: A completely empty vessel apart from his own fame. We just don't know, because we're never allowed to see beyond the surgically altered face."

Despite his legal troubles and declining record sales, Michael's ego, from all reports, had expanded greatly. Associates, even if speaking off the record, began to weigh in with informed opinions. One executive claimed that "Jackson wants to be in that pantheon that includes Mozart, Walt Disney, Elvis Presley—and let's throw in Fred Astaire and Gene Kelly for good measure."

Michael was reported to have said, "The rules that apply to common folk don't apply to me. I can get away with whatever I want because I'm Michael Jackson. I not only walk forward, but I can walk backward as well."

In December, after the September 11 attacks, *National Enquirer* reported that, "A bizarre-acting Michael Jackson is hooked on drugs and booze and his frightened family flew across the country to save his life." It was then reported that Michael had rejected his family's plea for him to seek treatment in a clinic such as Betty Ford that Elizabeth Taylor had previously recommended. "Michael is succumbing to drugs and alcohol," one source reported. He was hooked on Demerol and "drinking vast bottles of Jesus Juice," (i.e., wine). Demerol was said to have made him so mentally sluggish that he was "walking around his hotel suite like a zombie."

When Bob Jones was told that one can't believe what one reads in *National Enquirer*, the publicist said, "Well, that is just not the case. Over the years, so-called insiders and Jackson family members themselves sold stories to the *Enquirer*. Michael Jackson even sold pictures to the tabloid."

As a good friend, Marlon Brando tried to intervene to help Michael, asserting that Michael's appearance as a high-profile film actor could generate millions, thereby resolving many of his financial woes. As a means of improving his acting technique, Brando invited Michael to attend an acting workshop that

Marlon Brando,
three years before his death

he was teaching.

Critics have chastised, or ridiculed, Michael for "cross dressing," but he learned what cross dressing really was when he, along with Sean Penn, went to an acting class in Los Angeles presided over by Brando, who was holding private invitation-only acting workshops for special VIPs in Hollywood.

On the first day of class, the curtain opened to reveal the corpulent star dressed as a woman. Under a long blonde wig with the kind of scarlet lipstick Betty Grable and Lana Turner wore in World War II movies, Brando conducted the improvisation class. "I didn't want my acting classes to be a drag!" Brando later quipped to Sean Penn.

Driving his teacher home in a limo, Michael confessed to what he called "some astonishing news." He shared with Brando the fact that he was about to become a father for the third time, and presumably told Brando how he'd come to acquire a second son in his life.

Mysteriously Michael presented this other son to the world in February of 2002. The world learned that the child's name was Prince Michael II. Against overwhelming evidence, Michael still insisted that his first two children had been born "the natural way"—that is, his having had sex with Debbie Rowe. But insofar as this new child was concerned, he confessed that Prince Michael II was the result of artificial insemination, although in one interview he contradicted himself, stating that "I had a personal relationship with the mother."

Changing that testimony, a few weeks later he said that his own sperm

cells were used with a surrogate mother. At one point he claimed that the mother was black, later stating that he didn't know the identity of the mother. It is highly unlikely that Prince Michael II is black, as the child is very blond, like a possible clone of Macaulay Culkin. Debbie Rowe testified that she didn't give birth to Michael's second son and that she doesn't know who his mother is.

The child became world famous in November of 2002 when Michael suspended the nine-month-old infant over the edge of a fifty-foot balcony at the legendary (and massively restored) Adlon Hotel in Berlin, where, during the 1920s, Greta Garbo and Marlene Dietrich had carried on a torrid affair.

Stunned fans watched in horror as Michael precariously held the baby with only one hand and lifted him over the railing. Clad only in a

MJ

romper suit, "Blanket"—his nickname—struggled to break free. A white cloth had been placed over his head to prevent the paparazzi and "crazed fans" from photographing him. Fortunately, Michael pulled the infant back to safety before he accidentally plunged to his death.

Responding to worldwide protests, Michael claimed that he'd held Blanket very tightly and that the infant was never in any real danger. "I got caught up in the excitement of the moment. I would never intentionally endanger the lives of my children."

Uri Geller, the psychic and Michael's friend, told the press that he suspected that Blanket wasn't really Blanket at all, but a fake child made of plastic. "Michael would never do such a thing like dangling a real child over that railing."

Liza Minnelli also rushed to Michael's defense. "I don't see a picture where he is dangling the child nervously. I see him holding him up above a railing for the press to say hello to the kid."

In California, child protection officers held secret talks to decide whether to inaugurate proceedings to determine if Michael were a fit father. They even debated the launch of a formal investigation. "Why on earth," reporter Alison Boshoff asked, "has this obviously disturbed man been allowed to father a brood of three 'motherless' children in the first place?"

At the time he was dangling "Blanket," over the edge of the balcony in Berlin, *The Independent Sunday* in London concluded "The last decade of Michael Jackson's life has hardly been the most glorious phase of his career, but the events of the last six months have seen him slide downwards at unprecedented speed. If Jackson was ever the 'King of Pop,' there seems little doubt that his crown has now been broken into small pieces."

On March 16, 2002, Michael stashed Blanket, along with his other two children, with nannies while he attended the most bizarre wedding of the year, the nuptials of his faithful friend, Liza Minnelli, who at the age of 55 was marrying David Gest, 48, another close friend of Michael's. Michael shared best man honors with his brother Tito. Elizabeth Taylor was matron of honor, sharing the position with Marisa Berenson.

The whole world knew who Minnelli was, of course, but Gest, the American TV producer and concert promoter, was little known outside the entertainment industry until his marriage to the great diva.

The couple met when Gest produced the 30th anniversary concert for Michael in New York in September of 2001. Three months later, and despite her track record in marriage, which had included an ill-fated union with the brilliant homosexual entertainer, Peter Allen, Minnelli was talking marriage once again.

Liza called Michael to tell him that, "I'm the happiest I've ever been. I

470

nearly died, but I'm alive and dancing my buns off. Fuck encephalitis. Fuck hip replacements. Everything I've been through was worth it to find David."

Gest had known Michael since he was a teenager, and had even picked up memorabilia from the pop star, including a rhinestone-studded glove which "Mr. Minnelli" two years later offered for sale on eBay for $250,000. In an interview he gave *Dateline NBC*, Gest revealed that he grew up in Encino with the Jackson family as his neighbors. He claimed that "we played together and did everything normal kids do."

Not only was Gest a close friend of Michael's brother, Tito, he'd even dated La Toya, or so he claimed. As teenagers, Gest, Michael, and some of the Jacksons used to go to DuPars on Ventura Boulevard in Los Angeles to eat pancakes. In the back seat, Michael would take a squirt gun and shoot at Gest.

Michael and Gest shared at least one love in common. It was reported that one entire section of Gest's New York apartment was devoted to Shirley Temple memorabilia, evoking Michael's special room for the moppet star at Neverland.

Many friends intervened to try to prevent Minnelli from marrying Gest, but Michael reportedly approved of the marriage of "my two best friends." A close friend of Minnelli claimed, "Gest is forever courting old-time actresses like Jane Russell and Janet Leigh. We hope that Liza won't be used to satisfy David's desire for stardom."

At the time of his marriage to Minnelli, the press speculated about Gest's sexual orientation, but he always maintained that he was straight, citing that he had at one time been romantically linked to Ruth Warrick. Ms. Warrick, a 1940s film actress and soap opera diva, died in 2005 at the age of 89. An intimate friend of the author of this biography, she confided that there was and had never been a romance between Gest and herself—and that privately, "I knew he was gay."

The website, "NNDB—Tracking the Entire World," lists Gest's sexual orientation as a "matter of dispute."

The timing of the Minnelli/Gest wedding at New York's Marble Collegiate Church on Fifth Avenue was held up by Elizabeth, who forgot her shoes. She arrived at the wedding without makeup and wearing slippers. The wedding ceremony was delayed because Elizabeth had to send for her shoes back at her hotel, refusing to take part in the ceremonies until she had the proper footwear.

After that, the ceremony went off with few hitches, even though Elizabeth seemed to struggle with the wedding rings until best man Michael intervened to help her.

MJ dangling his child over a balcony in Berlin

Before entering the church, Michael, Elizabeth, and the other invited guests were searched for hidden cameras. Apparently, Gest and Liza had left word to search *all* guests, failing to provide an exemption for the famous best man and matron of honor. A full unit security team blanketed the wedding.

Hundreds of rubber-neckers lined Fifth Avenue to watch fleets of black limousines arriving with such guests as Gina Lollobrigida, Petula Clark, Tony Franciosa, Robert Wagner, Joan Collins, Carol Channing, Lauren Bacall, Janet Leigh, Mia Farrow, Patricia Neal, and Diana Ross. Turning down Liza's invitation were Elton John, Michael Douglas, and Liam Neeson.

"As long as David and Liza keep trying, they will make it," said actor Mickey Rooney, a long-time friend of Liza's mother, Judy Garland. "I wish them the best of luck." The bride walked down the aisle to the sounds of "Unforgettable," sung by Natalie Cole.

Liza had seventeen bridesmaids, Gest making do with only fifteen groomsmen. Performers at the reception ranged from an aging Tony Bennett to a troubled Whitney Houston.

The private planes rented, the hairdressers, the champagne, and buckets of Beluga caviar were paid for by a $600,000 offer from *National Enquirer* for exclusive photo coverage and a deal struck with a British tabloid. One source was quoted as saying, "Tabloid star darlings may poo-poo the supermarket rags, but their checks never bounce!"

As predicted, the Gest/Minnelli marriage didn't survive long, lasting a year and a half. In October of 2003, Gest sued his former wife for $10 million, claiming that she had "been violent and physically abusive" during their marriage, blaming it on her "persistent alcoholism," according to his affidavit. Minnelli denied the accusations, claiming that Gest was simply after money.

During the breakup of the Minnelli/Gest marriage, Michael was torn in his loyalties between his two friends, listening patiently to both sides of their stories. Gest returned that loyalty to Michael, maintaining his faith in Michael during the pop star's child molestation trial in 2005. Gest even wanted to produce yet another documentary, a TV special showing the accused child molester's "world." The estranged husband of Minnelli also vowed to be a friend to Michael whatever the outcome of his trial. "I can't just turn on him," Gest told the press. "I would feel very sad if Michael is convicted. I'm not gonna turn my back on him—that's not my style. Never has been."

But by May of 2006, Gest might have been wavering in his loyalty, as he announced that he was going to expose "some shocking revelations" about Michael in a forthcoming autobiography. He announced that among his upcoming "bombshell revelations," he knew "where the skeletons of the past are buried."

In his tell-all Gest promised to reveal "secrets regarding Michael

Jackson's sex life." Gest's co-author, Mark Bego, told the press that Gest is going to reveal such tidbits as Joe Jackson paying a prostitute to have sex with his son and young Michael being propositioned for sex by a male record executive. After some of the other international headlines and revelations about Michael, these so-called "revelations" seemed Sunday school tame.

As for Minnelli, Gest said, "I know stories, but I don't know what will make it into print."

A wacko story released by the *New York Post* on July 12, 2006, was headlined GEST'S BED IS STRAIGHT. In it, Gest's burly British bodyguard, Imad Handi, claimed that his boss likes African-American women. "He would talk about what he did with women, and that he likes to use whipped cream and cherries," Handi told *Post* reporter Dareh Gregorian.

Handi issued these statements in reaction to a lawsuit filed by Charles Beyer in federal court. Beyer claimed that Gest and Handi sexually harassed him, charging Gest with making crude comments about his manhood: "I bet you have a small penis." Beyer also charged that Gest sent him lewd written communications which included the words: "Shake my penis, make sure it feels good, wash it in hot water and dip it in chocolate fudge." Beyer also charged that "Mr. Minnelli" grabbed "my rear end on several occasions and once grabbed my crotch." In spite of the *Post* headline, the story did little to convince New Yorkers that Gest was indeed as straight as he has claimed.

When Michael returned to New York later that summer, it was not to attend a wedding but to launch "the press war of 2002." Bitterly disappointed over his declining record sales, he took on Sony in a counteroffensive. First, he made the false accusations that Sony had demanded $200 million "to pay them back for marketing costs." Sony had done no such thing—in fact, Sony had invested millions of its own funds in what could only be called a disappointing comeback for Michael.

Stewing in his juices, Michael struck back a few weeks later, viciously attacking Sony mogul, Tommy Mottola.

Earlier in the day, in Harlem, Michael had denounced Tommy Mottola as a racist. "He's very, very devilish," he charged. Michael brandished a poster of Mottola with horns superimposed on his head, a tail on his posterior, and a pitchfork in hand. He also claimed that Sony had not "done enough" to back *Invincible* because Michael was black. "That's the first time I ever heard Michael call himself black," said a music critic for *Rolling Stone* magazine.

Many singers who had previously signed with Sony, including Ricky Martin and Mariah Carey, defended Mottola. But members of the Jackson clan backed Michael, claiming that racism had ended their professional relationship with Sony.

The charges of racism were ridiculously false. Mottola had previously been married to Mariah Carey, who is part black.

For support Michael picked up such heavyweights as the Rev. Al Sharpton and his former attorney, Johnnie Cochran. The pop star was demanding that a commission be set up to investigate all record companies—not just Sony—to see if they were exploiting black recording artists.

Sharpton later said that when he made the appearance with Michael, he didn't know the pop star would attack Mottola as racist. Privately Sharpton didn't seem to agree with Michael's slander. Sharpton claimed that Mottola had "always been supportive of the black music industry."

"Music moguls are liars," Michael claimed. "They manipulate history. If you go to the record store at the corner, you won't see one black face. You'll see Elvis Presley and The Rolling Stones. The attack on me began after I broke Elvis's sales and The Beatles's sales. It's a conspiracy. I was called a freak, a homosexual, and a child molester."

Only 150 rag-tag but diehard fans in New York joined Michael in his pathetic protest. At one point Michael falsely accused Mottola of using "the N-word."

Sony shot back, calling Michael's remarks, "ludicrous, spiteful and hurtful." Nonetheless, allegations of racism by Michael put pressure on Sony to sever ties with Mottola. By January of 2003, he was no longer head of Sony Music Entertainment.

After attacking Sony, Michael decided to pitch a sequel of *Moonwalk* to a group of publishers meeting in Stamford, Connecticut. In a new autobiography he was envisioning, he would "set the record straight," perhaps another one of his Freudian slips.

He bitterly attacked the interview Diane Sawyer had done with him for *ABC's Primetime.* This startled the publishers, because Sawyer had herself been attacked for a "candy ass" interview in which she'd "sucked up" to Michael, allowing him to deliver his version of the child molestation questions.

One of her rivals, who didn't want to be named, accused Sawyer

The wedding party: David Gest, Liza, MJ, & Liz

of "ass-kissing. For an exclusive interview, Sawyer sacrificed her journalistic integrity. I didn't believe a word Michael said. He should have paid ABC and put Sawyer on his payroll."

"How could Sawyer do that to me?" Michael asked the assembled publishers. "She should have categorically denied that I was a pedophile on nationwide TV." What was not asked was how could Sawyer know if Michael were a pedophile or not?

Before the publishers departed from his hotel suite, Michael assured them, "I'm just a regular all-American guy. Nothing more, nothing less." The stunned publishers filed out, heading for the hotel bar.

The next day Michael told an executive at Simon & Schuster that he was considering retiring from the music world and devoting the rest of his life to writing children's books. The publisher assured him that S&S would be delighted to look at any children's book that he might write.

After the Stamford meeting, no publisher got back to Michael with an offer to print his second installment of memoirs. Michael was shocked by the lack of interest, having told associates that "my new memoirs will make millions." The project died.

Michael felt humiliated at the rejection. Later that summer, on August 29, 2002, more embarrassments were on the way, some of them exhibited and played out in public. At MTV's Annual Video Music Awards, Britney Spears presented Michael with a birthday cake, making an offhand remark that he was "The Artist of the Millennium."

In a rambling acceptance speech, Michael accepted a trophy that was meaningless. Everyone on stage received the same trophy. Nonetheless, Michael seemed to assume that he was actually being honored as "Artist of the Millennium." In a subsequent remark allegedly delivered by Spears, she may have said, "Michael Jackson should be singing 'Fly Me to the Moon.' He's already on Jupiter."

Michael faced more rejection and ridicule when writers filed their reports of the event. MTV quickly announced that Michael was mistaken, claiming that the channel had "merely wanted to wish him many returns on his birthday." More media attacks were on the way.

Forbes called his career "a franchise in demise." Soon his critics were calling him "Pop's Lost Boy." Rabbi Shmuley Boteach, on CNN, said, "My criticism of Michael is his self-absorption. The whole celebrity thing, where he needs to feel like he's worshipped." As one former fan on the web said, "Michael Jackson loves fairy tales. He's become a fairy tale and even Neverland can't contain him as he wanders over the rainbow. Sorry, Michael, but that pot of gold has eluded you now."

Michael's troubled year of 2002 concluded on a sour note. The magazine,

People, named him "the biggest loser" of 2002. The pop star beat out George Michael (arrested in a men's toilet) and Robert Blake (charged with the murder of his wife) as the winner of that dubious honor.

People wasn't the only magazine causing trouble for Michael. Unknown to him, additional revelations about his private activities were being investigated for publication in *Vanity Fair*.

Just when the world thought it had heard every bizarre story ever associated with Michael Jackson, along came "Michael watcher" Maureen Orth. *Vanity Fair*'s April, 2003 issue contained an article she had authored. In it, she revealed that Michael had paid $150,000 for the activation of a "voodoo curse" to kill former friends—now "A-list enemies"—Steven Spielberg and David Geffen.

The actual voodoo ceremony, according to Orth, occurred in 2000. In Switzerland Michael was said to have undergone a "blood bath" as part of the ritual. Presumably "blood bath" meant that Michael had actually bathed in blood. One can only speculate in wonder at that claim. In a separate lawsuit that Myung-Ho Lee, the star's former business manager, filed it was revealed that Michael ordered him to wire the $150,000 to a bank in Mali, into an account controlled by a voodoo chief named "Baba." Baba was expected to sacrifice forty-two cows as part of an extended ceremony, *Vanity Fair* reported.

The story left a lot of unanswered questions. What was the link between Switzerland and the voodoo priest in Mali? Where did the killing of the cows take place? Presumably in Mali. Or one might ask an even more provocative question. Is this widely published story really true?

The witch doctor was said to have intoned a series of chants during the massacre of the cows. The individual name of each recipient of the curse was articulated before a cow's head was chopped off. "David Geffen be gone! Steven Spielberg be gone!"

In the *Vanity Fair* article, it was revealed that twenty-five persons made Michael's list of people he wanted dead. He was assured by the voodoo witch doctor that everyone whose name appeared on the list would "soon be dead." An immediate mass demise of everyone on the list never happened, according to reports, but we can't be sure about the long-term affects of the blood-drenched voodoo ceremony. After all, only the names of Geffen and Spielberg were revealed in the article. It is not known who the other 23 intended victims were, but surely it

Tommy Mottola

included some prosecutors in the Santa Barbara area.

Shortly thereafter appeared yet another bizarre story in *Vanity Fair*, alleging that Michael, in addition to placing curses on perceived enemies, had made several serious (at least for him) attempts to create money "out of thin air." A mysterious Egyptian woman, claiming links to the ruling elite of Saudi Arabia, appeared in Michael's life.

The Egyptian woman, once called "a modern-day Cleopatra," was identified only as "Samia." She is alleged to have escorted Michael to a basement apartment in the Swiss city of Geneva where she reportedly showed him $300 million in cash. She promised him that he could have the money and a multi-million-dollar yacht stashed at a port on the French Riviera, plus a spectacular European villa "if you do what I ask."

Her demands were articulated in detail when three of her male associates flew into Los Angeles where they were driven to Neverland for a private meeting with Michael to discuss the deal. At the meeting, according to Myung-Ho Lee, Michael was ordered to produce one million dollars in cash. Lee also testified that he paid $20,000 to an armored truck company to deliver the million dollars. Of course, if someone had $300 million in a bathtub, stashed away, why would they need a million from Michael? It seems insane that someone would give Michael $300 million, plus a yacht and villa, in exchange for a million in cash.

It is not known if Michael turned over the money that day or not. According to Lee, he was flown by Michael back to Geneva to consult yet another voodoo doctor who put on a "show of sound, lights, and pigeons" before opening the door to reveal a bathtub filled with $50 million. According to testimony, this new voodoo man said that the money would disappear unless Michael paid "thousands of dollars for the slaughter of poultry and other animals." Again, this story raises far more questions than it answers. It, in fact, makes no sense at all.

MJ whispering to the Rev. Al Sharpton

Perhaps the voodoo story would never have surfaced if Lee hadn't brought a lawsuit against his former employer. Lee's lawsuit was inaugurated at the same time that approximately fifty legal procedures were being filed against the pop star annually. By 2000, Michael had become the most frequently sued performer in the history of the entertainment industry. Aside from child molestation charges, most persons suing Michael charged him with unpaid bills.

In an interview on *The O'Reilly Factor* for Fox News Network, Bill O'Reilly questioned Maureen Orth. After reviewing, on camera, the voodoo charges she had raised in *Vanity Fair,* she then cast doubt on Michael's much-lauded charity work. "I think he's manipulating his own image," Orth said. "He's declaring he's a champion of children and children's charities, but the charities aren't raising any money. There's $100,000 that was given to one charity, shuffled over to another, that is now being investigated for not being reported properly."

More and more people, not just *Vanity Fair*, were realizing there was money to be made in exposing the private life of Michael.

Within the passenger compartment of a private jet flying from Las Vegas to Santa Barbara, two "buggers" filmed and recorded Michael during private conversations, perhaps hoping to sell the footage to the tabloids. It was revealed that the owner of XtraJet, Jeffrey Borer, had instructed Arvel Jett Reeves, owner of Executive Aviation which provided maintenance for the fleet, to install the secret video equipment.

It is not clear how the secret recording came to the attention of law enforcement officials. Perhaps an employee of the airline tipped off authorities, who investigated and found that indeed an illegal recording device was used. In March of 2006, within a Los Angeles courtroom, each of them pleaded guilty to one felony count of conspiracy. Borer was sentenced to six months of home detention and fined $10,000. Reeves was sentenced to eight months in prison and ordered to spend six additional months in a halfway house—and to pay a $1,000 fine.

Michael's biggest exposé was yet to come, this time on television.

On February 6, 2003, ABC broadcast a two-hour documentary produced by Britain's Granada Television, featuring correspondent Martin Bashir, the British television journalist known for a notorious interview he had inaugurated with Princess Diana. In that interview, Di had spoken of her lover, James Hewitt, and her husband's mistress, Camilla Parker Bowles.

Bashir's interview with Michael was one of the most controversial TV shows ever aired and it would have devastating

MJ presented with an award by Britney Spears

effects on the pop star's personal life. In one of the most foolish decisions of Michael's life, he granted Bashir "unfettered access" to many aspects of his private life for an astonishing total of eight months. After watching the broadcast in horror, Michael immediately filed complaints with the Broadcasting Standards Commission and Britain's Independent Television Commission.

When the TV show was aired in Britain in February of 2003, some 15 million Brits had tuned in. To be granted air rights Stateside, ABC paid anywhere from $4 to $5 million.

In tears, Michael confessed that the raw wound of his father's alleged sadism made Michael "regurgitate" whenever he saw him.

Bashir went on to question Michael about plastic surgery. In an astonishing statement and in spite of overwhelming evidence to the contrary, Michael still insisted that he'd had only two operations on his nose to help him breathe better so that he could hit the high notes of his vocal range.

Teresa Wiltz, writing in *The Washington Post*, said, "Perhaps the most poignant is the scene where Michael sits with Bashir in his movie screening room, watching old television of himself performing 'I Want You Back' with The Jackson 5. The camera jumps from the young Michael—cute, brown, innocent—to the middle-aged Michael—ravaged, white, and clinging to the illusion of innocence, and that moment says more than nearly two hours of shock TV that comprises *Living With Michael Jackson*."

Michael admitted that he'd wanted children so badly that he often walked compulsively around Neverland, playing with baby dolls.

But, like any other parent, he also showed that he could become annoyed with his child. When Blanket cried, Michael brusquely shoved a baby bottle in the veiled infant's mouth to shut him up.

In the interviews with Bashir, Michael freely admitted that he slept with young boys in his bed. As an afterthought, he added that "little girls were also included." According to staff members at Neverland, there is no evidence that Michael ever slept with young girls.

One of MJ's victims?

In the most astonishing of the interview's footage, Gavin Arvizo, a 12-year-old cancer survivor who would later bring charges against him, sits cuddling with Michael, his head nuzzling against the star's shoulder. Gavin clutches Michael's hand, relaying testimony about spending many a night in Michael's bed, and seemingly not aware at the time of how damning these revelations were.

"Why can't you share your bed?" Michael asked on the program. "The most loving thing is to share your bed with someone. I am Peter Pan."

Bashir reminded him that "you're Michael Jackson." "I'm Peter Pan in my heart," Michael countered.

On camera, Bashir also documented Michael's big-spending habits that showed very few signs of slowing down, despite his dwindling cash reserves. On camera, Michael was shown spending $100,000 in two hours on clothing in a New York store. But the most astonishing footage showed him spending $6 million in Las Vegas on art objects which included antique urns, vases, and a marble chess set.

The broadcast was seen by 27 million viewers around the world. Later, Michael claimed that the footage was deliberately edited to portray him in a bad light.

This set off a feeding frenzy among the media, Fox alone offering $5 million to broadcast out-takes. The out-takes were eventually shown, with Marc Schaffel, the gay porn producer, emerging as the orchestrator of the deal. On that show, Michael claimed—once again—only two trips to the plastic surgeon, but later, on NBC's *Dateline,* partly in reaction to that statement, a plastic surgeon was interviewed, insisting that the star had had as many as 50 separate operations on his face.

In November of 2003, Michael needed money, but seemed to be in no shape to release an all-new album. He was not above cannibalizing his past when he agreed to release his *Number Ones* album of previous hits.

The album recycled such by-now-familiar songs as "Beat It," "Billie Jean," and "Don't Stop 'Til You Get Enough." It also included the previously unreleased R. Kelly ballad, "One More Chance," which was sung by Michael. One of Michael's fans posted his reaction to this new release on the web. "R. Kelly should have kept the song to himself."

R. Kelly, of course, was one of the biggest-selling male vocal artists of the 1990s. Like Michael himself, Kelly frequently wears a mask, a Zorro mask. And also like Michael, he's had his problems with child molestation issues. In 1994, when he was in his 20s, he married R&B singer/actress Aaliyah, who was only 15 at the time, but the marriage was subsequently annulled. On August 25, 2001, Aaliyah and eight other people died when their plane crashed in The Bahamas.

In June of 2002, Kelly was arrested in Winter Haven, Florida, after prosecutors in Chicago indicted him on 21 felony counts of child pornography. The soul star was led away in handcuffs as fans gathered to shout "We

Maureen Orth

love you," in much the same way they'd reacted to Michael. Kelly was eventually acquitted of the charges. Had he not been, he might have faced up to 15 years in prison.

Of course, Kelly's arrest had nothing to do with the sales of Michael's *Number Ones* album. It was Michael's own arrest that may have hurt sales. From reports, it appeared that Michael was too weak to produce an entire new album and was forced to cancel the announced *Resurrection*, which was to be the follow-up album to *Invincible*. Wanting to get something on the market, he released *Number Ones* instead, filled with recycled songs from his previous all-too-familiar repertoire.

Even though the songs it contained were recycled from earlier albums, the *Number Ones* album sold six million copies worldwide. Michael, who had predicted that at least forty million copies would be sold, defined this figure a great disappointment.

On November 16, 2003, Joe Jackson gave a now-infamous TV interview with Louis Theroux in which the father—often called a "ruthless Svengali"—became furious at the suggestion that his famous son might be homosexual. "I can't stand gays!" Joe shouted. He was also asked if he'd like to see Michael settle down with a partner. Joe shot back, "What do you mean by 'partner?'"

"A boyfriend or a girlfriend," Theroux replied.

The question seemed to infuriate Majestik Magnificent, Michael's former personal magician, who'd accompanied Joe to the interview. "He is Michael's father and you're going to sit there and say he has got a boyfriend. How much more disrespectful can you be? You should just say a girlfriend or wife, not insult Mr. Jackson."

When Theroux, on camera, asked why the question was disrespectful, Joe interrupted him. "Because we don't believe in gays. I'm sitting here saying right now, he's not with no boys. OK?"

Majestik then continued to object, on camera, protesting loudly, "Michael's not gay...You have to be gay to have a boyfriend and I'm telling you, Michael is not gay!"

Before walking angrily off the set, prior to the scheduled end of the interview, Joe claimed that he had never beaten his son. "You beat someone with a stick. I whipped him with a switch and a belt."

Two days after his father's interview, Michael was at the Mirage Hotel and Casino in Las Vegas, where he'd gone to shoot the video for R. Kelly's "One More Chance."

For nearly a month, Michael had been holed up at the hotel where a waiter reported that nearly three dozen boys, some of them "German or Austrian" were seen coming and going at all hours of the day and night. Inside his lavish suite, Michael was said to be drunk or drugged and hadn't dressed for three weeks, appearing in a long dashiki robe dyed a deep, almost purplish scarlet.

On the morning of November 18, 2003, an assistant manager of the hotel sent Michael an urgent message, asking him to evacuate the hotel that night. The other, usually affluent, residents of the hotel had lodged several complaints about the noise level, especially the blasting rap music heard day and night.

R. Kelly

"Somebody on Michael's staff seemed to be recruiting good-looking boys from the Strip," claimed a waiter. "All of them looked to be around sixteen, maybe older—none really very, very young."

Michael had demanded that food from room service be left at the door. But the assistant manager wanted to see firsthand the condition of Michael's suite to assess damages before evicting him from the hotel. Using a pass key he entered the suite to witness a scene of devastation. "It looked like a hurricane had blown through," he later said.

Elegant sofas and armchairs had been burned by cigarette butts. Liquor bottles were scattered everywhere. And since room service waiters weren't allowed in, rotting food had never been removed. Broken glasses with stale booze were seen everywhere. At first glance, it appeared that Michael would have to pay at least $50,000 in damages, maybe more. About seven young boys, some in jockey shorts, were sprawled about the suite.

From the bedroom, the assistant manager heard Michael's whispery voice. He appeared to be sobbing. "Oh, God, no!" Finally, he raised his voice in a bellowing rage. "Not again!"

It was only later that the assistant manager learned the news that Michael was hearing on the phone. Once again, Federal authorities had raided Neverland, based on allegations made by the 12-year-old boy, Gavin Arvizo, who had appeared all cuddly with Michael on the Martin Bashir TV documentary. Soon radio and television stations were carrying the news that an arrest warrant for Michael had been issued based on multiple charges of child molestation.

"Here we go again," Bob Jones said. "Only this time Michael may not escape the noose tightening around his neck."

"He loves genres that emphasize mutable identities, carefree cartoons and horror tales. And it's mutability that makes his dancing so special. That ability to turn a James Brown funky chicken smoothly into Josephine Baker's knock-kneed Charleston. He has the ability to be liquid and percussive all at once, to create an aura of suspense and improvisation."

--Margo Jefferson

"He understands the value of copyrights and that his public eccentricities—pajamas, umbrellas, sunglasses, top hats, children in masks, etc., going right back to hyperbaric chambers and the Elephant Man bones—are all part of a well-choreographed game to keep the public interested in his fading celebrity."

--Roger Friedman

"We have watched as we have been vilified and humiliated. I personally have suffered through many hurtful lies and references to me as 'Wacko Jacko.' This is intolerable and must stop. The public depiction of us is not who we are or what we are."

--Michael Jackson
Responding to a TV movie about his family's troubles

"Given Mr. Jackson's having shared his bedroom with boys, while not illegal in itself, was deeply troubling. Given the fact he was acquitted, but still highly suspected by many adversaries, he must never again submit himself to the appearance of wrongdoing. He really has to make that modification—and substantially so—and I think he will. I don't know any of his fans who would not advise him now to please avoid the appearance of impropriety."

--The Rev. Jesse Jackson, June 2005

Chapter Fifteen

On November 18, 2003, some 70 investigators from the Santa Barbara County sheriff's and district attorney's offices stormed Neverland. A cabal of 20 officers were assigned to search the 2,700-acre ranch as part of an ongoing criminal investigation. No immediate arrests were made, and Michael remained in seclusion in Las Vegas. In case Michael had actually been in residence at Neverland, police also had an arrest warrant in addition to a search warrant.

Police officers spent two full days crawling over the ranch, looking for videos and photographic evidence. In Santa Barbara, Tom Sneddon, the district attorney, urged Michael to "get over here and get checked in." At the time, Michael was still in Las Vegas.

Michael charged that the raid on Neverland was deliberately timed to sabotage the release of his new album, *Number Ones*. Sneddon claimed he knew nothing about the release of any album. "Like the sheriff and I are into that kind of music," he said sarcastically.

Sneddon, who had failed to build a case against Michael in the Jordie Chandler scandal, seemed determined not to let that happen again. He told associates that "Jackson won't be able to moonwalk his way clear of the long arm of the law this time." Since 1993, California law had changed, and it was now permissible for prosecutors to force alleged child abuse victims to testify against their accused molesters. "The Jordies of the future can't be silenced with millions," Sneddon said.

Michael faced a formidable foe in Sneddon, who was serving his sixth term as the county district attorney. Sneddon had such a reputation for tenacity that he was called "Mad Dog" by his associates.

Michael had even written a song about the prosecutor calling it "D.S.," changing Sneddon's name to Dom Sheldon. The lyrics of Michael's song said he was being sought "dead or alive."

You know he really tried to take me
Down by surprise
I bet he missioned with the C.I.A.
He don't do half what he say
Dom Sheldon is a cold man
He out shock in every single way
He'll stop at nothing just to get his political way.

As news of the latest allegations of child molestation were leaked to the press, Stuart Backerman, spokesman for Michael, blasted them as "outrageous, false, and scurrilous. When the evidence is presented and the allegations proven to be malicious and wholly unfounded, Michael will be able to put this nightmare behind him."

Most of Michael's celebrity friends ran for cover when charges of child molestation were once again leveled against him. Not so 71-year-old Elizabeth Taylor, who slammed the media for acting "abominably" toward the entertainer. "I thought the law was 'innocent until proven guilty.' I know he is innocent, and I hope the media all eat crow. I believe Michael will be vindicated."

Earlier in 2003, Elizabeth's friendship with Michael had been shaken when he didn't turn up for a date with her at Neverland. In anger, she refused to invite him to her star-studded birthday bash. But he repaired the fractured relationship when he sent her 1,000 sterling silver roses.

The question on everybody's lips was, "Is it possible for a grown man to share his bed with pre-pubescent boys and not be guilty of something?" Oliver James, a psychologist, weighed in with his opinion: "It's quite clear that he has a kind of pedophile personality. The idea that he is regressed and is arrested in his development is one way of thinking about it, but if you want to know why he repeatedly has young boys in his home, that doesn't explain it. You have to look at the trauma that he suffered—physical abuse, being beaten up in a really vicious way, combined with some kind of sexual abuse."

Although some press reports main-

MJ's mugshot from the
Santa Barbara County jail

486

tained that Michael's cohorts had placed him on "a suicide watch," he managed to pull himself together and fly on a leased Gulfstream IV plane from Las Vegas to Santa Barbara, where he was driven to the county jail.

On November 20, Michael, his hands cuffed behind his back, was led into the county jail and booked on charges of child molestation. Inside the Inmate Reception Center, he was fingerprinted and photographed. Later, before a field of microphones, he referred to the allegations against him as "a big lie."

Before his release, Michael posted $3 million bail and surrendered his passport. An arraignment was set for January 9, 2004, before a judge in the Santa Barbara Superior Court.

After the sheriff's department posted Michael's booking photograph on its website, Michael's dilemma became the most famous celebrity arrest in the history of entertainment, even more so than the time police arrested Frank Sinatra.

In the mug shot, Michael's heavily made up head tips to the right and his eyebrows are sharply arched. His wide-open eyes were later compared to those of Joan Crawford. He'd painted his thin lips a scarlet red, and his nose looked chiseled, the result of countless plastic surgeries.

Specific charges against Michael were not defined with any specific detail or legalese at the time, but police revealed that they would include multiple counts of "lewd and lascivious acts with a child under the age of 14."

Emerging from the jail after his booking, Michael waved and flashed a V-for-victory sign at screaming fans. He blew a kiss to photographers before stepping into a dark Chevrolet Suburban with opaque windows. He was then driven to the airport for his return to Las Vegas.

Back in Las Vegas, he moved into the penthouse suite of the Regency Tower at the Las Vegas Country Club, the same building where sister La Toya

MJ's fans with gestures of support

has a condo. En route to Nevada, Michael dressed in drag—black flowing clothes and a dark hat as well as a veil.

Katherine Jackson angrily responded to the charges, claiming that "there are two sets of rules in this country—one for the white people and the other for the black people."

His mother wasn't the only family member weighing in on the side of Michael's defense. In an interview with CNN, Jermaine proclaimed Michael's innocence. "I'm sick and fucking tired of people," he angrily said. "This is nothing but a modern-day lynching."

In the wake of his arrest, the damage to Michael's singing career was immediate. In February of 2003, ABC, NBC, and Fox had each won huge ratings by exposing bizarre aspects of Michael's private lifestyle to the world at large. But in November of the same year, following the latest police raid on Neverland, intense pressure was put on CBS to cancel a music special which had been scheduled for airing on November 26 and linked to Michael's latest album, *Number Ones*, his collection of previous hits.

In an article that appeared in *The New York Times*, Alessandra Stanley predicted that if CBS had actually gone ahead and shown the program, "many millions would certainly watch. His fans aside, people watch Mr. Jackson for the same reasons they watched O.J. Simpson's Bronco ride, forest fires in California, and the finale of *The Bachelor*. It's scary, grotesque, and fascinating."

As his defense attorney, Michael hired Mark Geragos, the son of an Armenian-American lawyer, who was at the time also handling the Scott Peterson murder case. Geragos insisted that he could easily juggle the two cases. Geragos had previously won two high-profile acquittals—one for Whitewater scandal figure Susan McDougal and another for Roger Clinton, Bill's half-brother, on a drunken driving charge. He'd also defended sticky-fingered actress Winona Ryder during her shoplifting trial.

In response to Michael's detractors, Geragos said, "What we have here is an intersection between a shakedown—someone who's looking for money—with somebody doing an investigation who has an ax to grind."

He was referring, of course, to Tom Sneddon's "ax." Geragos claimed that the boy fabricated the kiddie sex story in the hopes of a payoff that was equivalent to the $25 million that was paid out to Jordie Chandler in 1993.

With the exception of Elizabeth, most celebrities, including Lisa Marie, issued a "No comment!" to the press, Virtually everybody else who had worked for Michael or been employed by him weighed in with an opinion as to his guilt or innocence.

Paul Barresi, a former legman for the controversial private investigator Anthony Pellicano, who at the time was in prison, revealed Michael's "modus operandi for entertaining children. First, he wins the parents over. They

Paul Barresi

become just as mesmerized as the kids. Then he puts the parents in separate buildings. He naps all day intermittently with the kids in the tepee or different places so that kids are well rested. Then he frolics and plays with the kids all through the night while the parents are sleeping."

At first the name of Michael's teenaged accuser, charging him with sexual molestation, was either not known to the press or else known but not revealed by the media because of his age.

But soon his name would become a household word. Gavin Arvizo was born in 1989 to David Arvizo and Janet Ventura-Arvizo in California. He had an older sister, Davellin, and a younger brother named Star. Ironically, Gavin's mother, who eventually would acrimoniously divorce her 37-year-old truck driver husband, David, would become "Janet Jackson" because of her marriage in 2004 to U.S. Army major Jay Jackson.

Born into a poor Latino family, Gavin lived with his parents, his brother, and his sister, in a rough urban neighborhood in East Los Angeles. Their home was a box-like studio apartment. At one point they were so poor they'd lived in a horse stable.

The question repeatedly asked by the media was how Gavin came to meet Michael in the first place. The Arvizos had read countless stories about Michael's involvement with Jordie Chandler, which could have alerted them to the potential danger associated with having their underage son hang out with the pop superstar.

Eventually the story of how Michael met Gavin came to light: In 2002,

Jaime Masada

Gavin lay in a hospital bed in Hollywood suffering from a cancerous tumor in his stomach. He was befriended by Jaime Masada, the owner of the Los Angeles comedy club, Laugh Factory, who also ran a summer camp for underprivileged kids. Masada promised Gavin that if he'd start eating and building up his strength, he'd introduce him to any star he wished to meet. Gavin listed Chris Tucker, Adam Sandler, and Michael Jackson in that order.

Masada managed to get Tucker and Sandler to visit Gavin, and eventually he even contacted Michael himself. Masada later expressed his regrets for having introduced Gavin to Michael. "You hate to think you may have brought the boy to the lion."

Michael called the hospital and spoke to Gavin when he was only 10 years old, shortly after

489

he'd had a 16-pound tumor removed from his stomach. The pair became friends and Michael invited Gavin, with his family, to Neverland. But the friendship did not last and calls from Michael eventually ceased. However, in 2002 Michael called Gavin again. "You want to be an actor, right? I'm going to put you in the movies." The "part," it turned out, was in the Bashir TV documentary. After appearing within the documentary, Gavin became Michael's beloved "Doo Doo Head," the star's nickname for his new pet.

Neverland staff member Talia Mandel reported on Gavin's appearance during his first visit to Neverland. "He was really sick-looking and pale. He was little and skinny and had no hair and no eyebrows as a result of cancer treatments. He told me that Michael was helping him recover from cancer, but I don't know exactly what he was doing."

According to Gavin's claims, Michael did not begin to abuse him until after his appearance in the Bashir TV documentary. The show was filmed in 2002 and was not aired until 2003.

During the very few months when Michael got to know his future enemies, Janet and her son, Gavin, they had the run of Neverland. As poor people from the ghetto, Gavin and Janet felt they'd arrived at paradise on earth. Just as Michael had seduced Jordie Chandler's family, so he set out to woo the Arvizos with a lavish lifestyle and expensive presents.

He paid for Gavin's mounting medical expenses, and he hired a limousine to take him to and from chemotherapy sessions. When Janet separated from her husband, David, Michael even leased an apartment in Los Angeles for her new boyfriend. Janet asked all her children to call Michael "Daddy" when "Sugar Daddy" might have been a more appropriate term.

The honeymoon ended after Gavin revealed during his statements on the Bashir TV documentary that he was sharing Michael's bed at night. Massive criticism, exacerbated by Gavin's cuddly appearance, followed in the wake of the program. Janet claimed that Michael had not secured permission from her for Gavin to appear on the show.

Later, Michael came to Janet and got her permission to allow Gavin to appear on Michael's own TV show, which was being produced as a formal "rebuttal" to the Bashir documentary. Consequently, Michael dispatched his videographer to tape an interview with the Arvizos, during which they would insist that Michael's relationship with Gavin was

Gavin Arvizo

innocent and pure.

During that taped interview, Janet issued a statement that would later be used against her at Michael's trial in 2005. "I'm appalled at the way my son has been exploited by Martin Bashir. The relationship that Michael has with my children is a beautiful, loving, father-sons-and-daughter one. To my children and me, Michael is part of my family."

In front of cameras, Janet went on to claim that Michael was "good to us—in no way were we unhappy with anything he has said or done."

"If Michael knew at the time that they were going to make these accusations, making this tape was obviously a crafty thing to do," Michael's personal videographer, Hamid Moslehi, later said.

At the time, Janet also signed an affidavit clearing the pop star of any wrongdoing. However, in November of 2003 she claimed that she was "confused and coerced" when she put her signature on the document.

On February 18, 2003, after being besieged with complaints from all over the country, the Santa Barbara Sheriff's Office began a formal investigation. The Santa Barbara District Attorney, Tom Sneddon, seemed only too willing to endorse a child molestation case against Michael again, having failed to inaugurate a trial in the Jordie Chandler case after the boy was bought off.

It has never been determined what went wrong between Michael and the Arvizos. One day they were singing his praises to authorities, but within weeks they turned on him. Janet consulted with attorney Larry Feldman, the lawyer who had represented Jordie Chandler in his case against Michael in 1993.

Then Feldman arranged for Gavin to be interviewed by Dr. Stan Katz, a psychologist. Gradually, during a series of interviews with the psychologist, Gavin related incidents of alleged child molestation by Michael. The case heated up when Katz, in compliance with the laws of California, was obligated to turn his reports over to state authorities.

Janet Arvizo Jackson

Katz told authorities that he believed that the Arvizo family had not been honest in their previous testimony and now were coming forward with the truth.

In April of 2003, the Santa Barbara County Sheriff's Department had more or less concluded its investigation without unearthing any really damaging evidence against Michael. But in June of that year, the Sheriff's Department received Katz's damaging report, in which allegations were made that child molestation had indeed taken place despite previous denials of wrongdoing from the boy's family. After the receipt of the Katz conclusions, members of the Sheriff's Department began interviewing family members, especially Janet and Gavin, for inconsistencies in their previous stories.

It was learned that the relationship between Janet and Michael had soured when she blew up after being told that he had served her cancer-stricken son wine, which she maintained "might have killed Gavin." Later, she would learn about more serious charges, including claims that Michael had masturbated her son and even taken nude pictures of him at Neverland.

During the course of their own pre-trial investigation, Michael's defense members discovered a scandal involving the Arvizo family. On August 27, 1998, they had been caught in a shoplifting sting in a JC Penney store in West Covina, California.

Both boys had been sent out of the store with concealed clothing which hadn't been paid for. Janet would later claim that her sons were modeling clothes for the chain, although there was absolutely no evidence of this.

Security detained both the father and mother, plus their two sons, including Gavin, age 8, charging them with stealing clothing. Both the Arvizos were arrested and charged with theft and battery, for allegedly hitting the security guards. The charges were dismissed on March 11, 1999 in Los Angeles Municipal Court.

In a counter offensive, Janet then filed a $3 million civil complaint against the store, charging that their boys were "beaten, battered, falsely arrested, falsely imprisoned and falsely accused of criminal conduct" by store personnel.

Two years later she added a new charge to her original complaint, claiming that during her arrest by two male security guards she was "sexually fondled on my breasts and pelvic area." A psychiatrist hired by the store claimed that she'd rehearsed her sons to back up this outrageous story that seemed "suddenly remembered" at the last moment.

In yet another outrageous claim, she charged that she'd suffered broken bones during the fray. Not only that, but that both Star and Gavin had also suffered broken bones during the

Gavin Arvizo with MJ

492

Michael's charges, claiming he was "treated with courtesy and professionalism throughout the arrest and booking process."

Michael wasn't the only Jackson family member involved in scandals. La Toya had created nationwide sensations when she'd posed in a state of partial undress for *Playboy* in March of 1989 and again in November of 1991. On February 1, 2004 sister Janet was involved in "Nipplegate" at Super Bowl XXXVIII in Houston, Texas.

During the Super Bowl's halftime show, Justin Timberlake and Janet reached the final line of their suggestive song, singing "I'm gonna have you naked by the end of this song." Timberlake theatrically, and unexpectedly, pulled off a strategic part of Janet's costume, revealing a view of her right breast to millions of viewers on live TV. The rather ample breast was adorned with a large, sun-shaped nipple shield, a piece of jewelry worn to accentuate the appearance of a nipple piercing. In horror, CBS producers immediately ordered their cameramen to cut to an aerial view of the stadium. But Janet's breast had already been broadcast around the world. In the aftermath, a record-breaking 200,000 Americans lodged complaints against CBS.

Both Janet and Timberlake stated that the exposure was a case of "wardrobe malfunction." No one believed them.

Reporter Keith Olbermann wrote, "Well, look at it this way. In an incredible role reversal, a Jackson is accused of having their clothes intentionally ripped off them by a boy."

Michael was reported to be either "horrified" at the incident, or else "amused." Take your pick.

Janet, après nipplegate

Michael's friend, Marlon Brando, wasn't one of the 200,000 people complaining. He told friends that "Janet had balls" to pull a stunt like that, revealing that one of his favorite pastimes when he was her age was "mooning."

Former friends had deserted Michael in the wake of his scandal, and he was sorry to hear that his sister's career had also been damaged. It was reported that soon after the incident, Lena Horne cancelled a project wherein Janet would have portrayed her in a filmed retrospective of her life. But, like Elizabeth Taylor, Brando remained a faithful friend to Michael until the very end.

Early in 2004, when Brando ventured out of his house for the last time, it was to visit Michael at Neverland and to sympathize with his plight. Reportedly, Brando warned Michael not to press the charge of police brutality too strongly because if he couldn't prove it, it might hurt his credibility later on as a witness in his own defense.

Apparently he said nothing to Michael about child molestation, but later expressed misgivings about Michael's relationships with young boys.

Whatever "misgivings" Brando might have had about Michael might have been revealed to confidants, but they were never revealed to California's legal authorities.

As part of what was referred to as "the biggest witch hunt since the Spanish Inquisition," the Los Angeles D.A.'s office called in Marlon Brando for questioning about what he knew of the sexual abuse charges leveled against Michael. Officers questioned the corpulent star for an astonishing seven hours before letting him go.

Michael was known to place long late-night calls to Brando, from whom he sought advice on personal matters. An officer in the D.A.'s office claimed, "We wanted to know just how personal those matters were and did they concern boy love." Reportedly, Brando denied knowing anything about Michael's sex life and claimed that the pop star had never confided "anything pertinent in the abuse case."

While at the D.A.'s office, Brando learned that Brooke Shields, who had "dated" Michael, had also been subpoenaed. Why she was called was not made clear, but she duly appeared without counsel, although there was no information that she had that was pertinent to the Arvizo case.

The final conversation between Brando and Michael was strictly private, but sources close to Brando reported that the actor made Michael a final promise. "If any of those child molestation charges ever stick to you, I'll get you out of the country and get you a safe refuge in Tahiti. Don't worry. I can do it!"

This was no idle promise on Brando's part. On June 5, 2003, the actor granted Michael sanctuary on one of the Pacific islands he owned "for the rest of Jackson's natural life." Brando transferred unrestricted use of a half-acre on the islet of Onetahi in the French Polynesian atoll of Tetiaroa to Michael.

Brando died of lung failure at the age of 80 on July 1, 2004. Some of the star's ashes, along with those of his long-time lover, Wally Cox, who had died in 1973, were scattered in Death Valley. The rest of Brando's ashes were spread in Tahiti where he maintained several real estate investments and a private island.

Michael was reported to have "cried for three days and nights" upon learning of the death of his beloved mentor.

After the actor's death, when news of Brando's "misgivings" about Michael's involvement with young boys was leaked to the press, some friends wondered if Brando's criticism of Michael wasn't a case of the pot calling the kettle black.

A former business manager for Brando, Joan Corrales, weighed in with an opinion. She'd been fired by "The Godfather" as co-executor of his will only 12 days before he died. Subsequently, she filed a $5 million wrongful termination suit in Los Angeles. She not only charged him with sexual harassment for exposing his genitals to her, but she claimed that he had a "disturbing" attraction to underage girls and vividly described his "terrible fixation" on minors.

"Brando derived pleasure from sharing his stories of sexual exploitation—including his sexual escapades with minors," Corrales charged.

In her testimony, she confirmed that the rotund recluse had deeded a Polynesian island sanctuary to Michael.

"Brando and Jackson were birds of a feather," said a source close to both men. "Both of them had an unnatural fixation on minors."

Michael kept his promise not to live at Neverland. In January of 2004, he moved out of the ranch and rented a nine-bedroom mansion built in 1991 in Beverly Hills, complete with a 36,000-square-foot ballroom and theater and two regulation-size bowling lanes. Owned by a Chinese painter, it was on the market for $20 million. When there were no takers, Michael rented the property for $70,000 a month as part of a one-year lease. The mansion was allegedly secured for him by Leonard Muhammad, the advisor of the Nation of Islam. Reporters couldn't help but note that the rented mansion overlooked a children's park and playground.

A few days later, on January 16, 2004, Michael, aged 45, arrived late for his arraignment in Santa Maria, California on child molestation charges. In a

Jermaine

whispery voice, he pleaded "Not Guilty." Inside, the courtroom was packed, and outside, some 3000 people, including hundreds of hysterical fans, waited shoulder-to-shoulder with news media from as far away as Norway and Japan. Some fans had crossed the deserts of Nevada in cars called the "Caravan of Love."

When Michael had arrived in a black sports utility vehicle, a roar had gone up for him. A huge black umbrella shielded his white skin from the California sun. One news reporter said he looked "like a cross between Mary Poppins and Mary Tyler Moore." He wore a silk armband and rhinestone-studded boots for his arraignment. Making a surprise appearance was his superstar sister, Janet, who only smiled as Michael repeatedly claimed, "I love my fans!" Brother Jermaine, Joe Jackson, and mother Katherine were part of his entourage.

Upon Michael's arrival, stern men in dark suits with walkie talkies were posted every few feet, forming a wall around Michael. These radical Muslims were from Louis Farrakhan's Nation of Islam.

Reporters worked overtime, investigating and subsequently filing stories about Michael's new link with the Nation of Islam and Louis Farrakhan.

During its turbulent history, the controversial black militant group has issued statements claiming that "whites are devils who must be destroyed." The group, whose membership is estimated at 20,000, has referred to Jews as

Mark Geragos

"bloodsuckers" and campaigned aggressively for a separate African-American state.

Journalist Geoffrey Wansell asked, "So has the androgynous former child star from Gary, Indiana, who spent years undergoing plastic surgery apparently designed to make him look white, suddenly decided to return to his roots? Or is it a final, desperate effort to stave off the long arm of the law? Michael will do anything—*anything*—that will keep him out of prison, one former colleague told me this week. He clearly hopes the Nation can help him do that."

Unlike his brother Jermaine, Michael had not become a Muslim. It was reported that he was still a Jehovah's Witness, but despite that detail, Farrakhan had stationed Leonard Muhammad, his son-in-law and chief of staff, within the Los Angeles office of Michael's lawyer, Mark Geragos.

In reaction to this, a member of Michael's staff, who refused to be named, resigned in protest at the Nation's increasing control over Michael. "These people are basically brainwashing him," the former employee charged. "They tried to do the same thing with Whitney Houston. They offer a false sense that they can control everything. Everybody is afraid of them. They pretty much keep Jackson semi-captive."

It has been suggested by Michael's worst critics that he wanted to align himself with Farrakhan—sometimes called "the black man's Hitler"—as a politically correct anti-racism stance, perhaps a last-minute attempt to win the support of black Americans, whom he'd frequently shunned. O.J. Simpson, who had courted white women throughout most of his life, had also solicited the Nation for support when he faced criminal charges of murder.

498

Michael was said to have prayed with Farrakhan and to have been fascinated by his story of being swept up into a UFO and taken to the larger mother ship. Michael wanted to know if these extraterrestrials looked like E.T. Farrakhan reportedly told Michael that the UFO "mother wheel" was piloted by a dozen young men who were in perpetual orbit above the Earth, prepared for a signal from Elijah Muhammad to unleash total destruction on all the "white devils" of Earth, but rescuing all people with black skin. The question is, does Michael still believe the words of his former hit single where he famously sang, "It don't matter if you're black or white"?

"With friends like Farrakhan and those boys from the Nation of Islam, Michael Jackson doesn't need enemies," or so claimed reporter David Keller, reportedly writing a book on the black militant group.

Back at the courthouse, as members of the Nation of Islam guard gazed ominously at the proceedings, Judge Rodney Melville fumed at the sight of Michael buzzing theatrically into the courtroom 21 minutes late. "Mr. Jackson, you have started out on the wrong foot with me," the judge said. "I will not put up with that. It's an insult to the court."

After leaving the courtroom, Michael headed for his SUV, hoisting himself up onto its roof. In doing so, he gave no indication of the shoulder injury he'd claimed to have received from police "manhandling." In the background, music blared from boom boxes. From his perch on top of the SUV and from under an umbrella, he blew kisses into the air and even performed a few dance moves, whipping the crowd into a frenzy.

Members of the Nation of Islam distributed invitations to fans, inviting them on the following day to a bash at Neverland "in a spirit of love and togetherness." Hundreds of fans showed up the next day for fried chicken, turkey dogs, and ice cream, but Michael was a no-show. His fans rode the Ferris wheel and stared in awe at the snakes. But their hope that Michael would appear was never realized.

MJ on top of the SUV

At the arraignment, news leaked that Gavin Arvizo, the accuser, was in poor health. He'd lost a kidney, his spleen, and an adrenal gland in surgery to remove a large, cancerous tumor. Gavin was reported to "be in hiding." A spokesperson claimed, "The boy and his family are very private people."

Even though Judge Melville had imposed a gag order, news still leaked from the courtyard to the press. It was learned that

Gavin had supplied police with drawings of Michael's genitals, just as Jordie Chandler had done in 1993. The boy also claimed that Michael stole his underwear during his visits to Neverland. It was also rumored that the star kept the underwear of many of his overnight guests, presumably as souvenirs, especially if they were urine- stained.

At the end of January, some details about Maureen Orth's upcoming piece in *Vanity Fair* was released to the press. In the article, she revealed that Michael allegedly seduced boys by giving them a Coca Cola can filled with white wine, calling it "Jesus Juice." Red wine was named "Jesus Blood."

In March, 2004 the grand jury convened to hear the child molestation charges against Michael. The key witness was, of course, 14-year-old Gavin Arvizo. The proceedings were secret, but many of the details of Gavin's testimony were revealed. The boy told the grand jury that he had been molested by Michael at least seven times early in 2003. Gavin said that Michael "loosened me up with Jesus Juice and showed me pictures of naked women before sexually molesting me at Neverland." Obviously this was a different Gavin from the boy who had appeared on the Bashir TV documentary cuddling with and praising Michael. The accuser's psychologist, Stan J. Katz, was also brought forward to testify.

In the months preceding the trial, as prosecutors worked day and night trying to secure young boys to testify that Michael had molested them during visits to Neverland, it was a 45-year-old man who leaked the news of a sexual relationship with Michael.

Scott Thorson had been the former lover of Liberace. He announced to the press that he'd also had an affair with Michael shortly before he split with the flamboyant piano player in the early 80s. The staff at the *National Enquirer* reported that Thorson had passed a polygraph test and was ready to testify in the singer's child molestation case. The former male model claimed that he could prove useful to prosecutors if Michael's attorneys claimed that he was thoroughly straight and had no interest in boys.

According to Thorson, he said that he'd met Michael in 1979 in Las Vegas, but that the two didn't have their first sexual encounter until a while later in an apartment in London. In his testimony, he charged that he was trying on some new clothes when "Michael motioned me over to the bed where he was lounging." Thorson said that they also had another sexual tryst the following

Judge Rodney Melville

500

evening after a dinner party.

"Michael felt comfortable enough to make the first move on me, and I didn't resist," Thorson claimed. "Michael begged me to leave Liberace, but I had to say no."

An attorney for Michael, Steve Cochran, claimed that Thorson's account is "total trash."

Thorson was evicted in 1982 from Liberace's home in Los Angeles after he became addicted to painkillers and other drugs. The former model later sued Liberace for palimony.

No sooner had headlines about Liberace's former lover faded than new headlines blared on April 22, 2004: GRAND JURY INDICTS JACKSON. There was no immediate official confirmation. The grand jury had spent three weeks hearing from witnesses.

Four days later, it was revealed that Michael had decided to replace his legal team. One of Michael's lawyers, Benjamin Brafman, a New York criminal defense lawyer, said that "serious conflicts had been brewing for weeks" among Michael's legal team, the members of which had also conflicted with Jackson family members. "Mark Geragos and I are stepping down—or, as the Jackson camp suggests, being replaced," said Brafman.

Still representing Scott Peterson for allegedly killing his pregnant wife, Laci, in late 2002, Geragos also claimed that "I will no longer represent Mr. Jackson."

A new defense team would be led by white-maned Thomas Mesereau Jr., a Los Angeles lawyer whose best-known recent client had been the actor Robert Blake, who had been charged with murdering his wife, Bonny Lee Bakley, three years previously. A 53-year-old, 6-foot-3-inch bruiser, Mesereau had boxed and played football at Harvard, and had also represented Mike Tyson during a 2001 California rape investigation.

Assuming control of Michael's defense, Mesereau flew to Orlando to meet privately with Michael, who at the time was visiting Disney World with his three children.

On April 30, 2004, in Santa Maria, Michael arrived in an SUV to greet a diminished crowd of only 150 fans. Facing new charges, he entered the courtyard flanked by his

Liberace with Scott Thorson

new lawyer. Gone were the Nation of Islam bodyguards, who had been supplanted by a small cadre of security guards.

He pleaded "Not Guilty!" to all 10 felony charges.

Count one was for conspiracy involving abduction, false imprisonment, and extortion, alleged to have occurred between February 1 and March 31, 2003. Counts two to five charged lewd acts upon a child under the age of 14. Counts four and five also alleged that a third person, "James Doe," witnessed the acts. This was an obvious reference to Gavin's younger brother, Star. Count six cited an "attempt to commit a lewd act upon a child under the age of 14," and counts 7 to 10 charged Michael with "administering an intoxicating agent" to Gavin to assist in the commission of child molestation.

Mesereau, in a brief statement, told reporters that the case was about "the innocence and the complete vindication of a wonderful human being named Michael Jackson." Before driving away in his SUV, Michael waved and flashed a peace sign.

In May of 2004, Michael's defense team sought for the reduction of his $3 million bail, claiming it was excessive and that it violated Santa Barbara County standards for bail. The prosecutor objected, arguing that the star might choose to live the rest of his life as "a wealthy absconder" rather than face a life term in a California prison. It was pointed out that Michael was known and "adored" in many countries in the Middle East and Africa, countries that had no extradition treaties with the United States. In June of 2004, Judge Melville refused to lower Michael's $3 million bail.

During this time, some reporters inaugurated a policy of posting daily bulletins about the Michael Jackson case. In lieu of hard news, rumors were printed, none more bizarre than stories circulating that Michael was dead.

These rumors grew and grew until Raymone Bain, Michael's new spokeswoman, was forced to declare, "My client is not dead. Michael Jackson is doing just fine." Bain wrote a "Michael Jackson Is Not Dead" press release. "I had been up since 3 in the morning getting phone calls from reporters all over the world! The rumors were rampant! It's my job to correct the record."

A Hollywood publicist told the *New York Daily News*, "When you have a client who is clearly three sandwiches short of a picnic, you need to protect him with grace and dignity. And a press release that announces to the world that your client is not dead certainly reinforces the notion that he's a total nut bar."

The sudden appearance of Bain as a spokesperson raised the question of "Whatever happened to Bob Jones?" Michael's long-time publicist. After 17 years of brilliant service, Jones had been dismissed by Michael. Two bodyguards showed up at Jones's residence to retrieve Jackson memorabilia. "He never betrayed Jackson," one source claimed, "although he easily could have, as he was the keeper of many secrets."

Jones was said to be "dismayed and shocked" at Michael's abrupt firing of him. Since Jones never signed a confidentiality agreement with MJJ Productions, that left him free to write a memoir of what it was like representing Michael.

One by one, most of the Hollywood elite during the summer of 2004 began to avoid Michael, not accepting his calls and not returning his urgent messages.

In the past, Michael had succeeded in getting a superstar like Madonna to go out on a "date" with him for publicity purposes. But in July of 2004, he struck out with another superstar, Nicole Kidman, 37. He called her and asked if she'd be his date at the upcoming MTV Awards, but the former wife of Tom Cruise politely declined.

"I had never even met him," Kidman told the press. "It was a little strange. I did decline but, hey, the way my love life is going I took it as a great compliment. I keep thinking of those photographs of Michael in a shocking wig at Disneyland looking ridiculous. So call me crazy, but it just didn't tempt me to want to accept." Some Hollywood wag facetiously suggested that Michael would have had better luck if he'd called Tom Cruise instead.

In August of 2004, the state attorney general's office concluded that Michael had not been "manhandled" by the sheriff's deputies who took him into custody. The findings were contained in a three-page letter which Martin A. Ryan, chief of the attorney general's California Bureau of Investigation, sent to Santa Barbara County sheriff Jim Anderson. Ryan's office had assigned a dozen people to investigate Michael's charges, and collectively, they spent more than 2,500 hours looking into them. A spokesperson in Ryan's office, who refused to be named, claimed, "It's pure and simple. Michael Jackson lied. He was treated with dignity and respect, something not always accorded to child molesters, especially when they go to prison, where they are often attacked by fellow inmates."

On August 16, 2004, Michael, dressed completely in white and accompanied by La Toya, Janet, Randy, Jackie, and Jermaine, watched prosecutor Tom Sneddon get grilled. During court proceedings, the district attorney lost his temper twice and was consequently rebuked twice by the judge. Watching it all, Michael giggled both times.

Michael was not required to attend the grilling, but apparently wanted to see his nemesis

Nicole Kidman

503

questioned. Michael believed that Sneddon nurtured "a vendetta against me."

As Michael emerged from his double-decker bus, he was greeted by cheering fans. He read a sign: IF MICHAEL JACKSON IS PETER PAN, THEN TOM SNEDDON IS CAPTAIN HOOK.

In a series of legal maneuvers, Mesereau was trying to get evidence that had been previously accumulated by private eye Bradley Miller tossed out of court. Mesereau claimed that in November of 2003, Sneddon had violated lawyer/client privilege when his men smashed their way into Miller's office, confiscating computers, documents, and papers pertaining to Michael. At the time, Miller had been a private investigator working for Geragos, who was Michael's original lawyer in the case.

During his 3½ hours on the witness stand, Sneddon clung to his claims that he was unaware of a professional relationship between Michael's former lawyer, Geragos, and the private dick, Miller.

During his interrogation on the stand, it was learned that Sneddon, in his search for damaging evidence on Michael, had also videotaped testimony from Janet Arvizo. Her testimony was recorded in the summer of 2003 in the wake of the disastrous fallout from the Bashir TV documentary. In front of investigators from the sheriff's department, Janet claimed that "Michael's henchmen" had pressured her family to relocate to a new home in Brazil, all at Michael's expense "because there was people that were gonna kill the children and me—um, mostly my children." On public TV in September of 2004, Janet appeared again to make more claims, asserting that she and her children "were chosen by God" to take on Michael. In a police video obtained by *The Insider*, Janet was shown telling people that "God knew that we weren't gonna fall for any of their money. That it was gonna be justice more than anything."

Even before the trial began, Michael had become the butt of jokes—in magazines, on talk radio, on television, and definitely in newspaper cartoons. He rarely responded to attacks. But in October of 2004, derision by a fellow performer made the pop star "hip-hoppin mad." In response, he issued a public attack, slamming Eminem's new music video, the controversial "Just Lose It."

In the music video, Eminem mocks Michael about the child sexual abuse allegations he was facing. In one scene Eminem is dressed up like Michael, sitting on a bed with little boys jumping up in the background. The lyrics say, "Come here little kiddie, on my lap. Guess who's back with a brand new rap? And I don't mean rap, as in the case of child molestation." Other scenes in the video mock Michael's nasal plastic surgery and hair-burning incident during the filming of the Pepsi commercial.

"I am very angry at Eminem's depiction of me in his video," Michael told

504

Eminem

radio host Steve Harvey. "I feel that it is outrageous and disrespectful. It is one thing to spoof, but it is another to be demeaning and insensitive."

Of course, Michael had far more than Eminem to worry about. Michael's attorneys had been desperately trying to get Judge Melville to dismiss charges or else throw out evidence. In his ruling of October 16, 2004, the judge refused, claiming that the police had acted properly when they'd searched Bradley Miller's office.

As Michael neared his trial date, more suspicions were aired about his past activities with young boys—many of them anonymous, but some of them minor celebrities in their own right. One such case involving "names" surfaced in November of 2004.

It was revealed that teen pop singer Aaron Carter had spent an unsupervised night with Michael, "my idol," at Neverland. Aaron was only 15 years old at the time. He'd gone to Michael's 45th birthday bash at Neverland with his older brother, former Backstreet Boy Nick Carter. The next day, Nick told his mother, Jane Carter, that Aaron refused to leave Neverland, so he left his younger brother there.

His mother claimed she was in panic until Aaron came home about 24 hours later, never giving his mother an explanation of what went on during his absence. "I don't know if he was alone with Michael," June claimed to celebrity interviewer Daphne Barak on *Access Hollywood*. June later said that prosecutors grilled Aaron about his time at Neverland. "I have no idea what he told them," June said.

Aaron did admit spending time in Michael's bedroom but mostly "we had innocent, fun-like dance lessons and rode around the ranch." Aaron reportedly also told his mother that Michael gave him a Bentley, but he never brought the vehicle home. Later Michael denied giving the teenager the expensive car.

When June called Michael, he reportedly told her, "Nothing happened. Absolutely nothing happened. All we did was hang out."

Michael's show-biz involvements were ground to a virtual halt as police grilled one boy after another. His upcoming trial dominated the headlines, which is why the world took little notice of the November 16, 2004 release of *Michael Jackson, The Ultimate Collection Box Set*, a flashy-looking assortment of five separate CDs. It contained 13 previously un-issued recordings dating back to as early as 1969 and forward to the post-millennium. It also

505

presented an unreleased 1992 live concert and contained 57 tracks of hit singles. But the glory days of *Thriller* sales were long gone.

On December 3, 2004, just weeks before Michael was scheduled to go on trial, police—armed with a search warrant—once again raided Neverland. Investigators entered the estate at 9 a.m., remaining there for three hours, but issued no statement as to the reason for the raid. Michael was leaving Neverland at the time of the raid, but did not stick around to see what the police were doing. When he heard about the raid, Mesereau raced more than 150 miles from Los Angeles to the Los Olivos ranch to monitor the search.

Within days, Mesereau filed a motion to dismiss the child molestation charges on the grounds of "vindictive prosecution and outrageous government conduct." The defense also asked Judge Melville to suppress all evidence seized at Neverland under the latest search warrants. According to reporters, Michael's lawyers even wanted a DNA sample taken from the star destroyed.

Around Christmas in 2004, private videos of Michael went on the market. The footage was shot in 1996 by Dr. Allan Metzger, who taped scenes from the *HIStory* tour as well as scenes from Michael's wedding to Rowe. Although in the wedding scenes Rowe looks more attractive than she usually does, Michael allegedly looks like a freakish goon. As for what the film contained, a source who'd seen the footage claimed, "You see Michael bitching and moaning about his fans. He says he doesn't like them to touch him and gets really upset when they storm his limo."

Metzger did not release the tapes himself and was "shocked and aghast" to find the video being peddled. He said he thought the tapes were locked in a safe. It was reported that an estranged member of Metzger's family managed to procure the damaging tapes.

More damaging video was on the way.

Directed by Helen Littleboy and narrated by Mark Strong, *Michael Jackson's Boys* aired on television in 2005. It used interviews with friends, family, journalists, and many young boys who had been involved with Michael over the years. Boys included Frank Cascio, playing himself. Jordie Chandler in archive footage also appeared as himself, as did the array of the "usual suspects," including Macaulay Culkin, Terry George, Emmanuel Lewis, Jimmy Safechuck,

Brothers, Aaron and Nick Carter

and others. Archival footage was also used of Lisa Marie and Brooke Shields.

Some fans immediately attacked the film as "very dangerous, one of the most biased pieces of television I've seen in a long time." The show clearly left the impression that Michael "grooms" young boys for a relationship but "rejects them once puberty hits."

The impending trial had all the elements for a great show business special. The defendant was arguably the most famous personality in show business, the only performer who rivaled Elvis Presley and The Beatles in worldwide name recognition. Charges of child molestation were expected to bring lurid testimony from shady accusers. Over-the-top courtroom histrionics could be expected. For defense witnesses there was talk of an all-star cast, including Dame Elizabeth herself.

In a perceptive article, journalist Amy Sohn wrote that Michael might as well be on trial for much more than child molestation, citing "body dysmorphia, bizarre wardrobe, narcissism, racial-identity disorder, transgenderism, makeup wearing, and poor parenting. Jackson is a walking set of contradictions between male and female, gay and straight, man and boy, abused and abuser."

Even as charges swirled around Michael, many parents defended the pop star, claiming the accusations were lies and asserting that it was still safe for their kids to visit Neverland if invited.

In Los Angeles, Gaynor Morgan told the press that she had no objection to her ten-year-old son, Alex, visiting Michael. "It'd be fine for him to stay and spend time . . . and you know, confident," Morgan said in a slightly awkward statement.

Sally Thomas of Dallas defended Michael, claiming that her five-year-old son, Travis, had visited Neverland as a participant in a Make-a-Wish Grant. "I don't think Michael sees himself as a middle-aged man when he's with these children, because he's out there playing just like they are," said Thomas.

One reporter concluded, "That leaves some to complain that Michael Jackson may be Peter Pan—but it's the parents who are in Neverland."

As defenders came forward to praise him, Michael saw his hopes dashed on January 31, 2005. His lawyers had been working feverishly behind the scenes to have charges against their client dropped, but 4,000 summonses had been mailed out to county residents. Jury selection had begun, as court officials hoped to find a dozen "impartial" jurors. Because of so much pre-trial publicity, nearly every prospective juror had already formed an opinion, and most of them seemingly believed that Michael was a child molester.

During the jury selection, everyone who was even remotely connected with Michael—real or fantasy wise—talked to the press. A resident of Phoenix, Hans Schmidt, came forward, claiming he had tapes in which

Michael asserted that he pined for "a woman to love." Schmidt maintained that these tapes would prove that Michael was straight.

On the tapes, the singer allegedly expresses his dislike for his nappy hair, calling it "nigger hair." He also mentioned his battle with anorexia. Even so, during the filming of these tapes, he was reported to have shared a dessert with a beautiful blond-haired boy. In the *New York Daily News*, columnists provocatively speculated: "Let's hope it wasn't the English dessert Jackson mentions a fondness for in another conversation: Spotted Dick."

Finally, the court selected 12 jurors, each of whom claimed that they wouldn't allow Michael's celebrity to affect their final decision as to his guilt or innocence. The jury of four men and eight women was made up mostly of whites. No jurors were black, but at least three appeared to be Hispanic and another Asian.

Some of the final jurors, ranging in age from 20 to 79, were Michael's fans; four parents of young children; a woman whose grandson had been convicted of a sexual offense, and a man who had visited Michael at Neverland when he was a child. Eight alternates were selected—four men and four women ranging in age from 19 to 81.

The trial that would last for 73 days began on March 1, 2005, and would involve the state calling 90 witnesses, the defense 50. Some 700 pieces of evidence, including pornography, would be introduced into the official record. But perhaps none of these exhibits was as bizarre as a collection of bare-breasted plastic "Barbies" in S&M gear.

As a means of demonstrating Michael's attraction to young boys, the prosecution introduced two books featuring nude prepubescent boys. The books had been seized during the 1993 raid on Neverland and never returned. The pictures were of boys who took part in the 1963 film adaptation of *Lord of the Flies*. One book, *The Boy: A Photographic Essay* featured many photos of nude boys, including some explicit depictions of genitalia.

In TV coverage, reporters Diane Dimond and Nancy Grace emerged collectively as Michael's

The perils of plastic surgery

508

bête noire. Each of them would later insist that Michael got away with some serious charges of child molestation, all of it coming at great cost to his music career and personal reputation.

Judge Rodney Melville ruled that witnesses, including young men, could be summoned to court to testify if Michael had ever sexually abused them. In most cases, evidence of past behavior had not been admissible against a defendant. However, in 1995, the California Legislature changed that, passing a law that in cases of child molestation, testimony from the past could be allowed. The judge cleared the way for the prosecution to introduce testimony that Michael had made moves on five other boys, including Macaulay Culkin. However, even before his appearance in court, Culkin had consistently denied that Michael ever molested him.

In pressing for the introduction of boys from Michael's past, Sneddon told the judge that Michael's actions with these youths were inappropriate, including "kissing, hugging, and inserting his hands into their pants." He also claimed that "there was a pattern of grooming," or preparing the boys for molestation, but did not elaborate.

Sneddon wanted testimony from Jordie Chandler, but the boy had refused to appear, reportedly fleeing the country. Nonetheless, the DA wanted the jurors to see the cute young boy with his dark hair and doe eyes. A larger-than-life photograph of Jordie was shown to jurors on an overhead projection screen. Attorney Larry Feldman, who previously had brokered Jordie's $25 million settlement with Michael, claimed that Jordie was much better looking than this photograph revealed. "I can tell you, at that age he was adorable," Feldman said. When the picture was shown in court, Michael did not look up at it but stared straight ahead.

Michael's critics suggested that both Jordie and Gavin represented a type, in that each had dark eyes, dark skin, short dark hair, and what was called a "pixieish look." Perhaps Sneddon was indeed hoping to prove that Michael had a type, although the dark looks of Gavin and Jordie wouldn't account for the blond-haired *Home Alone* allure of Macaulay Culkin.

The most crucial day was March 10 when the jury got a look at Gavin Arvizo for the first time. All courtroom observers agreed that the case against Michael would hinge on this teenager's testimony. At the time of his court appearance, Gavin was 15 years old.

Astonishingly, the defendant himself did not show up on this crucial day, as noted by Judge Melville who took the bench at 8:35 a.m.

Michael's attorney, Tom Mesereau, explained that he was in Cottage Hospital in Santa Ynez being treated for a serious back injury. Melville came down harshly. "I'm going to issue a warrant for his arrest. I'm forfeiting the bail."

Michael got the message loud and clear. His motorcade came screaming up to the courtyard. Getting out, Michael shuffled in slowly, wearing designer pajamas. Seated in the courtroom in these pajamas, he had to face Gavin accusing him of taking him to bed. Without emotion he sat rigidly, listening to Gavin claim that Michael had told him it was necessary to masturbate or else he "might rape a girl."

As Gavin sat across from Michael, the boy was being carefully screened by the jury. With his closely cropped hair, he looked older, bolder, and stronger than in previous pictures. In all, he cut a sympathetic figure and had a pleasing demeanor.

He stared straight at Michael as he made his charges, explaining that "I was kind of hypnotized by Michael and Neverland when we met in 2000."

Michael set ramrod straight as he stared back at the teen. Gavin testified that on his first night at Neverland he was invited to sleep in Michael's bedroom with both Michael and Frank Cascio.

He testified that Cascio, now calling himself "Frank Tyson," surfed the web for porn that featured women between the ages of 15 and 25. Gavin testified that Michael masturbated him and tried to get him to touch his genitals. "He grabbed my hand but I pulled my hand away because I didn't want to do it," Gavin claimed.

Adult materials found at Neverland included some 75 magazines of straight porn, as well as four gay-themed books. Some of these publications had the fingerprints of the two Arvizo brothers on them, both Star and Gavin. Both boys claimed that Michael showed them these adult materials, alleging it was for the purpose of lowering inhibitions to sexual behavior, a charge Michael denied, but not on the stand.

Allegedly, Michael showed the boys pictures of topless women while asking, "Got milk?" He was also said to have leaned in and whispered to Prince Michael II, who was sleeping nearby, "Prince, you're missing some pussy."

Gavin also charged that Michael not only showed him porn, but got him intoxicated on wine as a prelude to seduction.

During police investigation into the case, Gavin had initially claimed that he'd been molested "five to seven times." But on the witness stand, he could only describe in detail two occasions where he claimed that the pop star had molested him.

MJ arriving at
his trial in pajamas

510

Under cross-examination, he grew argumentative with the defense, especially when he was painted as a juvenile delinquent with behavioral problems, who had been schooled by his mother to lie under oath for financial gain and to pester celebrities for money. The jury seemed to waiver between sympathy for Gavin as a cancer victim and exasperation at the venality of the entire Arvizo clan.

His sister, Davellin, 18, had stubbornly denied that Gavin had disciplinary trouble at his school. Yet nine teachers, according to school records, claimed he was a "classroom nightmare," citing such offenses as fighting, disrupting class, refusing to obey teachers' orders, and being defiant. Gavin did admit that he often misbehaved in class and never did his homework.

Gavin was forced to admit that he had twice told a school official that the King of Pop never molested him. Wincing, Gavin was forced to recount a conversation he'd had with Dean Jeffrey Alpert at his school in the spring of 2003. "I told Dean Alpert he didn't do anything to me," Gavin admitted.

In another coup for the defense, the boy admitted that many of the glowing things the Arvizos had said about Michael in a 90-minute rebuttal video, filmed on February 19, 2003, were true. Then both Star and his sister claimed that the family was coerced into making the rebuttal video. News accounts carried on March 15 said that Gavin "lost his halo" in court.

In rebuttal, Gavin claimed that "I didn't spill my guts" to the dean because "I feared cruel taunts from my classmates if word got out."

Under questioning by Sneddon, Gavin claimed that after the Bashir documentary was aired, showing him holding hands with and nuzzling the pop star, he was "mercilessly ridiculed by schoolmates. Kids would laugh at me and say, 'That's the kid who got raped by Michael Jackson.'" According to testimony, Gavin was repeatedly called "a faggot" by his classmates.

Mesereau was successful in getting Gavin to acknowledge that he and his family came and went at their leisure from Neverland, refuting his mother's previous claims that they had been held at the ranch against their will.

After 13 hours on the stand, Gavin was asked how he felt about Michael today. "I don't really like him anymore. I don't think he's deserving of the respect I was giving him as the coolest guy in the world."

The prosecutor, Sneddon, attacked Mesereau in his defense of Michael, calling it "a scorched-earth, take-no-prisoners approach." Sneddon alleged that Mesereau was particularly caustic in his cross-examination of Gavin. "He left the boy bewildered and stammering contradictions over three days of testimony. Mr. Mesereau was as abusive, as mean, as obnoxious as you could be to a child witness," Sneddon told the judge. "Victims don't want to show up because they don't want to go through what the accuser experienced."

After Gavin's testimony, Michael made a rare appearance on the Rev.

Jesse Jackson's Sunday TV show. The star claimed that he was a victim of conspiracy "just like other black luminaries," citing Nelson Mandela as an example. He noted that some of the press had noticed that he was crying when hearing Gavin's testimony about child molestation. "I was in a great deal of pain," Michael said. "I was coming out of the shower and I fell and all my body weight, I'm pretty fragile, all my body weight fell against my rib cage." It was physical pain, not emotional pain, that caused him to tear, he claimed.

In April of 2005, in the midst of the trial, Michael managed to attend the funeral of attorney Johnnie Cochran Jr.

Michael joined O.J. Simpson, along with other celebrities who included the Rev. Jackson, in paying tribute to the controversial lawyer. It is not known what words O.J. Simpson and Michael exchanged with each other, but both Michael and O.J. could thank Cochran for extricating them from sticky messes—O.J. for an alleged double murder, and Michael for getting Jordie Chandler and that earlier issue about child molestation off his back. Cochran died on March 29, 2005, at his home in Los Angeles, where he'd been suffering from an inoperable brain tumor.

The Rev. Calvin Butts, pastor of the Abyssinian Baptist Church in Harlem, referred to Cochran "a great warrior for justice." In a dissenting voice, writer Paul Stefani in 2006 said, "I guess he was all that if you call helping a wife murderer and a child molester beat the rap."

Back at the trial, Davellin Arvizo testified that she saw Michael kissing her brother on the cheek and head while her family lived at Neverland during February and March of 2003. "When I was in his bedroom one time, he had his arm around Gavin and they were hugging over and over, and kissing over and over," she charged.

Gavin's younger brother, Star, was also called to the witness stand. While on the stand jurors learned that Michael had nicknamed him "Blowhead." Star told the court that on two occasions he'd seen Michael lying on his bed at Neverland, groping Gavin with his free hand while Michael played with himself. On yet another occasion, Star claimed that he and Gavin were on Michael's bed watching TV when Michael walked in with a full erection. "It's natural," Michael was alleged to have told the two brothers.

At one point, Star claimed, Michael grabbed the mannequin of a little girl and pretended to hump her in front of the brothers.

Star indicated that when he saw Michael fondling Gavin, both his brother and Michael were unaware of his presence. "I saw directly into the bedroom, and my brother was on top of the covers," Star claimed. "I saw Michael's left hand in my brother's underwears and his right hand in his underwears." He said he saw the alleged molestation as he climbed a stairwell leading to the pop star's bedroom.

Prosecutors bolstered Star's account by proving that the boy would have had a line of sight to Michael's bed from the top of the stairs.

On the stand, Star also testified that Michael had shown Gavin and him copies of such porn as *Barely Legal* and *Juicy, Ripe and Ready.*

When Mesereau cross-examined Star, the attorney scored points by revealing that the magazine, *Barely Legal,* seized in a raid on Neverland, was actually published in August of 2003, months after Michael allegedly had "shown" it to Gavin and Star. The teen also couldn't explain why the door to Michael's bedroom had been left unlocked or why no alarm had been triggered by his secret approach. Previously he had claimed that there was a system of keypad locks and a warning bell in the hallway leading to this very private master bedroom.

Star testified that for amusement Michael, acting like an overgrown teenager, made obscene crank calls to anonymous people. When one woman answered her phone, Michael, according to Star, asked her about the size of her genitals.

The boy was forced to admit that he'd lied during previous depositions, including one taken in 2000 as part of a lawsuit the Arvizos filed against JC Penney. Star claimed that his father never hit him and that his parents never fought. Under Mesereau's stern questioning, the boy was forced to concede that he'd committed perjury.

The teen was also forced to admit that he'd given conflicting accounts in previous statements to a psychologist. Very forcefully, Mesereau pointed out that Star had given three different versions of what he claimed he witnessed Michael doing to Gavin's body. The attorney said, "In one version, Mr. Jackson's hand was outside the boy's clothes; in another, it was inside, and in a third Mr. Jackson was 'rubbing his penis' against the boy's buttocks."

O.J. Simpson

If Star appeared to be an inconsistent witness, his mother, Janet, was even worse on the stand. In retrospect, some court observers claimed that her appearance on April 3 lost the case for the Arvizos. Even before she appeared in court, the defense had sought to portray both her and her family as "gold diggers who saw Mr. Jackson as a celebrity fall guy to be milked for cash."

On the stand, Janet was a loose cannon and, thanks to her erratic courtroom outbursts, the most explosive witness in the case. A mercurial character, she rarely gave a straight answer to any of the defense team's questions. She repeatedly said, "It's burned inside my memory" or "money doesn't buy happiness." It was also claimed that she exploited her cancer-stricken son for money and at one time spent $7,000 shopping and dining out at the same time she alleged that Michael was keeping both her and her family "captive."

In five days on the stand, the mother "ranted, raved, and refused to answer questions." Many of her replies were nonsensical. The 36-year-old woman kicked off her testimony by invoking her Fifth Amendment right against self-incrimination on questions about alleged welfare fraud. She admitted that she'd lied under oath in an unrelated court case.

Dressed in pink, Janet was often sarcastic in court but at one time she broke down on the witness stand, asking those in the courtroom, "Please don't judge me." In her testimony she claimed that she'd seen Michael lick her son's forehead like a cat. She alleged that the head-licking incident occurred on a charter flight from Miami to California in February of 2003.

At the time, she did not intervene to stop it. "I thought I was seeing things."

She also testified that Michael and his "henchmen" told her that there were unnamed "killers" out to get both her and her children in the wake of the damaging Bashir TV documentary in 2003.

Mesereau was known for trying to box accusers in with "yes" or "no" answers. Defiantly, Janet made rambling speeches to the jury instead. At one point she looked at Michael across the courtroom and said, "He managed to fool the world. Now, because of this criminal case, people know who he really is. He really doesn't care about children. He cares about what he was doing with children."

In a combative day on the stand, she was forced to admit that she'd once told sheriff's deputies that she feared Michael had a plan for her and her family to "disappear from his Neverland ranch in a hot air balloon."

There were times such as this when the court erupted in derisive laughter at her answers.

Janet had claimed that she was being held against her will at Neverland, but defense witness Angel Vivanco, a chef, claimed that Janet got a deluxe body wax at a spa and sipped champagne with one of her "captors." Vivanco charged that Janet was a "flirtatious mom," who downed bubbly with Michael's "henchman," Dieter Wiesner, at the kitchen bar at Neverland. According to Vivanco, the pair left together "for parts unknown." Vivanco's charge of Janet's cozy session with Wiesner flew in the face of her

Thomas Mesereau

previous testimony when she described Wiesner as one of the two threatening men she called "Germans," who made "my life hell at Neverland."

To help the defense's case, an employee, Kate Bernard, asserted on the stand that she drove Janet to the Bare Skin Aromatherapy Day Spa in Los Olivos for a deluxe body wax. It was suggested that if Janet were indeed being held "captive," she could have escaped at any time.

Joe Marcus, ranch manager at Neverland, also countered Janet's testimony, stating that the Arvizos were "happy" to be at Neverland. When he would take Janet out on a shopping trip, he claimed that she was always anxious to get back to Neverland. Marcus also said that Janet and Gavin "never complained about anything." Marcus was part of a string of current and former Neverland employees called by the defense to counter disgruntled former staff members who testified against Michael for the prosecution.

Prone to emotional outbursts wherein she would snap her fingers at jurors, Janet could not explain why, if held hostage at Neverland, she didn't call the police, since it was shown that she had unrestricted access to a telephone. She also couldn't give a reason why she never called for help when Michael's aides took her to public places such as restaurants, beauty salons, stores, and even government offices where she repeatedly encountered law enforcement officials and said nothing.

To counter charges of kidnapping, defense attorney Robert Sanger produced the gate log at Neverland, naming Brian Barron as the guard on duty February 12, 2003, when the Arvizos left the property at 1:38 a.m.

A tall, red-haired cop, Barron moonlighted at Neverland for five years. He'd also noted that the Arvizo family returned voluntarily a few days later. In other tantalizing tidbits, not related to the case, Barron recorded a secret visit of the Rev. Al Sharpton on June 23, 2002, and from Ed Bradley, the *60 Minutes* correspondent, on February 8, 2003. A visit by Elizabeth Taylor had been scheduled but she never showed up.

After these revelations, Sanger tore into the mother. "She lies for gain. She's lied and cheated her way through life—that's what she does."

Janet claimed that in the wake of repeated death threats, she'd become so afraid for herself and her children that the Arvizos escaped "in the dead of the night" in one of Michael's Rolls-Royces. They were not to see Neverland again and future encounters with Michael would occur in court.

Janet was the big loser at the trial. She not only lost her case against Michael but later faced charges of welfare fraud and perjury. A five-count felony indictment against her came down in October of 2005. She was charged with a single fraud count and four instances of lying to secure nearly $19,000 in welfare payments to which she was not entitled. During the Jackson trial, she'd refused to answer questions about how she'd obtained welfare payments despite having more than $30,000 in the bank.

On November 13, 2006, Janet, aged 38, was found guilty of welfare fraud. As part of a plea bargain, she agreed to repay $13,606 to the State of California.

She was ordered to repay the rest of the money she'd illegally acquired and to complete 154 hours of community service before April 27, 2007. If she complied, the felony charge would be reduced to a misdemeanor and she'd not have to go to prison.

After Janet's appearance, legal experts weighed in on Michael's trial, even before the prosecution had wound up its case. Michael Cardoza, a defense lawyer and former Alameda County (CA) prosecutor, predicted that "Jacko may moonwalk over the DA's weak case." At the worst, a hung jury was predicted. "I wouldn't have let her anywhere near my case," said Cardoza, referring to the accuser's wacky mom. "Her testimony hurt more than it helped."

It wasn't just Janet's testimony that came under fire. The defense called witnesses to counter some of Gavin's claims, especially a charge that Michael had supplied him with alcohol during a cross-country flight from Los Angeles to Miami.

The defense called a corporate flight attendant for Xtra-Jet International, Cynthia Ann Bell, to the stand. She disputed the accuser's claim that Michael had urged Gavin to "tank up on Jesus Juice" to shake off his fear of flying aboard a February 7, 2003 flight to Miami. She maintained that the King of Pop never shared his soda can of wine with Gavin, claiming that she'd kept an eye on both Michael and Gavin throughout the flight.

The pretty blond jet hostess did admit that Michael was a "very private drinker," who downed almost two bottles of white wine, hidden inside a diet Coke can, during the cross-country flight.

She also testified that she never saw Michael "inappropriately touch the accuser or any child." Gavin had testified that he had drunk "at least a whole can worth of wine from Jackson's Diet Coke container" during the flight. His sister also testified that she saw Michael pass the can to her brother. "They were sipping it back and forth."

Bell also attacked Gavin for being "a rude and discourteous loudmouth, who threw mashed potatoes and raised a ruckus when his chicken wasn't warm enough." In her testimony, she also said that Gavin showed off an expensive watch Michael had given him. She quoted the boy as bragging to her, "Jackson will buy me anything I want."

It had been announced that many big names would appear in court for the defense. Most of them, such as Elizabeth Taylor, were never summoned. Judge Melville barred "bombshell" testimony from CNN talk show host Larry King. With jurors out of earshot, the CNN host testified that the attorney,

Larry Feldman, who at one time represented the accuser, told him that the boy's mother was a "wacko," a term most often used for Michael himself—and "that she was just in it for the money." Melville ruled that this was "hearsay" testimony and was inadmissible.

As a key witness for the prosecution, Dr. Stan Katz took the stand. He was the one who had transmitted Gavin's allegations against Michael to authorities in June of 2003 when the boy was only 13.

On the stand, the psychiatrist claimed that, "It would be highly unusual for a 12- to 13-year-old boy to make false accusations against a male," Katz claimed, although there is massive evidence to dispute that.

Katz was known to TV audiences for his appearances on the NBC-TV reality show, *Starting Over*.

Mesereau attacked Katz's credibility by citing a book he'd written, in which the psychiatrist claimed that forty percent of child abuse claims are false.

Surprisingly, when comedy club owner Jaime Masada took the stand, he bolstered the claim of Janet. He testified that the mother, in a hysterical phone call, claimed, "I can't leave Neverland Ranch. They're holding me and my kids against my will." He remembered the call as coming through early in 2003. He quoted Janet as shouting, "Oh my god, they're holding me here." As Masada remembered it, she was sobbing.

Masada claimed that it was not Janet but the father, David Arvizo, "who was the one who pestered me for cash when the boy had cancer in 2001 and 2002." According to Masada's testimony, David, then unemployed, often "hit me up for gasoline money or rent."

Masada is accredited with setting into motion the meeting between Michael and Gavin. In court he disputed the defense contention that the mother was a scam artist. Masada is the owner of the Laugh Factory Comedy Club on Sunset Strip. Arriving in America from Iran when he was 14 years old, Masada built a comedy empire in Los Angeles. He met Gavin in 1999 at a comedy camp he sponsored for disadvantaged children. At Gavin's request, Masada put him in touch with Michael.

George Lopez, the star of the ABC sitcom, *George Lopez*, was called as a witness for the prosecution. He recalled that he met Gavin's family in 1999 at a Sunset Strip comedy club and became close to them when he learned of the boy's illness. "I was invested in them," he testified, "and I saw a lot of myself in that family." But he said that the father kept calling him asking him for money. At one point, the father accused Lopez of stealing $300 from Gavin's wallet, which had been left behind at the comic's house. Obviously the relationship soured after that. "What am I supposed to tell my son?" David asked Lopez. The comedian curtly replied, "Tell him that his father is an extortionist."

A pivotal moment in the case came when the judge ordered Michael to remove his trademark surgical mask. For all the world to see, Michael was hardly ready for Norma Desmond's famous close-up. Photographs revealed scarred lips and a nose seemingly held together by Elastoplast. One reporter called the look one of a "borderline sci-fi scenario."

Throughout the trial Michael looked pale and frail under a pageboy haircut. He often wore military jackets with a red armband and a pocket crest. He always painted his mouth scarlet and wore dark sunglasses. As one juror later said, "If I was being charged with molesting a young boy, I would have left the tube of lipstick laying on my vanity table."

On May 11, jurors saw two videotaped interviews which described Michael's pure love of children, comparing himself to Princess Diana, the Rev. Dr. Martin Luther King Jr., Mohandas K. Gandhi, and Mother Teresa. "Since these figures are dead," Michael said, "there's not a voice for the voiceless, and I've been doing it for many years."

On May 18, Rijo Jackson, Michael's 12-year-old cousin, took the stand. His testimony cast grave doubt on the innocence of the Arvizo brothers. Rijo stated that he saw Gavin steal wine and money and secretly watch porn on TV while masturbating. Rijo also testified that Star took part in misbehaving during visits to Neverland. He said both brothers asked him to join them in masturbation as they watched an X-rated TV channel showing naked women cavorting. Rijo said that he went to tell Michael what the boys were doing. "But he didn't believe it," Rijo claimed.

Brushing aside tears, the doe-eyed boy described his X-rated encounter with complete believability as he told of Gavin and Star "doing nasty stuff." The pony-tailed cousin's account was important because Gavin had testified that he never looked at porn or engaged in sexual conduct unless Michael was there "to coach me."

The testimony of Jay Leno on May 23 was a disappointment. Michael's lawyers hoped that Leno would take the stand, accusing the Arvizos of trying to weasel money out of him. But he testified that he was never asked for money.

Headlines claimed that Leno had bombed and that the *Tonight Show* funnyman was no stand-up guy for Michael. His testimony appeared to contradict statements that he had made earlier to investigators for the Santa Barbara sheriff's department. During that session, the 55-year-old comedian claimed that the Arvizos were "sort of looking for money" and that he felt he'd been targeted as their next "mark."

The following day Michael's defense team concluded their case without bringing the pop star to the stand. The prosecution had two and a half months

Psychiatrist Dr. Stan Katz

to summarize their case, the defense resting after less than three weeks. Michael did speak on videotape, referring to himself as "a childlike spirit surrounded by adults who have deceived and betrayed me."

The final witness for the defense was comedian Chris Tucker, who called the Arvizos "cunning and relentless in the pursuit of money, gifts, and free trips" from himself and other celebrities.

On May 26, prosecutors lost a bid to show the jury photos of the pop star's allegedly spotted penis. The bid had called for presentation of those photos alongside Jordie Chandler's illustration of a distinctively marked penis that was alleged at the time to have been inspired by Michael's penis. Judge Melville said, "I'm going to deny bringing in evidence of the blemished penis. I find the prejudicial effect would far outweigh the probative value."

In his argument for the prosecution, Ron Zonen claimed that Michael had a discolored spot on the underside of his penis which could only have been seen if the penis were erect.

The jury did not get to see pictures of Michael's penis, but a number of other curious parties did—but only if willing to pay big bucks for that dubious privilege. As early as October of 1994, *The Amsterdam News* in New York was reporting that photos of Michael's genitals were floating around Hollywood. "They're either duplicate photos of those held by the D.A., or fakes, according to our sources," claimed reporter Abiola Sinclair. One source, who requested anonymity, said that the pictures were smuggled out and that the negatives are on the market.

Another anonymous source, who had seen the actual photographs of the nude Michael and also the pictures being hawked as the real thing, claimed off the record that "They're the genuine article—that's Jackson's dick all right! But I don't know how copies became available. Just too many people have seen and dealt with these photos. After all, if Tom Sneddon had had his way, not only the jurors would have seen Michael's prick, but in time the entire world. As has been shown time and time again, it's hard to keep pictures private if a star poses nude or makes a sex video. It's going to get out. Take Paris Hilton, whomever."

In their closing arguments on May 27, prosecutors were allowed to show a 70-minute video of Gavin's first interview with the police on July 7, 2003. In denim shorts and wearing a blue shirt, Gavin claimed, "He put his hands in my pants. He started masturbating me. I told him I didn't want to do that and he kept on doing it. I told him no. He said he wanted to show me how to masturbate. I said no. Then he said he could do it for me. He grabbed me. My private area. He touched me for a long time."

On June 3, in closing arguments, Zonen, for the prosecution, once again dragged out Michael's porn collection, showing the jurors the cover of a book called *A Sexual Study of Man*. "It shows everything one man could possibly do to another man," Zonen told the panel of eight women and four men.

George Lopez

On June 3, during closing arguments, the defense claimed that the Arvizos were "con artists, actors, and liars." Prosecutors claimed that Michael had lured the vulnerable cancer survivor "into the world of the forbidden in his bedroom and molested him." Zonen charged, "The lion on the Serengeti doesn't go after the strongest antelope. The predator goes after the weakest."

On the dawn of the jury's verdict, journalist John M. Broder accurately predicted that regardless of the outcome Michael's "secrets have been laid bare and his psyche picked apart as if by carrion birds. Even if he is acquitted, many people will continue to believe that he harbors an unhealthy fondness for young boys."

En route to court on June 13 to hear the verdict, Michael rode with his family with a Bible open on his lap. He was rocking back and forth, saying, "They tried to do this to Job. Now they are trying to do it to me. Why me?"

On 2:25 p.m. that day, the jury of the Superior Court of the State of California determined that Michael was not guilty on all counts.

As he heard "not guilty" seemingly repeated endlessly, Michael sat motionless for five minutes as the possibility of nearly 20 years behind bars was finally lifted.

Judge Melville declared, "Mr. Jackson, your bail is exonerated and you are released." Wiping tears from his eyes, Michael walked out of the courtroom after exchanging joyous hugs and handshakes with his attorneys. Tom Mesereau said, "Justice was done. The man's innocent and always was."

Fans celebrated outside the courthouse, cheering and waving signs. Both the investigation and trial had lasted an astonishing 574 days.

Outside the courthouse Michael, weak and frail, walked slowly with a solemn face.

One loyal female fan released one white dove for each count on which Michael was acquitted. Confronting his fans, Michael blew kisses to them before disappearing into a black SUV for the trip back to his fantasyland estate. This time there were no dances of victory atop the van.

Foiled in his second attempt to bring Michael to "justice," Sneddon was clearly angered at the verdict. "No comment!" he snapped at reporters.

One woman juror said she was offended at Janet Arvizo "snapping her fingers at us. 'Don't snap your fingers at me, lady,' I said to myself."

On the east coast, hundreds of people, both anti-Michael and pro-Michael, gathered in Times Square, where a giant screen heralded news of the star's acquittal.

Elizabeth Taylor issued a statement. "Thank God Michael is vindicated for all time. Now maybe people will leave him alone."

After Michael's victory, his attorney, Mesereau, told Barbara Walters in an ABC interview, "I may have saved Michael's life. I don't think he would have survived prison."

In yet another statement, the attorney went on to say that Michael had learned a valuable lesson. "He's not going to make himself vulnerable to this kind of thing anymore."

Robert M. Sanger, another defense lawyer, reported visiting Michael at Neverland a few hours after the verdict came in, finding him extremely grateful that the trial turned out as it did.

"There was a strong sense that the charges were preposterous and that it would be bizarre for a jury to believe these people were telling the truth, let alone beyond a reasonable doubt." Having represented Michael for 12 years, Sanger claimed that the trial was a "long, long battle for Michael to clear his name. He's finally gotten a resounding acquittal, an exoneration!"

As Michael was driven back to Neverland, loyal fans had gathered at the gates to greet him. ALL OF US HERE AND MILLIONS AROUND THE WORLD LOVE AND SUPPORT YOU.

The next day the number of fans had dwindled to only a few loyalists, but an estimated 200 members of the media lined the rural road, watching as cars

Jay Leno

came and went through the guarded gate. Everybody wanted to see Michael leaving Neverland but had to settle for Joe Jackson instead. He claimed that his son was "exhausted and resting" before his vehicle disappeared inside the gates.

This may have been Joe Jackson's last visit to Neverland. For public relations purposes, Michael had wanted a show of solidarity from the Jackson family. But sources close to the pop star claimed that once the trial ended, he didn't want to see any of them. And in the wake of the trial, after he'd fled the country, it was claimed that he no longer accepted their phone calls, even those from his pleading mother, Katherine.

In a post-verdict interview, juror Raymond C. Hultman, a civil engineer, said, "I would tell him not to sleep with boys. It's not something that's normally acceptable in this society." Hultman said that he believed Michael might have molested boys in the early 90s, but that the "prosecution in the latest case had failed to provide sufficient evidence. I had what I thought were some valid reasons to believe this child had been molested, and his demeanor seemed genuine." But Hultman felt that the "prosecution's timetable did not make sense."

Even though he was found not guilty by a jury of his so-called peers, Michael seemed disgusted and even furious at what he'd been put through in America. He vowed never to set foot on American soil again. Two weeks after his acquittal, he flew to distant Bahrain, an island nation in the Persian Gulf, one linked to Saudi Arabia by a bridge.

If Michael thought interest in him had waned, he was mistaken. Beginning in the summer of 2005 and lasting through the year of 2006, he made more blaring headlines around the world than any other person in the entertainment business, exempting the fluffy coverage of the Brad Pitt/Angelina Jolie romance.

Almost everything Michael did—known or perceived—merited a headline.

In Bahrain, Michael was the guest of the royal family, specifically Abdullah bin Hamad Al-Khalifa, the son of Bahrain's king, Sheik Hamad. His Majesty reportedly didn't welcome Michael and resented his son's fascination with the superstar. Unlike the prince, the ruler reportedly didn't like the media coverage and notoriety the disgraced pop star would bring to his tiny country.

Local news accounts reported that Michael's home in Bahrain was filled with "personal boy servants," and that he constantly had an "entourage of several young boys wherever he went." Michael was said to have been delighted to discover that Bahrain has a branch of Toys 'R Us.

Michael's attorney, Tom Mesereau, refused to say if his client would relinquish his U.S. citizenship and seek immigrant status in Bahrain.

Rashid Bin Abdulrahman Al-Khalifa, an officer in the ministry of information, predicted that Michael would not be given citizenship. "Citizenship," he said, "is not easy to get here in Bahrain—even for Michael Jackson. But he may stay indefinitely as long as he owns property here."

The local press in Bahrain claimed that Michael had invested $1.5 million in two villas and a plot of land in the country's manmade Amwaj Islands.

The Amwaj Islands are popular with Bahrain's oil-rich set, many of whom maintain second homes here. It's a secluded area within eyesight of mainland

Bahrain. There's even a posh private school for Michael's sheltered, veil-wearing kids.

In 2005, papers were publishing stories about "the curse of the Jacksons," as newspaper reporters who included Patricia Shipp were updating the public on the famous and once-rich family. Much of the data had already been published and made known for the public, and the financial plight of Michael himself had been extensively written about. Of all the family members, Janet seemed in the best financial shape. Both Joe Jackson and Katherine Jackson were perceived as being in "financial peril."

It was reported that Marlon, at the age of 48, was having trouble keeping up the $9,000 monthly mortgage payment on his $2.2 million California mansion. Back in 2001, Randy, 44, admitted to bankruptcy fraud when he failed to list his ownership of a sports utility vehicle in filing his claim. After a string of flop solo albums, Jermaine at 51 had moved back into the Encino house but reportedly traveled to the Middle East to meet with leaders of the Muslim faith. Tito at 52 was appearing at small venues performing on his blues guitar. Jackie turned 54 in 2005 but had not appeared in public since 1989, when he released a solo album that bombed.

Even though he lived in exile in Bahrain, the lawsuits against Michael continued. The most bizarre and most high-profile of the lot was filed in Los Angeles by Marc Schaffel. It offered additional embarrassing insights into Michael's private life, much of which had already been laid bare during the Arvizo case.

Michael had long been known for his "odd couple" relationships, and none was more exotic than his hookup with a gay porn producer, Marc Schaffel. Their link originated in October of 2001 for a performance of "What More Can I Give?" at the *United We Stand* charity concert for victims and survivors of the September 11 terrorist attacks. Performing in Washington, DC, 27 artists joined together onstage for the observance, including such big names as Ricky Martin, Julio Iglesias, Mariah Carey, Celine Dion, and Justin Timberlake. The event raised $3 million.

Tom Sneddon:
District Attorney

"What More Can I Give?" was available for paid download on the Internet and a video was shot of it. However, the single was never commercially released as had been planned. Michael blamed Sony's Tommy Mottola, his favorite target, for the single's cancellation. But the release may have had more to do with Michael's involvement with Schaffel. Later a catalogue featuring the song, "What More Can I Give?: Michael Jackson and Friends," was released instead.

"What More Can I Give?" was expensive to produce but was cancelled by Sony when its executive producer, Schaffel, was revealed to have a background in gay porn. As Michael tried to distance himself from Schaffel, various corporations, including McDonald's, claimed only minimal involvement in having sponsored the song.

Michael's involvement with Schaffel—not only in association with the charity recording, but in other projects as well—came to light during the autumn of 2005 when Schaffel sued Michael, threatening to "tell all" in court. In the producer's suit, he claimed that Michael owed him $800,000 for producing two TV specials in 2003 and $2.3 million for personal loans he'd made to the star during the previous two years.

In his lawsuit, Schaffel alleged that he had been promised twenty percent of the gross returns on the TV specials he produced and which had been aired on Fox in rebuttal to the damaging Bashir TV documentary of 2003. The Fox specials produced by Schaffel were sold to a British TV station for $10.6 million. Schaffel's documentaries of Michael were flattering portraits. Schaffel went on to claim that the pop star had used them to repair some of the damage to his reputation caused by the Bashir TV show.

Michael's attorney countersued on October 18, 2005, claiming that Schaffel had failed to pay costs related to the production of the charity song, "What More Can I Give?" The producer was also charged with keeping $250,000 worth of sculptures and paintings that belonged to Michael. Michael's lawyer, Brent Ayscough, also claimed that the porn producer had tried to get a lien placed on Neverland. In all, Michael charged that Schaffel owed him $600,000.

Michael had "divorced" himself from Schaffel after learning about the producer's previous background in gay porn. In testimony that was videotaped—Michael never appeared in court himself—the pop star said that he had been

MJ in a burqa with one of his sons

524

shown a film directed by Schaffel, depicting "two guys naked from head to toe. Schaffel was telling them what to do with each other. They were touching their penises." After seeing the film, Michael claimed that he wanted to distance himself from Schaffel and his X-rated movies because "I'm no fan of gay porn."

Michael's videotaped deposition was shown to jurors in July of 2006. "I just thought this association with Schaffel wouldn't vibe with the charitable work I've done," Michael claimed in his testimony. "I wanted to be diplomatic about it. I didn't want to embarrass him."

In the video, Michael claimed, "I'm sure he got money," referring to Schaffel. When asked how he could be so sure, Michael said, "Because he always seemed to be happy." The lawyer responded, "Money doesn't buy happiness."

In court, Schaffel countered by dishing the dirt on Michael, claiming that he flew to Brazil on several occasions to try to adopt boys for Michael. In his testimony, he charged that these "boy searches" occurred twice a year between 1999 and 2001. "I would go between Thanksgiving and New Year's. Mr. Jackson definitely wanted to adopt some boys."

In other testimony, Schaffel charged that in addition to the "adopt scheme," he flew to Buenos Aires to pay $300,000 in "hush money" to prevent another child molestation scandal. It was alleged at the time that a Ruby Martinez and her son, David, had "knowledge of past abuse allegations against Jackson dating back to the 90s."

Schaffel initially sued for $3.8 million but his claims were eventually cut by his attorney to $1.4 million before his client actually appeared in court.

In all, Schaffel claimed that he'd paid out $8.9 million for Michael since 2001 but had been repaid only $6.3 million. He also stated that he wanted to get paid while Michael might still have the cash "because he's a ticking financial time bomb." In Schaffel's suit, he alleged that all payments to him stopped once Randy Jackson took control of Michael's finances in June of 2004.

Marc Schaffel

In his complaint, Schaffel alleged that the pop star's need to borrow money "accelerated when Jackson's increasingly more frequent and excessive use of drugs and alcohol impelled him into irrational demands for large amounts of money and extravagant possessions." On an interview with ABC News on *Good Morning America*, Schaffel speculated that Michael's dependency on painkillers and pain medication led him to "call me in the middle of the night seeking loans for one of his spending sprees."

"When Michael would be on drugs, he would call me at two, three, or four in the morning. Very distorted. And he would say, 'Oh, can you give me $70,000 tomorrow? There's this table I saw. I gotta have it for my living room.'"

Schaffel even brought Marlon Brando and Elizabeth Taylor into his trial. He claimed that Michael asked him to raise $1 million to pay Brando for appearing in a music video and on stage at Madison Square Garden. Schaffel said he was also asked for $600,000 as a loan to buy Elizabeth Taylor a piece of jewelry in exchange for her appearing on Michael's behalf. That exact appearance by Dame Elizabeth was not specified.

Schaffel's own appearance on ABC led to more speculation that Michael was indeed "buying the friendship" of Elizabeth, as had been alleged so many times in the past. Schaffel also claimed that he'd lent Michael at least $100,000 to finance shopping sprees and help him make payments on a Rolls-Royce Phantom and a Bentley Arnage.

There were more claims. In 2001, after the September 11 attacks in New York, Michael called the producer wanting half a million dollars in cash for access to an underground shelter to protect "my loved ones," which the public learned in this case was Elizabeth and Marlon Brando, not the Jackson family members who were also in New York at the time.

Attacking back, Michael's spokeswoman, Raymone Bain, denied the ABC show, calling Schaffel's remarks "slanderous" and claiming he could not be trusted because of his close ties with the porn industry.

During the Schaffel trial, a tantalizing tidbit emerged. In a raid on Neverland preceding the Gavin Arvizo trial, sheriff's deputies also raided the Calabasas, California home of Schaffel. The speculation was that the gay porn producer had videos that he'd taken of Michael in sexual situations with young boys. The confiscated items were loaded into a police van for investigation, but "no smoking gun" was found. A lot of gay porn was discovered, but none featuring Michael.

At the actual Arvizo trial, Schaffel was named as one of the un-indicted "co-conspirators," who had "tried to quiet" Gavin Arvizo and his family.

The jury in the Schaffel/Jackson trial listened to phone messages Michael left for the producer. In one such message, jurors heard the very high-pitched voice of Michael saying, "I like you. I love you . . . I really want us to be friends and conquer the business world together."

Attorney Thomas Mundell, representing Michael, put up a vigorous defense, at one point claiming that Schaffel pocketed $400,000 from a Japanese company for rights to the charity record and that he used the funds as a down payment on a house.

Mundell also read to jurors a voice mail message from Michael to Schaffel. "Marc, please, please never let me down. I have been betrayed so much by people. Be my loyal, loyal friend." In conclusion, Mundell went on to say, "Members of the jury, Marc Schaffel was not Mr. Jackson's loyal friend. I ask you to send him from this courtroom with nothing."

The battling attorneys were bitter in their closing words to the jury, Schaffel's lawyer, Howard King, called Michael a "cagey, calculating witness" who took advantage of the producer. The pop star's attorney, Mundell, countered that Michael was the "victim of financial manipulation" by a former associate. "I resent that Mr. Schaffel is portrayed as some sort of parasite hanging on to Mr. Jackson," King said angrily.

Mundell shot back: "I don't see the evil, conniving puppet master he saw. I see the gentle, easily influenced artist who pays little attention to business matters."

In July of 2006 a jury of twelve, equally divided among men and women, deliberated for nine hours after hearing ten days of testimony. In their verdict, they granted Schaffel $900,000, citing Michael's breach of contract with the producer. The jury also granted Schaffel $300,000 for his out-of-pocket expenses in flying to Buenos Aires to offer hush money to a family with dirt on the pop star. But in a split verdict, they also awarded Michael $200,000 believing that Schaffel skimmed that amount from the proceeds of the unreleased charity recording of "What More Can I Give?"

In November of 2005, in the midst of the Marc Schaffel brouhaha, a new eruption occurred when Michael faced headlines accusing him of anti-Semitism. These were old charges first aired in 1995 when he released the song, "They Don't Care About Us," in which he referred to Jews as "kikes."

A Jackson family attorney, Brian Oxman, responded that anti-Semitic messages, which were later broadcast on TV, were actually "telephone conversations recorded without permission." The phone messages were recorded in 2003 but not leaked to the press until 2005.

Michael's words were broadcast on ABC's *Good Morning America*. In the recording, Michael states that Jews rob performers of their money. His exact words were, "They suck them like leeches." The message was left for Dieter Wiesner, who had filed a $64 million lawsuit against Michael, claiming fraud and breach of contract. Wiesner, as Michael's former business advisor, was one of the un-indicted "co-conspirators" involved in Michael's child molestation trial.

"I have been with the Jackson family for 15 years," Oxman said. "And I'm Jewish. I have never once seen anything anti-Semitic from him or from his family."

The day after ABC aired the telephone answering machine message, the

Anti-Defamation League demanded that Michael apologize. "Michael Jackson has an anti-Semitic streak and hasn't learned from his past mistakes," said ADL director Abraham Foxman.

More unwanted publicity came late in 2005 in the form of a book by Pulitzer Prize winner, Margo Jefferson, who published a short treatise on the star. Only 138 pages, *On Michael Jackson* claimed that the performer "speaks to and for the monstrous child in us all." An African-American, Jefferson has long been an admirer of Michael's. But she also paints a devastating portrait of the entertainer. She raises some disturbing questions about sexual desires in young boys, particularly at the ages of 12, 13, 14, and 15. Such boys are not necessarily "innocent," she said, noting that "they are curious, they have sexual desires, as well as impulses, and they want to act on them. I am not trying to turn Michael's accuser, Gavin Arvizo, into a youthful seducer. I am simply trying to say there was almost no public acknowledgment of these everyday facts, known to anyone who has had a child, spent time with children, or remembers being a child."

Those children that Michael had once befriended—at least most of them—had turned into adults. In the fierce sun of Bahrain, Michael had plenty of time to acknowledge Sean Lennon, son of John, as he turned thirty in 2005. Sean, a holdover from Michael's "boy crazy days," had grown into a man, although Michael reportedly had been disappointed that Sean had not realized his dream in music. "How could anyone, even a son, follow in the footsteps of a father like John Lennon?" Michael asked. "My own father, Joe, was a failed musician, so I didn't have to compete with his record like poor Sean has to do. It's the same with Lisa Marie. She's no female Elvis—let's face it."

Although a multi-millionaire and the reasonably attractive son of a music legend, Sean stunned the world when he virtually advertised for a lady companion. He told the press that it could be, "Any girl who is interested but she must be born female and between the ages of 18 and 45. She must have an IQ above 130 and must be honest. She must not have any clinical, psychological disorders . . . and a kind heart. Clearly beautiful—but beauty on the inside is more important—but no deformities, third legs, fifth nipples." In a statement so bizarre as to seem unbelievable, the rich singer/songwriter claimed that, "I'm completely alone and I'm completely miserable."

When Michael read this astonishing statement, he reportedly said, "I'm in the same boat as Sean." As an afterthought, he added, "Of course, I have the children, but sometimes even they are a mixed blessing. As I get older, I realize that parenting can be an annoying task at times."

Taking over most of that parenting for Michael in Bahrain was Grace Rwaramba, a native of Rwanda, who was the nanny to his kids. The rumor mill swirled around Michael and the nanny when the press reported that Michael was planning to wed Grace so that she could become the actual mother—not the stand-in—for his kids.

The trouble with that report was that Grace was already wed, having married Stacey M. Adair in Las Vegas on February 26, 1995. The couple had not lived together, however, for years.

Adding to the tabloid fodder, it was rumored in the press that Grace had also been involved in "romances" with two of Michael's brothers, Jermaine and Randy. Grace has denied introducing Michael to the Nation of Islam and has blamed his problems on Satan.

It was believed that Michael considered marrying Grace when a California appellate court restored Debbie Rowe's parental rights. If he were in a marriage, or so it was believed, it would help his legal status as a parent and sole custodian for his three children.

Reporter Roger Friedman claimed that, "Rwaramba is widely disliked by the Jackson camp, by nearly all of his family members, and his remaining two or three employees. They see her as a social-climbing gold-digger who wants what's left of Jackson's money."

Friedman had reported in 2005 that Grace was "drugging Jackson and keeping him isolated from family and friends." She's been with Michael and his three kids since he fled to Bahrain. "Family members and business associates who want to speak with Jackson must call the nanny, who decides what calls are put through to the abundantly weird singer," Friedman claimed.

Because of his ties to Grace and her links to the Nation of Islam, and because of Michael's previous links to that group, rumors also circulated that he was prepared to convert to Islam, as had his brother Jermaine, who was also said to be urging his brother to convert. It was even claimed that Michael was planning to erect a mosque in Bahrain.

A spokesman for Islamic causes said, "Thousands of people are embracing Islam. Michael Jackson is just one of them." Michael's spokesperson, Raymone Bain said, "Michael is looking to give something back to the country that has welcomed him so openly."

Michael caused a media storm when he entered the women's restroom in a shopping mall in Bahrain. A representative claimed that the singer did not understand the Arabic sign and mistook the bathroom for a men's room.

Bain claimed that Michael left the women's room as soon as he discovered what it was. But witnesses said that he did not leave the toilet at once and was spotted applying makeup in the mirror. Upon his exit, he was recognized and a mob began to gather. He hid out in a bookstore until the police arrived to escort him out of the mall.

Relations with Bahrain soured when he was pilloried for appearing in a

Muslim *abaya* robe, garb which is traditionally worn by females.

Every time Michael appears in public, including a surprise visit to the water park in Dubai, it is widely reported in the press. He rented the entire Wild Wadi Park and appeared here in a white Lycra body suit that exposed just his nose and eyes. A lifeguard told the British tabloid, *The Daily Express*, "He looked even stranger than usual. His body is very skinny and Lycra does him no favors."

Although in exile and cut off from family members, Michael was believed to have stayed in contact with brother Jermaine, who was reportedly flying to Bahrain to see friends there. In fact, Jermaine, a Muslim, was believed to have been responsible for Michael's move to that country in the first place. But while Jermaine was still publicly defending his brother, reports reached Michael—and later the press—that he was actually shopping a book, hoping to cash in on Michael's trial and subsequent notoriety.

Allegations made by Jermaine were leaked to the New York press. In the never-published book, *Legacy: Surviving the Best and the Worst*, Jermaine claimed that a "sperm donor" was responsible for the birth of Michael's two children with Debbie Rowe in spite of the pop star's insistence that the kids were fathered in "the natural way."

"It was like a sanctioned black market," Jermaine claimed. Michael's brother did not explain how Michael acquired his third child, Prince Michael II. The mother of "Blanket" has never been identified.

In his book proposal, Jermaine is alleged to have suggested that daughters Rebbie and La Toya may have been molested by Joe Jackson and that young Michael himself may have suffered abuse from an "important businessman."

Jermaine, according to news reports, even suggested his father "may have set up Michael to be somehow victimized by older men."

Jermaine also claimed that all of Michael's brothers feared he was gay when they toured as The
Jackson 5. He noted that all the other brothers fell in
love with women. "But, Michael, well, he wasn't
interested," Jermaine said. "We used to quietly say
that we couldn't have a gay brother."

Other allegations by Jermaine accused Michael
of being "devious and calculating" in squashing the
brothers' solo musical careers and paving the way for
himself alone. Jermaine said that Michael hated Jews,
including David Geffen, Steven Spielberg, and
Jeffrey Katzenberg, because "They stole the idea for
Dreamworks from me, including the boy-on-the-
moon logo."

Sean Lennon

530

Jermaine said that Michael preferred such drugs as Demerol, his eternal favorite, but also Vicodin, codeine, cocaine, Percocet, red wine, and good ol' Jack Daniels. Giving us an insider look at the troubled star, Jermaine's still unpublished book was drafted by Stacy Brown, who had co-authored with Bob Jones the book, *Michael Jackson: The Man Behind the Mask*.

If Jermaine is to be believed, his brother's behavior with his own nephews had left the family shaken. In one incident recalled, Michael was found sitting on a bed with Tito's young sons and "holding them in a disturbing manner" following the death of their mother in the mid-90s.

The bombshell proposal also alleged that Jermaine feared Michael might be guilty of child molestation but backed him at the trial because he thought the pop star "would commit suicide in prison." He also alleged in the eight-page proposal that Michael was "an out-of-control drug and booze abuser with a calculating mean streak and a thing for young children."

"With all those drugs in his system, does Michael really know what he does with these kids?" Jermaine asked. "I don't want to tell you my brother's innocent. I am not certain that he is."

Most of the so-called revelations in Jermaine's proposal, including far more devastating ones than he outlined, had not only been heard but often published before. One publisher who looked at the manuscript said, "There's nothing new here."

In New York, news was leaked that publishers who'd seen the proposal turned it down when Jermaine refused to say definitely if Michael were guilty in his kid-sex case. HarperCollins and St. Martin's were two publishers who reportedly "passed" on the badly written proposal.

Reporter Michelle Caruso had a different spin, claiming that "Jermaine pulled the plug on the book after Michael got wind of it and went ballistic, threatening to sue and toss Jermaine out of the family home."

Even that family home was under threat.

By the summer of 2006, four notices of pending foreclosure were delivered at the Encino home of the Jackson family. Hayvenhurst is listed on the real estate market as being worth about $7 million. Michael had failed to make a $2 million mortgage payment on the property, and the Jacksons did not have that much cash. Janet finally came through for her parents, delivering the money to pay the back mortgages.

Journalist Roger Friedman said that, "A pattern has developed in which Michael Jackson refuses to pay a bill—or get someone to pay it for him—until legal action of some kind has been commenced against him."

That was certainly the case at Michael's once-beloved Neverland.

By March of 2006, Neverland had gone dark. No more laughing children. No more arcade pulsing with rap music. No one waiting at the gate with ice cream for the kids. "I don't think he'll be back any time soon," said a security guard at the gate to Peter Pan's Castle. He refused to give his name. "I signed a confidentiality agreement," he claimed.

In June of 2006, the animals at Neverland were moved to new homes, the two tigers, Sabu and Thriller, were being cared for by actress Tippi Hedren, animal rights activist and former star of Alfred Hitchcock's *The Birds*. Her fiancé, Dr. Martin Dines, Michael's long-time vet, said that the animals are all being moved out into "happy new environments." Despite reports that the animals were being mistreated, Dr. Dines insisted that they were in good condition, including four giraffes and two orangutans remaining. "I visit once a week," he said. "There has never been a lapse in the care and feeding of the animals."

The doctor's reports contradicted other claims. A former employee at Neverland said, "The poor underfed animals are looking as sickly as Jacko himself." Animal rights groups became enraged at these charges and demanded action from state officials.

Those state officials, especially in the California labor department, were moving in on Michael on yet another front, fining him on March 9, 2006 $169,000 for failure to cover workers' employment insurance.

Michael not only paid this fine, but shelled out another $306,000 to Neverland employees for back pay. By coming up with the funds, Michael escaped court action. He ordered that Neverland be closed except for a skeletal crew he's forced to keep on. Today, Neverland is in search of a buyer.

In March of that year, stories about the collapse of Neverland weren't the only headlines making the news. In the past, Michael's critics had often accused him of being an extraterrestrial. Although said in jest, those claims took on a more serious face that spring.

Mike Luckman, director of the New York Center for Extraterrestrial Research, claimed that Michael, late in 2003, "indicated to me that he is open to making contact with otherworldly beings." The revelations reportedly occurred in the famous magic store, Abracadabra, on 21st Street in New York's Chelsea district.

Luckman also claimed that Michael wanted to build an airport for aliens, perhaps set up the landing strip in the Nevada desert. "Michael wants to welcome the extraterrestrials to earth and film the landing." According to Luckman, the pop star also confided to him that, "I am from another planet myself." Luckman quoted Michael as identifying his home planet as "A Capricious Anomaly in the Sea of Space located just beyond our solar system."

In July of 2005, Luckman had revealed that Michael had been so afraid of dying in prison that he planned to have his body frozen. "Michael discussed having his remains cryogenically preserved so that he might be brought back to life," according to Luckman. Michael, or so it was said, has taken GH3, the Romanian-developed drug said to make you live longer. It was also claimed that Michael had invested millions in DNA research in the hope of engineering perfect offspring. "Michael has gone to extreme lengths to achieve immortality," Luckman claimed.

Raymone Bain, spokesperson for Michael, called Luckman's account "pure bull."

Luckman only raised more charges of "Wacko Jacko." But Elizabeth Taylor, appearing on CNN's *Larry King Live* in May of 2006, defended Michael, as always. She startled viewers, however, by admitting that she once frolicked in bed with Michael and his nephews, claiming "there was nothing abnormal about it. We were all in bed watching Disney movies on TV."

On the show, his close pal erroneously predicted that Michael probably would never return to the United States. "Really, why should he?" she asked. "He's been treated like dirt here." On the show she also denied reports that she was suffering from Alzheimer's.

Reportedly, Michael was delighted at Elizabeth's appearance, which he hoped would help counter the constant newspaper cartoons, routinely depicting him as a pedophile. He showed his old anti-media hostility when *GQ* magazine ran a picture in its May edition of a look-alike wearing a Bedouin outfit. The imposter is shown wearing one white glove and with his head shrouded standing on a sand dune. Michael wanted *GQ* to apologize and withdraw the edition from newsstands. The baffled editors responded that the image was clearly satirical.

That same month, Michael, in an attempt at the rehabilitation of a failed career, made his first public appearance. He flew to Japan to greet fans, launching his return at a bash at Tokyo's Yoyugu Olympic Stadium. "I look forward to saying hello to my huge fan base in Japan," Michael said before his arrival in Tokyo.

In Tokyo, Michael visited an orphanage where he told 140 kids that, "I love you." He wore sunglasses and a white T-shirt under a black double-breasted suit with gold buttons and a red armband. He shook hands and signed autographs at his first public appearance since his acquittal of child molestation charges.

While in Tokyo, he accepted MTV Japan's "Legend Award" during a Yoyugu Olympic Stadium ceremony.

If Michael did indeed want to re-launch a faltering career, Japan was a wise choice as a venue, because his fans there reportedly had remained the most loyal, while millions of other former admirers, especially in America, had deserted him in favor of other singers such as Britney Spears and Justin

Timberlake.

Back in Bahrain, Michael dramatically severed his ties with his Bahraini lawyers, accountants, and business managers and hired a New York-based firm "known for restructurings and turnarounds." Publicist Raymone Bain announced that she had been named general manager of the new Michael Jackson Company, which replaced the old MJJ Productions. Through Bain it was also announced that Michael would be leaving Bahrain and settling in Europe, perhaps Ireland or maybe France.

What had gone wrong?

The Bahrain dream had actually ended in February of 2006 when it was reported that Michael had a falling out with Sheik Abdullah bin Hamad Al-Khalifa.

Reports coming out of Bahrain in the late summer of 2006 claimed that the Prince's father didn't like Michael hanging out in the Bahraini capital when his son wasn't there to play host to him. King Hamad was 57 years old in 2006, but the young prince was only 31 years old. Michael turned 48 in Bahrain so he's closer in age to the King than he is to the Prince.

King Hamad was reportedly angry that his son had spent millions of dollars entertaining Michael and his entourage and not one bit of money had been earned from their record company, Two Seas, which the two men had set up.

Within days of news stories that the welcome sign had been removed for Michael in Bahrain, the pop star claimed he'd discovered a conspiracy among his former attorneys to force him into financial ruin. His spokesperson, Raymone Bain, claimed that the pop singer had discovered documents that detailed the conspiracy to drag him unwillingly into a bankruptcy court.

Bain did not name the former attorneys charged with conspiracy to bring Michael down. She also refused to state who provided these secret documents to Michael. It wasn't clear why Michael's former associates would want to force bankruptcy onto him—or what they had to gain from such a maneuver.

"That's what we'd like to find out," Bain said. "Michael has always been suspicious that some of those whom he entrusted to act on his behalf may not have acted in his best interest."

To stage his "spectacular pop comeback," Michael decided that he wanted a "hot new manager," and found one in Guy Holmes, who had helped launch the "Crazy Frog," an audio/animated cell phone ringtone that soon after became one of the most popular mobile phone accessories in America.

Michael had become fascinated with Axel F.,

Raymone Bain

the animated cartoon frog character. Holmes said that though Crazy Frog had originally been mainly for kids, "it seems to be that it also attracts a lot of adults who haven't grown up," which might—just might—include Michael.

Cellular News asked a provocative question, "Will we get a duet between Crazy Frog and the so-called King of Pop?"

In Britain, another headline asked CAN CRAZY FROG REVIVE A CAREER THAT CROAKED?

Michael was reported to have signed an exclusive recording agreement with the Bahrain-based Two Seas Records, and Holmes was tapped to be the CEO of the Two Seas label while still remaining chairman of Gut Records.

A music industry insider claimed that "Holmes is a genius for helping older acts stay in the limelight," citing how he masterminded Tom Jones's pop makeover with the 1991 album *Reload*.

Holmes flew to Bahrain to sign the star at the age of 47. Michael announced, "I am incredibly excited about the new venture and I am enjoying being back in the studio making music." He announced that his new album would be ready for release in 2007.

While preparing for a comeback in Bahrain, Michael was interrupted at his studio with an urgent call from his California lawyers. New charges of child molestation had been filed against him in the Orange County Superior Court in California. In papers filed, a twenty-year-old man charged that the pop star had "plied me with drugs and alcohol and then molested me." The man's name was not released to the newspapers at the time.

Charges leaked to the press cited Michael for "repeatedly and forcefully" sexually molesting the boy beginning when he was only two years old. In addition, charges accused Michael of "burning and torturing me."

The plaintiff also claimed that Michael "forced me to undergo unnecessary plastic surgery." The young man's lawyer, Michael Mattern, said the most

glaring surgical procedures performed on his client gave him "noticeably red lips, resembling the garish makeup Jackson often wears in public, and a pronounced cleft chin."

There was more. The plaintiff also charged that both Michael and Sony stole his song ideas and lyrics.

The plaintiff's name wasn't new to the police. During the raid on Neverland in 2003, Santa Barbara County authorities announced that they wanted any "past or new Jackson accusers to step forward." The young man surfaced at the time and was interviewed by police at length. But reportedly

Larry King

the law officials didn't believe that the boy's story would stand up in court.

Michael's lawyer, Tom Mesereau, denounced the charges as "ridiculous on their face—they will be vigorously defended." It was doubtful if the case would even come to court since a judge might refuse to hear it unless he felt the charges had some validity.

This Orange County case was just one of many that would be filed against Michael in 2006 by plaintiffs seeking damages for alleged molestation. Jordie Chandler walking off with $25 million in 1993, a story repeated endlessly in the Gavin Arvizo trial, had obviously attracted a lot of attention among future plaintiffs.

With Gavin Arvizo's name being mentioned again in the papers in the wake of this rather ridiculous new molestation case, the question was raised, "Whatever became of Gavin Arvizo?"

He was found in Orange County living under an assumed name, hoping to escape death threats leveled at him by crazed Michael Jackson fans.

The cancer survivor told reporters that the "day Jackson was acquitted was the worst day of my life. I thought on that day that my life couldn't get any worse. Why didn't they believe me? I told the truth. Why didn't they believe me?"

Gavin, at the age of 16, also confided to a reporter that his own mother, Janet, had "turned her back on me. She blames me, not herself, for the court-room loss." Reportedly, she even blamed Gavin for the welfare fraud charges filed against her, since his claims about Michael led to the discovery of her own misdeeds.

Gavin was still living with his mother, but he said that she treated him "like dirt and won't let me go to counseling to deal with my trauma."

One source reported that Janet screams at her son. She was quoted as saying, "You allowed him to touch you. You allowed him to do it. It was your fault the jury didn't believe you."

Unlike Jordie Chandler, who was enjoying the life of a rich young man, Gavin in the summer of 2006 rode to work across town on his bike where he was employed in a fast-food joint. He buys his own food because Janet allegedly refuses to cook for him. With Jay Jackson, her new husband, she had two more children.

In a press interview, Gavin said, "I wish I had never met Michael Jackson. He ruined my life, and I've nothing to show for it except trouble."

His brother, Star, said, "I am just plain angry at the world. I saw Michael Jackson molesting my brother!"

Back in Bahrain, in a surprising story, it was reported that Michael was undergoing a major revamp to make himself appear more macho, at least according to author Michael C. Luckman who wrote: *Alien Rock: The Rock*

536

'n' Roll Connection. "He's been seen working out, wearing shorter wigs and less makeup," Luckman said. It was also reported that Michael was holding talks with a Las Vegas hotel about a long-term performing deal similar to what Celine Dion has.

But when Michael was spotted with his children touring England, France, and Ireland, there was no evidence that he'd become a "macho man." In Ireland, he was reported to be considering linking his name with a theme park aimed mainly at children, although why investors would want a man accused of child molestation linked with a kiddie theme park remained a mystery. That can be filed alongside reports from Stockholm in 2003 that Michael had once been "seriously considered" for the Nobel Peace Prize.

If Michael indeed moved to Ireland, he might have a companion, as it was reported that he'd acquired a genuine Irish ghost trapped in a bottle. According to BBC News, the century-old ghost was bricked up in a window by a priest following a failed exorcism. An agent representing Michael did the bidding for him, managing to secure the ghost on eBay for only $473.33.

News of the Irish theme park was but one of several multi-million dollar projects Michael was said to be considering. News of these never-to-be projects were coming at the press so fast that Michael was held up for ridicule.

Tim Nelson of the *St. Paul Pioneer Press* greeted Michael's Irish pronouncement with the skepticism that was due. When hearing that Michael was taking the helm of a $100 million Korea-based venture fund that will invest in entertainment-oriented Internet companies, Nelson listed nine other Jackson projects that went belly up. "Coming soon to a vacant lot near you!" he wrote.

Among the failed projects of "Neverland Pictures" was the filming of *The*

MJ with Guy Holmes

Nightmare of Edgar Allan Poe, with Michael as the star. That went the way of the giant resort near Victoria Falls in Zimbabwe and the huge "Majestic Kingdom" theme park in Detroit.

No one got to drink the new soft drink, Mystery, that was going to wipe out Pepsi, Michael's old alma mater.

In partnership with Saudi Prince Al-Waleed bin Talal, Kingdom Entertainment never got launched as a "family values" global entertainment empire with a theme park that could be a home for cattle afflicted with mad cow disease.

That $500 million World of Children Amusement Park was never built in Poland. A few projects got off the ground, including a German manufacturer who produced flat stereo speakers with

Michael's image on them. They were priced at $620. Only they didn't sell. No one wanted one.

While Michael and his children lived in luxury at the former home of the Astor family, Cliveden, in the English countryside, his "comeback" was announced. His highly anticipated first stage appearance since his trial was scheduled for November of 2006 at the World Music Awards in London.

Traveling by limousine to London with his trio of kids, Michael ensconced himself at the pricey Hempel Hotel where his entourage was charged $100,000 a night.

On the night of the presentations, Michael arrived at the auditorium two hours late. Emerging from the limousine, he waved and blew kisses at fans who were angry for having to wait so long for a glimpse of The Gloved One. The words he mumbled to the press were barely comprehensible.

At the ceremony, Jon Bon Jovi, the New Jersey rocker, snubbed Michael and didn't want to present him with an award "because of the stigma of his child molestation trial."

Forever the diva, and much to the disappointment of his still-loyal fans, Michael came on stage and sang only two verses of "We Are the World" before the music went dead. He was backed up by an army of apple-cheeked children. The fans had been told that Michael was going to sing "Thriller" instead. Chris Brown, wearing the familiar red leather of the original video, sang "Thriller" onstage, but he failed to placate the angry crowd. Boos were heard across the auditorium.

"However many times he told us he loved us—and there were too many— and however much we yelled and screamed and pinched ourselves, his performance was a shambles," said a disappointed London fan. Even so, one loyalist held up a banner that read THE KING IS BACK.

The reclusive King of Pop received a Diamond Award given to artists who sell more than 100 million albums. At the last minute, the host of the show, Lindsay Lohan, presented the "Diamond" to Michael.

It was later reported that Beyoncé even had to go to Michael's dressing room and persuade him to come onstage. "He didn't want to come out of his room," Beyoncé later told reporters. The delay caused her to miss her trans-Atlantic flight home.

Her greatest fame would come just months after she stood at the door to Michael's dressing room with the release of *Dreamgirls*, the film adaptation of the hit 1981 Broadway musical about a 1960s singing group loosely based on Motown's Supremes.

Beyoncé was cast as the Diana Ross-based character, Deena Jones. After her "rescue" of Michael, he later said, "I know the *real* Diana Ross, not the mock version."

538

She had her own comeback to Michael, "Don't you think it's scary that you rarely meet celebrities who are normal? I do normal things, walk in the park. I don't want to be off on my own diva planet. I want to be on earth."

Could meeting Michael possibly have triggered that quote?

Breaking his vow about never returning to America, Michael in the closing hours of 2006 flew to Atlanta, Georgia, where he traveled by limousine to Augusta for the funeral of his beloved mentor, James Brown.

With hugs for the Rev. Al Sharpton and the Rev. Jesse Jackson, Michael joined 9,000 other

Beyoncé

mourners, including the squabbling members of Brown's family, to pay his respects at the gold-plated coffin. Michael bent down and seemed to place a gentle kiss on Brown's forehead.

Michael later said, "James Brown is my greatest inspiration ever since I was a small child. When I saw him move, I was mesmerized. I've never seen a performer perform like James Brown, and right then and there, I knew that was exactly what I wanted to do for the rest of my life."

Sharpton told Michael that Brown got his start in Augusta "shining shoes and dancing for pennies. Nobody started lower and went higher."

Reports leaked out that Michael, ending his self-imposed exile, was settling in Las Vegas—that "forgiving town"—to revitalize a dormant career.

If his appearance at the posh shopping mall at Caesars Palace in December was any indication, Michael can still cause a mini-riot, which is just what he did when he appeared here on one of his famous shopping binges. In a black leather jacket, protected by three hotel security guards, Michael was surrounded by hundreds of fans or else rubber neckers.

"Yes, he's here, and, yes, we're working on projects," said Jackson pal and entrepreneur Jack Wishna. "But we're not willing to disclose anything yet."

Jeff Beacher, a savvy observer of the Nevada scene, said that "Jackson's best shot at jump-starting a dead career is Vegas. Vegas is about wild, weird, and crazy. If Michael Jackson is going to come back, this could be the place to do it."

Wishna hinted that the fallen star is seeking to score a "long-term hotel showroom deal like Celine Dion."

Reporter Bob Shemeligian quoted an anonymous Vegas producer as saying, "Jackson has no known offers and is here with hat in hand, looking to generate any buzz he can."

"I believe America likes a comeback story," Wishna claimed.

At least one idea for raising money was activated by Michael in January of 2007. He announced a pair of upcoming "fan appreciation events" in Japan, where his admirers tend to remain the most loyal. If a fan is willing and can afford it, he or she would be allowed to pay $3,300 for an up-close-and-personal 30-second moment with the Gloved One himself. Guests who shelled out this kind of money would also be invited to a "platinum VIP party" that would include dinner and an autographed photo of Guess Who?

The American novelist, F. Scott Fitzgerald, once wrote that "There are no second acts" in America. But is that really true? A failed, fading, and nearly broke mediocre actor named Ronald Reagan proved Fitzgerald wrong, and there have been countless other examples.

The question is often asked, "Can Michael Jackson reinvent himself to achieve the universal acclaim he enjoyed in the 1980s?" The answer to that is, "Of course not!"

Yet a more modest comeback is highly likely for an unimaginably famous performer reaching his half-century mark. Michael has surprised and shocked the world many times in the past.

His story is hardly over. Of course, there will be future headlines, both favorable and destructive.

After all, he *is* Michael Jackson.

With The Gloved One, anything seems possible.

MJ's new home in Las Vegas

A Cast of Thousands
(Author's Epilogue)

Compiling Michael Jackson's life history with any degree of fairness and accuracy is a daunting task. During the past thirty years, he's been the most written about and talked about celebrity in the entertainment industry. A comprehensive bibliography listing everything ever written about him would require a massive encyclopedia of its own.

In my assessment of the source material associated with the life of the entertainer, I depended on what I hoped were reliable witnesses. Regrettably, some of the sources closest to Michael Jackson, for reasons of loyalty or self-interest, were sometimes deliberately misleading, often uttering statements that shed favorable light on situations that by anyone's estimate were either embarrassing or legally compromising.

Complicating matters, Michael himself has sometimes opted to camouflage details about his personal life, contributing in the process to the mountains of misinformation that now litter the MJ moonscape. In some cases, Jacko seems to have done this almost obsessively, despite his protests about the "lies" (his words) which have subsequently appeared about him in the press.

About 30 years ago, I became fascinated by Michael, the Jackson family, and their collective talents, and consequently began compiling information pertaining to their metamorphoses into American legends. Since then, a great number of people—some celebrated, some unknown— provided valuable insights into what tended to happen whenever The Gloved One removed that glove. People from all walks of life, from executives to service personnel, offered information about what was going on behind the carefully guarded doors of the houses and hotel suites Michael occupied throughout his hectic life. Members of Michael's domestic and professional staff also presented intriguing stories to me. Some of them spoke publicly; others preferred the security of anonymity as if still—long after the termination of their employ-

541

ment—they feared retribution.

Lawyers, celebrities, show business executives, friends, enemies, other reporters, alleged lovers, classmates, teachers, and cultural critics, many with contradictory opinions, have also weighed in heavily during the compilation of this biography. In some cases I quoted their words as they appeared in previously published articles; sometimes I quoted them after direct encounters and interviews with me.

As for bias in the wacko task of documenting Jacko, whenever it was perceived that a source might be self-serving or deliberately misleading, I quoted that source directly, so that his or her point of view would be presented merely as an opinion and not as a definitive conclusion from a historian. Over the years, based on my perception that they were unreliable, I've discarded dozens of "I-had-a-close-encounter-with-Michael" stories. And as might be expected, the stories included those that praised and those that damned. Some were brutally and unrelentingly negative; others were phrased like mystical tributes from life-long fans. Some, including a few from Elizabeth Taylor, were effusive to the point of being suspect in and of themselves.

Since so much of Michael's life has been played out on the world stage, my researchers, especially Monica Dunn, and I have tried to focus on stories that had previously not been widespread.

The biographer's role is never easy, and determining the "truth" in matters of history and the human heart is always, at best, subjective. But within these pages, I've done my best to portray, as fairly and objectively as possible, the life of Michael Jackson.

Darwin Porter
New York City
February 2007

BIBLIOGRAPHY

Adler, David, and Ernest Andrews. *Elvis My Dad: The Unauthorized Biography of Lisa Marie Presley.* New York: St. Martin's Paperbacks, 1990.

Aldridge, John. *Satisfaction: The Story of Mick Jagger.* New York: Proteus Books, 1984.

Amburn, Ellis. *The Most Beautiful Woman in the World: The Obsessions, Passions, and Courage of Elizabeth Taylor.* New York: Cliff Street Books, 2000.

Andersen, Christopher. *Barbra: The Way She Is.* New York: HarperCollins Publishers Inc., 2006.

_____, *Citizen Jane: The Turbulent Life of Jane Fonda.* New York: Dell Publishing, 1990.

_____, *Jackie After Jack: Portrait of the Lady.* New York: William Morrow and Company, Inc., 1998.

_____, *Jagger: Unauthorized.* New York: Dell Publishing, 1993.

_____, *Madonna: Unauthorized.* New York: Simon and Schuster Inc., 1991.

_____, *Michael Jackson: Unauthorized.* New York: Simon and Schuster Inc., 1994.

Astaire, Fred. *Fred Astaire: Steps in Time.* New York: Harper & Row Publishers, 1959.

Barbieri, Paula. *The Other Woman: My Years with O.J. Simpson: A Story of Love, Trust, and Betrayal.* Toronto, Canada: Little, Brown and Company, 1997.

Bego, Mark. *Michael!* New York: Pinnacle Books, 1984.

____, *On the Road Michael!* New York: Pinnacle Books, 1984.

Berg, A. Scott. *Kate Remembered.* New York: G.P. Putnam's Sons, 2003.

Bergin, Michael. *The Other Man: A Love Story, John F. Kennedy Jr., Carolyn Bessette, & Me.* New York: Regan Books, 2004.

Bishop, Nick. *FREAK!: Inside the Twisted World of Michael Jackson.* Boca Raton, Fl.: AMI Books, Inc., 2003.

Black, Shirley Temple. *Child Star.* New York, McGraw-Hill Book Company, 1988.

Bockris, Victor. *Warhol: The Biography.* London, England: Da Capo Press, 2003.

Bonderoff, Jason. *Brooke.* New York: Kensington Publishing Corp., 1981.

Breskin, David. *We Are the World.* New York: Perigee Books, 1985.

Brown, Geoff. *Michael Jackson: Body and Soul.* New York: Beaufort Books, 1984.

Buckley, David. *Strange Fascination: David Bowie: The Definitive Story.* London, England: Virgin Publishing Ltd., 2001.

Burrell, Paul. *A Royal Duty.* New York: G.P. Putnam's Sons, 2003.

Burton, Humphrey. *Leonard Bernstein.* New York: Doubleday Publishing, 1994.

Campbell, Lisa D. *Michael Jackson: The King of Pop*. Boston, MA.: Branden Publishing Company, Inc., 1993.

_____, *Michael Jackson: The King of Pop's Darkest Hour*. Boston, MA.: Branden Publishing Company, Inc., 1994.

Capote, Truman, and Gerald Clarke. *Too Brief a Treat: The Letters of Truman Capote*. New York: Random House Publishing Group, 2004.

Chandler, Raymond. *All that Glitters: The Crime and the Cover-Up*. Las Vegas, NV.: Windsong Press, Ltd., 2004.

Chaplin, Charles. *Charles Chaplin: My Autobiography*. New York: Simon and Schuster Inc., 1964.

Clarke, Gerald. *Capote: A Biography*. New York: Simon and Schuster Inc., 1988.

Clayson, Alan. *Mick Jagger*. London, England: Sanctuary Publishing Ltd., 2005.

Colacello, Bob. *Ronnie & Nancy: Their Path to the White House 1911 to 1980*. New York: Warner Books, 2004.

Cornwell, Jane. *Janet Jackson*. London, England: Carlton Books, 2001.

Culkin, Kit. *Lost Boy.2005.Kit Culkin: The Official Site*. 9 May 2005 <http://lost-boy.kitculkin.com>.

Cummings, Katharine. *Sex, Drugs & Rock 'n' Roll: The Lisa Marie Presley Story*. Boca Raton, Fl.: AMI Books, 2004.

Dannen, Fredric. *Hit Men*. New York: Vintage Books, 1991.

Davis Jr., Sammy, and Jane, and Burt Boyar. *Yes I Can: The Story of Sammy Davis Jr.* New York: Pocket Books, 1972.

Deaver, Michael K. *Nancy: A Portrait of My Years with Nancy Reagan*. New York: HarperCollins Publishers Inc., 2004.

Degnen, Lisa. *Prince William: Prince of Hearts*. New York: Warner Books, Inc., 1998.

Dimond, Diane. *Be Careful Who You Love: Inside the Michael Jackson Case*. New York: Atria Books, 2005.

Dineen, Catherine. *In His Own Words: Michael Jackson*. London, England: Omnibus Press, 1993.

Edwards, Anne. *Shirley Temple: American Princess*. New York: William Morrow and Company, Inc., 1988.

Eliot, Marc. *Cary Grant: A Biography*. New York: Harmony Books, 2004.

Fishgall, Gary. *Gonna Do Great Things: The Life of Sammy Davis, Jr.* New York: Scribner Publishing, 2003.

_____, *Gregory Peck: A Biography*. New York: Scribner, 2002.

Fonda, Jane. *My Life So Far*. New York: Random House Publishing Group, 2005.

Freedland, Michael. *Gregory Peck*. New York: William Morrow and Company, Inc., 1980.

Gaines, Steven. *Simply Halston: The Untold Story*. New York: G.P. Putnam's Sons, 1991.

_____, and Sharon Churcher. *Obsession: The Lives and Times of Calvin Klein*. New York: Carol Publishing Group, 1994.

Gallick, Sarah, and Nicholas Maier. *Divinely Decadent: Liza Minnelli: The Drugs, the Sex & the Truth Behind Her Bizarre Marriage*. Boca Raton, Fl.: AMI

Books, 2003.

George, Nelson. *The Michael Jackson Story*. New York: Dell Publishing Company, 1984.

Giles, Sarah. *Fred Astaire: His Friends Talk*. New York: Doubleday Publishing Group, 1988.

Goldman, Albert. *Elvis*. New York: McGraw-Hill Book Company, 1981.

———, *The Lives of John Lennon*. New York: William Morrow and Company, Inc., 1988.

Gordy, Berry. *Berry Gordy: To Be Loved: The Music, the Magic, the Memories of Motown*. New York: Warner Books Inc., 1994.

Grant, Adrian. *Michael Jackson: Making HIStory*. London, England: Omnibus Press, 1998.

———, *Michael Jackson: The Visual Documentary*. London, England: Omnibus Press, 1997.

Graves, Karen Marie. *People in the News: Michael Jackson*. San Diego, CA: Lucent Books. Inc., 2001.

Guralnick, Peter. *Careless Love: The Unmaking of Elvis Presley*. New York: Little, Brown and Company, 1999.

Gutierrez, Victor M. *Michael Jackson Was My Lover: The Secret Diary of Jordie Chandler*. Santiago, Chile, 1997.

Haden-Guest, Anthony. *The Last Party: Studio 54, Disco, and The Culture of the Night*. New York: William Morrow and Company, Inc., 1997.

Haining, Peter. *Elvis in Private*. New York: St. Martin's Press, 1987.

Haskins, James, and Kathleen Benson. *Lena: A Biography of Lena Horne*, 2nd ed. Chelsea, Mich.: Scarborough House Publishers, 1991.

Haney, Lynn. *Gregory Peck: A Charmed Life*. New York: Carroll & Graf Publishers, 2003.

Hefner, Hugh M., and Bill Zehme. *Hef's Little Black Book*. New York: Harper Collins Publishers, Inc., 2004.

Heston, Charlton, and Jean-Pierre Isbouts. *Charlton Heston's Hollywood: 50 Years in American Film*. New York: GT Publishing Corporation, 1998.

———, *In the Arena: An Autobiography*. New York: Boulevard Books, 1997.

Heymann, C. David. *A Woman Named Jackie: An Intimate Biography of Jacqueline Bouvier Kennedy Onassis*. New York: Lyle Stuart Inc., 1989.

———, *Liz*. New York: Carol Publishing Group, 1995.

Hirschhorn, Clive. *Gene Kelly*. Chicago, IL: Henry Regnery Company, 1974.

———, *Gene Kelly: A Biography*. New York: St. Martin's Press, 1984.

Horne, Lena, and Richard Schickel. *Lena*. New York: Signet Publishing, 1965.

Hughes, Geraldine. *Redemption: The Truth Behind the Michael Jackson Child Molestation Allegations*. Radford, VA.: Branch and Vine Publishers, LLC., 2004.

Jackson, Katherine, and Richard Wiseman. *My Family: The Jacksons*. New York: St. Martin's Paperbacks, 1990.

Jackson, LaToya, and Patricia Romanowski. *LaToya: Growing Up in the Jackson Family*. New York: Penguin Group, 1991.

Jackson, Laura. *Heart of Stone: The Unauthorized Life of Mick Jagger*. London, England: Blake Publishing, Ltd., 1998.

Jackson, Margaret Maldonado, and Richard Hack. *Jackson Family Values: Memories of Madness*. Beverly Hills, CA.: Dove Books, 1995.

Jackson, Michael. *Dancing the Dream: Poems and Reflections*. New York: Doubleday Publishing, 1992.

_____, *Michael Jackson: Dangerous*. Secaucus, NJ.: Warner Bros. Publications Inc., 1992.

_____, *Moonwalk*. New York: Doubleday Publishing, 1988.

Jefferson, Margo. *On Michael Jackson*. New York: Pantheon Books, 2006.

Jones, Bob, and Stacy Brown. *Michael Jackson: The Man Behind the Mask*. New York: Select Books, Inc., 2005.

Jones, Quincy. *The Autobiography of Quincy Jones*. New York: Doubleday Publishing, 2001.

Katz, Robin. *Michael Jackson*. New York: Multimedia Publications, 1984.

Kelly, Sean, and Chris Kelly. *Herstory: Lisa Marie's Wedding Diary*. New York: Villard Books, 1996.

Kelley, Kitty. *Elizabeth Taylor: The Last Star*. New York: Simon and Schuster, 1981.

_____, *Jackie Oh!*. Secaucus, NJ: Lyle Stuart Inc., 1978.

_____, *Nancy Reagan: The Unauthorized Biography*. New York: Simon and Schuster, 1991.

King, Tom. *The Operator: David Geffen Builds, Buys, and Sells the New Hollywood*. New York: Random House Publishing, 2000.

Kluck, Ted A. *Facing Tyson: Fifteen Fighters, Fifteen Stories*. Guilford, Conn.: The Lyons Press, 2006.

Latham, Caroline. *Michael Jackson Thrill*. New York: Kensington Publishing Corp., 1984.

Leamer, Laurence. *Sons of Camelot: The Fate of An American Dynasty*. New York: William Morrow and Company, Inc., 2004.

Leigh, Wendy. *Prince Charming: The John F. Kennedy, Jr., Story*. New York: Penguin Group, 1993.

Lewis, Jel D. *Michael Jackson: The King of Pop: The Big Picture, The Music! The Man! The Legend! The Interviews! An Anthology*. Phoenix, AZ: Amber Books 2, 2005.

Luft, Lorna. *Me and My Shadows: A Family Memoir*. New York: Pocket Books, 1998.

Lynn, Kenneth S. *Charlie Chaplin and His Times*. New York: Simon and Schuster Inc., 1997.

Mabery, D.L. *This Is Michael Jackson*. Minneapolis, MN: Lerner Publications Company, 1984.

Maddox, Brenda. *Who's Afraid of Elizabeth Taylor?*. New York: M. Evans and Company, Inc., 1977.

Manso, Peter. *Brando: The Biography*. New York: Hyperion, 1994.

Marsh, Dave. *Trapped: Michael Jackson and the Crossover Dream*. New York:

Bantam Books, Inc., 1985.

Mecca, C. *Michael Jackson: American Master*. Millbrae, CA.: Cam Publishing, 1996.

Miles, Barry. *Paul McCartney: Many Years From Now*. New York: Henry Holt and Company, LLC, 1997.

Millman, Selena. *Loving Michael Jackson*. Prospect, CT.: Biographical Publishing Company, 2001.

Morton, Andrew. *Diana: Her New Life*. New York: Simon & Schuster, Inc., 1994.

_____, *Madonna*. New York: St. Martin's Press, 2001.

Mulvaney, Jay. *Diana & Jackie: Maidens, Mothers, Myths*. New York: St. Martin's Press, 2002.

_____, *Diana: Her True Story*. New York: Pocket Books, 1992.

Munn, Michael. *Charlton Heston: A Biography*. New York: St. Martin's Press, 1986.

Nathan, David. *The Soulful Divas*. New York: Billboard Books, 1999.

Nicholson, Lois P. *Michael Jackson*. New York: Chelsea House Publishers, 1994.

O'Neal, Sean. *Elvis Inc.: The Fall and Rise of the Presley Empire*. Rocklin, CA.: Prima Publishing, 1996.

O'Neal, Tatum. *A Paper Life*. New York: Harper Collins Publishers, Inc., 2004.

Parish, James Robert. *Katharine Hepburn: The Untold Story*. New York: Advocate Books, 2005.

_____, and Jack Ano. *Liza!*. New York: Pocketbooks, 1975.

_____, and Steven Whitney. *Vincent Price Unmasked: A Biography*. New York: Drake Publishers Inc., 1974.

Pasternak, Anna. *Princess In Love*. New York: Penguin Books Ltd., 1994.

Peyser, Joan. *Bernstein: A Biography*. New York: Beech Tree Books, 1987.

Pinkerton, Lee. *The Many Faces of Michael Jackson*. Suffolk, England: Ozone Books, 1997.

Presley, Lisa Marie. *I, Lisa Marie: The True Story of Elvis Presley's Real Daughter*. 1998.

Price, Victoria. *Vincent Price: A Daughter's Biography*. New York: St. Martin's Griffin, 1999.

Reagan, Nancy and William Novak. *My Turn: The Memoirs of Nancy Reagan*. New York: Random House Inc., 1989.

Regan, Stewart. *Michael Jackson*. London, England: Greenwich House, 1984.

Ross, Diana. *Memoirs: Secrets of a Sparrow*. New York: Villard Books, 1993.

Rowland, Mark. *The Totally Unauthorized Michael Jackson Trivia Book: Every Little Thing You Want to Know*. New York: Dell Publishing Company, Inc., 1984.

Sandford, Christopher. *McCartney*. New York: Carroll & Graf Publishers, 2006.

_____, *Mick Jagger: Primitive Cool*. New York, Cooper Square Press, 1999.

Scaduto, Tony. *Mick Jagger: Everybody's Lucifer*. New York: Berkley Publishing Corporation, 1974.

Schofield, Carey. *Jagger*. London, England: Methuen London Ltd., 1983.

Seward, Ingrid. *The Queen & Di*. New York, Arcade Publishing, 2000.

Simmons, Simone and Ingrid Seward. *Diana: The Last Word*. New York: St.

Martin's Press, 2005.

_____, and Susan Hill. *Diana: The Secret Years*. New York: The Ballantine Publishing Group, 1998.

Summers, Anthony. *Goddess: The Secret Lives of Marilyn Monroe*. New York: Macmillan Publishing Company, 1985.

Swanson, Gloria. *Swanson on Swanson*. New York: Random House Inc., 1980.

Taraborrelli, Randy. J. *Call Her Miss Ross: The Unauthorized Biography of Diana Ross*. New York: Carol Publishing Group, 1989.

_____, *Michael Jackson: The Magic and the Madness*. New York: Carol Publishing Group, 1991.

_____, *Motown: Hot Wax, City Cool & Solid Gold*. New York: Doubleday & Company, Inc., 1986.

Taylor, Elizabeth. *Elizabeth Taylor*. New York: Harper and Row Publishers, 1965.

Thomas, Bob. *Astaire: The Man, The Dancer*. New York: St. Martin's Press, 1984.

_____, *Liberace: The True Story*. London, England: Weidenfeld and Nicolson Ltd., 1987.

Thumbtzen, Tatiana Y. *The Way He Made Me Feel*. WII Books.

Tremlett, George. *David Bowie: Living on the Brink*. New York: Carroll & Graf Publishers, Inc., 1996.

_____, *The Rolling Stones*. New York: Warner Books, 1975.

Wallner, Rosemary. *Michael Jackson: Music's Living Legend*. Minneapolis, MN: Abdo Consulting Group, Inc., 1991.

Warhol, Andy, and Hackett, Pat. *The Andy Warhol Diaries*. New York: Warner Books, 1989.

Wegner, Robert W. *My Three Years Working for Michael Jackson: Dec 1990-Dec 1993*. 2002.

White, Charles. *The Life and Times of Little Richard: The Quasar of Rock*. New York: Da Capo Press, 1994.

Wolfe, Donald H. *The Assassination of Marilyn Monroe*. London, England: Little, Brown and Company, 1998.

Yetnikoff, Walter, and David Ritz. *Howling at the Moon*. New York: Broadway Books, 2004.

Yudkoff, Alvin. *A Life of Dance and Dreams: Gene Kelly*. New York: Back Stage Books, 1999.

Zec, Donald. *Sophia*. New York: David McKay Company, Inc., 1975.

INDEX

If you've enjoyed this biography,

Please consider these other fine products from

Biographies and film guides that change how
America interprets its entertainers

www.BloodMoonProductions.com

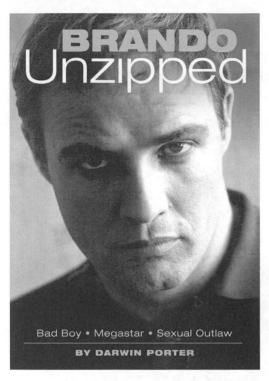

"**Brando Unzipped** is the definitive gossip guide to the late, great *actor's life*"
New York Daily News .

"*Entertainingly outrageous*"
Frontiers

Yu*mmy!*...*An irresistibly flamboyant romp of a read.*"
Books to Watch Out For

Lurid, raunchy, perceptive, and certainly worth reading"
The Sunday Times (London)

"*Astonishing. An extraordinarily detailed portrait of Brando that's as blunt, uncompromising, and X-rated as the man himself.*"
Women's Weekly (Australia)

"*This shocking new book is sparking a major reassessment of Brando's legacy as one of Hollywood's most macho lotharios.*"
Daily Express (London)

Brando Unzipped
by Darwin Porter.   ISBN 09748118-2-3
©2006   Hardcover,
624 pages, with hundreds of photos. $26.95

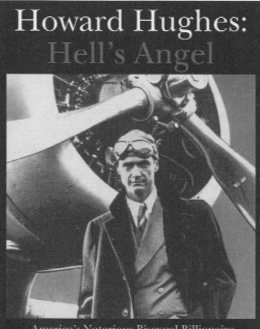

"Thanks to Darwin Porter's biography of Howard Hughes, we'll never be able to look at the old pin-ups in quite the same way"

THE TIMES of London

"Darwin Porter grew up in the midst of Hollywood Royalty. His access to film industy insiders and other Hughes confidants supplied him with the resources he needed to create a portrait that both corroborates what other Hughes biographies have divulged and go them one better."

FOREWORD MAGAZINE

"According to a new biography by Darwin Porter, Hughes's attitude toward sex, like the Emperor Caligula, was selfish at best and at its worst, sadistic. He was obsessed with controlling his lovers and, although he had a pathological fear of relationships and marriage, he proposed to countless women, often at the same time. Only three people successfully resisted Hughes's persistent advances: Elizabeth Taylor, Jean Simmons, and Joan Crawford. Of the three, it was Crawford who most succinctly revealed her reasons for refusing Hughes's advances, "I adore homosexuals, but not in my bed after midnight."

LONDON's SUNDAY EXPRESS

The Secret Life of HUMPHREY BOGART
The Early Years (1899-1931), by Darwin Porter

Bogie was America's most famous male movie star, but until the release of this biography, very little had ever been published about his early career and youthful emotional entanglements.

"Porter's biography uncovers scandals within the entertainment industry of the 1920s and 30s, when publicists from the movie studios deliberately twisted and suppressed inconvenient details about the lives of their emerging stars."

Turner Classic Movie News

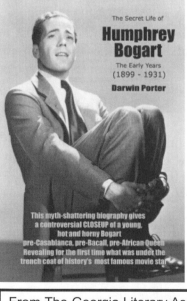

"Humphrey Bogart was one of Hollywood's most celebrated lovers, his romance with Lauren Bacall hailed as one of the greatest love stories of the 20th century. But before they met, he was a drug-taking womanizer, racking up a string of failed marriages and broken relationships with some of the world's most beautiful women. In this extraordinary biography, drawing on a wealth of previously unseen material, veteran showbusiness writer Darwin Porter, author of *Hollywood's Silent Closet,* reveals the truth about Bogart's shady past."

The Mail on Sunday
(London)

From The Georgia Literary Association
(an affiliate of Blood Moon Productions)
ISBN 0966-8030-5-1
528 pages, plus 64 photos. $16.95

Here, assembled into one comprehensive volume, is a rundown of the year's most intriguing Gay, Lesbian, and Transgendered films, an illustrated guide that's Out, Outrageous, Provocative, and Proud. This guide is radically revised and re-issued every year, reflecting an updated roster of the year's best films.

"Authoritative, exhaustive, and essential, *Blood Moon's Guide to Gay and Lesbian Film* is the one-stop resource for what to add to your feature-film queue. The film synopses and the snippets of critic's reviews are reason enough to keep this annual compendium of cinematic information close to the DVD player. But the extras--including the Blood Moon Awards and commentary on queer short films--are butter on the popcorn."

Books to Watch Out For

"This compilation of everything fabu in the year's movies is essential, comprehensive and entertaining, with over 135 feature films and 60 shorts discussed. Scattered throughout the listings are "Special Features," tongue-in cheek essays about the best and worst mishaps in film last year. Blood Moon plans on publishing a new edition every year, so here's hoping for a good, gay 2007.

Bay Windows (Boston)

ISBN 978-0-9748118-4-X (First Edition) and
978-0-9748118-6-6 (Second Edition, available June, 2007)
All this and more from   **www.Blood Moon Productions.com**

About the Author:

In addition to *Jacko: His Rise and Fall*, **Darwin Porter** has penned at least four other unauthorized biographies. Each of these has salvaged the otherwise forgotten oral histories of America's entertainment industry, and each of them has appeared in serialized form in major newspapers of Britain. They include *The Secret Life of Humphrey Bogart: The Early Years (1899-1931)*; *Howard Hughes: Hell's Angel*, a book about the Hollywood involvements of an American emperor; *Brando Unzipped*, a "lurid, raunchy, and perceptive" biography of Marlon Brando that's "as X-rated as the man himself"; and *Katharine the Great*, a starkly unapologetic exposé of the life and personal quirks of *über-diva* Katharine Hepburn.

Porter is a long-time associate of **THE FROMMER TRAVEL GUIDES**, the author of a regularly scheduled Florida-based newspaper column about the entertainment industry ("Hollywood Remembered"), and a frequent guest on radio talk shows. When not traveling (which is rare), he lives in New York.